Urban Planning Analysis:
Methods and Models

Urban Planning Analysis:
Methods and Models

DONALD A. KRUECKEBERG
Associate Professor of Urban Planning and Policy Development,
Rutgers University

ARTHUR L. SILVERS
Urban and Regional Economist, Latin American Program in Brazil
Resources for the Future, Inc.

JOHN WILEY & SONS, INC., New York · London · Sydney · Toronto

Library of Congress Cataloging in Publication Data

Krueckeberg, Donald A
    Urban planning analysis: methods and models.

    Includes bibliographies.
    1. Cities and towns—Planning—1945–   2. Cities and towns—Planning—Mathematical models. I. Silvers, Arthur L., Joint Author. II. Title.
HT166.K78   309.2'62   74-7087
ISBN 0-471-50858-6

Printed in the United States of America

10 9 8 7 6 5 4 3 2

Preface

This book is an introduction to the basic quantitative techniques of urban planning and policy analysis. The development and diffusion of these techniques within professional practice have been limited by historical factors. Modern city and regional planning originated in a loose collaboration among a diverse group of urban reformers during the late nineteenth and early twentieth centuries. It included housing economists, public health officials, zoning lawyers, local government reformers, civil engineers, urban sociologists, geographers, architects, and landscape architects. But as universities began to train professionals for this movement, their programs of study did not fully succeed in spanning this multidisciplinary foundation. Professional training became mainly the province of the design professions of architecture and landscape architecture, neither of which had the strong bookish habit of theory building, characteristic of most of the sciences. Thus, while urban theory and analytic methods were generated primarily by economists, sociologists, and geographers, the tools that they developed were added very slowly to the mainstream of city planning. The profession's centers of training did not become the national centers of urban theory and scientific research. The gap that developed between practice and theory, between urban action and urban analysis, became so broad that a pressure of almost revolutionary proportion was necessary to close it. This revolution came in the late 1950s and throughout the 1960s. The increased pace of quantification in the social sciences, together with a shift in governmental and academic priorities toward a more intense concern for urban problems, precipitated radical changes both in planning practice and the education of practitioners.

In the field of practice we have witnessed a tendency for analytic techniques to exhibit a leapfrogging behavior, jumping from the stages of initial invention, over the heads of the main body of the profession, directly to very high levels of abstraction. The effect has been a kind of capitalistic monopoly of technical knowledge, maintained in the language of higher mathematics by persons who know how to use it. Partly as a result of this process, many very expensive mistakes have been made in the name of the planning profession by selling to the public, at an enormous cost, models of analysis that have been mainly untested and that have proved to be highly impractical.

In academic settings, where these sophisticated techniques have been introduced into the intellectual traditions of planning, the language and culture of professional training has tended to replace one very esoteric language—the traditional language of architectural taste and design—with another, the new language of mathematics and statistics. Intellectual leadership within the field, to use a social analogy, has simply been transferred from one elite to another.

Neither the traditions of social science nor the traditions of planning practice have been very successful in dealing with the problems of urban policy development. Therefore, we believe that leaping back and forth from one to the other is not a solution. One of our basic objectives is to help establish a middle ground, the common foundation on which planners and social scientists, in concert, can build more suitable and stable extensions of urban analysis to enhance the efficiency of public policymaking.

Students and professionals who have come to the study of urban systems with no familiarity with and/or facility for quantitative procedures have found almost no opportunity, in this highly interdisciplinary field, for sympathetic instruction at an elementary level. This has been true for both those in the academically oriented social sciences in search of fields of application, and for those in the field of planning in search of analytic discipline. For students with a natural skill in mathematics, this has not necessarily been a problem. They have been able, in many cases, to refer to textbooks of sociology, business administration, economics, and engineering and, with considerable effort, have been able to make the transition from those contexts into the area of urban applications. Our efforts here are directed toward students who find such a procedure inefficient and to those who pursue mathematics and statistics with uneasy hesitation or even a sense of fear. We have found that most people attempt to understand quantitative analysis, not because they are attracted by the elegance of mathematics and logical reasoning, but because they want to understand a specific practical problem concerning, for example, housing, education, transportation, or health. Quantitative analysis in this practical context is a means to an end, not an end in itself—and a bothersome one in many instances. The basic methods and models of planning are fundamentally quite simple. Yet, ignorance of these techniques not only can be an obstacle but also can leave one vulnerable to exploitation. People and communities can be exploited by their public servants, public planners can be exploited by private interests and expert consultants, and research centers and university professors can exploit almost everybody, including each other. Everyone is vulnerable. The lessons of the past tell us all too clearly that well-intentioned humanists will continue to lose the battles for people, cities, and the environment until they come to terms with these instruments and their role in these struggles. We believe that all planners should acquire a knowledge of these tools, should know their strengths and weaknesses, and should then use them judiciously to get on with the work.

For these reasons we always attempt here to begin our presentations and discussions from the position of realistic problems and decisions and, then, to show how particular techniques can be brought to the analysis of those problems and can contribute to their solution. Some topics are not included here that some readers may feel should have been included. Mathematicians and statisticians may wonder why we do not introduce set theory as a foundation for probability theory, or why calculus is not used to describe probability distributions or to find the least-squares solution in regression analysis. Our intention has been to include only the concepts and computations that have a genuine and direct application to problems in urban planning analysis—not those that we and other theoreticians may feel should be applied, but those that, indeed, are in daily application.

In attempting to avoid the difficulties and pitfalls of speaking strictly from within the disciplinary framework of mathematics and statistics, we may leave an impression that the methods and models we present are not of a general nature and, therefore, are not applicable to a broad spectrum of problems beyond the particular problem on which we have chosen to demonstrate each technique. All of the analytic procedures discussed here are, in fact, quite general in nature and can be applied to a wide range of decision problems. We risk being misinterpreted on this point because we are too familiar with the alternative gamble in which students are presented with general theories and abstract methods that usually cannot be translated into the students' own practical context. The difficulty with general mathematical and statistical theory, at this stage of learning, is that it requires, in order to present a coherent chain of logical reasoning and proof, the introduction and exercise of numerous concepts and operations that simply do not translate directly into real problem solving. Thus the cautious and, perhaps, fearful reader of such a treatment finds it too easy to indict the whole system of quantitative analysis as being irrelevant and ungrounded in his practical experience. Of course, such a conclusion is largely correct. That is why we have tried to derive the structure and development of our presentation from the structure of urban problems and from the development of planning and decision processes, rather than relying exclusively on the traditional modes of mathematical presentation.

DONALD A. KRUECKEBERG
ARTHUR L. SILVERS

Use of the Book

This book is divided into two parts. Part I is comprised of seven chapters and is a sequential treatment of the various stages of a rational planning process. It begins with the definition of the planning process, the role of standards and goals, and the structuring of problems, and progresses through information gathering, the specification of alternative solutions and outcomes, the estimation of the impacts of solutions on goals, program evaluation and selection and, finally, the management of program implementation. The principal analytic tools introduced throughout this sequence include the calculation of need gaps, causal diagrams, sampling and survey research methods, data tabulation, descriptive statistics, hypothesis testing, correlation and regression analysis, cost-effectiveness and cost-benefit analysis, program evaluation and review technique, and critical path analysis.

Part II presents models of urban systems that are widely used in planning analysis. Simple and complex models of population projection, models of location and travel behavior, and the simulation of large-scale transportation systems are discussed in Chapters 8 to 10. Chapter 11 is a slight exception in format. At this point, if not sooner, most readers can easily understand the need for a more manageable algebra for handling the data and computations of these complex models. Linear algebra, or matrix algebra, is introduced to fill this need. The final chapter presents models of regional income and employment analysis.

This work is intended for three groups: (1) upper-level undergraduate students in urban studies or the social sciences who have had some preparation in the nature of urban systems and social policy questions; (2) graduate students either directly in the field of urban and regional planning or in related professions who may wish to explore the field of urban policy analysis; and (3) practicing planners who either have had no adequate opportunity to study these methods and models or who feel the need for renewing or restructuring their knowledge in this area. We assume, by way of mathematical preparation, only training in high school algebra or a first-year college course in algebra for nonmathematicians and nonscience students. In fact, we even assume that most of that study will have been forgotten. In the process of writing this book, with the help of some of our colleagues, we used all of the book's material in both undergraduate and graduate classrooms and found this to be of invaluable assistance, leading to beneficial rewritings, reorganizations, and some corrections. As a textbook, we suggest that the book be used for a full academic year course or sequence of courses. This can be done for either undergraduate or graduate classes, depending on their abilities.

More difficult sections often can be passed over without losing continuity, such as the section on the binomial distribution in Chapter 3 and some of the later sections of Chapters 6, 11, and 12. Where students are able to proceed through the material at a fairly rapid pace, as we find to be true of some undergraduates as well as graduates, it is beneficial to supplement the chapters with the suggested additional readings in both computational theory and practical application. We also find it easy and useful to introduce computer usage at several stages in the learning process. For example, we define research projects that require the selection of a sample, keypunching, and simple data description with the use of packaged computer programs and find this to be a stimulating aid in the study of Chapters 2 and 3. Also, we ask students to take the same sample of data and to analyze it further through the use of packaged statistical programs for regression and correlation analysis on the computer in conjunction with Chapters 4 and 5. This can be easily accomplished with programs from the Biomedical Computer Programs or the Statistical Package for the Social Sciences. The importance, in a subject like this, of learning by doing and of comparing hand calculations with machine calculations can hardly be overemphasized.

Our concerns for planning practice again have caused us to emphasize not only the theory of various models but also to spend a considerable amount of time demonstrating the procedures for estimating and fitting these models—procedures often neglected or obscured in the available literature. Sets of problems and selected bibliographies accompany each chapter. We have tried to keep down the items in each bibliography to a reasonable number, considering balance with respect to theory and practice, elementary versus advanced treatments, and complementary versus supplementary materials. Of course, there are many excellent items in the literature that have not been cited and that could easily be substituted for the ones we included.

Because of space limitations, we have not introduced some of the newer techniques, such as linear programming (although we do sneak in a little here and there), models of natural resource systems, social area analysis, social indicators, management information systems, models of the design process, and the like. This has been done not because we are unaware or unsympathetic to any of these areas of analysis, but because we believe that a comprehensive survey format would force other compromises in depth of treatment and would simply create an information overload for those to whom the book is primarily addressed.

D. A. K.

A. L. S.

Acknowledgments

Lawrence D. Mann provided the strong organizational and intellectual support that we needed when we undertook the writing of this book. We owe him a great deal. Formerly our chairman at Rutgers University, he is now at Harvard.

Many of our colleagues also gave helpful criticism and suggestions, and in several instances contributed exercises to chapters based on their use of the book in their courses. Others read drafts and helped us to work out our ideas in discussion. We especially thank Richard K. Brail, George W. Carey, Salah El-Shakhs, Susan S. Fainstein, Arthur Getis, Michael R. Greenberg, Jerome C. Harris, William B. McCullough, and George Sternlieb. Our special thanks go to Robert Thomas Crow of the State University of New York at Buffalo.

We are grateful to the students of Livingston College and The Graduate School at Rutgers who, over the past several years, have studied various drafts of the manuscript and have expressed encouraging and helpful comments. They, through their reactions both in the classroom and out, must be credited with a very large portion of whatever works well in this book.

We thank the faculty and students of CEDEPLAR, Centro de Desenvolvimento e Planejamento Regional, Universidade Federal de Minas Gerais, Brazil, who provided much useful feedback on Chapter 12.

We are fortunate to have had several excellent managers of the typewriter, duplicator, and various other office devices that played a vital role throughout. Our thanks go to Ronnie Fernandez, Stephanie Ross, Laura Sesta, and most especially to Vera Lee. Vera's energy and dedication has been like that of an author.

We acknowledge the assistance of The Research Council of Rutgers

University, which provided us with small grants that were helpful in the early stages of our undertaking.

We are also grateful to Barbara Silvers and Lee Krueckeberg who contributed numerous bright ideas to the book, as well as unrepayable loans of courage and patience.

D. A. K.
A. L. S.

Contents

6   EVALUATING AND SELECTING PROGRAMS

7   PROGRAM SCHEDULING

Urban Planning Analysis:
Methods and Models

PART I
Methods

CHAPTER 1

Planning, Goals, and System Structure: Elementary Analysis

1.1 THE PLANNING PROCESS IN PRACTICE AND THEORY

In a community, within the core area of a large city, several dissatisfied citizens meet to discuss the low quality of health services available to the local population and to determine some action alternatives to remedy that situation.

They enumerate the kinds of health care needs that have not been adequately treated by the existing health care facilities. Based on their experience with these institutions, they point out the reasons for these inadequacies. Among these reasons are the many health care clinics that are located downtown, away from their community, making access to them difficult for elderly people and for young children. In the facilities that are nearer, such as private doctor's offices and hospitals, the costs of health care are too high in comparison with the low incomes earned by most of the community's residents. And, even if income were not a factor, the existence of race and language differences, as well as numerous rules of eligibility, has greatly inhibited local residents from obtaining the health services that they need. Finally, in considering the resources available for health care, they indicate that a major factor in the current situation is the lack of public funds for the construction of facilities and for improved services, the result of conflicting priorities among government legislators at both the federal and the municipal levels.

With this structure of the health system in mind, the small group of citizens selects the following set of action proposals, subject to more detailed evaluation. They propose that a small health care facility be established in the

3

community, within easy access to all residents. They propose to staff the facility with local residents, and to equip it with manpower training programs to teach the unskilled much of the range of skills needed to operate the facility. Where the needed skills cannot be readily taught, and where local residents cannot provide them, they propose to hire staff from outside the community at competitive wages until it can be secured locally. By selecting these actions, they hope not only to improve medical services and facilities in the community but to reduce the time and money spent on travel, to increase local employment, and to provide a stimulus to community education services—in short, to contribute to the solution of several problems at once.

To implement their scheme they outline several immediate actions aimed at raising funds for the program, recognizing that in all probability one or more of them will not succeed. First, they will request funds from federal agencies that are legislated to support community health services. Second, they will impose a service charge for those residents who can afford to pay. Third, they will raise funds from the savings of local residents through an ongoing fund raising campaign. Fourth, they will attempt to influence the priorities of the municipal government so as to channel a larger share of the municipal budget into community health services, through voter registration drives, through publicity campaigns and organized demonstrations, and by running local candidates for public office. Finally, to assure that the health services provided by the new facility continue to meet their needs, even as the population and needs of the community change over time, the group propose that the management and administration of the facility be under the exclusive control of local residents. As part of the facility's control structure, information on its performance in meeting the health care needs of the community will be regularly fed back to the facility's managers for use in making new management and planning decisions pursuant to the community's goals.

All carefully developed plans will be based in a format similar to the set of planning tasks implicit in the above process. This process can be separated into four parts, or tasks:

1. *The statement of goals.* An agreement must be reached to give priority to the solution of a general problem or the attainment of some ends.
2. *An analysis of system structure.* The dimensions or parts of the problem or goal must be specified as well as their causal interrelationships.
3. *An evaluation and selection of possible solutions must be made.* Commitment must be made to a plan of changes expected to achieve the goals in the most effective or efficient manner.
4. *The design of an implementation procedure.* The steps to be taken to accomplish the planned solution must be specified.

The amount of time and resources required to complete these tasks depends on the magnitude of the problem at hand and the resources available. These tasks can sometimes be accomplished through an evening's perceptive discussion where the problem is well understood by the participants in the planning process. But many planning situations are beset with a multitude of goals, some of which are in conflict and many of which are vague, and with sets of causal environments that are so complex as to require the attention of a team of trained professional analysts with advanced technical tools for a period of many months. As problems become relatively complicated, rather large quantities of information must be organized to accomplish the tasks of goal formulation, system specification, plan selection, and program implementation.

The four-stage planning process we describe is shown in Figure 1.1 as a sequence of planning tasks that interact with each other and with the community of the real world in which the problem lies, and where the persons, institutions, and characteristics exist that are both the sources of the problems and of their solution. The planning effort of the small group of dissatisfied citizens, described above, can be systematically understood in terms of Figure 1.1. Goal formulation took place through the interaction of people's experiences and perceptions of health problems in their community and their common commitment to give priority to a solution of this problem. The interaction (represented by the arrows, in Figure 1.1, between goal formulation and the community situation) took the form of questions put to the problem and of answers fed back, in this case, simply a discussion. These interactions can also be interpreted in terms of exchanges of perception and response, responsibility and commitment, authority and leadership, information and decision, and so forth, finally moving on to the second stage of analysis.

The analysis of system structure produced, from further probing of the problem and its environment, a structural picture of the elements involved in the problem: the location of facilities, the costs of care, incomes, the barriers of race and language, sets of administrative procedures, public budgets, and federal and local public policies. This system description constitutes what we will call a model of the problem. It is a smaller than real life, less detailed, picture of the problem that nonetheless contains the salient factors affecting the goal. By manipulating the model, that is, by considering changes in some of the parts of the system and different configurations of the elements we can perform mental or paper experiments. We can consider, for example, leaving the location of facilities downtown, as they now are, and improving the transportation services. Alternatively we might leave the transportation services as they are but move the facilities nearer to the community. By examining, systematically the advantages and

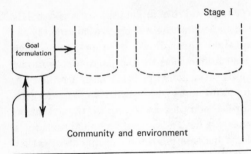

Stage I

Goal formulation takes information on preferences, demands, supply, standards, and problem symptoms to form a structured commitment to the solution of a problem, and its definition in a form sufficient to facilitate movement toward solution.

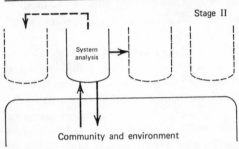

Stage II

System analysis takes the defined problem and structures a model of the problem variables and their interrelationships, based on gathered data and their careful analysis, to calibrate the effects of various control and change strategies on the goal and need variables.

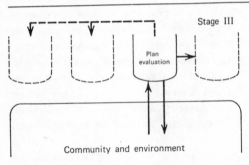

Stage III

Plan and program evaluation draws upon the analysis of system structure to select a finite set of alternative actions that can take on the form of programs or projects, and then evaluates the effects and costs of each program in terms of the long- and short-run effects to select the most effective program.

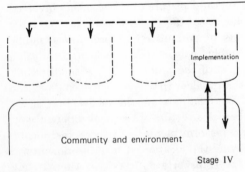

Program implementation takes the program or project of choice and sets out the specific activities and actions, in sequence, that must be undertaken to implement the plan, and analyzes the allocation of resources to the steps of implementation, as well as dealing with the long-run problems of program monitoring, feedback, and replanning.

Stage IV

FIGURE 1.1 The process of planning analysis in four stages.

disadvantages of imagined reconfigurations of the system, alternative proposals and schemes for reaching the goal of improving health services can be evaluated.

The third task is the formal evaluation of alternative proposals. By using the model from the prior step and gathering and estimating further the impacts and costs of various proposals, we can attempt to choose a plan that will most effectively accomplish the goals. These citizens' particular choice was the establishment of a new, small health care facility within the community, incorporating several programmatic and managerial innovations.

The fourth task is to make even more detailed and specific the sequence of actions that is needed to implement the program and to manage its installation and continued operation in the community.

In reality, planning is done in a city or a region, at any given point in time, by many groups and organizations, both public and private, individual and governmental, all of which have many goals. The planning and decision processes of each are in varying stages of progress and often intersect with each other. Common goals for two groups may lead to separate models of the problem. Separate goals may converge to common program choices and measures for implementation. The organization and proper coordination of all of these separate decision processes are most significant. At the root of political and economic philosophy, they pose the fundamental question. We do not directly try to answer this question, but the contributions of this book do relate to it in focusing on the tools of quantitative analysis that can be brought to bear in a planning process by those who are doing the planning.

In the following sections of this chapter we consider problems and techniques of goal formulation and the structuring of problem definitions around goal statements that lead toward manageable procedures for the analysis of system structure and model building. It may already be evident, and will become clearly obvious, that the various stages of the planning process we have defined blend into one another in their practical execution.

1.2 THE DEFINITION OF GOALS AND NEEDS

In most planning situations that are intended to serve the needs of a diverse array of socioeconomic groups, the task of stating goals is by no means as straightforward as in the health planning effort described above. Even there, the array of health needs of the community's diverse age groups and income groups requires that the statement of health goals be made more specific if a health facility is to be designed that meets the community's needs. For example, if we examine the age distribution of the population and find that it has a large proportion of women of childbearing age and also a large low-income Spanish-speaking elderly population, the health facility must reflect these population attributes by being oriented to the special needs of these groups. But it must also be designed to allow flexibility in the array of health care services over time as the processes of birth, death, and migration further alter the population mix.

We see that differences within the community population require that an overall goal such as "achieve better health" must be divided into a series of subgoals that define whose health is to be improved—the young, the elderly, the poor, and the like. Furthermore, since health has many attributes, a health goal must also be divided according to what aspects of health are to be treated—child care, terminal illness, narcotics treatment, out-patient care, and advanced surgery. But even answering the question of what aspects of health care should be given priority in the community health program does not completely solve the problem of defining goals. Certain health needs are, from a professional medical standpoint, obvious candidates for a community health center, such as well-baby clinics and care for the elderly. Other needs may be viewed as essential from the standpoint of community leaders because of their popular demand in the community, and these, too, may be included in the health program, even though they may not be "medically" critical. For example, a special clinic to provide services to unwed mothers may be regarded as extremely high in demand by the community residents but may not be viewed as a pressing need by medical experts. Only if the community is successful in making their felt needs known to the local health program administrators is such service likely to be included.

The existence of these felt needs, in constrast to those that are scientifically or professionally recognized, raises the question of human values and of their communication. These difficulties would, no doubt, be quite obvious to our small group of citizens meeting to plan a community health program. In fact, they may be the very factors that have led to the meeting. In large cities with massive governmental bureaucracies, city hall is often far removed from each small community, especially where the community does not have power or regular channels of communication with the municipal power structure. The result is that the values and needs of low income communities are often underrepresented in the municipal decision-making process, with city hall persistently giving priority to the needs of the more articulate and powerful groups and communities in the city. In seeking local control over health services, the small community group may see a means to assure that their needs are more adequately satisfied.

To summarize, goals must be specified in terms of *what* needs are to be served as well as *whose* needs are to be served. Furthermore, the array of needs includes not only those *judged* as essential by professional decision makers but also those *felt* as essential by the community population. To articulate the popular felt needs of all community groups, information feedback mechanisms must be built into planning processes to provide data to decision makers on the array of needs of all of the socioeconomic groups of a community.

The ultimate decision makers, guided by this planning process, will want to reduce the many needs of the community's population groups into a consolidated, well-defined list of needs that they, as decision makers, are willing and able to implement. Selected felt needs, plus perhaps less popular needs that are believed by the decision makers to be essential, will become the decision makers' statement of policy goals. In many real cases the decision maker who is an adroit politician may refuse to reveal the true list of goals that he intends to pursue. Nevertheless, whether he reveals them or not, he must somehow aggregate or reduce the many needs that are expressed into a manageable statement that he intends to support as his goals. We will assume that his goals are made explicit and are made known, if not to the entire community, then, at least, to those who participate in the planning process.

Suppose that the decision maker either desires or is required to aggregate the felt needs of all the different population groups in a way that is fair and not arbitrary. This task is more difficult than one might at first imagine. To understand why this is so, let us suppose that there are only two population groups in the community, groups A and B, and that there are three needs; a park, a firehouse, and a health center, which are valued independently by each group. These values can be expressed in relative terms by having each group simply rank them in decreasing order of preference, with the result as shown in Table 1.1. Since both groups rank the firehouse first, it is clear and fair to conclude that for the community as a whole this has first priority. What is not clear is a community-wide ranking for the other two needs. It could be that group A places no real value at all on the health center, which it prefers least of all, and that, although group B ranks the health center second, it in fact values the park nearly as much as the health center. In this instance it might seem fair that, for community-wide decision making,

TABLE 1.1
Three Needs Ranked by Two Groups

Preferences	Group A	Group B
First	Firehouse	Firehouse
Second	Park	Health center
Third	Health center	Park

TABLE 1.2
Three Needs Ranked by Three Groups

Preferences	Group A	Group B	Group C
First	Firehouse	Health center	Park
Second	Park	Firehouse	Health center
Third	Health center	Park	Firehouse

the park should get second priority and the health center third priority. But such a clear-cut case may not exist. It is essentially not possible to determine how much more a population group values a certain need than does another group. Therefore, in general, there is no definite way to arrive fairly at an aggregated need ranking for a community as a whole. To consider a more extreme example, let there be a third group in the community, group C, and suppose that instead of the rankings for groups A and B given above, the three groups make their selections according to the preferences shown in Table 1.2. Here it is impossible to establish a community needs ranking, since there is not a single point of agreement in the three groups' rankings.

These examples indicate that it may not be possible to devise a fair basis for aggregating the diverse needs of differing population groups in a community into a single community-needs ranking in an objective and analytical manner. Instead, in practice the decision maker may represent a coalition of groups and be arbitrarily applying his own values when defining goals, values that may be known and acceptable to the coalition, on the whole. Here, the values placed on needs by those groups not included in the coalition or party will very likely be ignored. In the private sector of a free enterprise economy the pure economic theory of the situation states that problems of goal aggregation do not have to be formally resolved. There is no need to define a single community-wide needs set because if a private need is found to exist even by only one group, a firm will arise and serve these needs so long as revenues are sufficient to cover costs. Whether or not this condition is satisfied is determined by conditions of supply and demand as mediated by prices. However, we do not live in a theoretical world, not to mention that we are concerned, in the main, with planning for the public sector, not the private.

In attempting to reduce the arbitrariness of the needs aggregation process, public planners often seek to establish need standards that can be applied to all population groups. For example, housing standards may be established that state the number of rooms that should be provided to each family according to the number of persons in the family. Standards may also state the lowest acceptable structural conditions for housing. Standards are often established to define the lowest acceptable amount of recreation space per family or food per family, of health care per person, and of pollutants per unit of water or air. In arriving at these standards, planners often seek the findings of scientific research for support. For example, if it is possible to determine that an amount of sulfur dioxide in the air exceeding "x parts per million" is a threat to life, this may serve as a minimum standard of air quality. But scientific information is unavailable for the setting of some standards. As in the case of housing density, overcrowding, and recreation space, the standards that are set are based on judgement and derive from the general standard of living in the society as a whole.

When certain standards have been accepted by either the courts, administrative practice, or just as working assumptions by planners, then need gaps may be computed for each population group in the community. This is often done by determining the population size of the group or community and multiplying that figure by a per capita standard, yielding a gross statement of need. For example, if there are 10,000 people in the community, and the open space standard is 2 acres per capita, then there is a gross need for 10,000 times 2 acres or 20,000 acres of open space. Suppose further that there are 5000 acres of open space already in existence in the community. They by subtracting the available open space from the gross need, we obtain the net need or the need gap for open space.

We can formulate this process of reasoning as a general procedure by using the notation below

$$G = (St \times P) - Su \qquad\qquad 1.1$$

where

$G =$ the community need gap
$St =$ a per capita standard
$P =$ population size
$Su =$ current supply

Thus our open space calculation takes this form:

$G = (2 \text{ acres per person} \times 10,000) - 5000 \text{ acres}$
$G = (2 \times 10,000) - 5000$
$G = (20,000) - 5000$
$G = 15,000 \text{ acres}$

Proceeding in this fashion, we can calculate a set of need gaps for the entire range of different needs for which standards can be established. It should be emphasized that for most types of need the need gap should be calculated for each socioeconomic group for whom the need exists. For example, it may be found that a city's need gap in housing units is 5000 units. If this aggregate measure is the only information provided, a program may in all likelihood be planned to construct 5000 two-bedroom apartments for small upper-middle income families. This is a likely result because the return on the financial investment, both to the private sector and to the public sector, is usually highest for this type of construction. But if the 5000 housing units are needed by 4500 families earning low incomes, half of which are large families requiring five or more rooms, and the other half of which are elderly people requiring special facilities, then the need gap must be stated explicitly in terms of these population groups for whom the need gap exists, so as to make certain that program plans are properly designed to fit them.

What does a statement of goals then look like and, once you have it, what can be done with it? The presentation of goals may take several forms. Some of them are:

1. A list of statements, such as "all residents of the community shall have housing of adequate size and quality." The list might cover a range of goals including housing, recreation, education, health, safety, jobs, transportation, and other service needs.
2. A list, like that just described, wherein a weighting or ranking of relative importance is assigned to items.
3. A set of standards and need gap calculations for each goal and community group. These may take the form of numerical tables.
4. A community map, or set of maps, on which graphs or symbols locate the types and magnitudes of need gaps as they are geographically distributed.

These are only some of the forms that goal statements can take. There are also many things that can and should be done with these statements, tables, and maps. Some of these uses are as follows:

1. They may form the basis of a political campaign, party platforms, or administrative statements of intent.
2. They may serve as a list of demands or as the basis for negotiations in conflict situations.
3. They may be capable of setting the structure of issues for an educational campaign for newspapers, radio, television, or other public media.
4. They may form the set of task definitions for a series of task forces or investigative commissions.
5. They may serve as the initial basis for defining community problems that require further analysis for the purposes of program evaluation.

Since our central interest is in methods of analysis, we now consider the last of these uses to see how goals and need statements like those we have discussed lead to the analysis of data and assist in the construction of more sophisticated and powerful models for program experimentation and evaluation through the specification of system structure.

1.3 GOALS AND NEEDS ARTICULATED WITHIN THE STRUCTURE OF SYSTEMS

To say that needs exist that are not being adequately satisfied is to say that there are problems in the existing system and that corrective changes must be made. To identify the potential points of change and their relative importance, we must extend needs analysis to an analysis of the system structure. Once this has been achieved, programs may be designed to correct problems to the extent that available resources permit. Goals can thus be attained.

Let us think of the elements of a system as a set of variable characteristics that are causally linked to one another in a way that can be identified. Among these variables we distinguish three types. One type is the needs variables defined through goal statements. Examples of two such needs variables might be the amount of preventive child health care and the amount of adult narcotics addiction treatment.

A second type of variable in the system is the subset of control variables. These variables are characteristics that are subject to direct control and manipulation by the community or decision makers and that either directly or indirectly affect the state of each of the needs variables. Third, the remaining variables of the system are called uncontrolled variables. These variables determine the magnitude or status of the need variables but are not directly under the control of community policies or decision makers.

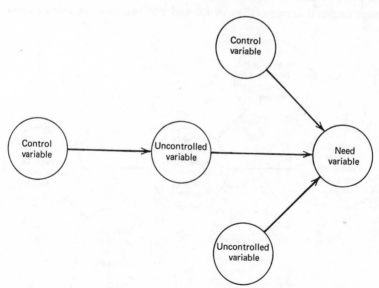

FIGURE 1.2   Relationships among types of variables in a system.

Although some of these may be indirectly affected by certain control variables, none can be directly controlled. A possible configuration of these types of variables is presented abstractly in Figure 1.2.

To illustrate these relationships less abstractly, let us continue with our health-care-system example. Underlying the need variable "amount of preventive child health care," let us say, are (1) the number of children in the community, (2) the number of trips made in the community to a child health care center, (3) the distance of the child-health-care center from the community, and (4) the income levels of the families with children in the community. These variables and the causal relationships among them are postulated in Figure 1.3.

In this system a control variable is available to the health care planners— the distance of the health care center from the community. If they plan to locate the center directly within the community, then the number of trips made to the center for preventive health care (an uncontrolled variable) is likely to increase, and the level of health care will be improved. The extent of improvement, however, also depends on the average family income level and on the number of children in the community. We assume that these are both uncontrolled variables, too. If the income level declines, then the community residents will be less able to afford transportation outlays, and as a result the number of trips will decline, further reducing the level of health care. Finally, if the number of children in the community increases, health care needs will increase.

These causal diagrams (Figures 1.2 and 1.3) can be considered as pictorial

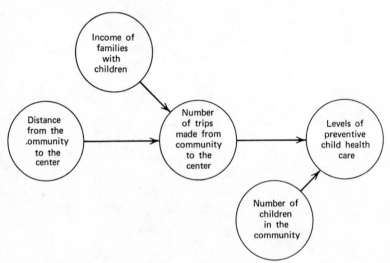

FIGURE 1.3   Determinants of the level of preventive child health care.

presentations of an elaborated needs gap equation. Recall that the needs gap equation (equation 1.1) states that

$$G = (St \times P) - Su$$

or, turned around,

$$(St \times P) - Su = G$$

As a causal diagram, this statement might appear as shown in Figure 1.4.

The difficulty with such a simple model, whether it be algebraic or diagrammatic, is that it gives little clue as to the real nature of the system in terms of controllable and uncontrollable causes. Assuming that little or nothing can be done about population size, this model presents only two ways of affecting the need gap: (1) by lowering the standard, which is counter to our purpose in setting the standard as part of the goal statement in the first place, or (2) by increasing the supply, which amounts to no more than a trite and redundant restatement of the original problem. We need to know what are the components, actions, and resources that can be manipulated to increase the supply. Thus the statement of Figure 1.4 is not untrue, it is just not very informative. It is helpful to recognize, however, at least in these initial stages of analysis, that one can use formulas and causal diagrams somewhat interchangeably. We can translate Figure 1.3, for example, into a general functional equation as follows:

$$H = f(D, T, I, C) \hspace{2cm} 1.2$$

where

$$D = \text{distance}$$
$$T = \text{trips}$$
$$I = \text{income}$$
$$C = \text{children}$$
$$H = \text{health care}$$

and $f(\ )$ indicates that some functional relationship exists among the variables arrayed within the parentheses. Whether that relationship is additive, logarithmic, or exponential, or the like is still not determined. That,

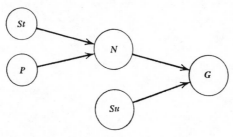

FIGURE 1.4   A diagram of the need gap equation.

in fact, is one of the questions about which the first half of this book is primarily concerned: given a set of variables, how can we determine their functional interrelations with one another as these affect a goal or set of goal variables. We shall consider this problem later.

Let us examine another example. Suppose that underlying the need variable, "amount of adult narcotics addiction treatment," are (1) the number of narcotics addicts in the community, (2) the degree of alienation among adults in the community, (3) the income level, (4) the amount of employable skills among adults, (5) the number of services offered at the center that are viewed by the addict as desirable, and (6) the addicts' likelihood of voluntary participation in a treatment center. A configuration of relationships among these variables is shown in the causal diagram of Figure 1.5. In this system there is one control variable available to the health planner, "the number of services seen as desirable by addicts." As this increases, more addicts will be encouraged to participate in the center's treatment program. If among the desirable services offered by the center is an effective job training program, then the quality of the addicts' employable skills will be improved and, as he obtains better employment, his income also will increase. With improved rewards from participating in the system, his sense of alienation from the system should decline, and his dependency on drugs should likewise decline, thereby reducing his need for treatment.

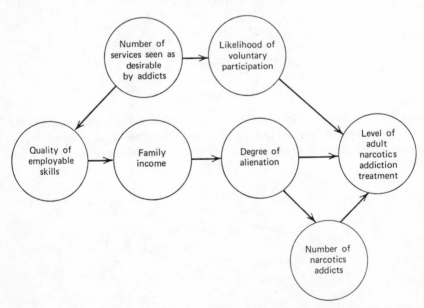

FIGURE 1.5   Determinants of the level of adult narcotics addiction treatment.

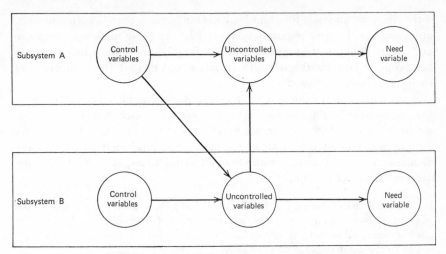

FIGURE 1.6   A simplified interdependent system of linked subsystems.

Now let us refer again to the two health systems we describe in Figures 1.3 and 1.5, preventive child health care and adult narcotics addiction treatment. Notice that the uncontrolled variable "family income" appears in both systems. But this variable can be affected by a control variable in the narcotics addiction system via the "employable skills" variable. Thus if the job training program is successful in achieving its *direct impact* on narcotics addiction in that system, it will also have an *indirect impact* on child health care in the other system. By taking account of these indirect impacts through the analysis of several systems or subsystems together, economies can be attained by planning programs so that the indirect impacts on goals, generated by each program, are anticipated and utilized.

A generalized portrayal of two systems that are linked to each other by shared variables is presented in Figure 1.6. Two linked systems of this kind, like our child health system and narcotic addiction treatment system, when considered together are often regarded as two subsystems within the larger community health system of which they are obviously a part. It is often quite difficult to determine where the boundaries of a system are, and this is part of the whole task of goal and problem definition. Some policy interests surely would say that narcotics addiction treatment is also linked to the whole system of law enforcement because the supply of narcotics clearly has a direct impact, and the needs for treatment and the control variables affecting supply are largely within the realm of the criminal justice and law enforcement system. Likewise, one could define the child health care system linkages to the educational system, as both child and adult education about nutrition and personal health practices are clearly control variables that could have direct impacts on goals for child health. Our point is that it is the interest, ambition, insight, and resources of those who use these models to influence and create policy and programs that will largely determine when a system has properly translated goals into variables and has set the boundaries of the system being analyzed.

We can ask now, of the system structure models we have been discussing, first, what are the final forms that these models assume and, second, once we have them, what is their practical value—how are they to be used? Just as was true of goal statements, these structural models, as we have demonstrated, can take on a number of alternate forms, each valid, yet each different. Some of them are:

1. A verbal model stating in words not just the general goal, but a goal variable or set of measurable and observable characteristics of the goal or need, as well as a set of controllable and uncontrollable factors that are considered to be causally linked to the need variable or variables.
2. A diagrammatic model that presents pictorially three basic types of variables in the system under consideration, and delineates the linkages among these variables and, perhaps, linkages to other systems and subsystems of importance.
3. A mathematical model stating in either generalized or specified terms and algebraic relations the variables and their interrelationships.
4. A physical model, a type that we have not demonstrated but that is used often in engineering and architecture and landscape architectural planning processes, in which an actual scale model of buildings, roads, public service location, and geographic conditions are represented in relation to one another in small-scale artifacts in three dimensions. A map, in fact, is considered such a model, but is only two dimensional. Many needs and goals cannot be adequately depicted in terms of a problem of physical dimensions, but it is a very rare goal that does not have some physically representable aspects of major significance.

The uses of these system models also parallel the uses of goal statements, which should be expected because, if properly done, system models are no more and no less than more detailed and elaborated restatements of goals and needs. Some of the uses of these models then are:

1. As a focus and discussion, either between planners and policymakers or between and among these groups and groups throughout the community, in an attempt to generate concern, information, support, or the redirection of action.
2. As a basis for decision, where this stage of analysis is either deemed adequate to inform decisions or where time, resources, and pressure prohibit further analysis.
3. As a basis for more penetrating research into the nature of the system and a more careful and informative specification of the model and the impacts of variables on each other as grounds for plan making and policy development evaluation.

1.4 GOAL INPUTS TO SUBSEQUENT STAGES OF PLANNING ANALYSIS

We have discussed, in the two previous sections of this chapter, first the definition of goals and their translation into need gaps at a very general level of analysis, and second the translation of these goal and need statements into more elaborate, but still general, causal models of problem systems. In this section we carry these goal formulations through the subsequent stages of planning analysis—system analysis, plan evaluation, and program management. We cannot, of course, do this in detail, as these tasks and the techniques for accomplishing them are the very purpose of the next six chapters. But what we will attempt to do is to create a scenario of what these subsequent tasks of planning analysis are and how they and goal formulation are linked to each other to constitute a rational process of planning analysis. We hope, thus, to create not only a wider context for what we have discussed in the earlier sections of this chapter but also to provide a fuller context for understanding what follows in the remaining chapters in Part I of this book.

1.4.1 SYSTEM ANALYSIS

The purpose of carrying the analysis of goals and needs further to a more detailed and rigorous system analysis is to attempt to verify whether or not the relationships among controllable, uncontrollable, and need variables that we postulated initially are in the real world factually true or false. If true, we attempt to measure more precisely the degree to which these assumed relationships tend to hold true and to make, where possible, quantitative estimates of the relative power of one variable, as a potential program instrument, versus another. We ask questions such as, if we change A, what impact will it have on B.

Suppose, for example, we consider only a part of the causal diagram that we posited in Figure 1.3 as the determining system of the level of preventive child health care. We deal with just the set of three variables shown in solid lines of Figure 1.7.

If we assume, for the time being, that a higher number of trips made to a health center will be associated with a higher level of health care, then we want to know whether, in fact, the number of trips made by a population is a function of their incomes (ability to bear the costs of making trips) or is a function of the nearness of the center, or possibly both, or neither. By looking at actual behavior we might find that, within certain extreme limits, income is not a factor, but that distance determines the convenience and willingness of people to use a health facility. Or we might find that income alone is the key factor, and that as long as income is adequate, distance can always be overcome with adequate finances. Or we may find that both are factors, in

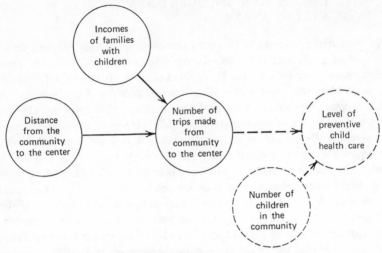

FIGURE 1.7   A subset of the child health care system variables.

which case we must ask if one is stronger than the other or if, in fact, their joint effect determines the number of trips made. Finally, we could possibly find no real connections, suggesting that we must look elsewhere for the true factors that affect travel to health centers.

How do we determine the answers to these questions? One way, which we discuss in detail in Chapter 2, is to conduct a sample survey of families, with children, of various income levels that live various distances from existing child health centers. If there are no such centers in our community, we may have to draw inferences from the behavior of other communities. The data might look like that in Table 1.3, although a real survey would certainly question more than six families.

Chapters 2 to 5 deal extensively with statistical methods for analyzing data, such as these, to determine whether or not there are distinct patterns of variation that support our hypothesized linkages among these variables. With just the small set of data we have here, even the untrained analyst can

TABLE 1.3
Sample Data on Family Behavior

Variables	Families					
	A	B	C	D	E	F
Income ($1000's)	15	4	9	4	3	8
Miles to center	3	1	5	6	4	2
Trips per month	3	6	2	2	3	5

probably see, after some thought, that an inverse relationship seems to exist between distance (miles to center) and trips per month. In family B, for example, the distance is very small while the number of trips is high. The same is true in family F. But in families C and D the inverse is true, distance is high and trips are few. It is very difficult, on the other hand, to detect any correlation between income and either of the other two variables. Does that mean that our assumption is wrong? Maybe. But we have not dealt with the possibility that our sample may not be drawn in a representative random manner, or the fact that it may not be large enough to be reliable. These are just a few of the statistical problems that empirical model construction must deal with. But let us suppose that we must base our decision on these data. Even the apparent inverse relationship between distance and travel could be just a product of chance. What is the probability that this happened by chance? And even if we were to find it reliable, would it not be better to be more precise about this relationship? Six trips for family B may not be high at all if family B happens to have eight children, just as two trips may not be low for a family with one child. Our paper experiment needs to control for other variables. Moreover, as we face questions of policy, just how close does the data indicate that a center must be before it attracts an adequate user response.

The analysis of the structural relationships among the variables of a system, at its best, brings many tools of quantitative analysis to bear on these questions. But let us suppose that our best analysis of the system's structure still strongly suggests that the location of the health center is a key policy control variable and that a system change of some kind is indicated. How can we evaluate alternative location patterns, since there may be several ways of accomplishing this change. At this point, we move on to another stage of planning analysis, that of plan and program evaluation.

1.4.2 Evaluating Plans and Programs

We are now into the third stage of the planning analysis process as it was defined in the first section of this chapter. We might imagine, now, that the results of our system structure analysis have been discussed extensively with policymakers and community organizations so that the alternative programs have been narrowed down to two feasible alternative locations: (1) a new health center located in the heart of the most densely populated area of the community, or (2) a new health center located in the lowest density area of the community. Both alternatives meet the general system criteria of putting the health facility within the community. But where in the community now becomes the question. Program evaluation at this point becomes a problem in the analysis of the effectiveness and costs of two quite specific alternatives. Among the problems we must investigate are the following.

First, we must consider the budget available. Land costs vary, and the high-density location will probably require more money for land, leaving less for construction and program operation—staff, equipment, and the like. We may be able to rely on the local bus system and walking to get people to the high-density area of the community, but the low-density location may require more room for parking, as more users will choose to drive. Funding sources, if they are linked with local banks, may prefer to have their money "invested" in the low-density area, and will thus offer a more favorable interest rate for that site than the other. A second consideration should be that of who will be better served. Poor families may find one site more accessible than middle income families, and these differential effects must be weighted. Third, there are a number of time considerations to be made. They include not only the investment costs and differences in capital outlays and interest returns, but may also include population growth trends and shifts in location of families that are foreseeable and that demonstrate long-run effectiveness to be quite different from short-run payoffs. The effect of the site on the scale of the center's operation must also be considered in terms of the feasibility of future expansion. The high-density site may not lend itself to expansion 10 years from now, while the low intensity (and cost) of land development near the other site may leave the center in a more flexible position. On the other hand, there may be certain external economies to the high-density location, such as nearness to a major hospital and its emergency, intensive care, and surgical facilities.

In some manner these criteria, and others, must be systematically applied to the two alternatives, and the results aggregated to conclude which alternative is the more beneficial. The techniques of cost/effectiveness analysis and benefit/cost analysis in Chapter 6 deal extensively with the tools of this process. Evaluation of this sort may, in fact, lead to further use of the models of system structure, at finer levels of detail than before, to resolve some of these questions. Many of the models presented in Part II of this book are in fact models that planners have actually found useful, over and over, in the analysis of some of the very questions we raise above.

But given the resolution of this choice problem, and a policy commitment to one of the alternatives over the other, the struggle to improve child health services is still not completely won. For now we must consider yet another set of problems in the arrangement and scheduling of the program's implementation.

1.4.3 SCHEDULING PROGRAM IMPLEMENTATION

We can view the implementation process from two points of view—the short run and the long run. Each perspective raises some important analytic problems.

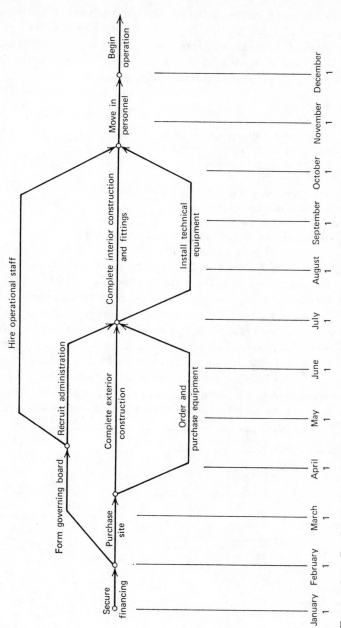

FIGURE 1.8   Implementation schedule for a community child health care center.

In the short run, the immediate future, the questions are: What do we do first, and then what do we do next, to get this health center operating? And how do we distribute our energies and resources to get the job done efficiently? We might, for example, make a list of jobs that need to be completed before the facility can open and begin operation. It might include:

1. Secure financing.
2. Purchase site.
3. Complete exterior construction work.
4. Complete interior construction work.
5. Order and purchase equipment.
6. Install equipment.
7. Establish a governing board.
8. Recruit an administrative staff.
9. Recruit an operating staff.
10. Move all personnel into quarters to prepare for opening.

Clearly, however, these things need not be done just one at a time. Although some must precede others, still others can be done in a parallel fashion, such as (3) exterior construction and (5) order and purchase of equipment. What is required is the sequential scheduling of these tasks in a manner that assists in the allocation of resources to their completion in order to complete the entire project within a desired period of time. An example of such a sequence is shown in Figure 1.8, spanning an 11-month period. We shall introduce techniques in Chapter 7 for constructing and analyzing schedules of this kind.

In the perspective of the long-run, other scheduling problems require solution. These are the problems of maintaining a continuous monitoring of

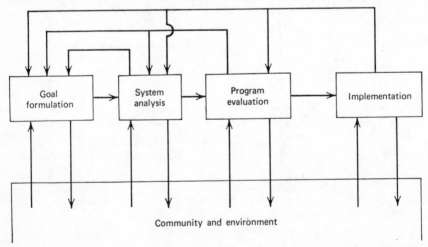

FIGURE 1.9   Information and feedback flows in the process of planning analysis.

the needs of the community and its various residents and of using this information to replan, reconstruct, and continuously adjust the programs, facilities, and services, through a continuing planning process. This continuous process of analysis and correction, originally shown in Figure 1.1 is portrayed again, here, in Figure 1.9.

PROBLEMS

1. By the year 1980 the city will need a total of 35 elementary schools. The city's present supply of elementary schools consumes 100 acres of land. By using an overall standard of 5 acres per school, how many additional acres of land will the elementary school system require by 1980?

2. The CBD (central business district) currently has a car parking capacity for 22,000 cars. There are an estimated two million sq ft of retail space in the CBD. At a standard of one parking space per 100 sq ft of retail space, what is the estimated current need gap in number of parking spaces?

3. The local newspaper editorial claims a current need for 425 additional hospital beds in the county. Given the present population of 85,000 and the standard of 10 beds per 1000 persons, what must the current supply of beds be?

4. The chairman of the regional parks commission claims that 16,000 additional acres of parkland are needed to bring the region up to standard. If there are three million people in the region and 20,000 acres currently in parks, what is the standard he is using?

5. The Conservation Association has recommended a standard for parkland of 10 acres per 1000 persons. In a township of 200,000 persons, which already has 400 acres of parkland, how many more acres would be required to bring the township up to the Conservation Association standard?

6. A local citizen group argues for a different standard for parkland for the central city area of the township. If the local group calculated a need gap of 300 acres for the central city area, given 20,000 persons in the central city area and its current supply of 100 acres, what standard are the local citizens using?

7. Draw a one-page schematic diagram or flowchart of the planning process that would be appropriate for presenting the process in clear, simple, and accurate terms in a public meeting.

8. In planning a community library system, it is found that the community's population can be divided into four groups of readers: (1) children, (2)

students, (3) leisure, and (4) technical. Assuming that no two groups read the same type of book, standards are established on the number of books per person required in an adequate library system for each type. These standards and estimates of the population and current stock of books in each group are given in the table below. Determine the need gap for

Population Group	Standard: Number of Books per Person	Estimated Population	Books in Stock Currently
Students	6	2,900	14,000
Children	4	2,100	9,500
Leisure	4	4,700	16,500
Technical	2	490	2,000

each population group. What is the total cost of books that would have to be purchased to bring all categories up to adequacy if the average purchase cost is $8.50?

9. Select one of the need variables mentioned in questions 1 to 5, or a different community problem of interest to you, and construct a causal diagram, based on your best knowledge and reasoning about the problem.

10. With reference to your causal diagram (problem 9), which variables are controllable by government? Which are controllable by private industry and business? Which are controllable only by individual consumer choice? Are any absolutely uncontrollable?

BIBLIOGRAPHY

Ackoff, Russell L. *Scientific Method: Optimizing Applied Research Decisions.* New York: Wiley, 1962.

Alexander, Christopher. *Notes on the Synthesis of Form.* Cambridge, Mass.: Harvard University Press, 1964.

Altshuler, Alan A. *The City Planning Process: A Political Analysis.* Ithaca, N.Y.: Cornell University Press, 1965.

American Public Health Association. *Planning the Neighborhood.* Chicago: Public Administration Service, 1948.

Arrow, Kenneth J. "Mathematical Models in the Social Sciences," in Daniel Lerner and Harold D. Lasswell (eds). *The Policy Sciences.* Stanford, Cal.: Stanford University Press, 1951.

Benson, Robert S., and Harold Wolman (eds). *Counterbudget: A Blueprint for Changing National Priorities 1971–1976*. New York: Praeger, 1971.

Blalock, Hubert M., Jr. *Theory Construction: From Verbal to Mathematical Formulations*. Englewood Cliffs, N.J.: Prentice-Hall, 1969.

Boyce, David E., Norman D. Day, and Chris McDonald. *Metropolitan Plan Making*. Philadelphia: Regional Science Research Institute, 1970.

Buchanan, James M., and Gordon Tullock. *The Calculus of Consent: Logical Foundations of Constitutional Democracy*. Ann Arbor, Mich.: University of Michigan Press, 1962.

Chapin, F. Stuart, Jr. "Foundations of Urban Planning," in Werner Z. Hirsch (ed). *Urban Life and Form*. New York: Holt, Rinehart, and Winston, 1965.

Chapin, F. Stuart, Jr. *Urban Land Use Planning*, second edition. Urbana, Ill.: University of Illinois Press, 1965.

Davidoff, Paul, and Thomas A. Reiner. "A Choice Theory of Planning," *Journal of the American Institute of Planners*, *28* (May 1962), 103–115.

Friend, J. K., and W. N. Jessop. *Local Government and Strategic Choice: An Operational Research Approach to the Processes of Public Planning*. London: Tavistock Publications, 1969.

Harris, Britton. "The Limits of Science and Humanism in Planning," *Journal of the American Institute of Planners*, *33* (September 1967), 324–335.

————. "Plan or Projection: An Examination of the Use of Models in Planning," *Journal of the American Institute of Planners*, *26* (November 1960), 265–272.

————. "The Uses of Theory in the Simulation of Urban Phenomena," *Journal of the American Institute of Planners*, *30* (November 1964), 317–322.

Lamanna, Richard A. "Value Consensus Among Urban Residents," *Journal of the American Institute of Planners*, *30* (May 1964), 100–109.

Leven, Charles L. "Establishing Goals for Regional Economic Development," *Journal of the American Institute of Planners*, *30* (May 1964), 100–109.

Lindblom, Charles E. "The Science of Muddling Through," *Public Administration Review*, *19* (Spring 1959), 79–88.

McLoughlin, J. Brian. *Urban and Regional Planning: A Systems Approach*. New York: Praeger, 1969.

Moore, Gary T. (ed). *Emerging Methods in Environmental Design and Planning*. Cambridge, Mass.: M.I.T. Press, 1970.

Mushkin, Selma J. (ed.) *Public Prices for Public Products*. Washington, D.C.: The Urban Institute, 1972.

President's Commission on National Goals. *Goals for Americans*. New York: Prentice-Hall, 1960.

Public Administration Service. *Action for Cities: A Guide for Community Planning*. Chicago: Public Administration Service, 1950.

Reiner, Thomas A. "The Planner as Value Technician: Two Classes of Utopian Constructs and Their Impacts on Planning," in H. Wentworth Eldridge (ed). *Taming Megaloplis*, Volume I. New York: Anchor Books, 1967, 232–248.

Urban Land Institute. *The Community Builders Handbook*. Washington, D.C.: Urban Land Institute, 1960.

Hare, Van Court, Jr. *Systems Analysis: A Diagnostic Approach*. New York: Harcourt, Brace and World, 1967.

Wheaton, William L. C., and Margaret F. Wheaton. "Identifying the Public Interest: Values and Goals," in Ernest Erber (ed). *Urban Planning in Transition*. New York: Grossman Publishers, 1970.

Young, Robert C. "Goals and Goal-Setting," *Journal of the American Institute of Planners, 32* (March 1966), 76–85.

Theories of rational planning are treated abstractly in the classic papers of Lindblom and Davidoff and Reiner. Theories of the process of planning analysis are found in the books of McLoughlin and Friend and Jessop. Altshuler and Boyce et al. present case material on the planning process in practice.

Problems of goal definition and aggregation at the level of general political and economic theory are treated extensively in Buchanan and Tullock. Professional practice relating to goals in urban planning is discussed in Chapin's "Foundations . . . ," Lamanna, Leven, Reiner, and Young. Examples of goal statements are the President's Commission on Goals, Benson and Wolman, and the Public Administration Service's *Action for Cities*. Examples of the use of standards in planning are found in the publications of the Urban Land Institute, American Public Health Association, and in Chapin's *Urban Land Use Planning*.

The concepts of models, control, and system structure are discussed nonmathematically in Van Court Hare, Jr., Alexander, and in the papers of Britton Harris. Partially mathematical presentations are found in Ackoff, Arrow, and Blalock. Some recent attempts to expand these ideas and applications are discussed in the large collection edited by Moore.

An alternative approach to need gaps is found in Mushkin which considers that standards and needs may be adjusted to take account of prices, congestion, and other kinds of costs.

CHAPTER 2

Planning Information

2.1 INTRODUCTION

A neighborhood association of parents wants the local school board to initiate a supplemental breakfast program in the neighborhood school. A few teachers have publicly claimed that too many students come to school without a breakfast and thus are doing poorly in reading and other academic tasks. Some parents claim, privately, that it is the problem of low income families. Spokesmen for several minority groups claim that the problem is not one of low income families but of undisciplined upper-income homes and poor teaching that lead to poor academic skills. The medical staff of the school board quotes research studies that fail to name the lack of a breakfast as a major contribution to malnutrition. The school board resists recognizing the problem.

Is there a problem? If so, what is it? Suppose that the community health planning center described in Chapter 1 faced this situation. What should it do? Clearly better information is needed. Of the many allegations and assertions that have been made, which ones are true? Is there a problem and what is its structure? The purpose of this chapter is to show how to conduct and to analyze a community survey, using this problem in education planning as a prototype.

First, we define the survey research process in general as the framework for considering the collection and analysis of planning information. Second, we discuss in detail the data collection process. Third, we demonstrate elementary statistical techniques for analyzing data and drawing conclusions. Throughout this chapter we focus on practical methods for analyzing the education problem posed above.

2.2 THE SURVEY RESEARCH PROCESS

The survey research process is composed of the following set of tasks.

I. Defining information needs and obtaining resources.
II. Collecting the data.
    A. Choosing the technique of observation.
    B. Defining the questions (variables).
    C. Determining the sample.
    D. Pretesting and conducting the survey.
III. Analyzing the data.
    A. Compiling and editing the raw data.
    B. Analysis of the distribution of response to a single question (variable).
    C. Analysis of the interrelations among variables.
    D. Interpreting the analysis.

The way in which information needs are initially defined determines much of the work that follows. Also, it largely determines how much in the way of resources is required to do the work. Simultaneously, of course, resource availability restrains the amount of information that can be gathered and generated from the analysis. Do we need to survey all students in the city elementary schools, or can our needs be filled with a sample of representative children from one classroom? Are complete physical examinations required to detect malnutrition or can the school nurse answer our questions from existing records? Do we need comprehensive, long-term case studies of specific children over a several-year period, or can a brief questionnaire administered to a cross section of students yield the data needed? Must a statistical consultant be hired, or can the entire process of collection and analysis be done by the staff of the local health planning agency? Do we need an electronic computer or a simple desk calculator?

The exact nature of these choices is presented in the following sections and is the substance of this chapter. They are raised above to emphasize that it is folly to decide to commit oneself to undertaking survey research without first, in some preliminary fashion, understanding what kind of data gathering and analysis is feasible with the level of resources available and then deciding whether those results are likely to be worthwhile.

One of the most frequent errors made in the initial planning of survey research is to spend too much time and money in gathering the data so that no resources are left to analyze them. Data collection and data analysis are not independent options. Obviously data cannot be analyzed if one does not first collect them. But not so obvious to many researchers, until it becomes too late to do anything about it, is that there is no point in collecting data if one does not then analyze them. Millions of dollars have been thrown away by so-called planning research by not understanding that collection of the data is only half the job and is useless by itself.

2.3 COLLECTING THE DATA

At the outset there are two kinds of data sources to which we might turn, primary data and secondary data. Primary data are first-hand information, gathered from original sources, for instance, through interviews, or going out and directly observing the phenomena that is being studied. Secondary data are second-hand data, data that someone else has gathered but that are available and may fit one's needs. Data collected by the United States Bureau of the Census, published and stored in the library, become a secondary source for everyone's use.

If there is any single criterion for distinguishing good data from bad data, it is summed up in the word "bias." Bias is what we are always trying to minimize and avoid. Bias means that somehow the data contain a systematic error and thus do not represent what we intended them to represent. Secondary data are often considered more likely to contain bias than primary data, causing them at times to be looked upon with suspicion. The data gathered in a first-hand survey are subject to many processes of definition and interpretation that may not fit the requirements of the secondary user. If the secondary user knows the technical procedures in which the data were gathered and finds them acceptable to his purposes, then there is no reason to claim bias. We now examine those technical procedures.

2.3.1 THE TECHNIQUE OF OBSERVATION

The technique of observation is the actual physical process by which the information is gathered. The choices may be classified as self-surveys, interviews, and direct inspection.

Self-Surveys

These are often in the form of questionnaires sent to respondents through the mail or of survey forms handed out to motorists or shoppers or inserted in newspapers and other publications. Mail-back questionnaires work fairly well in middle-income communities. Returns in excess of 50% are rare. They do not work well in low-income and high-income neighborhoods. The number of questions must be small in any case, and the possible answers must be few and uncomplicated. Essay questions do not work well.

Interviews

They can be face-to-face or by telephone. Face-to-face interviews are perhaps the more accurate technique, but any sort of interviewing is expensive. Interviewers must be trained and, since one-shot surveys cannot hire full-time interviewers, staffing a survey is difficult. In these circumstances, survey research centers, often affiliated with universities or with large businesses with full-time experienced staffs, are frequently used for major survey research jobs.

Direct Inspection

The direct inspection of conditions or activities is employed in making traffic counts, recreation area use surveys, housing quality studies, and many other kinds of surveys where human communication is not required to elicit the information directly. This is not always as easy as it sounds. Consider the problem of counting the number of rooms in a dwelling unit. We are faced with deciding when a space is so large that it is no longer a closet, but should be considered a room. Suppose the room has no roof. Is it still a room? Are the number of walls and the material from which they are made important? Is a tent a room? These become quite serious problems in, for example, an international survey of housing, and even in a national survey such as the United States Census of Housing where the conditions of climate and wealth vary widely throughout the population being surveyed.

Another well-known direct technique is participant-observation. The technique was developed by anthropologists in the study of community life. The surveyor becomes a resident of the community and lives among the people, learning their way of life by participating in it. It has been very effectively used by some social scientists in contemporary western cities to investigate problems of middle class and ethnic life.

What techniques of observation would be appropriate in the survey for our education problem? We want to know if a child eats breakfast every morning before going to school. We could telephone the parents to ask, but who would dare to respond that they do not give their children breakfast? We could mail a questionnaire to the parents on eating habits, or we could ask the children directly. We could even try to observe them at home, which would probably be very expensive, directly in terms of time and care required, and indirectly in terms of the delicate question of the invasion of privacy that would no doubt be raised. There is also a good chance that by interjecting ourselves we would change the reality we want to observe. The question of choice of techniques of observation rests primarily on these two criteria—*bias* and *cost*, both of which we always want to minimize but which are frequently interrelated in such a way that reducing one results in increasing the other. The choice of technique, then, is a problem of striking a balance of these two criteria.

Not all questions of information are open to so many different modes of observation. The question of a child's reading ability has been subjected to a great deal of analysis, and a reading test of some sort is widely considered superior to asking the parents of the child to score the child's reading skills. Thus the mode of observation is often largely determined by either the form or the substance of the question being asked.

2.3.2 DEFINING THE QUESTIONS

The questions of a survey are also called the variables of the survey. This means that each question constitutes an item for which we seek information about variation in the population being surveyed. Family income, as a variable or question in a survey, tells us how family income varies among those being surveyed. There are three basic structures of variation that are used in structuring the questions of a survey. These three structures are the three basic kinds of measurement scales: nominal, ordinal, and interval. We define each type, giving some examples of each, and then structure some questions for our education problem survey.

Nominal Scales

These are sets of names. Nominally scaled variables are those whose various possible answers are categories of different names. A question to which the answer is either "yes" or "no" is a nominally scaled question. Some examples of nominal scales are:

Sex	male, female
Color	black, red, white
Profession	doctor, lawyer, politician, clergy,
Armed service	army, navy, air force
Industry	oil, steel, auto, insurance

Nominal scales have no inherent order among the alternative responses. The requirements of a nominally scaled question are that the allowable responses be mutually exclusive, exhaustive of the possible relevant responses, and that the categories be constructed to best represent the levels of differentiation required by the problem being investigated in the survey.

Ordinal Scales

They put things in a ranked order. In the ranking of goals discussed in Chapter 1, we employed ordinal measurement. Some examples of ordinal scales are:

Priorities	1st, 2nd, 3rd, 4th, 5th
Social class	upper, middle, lower
Housing condition	Good repair, needs minor repair, needs major repair
Climate	cold, cool, warm, hot
Politics	radical, liberal, moderate, conservative

These are all examples of strong orderings. There can also be a weak ordering. Suppose a question asks you to rank four projects for your community: a park, a hospital, a street widening, and a library. If you are able to rank them, 1, 2, 3, 4, then you have a strong ordering. If you are indifferent among some of them, you have a weak ordering: for example, the hospital is of first priority and the street widening is least important, but the park and library are equally of secondary importance after the hospital.

Interval Scales

They provide a yardsticklike set of numbers for measuring the intervals between ordered responses. This is the most common everyday means of measurement. Dollars, distance, age, temperature, years of education, test scores, and weight are all usually measured on interval scales of numbers.

The full impact of the choices of measurement scales will be apparent when we begin to analyze data later in this chapter. What is important now is to recognize that each question in a questionnaire must be geared to one of these scale types. The type of scales chosen will set basic limits on the kinds of analysis that can be performed later. Thus, each question must be unambiguous as to its scale type. This is a prerequisite for nearly all forms of quantitative analysis. There are other forms of analysis that are nonquantitative and these, of course, can utilize surveys of unscaled, often called open-ended, questions. But techniques for the analysis of these data are a very complicated subject that we will not consider here.

Now, let us look at our problem and construct a questionnaire. We limit ourselves, arbitrarily, to four questions. These questions, drawn from our initial problem statement, are:

1. Does the student miss breakfast?
2. Is the student malnourished?
3. What is the family's income?
4. What is the student's reading ability?

We have already explored some of the observational difficulties of question one. But in addition to these, there is the problem of scaling the question. We could consider any of the following forms, each of which implies a different scale for question 1.

Nominal 1. Does the student come to school without breakfast?
　　　　　　　　　　　　　　_____Yes 　　_____No

Ordinal 1. How often does the student come to school without breakfast?
　　　　　　　　　_____Frequently,_____Occasionally, _____Never

Interval 1. How many times in the past six weeks has the student come to school without breakfast?
　　　　　　　　　　　　　　　　　　　　_____times.

The nominal form is quite ambiguous. Suppose the question is being posed of the students' morning teacher. Does the question mean to ask if the student ever has come to school without breakfast, or does it mean to ask if the student usually comes to school without breakfast. Even in the latter case, the question of defining "usually" is left up to the respondent. The ordinal form of the question also leaves a great deal of judgement in the hands of the respondent, but is more precise. The interval form is quite precise, but it may be too difficult in requiring a degree of precision that is beyond the competence of simple judgements. To answer the interval form responsibly might require six weeks of carefully interviewing the students each morning. This might actually end up in seriously biasing the responses as it might raise the level of consciousness of the students to the point that accurate answers would no longer be forthcoming. It also might take so much time out of the classroom teaching that the survey could be reducing the time the child learns to read, thus contributing to the very problem it is trying to help solve.

This range of alternatives, and their advantages and disadvantages, illustrates again the balance that must be sought in survey work between accuracy and effects, between bias and cost. Another good example of this problem in question design is illustrated in attempting to determine family income. Here are three alternate forms of question 3.

Nominal 3. Is the family poor? _____Yes, _____No.
Ordinal 3. Which annual income category is the family in?
_____Below $4000, _____$4000 to $10,000, _____above $10,000.
Interval 3. What is the family's annual income? _____

Here the different forms of the question vary in terms of precision and difficulty also. It should be noted that the interval scaled form still is not unambiguous. Are we looking for a dollar figure of precision down to the penny, the dollar, or is an answer rounded to the nearest thousand accurate enough? Furthermore, it is not clear whether we want to know the family's income for the past year or some average over several years. And none of these questions face the fact that the answer will have very different implications depending on the size of the family, their debts and savings, and other factors affecting their economic status apart from income alone.

To continue our demonstration of method, we assume that the following four questions are to be used in a survey of students.

1. How often does the student come to school without breakfast?
_____Frequently, _____Occasionally, _____Never.
2. Does the student exhibit physical signs of malnutrition?
_____Yes, _____No.
3. What was the income of the child's family during the past year?
$_____ (in 1000's)
4. What is the child's reading score? _____

We attempt to gather observations on a representative set of students by asking question 1 directly of the students, by asking question 2 of the school nurse, by asking question 3 of the parents, and by asking question 4 of the teachers, presuming a standard and fair reading test has been or will be administered. We now must consider selecting the sample.

2.3.3 SELECTING THE SAMPLE

In many surveys it is unnecessary and far too expensive to poll or interview everyone. That raises two problems: defining everyone, and selecting a sample from among them.

"Everyone" is usually termed—the population. It may be a population of people, houses, schools, industries, and the like. It is that set of entities about which one wants information. The population is usually defined as those items on a master list or map.

A sample, properly chosen, of some fraction of the whole is usually adequate to estimate the information accurately for the whole population. Where estimates from samples cannot be trusted, and adequate resources are available, the whole population can be surveyed. This is called a 100% sample. But a smaller sample is often the only feasible alternative. The problem is to make certain that the sample accurately represents the population. A sample that is not representative is called a biased sample. We discuss four alternative sampling techniques and their use in avoiding biased results.

Simple Random Sampling

Simple random sampling is the fundamental technique of sampling. Other kinds of sampling are variations on this method. It is the kind of sampling we do if we pick a card from a well-shuffled deck of cards. To be fair and accurately representative, every person or item from among those to be sampled must have an equal chance of being picked for the sample, and all combinations of individuals must have an equal chance of appearing. An interview technique called "snowballing," for example, violates these assumptions. It works like a chain letter; a person is interviewed and then is asked to recommend two more people to be interviewed, and so on. It is an effective way of studying a chain of personal linkages, but it is not a simple random sample.

Suppose we want a sample of the characteristics of 100 school children in, say, the third grade. First, we need a list of them. In the beginning, since we are picking at random, each has a 1 out of 100, or 1% chance of being chosen. After we have chosen one at random, 99 remain. For the second choice, each student has a 1 out of 99, or 1.01% chance of being chosen. For the third, each has a 1.02% chance. Can we truly say, then, that in a sample of 10 of them, everyone always had an equal chance of being chosen? No. But since our population is fairly large, we and statisticians agree that we need not worry very much about it. It is called sampling "without replacement." To keep the probabilities always equal, we would have had to replace the name of each student after it was chosen, thus making it possible (but not very highly probable) that some student would have been named in the sample more than once. "Simple random sampling," the standard name for the procedure we have just described, is usually assumed to be performed "without replacement."

Now, there are two things we have not really discussed, and they are vitally important. Where do you get lists of populations from which to sample, and how do you choose "at random?" Finding the right list, ready-made, is sometimes possible, but more often you must create your own. City directories, telephone books, motor vehicle registration lists, and the like, are often good sources of lists. They must be used carefully since lists of this kind are often out of date or are seriously biased by systematically excluding the poor, the young, and the aged who are less likely to have phones or cars. The point is simply that you must be very careful about having a list that really includes everyone you are going to draw conclusions about, or one that excludes people in an unbiased manner. The other techniques of sampling discussed below—systematic, stratified, and cluster sampling—are designed primarily to simplify the difficulties of lists.

Random choice can be accomplished with a variety of mechanical devices. The federal draft lottery, for example, chose birthdays in a random order by putting birth dates on blocks, mixing them in a tumbling cage, and then picking them blindfolded. The first list, you may recall, was not truly random though, because the mixing had not been thorough. Fortunately, such elaborate public demonstrations are not usually necessary. Statisticians have produced books full of tables of random numbers, and they are all you will probably ever need. A section of one of these tables is reproduced in Table 2.1. A larger table is given in Appendix II. Any reading of these tables down a column or any sets of columns, across a row or a set or rows, constitutes a random series of numbers. You simply open a book of these tables to an arbitrary page, arbitrarily pick a row or column and begin your selection. For example, with our students, there are 100 of them. While the number 100 is a three-digit figure, we only need a column of two-digit random numbers. Why not three? Because the one-hundredth student on the list can be represented by the two digits 00. Suppose we take the first two digits of column 1 in Table 2.1 and read down the column. The first line tells us to put student number 03 in our sample; the second line, student 38, and so on. This procedure would select a sample of six, including students numbered 03, 38, 17, 32, 69, and 24. Suppose we were to enlarge our sample. When we get

TABLE 2.1

Random Numbers

Line	Column			
	1	2	3	4
1	03991	10461	93716	16894
2	38555	95554	32886	59780
3	17546	73704	92052	46215
4	32643	52861	95819	06831
5	69572	68777	39510	35905
6	24122	66591	27699	06494
7	61196	30231	92962	61773
8	30532	21704	10274	12202
9	03788	97599	75867	20717
10	48228	63379	85783	47619
11	88618	19161	41290	67312
12	71299	23853	05870	01119
13	27954	58909	82444	99005
14	80863	00514	20247	81759
15	33564	60780	48460	85558
16	90899	75754	60833	25983
17	78038	70267	43529	06318
18	55986	66485	88722	56736
19	87539	08823	94813	31900
20	16818	60311	74457	90561

down to line nine, number 03 appears again. What do we do? We skip it because we are sampling without replacement. That's all there is to it.

Systematic Sampling

To take a systematic sample is to take every kth element from a list, say every tenth student or every fourth house on a block. Suppose, for example, we had an alphabetical list of the 100 students, and we wanted a sample of 6. We would do the following. First, we must find out how many times 6 divides into 100. The answer is 16 plus a fraction, but we must use whole numbers and always round down to the smaller number, 16, instead of using 17. This tells us to use every sixteenth student on the list. But there must be a starting place. Hence, to choose the starting place, we use a random number table to pick one of the first 16 students on the list, say, number 10. We then begin with number 10 and choose every sixteenth student until we have our sample of six. We would get students 10, 26, 42, 58, 74, and 90.

Notice that if, when we divided 6 into 100, we had rounded the answer up to 17, and if we also happened to choose number 17 in the first random choice, we would be stuck. Our sample would be 17, 34, 51, 68, 85, and 102. But there is no 102.

The technique of systematic sampling satisfies the requirements of a truly random sample as long as there is no bias in the ordering of the original list. Its great advantage is that it saves time and costs over simple random sampling. It is used, for example, in sampling from large unnumbered lists such as the telephone book, where simple random sampling would require first numbering every person in the book. Since the average number of persons on a page does not vary significantly, it is common to select a column and row at random, and then systematically take the person in that column and row on every page, or every fifth page, and the like, depending on the sample size.

Stratified Sampling

The technique of stratification is used to insure the representativeness of a sample where it might otherwise be unlikely. We might be interested, for example, in different evaluations of a community service by blacks, Puerto Ricans, and whites in a neighborhood that is 80% white, 18% black, and only 2% Puerto Rican. A small simple random sample might very well not include any Puerto Ricans and could easily contain an underrepresentation of blacks. To insure fair representation by using simple random sampling, we would have to make the sample size very large, and thus greatly increase the costs of the survey.

Stratification would deal with this problem by defining separate groups or lists, which are homogeneous, and then would take simple random samples or systematic samples from each group. The size of the sample taken from each group may be proportional to group size or disproportioned, depending on the information needs of the problem being studied. What constitutes a homogeneous group also depends on the survey objectives. In our school problem survey, for example, we might wish to be sure that males and females are equally represented, since there is a tendency for girls to differ from boys in their rates of physical and intellectual skill development. We could stratify our sample by sex in this case.

Cluster Sampling

Cluster sampling is very similar to stratified sampling, but the groups that are defined are heterogeneous. It is an alternative means for keeping the sample size small, thus keeping the costs down while insuring representativeness in the sample. Suppose that we are again in need of evaluations of a community service in a neighborhood, and we wish to insure a balanced view with respect to racial and ethnic groups. The lists that would be needed to stratify may be impossible to obtain. An alternative is to select clusters of blocks in the neighborhood such that the population in each cluster represents a balanced cross section of the neighborhood population. If these clusters can be identified, then either systematic or simple random sampling (or even stratified sampling) can be conducted within each of a few clusters. It will reduce costs considerably over other techniques and may be sufficient to yield a representative sample. For our school problem survey we might consider a particular class or grade within a school as a representative cluster of students.

What about sample size? How large should a sample be? There are some quite technical and fairly precise answers to these questions that will become clear in Chapter 4 when we discuss the role of sample size in tests of significance and the levels of confidence one can have in survey results as evidence. For the present, we can only state some general principles that are true and fairly useful.

1. The more disastrous the effect of poor information would be, the larger the sample required.
2. The more varied the responses are expected to be, the larger the sample required.
3. The larger the total population being sampled, the smaller the proportion of it that is required in the sample.

Each of these rules pertains only when other things are equal.

2.3.4 ADMINISTRATION OF THE SURVEY

Before the survey questionnaire is printed or the forms are run off, a presurvey test should be made. This should simulate real conditions. If the population to be surveyed is very large and the sampling proportion is small, then the test can be done with the target population. Otherwise, so as not to bias the real sample, an alternate but similar population should be used for the test. The test run will allow one more accurately to estimate costs in terms of time per interview or per question, allowing final adjustments in sample size or number of questions. It will also help one to spot the ambiguous questions, areas of misinterpretation, poor layout on the forms, and will help in formulating the special instructions and training that must be given to the survey personnel.

When surveys are conducted by a staff of interviewers or observers, some system of monitoring their performance is advisable to discourage and eliminate improper practices. It is not entirely uncommon to discover an interviewer who, being paid to walk the hot streets to collect his data, decides, instead, to spend the day in some pleasant form of relaxation while filling out the forms with make-believe answers.

2.4 ANALYZING THE DATA

Do not be misled by the title of this section. This entire book is devoted to various means of data analysis for planning. At this point, we are only introducing some of the most elementary and most widely used and general methods of data analysis. For some survey analysis, these techniques are sufficient. But for more specialized research, more advanced methods and models are required. We begin by looking at a set of raw data as it might be compiled in a small sample survey for our education problem. We then proceed to analyze these data, demonstrating various techniques appropriate for studying, summarizing, and drawing conclusions from them.

2.4.1 THE RAW DATA

Previously, in our discussion of the education problem survey, we defined four questions as our study variables. For short, we call these variables (1) missing breakfast, (2) malnutrition, (3) income, and (4) reading. Suppose, then, that we have conducted our survey and have gathered our data on six students. Let us call the students Art, Gabriel, John, Lee, Jessica, and Barbara. The raw survey data are shown in Table 2.2. This information is called raw data because nothing has been done to it. It is extremely important, when judging and evaluating the results of surveys, to know when one is looking at the original data and when one is looking at someone's subsequent manipulations. Even if one can be sure that the original questions in the survey and the raw data gathered with them are impeccably unbiased and perfectly in accord with the survey's intentions, a great deal of opportunity to sabotage the survey exists in manipulation and presentation.

2.4.2 ANALYZING THE DISTRIBUTION OF A VARIABLE

We first look at techniques for studying the characteristics of a variable as it stands alone. This requires the construction of a frequency distribution and the analysis of its properties.

TABLE 2.2
The Raw Data

	Art	Gabriel	John	Lee	Jessica	Barbara
Missing breakfast	Never	Frequently	Occasionally	Occasionally	Occasionally	Never
Malnutrition	No	Yes	No	Yes	Yes	No
Income	15,000	6,000	4,000	7,000	9,000	7,000
Reading	90	45	65	80	55	75

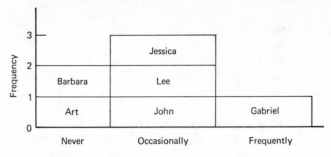

FIGURE 2.1 Frequency of missing breakfast.

Frequency distributions display the array of responses to a variable and indicate the frequency of each different response. Sometimes this can be easily stated verbally. For example, we can see by inspecting the raw data table that in response to the missing breakfast question there are two "nevers," three "occasionallys," and only one "frequently." With respect to malnutrition there are three yeses and three noes. The income and reading responses are nearly all different, however. They are best displayed graphically. In fact, all four variables can be easily displayed graphically. This is done in Figures 2.1 to 2.4 in the form of bar charts, also called histograms. The vertical scales up the left-hand side of each graph indicate the frequencies of responses. The horizontal scales indicate the distribution of possible responses on the measurement scale. Hence, the name—frequency distribution.

Central tendency is a property of frequency distribution that indicates the middle of the distribution or average response. There are three slightly different central tendency statistics, each defining the center in a different way. They are the mean, median, and mode.

The mean of a variable refers to the numerical average. It is determined by summing all of the response scores and dividing by the number of responses.

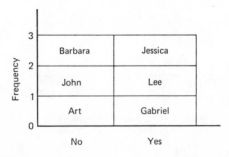

FIGURE 2.2 Frequency of malnutrition.

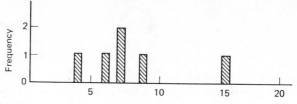

FIGURE 2.3   Frequency of income (thousands).

Thus the mean reading score is $90 + 45 + 65 + 80 + 55 + 75$ or 410 divided by 6, which is 68.33.

The median of a distribution is the point along the scale that divides the observations into two groups of equal numbers like the median strip of a highway.

In the reading variable, for example, the 70 value on the scale puts three people on either side. In this particular instance there is no precise definition of the median. In fact, any location between the scores of 65 and 75 would suffice, although the midpoint is usually taken in such a case. The case of the income variable is slightly different. Here the value of 7000 is the median because it divides the remaining four observations into groups of equal size—two below and two above.

The mode of a distribution is that value that occurs most frequently. For the income variable the mode is 7000, the same as the median. For the reading variable there is no mode, which is sometimes the case.

We have intentionally avoided discussion of the central tendency of the missing breakfast and malnutrition variables because the mean, median, and mode are all quite simple to apply to interval scaled variables, such as our income and reading variables, but their application to nominally and ordinally scaled variables is slightly more complicated. Let us look at the ordinally scaled missing breakfast first. A mean rank can be calculated, but it requires introducing a new and strong assumption. We can assign numerical values to the ranks, saying, for example, that never = 1, occasionally = 2, and frequently = 3. The choice of numbers is arbitrary and asserts an equal distance interval between ranks, which is equivalent to converting the order to an interval scale. Given these numerical assignments, we can calculate a

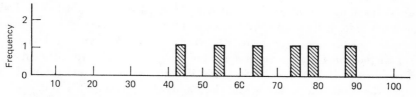

FIGURE 2.4   Frequency of reading scores.

numerical average as $1 + 1 + 2 + 2 + 2 + 3$ or 11 divided by 6, which is 1.83. This says that the mean is .83 greater than never or .17 less than occasionally but, since our raw data did not define occasionally as a number, the precision of 1.83 is misleading if it is taken literally. It is helpful because it indicates that the central tendency is closer to never than it is to frequently, but this is a kind of manipulating of the raw data that must be studied very carefully.

Similarly, the median of missing breakfast is ambiguous. We can see that it is somewhere within the range of occasionally, but exactly where is impossible to define. The mode, on the other hand, is very clearly occasionally. Now you can begin to understand why several different ways of describing the central tendency of a distribution are needed in statistical analysis.

The difficulties of specifying central tendency in nominal distributions are even further limited than in the ordinal case. When the nominal variable has only two possible values (called the binary case), it is sometimes legitimate to think of the two values as a continuum and convert it to an interval scale, such as setting no $= 0$ and yes $= 1$. If we did this in the malnutrition variable, we could speak of the mean and median as equal to .5. The problems of interpretation are similar to the ordinal case. But the binary case is the only situation in which this can be done. Since, by definition, there is no order in a nominal scale (such as a land use classification that might read as industrial land, commercial land, and residential land), it is truly meaningless to talk about a mean or median in such cases. The mode, however, is perfectly applicable. In our data on malnutrition there just happens not to be a modal value. Distributions such as our malnutrition and our reading data that have no modes are called flat or rectangular distributions.

The shape of the distribution is one of the important pieces of information we often look for. We want to know how most of the people scored or responded and what the range of their answers was; the frequency distribution gives us that information. Figure 2.5 illustrates some of the common variations in shapes of distributions that are encountered in data, classified according to type of measurement scale. There are several different ways of portraying some of these distributions, particularly the multimodel distributions.

Dispersion of the observations in a distribution is also a key characteristic of the distribution that is commonly defined in a formal way, just as central tendency is formally defined by the mean, median, and mode. The most used measures of dispersion are called the variance and the standard deviation and are measures of the average spread of the observations around the mean of the distribution. We introduce some algebraic notations that are used to define the mean, the variance, and the standard deviation. This simple form of notation is used almost universally in statistical work, and we use it

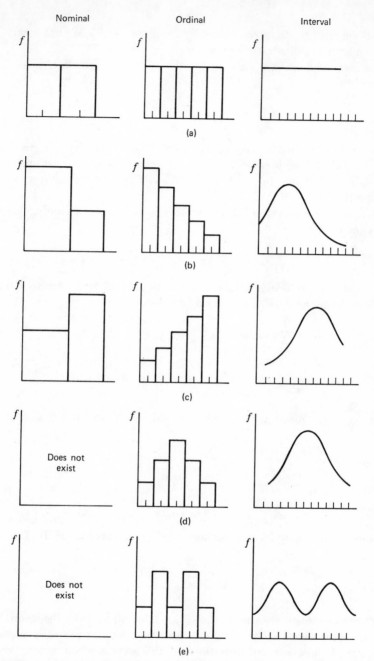

FIGURE 2.5 Common shapes of frequency distributions. (a) Rectangular or flat distribution. (b) Skewed distribution to the right. (c) Skewed distribution to the left. (d) Symmetrical or "normal" distribution. (e) Bimodal distribution.

extensively in later chapters, especially Chapters 4 and 5. We use our data on reading scores to illustrate the concepts.

The mean is defined in algebraic symbols as $\bar{x}$. Its formula is

$$\bar{x} = \frac{\sum\limits_{i=1}^{n} x_i}{N} \qquad\qquad 2.1$$

This says that the mean is equal to the sum ($\sum$), denoted by this greek letter sigma, of all of the observed values (x_i), beginning with the first one ($i = 1$) through the last one (n), and this sum is divided by the total number of observations (N).

Here is how it works. If there are six observations, six reading scores in our case, then

$$\sum_{i=1}^{6} x_i = x_1 + x_2 + x_3 + x_4 + x_5 + x_6$$

The numbers 1 to 6 index the people in our sample, from Art to Barbara. Therefore, for the reading scores we find that

$$\sum_{i=1}^{6} x_i = 90 + 45 + 65 + 80 + 55 + 75$$

or

$$\sum_{i=1}^{6} x_i = 410$$

Now to get the mean we just divide the sum by N, which is 6, so that

$$\frac{\sum\limits_{i=1}^{6} x_i}{N} = \frac{410}{6}$$

or

$$\bar{x} = 68.33$$

Now we are ready for the variance which is denoted as S^2. Its formula is

$$S^2 = \frac{\sum\limits_{i=1}^{n} (x_i - \bar{x})^2}{N - 1} \qquad\qquad 2.2$$

The numerator is the sum of the squared deviations from the mean. If the denominator were N, it would be clear that we are taking a numerical average of those squared deviations. If this were a whole population and not a sample of one, we would, in fact, use N in the denominator. But since it is a sample, and a small one at that, we can expect that the variance of the whole population of students that we are interested in contains more deviation than our small sample reveals. Thus to compensate for the tendency for a sample to underestimate the variance of a population, we use a denominator of $N - 1$ to enlarge our estimate of the variance over what we would get if we used N.

Squaring the deviations has two effects. Since some of the observed values are below the mean, subtracting the mean from them gives us a negative number. If we try summing these deviations from the mean, we find that they always add up to zero, which is not very informative about the dispersion of the distribution. Therefore, the first effect of squaring the deviations is to get rid of the negative signs, since any negative number, when squared, yields a positive number, for example, $(-3) \cdot (-3) = +9$.

The second effect of squaring the deviations is to give added weight to the larger deviations. A deviation of 2 from the mean will add 4 to our sum in the numerator. But a deviation of 3 will add 9. The 2 was doubled but the 3 was tripled. The squaring increases the effect of large deviations on the whole measure of variance.

The variance of our reading data is calculated as follows. Abstractly we know that the formula for the variance says that

$$S^2 = \frac{(x_1 - \bar{x})^2 + (x_2 - \bar{x})^2 + (x_3 - \bar{x})^2 + (x_4 - \bar{x})^2 + (x_5 - \bar{x})^2 + (x_6 - \bar{x})^2}{N - 1}$$

Since we have already calculated the mean $(\bar{x})$, which we round off to just plain 68, and we know the six reading scores and that $N = 6$, we can now write:

$$S^2 = \frac{\begin{array}{c}(90 - 68)^2 + (45 - 68)^2 + (65 - 68)^2 \\ + (80 - 68)^2 + (55 - 68)^2 + (75 - 68)^2\end{array}}{6 - 1}$$

$$S^2 = \frac{(22)^2 + (-23)^2 + (-3)^2 + (12)^2 + (-13)^2 + (7)^2}{5}$$

$$S^2 = \frac{(484) + (529) + (9) + (144) + (169) + (49)}{5}$$

$$S^2 = \frac{1384}{5}$$

$$S^2 = 276.8$$

Since the variance usually turns out to be a rather large and awkward number, its square root, the standard deviation is more commonly reported in statistical studies. The standard deviation is denoted by the letter S, when

$$S = \sqrt{S^2}$$

The standard deviation for our reading data is then

$$S = \sqrt{276.8}$$

which is approximately $= 16.6$. With respect to our reading scores, we now can say that the mean observed score is approximately 68 and the standard deviation from the mean is about 17 points, which is a standard index of the degree of dispersion in the distribution. The principal formulas to remember are two: the mean and the standard deviation of a sample. To reiterate, they are

$$\bar{x} = \frac{\sum_{i=1}^{n} x_i}{N} \qquad 2.3$$

and

$$S = \sqrt{\frac{\sum_{i=1}^{n} (x_i - \bar{x})^2}{N - 1}} \qquad 2.4$$

It is common in statistical survey reports, where many variables have been studied, to include a table that gives the mean and standard deviation of each variable, instead of the actual graphic displays of each frequency distribution. Keep in mind, however, that these tables are only rough indicators of the character of the distributions and do not tell us if the distribution is flat, skewed, symmetrical, or multimodal. Do not be misled by fancy statistics. The sure way not to be misled, while still using statistics as a tool, is to understand how these indicators of distribution are derived.

2.4.3 ANALYZING THE RELATIONSHIPS AMONG VARIABLES: CROSS TABULATION OF FREQUENCY DISTRIBUTIONS

While the distributions of variables are interesting and informative, the key questions usually focus on the interrelationships among variables. Our initial questions were about the effect of income on breakfast habits, the relationship of malnutrition to breakfast, and the effects of these variables on reading scores as a general indicator of academic performance. We now consider some graphic techniques for exploring these relationships, in the form of two-way frequency distributions.

Let us begin with our first two variables: missing breakfast and malnutrition. Do they appear statistically related? The data are given in raw form in Table 2.3.

TABLE 2.3
Raw Data on the First and Second Variables

	Art	Gabriel	John	Lee	Jessica	Barbara
Missing breakfast	Never	Frequently	Occasionally	Occasionally	Occasionally	Never
Malnutrition	No	Yes	No	Yes	Yes	No

We construct a table that reveals this coincidence or combination of scores jointly on the two variables. This is done in Table 2.4. We enter the names of the students in the cells that represent their scores on both variables.

In the usual display of such a cross tabulation we enter in each cell the frequency with which observations are found in that combination. This is shown in Table 2.5.

After constructing the table, our next task is to interpret it. We want to consider the patterns of all frequencies. Table 2.5 suggests a fairly strong pattern of correlation between the two variables—as the absence of breakfast increases, so does the incidence of malnutrition. If there was no evident relationship among the variables we would have expected a more uniform distribution over the cells, with perhaps a one in each cell, or some seemingly random pattern.

Is family income a factor that is correlated with malnutrition? Let's look at a cross tabulation of our second and third variable, shown in raw form in Table 2.6.

We immediately encounter a technical difficulty. Income is a continuous interval scale. To construct a table with income as one dimension we must

TABLE 2.4
Cross Tabulation of Malnutrition and Missing Breakfast

Malnutrition		Never	Occasionally	Frequently
	Yes		Lee Jessica	Gabriel
	No	Art Barbara	John	
			Missing breakfast	

TABLE 2.5
Cross Tabulation of Malnutrition and
Missing Breakfast, Standard Form

Malnutrition	Never	Occasionally	Frequently
Yes		2	1
No	2	1	

Missing breakfast

somehow break it up into categories. One alternative we might try is to divide income responses into high and low, using the mean value, which is $8000, as the dividing point. This gives us Table 2.7.

The distinct impression given by this table is that there is no relationship between the variables. Half of the low income children are malnourished, and half are not. The same is true of the children from high income families.

TABLE 2.6
Raw Data on the Second and Third Variables

	Art	Gabriel	John	Lee	Jessica	Barbara
Malnutrition	No	Yes	No	Yes	Yes	No
Income	15,000	6,000	4,000	7,000	9,000	7,000

But what if we divided the income scale up in a different fashion? Could the appearance of these data change? It certainly could, and that is why it is so important to be able to distinguish raw from processed information, and properly processed from improperly processed data. Suppose, for example, we divided income into high, medium, and low. A reasonable way to do this

TABLE 2.7
Cross Tabulation of Income
and Malnutrition

Income ($\bar{x}$ = $8000)	No	Yes
High	1	1
Low	2	2

Malnutrition

TABLE 2.8
A 3 × 2 Cross Tabulation of Income and Malnutrition

Income		No	Yes
	High ($11,795)→	1	
	Medium ($4,205)→	1	3
	Low	1	

Malnutrition

would be to calculate the standard deviation of the income data from the sample we have been discussing, which is about $3795. We could then say that any observation that is within $3795 of the mean, on one side or the other, will be considered medium income. Those more than $3795 above the mean will be considered high, and those more than $3795 below the mean will be considered low. Now we obtain a table such as Table 2.8.

Now a clear pattern emerges. Among the extremes of both low and high income there is no malnutrition. But three out of the four medium income students show signs of malnutrition. The data suggest that the parents who were accusing the poor and the rich, respectively, for causing the problem were in both instances quite wrong.

The cross tabulation of missing breakfast and reading scores also shows a fairly strong correlation. Two alternative ways of tabulating this are shown in Tables 2.9 and 2.10. One table uses the mean to divide reading scores into high and low, the other uses the standard deviation, just as we did with income, to make three categories of reading scores.

TABLE 2.9
A 2 × 3 Cross Tabulation of Reading and Missing Breakfast

Reading		Never	Occasionally	Frequently
	High $\bar{x} = 68$	2	1	
	Low		2	1

Missing breakfast

TABLE 2.10
A 3 × 3 Cross Tabulation of Reading and Missing Breakfast

Reading		Never	Occasionally	Frequently
	High (85)	1		
	Medium (51)	1	3	
	Low			1

Missing breakfast

Using the two alternative partitions of income again, we show the relation of income to missing breakfast in Tables 2.11 and 2.12. In neither case does there appear to be a very clear relationship.

The relation of malnutrition to reading is shown in Table 2.13.

We have looked at all combinations of variables in our survey except one—reading and income. In this instance we have two interval scale variables. A scatter diagram is usually used to display graphically two variables of this sort, which avoids the difficulties and pitfalls of setting up class intervals as we previously did, dividing the scores into high, medium, or low categories. Figure 2.6 shows the scatter diagram for these variables, each dot representing one observation. The name of the observation is printed near each dot.

Again, we can see a trend of correlation between the variables, as the dots are scattered from the lower left to the upper right of the graph.

2.4.4 INTERPRETING THE ANALYSIS

Finally, what can we conclude from our analysis? Is there a problem? If so, what is it? We undertook our survey and analysis in response to a proposed

TABLE 2.11
A 2 × 3 Cross Tabulation of Income and Missing Breakfast

Income		Never	Occasionally	Frequently
	High ($\bar{x} = \$8000$)	Art	Jessica	
	Low	Barbara	Lee John	Gabriel

Missing breakfast

TABLE 2.12

A 3 × 3 Cross Tabulation of Income and Missing Breakfast

Income	High ($11,795)	Art		
	Medium	Barbara	Lee Jessica	Gabriel
	($4,205)			
	Low		John	
		Never	Occasionally	Frequently
			Missing breakfast	

school breakfast program and a flurry of allegations as to what might be the contributing causes of poor reading skills in some students. Can our data help us now to sort out the true from the false hypotheses and to suggest what effects we might reasonably expect from a breakfast program if it were instituted? There are no formulas for interpreting our analyses. The procedure we use, as an example, is: first, to look at some of the potential interrelations of our variables; second, to look at the actual interrelations found in the data; and third, to draw some conclusions about the policy implications of the findings.

In the world of pure abstraction and speculation each of our four variables is potentially related to all of the others, and this network of interconnections can be portrayed as is shown in Figure 2.7. Figure 2.7 represents one extreme state of the system. If, in reality, all variables were interlinked in this way, it would pose an extremely difficult situation to handle. It would virtually be impossible to predict what would happen if we began a breakfast program.

TABLE 2.13

Cross Tabulation of Reading and Malnutrition

Reading	High ($\bar{x} = 68$)	2	1
	Low	1	2
		No	Yes
		Malnutrition	

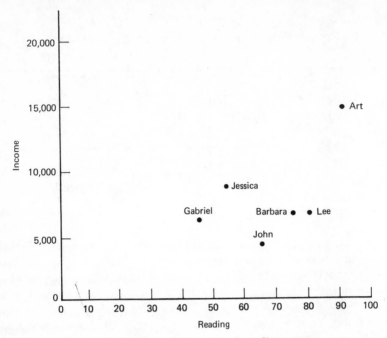

FIGURE 2.6 A scatter diagram of income and reading scores.

An alternate extreme situation would be one in which no linkages existed whatsoever. We believe, however, that reality is somewhere in between these two extremes and that there is some order to these linkages which, of course, is why we have undertaken the survey in the first place.

A highly believable hypothesis, intermediate between these extremes, might be the one shown in Figure 2.8, which suggests that low income leads

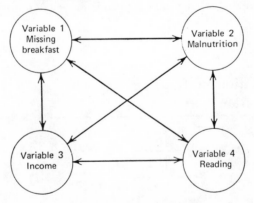

FIGURE 2.7 All potential linkages among the variables.

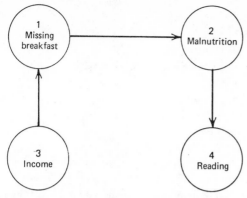

FIGURE 2.8. A believable hypothesis of linkages.

to deficiency in breakfasts which leads to malnutrition which leads to low reading scores.

Now let us look at the findings of our analysis and see what they suggest. As we can see from our diagram of all potential linkages (Figure 2.7), there are six possible pairings of the variables in relations with one another. They are variables 1 and 2, 1 and 3, 1 and 4, 2 and 3, 2 and 4, and 3 and 4. Table 2.14 lists each of these possible pairings, and beside each potential relationship we have written a judgement as to whether the relationships in our data reveal the link to be strong, weak, or none.

The reader may not agree with our judgements. They were made from studying the two-way frequencies in Tables 2.4 to 2.13 and in Figure 2.6. He should check his judgement against ours. Later chapters introduce more systematic and less arbitrary methods for making judgements like these. There are some very sophisticated tests of relationship but, since we are not assuming knowledge of them yet, we must rely on our judgements. Accepting

TABLE 2.14
Found Strength of Relations

Potential Relations Among Variables	Judged Strength of Found Relations
1 and 2	Strong
1 and 3	None
1 and 4	Strong
2 and 3	Weak
2 and 4	Strong
3 and 4	Weak

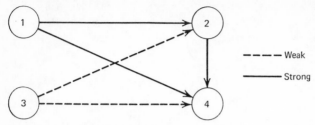

FIGURE 2.9   Graph of found relations.

these found relations, we can now portray our linkages, as revealed through our analysis in Figure 2.9.

We have, in fact, made another judgement, which is shown in the graphed relations, about the direction of the relation. There is nothing in the data that shows that malnutrition caused poor reading scores. Many philosophers would argue that we have no grounds for putting the arrow going in one direction and not in the other. We have indeed no statistical grounds in our data. For this we must rely on our other knowledge of the system that we are studying.

Can we now draw any policy conclusions from our analysis? Accepting, at least for the sake of the demonstration, that Figure 2.9 represents sound information, we can see that several things affect reading. Income affects it slightly and missing breakfast affects it directly, as does malnutrition. One difficult problem, at least with our limited data, is the question of whether malnutrition is, in fact, having an effect all its own or whether it is operating only as a direct consequence of the missing breakfast variable in concert with the (weak) effects of income. To answer that question is very difficult, especially since we have such a small number of observations. But even within the confines of our limited data and statistical techniques, we can say that a breakfast program can be expected to have good effects on reading scores. We can also say no, that income is not the key to the breakfast problem, while it does weakly affect reading. And malnutrition probably will continue to have a debilitating effect on reading performance, even if a breakfast program is established. Income producing programs and direct health services to the malnourished also would clearly improve the situation. A breakfast program is only, perhaps, a beginning.

PROBLEMS

1. Pick a simple random sample of a type of business establishment from the Yellow Pages of your telephone directory, for example, a sample of 15

drugstores. Study the sample of the population. Does the sample seem to be representative? On what criteria do you base your answer?

2. What level of measurement is implied in the following variables?
   (a) Human age, in years.
   (b) Sex: male or female.
   (c) Human age: young, middle-aged, old.
   (d) Color: red, green, yellow.
   (e) Construction material: brick, steel, wood, glass.

3. What type of sample is being taken in each of the following situations?
   (a) Sampling from two groups, males and females, such that the proportions of males and females in the sample are the same as in the population as a whole.
   (b) Beginning from a random place, take every fifteenth name from a list.
   (c) Assign a number to every industry in the region and, using a column of random numbers, select a sample of 10.

4. In Elgin County there are 20 municipalities. The number of fire stations in each municipality is given in the table below.
   (a) Plot a frequency distribution for these data.
   (b) Determine the mean.
   (c) Determine the median.
   (d) Determine the mode.
   (e) Determine the range.
   (f) Determine the standard deviation of the population.

Town	Number of Stations	Town	Number of Stations
1	3	11	3
2	10	12	6
3	2	13	5
4	1	14	2
5	7	15	1
6	3	16	3
7	6	17	0
8	0	18	5
9	2	19	1
10	8	20	12

5. A raw data table is given at the top of page 58.
   Problem: Construct frequency cross tabulations among all possible pairs of these four variables, partitioning the interval scales at their means.

		CENSUS TRACTS					
	VARIABLES	A	B	C	D	E	F
W	Average number of persons per residence	1	5	2	4	7	3
X	Average number of rooms per residence	3	6	4	5	6	2
Y	Housing quality (1 = high, 2 = medium, 3 = low)	1	3	2	2	3	1
Z	Is bus service adequate?	No	Yes	No	Yes	No	No

Use the original partitions of the ordinal and nominally scaled variables. Interpret, in a sentence, each cross tabulation.

6. A random sample of voters in a county were asked whether or not they would vote for an environmental quality bond issue. As technical consultant to the local environmental group, ECOALITION, you have been asked to analyze the following data and answer the questions below.

RESPONDENT	PREFERENCE REGARDING BOND (F = FOR, A = AGAINST)	INCOME LEVEL (H = HIGH, L = LOW)	PARTY AFFILIATIONS (R = REPUBLICAN) (D = DEMOCRAT)
1	F	H	D
2	F	H	R
3	F	L	R
4	A	L	R
5	A	H	R
6	F	H	D
7	A	L	R
8	F	H	D
9	F	L	R
10	F	H	D
11	A	L	D
12	A	H	R
13	A	L	D
14	A	H	R
15	A	L	D
16	F	H	D

Question 1. Is there any relationship between income and voting preference? If so, what is it?

Question 2. How does party affiliation affect the relationship between income and voting preference?

Question 3. ECOALITION would like to know on which of the different income and party affiliation groups they should expend their resources in hopes of generating more support for the bond. Assuming that the sample accurately reflects the population, rank the various groups in order of priority. Write a brief memo outlining priorities in terms of groups, estimating in percentages what portion of resources should go to each of the different groups.

BIBLIOGRAPHY

Berry, Brian J. L., Sandra J. Parsons, and Rutherford H. Platt. *The Impact of Urban Renewal on Small Business: The Hyde Park-Kenwood Case.* Chicago: Center for Urban Studies, University of Chicago, 1968.

Blalock, Hubert M., Jr. *An Introduction to Social Research.* Englewood Cliffs, N.J.: Prentice-Hall, 1970.

———. *Social Statistics,* second edition. New York: McGraw-Hill, 1972.

Bogue, Donald J. *Skid Row in American Cities.* Chicago: Community and Family Study Center, University of Chicago, 1963.

Burton, T. L., and G. E. Cherry. *Social Research Techniques for Planners.* London: George Allen and Unwin Ltd., 1970.

DuBois, W. E. B. *The Philadelphia Negro: A Social Study.* New York: Schocken Books, 1967. First published in 1899.

Heer, David M. (ed). *Social Statistics and the City.* Cambridge, Mass: Joint Center for Urban Studies of the Massachusetts Institute of Technology and Harvard University, 1968. Distributed by the Harvard University Press.

Holleb, Doris B. *Social and Economic Information for Urban Planning,* Volume 2. Chicago: Center for Urban Studies, University of Chicago, 1969.

Hyman, Herbert. *Survey Design and Analysis: Principles, Cases, and Procedures.* New York: The Free Press, 1955.

International City Management Association. *The Municipal Year Book 1971.* Washington, D.C.: International City Management Association, 1971. Published annually.

Kish, Leslie. *Survey Sampling*. New York: Wiley, 1965.

Labovitz, Sanford, and Robert Hagedorn. *Introduction to Social Research*. New York: McGraw-Hill, 1971.

Rainwater, Lee, and William L. Yancey. *The Moynihan Report and the Politics of Controversy*. Cambridge, Mass.: The M.I.T. Press, 1967.

Sternlieb, George. *The Tenement Landlord*. New Brunswick, N.J.: Urban Studies Center, Rutgers University, 1966.

Sudman, Seymour. *Reducing the Cost of Surveys*. Chicago: Aldine, 1967.

United States Department of Commerce, Bureau of the Census. *The 1970 Census User's Guide*, Part I. Washington, D.C.: U.S. Government Printing Office, 1967.

————. *County and City Data Book, 1972*. Washington, D.C.: U.S. Government Printing Office, 1973.

————. *Directory of Federal Statistics for Local Areas: A Guide to Sources, 1966*. Washington, D.C.: U.S. Government Printing Office, 1966.

————. *Statistical Abstract of the United States, 1970*. Washington, D.C.: U.S. Government Printing Office, 1970 (revised annually).

Warren, Roland. *Studying Your Community*. New York: The Free Press, 1955.

The studies by Bogue, Berry, DuBois, and Sternlieb are prototypes of superior work in the application of survey research methods, as they are described in this chapter, to urban policy problems. Each study contains documentary materials on how the survey was conducted, including copies of the questionnaires used, and carries the analysis through to the policy implications of the research. The book by Rainwater and Yancy is a careful documentation of the history of a famous policy report and the events surrounding its publication.

Some excellent reference works containing secondary urban data are the *County and City Data Book, Directory of Federal Statistics for Local Areas, The 1970 Census User's Guide, Part I, The Municipal Year Book*, and *Statistical Abstract of the United States*. An important set of papers is contained in the book by Heer, critically documenting the deficiencies of the 1960 United States census, especially in its mistreatment of minority population groups. An extensive reference guide to data sources for urban planning is the work by Holleb, in which abstracts of contents are listed covering data on population, housing, transportation, economics, education, social welfare, health, public safety, environment, and leisure.

Blalock (1970) and Labovitz and Hagedorn are introductions to survey methods and their role in research. Warren's book is an exhaustive review of the questions that are relevant to community surveys, covering nearly every aspect of community life. Blalock (1972) is an excellent handbook on statistical methods, and Hyman is the standard general reference on survey research. Kish and Sudman are excellent but very advanced reference works on the technical aspects of surveys. The short volume by Burton and Cherry is a nonmathematical presentation of survey research techniques which is especially directed to urban planners in Great Britain.

CHAPTER 3

Decision Models of Choice and Chance

3.1 INTRODUCTION

In this chapter we present several techniques of analysis taken from probability theory and demonstrate their use in the analysis of policy decisions. We examine the techniques through the analysis of two typical planning problems. The first is that of defining alternative policy choices for regional urban development. The second deals with the question of whether or not to provide a traffic accident service in a resort community.

The first problem is very general in nature. We presume that the governor of a large urbanized state and the mayors of the major cities of the state have agreed to come together to discuss alternative future patterns of urban expansion and to seek a common ground for concerting urban development policy. They are concerned with industrial location, the development of governmental projects in recreation and transportation, and the limitation of overcrowding in central cities. Our problem is to devise a systematic presentation of development alternatives that provides a focus for this discussion and assures that each of the various criteria for policy consideration is treated in the context of the whole pattern of urban development.

The second problem also deals with choices but in more particular detail. A summer resort community is faced with serious problems of traffic accidents and jams because of disabled vehicles. The town council is faced with the question of whether or not to contract for a traffic accident service to handle these problems over weekends. We have available certain information about the probabilities of accidents and the costs and inconveniences of not having an accident service. Our task is to analyze the situation to determine whether or not the town should purchase such a service and, if so, how much they should be willing to pay.

Both of these problems have at their bases the analytic problem of describing alternative outcomes. We begin with the introduction of decision trees and their use in constructing alternatives, leading to the fundamental principle of counting. We then turn to the assignment of probabilities to events and outcomes and the problems of assessing the interdependence of events. This probability problem also allows us to understand further several concepts introduced in Chapter 2. We then combine the use of decision trees and the probabilities of events in the analysis of a particular probability process leading to the binomial distribution and, finally, to the unit normal probability distribution, one of the most general and pervasive concepts in the field of probability and statistical analysis.

3.2 CONSTRUCTING ALTERNATIVE PLANS

We first examine a tool called the decision tree and use it to construct alternative plans from among a variety of plan components. Our problem, as sketched in the introduction above, is to present broad general alternatives to the governor and the mayors for the discussion of urban growth policy coordination. Our procedure will be (1) to identify the salient components of urban growth policy that are relevant to the kinds of decisions the policy-makers want to consider coordinating; (2) to specify the alternative forms of each component that should be considered; and (3) to systematically combine these component alternatives into alternative plans through the use of a decision tree graph.

Let us initially look at only two components of urban development—the land use pattern, and the pattern of major transportation routes. By land use pattern we mean the form of relatively dense urban use of land. The transportation system, for our purposes, will be defined as the principal pattern of major highways over a metropolitan area. Each of these components of urban development are subject to considerable public policy influence from both the regional and local levels of government.

Our second step is to define alternative values of each of these components or variables. With regard to land use we might suggest two alternatives; one is continuous expansion which is the current trend of development, and the other is nucleated expansion which might represent a new town program. These two alternatives are depicted in Figure 3.1.

With regard to transportation we might consider either a radial system of highways or a grid system of highways, as is depicted in Figure 3.2.

Perhaps everyone can intuitively grasp at this point that there are four possible combinations of land use and transportation patterns in our analysis. But we want to make use of a formal technique that allows us easily to define much larger choice problems of this sort that cannot be grasped

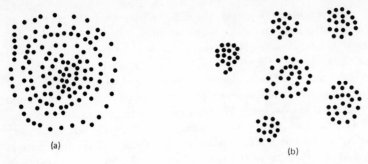

(a)

(b)

FIGURE 3.1 Land use alternatives. (a) Continuous expansion. (b) Nucleated expansion.

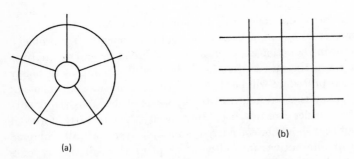

(a)

(b)

FIGURE 3.2 Transportation alternatives. (a) Radial highway pattern. (b) Grid highway pattern.

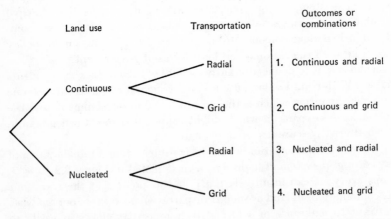

FIGURE 3.3 A decision tree of combined metropolitan growth alternatives.

FIGURE 3.4   Star-shaped expansion.

intuitively. Our technique is a tree graph or decision tree. The decision tree that combines our metropolitan growth alternatives is shown in Figure 3.3.

Suppose, now, that we were to add another alternative to the land use set—a star-shaped pattern of growth (Figure 3.4), combining some of the feature of both continuous and nucleated expansion. Our new decision tree will now look like Figure 3.5. Notice that introducing one more alternative element produced two new alternative combinations. Incidentally, we have also transformed the nature of the land use variable from a nominal scale to a scale that could be interpreted as being ordinal.

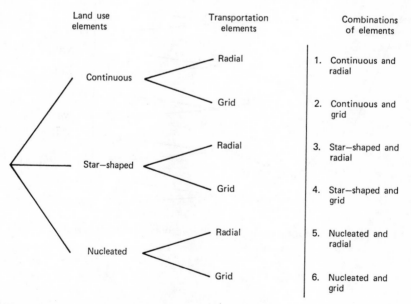

FIGURE 3.5   Six metropolitan growth alternatives.

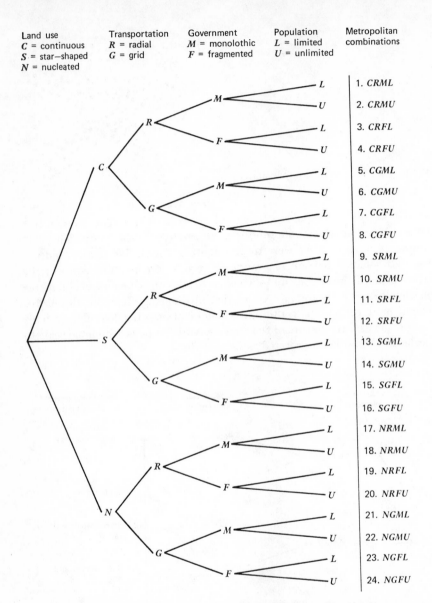

Land use	Transportation	Government	Population	Metropolitan
C = continuous	R = radial	M = monolothic	L = limited	combinations
S = star–shaped	G = grid	F = fragmented	U = unlimited	
N = nucleated				

1. CRML
2. CRMU
3. CRFL
4. CRFU
5. CGML
6. CGMU
7. CGFL
8. CGFU
9. SRML
10. SRMU
11. SRFL
12. SRFU
13. SGML
14. SGMU
15. SGFL
16. SGFU
17. NRML
18. NRMU
19. NRFL
20. NRFU
21. NGML
22. NGMU
23. NGFL
24. NGFU

FIGURE 3.6   Twenty-four metropolitan alternatives combinations.

Suppose, further, that we were to add some additional variables to be considered in the whole combined pattern of metropolitan development, such as the pattern of political jurisdictions governing each metropolitan area and the population size of these metropolitan agglomerations. With regard to government, for example, we might consider a monolithic metropolitan government versus a fragmented pattern of many little governments. With regard to population size we might consider limiting the growth of each metropolitan area or not limiting it. Each of these options could be encouraged by the right combinations of state and local policies. These variables, when merged with the previous considerations of land use and transportation, can be depicted in the decision tree of Figure 3.6.

Notice again how the number of final combinations increases as we add new considerations. There is a formal rule for computing the number of logically possible outcomes or combinations in problems of choice such as ours. The rule is known as "the fundamental principle of counting." It says: if one choice or task can be completed in n different ways and a second choice or task can be completed in m different ways, then both choices or tasks can be completed in a given order in $n \times m$ different ways. In terms of our earlier example, if land use can be developed in three different ways and transportation can be developed in two different ways, then they both can be developed, in that given order, in 3×2, or 6 ways. This principle is shown for our larger example in Table 3.1.

We might consider our analysis of the choices for metropolitan growth to be complete and thus ready to be offered to the conference of the governor and the mayors so that they can discuss the alternatives and hopefully select an outcome that they consider most preferable. While we may be tempted to do this, two problems immediately arise. First, it is virtually impossible for any person or group of persons to confront 24 alternatives simultaneously and to be able to evaluate them. Twenty-four is too many. You may argue

TABLE 3.1
Counting Metropolitan Alternatives

Variables	Number of Choices for Each Variable				
1. Land use	3				
2. Transportation		$\times$ 2			
3. Government			$\times$ 2		
4. Population				$\times$ 2	
Total number of alternatives	3	$\times$ 2	$\times$ 2	$\times$ 2	$= 24$

that if we were to increase the complexity and number of variables to some number more closely approaching reality, in fact, there would be several thousand alternative combinations. You would be right. But it is also nonetheless true that the unassisted human mind, alone or in groups, cannot meaningfully handle so many alternatives.

Second, it would immediately become apparent that some of these alternative combinations are trivial or nonsense and not worth considering because they are either totally infeasible or undesirable. The transportation routes must match the land use pattern in some way. There are, at least, extreme cases that one would obviously want to avoid, such as the highway that goes nowhere, and the land development with no access (although neither of these mistakes is so obvious that they have not happened in real life). Furthermore, we know that access tends to generate land use development. We would want to consider, then, the extent to which certain combinations of choices are causally or functionally linked or unlinked with one another. These linkages may be due to political, economical, technological, or social causes. The point is that we know that they exist. Thus we know that the number of realistic alternatives is fewer than the number of logical alternatives.

Both of these problems, the capacity of the human mind to consider only a few alternatives, and the need to eliminate unrealistic alternatives, lead us to techniques for reducing the range of logical choices and the need to evaluate the probability of combinations of events.

3.3 CALCULATING PROBABILITIES

To facilitate the orderly presentation of the further analysis of this problem, we limit our example to the original simple set of alternatives, presented again in Figure 3.7.

What we want to ask is whether each of these alternatives is equally feasible, given the current and foreseeable abilities and constraints of law, economy, politics, and society. In other words, can the policymaker choose among these alternatives as though they were in some sense equally available. One way that we can approach an answer to this question is to look at past, historical metropolitan growth patterns and their present manifestations to determine if, in fact, certain patterns and combinations of urban form elements are dominant. Such data do not tell us why the patterns exist, but they do suggest that, given no major changes in conditions and policies what patterns are most likely to evolve in the future. The estimation of the probability of events that is concerned with historical occurrences is called the frequency concept of probability. The notion of projecting historically estimated probabilities into the future or, simply, nonempirically, judging

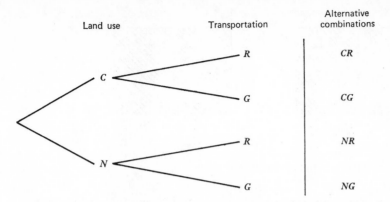

FIGURE 3.7   The initial four alternative combinations.

the probabilities of future events, is called the subjective concept of probability, and is the more general and all-encompassing concept.

Now, specifically, we want to know if there is evidence that some land use patterns are more probable, given our societal conditions, than others. Also we wish to know if one transportation system is more probable than another. Furthermore, we want to know if certain combinations of land use and transportation patterns are more common, and if others are more rare. To answer these questions we study the frequency of these alternative events in a sample of existing metropolitan areas.

Suppose that we select a random sample of 100 metropolitan areas in the United States and from an inspection of maps and aerial photographs determine for each metropolitan area which transportation pattern and which land use pattern each area most closely approximates. In reality this may not be very easy to determine, but we assume that with competent geographical assistance we are able to come up with a raw data table of the form of Table 3.2.

Let us presume that our initial analysis of these data yields the one-way frequency distributions of Figure 3.8.

TABLE 3.2

Raw Data Table, 100 Metropolitan Areas

	Metropolitan Areas			
	1	2	3	100
Variables	(Ann Arbor)	(Baltimore)	(Cincinatti) . . .	(Washington D. C.)
Land use	C	C	N	N
Transportation	G	R	G	R

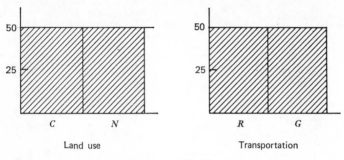

Land use   Transportation

FIGURE 3.8   One-way frequency distributions.

Based on this evidence we would be inclined to say that the chances of finding each land use pattern are fifty-fifty or equal and that the same is true for each transportation scheme. In probability terms we would say that the chance of selecting a metropolitan area at random and of finding that its land use pattern is continuous is one half or .50. The probability that it would be nucleated is also one half or .50. In other words, one half of the time we would expect one outcome and one half of the time the other outcome.

The probability of an event is defined as the relative proportion of times that the event occurs, relative to the total number of observations. We write our above results as

$$P(C) = .50 \quad \text{and} \quad P(R) = .50$$
$$P(N) = .50 \quad\quad\quad\quad P(G) = .50$$

Thus the probability of an event is always expressed as a fraction between zero and one unless, that is, we are totally certain that it will always happen, in which case its probability is $= 1.00$ (unity); or we are completely certain it will never happen, in which case its probability is $= .00$. Stated formally, this first rule of probability says that the probability of an event (x) is greater than or equal to zero and less than or equal to one. It is written as

$$0 \le P(x) \le 1$$

A second rule of probability says that if the probability of an event (x) is .60, then the probability that that event will *not* happen (x') is $1-.60$ or .40. Notice the sum of the probability of these mutually exclusive and exhaustive alternatives, (x) and (x'), is equal to 1.00, implying that it is absolutely certain that one or the other is going to happen.

Now what we are perhaps most interested in is the joint, or compound probabilities that result from looking at the combined occurrence of land use and transportation patterns. If the two factors, land use and transportation, are truly unrelated and independent, we can use the probabilities

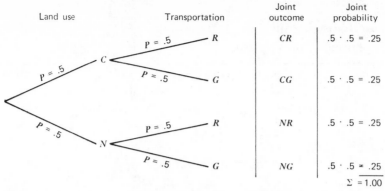

FIGURE 3.9   Joint probabilities assuming independence.

derived above and enter them into the decision tree with the results of Figure 3.9, using the following rules for calculation.

In a case of two independent events, if the probability of the first occurring is P_1 and the probability of the second occurring is P_2, then the probability of both occurring together is $P_1 \cdot P_2$. Thus, in our case, when the $P(C) = .5$ and $P(R) = .5$, then, assuming independence, $P(C, R) = P(C) \cdot P(R) = .5 \cdot 5 = .25$.

This set of four logically possible outcomes of the decision tree is also known, in the terms of sampling theory, as the *sample space*. Any sampling unit will fall somewhere in this space or set of outcomes. Thus, there is a direct conformance between the tree graph in Figure 3.9 and a two-way cross tabulation of the type we developed in Chapter 2. In fact, if our assumption of independence between our two variables is correct then, by cross tabulating the raw data in our survey of metropolitan areas, we should get a result like that of Table 3.3. Compare Figure 3.9 and Table 3.3.

TABLE 3.3
Two-way Cross Tabulation Illustrating
Independence of Variables

| | | Transportation | | |
		R	G	Row totals
Land use	C	25	25	50
	N	25	25	50
Column totals		50	50	$\sum = 100$

Table 3.4
Two-way Cross Tabulation Illustrating
Interdependence of Variables

		Transportation		Row totals
		R	G	
Land use	C	0	50	50
	N	50	0	50
Column totals		50	50	$\sum = 100$

Suppose, however, that we got the result of Table 3.4 instead of the result of Table 3.3. Notice that the marginal sums are unchanged from Figure 3.3, but the joint distribution shows a clear intercorrelation, or interdependence, between the variables. The probability tree corresponding to these data is that of Figure 3.10.

Thus while it is true that, when considered alone, without conditions, there is a probability of .5 of selecting a metropolitan area with a radial system, the conditional probability of getting a radial system, given a continuous growth pattern, is .00. We write these conditional probabilities as follows:

In Notation	In Words
$P(R \mid C) = .00$	The probability of R, given C, is zero.
$P(G \mid C) = 1.00$	The probability of G, given C, is one.
$P(R \mid N) = 1.00$	The probability of R, given N, is one.
$P(G \mid N) = .00$	The probability of G, given N, is zero.

When two events are not independent, their joint probability is found by multiplying the probability of the first, times, the conditional probability of the second, given the first. This is what is done in Figure 3.10.

We can now state these results in the form of rules for the probabilities of compound events. If two events A and B are independent, then $P(A, B) = P(A) \times P(B)$. But if two events are not independent, then $P(A, B) = P(A) \times P(B \mid A)$. The extension of these rules to more than two events is straightforward.

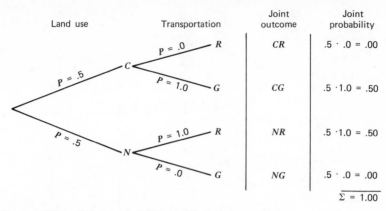

Land use	Transportation	Joint outcome	Joint probability

FIGURE 3.10   Joint probabilities with interdependence.

To illustrate further the notions of probability, independence, inter-dependence, joint probabilities, and the relation of probability trees to other modes of graphic presentation we present Figure 3.11. A wide range of alternative relationships between two variables or events is illustrated by cross tabulations, trees, and scatter diagrams. In the legend are names of eight different relationships possible between the two variables X and Y. The first column illustrates each of the eight by means of a cross tabulation in which the cell entries represent the percentage of the observations found in that cell. The next column represents exactly the same data in the form of a probability tree. The last column shows what each relationship might look like if the data were intervally scaled and plotted on a scatter diagram. In the case of the probability trees, of course, there are two possible ways of drawing each tree, depending on which variable is taken first. The resulting joint probability distribution, when order is disregarded, can be shown to be equivalent, no matter which variable is taken first. The reader should try this for himself to see that it is true.

Let us now return to our practical problem and determine what we have been able to develop in the way of techniques for decision making. First, we have been able to use a tree diagram as a technique for combining and counting, using the fundamental principle of counting, alternative sets of events or decisions that might represent alternative sets of policies or alternative plans. Second, we have reviewed a set of techniques for studying and defining the frequency of events and their interrelationships in proba-bilistic terms. We now consider our second major policy problem of this chapter in order to extend the concepts we have developed. The substantive issues of land use and transportation raised on a superficial level in this chapter are examined in much greater depth and technical detail in Chapters 9 and 10.

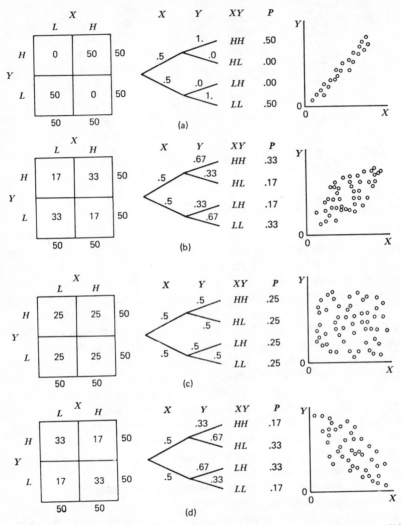

FIGURE 3.11 Cross tabulations, trees, and scatter diagrams of eight different relationships between two variables X and Y. (a) Strong positive or direct relation. (b) Weak positive or direct relation. (c) No relation, no interdependence. (d) Weak negative or inverse relation. (e) Strong negative or inverse relation. (f) No relation. (g) Curvilinear relation. (h) No relation.

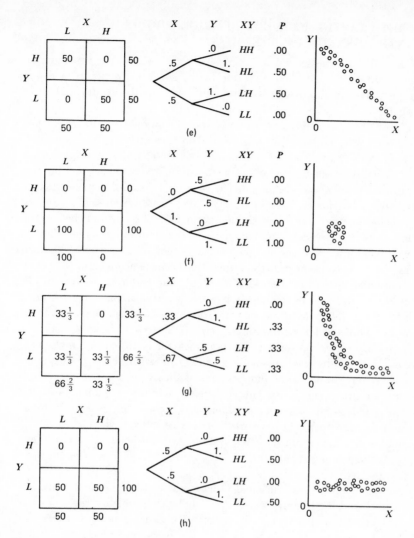

FIGURE 3.11 (continued)

Decision Models of Choice and Chance   75

3.4 THE TRAFFIC ACCIDENT SERVICE PROBLEM: INTRODUCING THE BINOMIAL

We now discuss the second policy problem sketched in the introduction to this chapter—the problem of traffic accident service policy in a resort community. We are now in a position to build more rapidly on our capabilities in probability theory.

The problem is as follows. A summer resort community is faced with a problem of traffic jams and accidents on the three days of the weekend, Friday, Saturday, and Sunday. The specific policy consideration is whether or not to contract on a regular weekend basis for emergency traffic and accident services. This would include the towing of disabled vehicles, taking water to overheated cars, and untangling traffic jams, as well as attending to the problems surrounding more serious accidents. The question before the community is: If they should prefer such a service, how much should they be willing to pay for it? Not having such a service is getting expensive. The town is losing business to other resort communities because people find that they waste too much time in it because of accidents and traffic jams. To build or expand the roads is out of the question. Some positive action is needed now.

We have the following data on which to build a recommendation. The probability of an accident (or major traffic jam) due to a serviceable vehicular failure on any given day of a three-day weekend is .20 or one fifth. This figure is based on observed frequencies and the event of an accident on any one of these days seems to be independent of the event of an accident on a preceding or subsequent day. The consensus of informed members of the community is that the cost, in loss of business, reputation, general aggravation, and damage to public property for a weekend on which one day of these major mishaps occurs is $10,000 dollars. A weekend of two accident days costs the community $25,000.00, and a weekend of three accident days costs $50,000.00.

The problem and the information we have about it is suitable for analysis as a special and well-known form of probability problem—the binomial process. Our first step is to lay out a tree of alternative events. Since the probabilities are the same each day, and the days are independent (their probabilities are independent), we can model the three-day weekend as a three-stage decision tree. The tree of possible weekends is shown in Figure 3.12.

This tree tells us that, selecting a weekend at random, the probability that it will have accidents on none of its days (outcome NNN) is .512, or about one half the weekends can be expected to be without incident. At the other extreme, the probability that a random weekend will exhibit incidents on each of its three days (outcome AAA) is .008, or eight times out of 1000. This means that about one half the weekends will cost the town nothing, and they will only be socked for $50,000 (three days of accidents) on eight out of a

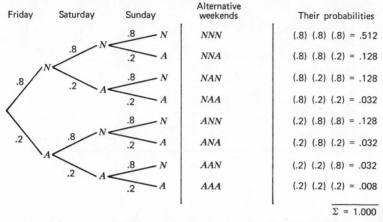

Friday	Saturday	Sunday	Alternative weekends	Their probabilities
		.8 — N	NNN	(.8) (.8) (.8) = .512
		.2 — A	NNA	(.8) (.8) (.2) = .128
		.8 — N	NAN	(.8) (.2) (.8) = .128
		.2 — A	NAA	(.8) (.2) (.2) = .032
		.8 — N	ANN	(.2) (.8) (.8) = .128
		.2 — A	ANA	(.2) (.8) (.2) = .032
		.8 — N	AAN	(.2) (.2) (.8) = .032
		.2 — A	AAA	(.2) (.2) (.2) = .008

$$\Sigma = 1.000$$

FIGURE 3.12   The three-day weekend probability tree and outcomes distribution; A = accident, N = no accident.

thousand or a little less than one weekend out of 100. The remaining 48% of the time they can expect some accidents at some cost, as indicated by the other outcomes and their probabilities.

Since the cost of a weekend is the same when there is only one accident on that weekend, no matter which day it falls on, three of the outcomes can be considered identical—NNA, NAN, and ANN. Each one costs the town $10,000. Thus the probability of a $10,000 weekend cost equals the sum of the probabilities of these three outcomes, which is $(.128) + (.128) + (.128) = .384$.

Similarly there are three outcomes in which there are two accident days, which means a weekend cost of $25,000. Thus the probability of a $25,000 weekend equals $P(NAA) + P(ANA) + P(AAN) = (.032) + (.032) + (.032) = .096$.

These outcomes, and the grouping of them, as we must estimate the probabilities of weekends with different frequencies of accidents, can be shown graphically as in Figure 3.13. On the right-hand side of Figure 3.13 is a graph of the resulting probability distribution turned on its side.

Now let us ask the question: On the average what does a weekend cost the community? We are asking, what is the mean of this distribution. We can find the mean of this distribution in the same manner that we found the means of the frequency distributions of Chapter 2. Treating our probabilities as measures of frequency, which by definition is precisely what they are, the mean can be found as follows:

$$(.512)\$0 + (.384)\$10,000 + (.096)\$25,000 + (.008)\$50,000 \qquad 3.1$$

$$= 0 + \$3840 + \$2400 + \$400 = \$6640 \qquad 3.2$$

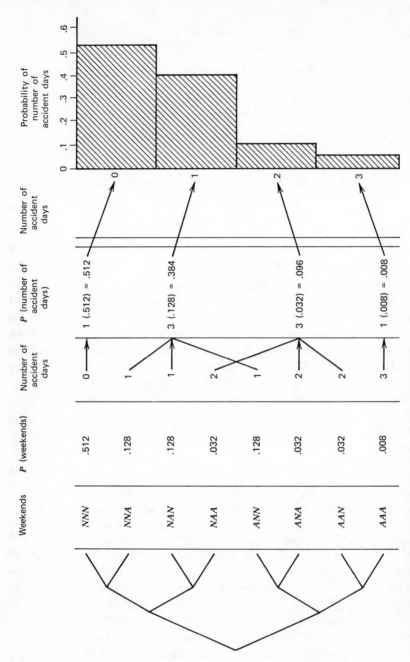

FIGURE 3.13   From probability tree to probability distribution.

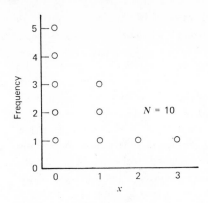

FIGURE 3.14   A common frequency distribution of $N = 10$.

But obviously our formula for calculating this mean is not exactly the same as the formula for the mean in Chapter 2, equation 2.3. The equivalence of the two can be shown as follows. Chapter 2 states the mean as

$$\bar{x} = \frac{\sum\limits_{i=1}^{n} x_i}{N} \qquad\qquad 3.3$$

This equation is normally applied to a frequency distribution such as Figure 3.14. Now to get the mean we must add up all of the values of X and divide by 10. Since there are five values of zero and three values of one, we write our computations as follows.

$$\bar{x} = \frac{5(0) + 3(1) + 1(2) + 1(3)}{10} = .80 \qquad\qquad 3.4$$

But this is the same as writing

$$\bar{x} = \tfrac{5}{10}(0) + \tfrac{3}{10}(1) + \tfrac{1}{10}(2) + \tfrac{1}{10}(3) = .80 \qquad\qquad 3.5$$

Now notice that the fractions $\tfrac{5}{10}, \tfrac{3}{10}, \tfrac{1}{10}, \tfrac{1}{10}$ are in essence probabilities by definition of probability as relative frequency. The mean of a probability distribution is usually called by another name, the *expected value* of the distribution. Thus to be perfectly correct we should rewrite equations 3.1 and 3.2 as follows for the expected value (in this case, expected cost).

$$E(C) = (.512)\$0 + (.384)\$10,000 + (.096)\$25,000 + (.008)\$50,000 \quad 3.6$$

$$E(C) = \$6640 \qquad\qquad 3.7$$

In most general form, the expected value of the probability distribution of a variable X (such as number of accident days) is calculated as

$$E(X) = \sum P(x_i)x_i \qquad\qquad 3.8$$

We now have a powerful application of decision theory. We can specify precisely how much the community should be willing to pay to alleviate the effects of the accident problem. If they can purchase a service at a price that is less than the average cost of the problem, which is $6640, then they would be economically wise to do so. But we know a good deal more than just the mean or expected value of this distribution. We know the character of the entire distribution and can use this knowledge further in the policy problem.

Suppose the local politicians took our advice and contracted for a season of, say, 15 weekends at say $4000 per weekend, thereby saving the community an average of $2640 per weekend. If the following season, just by chance, turned out to be accident free, our politician could look pretty silly. And anyone who has played games of chance knows that such a thing can happen. You could, in fact, calculate the probability of this with a 15-stage probability tree. The probability of this happening in our case can be shown to be $(.512)^{15}$, a very small but definite probability. Knowing this to be true, any smart politician would probably want to hedge his odds and not play a fifty-fifty game, which is what he plays if he uses the mean or expected value figure of $6640 per weekend. He would want to pay much less.

Furthermore, consider the whole problem from the point of view, not of the politician and his community but, from that of the supplier of the service. An unusually high number of accidents in a summer is also possible, and those probabilities could be calculated. If he were to contract on the basis of simple expected value, a really bad summer could send him into bankruptcy. He, therefore, would prefer to hedge the odds in his direction and ask for more than $6640.

To strategize intelligently, both of these parties would want to know, then, not just the mean cost or expected value. They would want to know the shape and character of all possibilities—the whole distribution.

3.5 THE GENERAL CASE OF THE BINOMIAL MODEL

There is yet another reason why the long process of analysis demonstrated in the preceding section is very important. The idea of constructing a model of a problem or process is not just to investigate one peculiar set of conditions. The objective is to be able to manipulate the model, once it is built, to determine in what ways its results are sensitive to changing the conditions of the problem. An architect builds a physical model of a future building so that he can experiment with it. He may change the location of walls, alter the location of doors and elevators and may experiment with different kinds of materials and colors to estimate the resulting effects on the total efficiency, beauty, and cost of the building. We have built a mathematical model of our accident problem so that now we can test the effects of varying some of the conditions or the parameters of the problem. In the process of doing so, we present the binomial model in its general form and then show the direct relationship between this binomial distribution process and an even more general case—the normal distribution.

There are two basic parameters or determinants of a binomial distribution. They are (1) the number of trials in the process, which is the number of days in a weekend in our case, and (2) the probability of a success, which is the probability of an accident (.20) in our example. These two parameters determine a probability distribution. Every time we change one or both of these conditions, we obtain a different distribution. In the general case we consider n = the number of trials and p = the probability of a success. The probability of a failure in each case is then called q and $q = 1 - p$, since $q + p$ must equal 1.

Now let us first look at what happens when we vary the number of trials. We might, for example, want to look at the probability distribution for our accident problem where the weekends consist in effect of only two days. Or we might wish to look at what our situation would be like if we considered the notion of a four-day weekend. Figures 3.15 to 3.17 represent the mechanical process of generalizing the trees for each alternative type of weekend—the two-day, three-day, and four-day. We set aside the specification of the probability of an accident and substitute the more general notation for simplicity. We say that

$$P(N) = q$$

and

$$P(A) = p$$

In studying Figures 3.15 to 3.17, the reader should carefully compare Figure 3.16, the three-day weekend, with our previous analysis of the three-day weekend in Figure 3.13. After he is certain that they are equivalent, he should then compare the three distributions of Figures 3.15 to 3.17 to see that, in fact, the same basic procedures are followed in each case. Finally, we study the right-hand column of each of these three distributions. One feature that becomes evident is a symmetry in the pattern of coefficients in this last column, the values (1, 2, 1) in the first; (1, 3, 3,1) in the second; and (1, 4, 6, 4, 1) in the last. Another pattern can be seen in the way the exponents (powers) of q and p shift as we move down each column. These patterns are so perfectly regular that any single term for a binomial expansion (this series of

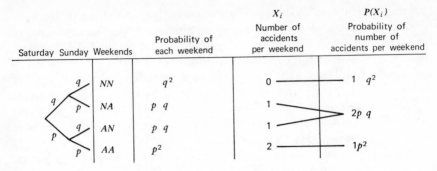

Saturday Sunday Weekends	Probability of each weekend	X_i Number of accidents per weekend	$P(X_i)$ Probability of number of accidents per weekend
NN	q^2	0	1 q^2
NA	$p\ q$	1	
AN	$p\ q$	1	2$p\ q$
AA	p^2	2	1p^2

FIGURE 3.15   The two-day weekend.

terms) can be calculated by a standard formula. This is most easily understood if we remember one simple rule from high school algebra. Recall that

$$(a + b)^2 = (a + b)(a + b) \qquad 3.9$$

or

$$(a + b)^2 = a^2 + 2ba + b^2 \qquad 3.10$$

We can reprove this to ourselves by substituting some numbers for a and b and proving that the two sides of equation 3.10 are equal. The similarity between equation 3.10 and the right-hand column of Figure 3.15 should be noted. To use this algebraic rule for expansion to produce the binomial probability expansion, we just substitute q and p for a and b. Thus we find that:

$$(q + p)^2 = q^2 + 2pq + p^2 \qquad 3.11$$

$$(q + p)^3 = q^3 + 3pq^2 + 3p^2q + p^3 \qquad 3.12$$

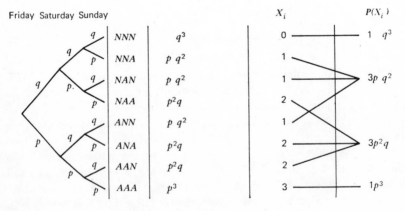

Friday Saturday Sunday		X_i	$P(X_i)$
NNN	q^3	0	1 q^3
NNA	$p\ q^2$	1	
NAN	$p\ q^2$	1	3$p\ q^2$
NAA	p^2q	2	
ANN	$p\ q^2$	1	
ANA	p^2q	2	3p^2q
AAN	p^2q	2	
AAA	p^3	3	1p^3

FIGURE 3.16   The three-day weekend.

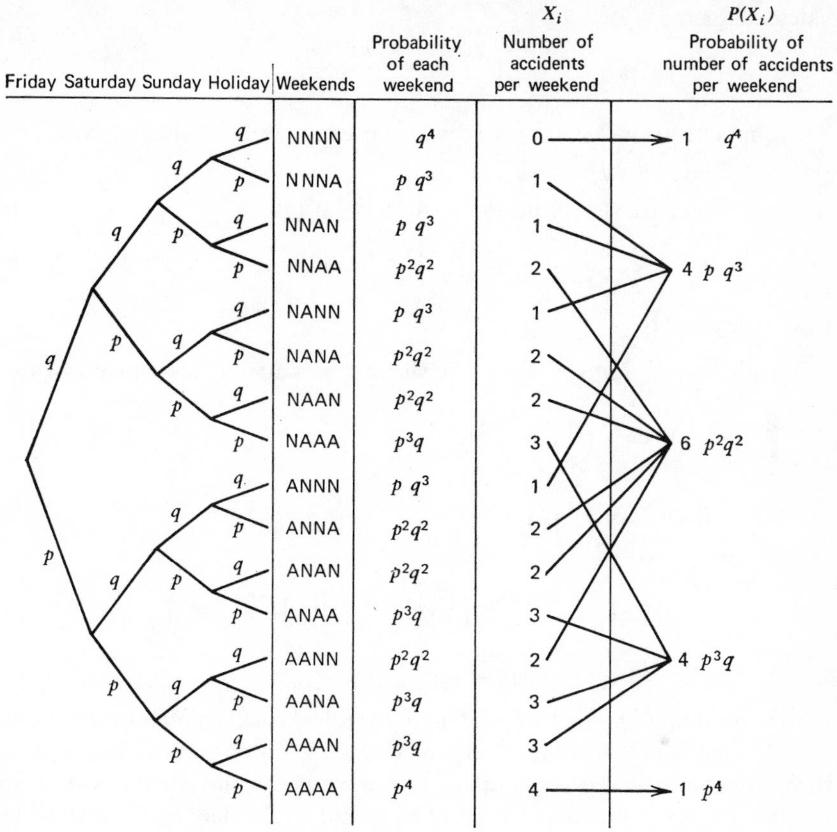

Friday Saturday Sunday Holiday	Weekends	Probability of each weekend	X_i Number of accidents per weekend	$P(X_i)$ Probability of number of accidents per weekend
	NNNN	q^4	0 →	1 q^4
	NNNA	pq^3	1	
	NNAN	pq^3	1	
	NNAA	p^2q^2	2	4 pq^3
	NANN	pq^3	1	
	NANA	p^2q^2	2	
	NAAN	p^2q^2	2	
	NAAA	p^3q	3	6 p^2q^2
	ANNN	pq^3	1	
	ANNA	p^2q^2	2	
	ANAN	p^2q^2	2	
	ANAA	p^3q	3	
	AANN	p^2q^2	2	4 p^3q
	AANA	p^3q	3	
	AAAN	p^3q	3	
	AAAA	p^4	4 →	1 p^4

FIGURE 3.17 The four-day weekend.

and

$$(q + p)^4 = q^4 + 4pq^3 + 6p^2q^2 + 4p^3q + p^4 \qquad 3.13$$

Since this is a probability distribution where $(q + p)^1 = q + p = 1$, then each of these equations must sum up to 1. This is, indeed, exactly what is the case in Figures 3.15 to 3.17. The exponent of $(q + p)$ is equal, in each case, to the number of trials.

The general equation for the binomial is

$$(q + p)^n = \sum_{x=0}^{n} \binom{n}{x} p^x q^{n-x} \qquad 3.14$$

The notation $\binom{n}{x}$ is read as the number of successes (x) in n trials. It is calculated as

$$\binom{n}{x} = \frac{n!}{x! \, (n - x)!} \qquad\qquad 3.15$$

The symbol (!) is called a *factorial* and, for example, is calculated as follows for 5 *factorial* and 3 *factorial*

$$5! = 5 \cdot 4 \cdot 3 \cdot 2 \cdot 1 = 120 \qquad\qquad 3.16$$

and
$$3! = 3 \cdot 2 \cdot 1 = 6 \qquad\qquad 3.17$$

$0!$ is always $= 1$

Thus we would write as follows, in the case of a 3-trial binomial expansion,

$$(q + p)^n = \sum_{x=0}^{n} \binom{n}{x} p^x q^{n-x}$$

$$(q + p)^3 = \sum_{x=0}^{3} \binom{3}{x} p^x q^{3-x}$$

$$= \binom{3}{0} p^0 q^{3-0} + \binom{3}{1} p^1 q^{3-1} + \binom{3}{2} p^2 q^{3-2} + \binom{3}{3} p^3 q^{3-3}$$

$$= 1q^3 + 3pq^2 + 3p^2q + 1p^3$$

It is no doubt more than evident that calculating binomial probability distributions is not something one would want to do very often. Fortunately there are standard statistical tables that have been calculated once and for all time for many different values of p, q, and n. But having presented the basic mechanics of the process, we now want to look at the actual probability distributions to deduce a very important characteristic of the binomial distribution.

Figure 3.18 presents the resulting binomial probability distributions for four different experiments or sets of trials. The probability of a success in each process is the same, $p = .20$, just as in our weekend problem. The number of trials in each process ranges from $n = 5$ in the upper distribution to $n = 40$ in the lower distribution. Notice what happens as n increases— the center (mean) of the distribution shifts to the right and the shape of the distribution tends to become increasingly symmetrical and flattens out.

Suppose we were to perform this exercise of increasing n for a different p, say $p = .80$. In fact, what we would get would be a left-to-right mirror image of these distributions. At $n = 5$, the skew would be in the other direction from that of Figure 3.18 and would gradually flatten and become roughly symmetrical at $n = 40$. As n increases even further, the two distributions would, in shape, become nearly indistinguishable. What would distinguish

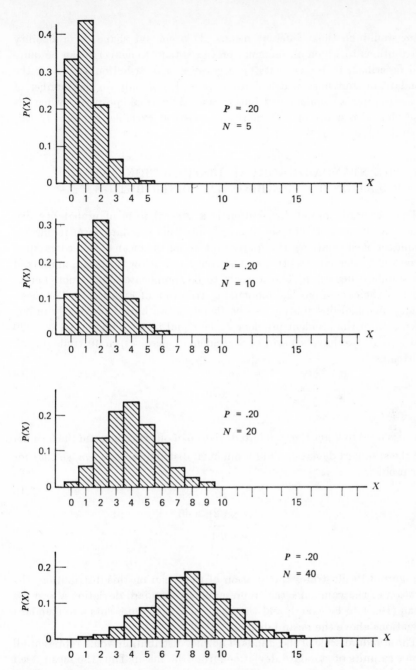

FIGURE 3.18 The binomial probability distributions for a constant $P = .20$ with N varying from 5 to 40.

them would be their different means. This general shape of probability distributions to which all binomial processes tend to converge can be quite well described, in terms of its properties, as a distribution known as the standard or unit normal distribution. Indeed, not only do the number of successes (x) in a binomial distribution take on "normal" properties when n is large, but also many other important statistical variables conform to this general distribution.

3.6 THE STANDARD NORMAL DISTRIBUTION AND ITS RELATION TO THE BINOMIAL DISTRIBUTION

The standard normal distribution is a general form of probability distribution. To convert any set of scores into this standard form requires a simple set of calculations. It requires that we set the mean of the scores equal to zero and then express other scores, above and below the mean, in units of the standard deviation. This appears to be complicated but is not. Let us consider the case of our last binomial distribution of Figure 3.18. The mean of any binomial distribution can be found, as we hinted previously in our discussion of the accident problem, to be equal to pn. Thus when $p = .20$ and $n = 40$ we have a mean of 8 accidents (successes) in 40 trials (days), written as

$$\bar{x} = pn \qquad\qquad 3.18$$
$$= (.20)40$$
$$= 8$$

We also need to know the standard deviation of our variable, and the formula for the standard deviation of any binomial distribution is $\sqrt{pqn}$, so that for our problem:

$$S = \sqrt{pqn} \qquad\qquad 3.19$$
$$= \sqrt{(.2)(.8)40}$$
$$= \sqrt{6.4}$$
$$= 2.54$$

Figure 3.19 illustrates the location of the mean on this distribution, the location of the value of x that represents one standard deviation above the mean (10.54 to be exact), and the value of x that represents two standard deviations above the mean (about 13).

The standard scale of the standard normal distribution would represent all scores as units of standard deviations from the mean. Thus the mean itself would be scored as zero. Our 10.54 would be scored as 1.00 and our 13.08 would be scored as 2.00.

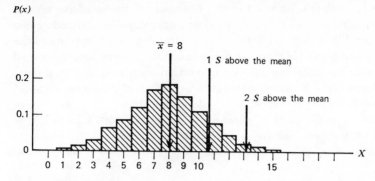

FIGURE 3.19 The illustration of the mean and standard deviation of the binominal when $P = .20$ and $N = .40$.

The general formula for converting any set of variable scores (x_i) into standard scores, also called Z scores is

$$Z_i = \frac{x_i - \bar{x}}{S} \qquad 3.20$$

Substituting equations 3.18 and 3.19 for the binomial, we get standard scores for the binomial as

$$Z_i = \frac{x_i - np}{\sqrt{pqn}} \qquad 3.21$$

Figure 3.20 illustrates our binomial of $p = .20$ with n raised to 100 trials.

Now the importance for our discussion, especially of the accident problem, is that with the knowledge that the binomial process approximates the

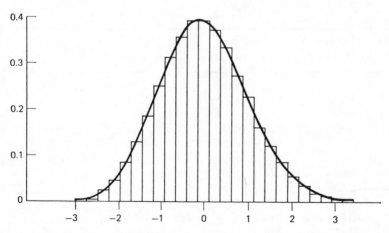

FIGURE 3.20 Normalized binomial for $P = .20$, $N = 100$.

normal when n is large, we can directly, from our knowledge of the normal curve, make a number of useful predictions and judgements without going through (again) that long and tedious process of calculating the terms of the binomial expansion. If, for example, our community policymakers discovered that what they thought was only a weekend problem was, in fact, a daily problem throughout the summer resort season of, say, 100 days, we could use our knowledge of the normal distribution immediately. The property of the standard normal that is especially interesting is that the probabilities that given values under the curve will occur are quite simple to determine from common tables. Table 3.5 summarizes the probabilities of values under

TABLE 3.5

Areas Under the Standard Normal Probability Curve, Between the Mean (0) and Various Values of Z from $Z_i = 0$ to $Z_i = \pm 3.0$

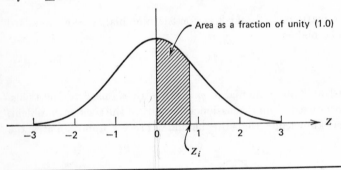

Area as a fraction of unity (1.0)

Z_i	Area Between Mean (0) and Z	Z_i	Area	Z_i	Area
.0	.0000				
.1	.0398	1.1	.3643	2.1	.4821
.2	.0793	1.2	.3849	2.2	.4861
.3	.1179	1.3	.4032	2.3	.4893
.4	.1554	1.4	.4192	2.4	.4918
.5	.1915	1.5	.4332	2.5	.4938
.6	.2257	1.6	.4452	2.6	.4953
.7	.2580	1.7	.4554	2.7	.4965
.8	.2881	1.8	.4641	2.8	.4974
.9	.3159	1.9	.4713	2.9	.4981
1.0	.3413	2.0	.4772	3.0	.4987

various segments of the normal. From it, for example, we can quickly see that the probability that (x), say, the number of accidents is more than three standard deviations above the mean, can be found. We know first that the probability of being anywhere below the mean of 20 accident days is .50 by definition. Furthermore, we can see that the area between the mean and $Z = 3.0$ (standard deviations) is .4987. Thus, in total, the probability of a given season's being picked at random and falling below $\tilde{x} + 3\sqrt{(pqn)} = 32$ accident days (out of a possible 100) is .50 + .4987, or $P = .9987$, and the probability of having more than that is 1–.9987 or .0013. The standard deviation of this distribution is $pqn = 4$, and the mean is $pn = 20$; hence, three standard deviations above the mean implies $20 + 3(4) = 32$ days of accidents.

A more complete table of values for the standard normal distribution is given in Appendix IV. This distribution is also called the unit normal distribution because the sum of the area or probabilities under the curve is equal to 1 — unity. In the next several chapters we make extensive use of this distribution and its properties.

PROBLEMS

1. York City and Jersey Town, lying on opposite sides of the West River are connected by several bridges and tunnels. Increased demand for transportation facilities has led the Transportation Authority to consider the following variables and alternatives.

VARIABLES	ALTERNATIVES
Crossing type	Bridge (B) or tunnel (T)
Capacity	Six lanes (SL) or eight lanes (EL)
Bridge type	Elevated (E) or draw (D)
Bus accommodation	Bus lanes (BL) or no bus lanes (NB)

Construct a tree diagram showing the possible combinations of alternatives being considered, giving a summary list of the combinations using the symbols.

2. If the probability of a one-hour traffic delay on Route No. 1 at a specified location is $p = .40$ for any given day of a three-day weekend, then:

(a) What proportion of these weekends might be expected to have one-hour delays on all days?

(b) What proportion of these weekends might be expected to have one-hour delays on none of the three days?

(c) What proportion of these weekends might be expected to have some number of days with one-hour traffic delays greater than 0 but less than 3?

3. A town's future employment status is uncertain and you want to know the possible changes that might occur to evaluate policy needs. You know that the probability the town's major industry will get a new federal contract and expand its operations is .25. If the contract is obtained, then there is a probability of .80 that a new manufacturing plant will move to your town. If the contract is not obtained, then the probability that the new industry will come is .50.

PROBLEM. Draw a tree diagram of these events, assign probabilities to all events, and list the alternative final outcomes and the probability of each. Finally, based on just this information, what is the probability that the employment situation in this town is not going to get worse.

4.

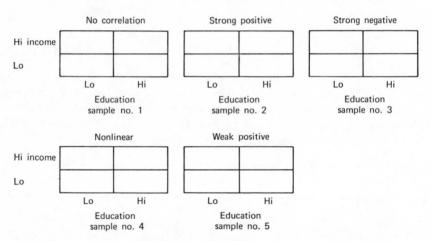

Above are five cross tabulations showing various hypothetical relationships between income and education for a sample of 100 counties. Fill in the cells of these cross tabulations so that the numbers conform to the indicated relationship. Then draw a probability tree corresponding to each sample, properly labeling each branch and outcome.

5. The local housing authority and the local community action agency frequently disagree. Each of the four major neighborhood organizations allies itself with one or the other of these two agencies on each major issue. A balance of power exists if each larger agency is backed by two smaller organizations—issues are then settled by prolonged negotiation.

Assumption. No organization abstains from taking sides on a major issue and organizational alignments are independent and equiprobable (meaning that the probability that any given organization will align with any given agency on a major issue is always = .5 and independent of the nature of the issue and independent of what other organizations do).

Question. Under these assumptions and conditions, what is the probability that a major issue gets settled without prolonged negotiation? (*Hint.* There are several different ways of doing this; one would be to begin from the point of view of each organization's alternative choices.)

6. The urban planner in Alphaville has available to him the following data on housing quality, household income, and ownership patterns for the 10 districts in the city.

DISTRICT	INDEX OF HOUSING QUALITY (1 TO 10)	INCOME LEVELS (L = LOWER, U = UPPER)	OWNERSHIP PATTERNS (PERCENTAGE OWNER)
1	3	L	30
2	2	L	40
3	7	U	20
4	10	U	90
5	3	L	80
6	3	L	40
7	4	U	60
8	8	L	90
9	7	U	20
10	9	L	80

a. Construct a two-by-two table of frequencies of the index of housing quality by household income. Use 5.0 as the breakpoint between low and high housing quality.

b. Can any relationship between housing quality and household income be ascertained? If so, what is it?

c. Draw a tree diagram of the two variables. Calculate the probabilities of the possible combinations that can occur.

d. Are the probabilities of the two variables independent of each other? Explain your answer.

e. Divide the ownership pattern variable into two categories—predominantly owner-occupied districts or predominantly renter-occupied districts, using 50% as a breakpoint. Using the ownership variable as a control, develop a three-way cross tabulation among the variables. What conclusions can you draw about the relationship between housing quality and income controlling for ownership?

7. This planner is also interested in a related issue. He knows from past records that, on the average, a serious fire in one of Alphaville's housing units breaks out on three of every 10 days. He also knows that only one serious fire will break out on a given day. The planner is concerned with determining the costs to the community on the average of the fires over a two-day period.

   a. Construct a tree diagram of possible combinations of events that can occur in a two-day period. Calculate the joint probabilities of the various combinations possible.
   b. What are the probabilities of a serious fire occurring on no days, one day, and both days of the two-day period?
   c. Each fire costs the city $10,000. What is the mean (expected value) of the probability distribution? That is, what does it cost the city on the average for each two-day period?

8. As planner for a citizens' group, you would like to assess the probabilities of a new rent subsidy program being approved by the city council and funded by various agencies. The council is currently split four-four on the issue. The one vacant seat on the nine-member council will be filled in an impending election by either Mumword or Greengardens. Current polls indicate that Mumword will win with 60% of the vote, with 40% of the vote going to Greengardens.
   However, Mumword is undecided as to whether to vote for the subsidy program. The best guess is that there is a fifty-fifty chance either way. Greengardens is 100% for the proposal.

   Problem 1. Lay out the alternative sequence of possible occurrences. What chance is there that the rent subsidy will pass the council, assuming that none of the eight current members change their vote and that either Greengardens or Mumword is elected for the ninth seat?

   Problem 2. If the rent subsidy passes, there is a 40% chance that the federal government will actually contribute its one-third share of the total cost and a 60% chance that the state will contribute its one-third share. The other one third comes from the city and would be allocated if the city council passes the rent subsidy. For your citizens' group, indicate the probabilities of having no funding, one-third funding, two-third funding, or full funding.

9. Convert the raw data scores below into standardized scores (Z scores).

SAMPLE OBSERVATIONS ON FIVE DWELLING UNITS

	1	2	3	4	5
Amenity score	9	7	4	6	3
$1000 assessed value	49	26	13	32	18

From a table of probabilities under the unit (standard) normal probability distribution, and by using the results above, determine:

(a) What is the probability of having an assessed value greater than $32,000?

(b) What is the probability of a raw amenity score less than three?

10. a. The federal standard for carbon monoxide for an eight-hour average is nine parts per million (ppm). Given that the eight-hour averages in the New Brunswick area are normally distributed about a mean of 4.2 ppm, with a standard deviation of 3 ppm, what is the probability that the New Brunswick area will exceed the federal standard for any eight-hour period?

b. The eight-hour mean for carbon monoxide in Denver, Colorado is 3 ppm. Your rich uncle is flying in from Denver. What is the probability that New Brunswick's carbon monoxide levels will be somewhere between Denver's mean and the federal standard?

BIBLIOGRAPHY

Alexander, Christopher. "The City is Not a Tree," *Architectural Forum*, Part I (April 1965), 58–62, and Part II (May 1965), 58–61.

———. *Notes on the Synthesis of Form*. Cambridge, Mass.: Harvard University Press, 1964.

Ayer, A. J. "Chance," *Scientific American* (October 1965).

Boyce, David, Norman R. Day, and Chris McDonald. *Metropolitan Plan Making*. Philadelphia: Regional Science Research Institute, 1970.

Bross, Irwin D. *Design for Decision*. New York: Macmillan, 1953.

Carnap, Rudolf. "What is Probability?" *Scientific American* (September 1953).

Chernoff, Herman, and Lincoln E. Moses. *Elementary Decision Theory*. New York: Wiley, 1959.

Downs, Anthony. "Alternative Forms of Future Urban Growth in the United States," *Journal of the American Institute of Planners, 36* (January 1970), 3–11.

Fisher, Sir Ronald A. "Mathematics of a Lady Tasting Tea," in James R. Newman (ed). *The World of Mathematics.* New York: Simon and Schuster, 1956, pp. 1512–21.

Friend, J. K., and W. N. Jessop. *Local Government and Strategic Choice.* Beverly Hills, Cal.: Sage Publications, 1969.

Goldberg, Samuel. *Probability: An Introduction.* Englewood Cliffs, N.J.: Prentice-Hall, 1960.

Kac, Mark. "Probability," *Scientific American,* (September 1964).

Kaufmann, Arnold. *The Science of Decision-making.* New York: World University Library, 1968.

Kemeny, John G., Arthur Schleifer, Jr., J. Laurie Snell, and Gerald L. Thompson. *Finite Mathematics with Business Applications.* Englewood Cliffs, N.J.: Prentice-Hall, 1962.

Krueckeberg, Donald A. "State Environmental Planning: Requirements vs. Behavior," *Journal of the American Institute of Planners, 38* (November 1972), 392–396.

Lessinger, Jack. "The Case for Scatteration," *Journal of the American Institute of Planners, 28* (August 1962), 159–169.

Magee, John F. "Decision Trees for Decision Making," *Harvard Business Review,* (July–August 1964), 126–138.

———. "How to Use Decision Trees in Capital Investment," *Harvard Business Review,* (September–October 1964), 79–96.

Mosteller, Frederick, Robert E. K. Rourke, and George B. Thomas, Jr. *Probability with Statistical Applications.* Reading, Mass.: Addison-Wesley, 1961.

Raiffa, Howard. *Decision Analysis.* Reading, Mass.: Addison-Wesley, 1968.

Schneider, Jerry B. "Doxiadis' Detroit: Forty-Nine Million Alternatives," *Journal of the American Institute of Planners, 38* (September, 1972), 332–333.

Scientific American. *Mathematical Thinking in the Behavioral Sciences: Readings from Scientific American.* San Francisco: W. H. Freeman, 1968.

Shaw, George Bernard. "The Vice of Gambling and the Virtue of Insurance," in James R. Newman (ed). *The World of Mathematics.* New York: Simon and Schuster, 1956, pp. 1524–1531.

Wallis, W. Allen, and Harry V. Roberts. *Statistics: A New Approach.* New York: The Free Press, 1956.

The items in the bibliography can be divided into three areas of concentration: (1) probability theory, (2) decision theory, and (3) elementary applications to urban problems.

The articles by Ayer, Carnap, Fisher, Kac, and Shaw are excellent, very well written explanations of the ideas of probability. The Ayer, Carnap, and Kac articles are reprinted in the Scientific American book along with several more advanced papers. Wallis and Roberts, Chapters 10 and 11, is a fine text with many examples and a minimum of mathematical usage. In order of increasing mathematical difficulty, we recommend also the works of Kemeny, Goldberg, and Mosteller, Rourke, and Thomas.

An excellent and highly readable introduction to statistical decision theory is the book by Bross. The papers of Magee are also good, well illustrated introductions. More advanced and thorough treatments are found in Kaufmann, Raiffa, and Chernoff and Moses.

A variety of applications of decision trees, systematic alternatives, and the like are found in Alexander, Boyce, Downs, Friend and Jessop, Krueckeberg, Lessinger, and Schneider. The citations here have been limited to applications that employ the ideas of this chapter at fairly elementary levels. Later chapters in this book deal extensively with more complex applications.

CHAPTER 4

Samples as Testable Evidence

4.1 SAMPLING TO ESTIMATE A PROPORTION

A well-known community leader in a large city decides that the only way to improve his community's share of the municipal budget is to gain representation in the municipality's decision-making process. Toward this end, he considers whether to run for mayor in the forthcoming election. In his opinion, if 20% or more of the registered voters currently support him, he can use a campaign budget of $250,000 to raise this proportion to the necessary 50% by election time. To gain information on how to make his decision, he hires an interviewer to go out into two local neighborhoods to bring back a sampling of voter opinion. The interviewer encounters 40 adults whom he determines are registered voters. To the question, "If Mr. Smith, the community leader, becomes a candidate for mayor, would you vote for him?" it is found that only 6 of the 40 persons interviewed, or 15%, would vote for him. Based on this evidence, Mr. Smith decides not to become a candidate Was this the proper decision?

From a broad point of view, we are not in a position to determine the "rightness" of Mr. Smith's decision. His decision may have been based in part on how he felt about intangibles such as pressing the people of his community for campaign contributions when only few could afford them; how strongly he evaluated the benefits of a larger share in what may in any event have been too small a municipal budget; and his optimism or conservatism in taking risks. These are questions that only Mr. Smith can evaluate. But we can evaluate other elements of his decision-making procedure: (1) whether he purchased good evidence for his money; (2) whether he used his evidence properly for evaluating his chances; and (3) whether he collected a large enough sample to take the results as sufficiently accurate evidence.

4.1.1 THE QUALITY OF SAMPLE EVIDENCE

Although Mr. Smith paid for 40 observations, we may suspect that in choosing only two local neighborhoods from which to draw his sample, the interviewer obtained biased evidence, perhaps, in this case, an overestimate of the actual percentage. We recall from our discussion of the techniques of random sampling in Chapter 2 that to obtain evidence about the voting behavior of the "typical" or average voter, it is necessary that each registered voter in the entire municipality have an equal chance of being included in the sample.

Of course, Mr. Smith may want additional more detailed information about specific voting groups or neighborhoods, but these additional requirements may still be satisfied within a framework of random sampling.

Mr. Smith might further object that such scientific procedures would be too expensive. But this objection is not valid. Sampled evidence has value for decision-making purposes only if its accuracy can be evaluated and, in this respect, his purchase of biased evidence may be of little or no value. A properly drawn sample will be only slightly more expensive, and its value will be much greater. But, as we shall learn, even a properly drawn sample will contain error, the magnitude of which can be reduced only by buying even more information—a larger sample.

4.1.2 MEASURING SAMPLING ERROR FOR SAMPLE PROPORTIONS

Let us assume now that a random sample was, in fact, obtained so that there is no reason to suspect that the information is biased. What should be Mr. Smith's expectations about the sample's accuracy? Let us assume that there are 10,000 registered voters in the city, and that 2000 or 20% of them actually intend to vote for Mr. Smith. This distribution is shown in the bar chart in Figure 4.1, where zero (0) indicates voters who do not intend to vote for Mr. Smith, and one (1) indicates voters who do intend to vote for him.

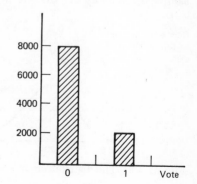

FIGURE 4.1 Distribution of votes for Mr. Smith.

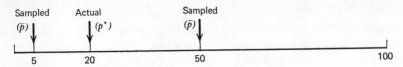

FIGURE 4.2   Percentage of observed vote for Mr. Smith.

If only 40 voters are randomly drawn from this distribution, because of the element of chance, there is a certain small probability that we shall draw a sample in which most of the sampled voters, say 50%, will indicate a vote for Mr. Smith. In contrast, 40 voters may have been drawn only 2 of whom intend to vote for Mr. Smith—a proportion of only 5%. In sum, although 20% of all voters actually intend to vote for Mr. Smith, it is probable (a very small probability) that a sample of 40 may indicate a vote as high as 50% or as low as 5%. These results are illustrated in Figure 4.2.

But these sampled results will not be the typical or expected sample result. We might imagine that 100 different interviewers were sent out, and that each obtained a different and independently drawn random sample of 40 voters. Most of these samples will yield an estimate that very closely approximates the true proportion of 20%. Only a few will yield results nearer to 10% or 30%, and perhaps only one or two will report a result as low as 5% or as high as 50%. The distribution of these outcomes is shown in Figure 4.3.

If we take an average of all 100 sample results, we should find that the average of the sample proportions ($\bar{p}$) is approximately equal to the true proportion ($p^* = 20\%$), a result that we state more formally as

$$E(\bar{p}) = p^*(= .20) \qquad\qquad 4.1$$

This is to say that Mr. Smith should have an expectation that his sampled proportion will equal the true proportion—a result that holds true only if the sample is randomly drawn. But he should also expect some error, recognizing

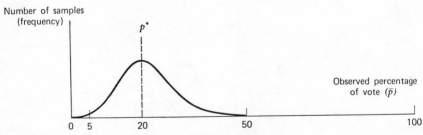

FIGURE 4.3   The distribution of sample proportions ($\bar{p}$).

that the probability of a large error ($\bar{p} = .05$ or $\bar{p} = .50$) is extremely small.

To calculate the probability of an error of a given magnitude, we use the techniques of Chapter 3. Recall from the traffic accident example that if 20% of all days had accidents ($p^* = .2$), and we "drew a sample" of three days ($n = 3$), it was possible to calculate the probability that all three days would contain an accident (e.g., $\bar{p} = 100\%$). There, we made use of the binomial expansion and found this probability was only .008, which is very small indeed. Recall further that we found that when the number of observations or, in this case, the sample size (n) becomes quite large, say $n > 30$, we could use the normal distribution to determine these probabilities instead of the binomial. We now apply the normal distribution for this purpose and, in so doing, we show how Mr. Smith should have used his sampled information for evaluating his chances of winning.

We first must employ a formula that provides a measure of what one should expect about a sample's accuracy. We refer to this measure as *the standard error of the sample proportion*, denoted by the symbol $\sigma_{\bar{p}}$. This measure is calculated from the following formula:

$$\sigma_{\bar{p}} = \sqrt{\frac{p^*(1 - p^*)}{n}} \qquad 4.2$$

where it is assumed that the total voting population from which the sample is taken is very large.[1] As we see, it is quite easy to calculate. In the case of Mr. Smith's sample of 40 where the true proportion of favorable votes is 20%, we have

$$\sigma_{\bar{p}} = \sqrt{\frac{.20(.80)}{40}} = \sqrt{\frac{.16}{40}} = \sqrt{.004}$$
$$= .064$$

If we both add and subtract this standard error from the true proportion ($p^* \pm \sigma_{\bar{p}}$), we obtain a range of values for the sample mean indicating the degree of sampling error that should be expected when the sample size (n) is 40 and the true proportion (p^*) is .20. In this case, the range is .20 $\pm$ .064 or from a low of 13.6% to a high of 26.4%. This is illustrated in Figure 4.4.

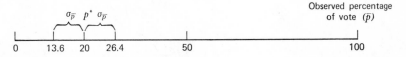

FIGURE 4.4 The true proportion plus and minus one standard error.

[1] Where the total population N is not large, the right-hand side of this formula must be multiplied by a reduction factor $\sqrt{(N - n)/(N - 1)}$.

However, this interval does not span the entire error range for estimates of p^*. As we have already indicated, sample estimates of p^* will be normally distributed, and with some very low probability, some samples may yield values of 5% or 50%. Instead, an interval of one standard error on either side of the true proportion p^* encompasses 68% or about two thirds of the results that can be yielded by random samples of a given size.

To see how we obtained this result, let us return to Table 3.5 (Chapter 3) which gives areas under the standard normal probability curve for various values of Z. Since we want to know the probability of all sample proportions ($\bar{p}$) lying one standard error from p^*, we look under $Z = 1.0$. We find that the probability of a sampled proportion $\bar{p}$ lying between p^* and $p^* + \sigma_{\bar{p}}$ (between $\bar{p} = 20\%$ and $\bar{p} = 26.4\%$) is .3413. Furthermore, the probability of observing proportions lying between $p^* - \sigma_{\bar{p}}$ and p^* (between 13.6% and 20%) is also .3413. Hence the probability of observing a sampled outcome lying in the range $p^* \pm \sigma_{\bar{p}}$ (13.6 to 26.4%) is .68.[2] But this implies that there is a probability of $1 - .68 = .32$ of observing sampled outcomes greater than one standard error from the true proportion p^*. As shown in Figure 4.5, the probability that a sample of size 40 will yield estimates of p^* of less than 13.6% is .16, and the probability of $\bar{p}$ greater than 26.4% is the same. Again, we see that the probability of observing $\bar{p}$ more than one standard error from the true mean p^* is $.16 + .16 = .32$.

Based on these considerations, we are now in a position to return to Mr. Smith's decision procedure.

4.1.3 Using Samples to Test Hypotheses About Proportions

Mr. Smith has stated that if the percentage of votes in his favor is less than 20%, he will not seek office. Conversely, if the true proportion is 20% or greater ($p^* \geq 20\%$), he will run. The difficulty in using a sample to estimate the true value of p^* is that even if $p^* \geq 20\%$, he will observe a sample proportion of less than 20% ($\bar{p} < 20\%$) quite frequently because of sampling

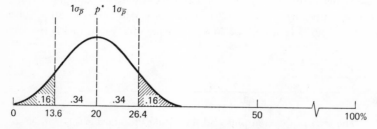

FIGURE 4.5   Distribution of observed percentage of vote $\bar{p}$.

[2] Rounded to two decimal places.

error. It will be our task to inform him when an observed $\bar{p}$ that turns out to be less than 20% could be simply the result of sampling error. For our analysis, we operate on the hypothesis that p^* is the lowest value consistent with a decision to run; that is, that $p^* = 20\%$.

After drawing a sample of size 40, it is found that $\bar{p} = 15\%$. We show that samples yielding $\bar{p}$'s at least this low will occur about 22% of the time when the true proportion is actually 20%. In light of this result we must conclued that Mr. Smith was too hasty in using the sample proportion $\bar{p} = 15\%$ as evidence that p^* is not at least 20%.

Let us now see how it was determined that $\bar{p}$ values of 15% or less would be observed 22% of the time when actually $p^* = 20\%$.

First, if $p^* = 20\%$ and $\bar{p} = 15\%$, there is a sampling error of 5 percentage points ($\bar{p} - p^*$). But a sample of only 40 observations has a standard error ($\sigma_{\bar{p}}$) of 6.4%, as we calculated previously. Therefore, the observed proportion $\bar{p}$ is less than one standard error away from the true proportion p^*. To be precise using the formula for Z, the number of standard errors that $\bar{p}$ lies from p^*, we have[3]

$$Z = \frac{\bar{p} - p^*}{\sigma_{\bar{p}}}$$

$$= -\frac{.05}{.064} = -.78 \qquad\qquad 4.3$$

This value, $-.78$, is the calculation for Z required to enter the normal probability table of Chapter 3.

Looking in Table 3.5 under $Z = .78$, we see that sample estimates lying up to .78 of a standard error below p^* occur approximately 28% of the time; this is illustrated in Figure 4.6 as the shaded area under the normal curve.

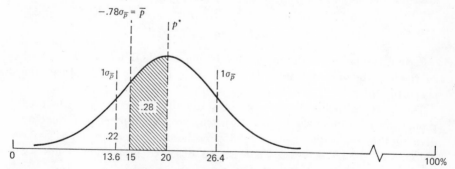

FIGURE 4.6   A probability distribution for a sample estimate p.

[3] Again, we must assume that the total population N is very large. Otherwise $\sigma_{\bar{p}}$ must be adjusted via the reduction factor indicated earlier.

Therefore, the probability of a sample estimate even lower than this is $.50 - .28 = .22$, as shown by the unshaded area lying between $\bar{p} = 0$ and $\bar{p} = 15$. Most people would, in these circumstances, agree that Mr. Smith was not using his sampled evidence properly in accepting the observed proportion of votes ($\bar{p} = 15\%$) as accurate—because if p^* were actually 20% as he had hoped, there is a probability of 22% that a sample of size 40 will yield $\bar{p}$'s of 15% or lower.

We now seem to be at an impasse. We went to the trouble to collect a random sample so as to be assured that the sample would be unbiased, but we now learn that the sampled evidence contains so much error that it cannot be used conclusively. What use, then, is all this effort to obtain a good sample?

In fact, the method we describe provides us with a very valuable tool. We are now able to evaluate the accuracy of our sampled evidence before we use it to reach important conclusions. As we have just seen, a random sample of size 40 that yields an observed proportion of votes for Mr. Smith of $\bar{p} = .15$ cannot be used to reject the hypothesis that the true proportion of votes is actually $p^* = .20$. We, therefore, have aided Mr. Smith by showing him that a decision not to run based on the sampled evidence would very likely be a poor decision. As we shall learn, what he needs is a much larger sample.

Suppose, on the other hand, that instead of a critical proportion of votes $p^* = 20\%$, Mr. Smith believes that the critical proportion is actually $p^* \geq 40\%$. Again, with a sample of size 40 he observes $\bar{p} = 15\%$. Let us now evaluate a decision not to run based on the same small sample.

As previously, we calculate the standard error of the sample proportion ($\sigma_{\bar{p}}$) by making use of equation 4.2.

$$\sigma_{\bar{p}} = \sqrt{\frac{(.40)(.60)}{40}} = \sqrt{.006}$$

$$= .077 \quad \text{or} \quad 7.7\%$$

Second, we calculate the magnitude of the sample difference $\bar{p} - \rho^*$ by subtracting the observed proportion $\bar{p} = .15\%$ from the hypothetical true proportion $p^* = 40\%$ to obtain $15\% - 40\% = -25\%$.

Third, we calculate the number of standard errors that the observed proportion $\bar{p}$ lies from the hypothetical true proportion p^*. This is done by dividing the sample difference of -25% by the standard error of 7.7%. We obtain $-25\%/7.7\% = -3.2$. That is, the observed proportion $\bar{p}$ lies 3.2 standard errors from the hypothetical true proportion p^*.

Fourth, by using $Z = 3.2$, we enter the table of the unit normal distribution in Chapter 3 to find the probability of observing such a large difference.

From Table 3.5, we find that the probability of observing a sample proportion of up to three standard errors ($Z = 3$) is $.5 + .4987 = .9987$, so that the probability of a sampling error of more than three standard errors is $1 - .9987 = .0013$. But since our observed Z score is even less than -3 (we calculated $Z = -3.2$), the probability of observing such a large sampling error is less than .0013—it is about .001. That is, if the true proportion actually were $p^* = 40\%$, then with a sample of size 40, only one such sample in a thousand would yield a $\bar{p}$ as low as 15%.

Fifth, we must now ask Mr. Smith to make a decision about using this sample as conclusive evidence. Realizing that so large a sampling error is extraordinarily unlikely, he will have very serious doubts that the true proportion p^* is actually 40%. Instead, he will undoubtedly decide that the sample difference $\bar{p} - p^*$ is not due to sampling error, but that it was the hypothesis $p^* = 40\%$ that was in error. Based on this probability test, he will therefore decide to accept the sample as conclusive evidence about the true size of the proportion p^*. He uses the sample to reject the hypothesis that $p^* \geq 40\%$. And it is here that we learn some important points about the nature of statistical sampling procedure.

First, the procedure cannot be used to accept an hypothesis—only to reject one. Our earlier experience with the hypothesis that $p^* \geq 20\%$ was not atypical. In that case, the sample difference was small enough that it might easily have been caused by sampling error. Therefore, it may well have been true that the hypothesis $p^* \geq 20\%$ was correct. But since the sample difference might also have been the result of an incorrect hypothesis, we see that just because we could not prove that the hypothesis was false does not mean that we have proved the hypothesis to be true. As shown in Figure 4.7, where the shaded area under the curve represents those sample proportions $\bar{p}$ that have less than 5% probability of occurrence when $p^* = 20\%$, if we observe $\bar{p} = 15\%$, although we do not reject the hypothesis, it may still be that the true sample proportion p^* is less than 20%. In sum, when we learn that the sample difference is small enough so that in all probability it may have been due to sampling error, all we are able to say is that *the sample does not constitute significant evidence for rejecting the hypothesis*. And this is what we said in the case of $p^* \geq 20\%$.

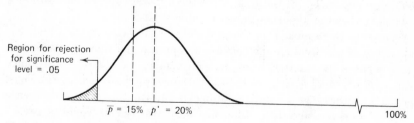

Region for rejection for significance level = .05

$\bar{p} = 15\%$ $p^* = 20\%$

100%

FIGURE 4.7   The rejection region.

However, when the sample difference $(\bar{p} - p^*)$ is so great that, in all probability, it could not have been due to sampling error, the sample provides the opportunity to draw a definite conclusion about the hypothesis— *the conclusion that it is false and should be rejected*. This is the result that was obtained in the case of $p^* \geq 40\%$.

It should be realized that the inability to use statistical sampling procedure for accepting hypotheses is not of great practical consequence. When we learn that a hypothesis should not be rejected, we learn that the sample should be rejected as significant evidence, and this is useful information. As in the case of Mr. Smith, to be able to point out to him that he should not use the sampled evidence is to prevent him from using it wrongly. When we learn that in all probability the hypothesis is false and should be rejected, we learn that the sample is significant evidence that can be used with confidence—and this is important for decision making. Finally, if the intent of the analysis is specifically to prove a hypothesis (for example, decentralized health clinics will result in increased outpatient care), one can proceed by seeking to reject conflicting hypotheses, and if all but the hypothesis of interest are rejected, we have "boxed in," for all practical purposes, our proof.

The next important point about decision making with samples can now be made. This is its subjective nature. We have repeatedly used the phrase "in all probability"—as in, "in all probability the sample difference is too large to have been due to sampling error." The question is at what probability level are we ready to make a definitive statement that a sample difference could not be due to sampling error. The answer is entirely subjective; it must be made by the decision maker; and it depends on the decision maker's attitudes toward risk. But once this probability level is decided on, it is a bench mark—a decision criterion—for accepting or rejecting each hypothesis being tested.

To see this, recall that when we tested the hypothesis $p^* = 20\%$, a sample difference of five percentage points was observed. It was learned that such a difference or more would occur 22% of the time when the hypothesis was true—too high a probability to reject the hypothesis. In contrast, it was learned that when $p^* = 40\%$, the resulting sample difference of 25% or more would occur only $.1\%$ of the time when the hypothesis was true—so low a probability that the hypothesis must be judged false.

Apparently there must be some probability level between 22% and $.1\%$ that serves as the dividing line between acceptance and rejection. Although this is a subjective matter, most decision makers use the 5% probability level, or *significance level* in statistical parlance, as the bench mark. Thus, when a hypothesis is set and a sample is drawn, the sample difference $\bar{p} - p^*$ is observed, and if the difference is so great that it would be caused by sampling error only 5% of the time or less, *the difference is said to be* *significant and not due to sampling error.* The sample is then accepted as evidence to reject the hypothesis.

The problem, of course, is that for those hypotheses that are rejected at the 5% significance level, 5% of the time they are true—the sample difference was due merely to sampling error—and they should not have been rejected. Here, there is, therefore, a 5% risk that decisions based on samples will be in error, a costly matter indeed. But how else are we to screen out those hypotheses that actually are false unless we accept some bench mark as a cutoff point? Although there is one alternative, but considerably less practical, hypothesis-testing procedure that avoids the use of such bench marks,[4] the only other alternative is to make decisions without sample evidence. Let us briefly consider this alternative.

The decision maker who has less than perfect information about those variables in the environment that he does not control and that may affect the payoffs to his decision must determine whether he wants more information prior to making his decision. Of course, if a wrong decision will not have very costly consequences, then he will not want to pay very much for information to avoid those costs. An example is a decision about which movie to see on Saturday night, or which secretary to hire. But when a wrong decision would be very costly, for example, a decision to invest in a manpower training program where the economic demand for the skills taught by the program might fail to materialize, it would pay to get more information first.

The decision maker who does not use a sample may (1) rely on information he already has at his disposal, nonquantitative information that he can obtain from acquaintances or consultants, or published secondary sources of information; or (2) attempt a complete enumeration of his target population. The first of these alternatives may well provide the information he needs, but he must be in a position to evaluate the degree of bias in such sources of information as well as the sampling error that those sources actually contain, since much of this type of information is in the nature of a sample. Here the risk of a wrong decision again appears, and this risk may be at least as high as in a well designed sample, but in contrast with the sample, the risk cannot be evaluated in advance.

[4] This is the procedure of statistical decision theory. To use this approach, the decision maker must be able to specify (1) the costs that he would bear not only if he were to reject a hypothesis when the actual "state of affairs" or "state of nature" was that the hypothesis was true, but also his costs for each alternative state of nature that might materialize; (2) the probability that each state of nature would materialize; and (3) his preferences for varying degrees of risk. One highly simplified example of this approach was given in the traffic accident example of Chapter 3, and another will be given in Chapter 11. However, since these three items are extremely difficult to obtain in practice, the use of the bench mark "significance level" is the more pragmatic approach. A list of references in decision theory is provided at the end of this chapter.

If the decision maker attempts a complete enumeration, for example, Mr. Smith attempts to interview every voter in the city, the cost of collecting and processing the data and the risk inherent in the mistakes that occur in coding and reporting that much data are very likely to exceed the combined cost of collecting a sample and the risk of wrong decision because of sampling error. And in many cases, a complete enumeration is not even possible. For example, to evaluate the life of very light bulb prior to a purchasing decision is to count the amount of time it takes each of them to burn out! Or in evaluating relatively new types of programs prior to financing a large number of them, a complete enumeration is, of course, impossible.

In light of all this, the decision maker may well see the wisdom of drawing a well-designed sample, knowing and accepting the condition that decisions with less than complete information are, to some extent, risky. We summarize the hypothesis-testing procedure for testing hypotheses about a proportion p^*.

---

1. State hypothesis that the proportion in question is true: $p^* \geq k$ or $p^* \leq k$. Use the equality $p^* = k$ for the test: where k is some percentage.

Comment. Our method operates by attempting to reject hypotheses. Therefore, we state the hypothesis as if it were true and attempt to use sample evidence to reject it. In the case of $p^* \geq k$, we set $p^* = k$ and attempt to show that $p^* < k$. In the case of $p^* \leq k$, we set $p^* = k$ and attempt to show that $p^* > k$. If hypothesis is $p^* = k$, then we attempt to show that $p^* \neq k$, for example, that $p^* > k$ or $p^* < k$.

2. State significance level below which hypothesis will be rejected, and collect sample of size n.

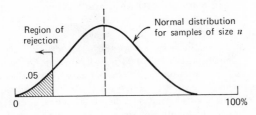

Comment. The significance level serves as the decision criterion for rejecting the hypothesis. Later, we consider another procedure that includes the determination of the sample size.

3. Calculate sample proportion $\bar{p}$.

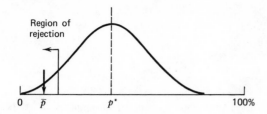

4. Calculate standard error of the sample proportion:

$$\sigma_{\bar{p}} = \sqrt{\frac{p^*(1 - p^*)}{n}}$$

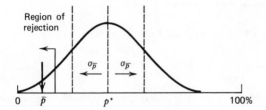

If the total population n is not large, multiply by $\sqrt{(N - n)/(N - 1)}$

5. Calculate the sample difference and convert into standard error Z:

$$Z = \frac{\bar{p} - p^*}{\sigma_{\bar{p}}}$$

6. Look in the table of the unit normal distribution for the probability that the sample difference $(\bar{p} - p^*)$ is up to Z standard errors below p^* for hypothesis that $p^* \geq k$ (or above p^* for hypothesis that $p^* \leq k$).

$$P(\bar{p} - p^* < Z\sigma_{\bar{p}}) = P(Z) + .5$$

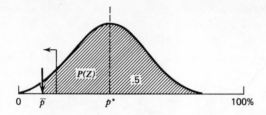

7. Determine the probability that the sample difference $\bar{p} - p^*$ is Z

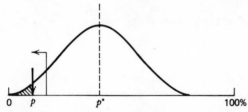

standard errors below p^* (or above—if hypothesis is $p^* \leq k$):

$$P(\bar{p} - p^* \geq Z\sigma_{\bar{p}}) = 1 - [P(Z) + .5]$$

8. If the probability of this sample difference is less than the significance level, reject the hypothesis. Otherwise, do not reject.

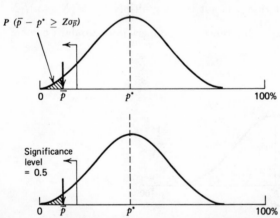

Comment. In our diagram, $P(\bar{p} - p^* \geq Z\sigma_{\bar{p}})$ is smaller than the significance level. We conclude that the sample difference $(\bar{p} - p^*)$ is too large to have been caused by sampling error. From our decision criterion (the 5% significance level) the sample is accepted as significant, and we reject the hypothesis.

We now apply our hypothesis-testing procedure to another example. Suppose that our prospective candidate, Mr. Smith, has been convinced about the virtues of sampling, and has 4000 registered voters interviewed. His hypothesis is that $p^* \geq 20\%$, and he decides to set the significance level at 5%. The sample proportion turns out to be $\bar{p} = 18\%$. Should he reject his hypothesis?

The standard error of the sample proportion $\sigma_{\bar{p}}$ is calculated and found to be .0064.

Step 4
$$\sigma_{\bar{p}} = \sqrt{\frac{.20(.80)}{4000}} = \sqrt{\frac{.16}{4000}} = \sqrt{.00004} \qquad \text{okay}$$

$$= .0064$$

Next, with a sample difference $\bar{p} - p^* = .18 - .20 = -.02$, the sample proportion is found to lie $Z = 3.1$ standard errors from the hypothetical true proportion p^*

Step 5
$$Z = \frac{.18 - .20}{.0064} = \frac{-.02}{.0064} = -3.1 \qquad \text{okay}$$

Referring to the table of the unit normal distribution in Chapter 3 under $Z = 3.1$, we find that the probability of observing $\bar{p}$ up to 3.1 standard errors below p^* is .499.

not okay $P(.02 < 3.1(s)$

Step 6 $P(\bar{p} - p^* < Z\sigma_{\bar{p}}) = P(Z) + .5 = .499 + .5$

okay

$$= .999$$

Therefore, the probability of observing a sample proportion that is greater than or equal to 3.1 standard errors below p^* is only .001.

Step 7 $P(\bar{p} - p^* \geq Z\sigma_{\bar{p}}) = 1 - [P(Z) + .5] = 1 - .999$

okay

$$= .001$$

Since this probability is less than his significance level (.001 < .05), he accepts the sample evidence as significant and concludes that $p^* < 20\%$— he rejects the hypothesis and presumably decides not to run.

This example provides some interesting information. Notice that although Mr. Smith paid for a sample 100 times as large as in the first example (where $n = 40$ and $p^* \geq 20\%$), his sampling accuracy did not increase proportionately. Our measure of sample accuracy, the standard error $\sigma_{\bar{p}}$, decreased from $\sigma_{\bar{p}} = .064$ with $n = 40$ to $\sigma_{\bar{p}} = .0064$ with $n = 4000$, an improvement in accuracy of only 10 times. There are, therefore, decreasing returns to increasing the sample size n. That this is generally true can be seen through a closer examination of the formula for the standard error:

$$\sigma_{\bar{p}} = \sqrt{\frac{p^*(1 - p^*)}{n}}$$

which may be written as

$$\sigma_{\bar{p}} = \frac{\sqrt{p^*(1 - p^*)}}{\sqrt{n}}$$

(assuming as before that the total population N is large).

With the hypothesis held constant (recall that p^* was 20% in both examples), the numerator remained constant as the sample size changed. Therefore, the standard error varies inversely with the square root of the sample size. For example, if the sample size is quadrupled, $\sigma_{\bar{p}}$ is reduced by 50%; if n is increased 100 times, $\sigma_{\bar{p}}$ is reduced by 90%. This relationship is illustrated in Figure 4.8.

Recalling the extremely low standard error that resulted when Mr. Smith increased his sample size 100-fold, it might be asked whether the great cost of this increased sample size was entirely necessary. One might suggest that with a significance level of only 5% and given the costs of sampling, a sample that yields a probability of less than 1% (.0064 to be exact) of observing the sample difference $\bar{p} - p^*$ is rather extravagant. A considerably less accurate sample would certainly be adequate, and a sizeable saving with the commensurately smaller sample would result. The question, of course, is how small a sample can be purchased to get just the specified degree of accuracy, and it is to resolving this question that we now turn.

4.1.4 Determining the Size of Sample for Estimating Proportions p

In determining an appropriate sample size, the first point to be considered, as we are by now well aware, is that samples provide estimates of the true

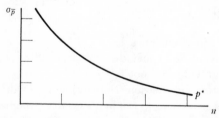

Figure 4.8 The relation between the standard error of the sample proportion and sample size.

sample proportion, and that some error must be expected. That is, samples provide "ball park" estimates of p^*. To be sure, the size of this "ball park" will be subject to the control of the decision maker—it can be measured in terms of standard errors and it can be reduced to any specified size by increasing the sample size. Nevertheless, the decision maker must first specify how large a ball park he is willing to accept. In making this decision, he must realize that on drawing the sample and observing the sample proportion $\bar{p}$, part of what the statistician will tell him is that the true proportion p^* lies between $\bar{p} - e$ and $\bar{p} + e$ where e is the sampling error. The range between $\bar{p} - e$ and $\bar{p} + e$ is his ball park, and he must be willing to use it and act on it as if it were the true proportion itself. In many instances, the decision maker might be able to put up with quite a large ball park. For example, in estimating how long it takes to fly from New York to Los Angeles, a decision maker might accept a result that is in error by plus or minus one half hour. In contrast, a race car driver intending to compete in the Indianapolis 500 may, in selecting a new engine, want an estimate of how long it would take to make one lap around the oval that is in error by no more than plus or minus two seconds.

Thus the first step in determining the right sample size is to determine the size of the "ball park" or, to return to more scientific language, he must determine his confidence interval. Suppose, in our election example, that Mr. Smith stipulates that he will accept the result of a sample that is accurate by plus or minus two percentage points. That is, whatever the sample proportion $\bar{p}$, he will be confident that the true proportion p^* lies in the range $\bar{p} - .02 < p^* < \bar{p} + .02$ (Figure 4.9).

But here is where he hears the other part of what the statistician has to tell him. That is that he cannot be 100% confident that this confidence interval will bracket the true proportion p^*. This is because sample proportions are approximately normally distributed about the true proportion, so that one sample proportion may be different from another. As a result, one confidence interval will span a different range of proportions than another as illustrated by samples A and B in Figure 4.10. Indeed, there is some small probability that a sample proportion $\bar{p}$ will be drawn that is so far from p^* that the confidence interval constructed around it will not bracket the true proportion. This is illustrated in sample C in Figure 4.10.

This is the risk counterpart to that encountered in hypothesis testing

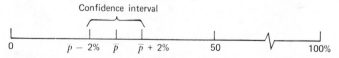

FIGURE 4.9   A confidence interval.

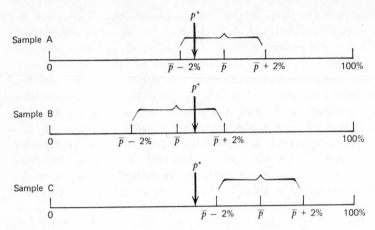

FIGURE 4.10 Variation in confidence intervals.

previously. It is what the decision maker wants to keep as small as possible, consistent with his other objective of keeping sampling costs low. Hence, although the decision maker cannot obtain 100% confidence that his confidence interval will bracket p^*, he can draw a large enough sample so that for 95% of all confidence intervals that could arise, that sample would bracket p^*. Or he could accept a sample that gives him only 90% or even 99% confidence. This *confidence level* is his to choose, and in so doing, he sets his risk of a wrong conclusion as well as his sample size.

Once the decision maker sets these two bench marks, the confidence interval and the confidence level, the determination of the sample size is straightforward. We have already supposed that Mr. Smith has decided on a confidence level that is plus or minus two percentage points about the sample proportion ($\bar{p} \pm .02$). This indicates that the largest error or *sample difference* he is willing to accept is $e = \bar{p} - p^* = .02$. From our formula for Z, we can write

$$e = \bar{p} - p^* = Z\sigma_{\bar{p}}$$

so that our error can be expressed in terms of the number of standard errors (Z) and the size of the standard error $\sigma_{\bar{p}}$. Furthermore, from our formula for $\sigma_{\bar{p}}$, where it is assumed that the total population is large, we may write

$$e = \bar{p} - p^* = Z\sqrt{\frac{p^*(1 - p^*)}{n}}$$

so that now our error can be expressed in terms of Z, p^*, and n. Since e has already been established in the confidence interval set by the decision

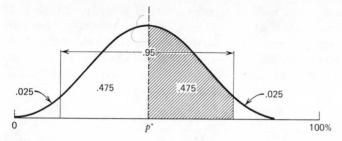

FIGURE 4.11   A 95% interval about p^*.

maker ($e = .02$), we need to know only the values of Z and p^* to derive the sample size n. We derive these in steps.

The value of Z can be obtained directly from the confidence level (.95) and from the table of the unit normal distribution. Notice that .95 establishes a probability limit on either side of and centered on the true proportion p^*, as illustrated in Figure 4.11. This leaves a probability of only .05 outside these limits, .025 in each tail. To use the table of the unit normal distribution, we want only the probability on just one side of p^*, which is illustrated as the shaded area under the curve in Figure 4.11. To obtain this probability, we simply divide the confidence level (.95) by 2 (.95/2) to get .475. Looking up this probability in Table 3.5, we find that such a probability occurs for a value of Z lying between $Z = 1.9$ and $Z = 2.0$. Interpolating (or more properly, using the detailed table of probabilities of Z in the Appendix IV of this book), we find that $Z = 1.96$. Now all we need to know is the value of p^*.

The problem is that p^* is unknown—it is the parameter that our sample is supposed to estimate. There are two pragmatic approaches for getting around this problem. The first is to use our sample proportion $\bar{p}$ in place of p^*. The other is to use that value of p that would result in the highest possible standard error. This approach is the most conservative, and will yield a sample size slightly larger than the minimum size. To find this value of p, note that the standard error of $\bar{p}$ rises as p^* approaches 50%, n assumed constant. For example, if $p^* = 20\%$, then $p^*(1 - p^*)$ in the formula for $\sigma_{\bar{p}}$ is $.2(.8) = .16$. If p^* rises to .4, then $p^*(1 - p^*)$ is $.4(.6) = .24$. If p^* rises to .5, then $p^*(1 - p^*)$ is $.5(.5) = .25$). This yields the highest value of $\sigma_{\bar{p}}$ since, we notice, when p rises beyond .5, the values for p^* and $(1 - p^*)$ simply become reversed. For example, if p^* rises to .6, we have $p^*(1 - p^*) = .6(.4)$ $= .24$, the same result as was obtained for $p^* = .4$. We use this approach, and set $p^* = .5$.

Now that we have obtained values for Z and for p^*, we can solve for n, the sample size. But, first, there is a nice simplification that we should recognize. If the decision maker's significance level is always .95, then Z will always be 1.96, while if p^* is always set conservatively at .5, then our values of both Z and p^* will be the same from sample to sample at $Z = 1.96$ and $p^* = .5$, respectively. The only item that would change is the decision maker's confidence interval. But once he sets this, we have all the information we need to calculate n. We do this now. We have

$$e = \bar{p} - p^* = Z\sqrt{\frac{p^*(1 - p^*)}{n}}$$

or

$$.02 = 1.96\frac{\sqrt{.5(.5)}}{\sqrt{n}} = 1.96(.5)/\sqrt{n}$$

Dividing both sides by $\sqrt{n}$ and by .02, we have

$$\sqrt{n} = \frac{1.96(.5)}{.02}$$

and, squaring both sides, we obtain our equation for n:

$$n = \left[\frac{1.96(.5)}{.02}\right]^2 \qquad\qquad 4.4$$

$$= \left(\frac{.98}{.02}\right)^2 = (49)^2$$

$$= 2401$$

Thus, if we are to obtain the confidence interval and confidence level stipulated by the decision maker, we need a sample of 2401 observations. Notice that this is considerably lower than the sample of 4000 drawn earlier by Mr. Smith. Let us generalize our formula for n. We substitute back into equation 4.4 the variables underlying the figures 1.96, .5, and .02; that is, we insert Z, $p^*(1 - p^*)$, and $\bar{p} - p^*$.

$$n = \left[\frac{Z\sqrt{p^*(1 - p^*)}}{\bar{p} - p^*}\right]^2 \qquad\qquad 4.5$$

Equation 4.5 represents the formula for general use in determining the sample size.[5] However, if the .95 confidence level and the conservative

---

[5] This approach is best applied where the sample size is large—say, 500 or more. If less, then the confidence interval will not be symmetric around the sample mean. Mr. Smith will therefore have to make use of the more laborious binomial distribution, or else refer to a more advanced text.

estimate of $p^*(p^* = .5)$ are always to be used, then we may simplify equation 4.5 to obtain

$$n = .96\left(\frac{1}{\bar{p} - p^*}\right)^2 \qquad\qquad 4.6$$

We use equation 4.6 for another example.

A program administrator in a certain community wants to know the proportion of families in his community that are poor—that is, that have incomes under \$4000 per year. He needs to know how large a sample he must collect to be within three percentage points of the true proportion with a 95 % confidence level. We insert .03 for $\bar{p} - p^*$ in equation 4.6 to obtain

$$n = .96\left(\frac{1}{.03}\right)^2 = .96(1109) = 1065$$

We have indicated at several points that this approach assumes that the total population is large. Suppose, now, that the administrator's community is actually quite small, containing, say, $N = 4000$ families. Here, the standard error of $\bar{p}$ must be adjusted downward by multiplying by a reduction factor $\sqrt{(N - n)/(N - 1)}$. Fortunately, however, instead of complicating the analysis, another simplified formula has been derived that takes account of the small total population.[6]

$$n = \frac{N}{1 + N(\bar{p} - p^*)^2} \qquad\qquad 4.7$$

Again, using the confidence interval $\bar{p} - p^* = .03$, we have

$$n = \frac{4000}{1 + 4000(.03)^2} = \frac{4000}{1 + 3.6} = 870$$

Finally, suppose our administrator wants to know not the proportion of people who are poor, a need that he is by now well equiped to fulfill, but the average family income in the community—a variable that is not a proportion. What techniques should he apply ? The answer is, the techniques described in the next section, of course!

4.2 SAMPLING TO ESTIMATE A MEAN

Our program administrator believes that the average family income in his community is no more than \$4000 per year. If this is true, then the community becomes eligible for federal financial assistance. After the application

---

[6] This formula also makes use of the conservative approach of setting $p^* = .5$. But instead of using $Z = 1.96$, it uses the slightly larger $Z = 2.00$, which results in the simplified equation. For its derivation, see Taro Yamane, *Statistics: An Introductory Analysis*, second edition (New York: Harper and Row, 1967), p. 581.

for eligibility is made to the federal government, the government has a sample survey done to determine whether the average family income level is, in fact, under $4000 per year. On drawing a random sample of 100, the government finds that the average income level is $4200, and on the basis of this evidence, rejects the administrator's application for eligibility and assistance. Should the program administrator agree with this finding, or should he argue that this high sample mean (denoted by $\bar{x}$) is merely the result of sampling error?

The logic of our earlier analysis of this chapter indicates that he must state the hypothesis that $\mu \leq \$4000$, where μ is the true mean family income of the community. He must then apply a statistical sampling procedure designed to reject the hypothesis. As we shall learn, this procedure is roughly the same as that used earlier in testing the accuracy of sample proportions ($\bar{p}$). After stating his hypothesis, and given that $n = 100$, he sets his significance level, calculates the standard error, determines Z, and tests the probability of Z relative to his significance level. However, the two procedures are not quite identical as we now indicate.

The difference between the two procedures revolves about the standard error—its roots, use, and calculation.

4.2.1 THE SAMPLING ERROR OF SAMPLE MEANS

Recall from Figures 4.1 and 4.3 that when we are sampling a variable that only has a zero or one value, the probability distribution of the sample proportion $\bar{p}$, although binomial, approximates the normal distribution when the sample size becomes large, say $n > 40$. Consequently, we could test for the probability of any number (Z) of standard errors ($\sigma_{\bar{p}}$) represented by a sample difference by using a table of probabilities under the unit normal distribution. But the variable x can take on any value and is, therefore, not binomially distributed; hence, the question arises of how we are to test for the probability of an observed number of $\sigma_{\bar{x}}$'s and thereby to test our sample evidence.

It develops that no matter what the distribution may be of the variable x, when we take a properly drawn random sample from this distribution, the distribution of *the sample means $\bar{x}$ will approach the normal distribution the larger the sample size n.*[7]

The rationale for this important result is shown in the following example. Our program administrator is interested in evaluating the mean value μ of the incomes x of all families in a certain community. Suppose that there are 2000 families in the community, and 500 of them earn under $2000 per year, 800

---

[7] This result is known as the central limit theorem and holds true as long as the variance σ^2 of the variable x is not infinitely large.

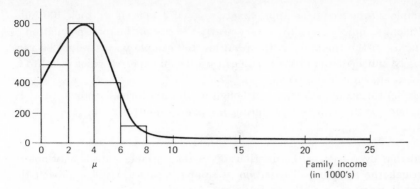

FIGURE 4.12 A distribution of family incomes.

earn between $2000 and $4000 per year, 400 earn between $4000 and $6000, 100 earn from $6000 to $8000 per year, and the remaining 200 families are scattered in intervals ranging up to $25,000 per year. This distribution of incomes is illustrated by the bar chart in Figure 4.12. This is clearly not a normal distribution but, as is shown by the curved line that approximates the height of the bars, it is sharply skewed to the right. The modal income level is between $2000 and $4000, and the mean income level is $\mu = \$4000$.

If only two independently drawn samples of 10 observations were drawn from this distribution, the first sample mean might be extremely low, say $\bar{x} = \$2200$ and the second might be extremely high, say $\bar{x} = \$6300$. But the probability of drawing such unrepresentative samples is very low. If, instead, 100 independently drawn samples of size 10 were drawn, most of them would yield sample means ($\bar{x}$) distributed much nearer to the true mean ($\mu = \$4000$). Similarly, if we were to draw 100 independent samples each of size 40, the resulting distribution of sample means would be approximately normal as shown by the bell-shaped curve in Figure 4.13, and the mean of all these

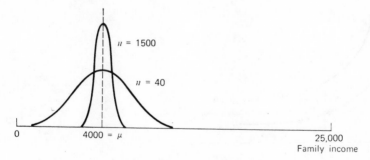

FIGURE 4.13 Distribution of sample means.

sample means would be approximately μ. Of course, if we took 100 independent samples of size 1500, very nearly the size of the total population of families in the community, the resulting 100 sample means would be very closely bunched around the true mean μ with an expected value equal to μ, also as shown in Figure 4.13.

From this example, we see (although we did not formally prove) that the expected value of the sample means is equal to the true mean

$$E(\bar{x}) = \mu$$

and that even though the distribution of the variable x itself may not be normal, the sampling distribution of sample means ($\bar{x}$) will approach the normal distribution as the sample size (n) increases.

Furthermore, just as was the case for the sampling distribution of $\bar{p}$ for a large sample size, the standard error of the sample mean $\sigma_{\bar{x}}$ is

$$\sigma_{\bar{x}} = \frac{\sigma}{\sqrt{n}} \qquad\qquad 4.8$$

(If the total population N is not very large, multiply $\sigma/\sqrt{n}$ by

$$\sqrt{(N-n)/(N-1)}.)$$

This is to say that the standard error of $\bar{x}$ depends both on the true standard deviation of the variable x, and on the size of the sample. The larger the standard deviation (σ) of x, the larger will be the standard error of $\bar{x}$; and the larger the sample size (n), the smaller will be the standard error of $\bar{x}$. These relationships are similar to those found for the standard error of $\bar{p}$, and are illustrated in Figure 4.14. We see that if a small sample $n(1)$ is drawn and the standard deviation of the variable x is small, say $\sigma(1)$, then the standard error of the sample mean will be $\sigma_{\bar{x}}(2)$. If we increase the sample size to $n(2)$, the standard deviation held constant, then we remain on

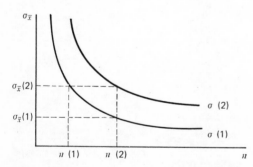

FIGURE 4.14 The effects of differences in σ and n on $\sigma_{\bar{x}}$.

the curve $\sigma(1)$ and find that the standard error has been reduced to $\sigma_{\bar{x}}(1)$. But if the standard deviation of the variable x were larger, say $\sigma(2)$, then at the larger sample size $n(2)$, the standard error would be read off the higher curve $\sigma(2)$, on which we find the larger standard error $\sigma_{\bar{x}}(2)$.

Given these results, we see that we are able to use essentially the same approach as we used for testing hypotheses about $\bar{p}$. For whatever the original distribution of the variable x, if our sample size is sufficiently large (say $n > 40$) we can make use of the standard error of $\bar{x}$ to test the probability that a given sample mean ($\bar{x}$) would be observed given an hypothesis about the size of the true mean μ.

A second difference between the procedures for testing hypotheses about p^* and μ concerns the calculation of the standard error. Recall that to calculate $\sigma_{\bar{p}}$, the only information needed was p^*, supplied in the hypothesis, and the sample size n, also given. But now, if we were to actually calculate $\sigma_{\bar{x}}$, we would need to know the income level (x_i) of each household (i) in the community. This information, of course, is not available, for if it were, the sample would not be needed—we could calculate the true mean directly. Consider the formula for σ in equation 4.9.

$$\sigma = \sqrt{\frac{\sum_i (x_i - \mu)^2}{n}}$$

4.9

We see what we have just said above, that the complete set of family incomes x_i is required for the analysis.

The best we can do short of this is to make use of the income of only the 100 families included in the sample to estimate σ. We, therefore, estimate σ by calculating S, the *unbiased sample standard deviation*.

$$S = \sqrt{\frac{\sum_i (x_i - \bar{x})^2}{n - 1}}$$

4.10

which depends only on the values of the incomes of the families x_i included in the sample. In sum, after calculating the sample mean $\bar{x}$ where, from Chapter 2,

$$\bar{x} = \frac{\sum_i x_i}{n}$$

We subtract $\bar{x}$ from each of the 100 x_j's, square each resulting difference or mean deviation to obtain $(x_i - \bar{x})^2$, and add all 100 squared deviations together. But instead of dividing the result by n, we divide by $n - 1$, a simple alteration which is all that is needed to assure that S will be an unbiased estimation of σ.[8] The result is the sample variance (S^2), from which S is obtained by taking the square root.

Once S is calculated, we then calculate the estimated standard error of $\bar{x}$, denoted as $S_{\bar{x}}$:

$$S_{\bar{x}} = \frac{S}{\sqrt{n}} \qquad\qquad 4.11$$

assuming as before that the total population N is large. This will serve as the basis for our hypothesis-testing procedure. Thus we see that although $S_{\bar{x}}$ is certainly easier to calculate than $\sigma_{\bar{x}}$, it required a lot more computational effort than was needed to calculate $\sigma_{\bar{p}}$, the standard error of $\bar{p}$.

But before we proceed, a problem that arises in using $S_{\bar{x}}$ instead of $\sigma_{\bar{x}}$ must be indicated. It arises after we observe a given sample mean $\bar{x}$ and obtain the sample difference $\bar{x} - \mu$. To determine the probability of observing this difference in terms of the number of standard errors, the ratio $(\bar{x} - \mu)/S_{\bar{x}}$ cannot be properly applied in conjunction with the table of the unit normal distribution. This is because this ratio is not a proper calculation for Z, the statistic required for entering this table. To calculate Z, we must use the true standard error $\sigma_{\bar{x}}$ as follows:

$$Z = \frac{\bar{x} - \mu}{\sigma_{\bar{x}}} \qquad\qquad 4.12$$

The ratio $(\bar{x} - \mu)/S_{\bar{x}}$ does not come from the unit normal distribution. It comes from a distribution that closely resembles the unit normal, but is more spread out. It is called simply, the "t-distribution."[9] However, as n becomes large, the t-distribution approximates the unit normal. In short, when we calculate this ratio, we do not obtain the statistic Z but, instead, the statistic t:

$$t = \frac{\bar{x} - \mu}{S_{\bar{x}}} \qquad\qquad 4.13$$

However, for large samples, and only for large samples, we ignore this distinction, although we return to it later when we consider the problem of hypothesis testing with small samples.

With this caveat firmly in mind, we proceed under the following rationale. It is that (1) since S is an unbiased estimator of σ, (2) since for increasingly large samples the error that is to be expected in using S in place of σ becomes increasingly small, and (3) since the t-distribution approaches the unit normal

---

[8] The proof of this assertion can be found in more advanced textbooks, such as Yamane, p. 503.

[9] For a given sample difference $(\bar{x} - \mu)$ and with identical standard errors $S_{\bar{x}} = \sigma_{\bar{x}}$, the probability of this sample difference will be slightly larger under the t-distribution than under the unit normal distribution.

distribution as the sample size increases, then for large samples the effects of using $S_{\bar{x}}$ in conjunction with the statistic Z and the unit normal distribution will, for all practical purposes, be negligible.

We continue now with our procedure for testing the hypothesis that the mean income level of our administrator's community is $\mu \leq \$4000$.

4.2.2 Testing Hypotheses About the Size of the Mean μ with Large Samples

Suppose our administrator sets his significance level at 5%. With a sample of 100 families having been drawn yielding $\bar{x} = \$4200$, he proceeds to determine whether such a large sample mean could have, in all probability, been observed when the true mean μ was actually no larger than $4000 ($\mu \leq \$4000$).

Suppose that the sample standard deviation is calculated and found to be $S = \$3000$. Then the estimated standard error of $\bar{x}$ is

$$S_{\bar{x}} = \frac{\$3000}{\sqrt{100}} = \$300$$

Since the sample mean ($\bar{x} = \$4200$) differed from the hypothetical true mean ($\mu = \$4000$) by $200, the number of standard errors (Z) represented by this sample difference is calculated as

$$Z = \frac{\$200}{\$300} = .67$$

or only two thirds of the one standard error. Looking in the table of the unit normal distribution under $Z = .67$, the probability that $\bar{x}$ could be as much as two thirds of a standard error above the mean is (rounded to two decimal places)

$$P(Z) + .5 = .25 + .5 = .75$$

Therefore, the probability of Z lying, at least, two thirds of a standard error above μ is

$$1 - [P(Z) + .5] = 1 - .75 = .25$$

Thus the administrator finds that if his hypothesis that $\mu \leq \$4000$ is true, as many as one sample out of four would yield a sample mean of $\bar{x} = \$4200$ or higher. Since this probability is much higher than his significance level ($.25 > .05$), the hypothesis that $\mu \leq \$4000$ cannot be rejected by the sample evidence. On the basis of this analysis, the administrator now has a strong case for arguing that his community should not be rejected as ineligible for federal aid.

We summarize our hypothesis-testing procedure for testing hypotheses about a mean μ with a large sample.

1. State hypothesis that the mean value μ of the variable x is true: $\mu \leq k$ or $\mu \geq k$. Use the equality $\mu = k$ for the test. No assumptions are required concerning the distribution of the variable x.

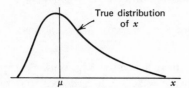

2. State significance level below which hypothesis will be rejected, and collect large sample of size n.

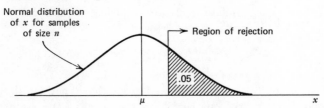

3. Calculate sample mean $\bar{x}$.

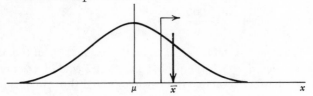

4. Calculate unbiased sample standard deviation S:

$$S = \sqrt{\dfrac{\sum\limits_{i=1}^{n} (x_i - \bar{x})^2}{n - 1}}$$

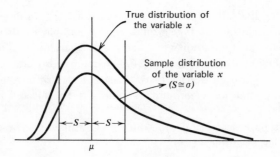

5. Estimate standard error of the sample mean $S_{\bar{x}}$:

$$S_{\bar{x}} = \frac{S}{\sqrt{n}} \quad \text{or} \quad \frac{S}{\sqrt{n}} \sqrt{\frac{N-n}{N-1}}$$

if N is not very large.

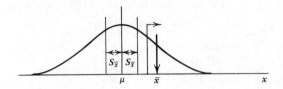

6. Calculate the sample difference and, using $S_{\bar{x}}$ as if it were $\sigma_{\bar{x}}$, calculate the number of standard errors Z:

$$Z = \frac{\bar{x} - \mu}{S_{\bar{x}}}$$

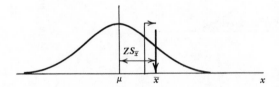

7. Look in table of the unit normal distribution for the probability that $\bar{x} - \mu$ is up to Z standard errors above mean (if hypothesis is $\mu \leq k$) or below mean (if hypothesis is $\mu \geq k$).

$$P(\bar{x} - \mu < Z\sigma_{\bar{x}}) = P(Z) + .5$$

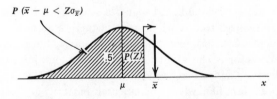

8. Determine probability that the sample difference $\bar{x} - \mu$ is Z standard errors above (or below—if hypothesis is $\mu \geq k$) mean μ:

$$P(\bar{x} - \mu \geq Z\sigma_{\bar{x}}) = 1 - [P(Z) + .5]$$

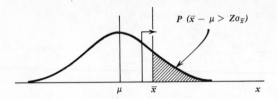

$$P\ (\bar{x} - \mu > Z\sigma_{\bar{x}})$$

9. If the probability of this sample difference is less than the significance level, reject hypothesis. Otherwise, do not reject.

If $P(\mu - \bar{x} \geq Z\sigma_{\bar{x}})$
$\begin{cases} \leq \text{significance level, reject hypothesis} \\ \\ > \text{significance level, don't reject} \end{cases}$

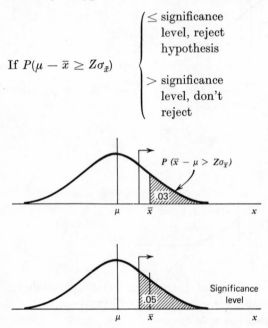

$$P\ (\bar{x} - \mu > Z\sigma_{\bar{x}})$$

Significance level

4.2.3 SMALL SAMPLE HYPOTHESIS TESTING: THE t-TEST

A member of a local community school board suggests a change in teacher-hiring policy. Although he realizes that a whole host of factors determines the educational achievement of the students in his community, he is convinced that one important factor is the ability of teachers to communicate with the students. Furthermore, since teachers who were raised in the same community would be more familiar with the cultural patterns of local students than would teachers from other communities, local teachers would be better able to communicate sympathetically with the students than would other teachers. Following this reasoning, he proposes as a matter of policy that teachers who have been raised locally be given preference for hiring.

Several other members of the school board object to this proposal, saying that it is "not where you come from," but "how much you know" that determines teacher effectiveness. In response, our board member agrees that the amount of academic training is another determinant of teacher effectiveness, but points out that it is not always easy to hire teachers with such credentials. He then asserts that the average teacher who has been raised in the community will have a better performance in class than will the average teacher raised elsewhere, and it is on this logic that his proposed new policy is based.

In effect, our board member is applying a somewhat more advanced line of reasoning than we have employed in this chapter heretofore. He is recognizing that a given dependent variable, in the case of teacher effectiveness, will depend on many independent variables. However, he can focus on the effect of the one variable, "where you come from," if this variable itself were unaffected by any of the other independent variables. With this assumption, he can ignore the effects of the other independent variables.[10] We proceed to analyze the problem at hand, making use only of the techniques that we have already described.

We state the hypothesis in a form that can be rejected and proceed, through an analysis of the significance of a sample, to attempt to reject it.

First, being interested in the proposition that the average "community-raised" teacher performs better than the average teacher, community of adolescence undifferentiated, we state the hypothesis that the true mean effectiveness μ of community-raised teachers is no greater than the true mean effectiveness of the undifferentiated teacher, the latter presumed already known. This, however, raises a question of measurement; that is, what we mean by and how we are to measure "teacher effectiveness."

Although by teacher effectiveness we could be referring to the degree of success of teachers in teaching students how to cope with life problems, we restrict ourselves to the less ambitious definition of "degree of success of teachers in raising the academic achievement of students." There are standardized examinations of academic achievement that are administered toward the completion of each student's high school education. We suppose that such an examination, culturally unbiased, has been administered by the local school board, and that annual average achievement scores are available for the school district as a whole. These achievement scores can range from a low of 200 to a high of 800. Suppose that in this school district the last average achievement score was 650. Then we state the hypothesis that the

---

[10] If there were reason to believe that this assumption is incorrect, our board member would have to worry about holding the other independent variables constant while considering the effect he describes. One technique for doing this will be described in the last section of Chapter 5.

achievement score of students taught by community-raised teachers is

$$\mu \leq 650$$

In addition, to avoid the complicating question of *weighting*, we assume that teachers have equal numbers of students in their classes.

Suppose now that a sample of nine teachers who were raised within the community is obtained, and that the achievement examination has already been applied to the students of their classes. The class averages for the nine teachers have been calculated, and will serve as the measure of each teacher's effectiveness x. These scores are shown in column 1 of Table 4.1. At the bottom of column 1 is the sum of these nine scores, and below that is the sample mean $\bar{x} = 668$. We now proceed to test whether this sample mean could have been, in probability, observed if the true mean score were actually no more than $\mu = 650$. However, because we are working with such a small sample, we cannot apply the Z-test as we did with large samples previously. Instead, we use a t-test. But as we indicated earlier, the use of the t-test requires that the true distribution of the variable x be normally distributed.

We show the distribution of the nine sample scores in Figure 4.15. It is believed that the true distribution of teacher effectiveness scores is normal

TABLE 4.1
A Sample of Teacher Effectiveness Scores

Observation	(1) x	(2) $x - \bar{x}$	(3) $(x - \bar{x})^2$
1.	626	−42	1764
2.	650	−18	324
3.	686	18	324
4.	650	−18	324
5.	674	6	36
6.	662	−6	36
7.	704	36	1296
8.	674	6	36
9.	686	18	324
$\sum$	6012	0	4464
$\bar{x} = \sum x / n$	668		
$S^2 = \sum (x - \bar{x})^2 / (n - 1)$			558

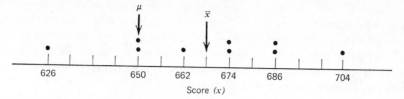

FIGURE 4.15   Distribution of teacher effectiveness scores.

and Figure 4.15, which shows these scores as rather more densely clustered near the sample mean, gives us no reason to suppose otherwise. We therefore continue under the assumption of normality.

We proceed to calculate the number of standard errors that the sample mean ($\bar{x}$) lies above the hypothetical true mean μ, and we take as our rejection criterion the significance level of .05.

First, we calculate the unbiased sample standard deviation S. In column 2 of Table 4.1, we show the deviation of each sample score from the sample mean $(x_i - \bar{x})$. The squared deviations are shown in column 3 $(x_i - \bar{x})^2$. At the bottom of this column, we have sums of the squared deviations $\sum (x_i - \bar{x})^2$ and below this is the average squared deviation $\sum (x_i - \bar{x})^2/(n - 1)$ or the sample variance S^2, which is equal to 558. We take the square root of this result, which gives S, the unbiased sample standard deviation

$$S = \sqrt{S^2} = \sqrt{558} = 23.62$$

Then, dividing this result by $\sqrt{n}$, we obtain the estimated standard error of the sample mean $S_{\bar{x}}$

$$S_{\bar{x}} = \frac{23.62}{\sqrt{n}} = \frac{23.62}{\sqrt{9}} = \frac{23.62}{3} = 7.87$$

or $S_{\bar{x}} = 7.87$. Finally, with a sample difference of $\bar{x} - \mu = 668 - 650 = 18$, we calculate the number of standard errors (t) that the sample mean lies from the hypothetical true mean as

$$t = \frac{18}{7.87} = 2.3$$

Until this point, we have followed the procedure used previously for calculating Z. But now we make use of the table of the t-distribution for completing the test. However, the use of this table is slightly different because one additional item of information is required. This is the number of degrees of freedom (denoted in the table as df) in the sample. This number is essentially the same as the sample size (n), but is adjusted to exclude the number of observations that could be derived given the additional statistics that are known about the sample. In this case, since we also know the sample mean $\bar{x}$ in addition to each of the nine observations, if any eight of these observations are known, then because we also know $\bar{x}$, we can derive the ninth observation arithmetically.[11] Hence, we deduct this observation froms the total. In the case of testing sample means, the number of observation that are free to vary, or the number of degrees of freedom, is

$$df = n - 1 \qquad\qquad 4.14$$

Now we are able to make use of the table of t-distribution, shown in Table 4.2. Notice that this table is set up differently than the table of the normal distribution—only a few probability values are shown, .05, .025, and .01. This is because, unlike the normal curve, there is a different set of probabilities under the t-distribution curve for each number of degrees of freedom. Since it would require a different table for each degree of freedom if all the probabilities were presented, only those most frequently used in conjunction with the significance level are presented.

To use the table, we set our level of significance (say, .05) and determine the degrees of freedom in our sample (df $= 9 - 1 = 8$). Then we look in the table and find the value of t, or number of standard errors $S_{\bar{x}}$, that would be observed in a sample of the size indicated by df where the probability of observing a sample difference is no smaller than the significance level.

This preset value of t, since it marks off the region of rejection, can be called the critical value of t and can be denoted as t^*. Hence, by looking in Table 4.2 in the column under .05 and in the row for df $= 8$, we find that $t^* = 1.86$.

We then compare t^* with the number of standard errors t that were actually observed in the sample difference $\bar{x} - \mu$. If t is smaller than t^*, then we cannot reject the hypothesis—that is, in this case the size of the sample difference as measured by t is small enough so that it could well have been due to sampling error. But if $t \geq t^*$, we reject the hypothesis, arguing that the probability of observing so many standard errors when the hypothesis is true is less than .05—so low that in all probability the hypothesis is false.

Returning to our hypothesis that community-raised teachers are no more effective than the average teacher (e.g., that $\mu \leq 650$), we have already found that the sample difference $\bar{x} - \mu$ measured in t-values was $t = 2.3$.

---

[11] For example, we take the first eight observations of x scores in the sample of Table 4.1 above and add them together. In addition, because we know $\bar{x}$ and n, if we multiply $\bar{x}$ by n, we get the sum of all nine observations. Finally, subtracting the sum of the first eight from the sum of all nine, we arrive at the value of the ninth observation.

TABLE 4.2

Selected values of t^* corresponding
to probabilities of the t-Distribution

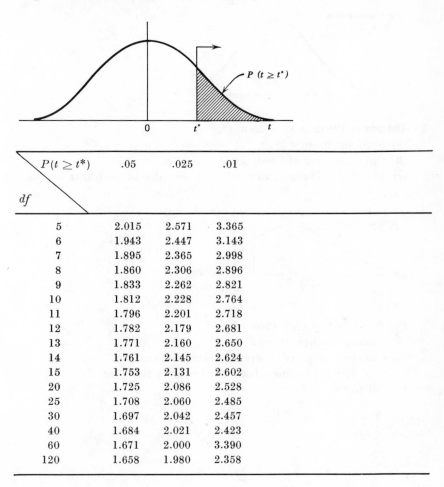

$P(t \geq t^*)$	.05	.025	.01
df			
5	2.015	2.571	3.365
6	1.943	2.447	3.143
7	1.895	2.365	2.998
8	1.860	2.306	2.896
9	1.833	2.262	2.821
10	1.812	2.228	2.764
11	1.796	2.201	2.718
12	1.782	2.179	2.681
13	1.771	2.160	2.650
14	1.761	2.145	2.624
15	1.753	2.131	2.602
20	1.725	2.086	2.528
25	1.708	2.060	2.485
30	1.697	2.042	2.457
40	1.684	2.021	2.423
60	1.671	2.000	3.390
120	1.658	1.980	2.358

But the largest value of t that could be accepted as consistent with the
hypothesis is $t^* = 1.86$. Since $t > t^*$, we must reject the hypothesis. Indeed,
we have provided evidence that substantiates our board member's assertion
that "where you have lived" has something to do with "how well you
perform," at least, where local education is concerned.

We summarize our small-sample hypothesis-testing procedure making
use of the t-test.

1. State hypothesis that the mean value of the variable x is true: $\mu \leq k$ or $\mu \geq k$. Use the equality $\mu = k$ for the test. Then collect sample of size $n \leq 40$. *The assumption is required that* x *is normally distributed.*

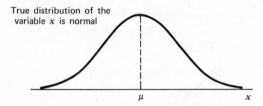

True distribution of the
variable x is normal

2. Determine the critical value of t^*:
   (a) State significance level.
   (b) Obtain degrees of freedom: df $= n - 1$.
   (c) Identify the critical value of t^* in the table of the t-distribution.

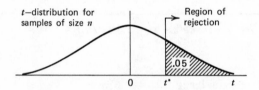

t–distribution for
samples of size n

Region of
rejection

.05

3. Calculate the observed value of t:
   (a) Calculate sample mean $\bar{x}$.
   (b) Calculate unbiased sample standard deviation S.
   (c) Calculate the estimated standard error of the mean $S_{\bar{x}}$
   (d) Calculate

$$t = \frac{\bar{x} - \mu}{S_{\bar{x}}}$$

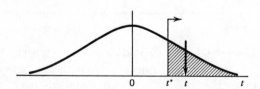

4. If $t > t^*$, reject hypothesis.
   If $t \leq t^*$, do not reject.

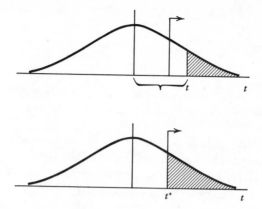

4.2.4 DETERMINING THE SIZE OF SAMPLES FOR ESTIMATING MEANS μ

Large Samples

Our procedure for determining the sample size for estimating a mean μ when the sample is to be large is similar to that used earlier for estimating a proportion p^*. First, we establish a confidence interval $\bar{x} \pm e$ about the sample mean that is expected to bracket the true mean μ, where

$$e = \bar{x} - \mu = Z\sigma_{\bar{x}} = Z\frac{\sigma}{\sqrt{n}}$$

assuming that the population is large enough so that the reduction factor is not required.

For example, our administrator who wants to estimate the average family income in his community may set a confidence interval of $\bar{x} \pm \$100$.

Next, a confidence level is set to establish the probability that the confidence interval will bracket the true mean. This fixes the level of Z. For example, if the confidence level is set at .95, the probability that the true mean μ will lie within the confidence interval but to just one side of the sample mean is $.95/2 = .475$. Then, looking in the table of the unit normal distribution under .475, we find that $Z = 1.96$. After rearranging the above equation for e to yield n,

$$n = \frac{Z^2\sigma^2}{(\bar{x} - \mu)^2} \qquad 4.15$$

we may insert the values of $e = \bar{x} - \mu$ and Z to solve for n. But we need one more item—the true variance of the variable $x - \sigma^2$. Not yet having taken the sample, we are unable to provide an estimate of the variance. If an estimate of this item can be furnished, perhaps through an analysis of similar but already published secondary data, then we can proceed. Suppose σ is, by luck, found to be $\sigma = \$3000$. Inserting into equation 4.15 this value as well as those of Z and $\bar{x} - \mu$, we have

$$n = \frac{(1.96)^2(3000)^2}{(100)^2} = 3455$$

which is a large sample indeed. But a confidence interval of $x \pm \$100$ is calling for a great deal of sampling accuracy and, of course, more accuracy is more expensive.

Now suppose that the administrator's community was actually quite small—only 4000 families. This time, the size of the total population ($N = 4000$) must be given a role in determining n via the reduction factor $\sqrt{(N - n)/(N - 1)}$. An equation that does this is[12]

$$n = \frac{Z^2\sigma^2}{(\bar{x} - \mu)^2 + \dfrac{Z^2\sigma^2}{N}} \qquad\qquad 4.16$$

Inserting the appropriate values, we have

$$n = \frac{(1.96)^2(3000)^2}{(100)^2 + \dfrac{(1.96)^2(3000)^2}{4000}} = 1855$$

Small Samples

Unfortunately, we cannot write a formula for directly determining the size of a small sample. Although we may substitute the critical value t^* or Z in equation 4.15, to find the appropriate level of t in the table of the t-distribution (Table 4.2), we not only must know the confidence level, we must also know the sample size n! Because we have not yet solved for n, instead of using equation 4.15, we may use the relation

$$\bar{x} - \mu = t^* \frac{S}{\sqrt{n}}$$

After first establishing the confidence interval for the left-hand side of this equation, we then must obtain an estimate of S, perhaps through a pilot sample of size n'. We may then "try" this number n' in the following way.

First, we establish the significance level, say .95, and subtract from one to obtain the probability that the confidence interval will *not* bracket the

[12] This is derived by multiplying the right side of equation 4.15 by $(N - n)/N$, leaving the -1 out of the denominator at no cost to the analysis, and rearranging terms.

true mean: $1 - .95 = .05$. Then dividing this result by 2, we obtain the probability that the true mean will lie beyond the confidence interval but to just one side of the sample mean: $.05/2 = .025$. Then, we look in the table of the t-distribution under this probability and along the line for which df $= n' - 1$. Suppose, for example, that we chose $n' = 9$. Then df $= 8$, and we find $t^* = 2.306$. Inserting this value in the above equation along with $\sqrt{n'} = \sqrt{9} = 3$, we calculate the resulting value of $t^*S/\sqrt{n}$ to see if it is equal to the value of the confidence level as indicated by $\bar{x} - \mu$. If the result is too low, we try a smaller sample size, and if the result is too high, we try a larger sample size. Continuing in this "trial and error" way, we try values of n until the equality is satisfied. At this point, we have obtained the size of our small sample.

To illustrate with our "teacher effectiveness" example, suppose that we have estimated $S = 4\%$, that our confidence interval is $\bar{x} \pm 2\%$, that our significance level is .95, which gives us the probability of .025 for use in Table 4.2, and that $n' = 9$. Then we have

$$2\% \neq 2.306(1.33)\% = 3.07\%$$

which is too high. We therefore must increase n. Suppose we now try $n' = 16$. This gives

$$2\% \neq 2.131(1)\% = 2.131\%$$

which now is just slightly too high. If we now choose $n' = 18$, we find that the equality is satisfied, as the reader should verify.

One point to remember, however, in using this technique, is that we must be confident about the assumption that the variable being tested is normally distributed.

PROBLEMS

1. The mayor of Deadrock County wants to participate in the federal highway program that will allocate sizeable government resources to the construction of a highway connecting the county seat to the interstate highway system. However, at a meeting of respected citizens, he is advised against this on grounds that a majority (more than 50%) of Deadrock residents would rather see the funds spent on mass transit. Believing that the advice is ill-founded and that such a majority does not really exist (that the proportion against is less than or equal to 50%), the mayor contracts with XYZ Research Associates to study the question. A random sample of 100 Deadrock residents of voting age is thereupon

taken, and it is found that 61% are against the proposed highway construction program. Since there are serious political ramifications, the mayor sets his significance level at .01.

(a) On the basis of this sample, should the mayor accept the advice of his respected citizens and scrap his program?

(b) What if his significance level were set at .05 instead?

2. A sample of 26 elderly families is surveyed to find out how much these families pay for rent. It is found that the average monthly rental is $\bar{x} = \$180$, with a sample standard deviation of $S = \$30$.

(a) Construct the confidence interval about this mean at the 95% confidence level, and interpret its meaning.

(b) What happens to this interval if the sample size doubles? If, instead, the standard deviation doubles?

3. A federal library agency is considering a program of grants for library construction in small towns. Believing that the average small town has four libraries, the agency has decided to offer grants only to those small towns having less than four libraries. A random sample of five small towns is drawn, yielding the following results:

Sample of five small towns

Number of libraries	6	3	9	7	3

Using the appropriate probability distribution, determine whether the sample mean is significantly greater than 4 at a significance level of .01; at a significance level of .10.

4. You have $2000 to spend on a survey of house prices in Cityville and want to know if there are enough funds to provide reasonably accurate estimates, given a confidence interval of $\bar{x} = \pm \$500$ and a confidence level of 95%. Each questionnaire administered costs $10. Finally, the best estimate of the standard deviation for all house prices in Cityville is $S = \$4000$.

(a) Can the survey be made for the $2000 budget?

(b) What variables would have to be changed to change the result of the preceding question?

(c) Suppose that the total number of houses in Cityville is only 2000. How does this additional information affect your conclusions?

5. Explain the reasoning behind the statement of Section 4.1.3 that the significance testing procedure "cannot be used to accept an hypothesis—only to reject one."

BIBLIOGRAPHY

Holton, Albert N., and Gerald W. Dean. *Decisions Under Uncertainty with Research Applications.* Cincinnatti, Ohio: South-Western Publishing Company, 1971.

Raiffa, Howard. *Decision Analysis: Introductory Lectures on Choices Under Uncertainty.* Reading, Mass.: Addison-Wesley, 1968.

Schlaifer, Robert. *Introduction to Statistics for Business Decisions.* New York: McGraw-Hill, 1961.

Tanur, Judith M., Frederick Mosteller, William H. Kruskal, Richard F. Link, Richard S. Pieters, and Gerald R. Rising (eds). *Statistics: A Guide to the Unknown.* San Francisco: Holden-Day, 1972.

Wonnacott, Thomas B., and Ronald J. Wonnacott. *Introductory Statistics.* New York: John Wiley, 1969.

Yamane, Taro. *Statistics: An Introductory Analysis,* second edition. New York: Harper and Row, 1967.

Wonnacott and Wonnacott, and Yamane are good references on statistical inference. Holton and Dean, Raiffa, and Schlaifer all deal in decision theory. The volume by Tanur et al. is an excellent collection of readings, classified by the statistical tools each paper employs. There are 44 papers included by leading analysts from a broad range of fields.

CHAPTER 5

Identifying Relationships Among Variables

5.1 INTRODUCTION

In Chapter 4, we learned in our "teacher effectiveness" example that the level of effectiveness that should be expected of teachers is a score of 650, as measured by the average achievement scores of their students. But if we place conditions on other characteristics of the teachers such as, for example, whether the teacher comes from the same community as the students or the amount of academic training in the teacher's background, then our expectation of the value of teacher effectiveness scores would be modified. Similarly, we learned in Chapter 3 that the probability that any given city would have a nucleated land use pattern might very well be conditional on additional information known about other characteristics of that city, such as the highway pattern type. However, if the type of land use pattern were independent of the type of highway pattern, then we would not expect the probability of observing a nucleated land use pattern to be conditional on the type of highway pattern.

Knowing that two variables are related or, conversely, that they are independent of each other can be extremely helpful to the planning process. For one thing, projections of one of the variables can be considerably refined if we know something about other variables that are related. For another, policy decisions can be greatly facilitated if we know something about the effect of a given policy on the behavior of certain variables that are connected to goals.

One difficulty in identifying relationships between variables is, as in Chapter 4, that most of our evidence is sampled. In consequence, what may

136

appear as evidence that two variables are related may be nothing more than the effects of sampling variability. The purpose of this chapter is to show how a number of statistical methods can be used with sampled evidence for testing whether two or more variables are independent, for measuring the strength of a relationship between them, and for refining an *expected value* for one variable (say $\bar{y}$) into a *conditional expectation*, given information about another related variable x (e.g., $\bar{y} \mid x$, read $\bar{y}$ given the value of x).

As we might expect, the more refined our measurement scales, the more we can find out about the kind, magnitude, and significance of a relationship. This is to say that the more sophisticated methods for analyzing relationships require that all variables be measured along interval scales. But this is not always possible: many important relationships often involve variables that are measured along nominal scales, as exemplified by our land use versus highway pattern problem. Thus we begin our discussion with a test for identifying relationships among two nominal-scaled variables (the chi-square test); then proceed to a method that tests the strength and significance among two ordinal-scaled variables (Spearman rank correlation); then, using "analysis of variance," we can readily measure the strength and significance of relationship, and the conditional expectation for an interval-scaled variable given a nominal or ordinal-scaled variable; finally, we describe how least-squares linear regression and correlation analysis can be used to give measures of strength, significance, and conditional expectations among two or among many interval-scaled variables, with adjustments automatically made that have the effect of holding constant all other variables save the two that are being related.

5.2 THE CHI-SQUARE TEST

Suppose, of the 100 cities sampled in Chapter 3, that 33 of them had a nucleated pattern and the other 67 had a continuous pattern. Similarly, imagine that 40 had a radial highway pattern, and 60 had the grid pattern. Furthermore, suppose that 28 had both the nucleated and radial patterns, which automatically indicates that 5 were nucleated-grid (we already knew that 33 were nucleated and 28 were nucleated-radial, so that $33 - 28 = 5$ with nucleated-grid); and likewise automatically indicates that 12 were continuous-radial and 55 were continuous grid. This information is shown in Table 5.1a, which is referred to as a "2×2 (two-by-two) contingency table." Dividing the observed frequency, n, in each cell of the table by the total number of observations ($N = 100$), we show in Table 5.1b the marginal probabilities for each highway pattern type, land use pattern ignored, and for each land use type, highway pattern ignored. We also show in the body of the table the observed joint probability that a given observation will have

TABLE 5.1a
A 2 × 2 Contingency Table

Land use pattern \ Highway pattern	Radial (R)	Grid (G)	Totals for Land Use
Nucleated (N)	28	5	33
Continuous (C)	12	55	67
Totals for highway	40	60	100

both a nucleated land use and a radial highway pattern, a nucleated and grid, or the like.

Now if the type of land use pattern is actually independent of the type of highway pattern, we recall from Chapter 3 that the joint probability that both variables will be observed in a given observation is the probability of observing a given value of one variable times the probability of observing a given value of the other. In the present example, the probability that the land use variable will take on the type "nucleated" (p_N) is .33; the probability that the highway pattern variable will be the type "radial" (p_R) is .40. If both variables were independent, then the probability of observing both a nucleated land use type and a radial highway type is

$$\bar{p}_{NR} = (p_N)(p_R) \qquad\qquad 5.1$$

$$= (.33)(.40) = .132$$

where $\bar{p}$ is used to denote the expected joint probability given independence.

TABLE 5.1b
Observed Joint and Marginal Probabilities for Contingency Table

Land use pattern \ Highway pattern	Radial (R)	Grid (G)	Marginal distribution for Land Use
Nucleated (N)	.28	.05	.33
Continuous (C)	.12	.55	.67
Marginal distribution for highway pattern	.40	.60	1.00

TABLE 5.1c

A 2 × 2 Table of Joint Probabilities Under Independence

Land use pattern	Highway pattern Radial (R)	Grid (G)
Nucleated (N)	.132	.198
Continuous (C)	.268	.402

That is, in the cell "nucleated-radial" in Table 5.1b, if both variables were independent, we ought to find the probability .132. The fact that the probability .28 was observed instead gives us some evidence that the two variables are not independent, they are related. Let us continue to fill out the "2 × 2 Table of Joint Probabilities under Independence" shown in Table 5.1c. Note that the sum of the probabilities down any column or across any row yields the observed marginal distributions shown in Table 5.1b. Clearly the joint probabilities expected under independence in Table 5.1c are quite different from those actually observed in Table 5.1b. But before concluding that the two variables are evidently not independent and therefore related, let us recall that the evidence comes from a sample: a different sample of 100 might have yielded different results and, in fact, a sample of 2000 might yield observed probabilities very nearly the same as those expected under independence. The question is: How can the sample size and the observed joint probabilities relative to the "expected" joint probabilities both be taken into account for evaluating whether the variables are independent? The method that is used is as follows.

First, for a given cell in our 2 × 2 contingency table, we subtract from the observed joint probability $\hat{p}$ the expected joint probability $\bar{p}$, square the result (which has the effect of getting rid of minus signs), and then divide by the expected joint probability, which gives $(\hat{p} - \bar{p})^2/\bar{p}$. Then we account for the effect of the size of sample simply by multiplying the above result by the total number of observations N. We repeat these calculations for each of the four cells in the 2 × 2 contingency table and sum the results. The resulting statistic is called "chi-square," and is denoted as χ^2. We will denote observed values of chi-square as $\hat{\chi}^2$. It is calculated as

$$\hat{\chi}^2 = N\frac{(\hat{p}_{NR} - \bar{p}_{NR})^2}{\bar{p}_{NR}} + N\frac{(\hat{p}_{NG} - \bar{p}_{NG})^2}{\bar{p}_{NG}}$$
$$+ N\frac{(\hat{p}_{CR} - \bar{p}_{CR})^2}{\bar{p}_{CR}} + N\frac{(\hat{p}_{CG} - \bar{p}_{CG})^2}{\bar{p}_{CG}} \quad 5.2$$

If we apply this formula to the percentages in Tables 5.1b and c, we find that:

$$\hat{\chi}^2 = 100\,\frac{(.28 - .132)^2}{.132} + 100\,\frac{(.05 - .198)^2}{.198}$$

$$+\ 100\,\frac{(.12 - .268)^2}{.268} + 100\,\frac{(.55 - .402)^2}{.402}$$

$$= 100\,\frac{.0219}{.132} + 100\,\frac{.0219}{.198} + 100\,\frac{.0219}{.268} + 100\,\frac{.0219}{.402}$$

$$= 16.59 + 11.06 + 8.17 + 5.44$$

$$= 41.26$$

Since we know that for this specific example $\hat{\chi}^2 = 41.26$, our next step is to ask whether so high an observed value could have occurred merely as the result of sampling error. Fortunately, there is a simple way to test this. After setting a significance level as we did in Chapter 4, and after determining the number of degrees of freedom, we merely look up the level of χ^2 in a table of the χ^2 distribution to determine how high χ^2 could be and still be generated by sampling error. We term this the critical value of χ^2, denoted as χ^2_*. If our observed chi-square exceeds the amount, then we say that the sample has provided sufficient evidence to reject the hypothesis that the variables being tested are independent.

In Table 5.2 below, we show a part of the table of the chi-square distribution: the columns associated with the 5%, 1%, and the .1% levels of significance, respectively, and the rows associated with from 1 to 10 degrees of freedom.

TABLE 5.2
The χ^2 Distribution

df	Level of significance		
	.05	.01	.001
1	3.841	6.635	10.827
2	5.991	9.210	13.815
3	7.815	11.341	16.268
4	9.448	13.277	18.465
5	11.070	15.086	20.517
6	12.592	16.812	22.457
7	14.067	18.475	24.322
8	15.507	20.090	26.125
9	16.919	21.666	27.877
10	18.307	23.209	29.588

To find the number of degrees of freedom, we use the formula:

$$df = (r - 1)(c - 1) \qquad\qquad 5.3$$

where r is the number of rows in the contingency table and c is the number of columns. For a 2×2 contingency table, we have

$$df = (2 - 1)(2 - 1) = 1$$

That there should be only one degree of freedom in a 2×2 contingency table makes sense when we recall that once we knew that the number of observations that had nucleated and radial patterns was 28, the other three cells of the contingency table were automatically determined.

If we set our significance level at .01, then we find in Table 5.2 our critical value of chi-square as $\chi^2_* = 6.635$; meaning that a chi-square level as high as 6.635 could occur due to sampling error alone. But our observed chi-square was 41.26, much too high to be the result of sampling error. Hence, we reject the hypothesis of independence, and presume a city's land use pattern type is related to its highway pattern type.

To show the effect of sample size, suppose that there were only 10 observations. We see in the equation for chi-square (5.2) that N may be factored outside of the four terms to be summed. If N were 10 instead of 100, we see that our calculations would have resulted in a chi-square of 4.126 instead of 41.26, a level that is no longer significant at the 1 % level. Conversely, we see that by sufficiently increasing our sample, it is usually possible to yield a sufficiently high χ^2 to reject the hypothesis of independence. What stands in the way, of course, is the degree to which our observed joint probabilities ($\hat{p}$) differ from the expected joint probabilities under independence ($\bar{p}$). If our sample of $N = 100$ yielded the observed joint probabilities in Table 5.3, for example, instead of the ones shown in Table 5.1b, then we should show that $\hat{\chi}^2$ would be the very low value of .55 which, at the 1 % significance level, is clearly not significant. The difference between the observed joint probabilities and the expected joint probabilities under independence could easily have been the result of sampling error. But, as we have just indicated, if the

TABLE 5.3
Alternative Observed Joint Probabilities

Land use pattern	Highway pattern	Radial (R)	Grid (G)
Nucleated (N)		.15	.18
Continuous (C)		.25	.42

sample size were increased sufficiently, a point would be reached that could be accepted as significant. In this case, if the observed joint probabilities remained as in Table 5.3, they would have had to have been generated by a sample no smaller than $N = 1207$ before the difference between the joint probabilities could be accepted as significant.

Before we generalize our chi-square test to contingency tables of any size, two points should be mentioned. First, the chi-square test does not place any requirements on the distribution from which the observed variables are sampled. Unlike the t-test, for example, chi-square does not require that the observations come from a normal distribution. For this reason, the chi-square test is referred to as a nonparametric test. Relative to methods that require the normality assumption, the chi-square test can be applied in a wider variety of situations. Note, in addition, that it is not restricted for use with nominal scales; its use is restricted to variables that can be categorized, and certainly both ordinal and interval scales can be stated in terms of categories (the category 0–10, 11–20, 21–30, etc).

The second point we wish to make is that the chi-square test we have used to test independence in contingency tables generates a statistic, via equation 5.2, that only approximates the true chi-square statistic. The true chi-square statistic cannot be applied to practical tests as readily because it is generated by an equation of slightly different form, but it is the one that is used to generate the table of the chi-square distribution shown in Table 5.2. Nevertheless, the approximating statistic used for making the chi-square test becomes almost identical with the true chi-square statistic as the sample size N becomes large. How large? A practical rule of thumb is that N should be just large enough so that no cell in the contingency table contains fewer than five observations. In our 2×2 contingency table (Table 5.1a), for example, we see that the cell containing cities that have nucleated land use and grid highway patterns has only five observations. This is the minimum that is acceptable if we are to use the chi-square test. If there were, instead, only four observations in this cell, we would be required to increase the sample size N, thereby increasing the number of observations in all the cells of the table, until the required fifth observation appeared in our deficient cell.

We now generalize our chi-square test to a contingency table of any size. Suppose we are working with one variable that has $i = 1, \ldots, r$ categories and with another that has $j = 1, \ldots, c$ categories. Then our contingency table will be of size $r \times c$—it will have rc cells with joint probabilities. We calculate $\hat{\chi}^2$ for such a table as

$$\hat{\chi}^2 = \sum_{i=1}^{r} \sum_{j=1}^{c} N \frac{(\hat{p}_{ij} - \bar{p}_{ij})^2}{\bar{p}_{ij}} \qquad 5.4$$

with degrees of freedom df $= (r - 1)(c - 1)$.

For purposes of making calculations, we may reduce the number of steps by recalling that our observed joint probability

$$\hat{p}_{ij} = \frac{n_{ij}}{N}$$

while our expected joint probability is

$$\bar{p} = p_i p_j = \frac{n_i}{N} \frac{n_j}{N}$$

Inserting these expressions for $\hat{p}_{ij}$ and $\bar{p}_{ij}$ in equation 5.4, and rewriting the term $N(\hat{p}_{ij} - \bar{p}_{ij})^2$ as $(N\hat{p}_{ij} - N\bar{p}_{ij})^2/N$, equation 5.4 becomes[1]

$$\hat{\chi}^2 = N \sum_{i=1}^{r} \sum_{j=1}^{c} \frac{\left(n_{ij} - \dfrac{n_i n_j}{N} \right)^2}{n_i n_j} \qquad 5.5$$

This equation is easier to use because we do not have to bother calculating the two joint probability Tables 5.1b and c—we only need to work with the actual magnitudes shown in Table 5.1a. The reader should apply equation 5.5 for calculating the chi-square statistic for Table 5.1a to see whether it comes out the same as before.

We now summarize the procedure for applying the chi-square test.

1. Determine r categories using nominal scale for first variable being related and c categories for second variable. Then collect sample of size N and distribute among the cells of the $r \times c$ *contingency table*. Be sure that N is large enough so that $n_{ij} \geq 5$ for all i and j.

n_{11}	n_{12}	$\cdots n_{1j} \cdots$	$\sum\limits_{j}^{c} n_{1j}$
n_{21}	n_{22}	$\cdots$	$\sum\limits_{j}^{c} n_{2j}$
$\cdot$	$\cdot$	$\cdot$	$\cdot$
n_{i1}	n_{i2}	n_{ij}	$\sum\limits_{j}^{c} n_{ij}$
$\cdot$	$\cdot$	$\cdot$	$\cdot$
$\sum\limits_{i}^{r} n_{i1}$	$\sum\limits_{i}^{r} n_{i2}$	$\sum\limits_{i}^{r} n_{ij}$	N

[1] In the case that df $= 1$, it has been found that the term in parentheses in equation 5.5 should be modified to read $(|n_{ij} - n_i n_j/N| - \frac{1}{2})^2$ to obtain a better approximation to the true chi-square distribution. The vertical lines before and after the term $n_{ij} - n_i n_j/N$ indicate that the absolute value of this expression is to be used (e.g., should the result be negative, we treat it as if it were positive), while the subtraction of $\frac{1}{2}$ from the result is termed a "continuity correction."

2. Determine critical value of χ_*^2:
   (a) State significance level.
   (b) Obtain degrees of freedom
       df $= (r-1)(c-1)$
   (c) Identify the critical value of χ_*^2 in
       the table of the χ^2 distribution.

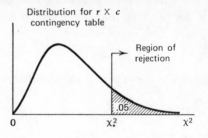

Distribution for $r \times c$ contingency table

Region of rejection

.05

$0 \qquad \chi_*^2 \qquad \chi^2$

3. Calculate the observed value of $\hat{\chi}^2$:

$$\hat{\chi}^2 = N \sum_{i=1}^{r} \sum_{j=1}^{c} \frac{\left(n_{ij} - \dfrac{\hat{n}_i n_j}{N}\right)^2}{n_i n_j}$$

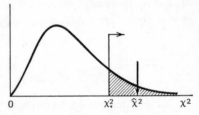

$0 \qquad \chi_*^2 \; \hat{\chi}^2 \qquad \chi^2$

4. Assume hypothesis of independence (e.g., no relationship among the variables). Then,

$\qquad$ if $\hat{\chi}^2 > \chi_*^2$, reject hypothesis;

$\qquad$ if $\hat{\chi}^2 \leq \chi_*^2$, do not reject.

5.3 THE SPEARMAN RANK CORRELATION TEST

The chi-square test that we have just described is useful for identifying whether or not a relationship exists among two variables. But we were not able to find out anything about the degree of strength in the relationship. What we would like to have is a statistic that takes on the value 1 if two variables are perfectly related, and 0 if there is no relationship at all. Such a statistic can then be used to relate any two variables and to show which pair is most strongly related.[2] In the course of this chapter, we show several statistics that can be used as measures of strength of relationship. The first of these, however, differs from the others in that, like the chi-square test, it is a nonparametric statistic. It does not require that the variables being tested come from normal populations. What it does require, however, is that both variables being tested be stated along an ordinal scale. This allows interval-scaled variables to be tested by this method, since any set of

---

[2] Actually, in the case of the 2×2 contingency table, we may divide the chi-square statistic by N to get a measure of strength $\phi = \chi^2/N$ that satisfies these requirements, that is, $0 \leq \phi \leq 1$. However, for larger contingency tables, ϕ may take on much larger values than unity and, therefore, loses meaning for comparative purposes.

observations that can be measured on an interval scale can also be ranked (for example, John is 6 ft 1 in tall, Jane is 5 ft 2 in and Harry is 5 ft 8 in; ranking these three in decreasing order of height places John first, Harry second, and Jane third). But it rules out variables that can only be measured on a nominal scale.

Our statistic is the Spearman rank correlation coefficient, denoted as r_s. It is calculated as

$$r_s = 1 - \frac{6 \sum_{i=1}^{N} D_i^{\,2}}{N(N^2 - 1)}$$

5.6

where D_i is the difference between the ith observation rank for the two variables being tested. For example, if Jane's rank among graduating seniors for the variable "height" is 3 and her rank for the variable "class academic standing" is 1, then the D measure for Jane is $3 - 1 = 2$.

The value of Spearman's r_s can lie between $+1$ and -1: It will be "plus one" if the two variables are perfectly and positively correlated; it will be "minus one" if they are perfectly negatively correlated (that is, as one variable increases, the other decreases); r_s will be near zero if there is no correlation. Let us consider this example.

A certain nation is experiencing increasing urban crime. One analyst believes that crime is caused by poverty, and that the proper way to deal with crime is to get at its causes. However, an incredulous official of a national crime control agency asks for evidence. Confident of his position, the analyst proceeds to gather data on "percent poor" and "crime rate per thousand" for a sample of 10 metropolitan areas of the nation. Furthermore, not having any basis for believing that either variable is normally distributed, the analyst wisely decides to use the Spearman rank correlation coefficient as his measure of the strength of relationship.

Suppose that the 10 metropolitan areas have the letter names A to J. Our analyst has ranked these 10 cities according to crime rate, with the highest crime rate city ranked first and the lowest ranked tenth. He has also ranked the 10 cities according to "percent poor," again ranking as first the city with the highest percent poor. These rankings are shown in columns 1 and 2 of Table 5.4. Shown in column 3 of this table is the difference D between the ranking, and in column 4 is D^2. At the bottom of column 4 is the sum of the squared difference $(\sum D_i^{\,2})$, which is the quantity to be inserted in equation 5.6. Inserting this value 74 for $\sum D_i^{\,2}$ and, with $N = 10$, the value 990 for $N(N^2 - 1)$ in equation 5.6, Spearman's r_s is calculated as

$$r_s = 1 - \frac{6(74)}{990} = 1 - \frac{444}{990} = .55$$

TABLE 5.4
Calculations for Spearman's Rank Correlation Coefficient

City	Rankings Crime Rate (1)	Rankings Percent Poor (2)	D (2) − (1) (3)	D^2 (4)
A	3	2	−1	1
B	6	1	−5	25
C	8	4	−4	16
D	10	9	−1	1
E	1	3	2	4
F	5	7	2	4
G	9	8	−1	1
H	7	10	3	9
I	2	5	3	9
J	4	6	2	4
$\sum D^2$				74

Although $r_s = .55$ is certainly larger than zero, we must remember that the correlation coefficient was calculated from sampled data. Therefore, there is always the possibility that a seemingly large value of r_s could occur merely as the result of sampling error. For this reason, it is always necessary to test for the statistical significance of the coefficient, that is, to be reasonably sure that an observed r_s as high as .55 could not occur when the true r_s is actually zero.

The test of the significance of r_s is greatly facilitated by the finding that when the true value of r_s is actually zero, the distribution of the sample value of r_s for sample sizes $N \geq 10$ is approximately normal with a mean value of zero. Thus we can test the significance of r_s via a technique very similar to that used for testing the significance of an observed sample mean $\bar{x}$ that we described in the preceding chapter. We calculate the number of standard errors (Z) that r_s lies from zero by dividing the sample difference ($r_s - 0$) by the standard error of r_s, denoted as σ_r:

$$Z = \frac{r_s}{\sigma_r} \qquad\qquad 5.7$$

Since we already have calculated r_s, we need only calculate σ_r to have our estimate of Z. Fortunately, the standard error of r is much easier to calculate than was $\sigma_{\bar{x}}$ in Chapter 4. Simply stated,

$$\sigma_r = \frac{1}{\sqrt{N-1}} \qquad\qquad 5.8$$

so that our equation for Z reduces to

$$Z = r_s\sqrt{N-1}$$

Our analyst calculates the observed value of Z, denoted by $\hat{Z}$, as

$$\hat{Z} = .55\sqrt{10-1} = .55(3) = 1.65$$

Assuming that he has also selected a .05 significance level, he next refers to the table of the unit normal distribution to find the critical value of Z, which we denote as Z^*.

Since our sampled r_s can be greater or less than zero when the true $r_s = 0$, our Z value can also take on positive or negative values. Hence, we want to know what range of Z values ($\pm Z^*$) could occur within our confidence level when the true $r_s = 0$. Since the table of the unit normal distribution excludes probabilities for negative Z values, we look up the probability associated with the positive half only. Since our significance level of .05 means that we will accept positive or negative Z values that could occur 95% of the time, it also means that we will accept positive values only that could occur .95/2 = 47.5% of the time (for future reference, this indicates that the significance test for r_s is a "two-tailed" test—it tests for values of r_s that could be positive *or* negative—in which case 1 - the significance level divided by 2 is used to enter the table of the unit normal distribution).

Our table of the unit normal distribution shows that we can expect Z values from zero up to 1.96 to occur .475 of the time when the true $r_s = 0$. Hence, our critical $Z^* = 1.96$.

Our analyst sees that his observed Z value of 1.65 is less than the critical value. Thus he cannot reject the hypothesis that the true $r_s = 0$, that is, that the high value of r_s he observed was not merely the result of sampling error. In sum, his sampled evidence concerning the relationship between urban crime rates and urban poverty cannot be accepted as significant. Should he give in to that incredulous official? Of course not. He should find better evidence instead, perhaps making use of some of the methods that we describe in the rest of this chapter.

We summarize the steps needed to calculate Spearman's rank correlation coefficient (r_s) and to test it's significance.

1. Collect sample size N, and assign ordinal (ranking) numbers to each of the $i = 1, \ldots, N$ observations for each of the two variables being related.

   Distribution of population of variates nonnormal or unknown.

2. Calculate the Spearman rank correlation coefficient r_s (where $-1 \le r_s \le +1$):

$$r_s = 1 - \frac{6 \sum_{i=1}^{N} D_i^2}{N(N^2 - 1)}$$

3. State hypothesis that the true $r_s = 0$ and seek to reject hypothesis via a test of the significance of Z, the number of standard errors that r_s lies from zero. This test makes use of the normal distribution, which is approximated by the distribution of r_s to the extent that N exceeds 10.

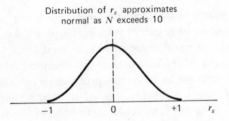

Distribution of r_s approximates normal as N exceeds 10

4. Determine critical value of Z^* (based on two-tailed test):
   (a) State significance level.
   (b) Determine the area under the positive half of unit normal distribution up to region of rejection

$$[1 - (\text{significance level})]/2$$

   (c) Use this value to enter the table of unit normal distribution to find critical Z^*.

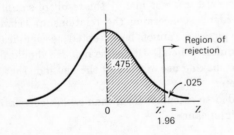

5. Calculate observed value of $\hat{Z}$:

$$\hat{Z} = r_s \sqrt{N - 1}$$

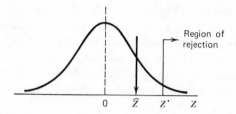

Region of rejection

0    $\hat{Z}$ Z^* Z

6. If $\hat{Z} > Z^*$, reject hypothesis that $r_s = 0$.
   If $\hat{Z} \leq Z^*$, do not reject, but state that the sample is not significant evidence for detecting a relationship between the two variables.

5.4 ANALYSIS OF VARIANCE

Instead of testing two nominal variables or two ordinal variables, suppose now that one variable, variable Y, is an interval-scaled variable, while the other, variable x, is nominal scaled (in which case, ordinal or interval scales can also be analyzed, since x can always be categorized down to a nominal scale).

5.4.1 THE MEAN OF y CONDITIONAL UPON x

If the variable x can be categorized into c groups $i = 1, \ldots, c$, then we would expect that for the observations in the ith group, the mean value of y for that group $(\bar{y}_i)$ will not only differ from the ungrouped mean $\bar{y}$, but will also differ from one group to the next, that is, the expectation of y conditional on x, $E(y \mid x)$, will differ from the expected value of y, $E(y)$, x not considered. Since the several group means $\bar{y}_i$ are easy to calculate, it is a simple matter to estimate our conditional expectations $E(y \mid x)$. In sum, if we already know the value of x_i, then it should be an easy matter to get a more accurate estimate of y than the one provided in Chapter 4 by $\bar{y}$. But there is one case when these estimates will not be more accurate. That is when y is unrelated to x. Here, knowing the value of x will not provide us with any more useful information about y than we already have: when x and y are independent, $E(y \mid x) = E(y)$. So in addition to estimating conditional expectations, or perhaps prior to making such estimates, it will be important to test for the significance of the relationship between y and x. The method we use for such a test is called "analysis of variance."

In addition to measuring conditional expectations, we may also want to measure the strength of the relationship between y and x. The measure we describe is called the "correlation ratio," E^2, and just as we found for the Spearman rank correlation coefficient, E^2 must be tested for significance. However, since the test is again via analysis of variance that may already have been used in testing whether the conditional expectations differs significantly from the expected value of y, it will not have to be repeated again. A point to be made about the analysis of variance test is that it requires the assumption that y comes from a normal distribution, that is, it is not a nonparametric test.

Let us now apply these concepts to the data shown in Table 5.5. Recall the

TABLE 5.5
Teacher Performance Scores Categorized by Community in which the Teacher Was Raised

(x_i) Location in which Teacher Was Raised	(y_{ij}) Performance Scores of the jth Teacher in the ith Subgroup.
x_1 Different state	440, 560, 380, 440, 320, 500
x_2 Different community	560, 440, 440, 500, 380, 500, 620, 500, 560
x_3 Same community	620, 740, 560, 620, 680, 500, 620, 680, 560

"teacher effectiveness" example from Chapter 4 in which we examined the issue of whether or not teachers who were raised in the same community in which they teach are more effective than the average. We now construct a more thoroughgoing analysis of this issue. Suppose that we randomly select 24 teachers from various communities and categorize them into three groups: group 1 includes teachers who were raised in a different state from the one in which they are currently teaching; group 2 includes teachers who were raised in the same state but in a different community than the one in which they are currently teaching; and group 3 includes teachers who were raised in the same community as the one in which they are currently teaching. The variable y_{ij} shows the performance scores for the jth teacher in the ith group, where these scores have a possible range of 200 to 800.

Noting that the performance scores only take on magnitudes that are 60 points apart instead of any magnitude between 200 and 800 (we did this on purpose so we could simplify our graphics), we form a frequency distribution of the scores for each group, as well as the overall frequency distribution for all 24 scores taken together. These distributions, together with the

TABLE 5.6
Frequency Distribution and Sample Means for Groups of
Performance Scores

Frequency f_{ij} / Score (y_{ij})	Overall Distribution	Group Distributions		
		Other State (x_1)	Other Community (x_2)	Same Community (x_3)
320	1	1	0	0
380	2	1	1	0
440	4	2	2	0
500	5	1	3	1
560	5	1	2	2
620	4	0	1	3
680	2	0	0	2
740	1	0	0	1
Sum of the Scores: $\sum_{j} (y_{ij})(f_{ij})$	12,720	2,640	4,500	5,580
No. Observations n_i	24	6	9	9
Group means $\bar{y}_i$	530	440	500	620

number of observations in each group (n_i) and the group means $(\bar{y}_i)$, are
shown in Table 5.6.

We can also present these distributions graphically, as is shown in Figure
5.1.

Looking at this figure, two conclusions can be drawn:

First, the values of the means for each group $\bar{y}_i$ are in each case different
from the overall ungrouped mean $\bar{y}$. Our calculations of the expected value
of y given x shows that as x shifts from x_1 to x_2 to x_3, the group means of y

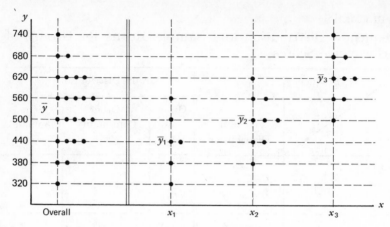

FIGURE 5.1 Frequency distributions of y given x.

increase, although by unequal amounts:

$$E(y \mid x_1) = \bar{y}_1 = 440$$
$$E(y \mid x_2) = \bar{y}_2 = 500$$
$$E(y \mid x_3) = \bar{y}_3 = 620$$

an increase of 60

an increase of 120

—it seems that how nearly a teacher teaches to the same community in which he was raised has a powerful effect on his teaching performance.

Second, it is evident that by grouping the 24 observations according to the value of "explanatory" variable x, we are able to obtain a more accurate estimate of y. This is in the sense that we can expect that the actual value of y will differ by a smaller amount from the estimate of y provided by the group means $\bar{y}_i$ than from the estimated value provided by the overall ungrouped mean $\bar{y}$. We can put this notion to use in the calculation of the strength of relation between y and x.

5.4.2 THE CORRELATION RATIO

For any observation that we might select, say the jth observation in the ith group, the error of the overall mean as an estimator of the y value (in this case, the performance of the ijth teacher) can be measured as $(y_{ij} - \bar{y})$. Instead, if the x variable is a meaningful explainer of y, that is, if a relationship exists between y and x, then we can get a more accurate estimate of y_{ij} by using the group mean $\bar{y}_i$ as the estimator. The improvement in accuracy will be $(\bar{y}_i - \bar{y})$, and the error will reduce to $(y_{ij} - \bar{y}_i)$. This is to say that the error $(y_{ij} - \bar{y})$ can be split into a part that remains unexplained and another part that is explained by the grouping:

$$(y_{ij} - \bar{y}) \equiv \underset{\text{unexplained}}{(y_{ij} - \bar{y}_i)} + \underset{\text{explained}}{(\bar{y}_i - \bar{y})} \qquad 5.9$$

$$\underset{\text{error}}{} \quad \underset{\substack{\text{unexplained} \\ \text{error}}}{} \quad \underset{\substack{\text{explained} \\ \text{error}}}{}$$

where the symbol $\equiv$ indicates that the expression is definitionally true. We can use this partitioning to show the effect of categorizing the N observations into groups based on the x variable by squaring both sides of the above expression and then summing over all the observations $j = 1, \ldots, n$ and $i = 1, \ldots, c$. It can be shown without great difficulty that the resulting expression is[3]

$$\underset{\text{total}}{\sum_i \sum_j (y_{ij} - \bar{y})^2} = \underset{\text{within groups}}{\sum_i \sum_j (y_{ij} - \bar{y}_i)^2} + \underset{\text{between groups}}{\sum_i n_i(\bar{y}_i - \bar{y})^2} \qquad 5.10$$

This says that the total sum of squares is split into an unexplained part, called the "within groups" sum of squares, and an explained part, called the "between groups" sum of squares. Suppose we subtract the within groups sum of squares from both sides and divide by the total sum of squares. The resulting expression is the fraction of the total sum of squares explained by the variable x. This fraction can be denoted as E^2, where

$$E^2 \equiv 1 - \frac{\sum_i \sum_j (y_{ij} - \bar{y}_i)^2}{\sum_i \sum_j (y_{ij} - \bar{y})^2} \qquad 5.11$$

and is called the correlation ratio. The ratio of the within groups to total sum of squares shows the fraction of the total sum of squares unexplained by the variable x, so that subtracting this fraction from one gives the fraction of the total sum of squares that is explained by x.

At one extreme, if x explains all the error so that the within groups sum of squares reduces to zero, $E^2 = 1$, while if x explains nothing—implying that the group means are all equal to the overall mean $\bar{y}$, the within groups sum of squares will equal the total sum of squares so that $E^2 = 0$. Thus the correlation ratio provides just the type of measure of strength of relationship that we discussed in introducing Spearman's rank correlation since $0 \leq E^2 \leq 1$.

[3] Squaring both sides of equation 5.9 and summing over all observations gives

$$\sum \sum (y_{ij} - \bar{y})^2 = \sum_i \sum_j (y_{ij} - \bar{y}_i)^2 + \sum_i n_i(\bar{y}_i - \bar{y})^2 + 2\sum_i (\bar{y}_i - \bar{y}) \sum_j (y_{ij} - \bar{y}_i).$$

In the last term on the right side, the summation within groups $\sum_j (y_{ij} - \bar{y})$ will be zero for each group. The entire last term therefore drops out, leaving equation 5.10.

A problem with this measure, however, is that for many kinds of relationships, it is possible to improve the value of E^2 just by increasing the number of categories for which group means can be calculated. This is to say that the correlation ratio should be adjusted to take account of the number of degrees of freedom. This can be done by multiplying the ratio of the within groups to total sum of squares by the ratio $(N - 1)/(N - c)$ where c is the number of categories. The resulting statistic is called the unbiased correlation ratio ε^2.

$$\varepsilon^2 = 1 - \frac{\sum_i \sum_j (y_{ij} - \bar{y}_i)^2}{\sum_i \sum_j (y_{ij} - \bar{y})^2} \left(\frac{N - 1}{N - c} \right) \qquad 5.12$$

As we shall see later, an advantage of both the E^2 and ε^2 measures is that they make no assumptions about the form of relationship between the variables, that is, whether the ratio is linear or quadratic, rising or falling, and the like. The relation between x and y can have any form, or even no form, and the correlation ratio can still be calculated. This is unlike the more popularly used coefficient of correlation, which we shall soon describe, that assumes linear relationships among the variables.

Let us use the data of Table 5.6 to calculate both E^2 and ε^2. By subtracting the overall mean $\bar{y} = 530$ (shown in the first column of Table 5.6) from each of the y_{ij} values (shown in the first row of Table 5.7), squaring the result (shown in the second row), and then multiplying (in the third row) these squared deviations by their frequency of observation f_{ij} (these frequencies are shown in the columns of Table 5.6), we obtain the total sum of squares $\sum_i \sum_j f_{ij}(y_{ij} - \bar{y})^2$ shown in the last column of the third row as 252,000.

Next, we calculate the sum of the squared deviations for each of the three groups. The calculations for the first group (teachers from other states) are shown in rows 4 to 6; for the second group (other communities) in rows 7 to 9; and for the third group (same community) in rows 10 to 12. The sums of the squared deviations within each of the three groups are shown in the last column of Table 5.7, rows 6, 9, and 12. Their sum, the within groups of squares, is

$$\sum_i \sum_j f_{ij}(y_{ij} - \bar{y}_i)^2 = 122{,}400$$

The correlation ratio is then calculated as

$$E^2 = 1 - \frac{122{,}400}{252{,}000} = 1 - .49 = .51$$

so that the variable x "explains" 51 % of the total sum of squares of y.

TABLE 5.7
Calculations for Sum of Squared Deviations

Score	320	380	440	500	560	620	680	740	Sum of Squares
1. $y_{ij} - \bar{y}$	−210	−150	−90	30	30	90	150	210	
2. $(y_{ij} - \bar{y})^2$	44,100	22,500	8,100	900	900	8,100	22,500	44,100	
3. $f_{ij}(y_{ij} - \bar{y})^2$	44,100	45,000	32,400	4,500	4,500	32,400	45,000	44,100	252,000
4. $y_{1j} - \bar{y}_1$	−120	−60	0	60	120				
5. $(y_{1j} - \bar{y}_1)^2$	14,400	3,600	0	3,600	14,400				
6. $f_{1j}(y_{1j} - \bar{y}_1)^2$	14,400	3,600	0	3,600	14,400				36,000
7. $y_{2j} - \bar{y}_2$		−120	−60	0	60	120			
8. $(y_{2j} - \bar{y}_2)^2$		14,400	3,600	0	3,600	14,400			
9. $f_{2j}(y_{2j} - \bar{y}_2)^2$		14,400	7,200	0	7,200	14,400			43,200
10. $y_{3j} - \bar{y}_3$				−120	−60	0	60	120	
11. $(y_{3j} - \bar{y}_3)^2$				14,400	3,600	0	3,600	14,400	
12. $f_{3j}(y_{3j} - \bar{y}_3)^2$				14,400	7,200	0	7,200	14,400	43,200

Inserting the correction factor, we calculate the unbiased correlation ratio as

$$\varepsilon^2 = 1 - \frac{122,400}{252,000}\left(\frac{23}{21}\right) = 1 - .53 = .47$$

5.4.3 THE F-TEST

Suppose that the true variance of the distribution of some variable is σ^2, and that two samples of size n_1 and n_2 are independently drawn. Although the variance of each sample

$$S_i^2 = \frac{\sum_j (x_{ij} - \bar{x}_i)^2}{n_i - 1}$$

will be an unbiased estimate of the true variance σ^2, we know that because of sampling error, the observed S_i^2 will in all probability differ from σ^2. Furthermore, the amount of difference that we should expect will be larger, the smaller is the sample size n_i. Suppose now that we form the ratio of the two sample variances S_1^2/S_2^2. If each sample variance were exactly equal to the true variance, then this variance ratio would, of course, equal unity. However, we expect again that the ratio will differ from one due to sampling error and that the extent of the difference is likely to increase, the smaller the size of the two samples (n_1 and n_2). But by how much might the variance ratio differ from one? If the variable being analyzed is normally distributed, then the answer to this, as we might imagine, has been worked out precisely. It is presented in what is referred to as the table of the F-distribution, where the F-statistic is the ratio of two independently drawn sample variances from the same normal distribution.

$$ F = \frac{S_1^{\ 2}}{S_2^{\ 2}} = \frac{\dfrac{\sum\limits_{j} (x_{1j} - \bar{x}_1)^2}{n_1 - 1}}{\dfrac{\sum\limits_{j} (x_{2j} - \bar{x}_2)^2}{n_2 - 1}} \qquad\qquad 5.13 $$

If the size of two independently drawn samples are given, then the probability that F will be a given amount can be shown on a curve such as is shown in Figure 5.2. The curve shows that if two samples are drawn of size $n_1 = 5$ and $n_2 = 10$, so that $df_1 = 4$ and $df_2 = 9$, then the probability that they will yield an F-value of 3.63 or higher is .05. Actually, curves such as this are not used in practice. Instead, a table of the F-distribution like that provided in the Appendix of this book is used. The table shows values of F for the .05 and the .01 significance levels for various values of df_1 and df_2. Looking in this table under df(numerator) = 4 and df(denominator) = 9 at the .05 significance level, we find that $F = 3.63$.

How can we make use of this F-statistic? We can and will use it to test whether the variances obtained from two independently drawn samples could have come from the same distribution. If, for a stated probability or significance level (such as .05 shown in Figure 5.2), the observed F-statistic denoted as $\hat{F}$—exceeds the critical F—denoted as F^*—found in the table of the F-distribution, then we can conclude that the two observed sample variances must have been drawn from different distributions. But if $\hat{F} < F^*$,

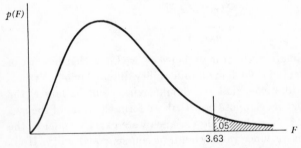

FIGURE 5.2   A probability density curve for the F-distribution for $df_1 = 4$ and $df_2 = 9$.

then we can say that the difference between $S_1{}^2$ and $S_2{}^2$ could well have been the result of sampling error and that we should not reject the hypothesis that they were drawn from the same distribution.

We shall find two uses for the F-test in this chapter. The first is to test whether, in grouping a set of observations for a variable y according to the nominal values of a variable x, the observed differences in the group means $(\bar{y}_i)$ could have merely been the result of sampling error rather than the result of an underlying relationship between y and x. This also tests the significance of the correlation ratio E^2. The second use of the F-test, which we shall encounter later, is in testing the significance of coefficients of multiple correlation (R). We shall apply the first use now in what is called the "analysis of variance," or ANOVA for short.

Recall that after calculating Spearman's r_s, we considered the possibility that if r_s were actually zero, a fairly sizeable r_s might still be observed because of sampling error. We then proceeded to test the significance of the observed value. The same problem arises here in the case of our correlation ratio, and it also arises in connection with our conditional expectations. If we can calculate a ratio of two independent variances from the distribution of the y values, then we can apply the F-test to determine whether by grouping the y values according to the values of x, we have significantly improved our ability to estimate y. It happens that if each of the several groups ($i = 1, \ldots, c$) of y values are drawn from the same normally distributed population, then the within groups sum of squares will be independent of the between groups sum of squares. This being the case, we can calculate two independent variances by dividing the two sums of squares by their respective degrees of freedom. The first is the *between groups variance*

$$S_b{}^2 = \frac{\sum\limits_{i}^{c} n_i(\bar{y}_i - \bar{y})^2}{c - 1}$$

and the second is the *within groups variance*

$$S_w{}^2 = \frac{\sum\limits_{i}^{c} \sum\limits_{j}^{n_i} (y_{ij} - \bar{y}_i)^2}{N - c}$$

(c degrees of freedom are lost: one for each of the c group means $\bar{y}_i$ used to make the calculation). If the n_i observations in each of the c groups all come from the same normal distribution, then the group means $\bar{y}_i$ will differ from one another because of sampling error and not because of a relationship between y and x (the group variances $S_i{}^2$ will also differ somewhat due to sampling error). As a result, the between groups variance $S_b{}^2$ and the within groups variance $S_w{}^2$ each provide independent and unbiased estimates of the true variance σ^2 of the distribution of y.[4]

So if we divide $S_b{}^2$ by $S_w{}^2$, the extent to which the resulting ratio will differ from one will be the result of sampling error. And the extent of the difference will depend on the degrees of freedom in each of the two variance estimates. In sum, the ratio of $S_b{}^2$ to $S_w{}^2$ is the observed value of F:

$$\hat{F} = \frac{S_b{}^2}{S_w{}^2}$$ 5.14

It should be noted that the between groups variance $S_b{}^2$ is always in the numerator. This is because if the groups are, in fact, not from the same distribution, but are due to a relationship between y and x, then $S_b{}^2$ will increase while $S_w{}^2$ will decrease. The F-value will then exceed unity by a considerable amount. Since the F-tables are set up to measure the amount by which F can *exceed* unity due only to sampling error, we assume that our observed F-statistic can be used with the F-tables by keeping $S_b{}^2$ in the numerator.

We can now apply the F-test to test whether we are significantly improving our estimates of y, "teacher performance," by taking account of the variable x, "where the teacher comes from." Since we have already calculated the within groups sum of squares from the data in Table 5.7. we can calculate the within groups variance by dividing by the degrees of freedom $N - c$.

$$S_w{}^2 = \frac{122{,}400}{21} = 5828$$

To calculate the between groups variance, we first must calculate the between groups sum of squares. This can be derived as a residual by using equation 5.10, since both the total and within groups sum of squares have been calculated, or it can be obtained directly as $\sum n_i(\bar{y}_i - \bar{y})^2$. The reader should verify that either method yields the quantity 129,600. Then dividing by the number of degrees of freedom $c - 1$

$$S_b{}^2 = \frac{129{,}600}{2} = 64{,}800$$

---

[4] If each group is an independent sample from the same distribution, then the expected value of the term $(\bar{y}_i - \bar{y})^2$ for each of the c groups in the between groups variance $(S_b{}^2)$ is the variance of the ith mean $S_{\bar{y}_i}^2 = S^2/n_i$ so that $n_i S_{\bar{y}_i}^2 = S^2$. That is, the expected value of each term $n_i(\bar{y}_i - \bar{y})^2$ is the overall variance S^2. There being c such estimates of S^2, if we divide by the number of degrees of freedom $c - 1$, the resulting $S_b{}^2$ gives an unbiased estimate of the true variance σ^2. The within groups variance $S_w{}^2$ also provides an unbiased estimate of σ^2 if observed differences between the $\bar{y}_i$ are due only to sampling error since, in this case, the variance around the observed mean value of each group will be unaffected by observed differences in the group means. Those who wish more precise proofs of these results should refer to C. E. Weatherburn, *A First Course in Mathematical Statistics*, second edition, Cambridge, Engl.: Cambridge University Press, 1962, pp. 210 and 236, example 1.

The observed F-value is then obtained as

$$\hat{F} = \frac{64,800}{5828} = 11.12$$

To test the significance of this observed F, we must find the critical value F^*. Looking in the table of the F-distribution (in the Appendix) under df(numerator) $= 2$ and df(denominator) $= 21$ for the .05 significance level, we find that $F^* = 3.47$. Since $\hat{F} > F^*$, we conclude that $\hat{F}$ is too high to have been merely the result of sampling error. (It should be noted that the F-test, in assuming that the grouped samples come from the same distribution, requires the group sample variances to be nearly equal—a requirement that is barely met in our example.) Our sampled observations are accepted as yielding significant evidence of a relationship between y and x.

What about testing the significance of the correlation ratio? If we divide E^2 by $1 - E^2$ and multiply by $(N - c)/(c - 1)$, the result is precisely equal to $S_b{}^2/S_w{}^2$, our $\hat{F}$ statistic:[5]

$$\frac{E^2}{1 - E^2}\left(\frac{N - c}{c - 1}\right) = \frac{S_b{}^2}{S_w{}^2} = \hat{F}$$

In other words, our F-test has already tested for the significance of E^2, and we have found that our observed value of $E^2 = .51$ is statistically significant at the .05 level.

We can now summarize the steps needed to calculate the correlation ratio E^2 and to apply the F-test for the analysis of variance.

---

1. Collect samples of size N for the interval-scaled variable y. Based on the nominal-scaled variable x_i, categorize the N observations into c groups of n_i observations each. Calculate:

   (a) The overall mean $\bar{y}$ $\bar{y} = \sum_i \sum_j y_{ij}/N$

   (b) The group means $\bar{y}_i$ $\bar{y}_i = \sum_j y_{ij}/n_i$

   (c) The total sum of squares $SS_T = \sum_i \sum_j (y_{ij} - \bar{y})^2$

   (d) The within groups sum of squares $SS_w = \sum_i \sum_j (y_{ij} - \bar{y}_i)^2$

   (e) The between groups sum of squares $SS_b = SS_T - SS_w$

---

[5] Write the "within sum" of square as SS_w, the "between sum" of square as SS_b, and the total sum of squares as SS_T.

$$\frac{E^2}{1 - E^2}\left(\frac{N - c}{c - 1}\right) = \left(\frac{SS_b}{SS_T}\bigg/\frac{SS_T - SS_b}{SS_T}\right)\left(\frac{N - c}{c - 1}\right) = \frac{SS_b}{SS_w}\left(\frac{N - c}{c - 1}\right) = \frac{S_b{}^2}{S_w{}^2}$$

2. Calculate the correlation ratio:

$$E^2 = 1 - \frac{SS_w}{SS_T}$$

3. Perform analysis of variance:
   (a) State null hypothesis that y is independent of x, and attempt to reject via F-test.
   (b) Assume that the interval-scaled variable y is normally distributed with constant group variances

   $$(\sigma^2_{y|x} = \text{constant})$$

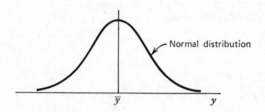

Normal distribution

$\bar{y}$ y

4. Determine the critical value F^*:
   (a) State significance level.
   (b) Obtain degrees of freedom
   df (numerator) $= c - 1$
   df (denominator) $= N - c$
   (c) Identify the critical value of F^* in the table of the F-distribution.

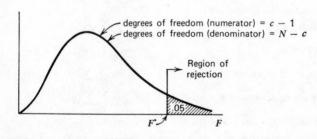

degrees of freedom (numerator) $= c - 1$
degrees of freedom (denominator) $= N - c$

Region of rejection

.05

F^* F

5. Calculate the observed value *of F:*

$$\hat{F} = \frac{S_b^2}{S_w^2} = \frac{SS_b/(c-1)}{SS_w/(N-c)}$$

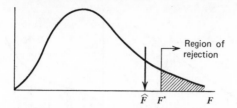

Region of
rejection

$\widehat{F}$ F^* F

6. If $\widehat{F} > F^*$, reject null hypothesis of independence.
    If $\widehat{F} \leq F^*$, do not reject, but state that the sample is not significant
    evidence for detecting a relationship between the two variables.

We have shown, in this section, how an interval-scaled variable (y) can be related to a single nominal-scaled variable (x). We have not extended our ANOVA methods to show how an interval-scaled variable can be related to two or more nominal-scaled variables, $x_1, x_2, \ldots$, even though it is possible to do so. The reason we have not extended the ANOVA approach to the *multivariate* situation is that, in social science research, ANOVA does not provide a practical means for this purpose. The difficulty is that the straightforward application of ANOVA to multivariate analysis requires the analyst to obtain his sampled data in such a way that there are an equal number of observations for each combination of the groups of the explanatory variables. For example, if variable x_1 has 3 groups and x_2 has 4, then there are 12 "subgroups" of x_1x_2 combinations. The number of observations of the y variable must be equal for all 12 subgroups. It is extremely rare that this requirement can be met in the kind of nonexperimental research possible in the social sciences. Instead, we leave multivariate analysis to consider the more mathematically tractable linear regression analysis, which is described in the remainder of this chapter.

5.5   LEAST-SQUARES REGRESSION AND CORRELATION ANALYSIS IN SIMPLE LINEAR MODELS

5.5.1   REGRESSION ANALYSIS

In the example of the preceding section, the conditional expectation of y given x_i varied in a rather irregular way as x varied. For example, for x_1, $\bar{y}_1 = 440$; for x_2, $\bar{y}_2 = 500$, an increase of 60; for x_3, $\bar{y}_3 = 620$, an increase not of 60 but of 120. In fact, this happens to be one of the advantages of the ANOVA approach as well as of the correlation ratio: they can be applied even when the expected value of the variable being estimated does not vary in a regular way with changes in the explanatory variable. Examples of such "irregular" relationships are shown in Figures 5.1 and 5.3a. Nevertheless,

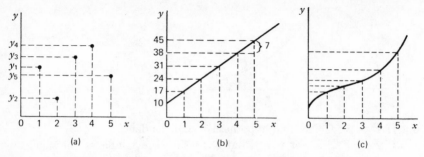

FIGURE 5.3   Different kinds of relationships between two variables.

certain analytic techniques require the relationships to be "regular"—
techniques that make use of mathematical model-building and that require y
to be a continuous function of one or more "explanatory" variables. Examples
of such continuous functions are shown in Figures 5.3b and c. Figure 5.3b
shows a linear relation between y and x, in which y increases by a constant
amount ($\Delta y = 7$) each time x increases by 1. Figure 5.3c shows a nonlinear
relation in which y increases by a predictable although not constant amount
each time x increases by 1.

However, the presence of a continuous relationship implies that the
explanatory variable x is neither of nominal nor ordinal scale, but of an
interval scale. Thus the methods to be discussed in the rest of this chapter
relate an interval-scaled variable to one or more variables that are also on
interval scales. (Techniques are available, however, that allow the methods
described to include nominal-scaled explanatory variables.)

The literature about these methods usually calls the variables being
explained the "dependent" variables, while the variables doing the explaining
are called "independent" variables. For example, in Figure 5.4a, x_1 and x_2 are
independent variables while y is the dependent variable. But the "independence" of x_1 and x_2 is a limited one. They may be independent in an

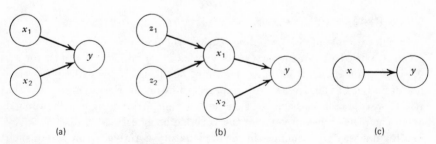

FIGURE 5.4   Examples of dependence and independence among variables.

162   *Methods*

analysis that seeks to explain only y, but in situations more typically encountered in planning situations, x_1 and x_2 might be part of a larger system in which policy controls available to decision makers cannot affect the independent variable y (in this case, a goal variable) directly. Instead, they must get to y indirectly by first affecting one or more variables such as x_1 and x_2 on which y directly depends. In Figure 5.4b, we show the variable x_1 as dependent on two other variables z_1 and z_2, with z_2 being subject to the control of policy. An analysis of the determinants of x_1, then, would now take x_1 as the dependent variable and z_1 and z_2 as independent variables. From the point of view of the decision maker who must use his policy z_2 to affect y, given all the other influences on y (in this case, z_1 and x_2), these distinctions are not so meaningful. At the level of a system such as is illustrated in Figure 5.4b, the variables z_1 and x_2 are said to be *exogenously* determined, that is, they are determined by unspecified factors outside the system: they are taken as given.

In this section, we do not work with a system of relationships such as is shown in Figure 5.4b. In fact, we limit ourselves to the simplest of relations: that between one dependent and one independent variable (Figure 5.4c). Furthermore, the form of the relation will be of the simplest type: the linear relation shown in Figure 5.3b.

The straight line relation between x and y in Figure 5.3b can be precisely represented by this equation:

$$y = 10 + 7x$$

This shows that y depends on the level of x multiplied by a slope coefficient (7), which shows the rate of change in y per unit increase in x, and on an "intercept" coefficient (10), which shows the point at which the straight line intercepts the y axis when the level of x is zero. Any equation that has this form is called a linear equation, since the relation between x and y can be represented by a straight line as in Figure 5.3b. If, for a given set of observations showing the values of two variables x and y, we can "fit" an equation such as the linear equation above, then, given the level of x, an estimate of the expected value of y is easily obtained.

The only difficulty in fitting a linear equation to a set of observations, however, is that there must be reason to assume that the relation between x and y is, in fact, linear. If this assumption is not warranted, then we do not benefit by using a linear equation.

But assuming that the true relation is linear, the expected value of y given x is easily obtained as

$$E(y \mid x) = \alpha + \beta x \qquad\qquad 5.15$$

In the present example, the intercept coefficient $\alpha = 10$ and the slope coefficient $\beta = 7$, so that if the value of x is given at 20, $y = 10 + 140 = 150$.

This is in contrast to the method of the preceding section used to estimate y, where all possible values of x had to be separately listed and the $E(y \mid x_i)$'s were itemized accordingly $[E(y \mid x_1) = 440; E(y \mid x_2) = 500;$ and $E(y \mid x_3) = 620]$.

Let us show how the coefficients α and β can be estimated by examining the following problem. A housing authority in a certain city is in the process of setting rental rates for the new housing it currently has under construction. One administrator wants to base these rates on the income and size of the families that are to occupy the housing. He asserts that the rental rates should be proportionate with the size of the family. However, a housing analyst familiar with the available data disputes the equity of the administrator's approach. He says that, in fact, on the average, family rent outlays increase less than proportionately with family size, and that the rental rates for public housing should, therefore, follow the pattern of the rest of the city by also rising less than proportionately. The administrator wants to have evidence that this "less than proportionate" relationship exists, and in case that it does exist, he wants to know by how much rents actually do rise as family size increases.

Let us now structure this issue from a quantitative point of view so that we can bring a meaningful statistical test to the problem. The administrator asserts a proportionate relationship between the dependent variable y (rent outlay per family) and the independent variable x (family size in number of persons per family). Such a proportionate relationship is shown in Figure 5.5a by the linear function F on which the ratio y/x remains constant. The housing analyst asserts a less than proportionate relationship between y and x. This is to say that as x increases from x_1 to x_2, the ratio y/x declines from $(y/x)_1$ to $(y/x)_2$ as is shown in Figure 5.5b—it is this declining ratio that indicates the less than proportionate relationship. One type of function that conforms to this type of relationship is a linear function in

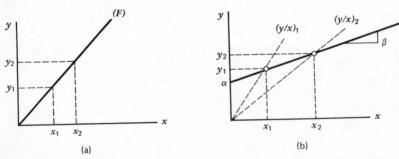

(a)

(b)

FIGURE 5.5 The relation between the coefficients of a linear equation and proportionality.

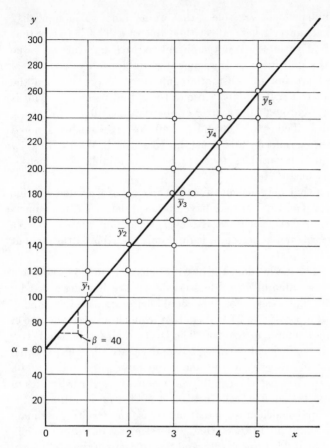

FIGURE 5.6 A scatter diagram of y given x.

which both the constant α and β (the coefficient of x) in equation 5.15 are positive. It will be our analyst's task to gather data and to use these data as evidence that both α and β are positive and to estimate their values. We accept as reasonable the assumption that y is a linear function of x.

Our analyst has gathered a sample of 24 observations (families) listing the amount of rent (y) currently paid and the number of people (x) currently in the family. A scatter diagram showing these observations is in Figure 5.6.

Let us suppose that the true values of the intercept and slope coefficients that relate y to x are $\alpha = 60$ and $\beta = 40$, respectively, shown in Figure 5.6 as the upward sloping straight line. However, very few of the observations actually fall on this line. There are two reasons that account for this. The first is that there may be many determinants of the dependent variable y, in addition to the independent variable x, that we have not taken explicitly into account but that, nevertheless, affect the value of y. This is to say that the single independent variable x is not sufficient to predict the actual value of y. However, if the multitude of the ignored variables fairly well cancel each other out and are not of substantial importance anyway, then the value of y predicted by x will be quite close to the actual value of y. This is what we observe in Figure 5.6: the scatter of observations all lie fairly close to the straight line described by $\alpha = 60$ and $\beta = 40$. Nevertheless, the ignored variables do have their effects, and must be considered. We do this by lumping all the ignored variables together as the variable ϵ_i, which is referred to as a "stochastic" term.

The second reason that may account for the variance of y around the line is measurement error. Our analyst may have obtained data that, for numerous reasons, are not perfectly accurate. However, we assume that the degree of measurement error is not serious and is randomly distributed throughout the observations.

A second point can be made about the observations in Figure 5.6. For each value of x_i, the mean value of y $(\bar{y}_i)$ does not lie on the line described by $\alpha = 60$ and $\beta = 40$. The reason for this should be anticipated: sampling error. Certainly a sample of size 24 will contain a much greater amount of sampling error than a sample of size 200. The larger the sample, the better we would expect the conditional means $\bar{y}_i$ to approximate the true expected values $E(y \mid x_i)$ that lie directly on the line given by $\alpha = 60$ and $\beta = 40$. For this reason, we do not use the conditional means $\bar{y}_i$ as our estimates of the conditional expectation $E(y \mid x_i)$. Instead, we attempt to estimate the true intercept and slope coefficients (α and β) and to use the resulting estimate of y given x as the conditional expectation. The estimates of the true coefficients are denoted as a and b, respectively, and the estimate of the conditional expectation $E(y \mid x)$ from the resulting equation is denoted as $\hat{y}$. Thus

$$\hat{y} = a + bx \qquad\qquad 5.16$$

is the equation we work with to estimate y given x. Our problem now is to find a method that uses the sampled observations of y and x to yield the most accurate unbiased estimates possible of a and b. The method that is used for this purpose is called *regression analysis,* and the line estimated by a and b is called the *regression line.* Similarly, the estimate a of the true intercept coefficient α is referred to as a *constant of regression,* while the estimate b of the true slope coefficient β is referred to quite simply as a *regression coefficient.*

To show how the coefficients a and b may best be calculated, it is useful to first introduce a new statistic, the covariance, which in the case of the two

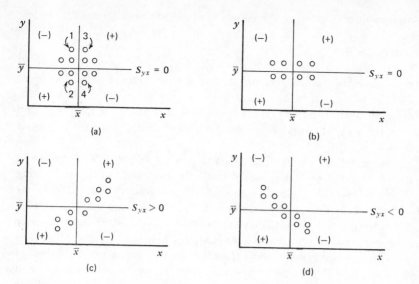

FIGURE 5.7 The relation between the pattern of observations and the covariance.

variables, x and y, is denoted as σ_{yx}. It may be calculated as

$$\sigma_{yx} = \frac{\sum\limits_{i}(y_i - \mu_y)(x_i - \mu_x)}{N}$$

if the true means μ_y and μ_x are known. If these values are estimated by a sample of size N, then the sample covariance is S_{yx}, calculated as

$$S_{yx} = \frac{\sum\limits_{i}(y_i - \bar{y})(x_i - \bar{x})}{N - 1} \qquad 5.17$$

which provides an unbiased estimate of σ_{yx}. To see what the covariance indicates, consider the diagrams in Figure 5.7. Figure 5.7a shows a scatter of observations in the shape of a ball. Notice that for observation 1, $(y_1 - \bar{y})$ is positive and $(x_1 - \bar{x})$ is negative, so that their product $(y_1 - \bar{y})(x_1 - \bar{x})$ must be negative. Likewise, for observation 2, since $(y_2 - \bar{y}) < 0$ and $(x_2 - \bar{x}) < 0$, the cross product $(y_2 - \bar{y})(x_2 - \bar{x}) > 0$. Furthermore, the two cross products will be of the same magnitude but, since the first is negative and the second positive, their sum is zero. This is also true of observations 3 and 4 and, in fact, for each of the remaining pairs of observations above and below the horizontal line $\bar{y}$. As a result, when all cross products are summed to obtain the numerator of the covariance, the result yields a zero covariance.

This argument is also true of the scatter of observations in Figure 5.7b which, although closely following a straight line, follow the horizontal straight line $\bar{y}$: again $S_{yx} = 0$.

This result does not occur in Figures 5.7c and d. In Figure 5.7c nearly all the cross products are positive, and the one negative cross product, being so close to the two mean values $\bar{x}$ and $\bar{y}$, has a very small value. As a result, the average value of these cross products, for example, S_{yx}, will be large and positive. By using the same argument for Figure 5.7d, S_{yx} will be large and negative.

Now suppose that we are confronted with a set of points as is shown in Figure 5.6. What straight line would be the best estimate of the underlying true linear relation that gave rise to these observed points? We take as our criterion for evaluating the "goodness of fit" of a regression line the requirement that the line must pass through the scatter of observations in such a way that the variation of observations around this line is minimized. But how can we translate this criterion into specific rules for calculating the values of a and b? To show this, consider first the set of six points in Figure 5.8a and the upward sloping straight line that is used as an approximation of the "best" regression line. Although this line follows the upward sloping trend of the six points, all six points lie above this line. In consequence, given x_i, the estimate y_i provided by this line will always be less than the observed value y_i. The difference between the estimated and observed values is a residual error, denoted as u_i

$$u_i = y_i - \hat{y}_i \qquad\qquad 5.18$$

and reflects the stochastic term ϵ_i referred to previously, as well as the error in fitting the straight line to the observed data. We show in Figure 5.8b the values of the six u_i generated by the regression line of Figure 5.8a. Since all six residuals are positive, the average residual $\bar{u}$ is shown as positive, so that the regression line is clearly generating more residual variation than is necessary. However, if we calculate the covariance S_{ux} about the mean values $\bar{x}$ and $\bar{u}$, we see that $S_{ux} = 0$, a result that indicates that the regression line is following the direction of the scatter very nicely.

Now let us evaluate the regression line shown in Figure 5.8c that has been "fitted" to the same six points. This regression line apparently does not follow the upward pattern of the six points very well. In fact, when we plot the residual u_i against the x variable, as we have done in Figure 5.8d, we can see that the covariance of the residual with x is strongly positive ($S_{ux} > 0$). Evidently, the slope of the regression line needs to be improved to eliminate the covariation between u and x. However, since the regression passes right through the center of the scatter of points (in fact, it can be visually determined that the line passes through a point at which $y = \bar{y}$ and $x = \bar{x}$), we

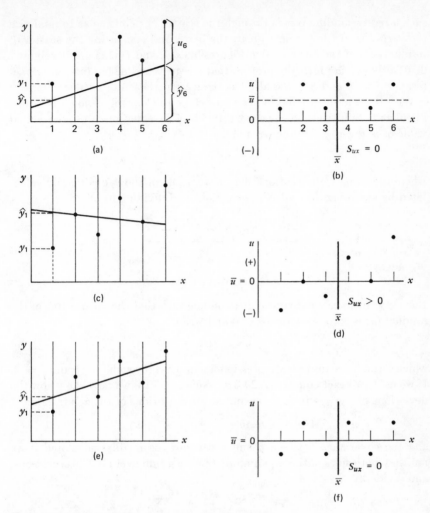

FIGURE 5.8 Criteria for fitting a regression line.

observe in Figure 5.8*d* that the average value of the residuals about this line is $\bar{u} = 0$.

Suppose the regression were to possess two characteristics that seem to be emerging: the average of the residual about the line is zero $[(1/n) \sum u_i = \bar{u} = 0]$ and the covariance between the residual and the independent variables is also zero $[(1/(n-1)) \sum (x_i - \bar{x})(u_i - \bar{u}) = S_{ux} = 0]$, as shown in Figure 5.8*f*. In this case, we see in Figure 5.8*e* that such a regression line would not only pass through the center of the scatter of points (thereby intersecting the point at which $y = \bar{y}$ and $x = \bar{x}$), it would also have the right slope. In consequence such a regression line passes through the scatter of points so as to minimize the variation of these points about the line.[6] And comparing the scatter of residuals about the line $u = 0$ in Figures 5.8b, d, and f, it is intuitively evident, although not formally proved, that a regression line having the characteristics $\bar{u} = 0$ and $S_{ux} = 0$ also has the least variation of residuals.

With these ideas in mind, we can now show how our regression line can be calculated. Substituting equation 5.16 for $\hat{y}$ in equation 5.18, the actual value of y_i given x_i may be written as[7]

$$y_i = a + bx_i + u_i \qquad i = 1, \ldots, n \qquad\qquad 5.19$$

where there are N observations. The mean value of the y_i's is readily calculated by summing over all N observations and dividing by N.

$$\frac{\sum_i y_i}{N} = \frac{Na}{N} + \frac{b \sum_i x_i}{N} + \frac{\sum_i u_i}{N}$$

or, more simply,

$$\bar{y} = a + b\bar{x} + \bar{u} \qquad\qquad 5.20$$

But we want to calculate our regression line such that the mean value of the residual ($\bar{u}$) is zero, so we set $\bar{u} = 0$ and write

$$\bar{y} = a + b\bar{x} \qquad\qquad 5.20'$$

which formally requires the regression line to pass through $y = \bar{y}$ and $x = \bar{x}$. If we next subtract equation 5.20 from equation 5.19, we may show how the deviations of the y_i's from $\bar{y}$ depend on the deviations of the x_i's from $\bar{x}$.

$$(y_i - \bar{y}) = b(x_i - \bar{x}) + (u_i - \bar{u})$$

and the covariance between y and x can now be readily calculated if we multiply both sides of this equation by $(x_i - \bar{x})$, sum over all N observations, and divide by $N - 1$

$$\frac{\sum_i (y_i - \bar{y})(x_i - \bar{x})}{N - 1} = \frac{b \sum_i (x_i - \bar{x})^2}{N - 1} + \frac{\sum_i (u_i - \bar{u})(x_i - \bar{x})}{N - 1}$$

or, more simply,

$$S_{yx} = bS_x + S_{ux}$$

which is to say that the covariance between y and x is equal to the regression coefficient b multiplied by the variance of the x_i values plus the covariance

[6] We shall define what we mean by "variation . . . about the line" shortly.

[7] Although for each value of x there are several values of y as is seen in Figure 5.6, suggesting that there should also be a subscript j on y, we have adopted a single subscript here, to simplify the presentation.

between u and x. But we want to calculate our regression line such that the covariance between the independent variable and the residuals (S_{ux}) is zero, so we set $S_{ux} = 0$ and write

$$S_{yx} = bS_x$$

Dividing both sides of this equation by S_x and noting that the $N - 1$ in S_{yx} and in S_x cancel out, the regression coefficient b is calculated as

$$b = \frac{\sum_i (y_i - \bar{y})(x_i - \bar{x})}{\sum_i (x_i - \bar{x})^2} \qquad 5.21$$

a task that is really no more difficult than the calculations required for analysis of variance, since we are again working with sums of squared deviations for N observations, where the y and x values for each of the N observations are already known.

Once b is calculated, the calculation of the constant of regression a is straightforward. Since $\bar{y}$, $\bar{x}$, and b are already known, the coefficient a is calculated, from equation 5.20', as

$$a = \bar{y} - b\bar{x} \qquad 5.22$$

Certain attributes of equations 5.21 and 5.22 that are used for estimating the true regression line $[E(y \mid x) = \alpha + \beta x]$ are worth noting. First, let us define a measure of the variation of the residuals u_i about the estimated regression line as the sum of the squares of the residuals

$$\sum_i u_i^2 = \sum_i (y_i - a - bx_i)^2 \qquad 5.23$$

which is analogous to the unexplained or "within groups" sum of squares in analysis of variance. When the method we have described is used for estimating the coefficients of the linear regression function, the resulting coefficients (a and b) are unbiased estimates of the true coefficients (α and β), and the straight-line regression has the characteristic that the sum of the squares of the residuals is minimized.[8]

It is in this sense that this "regression analysis" yields the straight line that best fits the given set of observations, and it is for this reason that the method is referred to as least-squares regression. And the assumptions

---

[8] We do not provide a proof that the residuals are minimized here, since some knowledge of elementary calculus is required. The reader who wants to see the proof is referred to T. H. Wonnacott and R. J. Wonnacott, *Introductory Statistics* (New York: Wiley, 1969), pp. 225–227 and p. 230, problem 11-4. The same reference provides proof that the coefficients a and b are unbiased (pp. 238–239).

underlying the regression are, to summarize, (1) that the true regression between y and x is linear; (2) that the residuals are independently distributed with mean $\bar{u} = 0$; (3) that the covariance between the residuals and the independent variable $S_{ux} = 0$; and (4) that the values of the independent variable x are given. It should be noted that we have made no assumptions about the form of the distribution of the dependent variable y and, therefore, about the residuals u. Specifically, we have not required "y given x" to be normally distributed.

Another attribute of least-squares regression is that it yields estimates of the coefficients a and b that will, themselves, have the least expected error. That is, least-squares regression is a minimum variance estimator of the coefficients of a linear regression equation.[9] In addition to the assumptions we have already cited, this result requires the assumption that variance of the dependent variable y, given the independent variable x, is constant over all values of x:

$$\sigma^2_{y|x_i} = \sigma^2_{y|x} \qquad \text{for all } i$$

Since the distribution of the residuals will differ from that of y only in that $\bar{u} = 0$, this assumption implies that the variance of the residuals given each value of x must also be constant over all values of x.

We now apply our method of least-square regression to calculate the coefficients of the linear regression equation that best fits the data shown in Figure 5.6. Our calculations are presented in Table 5.8, with the y and x values of the 24 observations shown in columns 1 and 2. The mean value of y, rent outlay per family, is $\bar{y} = \$185$, while the mean value of x, number of persons per family, is $\bar{x} = 3$. The deviations of the y and x values for each observation from their respective mean values are shown in columns 3 and 4. The cross product of the mean deviations for each observation is shown in column 5, and the sum of the cross products is shown at the bottom of this column as 1360. The squared deviations for y and x are shown in columns 6 and 7, and the sum of the squared deviations for each variable is shown at the bottom of each column, with $\sum (y_i - \bar{y})^2 = \$67,400$, and $\sum (x_i - \bar{x})^2 = 34$.

The coefficient b is calculated from equation 5.21 as

$$b = \frac{1360}{34} = 40$$

and the coefficient a is calculated from equation 5.22 as

$$a = 185 - (40)(3) = 65$$

[9] The proof of this result is known as the Gauss-Markov theorem, and is shown in R. J. Wonnacott and T. H. Wonnacott, *Econometrics* (New York: Wiley, 1970), pp. 48–51.

TABLE 5.8

Calculations for Regression and Correlation Analysis

y_i (1)	x_i (2)	$y_i - \bar{y}$ (3)	$x_i - \bar{x}$ (4)	$(y_i - \bar{y})(x_i - \bar{x})$ (5)	$(y_i - \bar{y})^2$ (6)	$(x_i - \bar{x})^2$ (7)
80	1	−105	−2	210	11,025	4
100	1	−85	−2	170	7,225	4
120	1	−65	−2	130	4,225	4
120	2	−65	−1	65	4,225	1
140	2	−45	−1	45	2,025	1
160	2	−25	−1	25	625	1
160	2	−25	−1	25	625	1
180	2	−5	−1	5	25	1
140	3	−45	0	0	2,025	0
160	3	−25	0	0	625	0
160	3	−25	0	0	625	0
180	3	−5	0	0	25	0
180	3	−5	0	0	25	0
180	3	−5	0	0	25	0
200	3	15	0	0	225	0
240	3	55	0	0	3,025	0
200	4	15	1	15	225	1
220	4	35	1	35	1,225	1
240	4	55	1	55	3,025	1
240	4	55	1	55	3,025	1
260	4	75	1	75	5,625	1
240	5	55	2	110	3,025	1
260	5	75	2	150	5,625	4
280	5	95	2	190	9,025	4
4,440 $\bar{y} = 185$	72 $\bar{x} = 3$	0	0	1,360	67,400	34

Thus, our least-squares linear regression equation that provides the best estimate of $E(y \mid x)$ is

$$\hat{y} = 65 + 40x$$

On the face of this result, it appears that our planner has made a strong case for his assertion that the relation between family rent outlays and family size is less than proportionate. The administrator, assuming a proportionate relationship, would have calculated the increase in family rental outlays per

unit increase in family size as

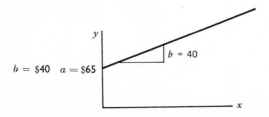

$$\frac{\bar{x}}{\bar{y}} = \frac{\$185}{3} = \$61.67$$

$61\frac{2}{3}$

whereas our analyst has shown that each time family size increases by one, rent outlays increase by

$b = \$40 \quad a = \$65$

$b = 40$

which is just under two thirds the quantity that the administrator would have used. But the administrator is not about to give up his rental plan so easily. Knowing something about statistics, he charges the analyst with trickery, insisting that a result of $b = 40$ could easily have been the result of sampling error, given that a sample size of only 24 was the sole evidence for the analyst's findings. Is the administrator correct in this charge? To find out, we must know how to evaluate the statistical significance of the regression coefficients. But before we do this, let us first consider the question of the strength of the linear relationship between y and x, which brings us to linear correlation analysis.

5.5.2 CORRELATION ANALYSIS

If we have reason to believe that the true relation between two interval-scaled variables is linear, then we can calculate a statistic called the "coefficient of determination," denoted as r^2, to measure the strength of the linear relationship. And if we have already obtained the data to calculate a regression coefficient, then the calculation of r^2 is an easy next step, since

$$r^2 = \frac{\left[\sum_i (y_i - \bar{y})(x_i - \bar{x}) \right]^2}{\sum_i (y_i - \bar{y})^2 \sum_i (x_i - \bar{x})^2} \qquad 5.24$$

That is, r^2 is the square of the covariance between y and x divided by the product of the variance of y times the variance of x (the degrees of freedom

$N - 1$ in these expressions cancel out, giving the form shown in equation 5.24).

Another way to calculate r^2 (which sheds more light on its nature but is too unwieldly for practical use) is very similar to the procedure used in analysis of variance for calculating the correlation ratio E^2 (see equation 5.11) But unlike the method for calculating E^2 in which the unexplained sum of squares was calculated from deviations from "within group" means $(y_i - \bar{y}_i)$, we now make this calculation from deviations about the regression line $(u_i = y_i - \hat{y}_i)$, so that our unexplained sum of squares is that given by equation 5.23 above. Proceeding as we did in calculating E^2, we divide the unexplained sum of squares by the total sum of squares and subtract the result from one:

$$r^2 = 1 - \frac{\sum\limits_i (y_i - \hat{y}_i)^2}{\sum\limits_i (y_i - \bar{y})^2}$$

Thus r^2 is interpreted as the percentage of the total sum of squares that is explained by the least-squares linear regression, and it is seen to have a range of $0 \leq r^2 \leq 1$. Its square root is called the *coefficient of correlation* (r) and has a range of $-1 \leq r \leq +1$. If either r or r^2 is zero, then we can say that the variables are not linearly related. Nevertheless, the variables might be strongly related via a nonlinear relation such as is shown in Figures 5.3a or c. In this case, it would be incorrect to use r^2 to measure the strength of relationship between two variables: the correlation ratio E^2 would be the appropriate measure.

It is useful to indicate the kinds of results that can be expected in terms of r^2's, E^2's, and the regression coefficients a and b, given various alternative patterns of observations for two variables. We present Figure 5.9 for this purpose, in which eight alternative patterns of observations are shown. The patterns on the left side of the diagram illustrate strong relationships, with the exception of Figure 5.9c. In this pattern even though the residuals about the regression line are extremely small, the total variance of the dependent variable y is also very small and is not at all reduced or explained by disaggregating the observations according to values of x. The patterns on the right side of the diagram all illustrate weak relationships. The bottom four patterns (e to h) all show negative relationships, although the bottom two (g and h) are nonlinear so that least-squares linear regression and correlation are inappropriate.

We now apply linear correlation analysis as indicated in equation 5.24 to calculate the coefficient of determination r^2 for the data shown in Table 5.8.

$$r^2 = \frac{(1360)^2}{(67,400)(34)} = \frac{1,849,600}{2,281,600} = .81$$

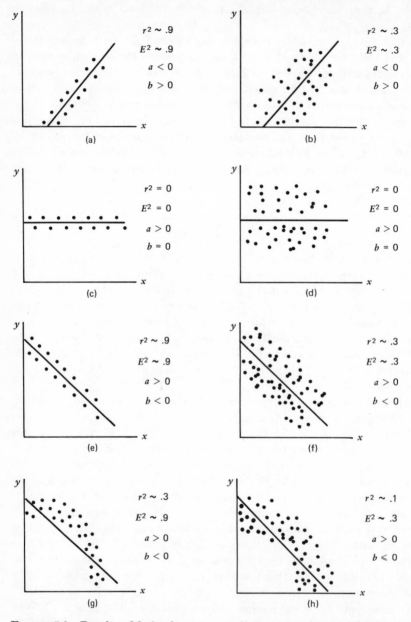

FIGURE 5.9   Results of fitting least-squares linear regression to eight alternative sets of observations.

That is, the use of a linear relation with x as the independent variable explains 81 % of the variation in y. We now consider the significance of the relation.

5.5.3 Testing the Significance of a Least-Squares Regression

We again ask the question whether a nonzero regression coefficient could have been calculated due merely to sampling error, given that the true regression coefficient is zero. The method for testing this question is similar to those used for testing the significance of several other statistics we have calculated, for instance, the mean $\bar{x}$ and Spearman's r_s. First, we calculate the standard error of the sample statistic; second, we find a probability distribution that describes the distribution of the sample statistic; third, we measure the number of standard errors that the calculated sample statistic lies from zero; and fourth, we determine the probability of observing this many standard errors and decide on this basis whether to judge the sample statistic as significantly different from zero.

To test the significance of the regression coefficient b, we first must calculate its standard error. This is

$$S_b = \sqrt{\frac{\sum\limits_{i} (y_i - \hat{y}_i)^2}{(N - 2) \sum\limits_{i} (x_i - \bar{x})^2}} \qquad 5.25$$

We see that the standard error of b increases as the unexplained sum of squares $[\sum (y_i - \hat{y}_i)^2]$ increases, and that it decreases as the number of degrees of freedom $(N - 2)$ increases or as the variation of the independent variable $[\sum (x_i - \bar{x})^2]$ increases.

It happens that if the dependent variable y is normally distributed, then the least-squares regression coefficient is also normally distributed and, in addition, the ratio of the regression coefficient to its standard error (as measured by equation 5.25) has the t-distribution.

$$t = \frac{b}{S_b} \qquad 5.26$$

This being the case, we can test the significance of the regression coefficient via the table of the t-distribution.

By setting a significance level of .05, we can determine the largest number of standard errors (t^*) that could be observed if the true regression coefficient β were zero. Since sampling error could result in an observed coefficient b that is either positive or negative, we use a two-tailed test. This means that we choose the column in the t-table as if the significance level were .025 instead of .05. We choose the row in the t-table that corresponds to the number of degrees of freedom, which in the case of simple least-squares regression corresponds to

$$df = N - 2$$

We find in the cell of the t-table, in the appropriate column and row, the critical value t^*. If the observed t value of equation 5.26, denoted as $\hat{t}$, exceeds the critical value (in absolute terms), then we reject the hypothesis that the true value of the regression coefficient is zero. If, however, $\hat{t} \leq t^*$, then we cannot reject the hypothesis that $\beta = 0$. This does not provide conclusive evidence that, in fact, $\beta = 0$ and that the two variables y and x are unrelated; instead, it requires us to conclude that the sampled data does not provide significant evidence that the two variables are linearly related.

Let us now test the significance of the regression coefficient that we calculated previously ($b = 40$). Selecting the column in the t-table (in the Appendix of this book) as if our significance level were .025, and selecting the row corresponding to df $= 24 - 2 = 22$, we find that $t^* = 2.074$. Next, using equation 5.25, we calculate the standard error of b. The calculations for the residual sum of squares are provided in Table 5.9. Inserting the result of this calculation, together with $(N - 2)$ and $\sum (x_i - \bar{x})$ (from Table 5.8) into equation 5.25, we find that

$$S_b = \sqrt{\frac{13,000}{22(34)}} = \sqrt{17.38} = 4.17$$

Since $b = 40$, the number of standard errors that b lies from zero is

$$\hat{t} = \frac{40}{4.17} = 9.6$$

This is certainly much larger than $t^* = 2.074$ and, hence, we reject the hypothesis that $\beta = 0$ and accept our sample as providing significant evidence that a linear relationship exists between y and x.

So far, so good. But remember that our planning analyst did not gather data just to learn that rent outlays are related to family size. He, as well as the administrator, were already quite satisfied that the relationship existed. The issue under contention was whether the relationship was proportionate or less than proportionate. We indicated earlier that the issue could be settled if, via regression analysis, we could show that both a and b are significantly greater than zero. However, because the calculation for the variance of a is somewhat more complicated than that for S_b and because, in the usual case, the significance of a is much less important than that of b, we avoid a test that requires the calculation of S_a and make use of a less complicated alternative.

TABLE 5.9
Calculations for Residual Sum of Squares

y_i (1)	x_i (2)	$\hat{y}_i$ (3)	$y_i - \hat{y}_i$ (4)	$(y_i - \hat{y}_i)^2$ (5)
80	1	105	−25	625
100	1	105	−5	25
120	1	105	15	225
120	2	145	−25	625
140	2	145	−5	25
160	2	145	15	225
160	2	145	15	225
180	2	145	35	1225
140	3	185	−45	2025
160	3	185	−25	625
160	3	185	−25	625
180	3	185	−5	25
180	3	185	−5	25
180	3	185	−5	25
200	3	185	15	225
240	3	185	55	3025
200	4	225	−25	625
220	4	225	−5	25
240	4	225	15	225
240	4	225	15	225
260	4	225	35	1225
240	5	265	−25	625
260	5	265	−5	25
280	5	265	15	225
				$\Sigma = 13{,}000$

Note that if x and y were proportionately related, then, since $\bar{y}/\bar{x} = 61.67$ as calculated previously, the values of a and b that ought to have been observed are $a = 0$ and $b = 61.67$. To test whether the relationship is less than proportionate, we can take the hypothesis that $\beta \geq 61.67$ and test whether our sampled data constitutes significant evidence for rejecting this hypothesis, that is, for concluding that $\beta < 61.67$.

At the .05 significance level, a one-tailed test with df = 22 gives $t^* = 1.717$. We then calculate the sample difference $b - \beta$ and determine whether this observed difference could have occurred due to sampling error. Thus

$$\hat{t} = \frac{b - \beta}{S_b} = \frac{21.67}{4.17} = 5.2$$

which again exceeds the critical value t^*. Hence, our planning analyst has a strong case in support of his argument.

At this point, we can summarize the procedures used in linear regression, correlation, and the test of significance of the linear relationship between two interval-scaled variables.

---

1. Collect sample of N independent observations for analysis of relationship between a dependent variable (y) and an independent variable (x), both of which are interval scaled. Assume that the error term u:
   (a) Has a mean of zero ($\bar{u} = 0$).
   (b) Has constant variance for all values of x ($\sigma^2_{u|x_i} = $ constant).
   (c) Is uncorrelated with the independent variable ($\sigma_{ux} = 0$).

2. Regression analysis: $y = a + bx$
   (a) Calculate
   $$b = \frac{\sum_i (y_i - \bar{y})(x_i - \bar{x})}{\sum_i (x_i - \bar{x})^2}$$
   (b) Calculate $a = \bar{y} - b\bar{x}$.

3. Correlation analysis:
   Calculate
   $$r^2 = \frac{\left(\sum_i (y_i - \bar{y})(x_i - \bar{x})\right)^2}{\sum_i (y_i - \bar{y})^2 \sum_i (x_i - \bar{x})^2}$$

4. Test of significance:
   (a) State null hypothesis that $\beta = 0$ and apply the two-tailed t-test in an attempt to reject null hypothesis; or hypothesis that $\beta \geq 0$ or $\beta \leq 0$ and apply the one-tail t-test in an attempt to reject null hypothesis.
   (b) Assume that dependent variable Y is normally distributed.

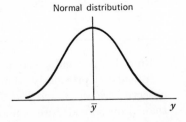
Normal distribution

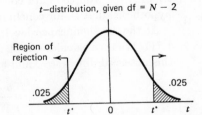
t–distribution, given df $= N - 2$

5. Determine critical value t^*:
   (a) State significance level for a one or two-tailed test.
   (b) Obtain degrees of freedom df $= N - 2$.
   (c) Identify the critical value of t^* in table of t-distribution.

6. Calculate the observed value of $\hat{t}$:

$$\hat{t} = \frac{b}{S_b}$$

where

$$S_b = \sqrt{\frac{\sum_i (y_i - \hat{y}_i)^2}{(N-2) \sum_i (x_i - \bar{x})^2}}$$

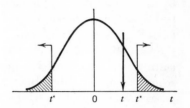

7. If absolute value of $\hat{t} > t^*$, reject null hypothesis. If $\hat{t} \leq t^*$, do not reject, but state that the sample is not significant evidence for detecting a linear relationship between the two variables.

5.6 MULTIPLE REGRESSION ANALYSIS IN COMPLEX LINEAR MODELS

5.6.1 IMPROVING THE EXPLANATION OF THE DEPENDENT VARIABLE

Consider a situation in which an agency of the federal government is responsible for improving the water supply facilities of rural regions that are unable to finance the needed improvements. The agency wants to be able to estimate the future water requirement of each of these areas so as to plan for the appropriate long-term investments that are needed.

A planning analyst working in this agency suggests that the increased demand for water (Δw) in these areas (j) depends linearly on increases in population and economic activity, which might be reasonably well measured by increases in the region's total income (Δy)

$$\Delta w_j = a + b\,\Delta y_j$$

After gathering data for 200 of these areas, he calculates the following simple regression:

$$\Delta w = 240 + 5\,\Delta y; \qquad r^2 = .67 \qquad\qquad 5.27$$
$$(1.25)$$

Noting that the standard error of the regression coefficient (shown in parentheses) is only 1.25, the resulting $t = 5/1.25 = 4$, statistically significant even at the .01 significance level, he concludes that his assertion that water demand and income are related is correct. Impressed by these results, the agency's decision makers nevertheless feel that the regression equation is not a sufficiently accurate estimator of water demand to serve as a basis for the planning of future water investments because it accounts for only two thirds of the variance in the water demand of these areas (i.e., $r^2 = .67$). Undaunted, the analyst suggests that estimation accuracy can be improved by using multiple regression analysis. This allows the introduction of several additional independent variables that might further explain the behavior of Δw.

Specifically, the analyst knows that these rural areas are largely agricultural and will use large quantities of irrigation water when rainfall is scant. Hence, on adding the new variable, change in area rainfall (ΔA_j), the analyst begins his work with a more complex model.

Models of this type, where there are two or more independent variables, can easily be estimated via multiple regression analysis yielding an equation of the form

$$\Delta w_j = a + b_1 \Delta y_j + b_2 \Delta A_j \qquad 5.28$$

All the calculations needed for the analysis are done on the computer via readily available "packaged programs" so that the analyst does not have to spend much time doing repetitive hand calculations. However, in addition to all the assumptions underlying simple regression, the analyst must rather explicitly confront some additional assumptions. We consider two of them. The first concerns the degree of correlation among the independent variables, and the second concerns the possibility that one or more of the independent variables might be simultaneously determined with the dependent variable. For the moment, we assume that all the independent variables have zero correlation with one another, and that they are, in fact, independent of the dependent variable, that is, not simultaneously determined with it. Such a causal structure is shown in Figure 5.10.

On arriving at the computer center, the analyst is told that his analysis has been run. The results are

$$\Delta w = 200 + 5 \Delta y - 12 \Delta A; \qquad R^2 = .95 \qquad 5.29$$
$$(1.0) \quad (2.0)$$

His knowledge of these areas has paid off: the variable "change in area rainfall" is negatively related to "change in water demand" and is highly significant. Furthermore, he is able to show how much of the original variance in the dependent variable is explained by the entire multiple regression via a

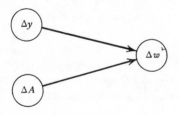

FIGURE 5.10 A causal structure with two independent variables.

statistic that has the same meaning as the coefficient of determination r^2, but that is referred to as the *coefficient of multiple determination* R^2. This shows that the variables Δy and ΔA, when linearly regressed on Δw, explain 95 % of the variance in Δw, an estimating accuracy that will be more than acceptable to the agency's decision makers.

Finally, to put the finishing touches on the analysis, our analyst is able to test the significance of R^2 via an F-test that is quite similar to the one used in analysis of variance.

The observed value of F can be calculated as

$$\hat{F} = \frac{\dfrac{R^2}{(c-1)}}{\dfrac{(1-R^2)}{(N-c)}} \qquad\qquad 5.29$$

with degrees of freedom, as in analysis of variance,

$$\text{df(numerator)} = c - 1$$
$$\text{df(denominator)} = N - c$$

where N is the number of observations and c is the number of coefficients in the regression equation, including the constant of regression. Compared with a critical value of F (at the .05 significance level) of 4.71 (found in the table of the F-distribution under df(numerator) $= 2$ and df(denominator) $= 197$), the observed value of F is

$$\hat{F} = \frac{.95/2}{.05/197} = \frac{.45}{.00025} = 1800$$

which is significant by anyone's standards.

This is all very fine. But now let us recall those two assumptions we alluded to earlier.

5.6.2 Coping with Estimation Bias

On showing these results to the policymakers, our analyst is unexpectedly confronted with some searching questions. The first one is stated as follows:

"Increased rainfall means more abundant crops, and that means increased income. It seems to me that the two independent variables Δy and ΔA are related. Wouldn't that ruin the estimates of the regression coefficients?"

What is being charged here is that, instead of the causal structure shown in Figure 5.10 or the rather simple recursive structure[10] of Figure 5.4b, we are really analyzing a more complex recursive system in which one of the variables that affects a dependent variable is itself partly determined by one

---

[10] It is recursive because none of the arrows emanating from any given variable loops back to affect one of the variables on which the given variable is itself dependent.

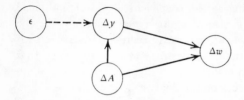

FIGURE 5.11   A more complex recursive structure.

of the other independent variables. If it were entirely determined by one of them (for example, if r^2 between Δy and ΔA were equal to 1.0), the issue would be much more difficult to resolve than is the approach we describe here. Thus we show in Figure 5.11 the variable Δy as being partly determined by the independent variable ΔA, and as being partly determined by other variables such as a nonzero stochastic term ϵ.

To understand the nature of the estimation problem produced by this kind of causal structure, we consider first the simple least-squares regression of equation 5.27. If the true causal structure is as shown in Figure 5.11, the simple regression equation 5.27 violates the assumption that the error term be uncorrelated with the independent variable (in our discussion of this assumption in Figure 5.8f, we showed $S_{ux} = 0$). Since the variable ΔA is contained in the residual (u) and is allegedly correlated with Δy, we see that this assumption is violated. What happens in consequence?

If, in fact, Δy increases as the excluded variable ΔA increases while Δw decreases as ΔA increases, then, when we relate Δy to Δw, we observe Δw increasing less than it would have, if the excluded variable somehow had been held constant. This is to say that the simple regression coefficient b calculated in equation 5.27 is an *underestimate* of the true coefficient.[11] This source of estimation error is known as specification bias, because it results from the analyst's failure to specify properly the variables and causal structure that comprise the system he is modeling. We show this effect graphically in Figure 5.12.

In Figure 5.12a, we show that the simple linear regression of Δw on Δy yields the regression line MM' with the slope b. If we want to take into account the variable ΔA, which is correlated, negatively, with only the dependent variable Δw, we can label the observations according to the value of ΔA. For example, points shown as A_1 have a lower value of ΔA than do points labeled A_2. If we hold the value of ΔA constant, say at A_1, and run the regression between Δw and Δy, the resulting regression line (the dashed line connecting all A_1 points) has the same slope b as the original regression line.

[11] If Δw were positively rather than negatively associated to ΔA, then the simple regression coefficient b would be an overestimate of the true coefficient.

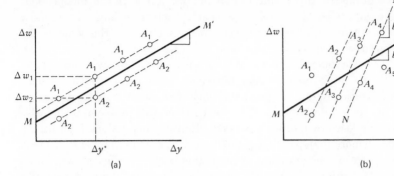

FIGURE 5.12 How correlation among independent variables causes estimation bias.

This is because the excluded variable ΔA is uncorrelated with the independent variable Δy, so that the estimated coefficient b remains unaffected even when the excluded variable ΔA is held constant. This is not true, however, in Figure 5.12b.

In this case, because ΔA is correlated with both Δw and Δy, when we mistakenly assumed $S_{u\Delta y} = 0$ we incorrectly attributed ΔA's affect on the dependent variable to Δy. Consequently, we obtained the regression line MM' with slope b. However, when we hold the values of ΔA constant (say at $\Delta A = A_4$), which is roughly what we do in multiple regression, we obtain the regression line NN' with a partial regression coefficient of $b_1 > b$.

Specification bias can usually be overcome by incorporating the heretofore excluded variable in a multiple regression. Then (the two exceptions are indicated below), the recalculated *partial regression* coefficient (shown as b_1 in equation 5.28 and in Figure 5.12b) will be adjusted upward,[12] thereby removing the specification bias.[13]

---

[12] Downward, in the case that Δw is positively rather than negatively correlated with ΔA.

[13] This result can be seen from the equation for the partial regression coefficient b_1, which can be written in terms of the simple regression coefficients between Δw and Δy, between Δw and ΔA, and between ΔA and Δy, denoted as b_{wy}, b_{wA}, and b_{Ay}, respectively:

$$b_1 = \frac{b_{wy} - b_{wA}b_{Ay}}{1 - r^2_{Ay}}$$

For this derivation, see A. A. Walters, *An Introduction to Econometrics* (London: MacMillan, 1968), p. 125. Since we have required Δy to be only partially dependent on ΔA, r^2_{Ay} is considerably less than one, so that the denominator is positive. Furthermore, since we have assumed $b_{wy} > 0$, but $b_{wA} < 0$, and $b_{Ay} > 0$, the term $b_{wA}b_{Ay} < 0$. In sum, our calculation will yield $b_1 > b_{wy}$. Similarly, if $r_{Ay} = 0$, then also $b_{Ay} = 0$ so that $b_1 = b_{wy}$, and specification bias is nonexistent.

The exceptions to this result are as follows. First, if the independent variables turn out to be unrelated so that specification bias was actually nonexistent, then the partial regression coefficient will be the same as the simple regression coefficient. This was the case shown in Figure 5.12a. Second if the two independent variables are perfectly correlated (e.g., the r^2 between them equals one) or very nearly so, then the partial coefficient could mathematically take on just about any value because mathematically, its value becomes indeterminate.[14] It was to avoid this problem, technically referred to as "severe multicollinearity," that we insisted in Figure 5.11 that Δy be no more than partly dependent on ΔA. Fortunately for diagnostic purposes, however, the standard error of this partial coefficient will be so high that its t-value will become unstable and very likely statistically insignificant.[15]

Now let us return to the question put to our analyst. If the two independent variables are correlated but not too much (if $r^2_{Ay} \geq .90$, it is probably too much),[16] then including them both in the same multiple regression will provide unbiased estimates of their regression coefficient that are superior to the estimate provided by simple regression which suffers from specification bias. If, however, we have a case of severe multicollinearity (r^2_{Ay} is too high), then the multiple regression provides inferior if not meaningless estimates of these regression coefficients.

Applying these points to our multiple regression equation 5.29, the inclusion of ΔA had no effect on the estimated value b_1 relative to that provided by the simple regression (thus, $b_1 = b = 5$). However, it did *reduce* its

---

[14] If $r^2_{Ay} = 1$ or very nearly so, then the denominator of the equation in the preceding footnote is $1 - r^2 = 0$ or nearly so, while $b_1 = \infty$ or nearly so and is extremely sensitive to slight sampling error in r^2_{Ay}.

[15] That this should occur can be seen from the equation for the standard error of b_1, which can be written

$$S_{b\,1} = \sqrt{\frac{S_u^{\,2}}{\Sigma\,\Delta y_j^{\,2}(1 - r^2_{Ay})}} \qquad \text{or, in words}$$

$$S_{b\,1} = \sqrt{\frac{\text{variance of }\Delta w\text{ unexplained by the multiple regression}}{\substack{\text{unexplained sum of squares of the independent variable}\\ \Delta y \text{ in the simple regression of }\Delta y\text{ on }\Delta A}}}$$

(derivations again from A. A. Walters, ibid, p. 153). By adding the excluded variable ΔA, since it is perfectly correlated with Δy, we add no new information to the regression, so that the unexplained variance of Δw (in the numerator of this expression) remains unchanged. But the denominator collapses to zero, causing $S_{b\,1} \to \infty$, so that if $S_{b\,1}$ rises faster than b_1, $t \to 0$.

[16] Actually, there is no clear cutoff point on how high an r^2 is too high.

standard error (from 1.25 to 1.0) so that its t-value increased and became even more significant.[17]

Evidently, the allegation that the two independent variables were correlated and that Figure 5.11 rather than Figure 5.10 correctly depicts the system being analyzed was incorrect. Thus specification bias was not present in the simple regression, and either equations 5.27 or 5.29 could be used for estimating the effect of Δy on Δw, with equation 5.29 preferred simply because it yields a higher R^2.[18]

As a final issue for this chapter, we consider the second source of bias. Our analyst's critic may have been placated concerning the issue of specification bias, but he is not yet ready to give up. He muses:

"Just last week I was over at the Agency for Economic Development, and they had a planning analyst who was explaining a regression he had just run. It showed how increases in water supply investments attract industry to those same depressed rural areas and thereby increase the income of these areas. The regression looked like this

$$\Delta y = a' + b' \, \Delta w \qquad\qquad 5.30$$

How do I know that that regression equation 5.29 that you're showing isn't really estimating Δw's developmental effect on Δy, rather than Δy's demand effect on Δw?''

What the critic is now postulating is that perhaps the causal structure being analyzed is neither that shown in Figure 5.10 nor in Figure 5.11, but is a simultaneous system such as we show in Figure 5.13.

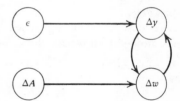

FIGURE 5.13 A simultaneous causal structure.

---

[17] That $b_1 = b$ indicates that $r_{Ay}^2 = 0$. Since $S_u{}^2$ in the numerator of the expression for $S_{b,1}$ (see footnote 15) decreased and the denominator remained the same, $S_{b,1}$ necessarily decreases.

[18] Readers may be interested in the related concept of "spurious correlation" in which the original independent variable (Δy in the present model) turns out to be unrelated to the dependent variable (Δw) even though $r_{wy} \neq 0$, but both are dependent on a third (excluded) variable (ΔA) which, on inclusion in multiple regression, causes the partial regression coefficient b_1 (relating Δw to Δy) to fall to zero. See Hubert Blalock, *Social Statistics*, second edition, (New York: McGraw-Hill, 1972), pp. 442–450, and Hubert Blalock, Jr., and Ann Blalock (eds.), *Methodology in Social Research* (New York: McGraw-Hill, 1968), especially Chapters 5 and 6.

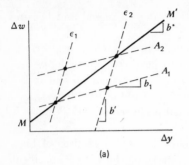 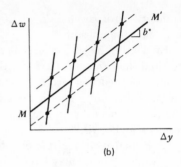

(a)   (b)

FIGURE 5.14   Identification bias in least-squares estimates.

Difficulties will indeed arise in using multiple regression analysis for estimating the impact of one variable on another when both are, in fact, simultaneously determined. The resulting estimate (b_1 in this case) will most likely be an averaging of the true regression coefficient connecting the two variables in each of the two equations (b_1 from equation 5.28 and b' from equation 5.30).[19] This effect is shown in Figure 5.14a where the lines marked A_1 and A_2 indicate the demand effect of equation 5.28 for different values of ΔA with a properly estimated slope of b_1, while the lines marked ϵ_1 and ϵ_2 indicate the developmental effect of equation 5.30 for different values of the stochastic term ϵ, the slope of these lines being $b' > b_1$. However, if we use multiple regression to estimate either of these coefficients, the result will be the regression line MM' with slope b^*, where $b_1 < b^* < b'$. In summary, we have failed to identify either the water demand or the developmental functions, and for this reason the resulting estimation error is called *identification bias*.

In most cases more advanced "simultaneous equations estimating methods" are needed to estimate these relations.[20] Nevertheless, is it ever possible to

[19] In general form, equation 5.28 with residual is

$$\Delta w_j = a + b_1 \Delta y_j + b_2 \Delta A_j + u_j$$

while equation 5.30 may be written in terms of b' w_j

$$b' \Delta w_j = \Delta y_j - a' - u'_j$$

Adding these two equations together and dividing by $(1 - b')$ gives

$$\Delta w_j = \frac{a - a'}{1 - b'} + \frac{1 + b_1}{1 - b'} \Delta y_j + \frac{b_2}{1 - b'} \Delta A_j + \frac{1}{1 - b'} (u_j - u'_j)$$

It is the coefficients to this equation and not the first equation that will be estimated by multiple regression when attempting to estimate equation 5.28. Instead of the coefficient b_1, the regression estimates the value of $(1 + b_1)/(1 - b')$.

[20] Refer to Wonnacott and Wonnacott, *Econometrics*, Chapters 7 to 9; and A. A. Walters, Chapters 7 and 8.

use least-squares regression when simultaneous causal structures are being analyzed? Under certain conditions, it is. For example, we show in Figure 5.14b a situation in which the steeper of the two equations is highly unstable because of the considerable variation in exogenous factors, while the flatter of the two equations is quite stable because of only slight variation in its exogenous variables. The result in this case is that the data will rather neatly trace out (identify) the stable equation. In fact, as shown in Figure 5.14b, the least-squares regression line MM' of slope b^* will be an unbiased estimate of the slope of the identified equation.

In our example, since it is the water demand equation 5.28 that has an exogenous variable (ΔA) known to vary quite a bit while the developmental equation has no additional variables, under ordinary circumstances in which both equations have reasonably acceptable total R^2's, we would suppose that it is the developmental equation and not the water demand equation that will be identified.

Our analyst, not yet ready to give up, asserts that there is one condition that will reverse this situation. He notes that if the simple r^2 between Δy and Δw is small enough to be statistically insignificant, then the simple regression coefficient b' in equation 5.30 will also be statistically insignificant. For example, if the observations were scattered as in Figure 5.14a, the resulting simple r^2 between Δw and Δy might well be small enough to accept the hypothesis that the true $r^2 = 0$. In this case, b' will also equal zero. Now, although this result will also hold true for the simple b of the water demand equation 5.27, if we have the situation described in Figure 5.11, the non-significance of b might be due to specification error. On the inclusion of ΔA, an unbiased, positive and significant value of b_1 will then be obtained via multiple regression, and it will be the water demand equation that will be identified.[21]

Just then, another person enters, introduces himself as the planning analyst from the Agency for Economic Development, and announces that he has just substantially improved his developmental equation by noting that in these rural regions, agricultural output, and thereby total income Δy, greatly improve when rainfall (ΔA) increases! His new multiple regression is plotted in Figure 5.15, which somehow looks like Figure 5.14b turned on its side. And, with the satisfaction that comes from discovery, he announces that his analysis has also identified the minimum water investment threshold as Δw^*, below which growth will not occur.

What will our water demand analyst say now? And what advice are we to give? Well, for one thing, we never said that statistics was not supposed

---

[21] Note in the last equation of footnote 19 that if $b' = 0$, the expression $-(a' + u'_j) = -\Delta y_j$ so that this equation reduces identically to equation 5.28.

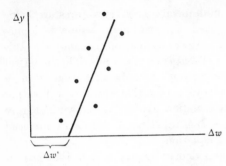

FIGURE 5.15   Who has identified what?

to be a difficult if not sometimes vexing activity to become enmeshed in. For another, we might note that we have just introduced the subject of econometrics, and that there are both courses and a multitude of books[22] that can help those who want to become involved in the business of unscrambling eggs.

PROBLEMS

1. It is believed that poverty and illiteracy are closely related. Data for 16 counties in the state of North Carolina are collected from the 1960 Census of Population, using "percentage of families earning under $3000 per year" as the measure of poverty, and "percentage of persons aged 25 years or older who have had less than 5 years of schooling" as the measure of illiteracy. The data are as follows:

POVERTY	ILLITERACY	POVERTY	ILLITERACY
21	14	59	20
38	15	55	24
51	16	30	11
54	22	29	18
61	18	24	16
58	18	31	18
59	21	53	10
64	23	35	11

[22] Three books we recommend are Ronald J. Wonnacott and Thomas H. Wonnacott, *Econometrics;* A. A. Walters, *An Introduction to Econometrics;* and Lawrence R. Klein, *An Introduction to Econometrics* (Englewood Cliffs, N.J.: Prentice-Hall, 1962).

(a) Determine whether these counties provide statistically significant evidence (at the 5% significance level) that poverty and illiteracy are, indeed, related (at least, in North Carolina). Use any test you like, but take into account that poverty is believed not to be normally distributed.

(b) Using this evidence, by how much should the State Education Agency reduce illiteracy if it wants to be 95% certain that county poverty rates will be reduced to under 50% (careful, don't be hasty).

2. An Economic Development Agency in North Carolina believes that county income levels are greatly affected by the type of industry located there. Using the following data for eight counties, it wants to know what kind of industry to attract. In column 1 is shown "median family income," in column 2 is shown "percentage employed in manufacturing," and in column 3 is shown "percentage employed in white collar occupations."

FAMILY INCOME (IN THOUSAND $'S) 1	% EMPLOYED IN MANUFACTURING 2	% EMPLOYED IN WHITE COLLAR 3
5.4	51	31
3.8	52	18
2.9	34	21
2.8	31	21
2.3	31	19
2.6	23	26
2.4	17	28
2.1	19	21

Determine which kind of industry is most strongly related with family income (use any measure you like). Although only two industries are shown, you can devise a third "all other industry" by adding columns 2 and 3 together and subtracting from 100%. To what industry does this "all other" category roughly correspond? Including this "all other" category in your calculations, what course of action would you single out for the Economic Development Agency as its "best bet" for increasing family incomes? (*Note:* it is believed that family income is not normally distributed. Include significance tests in your results.)

3. Using the data from Table 5.6, set the values of $x_1 = 1$, $x_2 = 2$, and $x_3 = 3$:

(a) Calculate the linear regression coefficient b and test its significance (at 5% significance level), compare it with $E(\bar{y} \mid x)$, and interpret it.

(b) Calculate the coefficient of determination r^2, compare it with the correlation ratio E^2, and interpret it.

4. Using the data of Table 5.8 in this chapter, calculate E^2, compare it with r^2, and interpret it.

5. (Optional.) Suppose a linear regression coefficient b were calculated for the data shown in the first of these problems above:

$$\text{Poverty} = a + b \text{ (Illiteracy)}$$

Give reasons why b may not be an unbiased estimate of the true coefficient. In your explanation, indicate specifically what other variables you think should enter into the analysis, the causal structure of the system, and how you would go about eliminating the estimation bias in b.

BIBLIOGRAPHY

Blalock, Hubert M., Jr., and Ann Blalock (eds). *Methodology in Social Research*. New York: McGraw-Hill, 1968.

Blalock, Hubert M., Jr. *Social Statistics*, second edition, New York: McGraw-Hill, 1972.

Klein, Lawrence. *An Introduction to Econometrics*. Englewood Cliffs, N.J.: Prentice-Hall, 1962.

Walters, A. A. *An Introduction to Econometrics*. London: Macmillan, 1968.

Weatherburn, C. E. *A First Course in Mathematical Statistics*, second edition. Cambridge, Eng.: Cambridge University Press, 1962.

Wonnacott, R. J., and T. H. Wonnacott. *Introductory Statistics*. New York: Wiley, 1969.

Wonnacott, T. H., and R. J. Wonnacott. *Econometrics*. New York: Wiley, 1970.

Yamane, Taro. *Statistics: An Introductory Analysis*, second edition. New York: Harper and Row, 1967.

CHAPTER 6

Evaluating and Selecting Programs

6.1 INTRODUCTION

6.1.1 Why Evaluate?

A plan may be viewed as a statement of programs recommended as best for achieving a certain set of goals, with the time period over which these goals are to be achieved and the resources required to achieve them properly indicated. In this chapter, we describe methods that can be used for deciding to recommend a given program for inclusion in the plan—or to recommend against its inclusion.

The methods are those of program evaluation (also of "policy analysis"), and their application is toward the program (or policy) selection decision. However, the methods to be described are all quantitative. Their use for evaluating a given program depends on the prior estimation, via tools such as are described in most of the chapters of this book, of the program's expected causal impacts on goals, and on costs over time. But the practical problem exists that the estimation of these requisite "impact coefficients" can, in many cases, be a most difficult and time-consuming activity, and it certainly has not yet been accomplished for the majority of programs that might be evaluated. In the meantime, problems abound that must be attacked immediately—this year, perhaps even next month—and program plans must be made accordingly. Thus, for most program plans to be made in the near future, the quantitative methods described in this chapter can be applied only selectively and with discretion.

For many planners who have come to value the information that quantitative analysis can provide, we are sure this warning comes as a disappointment (we recall how eager planners were, in the early 1960s, to apply some of the most complex quantitative theories to behavioral processes about which practically nothing had been yet systematically observed). But of greater importance to plan making is the "do-ability" of the work-plan used for making the plan. If the work-plan is loaded with methods that cannot possibly be carried through within the planning period, the information provided by these methods will not be useful because of the incompleteness or because of the estimation errors in the results. In consequence, the program plan suffers, and the erroneous impression is created that these methods are no good. How then, should program evaluation methods be used?

Aaron Wildavsky has persuasively argued that program evaluation activities are, in fact, of great importance for planning, and that considerable research effort should be concentrated on those few key policy issues that a decision maker must confront. As the results of these evaluations become available,[1] they can be incorporated into program selection decisions, but the planner should be aware that six months to two years or more may be required to yield such results. Thus quantitative program evaluation methods should be applied on a selective basis and, for the foreseeable future, certainly not on an across-the-board basis that tries to evaluate all the program alternatives of a plan.

But even for the rest of the programs that might be included in a plan, the principles that underlie quantitative program evaluation can and should be applied, and as explicitly as is reasonable. And what are these evaluation principles? In essence, they are (1) that the various impacts of a program over time be identified, (2) that the seriousness of these impacts be judged (in terms of how "good" or "bad" they are), and (3) that the resource needs (costs) over time of the program be considered in light of the availability of such resources.

In practice, these three evaluation principles are usually included in the program selection decision whether or not the planner has taken them explicitly into account (and, more often than not, he has not). What happens, too many times, resembles the following. First, the planner, mindful of how well a certain program reflects certain goals, decides to include the program in his plan (for example, the program might involve the construction of an industrial park on land now occupied by residents of badly deteriorating housing, or it might involve the construction of an air polluting highway through such a neighborhood.) Next, residents of the targeted neighborhood, on learning of the plan, use certain, by now, familiar audiovisual aids to

[1] Aaron Wildavsky, "Rescuing Policy Analysis from PPBS," *Public Expenditures and Policy Analysis*, Robert Haveman and Julius Margolis (eds.) (Chicago: Markham Publishing, 1970), pp. 461–481.

show how the program interferes with several additional goals formerly not of much concern to the planner. Finally, when the program is included as part of a plan presented to a local budgeting agency, it is so severely cut back on the grounds of excessive cost requirements that the original objectives of the "revised" program are lost.

Even when the goals that are taken into account in the program selection decision are broad and equitable, how many imaginative and even "visionary" plans have become "dust-collectors" or, in being revised so as to compromise with certain neglected realities, have severely disillusioned those who were told of the great benefits that they could expect? And is the budgeting agency, that no doubt is cast as the heartless culprit, the source of the problem? In numerous cases it is, but often, where a genuine desire exists to allocate the available budget on an equitable and goal-oriented basis, the budget agency has a responsibility to keep overall costs within the bounds of available budgetary resources. In such instances, the source of the problem lies with the planner, who is guilty of producing an infeasible plan. And this, in turn, is due to the not uncommon practice of basing program selection decisions on evaluations that include only direct program contributions to goals and that sidestep the explicit consideration of program costs. True, a plan that takes the "economic problem" into account may have quite a different program mix than the one that is created free of such constraints. Very likely, it will not attract the imagination in quite the same way. But this should not be surprising: expensive things that are free are nearly always more appealing to the imagination.

Rather than intentionally walking into a program selection process in which a plan can expectedly be cut to ribbons either by negatively affected outside groups or by the budgeting process, the more thoughtful approach and the one requiring even more creativity is an approach that creates and selects programs that are evaluated to contribute maximally to goal attainment within the various constraints of reality.[2]

6.1.2 OFFICIAL SUPPORT: BENEFIT COST ANALYSIS AND PPB

During the last four decades, governments have been officially seeking the use of systematic and quantitative methods of program evaluation in the project-selection process. Academically oriented analysts, of course, have

---

[2] In this sense, John Friedmann's feeling that innovation and allocation in the planning process are mutually exclusive and ought to be dichotomized is unfortunate. See John Friedmann, "Planning as Innovation: The Chilean Case," *Journal of the American Institute of Planners, 32* (July 1966), 194–204.

been devising and advocating the use of these methods for a much longer period.[3]

Congress made its official entry into program evaluation activity via the Flood Control Act of 1936,[4] which established the requirement that water-resource development projects (for flood control, navigation, hydropower, etc.) could not be selected unless evaluation showed that a project's expected "benefits to whomsoever they may accrue (be) in excess of the estimated costs." From this, the technique known as benefit-cost analysis[5] has been applied in thousands of program evaluations, including not only water, resource programs[6] but also human resource (training and education)-urban renewal, transportation, and health programs.[7]

The measure that is typically calculated for project evaluation is the benefit-cost ratio B/C, where B measures the anticipated benefits to be generated over time by a given program, and C measures its costs over time. A program is selected for inclusion in a plan if benefits exceed costs, which is to say if $B/C > 1$. In a typical application, the measure is stated in money terms and indicates the contribution of a given program toward the sole goal of economic efficiency, leaving aside questions of income distribution goals and the distribution of certain nonmarket goods such as parks, roads, and welfare services. Margolis, for instance, notes that the benefit measure used by the United States Bureau of Reclamation for evaluating water-resource

[3] One of the earliest and still one of the more sophisticated methods was devised in 1844 by a French bridge and highway inspector, Jules Depuit, "De la Mesure de l'Utilite des Travaux Publics," reprinted in its English translation as "On the Measurement of the Utility of Public Works," *Readings in Welfare Economics* (ed.), K. Arrow, and T. Scitovsky (Homewood, Illinois: Richard D. Irwin, Inc., 1969), 225–283. Work on the subject has continued to be of particular concern to economists and to operations researchers. A good introduction to the field of "public expenditure economics" is Robert Haveman, *The Economics of the Public Sector* (New York: Wiley, 1970). The operations research approach is nicely presented by Fred Hanssmann, *Operations Research Techniques for Capital Investment* (New York: Wiley, 1968).

[4] 49 Stat. 1570.

[5] See especially A. R. Prest, and R. Turvey, "Cost-Benefit Analysis: a Survey," *Economic Journal* (1965), 683–735; also Haveman, Chapter 8.

[6] Otto Eckstein, *Water Resource Development* (Cambridge, Mass: Harvard University Press, 1958); John V. Krutilla and Otto Eckstein, *Multiple Purpose River Development* (Baltimore, Md.: Resources for the Future, Johns Hopkins Press, 1958); and Allen V. Kneese, and Blair Bower, *Managing Water Quality: Economics, Technology, Institutions* (Baltimore, Md.: Resources for the Future, Johns Hopkins Press, 1968).

[7] In the order indicated, see the benefit-cost studies by Weisbrod, Rothenberg, Mohring, and Klarman in Robert Dorfman (ed.), *Measuring Benefits of Government Investments* (Washington, D.C.: Brookings Institution, 1965). See also the numerous summaries of benefit-cost studies in Prest and Turvey and in Werner Hirsch, *The Economics of State and Local Government* (New York: McGraw-Hill, 1970), pp. 236–247.

projects is "the difference in national income with and without the project'[8].

This definition of program benefits is, of course, much too limited for use in evaluating the kinds of programs usually implemented at the urban level where public housing, health, education, park, and transportation programs are implemented precisely because they contribute to income redistribution goals, or because they are not normally produced via market processes. This is not to say that benefit-cost analysis cannot be broadened to reflect these questions: it can and has been applied to the evaluation of these kinds of programs, as we have already indicated. But in broadening the measure, benefit-cost analysis becomes a considerably more complicated affair, and requires the explicit treatment of several issues such as program externalities, the incidence of program costs, and multiple goals.[9] We therefore begin our discussion of program evaluation methods with the simplest evaluation approach, and progress by introducing the various complications one at a time, concluding the chapter with an evaluation approach that captures most of the issues of a thoroughgoing benefit-cost analysis.

But before we begin this effort, there is another development in official government program evaluation and selection methods that we should discuss, and that is PPB—the Planning, Programming, and Budgeting system that has captured the imagination of almost every public administrator in federal, state, and local government. The "capture" occurred rather rapidly following the signing of an executive order in August 1965 by President Lyndon B. Johnson which instructed all executive agencies of the federal government to implement the PPB system. Its popularity among municipal governments was even more enhanced in 1966 when the Model Cities program[10] required participating cities to incorporate program evaluation in their grant-administration process.

What PPB tries to do is to require governmental agencies to do just what we have been suggesting: incorporate program costs and budget constraints directly into the program evaluation and selection process. The usual budgeting practice is to split annual agency-wide or municipality-wide costs into a capital and an expense budget, showing cost totals, on a "line item" or input basis (for example, total salaries and wages, equipment purchases, repairs and maintenance, etc). In contrast, PPB requires annual costs to be stated in terms of the programs that have been selected for inclusion in the budget. Furthermore, these costs must be projected into the near future so that future cost implications of current programs can be known. Once the

---

[8] Julius Margolis, "Secondary Benefits, External Economies, and the Justification of Public Investment," *Review of Economics and Statistics* (1957), 284–291; reprinted in Arrow and Scitovsky.

[9] See Haveman, pp. 157–159.

[10] Demonstration Cities and Metropolitan Development Act of 1966, 80 Stat. 1255.

budget is in program terms, the total costs of a given program can then be disaggregated by type of input. PPB also requires that programs be grouped into categories (referred to as the "program structure") that reflect a certain goal to which the included programs are supposed to contribute. That way, the program costs within each category can be totaled to indicate the amount of funds that the agency or municipality has committed toward the achievement of a given goal. To set up these categories, however, the budgeting agency must first be able to articulate the goals that it wants to attain and that the various programs have in common; and this is often a novel activity in many government agencies.

A second requirement of the PPB system is that explicit measures of annual program outputs be quantified for each and every program. For example, an output measure for an addict rehabilitation program might be "number of addicts successfully rehabilitated"; an output measure for a job training program might be "number of trainees effectively trained."

The task of deciding what these output measures are, on a program-by-program basis, and of actually quantifying them, is also a new and frequently difficult one for agency staff who are accustomed to measuring program activity levels by inputs used rather than by outputs produced. For example, the activity of a health program would traditionally be measured by "number of hospital beds" or "number of doctors or nurses" rather than by "number of persons made healthy." And there may occur considerable resistance in getting the agency official to come up with the new program output measures. After all, it is not that difficult to spend budgeted money and, hence, his performance, when measured in terms of "numbers of new hospital beds installed" or "new teachers hired," is much easier to defend than performance measures such as "number of low income persons made healthy" or "low income persons successfully trained."

Once these program output measures are regularly collected and neatly listed in the agency's new "management information system," the agency can produce periodic reports available to managers and officials for the purpose of monitoring ongoing program operations. This provides the managerial function with "information feedback" (which, in practice, often means massive reams of computer printout) so that timely control is, in theory at least, possible. Furthermore, regular collection of program output data provides the basic measures required for program evaluation. The measure E/C, the "effectiveness-cost ratio" that shows actual program output relative to program cost is readily calculated and, if properly stated, can be used for program evaluation.[11]

[11] An excellent introduction to PPB at the local level is given by Selma J. Mushkin, "PPB for the Cities: Problems and the Next Steps," *Financing the Metropolis*, Vol. 4,

As we have indicated, efforts to implement this highly reasonable Planning, Programming, and Budgeting system have already been undertaken by numerous state and local governments. However, the payoff of this activity is not always evident. Although the system should help the program evaluation and selection process by requiring agencies to clarify goals and to backup their program selection decisions with comparative information on program-cost and effectiveness measures, in many instances the cost of generating this information is simply too great, and in others the elaborate data generation activity generates more confusion and alienation than useful information.

What are the main problems? We describe three of the more obvious ones.

First, there are resource scarcities due to the difficulty of obtaining the necessary program effectiveness measures. (Even the hospital that directly treats a target population does not keep records on the number of patients it has successfully made healthy, so how is the official responsible for the city-wide health program supposed to measure program output?)

Second, there are a number of conceptual problems associated with the program analysis (evaluational) side of the system. We mention first that many programs may contribute directly to more than one goal and certainly will indirectly contribute to many goals. The use of program categories in which a given program is shown as contributing just to the goal of the category in which it is listed seems arbitrary and limiting (an employment program, for example, may contribute to a dependency-reduction goal and also to housing, health, and education goals that families can purchase directly with increased family income). Further, if the program's entire costs are attributed to the single goal, the resulting evaluation measure will represent the program as inefficient. On the other hand, if program costs are apportioned to each of the various goals it produces, the conceptual error arises that if the program effectively contributes to one goal but ineffectively to another, one might be led to the conclusion that the ineffective activity should be cut back. But since a program producing toward multiple goals (joint production) may be yielding them in unchangeable proportions, there is no way to cut back on one impact and to increase the other.[12] Instead of

Urban Affairs Annual Review, John P. Crecine (ed.) (Beverly Hills, Cal.: Sage Publications, 1970). Also in the same volume, see Donald Borut, "Implementing PPBS: A Practitioner's Viewpoint," and the dissenting view of Arnold Meltsner and Aaron Wildavsky, "Leave City Budgeting Alone!: A Survey, Case Study, and Recommendations for Reform." Also recommended is Haveman and Margolis, Chapters 15 to 25.

[12] Refer to the treatment of joint impacts by Russell Ackoff, "Toward Quantitative Evaluation of Urban Services," *Public Expenditure Decisions in the Urban Community* (Washington, D.C.: Resources for the Future, Johns Hopkins Press, 1963).

devising a cost-effectiveness ratio for each goal, the multiple goal impacts should be weighted and summed, and then should be related to total program costs. Another conceptual problem is that to be properly used for program evaluation, the effectiveness measure should reflect the change in the status of a given target group (say, the health of the low income elderly) that resulted from the program itself and not from changes in external conditions. To generate this "causal" effectiveness estimate will require, in a great many instances, the kind of intensive and selective analytic effort that, as is indicated previously (following Wildavsky's thinking), should characterize proper program evaluation work. It should be noted, however, that good program evaluation usually incorporates the refinements we have pointed out, but in so doing, it moves up to the more complex version of benefit-cost analysis that we encounter, by stages, in this chapter.

A third type of problem associated with PPB is the lack of support for its implementation that is often encountered among agency officials or staff. Frequently, this is merely a reflection of defensive behavior by those who want to avoid having their work evaluated. But in other cases it reflects a sincere impatience with attempts to impose what may be (1) an inflexible and often arbitrarily defined format for evaluating complex activities, and (2) a costly and seemingly make-work data collection and computerization effort that yields vast quantities of useless computer printout, all of which could lead right back to the very self-defending bureaucratic inflexibilities that have given rise to demands for reforming agency decision processes.

For these reasons, although the methods that we describe in this chapter can be used in conjunction with a PPB system, their presentation should not be viewed as a blanket recommendation of the system. The implementation of program evaluation methods either in formal quantitative analysis, or in principle to guide a more qualitative analysis, certainly does not require the prior adoption of PPB. But when the situation is appropriate for PPB then, of course, it is recommended as a means for formally incorporating program evaluation procedures into the program selection decision.

In what follows, we begin by showing how alternative programs may be evaluated in light of a budget constraint so that the program leading to the most effective goal attainment is selected. The simplifying condition is temporarily maintained that programs have only short-term cost and effectiveness-cost ratios. We show how the existence of project indivisibilities can introduce error in program-selection decisions based on such ratios. We then successively introduce a number of complications to the analysis, including project complementarities, differential incidence of program impacts among target populations, externalities and multigoal programs, and multiple goals treated as program constraints. We then introduce programs that have long-term cost and effectiveness impacts. After we show how discounting is used to weight impacts over time, we then describe program evaluation under conditions that are quite the same as benefit-cost analysis.

6.2 COST EFFECTIVENESS ANALYSIS FOR SHORT-TERM PROGRAMS

6.2.1 Maximizing Program Effectiveness Subject to a Fixed Budget

Consider the following example. It is discovered that a health hazard to children exists in a certain community that has been responsible for several recent hospital admissions due to lead poisoning. The goal is to once and for all eliminate illness due to this hazard and several programs are proposed for this purpose. Specifically, the hazard is in the form of a lead-based paint used many years ago to paint local housing. The paint is now peeling from the walls and is being ingested by youngsters, thus causing the lead poisoning. The alternative programs with potential for achieving the goal are as follows:

Program A   Repaint local housing with nonlead-based paint.
Program B   Educate children not to eat paint.

Suppose that it is determined that the potential effectiveness of program A can be estimated via techniques like those of Chapter 4. Two samples of 10 buildings each are obtained, the first consisting of buildings with lead-based paint and the second consisting of buildings with nonlead based paint. The number of cases of lead poisoning during the past year among children living in the housing of each sample is obtained from local hospital records, and the sample mean number of cases is calculated. It is found that the "with lead" sample mean is 4.0 per building while the "without lead" sample mean is one per building, a difference of 3.0, which is found to be significant at the .99 confidence level.

From this analysis, we state as our measure of the potential effectiveness of program A that to paint the lead-based painted buildings will reduce the number of cases of lead poisoning by three for each such building that is painted. Furthermore, we estimate that it will cost $1000 to paint each building.

We now evaluate program B. First, it is necessary to determine the average number of children living in each building with lead-based paint so as to calculate the cost and effectiveness of educating the children of each building. From studies that have been made in the past, we learn that by using a one-week program, teachers can effectively educate the children that they teach to be aware of and to avoid dangerous situations with a probability of 25%. This would reduce the number of lead poisoning cases by one. However, it will cost $200 to teach the children of each building.

TABLE 6.1
Cost-Effectiveness Analysis

Program	Effectiveness per unit	Cost per Unit	Maximum No. Units within Budget	Program Effectiveness
A	3	$1000	100	300
B	1	$ 200	500	500

Clearly, if we are able to base our decision on program effectiveness alone, since program A is three times as effective as program B, it is the program of choice. But suppose there are 500 buildings in the community that have lead-based paint, and our program budget is no more than $100,000. Now, recalling that it costs $1000 to paint each building, we see that program A can be applied to no more than 100 buildings, and at an effectiveness rate of three cases per building, the overall effectiveness of program A will be a reduction in lead poisoning cases by 300. In contrast, at $200 per building for program B, we can treat all 500 buildings in the community, and at an effectiveness rate of one per building, the overall effectiveness of program B is 500 fewer lead poisoning cases. With costs and budgets taken into account, together with measures of effectiveness, we now see that program B is the program of choice. This analysis is summarized in Table 6.1, and also in equations 6.1a, 6.1b, and 6.1c.

Maximize

$$E = 3x_A + x_B \qquad\qquad 6.1a$$

subject to

$$\$1000x_A + \$200x_B \leq \$100,000 \qquad\qquad 6.1b$$

and

$$x_A, \quad x_B \geq 0 \qquad\qquad 6.1c$$

Equation 6.1a is called the objective function, and states that we wish to maximize a quantity E, a measure of program effectiveness that represents the reduction in the number of lead poisoning cases resulting from our selection and implementation of a program. The maximum level of effectiveness (E) depends on the number of units of program A to be selected (x_A) multiplied by the effectiveness rate per unit of program A, plus the number of units of program B selected (x_B) multiplied by the effectiveness rate per unit of Program B.

Equation 6.1b is the constraint inequality. It states that the number of units of program A (x_A) times its cost per unit ($1000) plus the number of units of program B times its cost per unit ($200) must not exceed the total budget available for the program ($100,000).

Finally, equation 6.1c simply is intended to assure that whatever the values of the two program levels (x_A and x_B) that may be mathematically derived, they must not be negative, or said another way, they must be greater than or equal to zero.

The problem in this analysis is to solve for the values of x_A and x_B that maximize program effectiveness (equation 6.1a) subject to the constraint (equation 6.1b) that program costs do not exceed the limited budget. In this type of cost-effectiveness problem where there is only one constraint inequality, the solution may readily be found by first setting all program levels but x_A equal to zero. That is, even if there are several alternatives instead of only two as we have here, we set all of the x_i to zero except for x_A. In this case, when x_B is set to zero, we get the inequality

$$\$1000x_A \leq \$100,000$$

and we may solve for x_A by dividing both sides by \$1000:

$$x_A \leq \frac{\$100,000}{\$1000} = 100$$

which is to say that if only program A is operated, the number of units may not exceed 100 in order that the budget not be exceeded. We find this number in the third column of Table 6.1. Now if 100 buildings are treated under program A and all other programs are operated at a zero level, we see in the objective function (equation 6.1a) that the program effectiveness (E) level will be 300 cases, as is found in the last column of Table 6.1.

The next step is to set all program levels except x_B equal to zero and solve for x_B by the same procedure we used to solve for x_A. The result is $x_B = 500$, as is shown in the second row, the third column of Table 6.1. If 500 buildings are treated under program B with all other programs operated at zero level, the objective function (equation 6.1a) indicates that program effectiveness E will equal 500, as is noted in the last column of Table 6.1.

If there are additional programs to be evaluated, the same procedure can be used. In this case, all programs have been evaluated, and it is found that program effectiveness E is maximized if x_A is zero and x_B is 500. It will not pay to set up a program using some of program A and some of program B, since as x_A is increased, the level of effectiveness will move downward from 500 toward the lower 300 level.

6.2.2 Using Effectiveness-Cost Ratios to Evaluate Programs

The same result may be obtained from a somewhat different procedure. If we calculate the level of effectiveness per dollar cost (E/C) for each program, we find that the effectiveness cost ratio of program B is greater than that of program A

$$(E/C)_A = \tfrac{3}{1000} = .003; \qquad (E/C)_B = \tfrac{1}{200} = .005$$

If we select the program with the highest effectiveness-to-cost ratio, which is program B, and operate it to the full capacity of the budget, we obtain the same maximum effectiveness level as was determined earlier. But there is one difficulty that is less readily perceived with this method than it is with the lengthier approach of Table 6.1 and in equation 6.1. The problem occurs where project indivisibilities exist.

6.2.3 PROGRAM EVALUATION WITH PROJECT INDIVISIBILITIES

In the health problem described above, the units of each program consisted of buildings; the units making up the program of choice consisted of 500 short education courses, one course for each building in the community. In many problems, however, the units of alternative programs may consist of large projects. For example, in a river basin development plan, one potential program to be evaluated may consist of at most only two projects, say, two small hydroelectric dams, and this program is to be compared with another potential program consisting of only one project: a highway. To consider another example, a municipal library plan may require the evaluation of a library facilities program consisting of a number of small new library buildings, each of which can serve 8000 people per year at an annual cost of $400,000 for each building, or of a program consisting of numerous book-mobiles, each of which can serve 300 people per year at an annual cost of $30,000 for each bookmobile. Let us evaluate these alternative programs assuming a program budget of $1 million, and ignoring all future costs and benefits other than those that occur during the first year immediately following program implementation. In Table 6.2, we show unit costs and unit effectiveness rates, as well as effectiveness-cost ratios.

From this analysis, we see that for each $100 allocated to the construction and operation of a new facility, two residents will be served, while for each

TABLE 6.2
Effectiveness-Cost Ratios for Programs with Indivisible Projects

Program	Effectiveness per Project	Cost per Project	Effectiveness-Cost Ratio
New facilities	8000	$400,000	$\dfrac{8}{400} = .02$
Bookmobiles	300	$30,000	$\dfrac{3}{300} = .01$

$100 allocated to the operation of a bookmobile, one resident will be served. Thus the facility construction program is the more efficient, and is the program of choice. Unfortunately, this is the only information that is yielded from an analysis consisting only of effectiveness-cost ratios: the most efficient program, the program with the greatest rate of return per dollar cost, is identified. But a most effective plan has not been defined. Recall that the program budget is limited to $1 million. Applying a constraint equation of the same form as equation 6.1b, we divide the unit cost of the library facility program ($400,000) into the budget ($1 million) and find that 2.5 facilities can be constructed. Now this is not a sensible result: these facilities are indivisible and one either constructs 2 facilities or 3 facilities, not 2.5 facilities. Therefore, in addition to the constraint inequalities of the type shown in equations 6.1b and 6.1c, an additional constraint is required.

$$x_i = \text{an integer for all } i \qquad\qquad 6.1d$$

Since the budget is not large enough to allow 3 facilities, only 2 new facilities can be included under the program of choice, at a total cost of 2($400,000) = $800,000. This leaves $200,000 of the budget still unused. Thus, if only the effectiveness-cost ratios were used for program evaluation, they would have yielded the most efficient program (.02 residents served per dollar cost); but, applying an equation of the same form as equation 6.1a, we show that it is not the most effective possible program (16,000 residents served): the remaining $200,000 should be allocated for the operation of 6 bookmobiles. Thus the optimal plan consists of a construction program comprised of 2 new library facilities and the acquisition and operation of 6 bookmobiles. Although the mixed program plan is less efficient (.018 residents served per dollar cost), it is the most effective (17,800 residents served). These calculations are summarized in Table 6.3.

Table 6.3
Cost-Effectiveness Analysis with Project Indivisibility

Programs	Cost per Project	Effectiveness per Project	Number of Projects in Budget	Efficiency Ratio	Program Effectiveness
A. New facilties	$400,000	8,000	2	$\frac{8000}{400000} = .02$	16,000
B. Bookmobiles	$30,000	300	33	$\frac{300}{30000} = .01$	9,900
C. Optimal plan			$A = 2;\ B = 6$	$\frac{17800}{980000} = .018$	17,800

TABLE 6.4

Cost-Effectiveness Analysis of Indivisible Projects with Complementarities

Programs	Cost per Project	Effectiveness per Project	Efficiency Ratio
Job training	$350,000	$300,000	.86
Access road	$550,000	$650,000	1.18
Industrial park	$850,000	$990,000	1.17

6.2.4 TREATMENT OF PROJECT COMPLEMENTARITIES

Let us consider a depressed rural region beset with widespread poverty. A budget of $1 million is available for allocation among specific projects. Three programs intended to increase incomes are proposed: a job training center, an access road, and an industrial park. An analysis of the potential effectiveness of these public facilities indicates that a job training center of the type proposed can increase the incomes of 600 wage earners by 20%. For the rural region in question, this means that the current annual family income of $2500 would be increased to $3000 for 600 wage earners, or an aggregate income increase of $500 × (600) = $300,000 for the region. By a similar analysis, it is estimated that the access road would increase aggregate regional income by $650,000 and, finally, that the industrial park would increase aggregate regional income by $990,000. These effectiveness measures are shown together with associated costs in Table 6.4.

In this case, no program contains more than one of a given type of project— programs with two or three training centers or with several access roads are not considered. Thus, to the constraints already described, this additional constraint must be added:

$$0 \leq x_i \leq 1 \qquad \text{(for all } i) \qquad \qquad 6.1e$$

If projects were selected on the basis of their effectiveness-cost ratios, or relative efficiency, the access road would be given highest priority, the industrial park second priority, and the job training center third priority. But, because the program budget is limited to $1 million, we cannot include the two highest ranked projects within the budget. Furthermore, if we were to include the first ranked project and the third ranked project, although the budget would not be exceeded, the total effectiveness indicated in the table would amount to $300,000 + $650,000 = $950,000, and this is less than the effectiveness of the second ranked project, which has an effectiveness level of $990,000. It, therefore, appears that only the second ranked project, the industrial park, should be included in the budget.

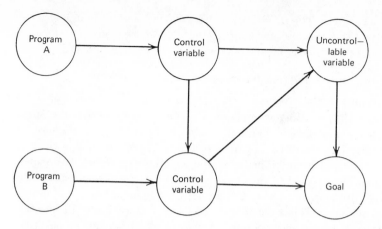

FIGURE 6.1 Causal relations among complementary programs.

It is clear at this point that the effectiveness-cost ratios have been of limited usefulness in determining which project should be recommended for maximizing program effectiveness subject to a limited budget. But the approach applied thus far has still failed to yield the most effective plan by assuming that the effectiveness of each project is independent of that of the others. For example, it is obvious that if the industrial park were developed together with the access road, more industries would be induced to locate in the industrial park while more users would benefit from the access road. The result is that the effectiveness of both projects taken together will be greater than the effectiveness of the two projects taken separately. This type of interdependence among projects that are intended to achieve a single goal is referred to as project complementarity. A flow diagram showing the relationships between programs and the goal is shown in Figure 6.1. The measure of effectiveness for each project is ignored if two or more complementary projects are being considered for inclusion in a single project package. Instead, the effectiveness of the overall project package is stated, which includes the effectiveness of each project separately plus their joint effectiveness.[13]

In the example we have just described, a program package consisting of an industrial park and an access road will exceed the budget and can, therefore, be ignored. In fact, the only such package that would not exceed the budget consists of the job training center and the access road. Suppose it is found that the access road will increase the number of wage earners who can attend the job training program and, as a result, the combined package generated total effects of $1,050,000 or $100,000 more than the two projects

[13] Refer to Russell Ackoff.

evaluated separately. The package will cost $900,000 and, although it is less efficient than either the access road or the industrial park alone, it is the most effective program that can be attained with the $1 million budget.

6.2.5 INCIDENCE OF PROGRAM IMPACTS

The measure of effectiveness used in evaluating the several program alternatives in the preceding example was the contribution of each alternative to aggregate regional income. For many purposes, such an aggregate measure is an appropriate indicator of program effectiveness. For example, if the goal of the program had been explicitly stated as "the expansion of economic output of depressed regions," then the aggregative measure would have been appropriate. But aggregate measures do not shed light on the social groups to whom program impacts were distributed; they do not answer the question of "who benefited from the program." For example, although the effectiveness of the industrial park referred to earlier was estimated as $990,000, it may be that most of this impact would have been incident to middle- and upper-income wage earners, with only a small proportion of the aggregate amount being incident to the poor. This information is not revealed by an aggregate income measure and for many types of programs, such as in this example of a program to alleviate poverty in depressed rural regions, the use of an aggregative measure will not be very useful for program evaluation. What is needed is:

1. A sharper definition of the program goal.
2. A more detailed analysis that provides information on the incidence of program impacts.

For example, a more explicit goal for the depressed rural region program would be "the reduction in the number or in the proportion of families located in depressed rural regions that are poor," where the word "poor" is defined by a dollar income measure. Such a goal statement requires not only a measure of the increase in aggregate regional income in the depressed areas that would be generated by each program but also a breakdown of the aggregative measure into the income groups to whom the increased income will be incident. From this information, it is possible to determine the number of low-income families that would benefit from the program. It is this measure and not the aggregative measure that should be used as the measure of program effectiveness.[14]

Suppose that the goal of a program is to generate program impacts for all population groups, but that impacts incident to certain groups are to be

[14] This approach is somewhat debatable. See Burton Weisbrod's illuminating discussion of this issue in his article "Collective Action and the Distribution of Income: A Conceptual Approach," in Haveman and Margolis.

given greater weight than are the impacts incident to others. In the library planning example, the measure of effectiveness was the total number of residents served by each program. But if service to residents with low-education levels is particularly important to program administrators, then the aggregative measure must be disaggregated so that "service to low-education residents" is measured. But to use this information for program evaluation, the actual weights to be given to service to each group must be indicated. If, for example, program administrators are able to agree that service to a "low-education resident" is three times as important as services to "all others," then the amount of service each program distributes to "low-education residents" will be multiplied by three (3), and the amount of service to "all other residents" will be multiplied by one (1). The aggregative effectiveness measure must now be disaggregated to indicate the number of residents of each education group that will be served by a unit of each program. Suppose it is found that of the 8000 residents served per unit of program A, 1000 are "low-education residents" and 7000 are "all others"; while of the 300 residents served per unit of program B, 250 are "low-education residents" and 50 are "all others." These measures of effectiveness, disaggregated by incidence group, together with the incidence weights, are shown in the second and third columns of Table 6.5. In the fourth column are shown the weighted effectiveness rates per unit of each program. These weighted effectiveness rates are obtained by multiplying the impact per unit of a given program incident to a given group by the incidence weight for that group, and then by adding the results for all incidence groups. For example, the impact per unit of program A incident to "low education residents" is 1000. This is multiplied by the incidence weight (3) to obtain 3000. Next, we multiply the impact per unit of program A incident to "all other residents" (7000) by the incidence weight (1) to give 7000. Adding the

TABLE 6.5

Cost-Effectiveness Analysis with Incidence Considered

Program	Cost per Project	Effectiveness per Project Weight=3	Weight=1	Weighted Effectiveness per Project	No. of Projects Within Budget	Weighted Program Effectiveness	Effectiveness-Cost Ratio
A. New facilities	$400,000	1000	7000	10,000	2	20,000	$\frac{10,000}{400,000} = .025$
B. Book mobiles	$30,000	250	50	800	33	26,400	$\frac{800}{30,000} = .0267$
C. Mixed program					$A = 2$ $B = 6$	24,800	$\frac{24,800}{980,0000} = .0253$

weighted program impacts of both groups gives 10,000, which is the weighted effectiveness rate per unit of program A. This is found in the first row, column 4, of Table 6.5. Following the same procedure, we find the weighted effectiveness rate per unit of program B which, as is shown in Table 6.5, is 800.

Column 5 of Table 6.5 shows the same information shown previously in the third column of Table 6.3: the number of units of each project that can be included within the program budget. This calculation, we recall, makes use of both the budget constraint (equation 6.1b) and the integer constraint (equation 6.1d).

Finally, to obtain the weighted effectiveness level for each program, we replace the aggregative effectiveness rates used in the earlier calculation with the weighted effectiveness rates that we have just derived. Multiplying the number of units of program A that can be included within the budget (2) by the weighted effectiveness rate (10,000), we obtain a weighted effectiveness level of 20,000. Repeating this procedure for program B, we obtain a weighted effectiveness level of 26,400. (*Note:* the effectiveness coefficients that would appear in the objective function, equation 6.1a, are accordingly replaced by the weighted effectiveness coefficients.)

Based on this "incidence-specific" cost effectiveness analysis, we now see that program B is the program of choice. Even if we recall that the integer constraint on program A results in $200,000 of the budget remaining unused, which could be allocated for six units of program B, the weighted effectiveness level of this "mixed program," shown in the last column of the third row in Table 6.5, is only 24,800, which is still less than that of program B. Finally, we observe in column 6 of Table 6.5 that the efficiency ratios for each alternative indicate that program B is the most efficient. In this case, the program-selection decision can be correctly made via the efficiency ratios.

6.2.6 EXTERNALITIES AND MULTIGOAL PROGRAMS

In the first example we describe in this chapter, both programs contribute to the goal of improving health by reducing the number of lead poisoning cases among children. But program A, repainting each building with nonlead based paint, not only contributes to the health goal but also contributes to the goal of housing improvement. In addition, program A helps reduce local unemployment, also a community goal, since local unemployed youth can easily be trained to paint the buildings that need repainting.

The point is that in addition to having impacts of the intended goal, a program typically will generate impacts incident to other goals. In the anti-lead poisoning example, these impacts are all favorable. But in the case of an electric power program, the air pollution produced by the power generating plant will negatively effect other goals—for example, the goal of maintaining a clean environment. Characteristic of these "external effects" is the condition that the program generating them is not compensated as the sine qua non for its positive contributions to external goals, nor does it compensate the other programs with goals that it negatively effects. These kinds of program impacts are referred to as "externalities" or "spillovers."[15]

The importance of taking externalities into account for the program-selection decision should be clear enough: programs that generate positive externalities should have a greater likelihood of getting included in a plan when their externalities are made an implicit part of program evaluation, and the reverse should be true for programs that generate negative externalities. But whether the more explicit accounting actually affects program selection is another matter. The difficulty is that a program administrator does not place any value on the externalities that his programs might generate: he does not get rewarded for generating positive externalities, and nobody seems to be requiring him to pay to injured third parties the costs caused by negative externalities. Thus the situation may arise in which he is faced with programs A and B and the effectiveness cost ratio for A exceeds that of B only if externalities are included. Under ordinary circumstances, the decision maker will choose B every time. The circumstances in which he will forego his "selfishness" are (1) our administrator is chosen for his job because he has known altruistic qualities or (2), on a less lofty plane, organizational arrangements make his cooperation in properly considering externalities the more profitable approach for his program and his career. Such arrangements include: sanctions placed on "suboptimal" behavior by higher level governmental or legal authority (federal air pollution legislation *requires* local governments to consider the polluting effects of their programs); actual transfers of funds paid to a program producing positive externalities by the parties that stand to benefit (a county library agency pays the central city library if the latter provides county residents with borrowing privileges); and the internalization of externalities by merging all programs that generate mutually beneficial or harmful impacts.

To be sure, none of these institutional arrangements are in widespread use, so that those responsible for program selection decisions have little incentive to properly take account of externalities. If anything, the contrary is true. How well-known is interagency rivalry; how often are agency administrators, in avoiding interdepartmental cooperation, accused of empire building? Nonetheless, because of the importance of externalities, we assume that the institutional arrangements have been resolved and that externalities are properly considered in program evaluation.

[15] For a theoretical introduction to the economics of externalities, see Haveman, pp. 35–43.

TABLE 6.6
Cost-Effectiveness Analysis with Externalities Considered

Evaluated Measure	Effectiveness per Unit				Weighted Effec- tiveness per Unit	Cost per Unit	No. of Units Within Budget	Weighted Program Effec- tiveness	Effectiveness Cost Ratio
	Health (No. of Cases)	Housing (No. of Bldgs.)	Unemployed (No. of Workers)	Education (No. of Years)					
Goal weight	1.0	.25	.5	1.0					
Program A	3	1	.5	0	3.5	$1000	100	350	.0035
Program B	1	0	0	−.2	.8	$ 200	500	400	.004

To undertake a cost-effectiveness evaluation of projects A and B with externalities explicitly considered, estimates of the unit impact of each program on each goal will be required. In many cases, it may be quite costly to obtain these estimates directly, if not impossible. For example, where the external goal is an intangible, such as the goal to "beautify our cities," it may be impossible to measure directly the effectiveness of a program in achieving such a goal. However, several indirect methods have been described in the literature.[16]

Let us suppose, now, that all externalities have been quantified, with measures of unit impacts on each goal shown in columns 1 to 4 of Table 6.6.

As in the evaluation based on the incidence of impacts, the treatment of externalities requires that there exist an agreement as to the relative import- ance of each goal, and that this be expressed numerically in terms of weight.[17] Suppose administrators agree that to put one unemployed worker to work is only one half as important as preventing a child from becoming ill; that an improved residential building is one fourth as important, but that the loss of the equivalent of a year of education (due to the transfer of the teachers from education to health) is just as serious as an illness.[18] These goal weights are indicated in Table 6.6. They are used in the same way as are the incidence weights in Table 6.5. That is, each weight (w) is multiplied by the impact (e)

---

[16] For example, Julius Margolis, "Shadow Prices for Incorrect or Non-Existent Market Prices," in Haveman and Margolis, pp. 314–329.

[17] Economists often use prices to represent these weights. Margolis' "Shadow Prices," presents a discussion of the rationale and estimation of these prices.

[18] Actually, the loss in education output is not a negative externality. In cases where the cost of hiring the teachers can be subtracted from the value of the antilead poisoning program stated in money terms (as a full benefit-cost analysis seeks to do), the negative effect on the education goal is automatically incorporated. But since our effectiveness rates are not stated in money terms, we include the effect of the teacher reallocation the same way as for externalities.

of a given program (i) on each goal (j) to yield the weighted effectiveness rate ($\bar{E}$) for that program:

$$\bar{E}_i = \sum_j w_j e_{ij} \qquad\qquad 6.2$$

Applying equation 6.2 to the data in the first four columns of Table 6.6, we obtain the weighted effectiveness rate for program A ($\bar{E}_A = 3.5$) and for program B ($\bar{E}_B = .8$) as shown in column 5. Then, since the cost per unit of program A is $1000 and the budget is $100,000, 100 units are feasible. Multiplying the number of units in a feasible program times the weighted effectiveness rate gives the weighted program effectiveness level. For program A, this is $(3.5)(100) = 350$. Following the same procedure for program B, we find that the weighted program effectiveness level is $(.8)(500) = 400$. We conclude that even with the externalities considered, program B still maximizes program effectiveness.[19] Observe in the last column of Table 6.6 that the effectiveness-cost ratios give the correct program selection decision.

Suppose that programs A and B are typically administered by a municipal government agency that is held responsible by the state government for achieving only health-related goals. Furthermore, it is never given credit by the state for any programs that generate positive or negative impacts on external goals, nor does the size of the budget made available by the state government take into account these externalities. The result, as we indicated earlier, is that the municipal agency will set all goal weights for external goals to zero, and the goal weight for its mandated goal will be set to one, so that the municipality ignores externalities when evaluating alternative programs. A similar result occurs where program impacts are incident to population groups residing in areas outside what the municipal agency considers its own target area. Such impacts, or spillovers, are simply disregarded.

Clearly, these practices lead to enormous inefficiency and duplication of services between both agencies and municipalities.

6.2.7 GOALS AS CONSTRAINTS

It often occurs that goal *weights* are not readily obtained but that required goal attainment *levels* can be stated. Recall from Chapter 1 that many types of goals could be stated in terms of a "need gap" that stipulates the minimum goal attainment level for a given goal (a lower constraint). Although the

---

[19] See the articles by Kneese, Weisbrod and Lichfield (Chapters 8 to 10) in Julius Margolis (ed.), *The Public Economy of Urban Communities* (Washington, D.C.: Resources for the Future, and Johns Hopkins Press, 1965).

method to be described can treat goals stated either as upper or lower constraints, we pose a problem containing the latter.[20]

Suppose two programs are being evaluated, each of which contributes to the goal of providing better transportation. One program is a highway network capable of transporting 5000 people by automobile for each mile of highway, and the other is a railroad system capable of transporting 2000 people for each mile of track. The highway network costs $1 million per mile while the railroad system costs $500,000 per mile. The total cost of the transportation system is constrained not to exceed the total available budget of $50 million.

However, each system generates air pollution, a negative externality. Suppose an index of air quality is constructed based on several types of pollutants that are emitted from transportation systems. It is determined that when this air quality index rises above a level of 10, a health hazard exists. Therefore, it is decided that whatever transport system is to be built, the overall emissions from the system must not cause the air quality index to rise above 10. Thus, in addition to a budget constraint, the degree of effectiveness that can be attained is now also subject to an air quality constraint.

Suppose that an analysis of the emission characteristics of each system indicates that each mile added to the highway system will cause the air quality index to increase by .4, while each mile added to the railroad system would cause the air quality index to increase by .05. This information is summarized in Table 6.7.

TABLE 6.7

Maximizing Program Effectiveness Subject to Two Constraints

Program	Effectiveness per Unit Transportation (No. Persons per Mile)	Cost per Unit (Mile)	Maximum No. Units Not Exceeding Budget ($50 Million)	Air Pollution Impact per Unit (Mile)	Maximum No. Units Not Exceeding Air Quality Index (10)	Feasible Program Effectiveness
Highway ($H = 25$)	5000	$1 Million	50	.4	25	125,000
Railroad ($R = 100$)	2000	$.5 Million	100	.05	200	200,000
Mixed program ($H = 16\frac{2}{3}$; $R = 66\frac{2}{3}$)						

[20] For a demonstration of the conceptual similarities between goals stated as weights, and goals stated as constraints, see Stephen A. Marglin, *Public Investment Criteria* (Cambridge, Mass.: The M.I.T. Press, 1967), pp. 23–32.

Let us proceed to evaluate the two alternatives based on effectiveness-cost ratios. We see that where more than one constraint exists, this method is inapplicable.

We find that the effectiveness per dollar cost on a per mile basis is greater for the highway network than for the railroad system. If we use this result as the criterion for evaluation, we would then multiply the highway effectiveness rate (5000) times the number of highway miles not exceeding the budget (50), to find that the program effectiveness level will be 250,000. This result would have represented the maximum feasible effectiveness level had the only constraint in the evaluation been the size of the budget. But now there is a second constraint, the air quality level. Because the highway system is relatively inefficient in terms of air pollution, we find that no more than 25 miles of highway can be included in the program and still not exceed the air quality constraint. Thus the number of highway miles used to calculate the program effectiveness level (50) far exceed the air quality constraint, and in this sense is infeasible. In fact, we see that no more than 25 miles of highway is feasible in terms of both constraints. Thus the best that can be attained with a feasible highway program is an effectiveness level of 125,000.

In contrast, we see that up to 100 miles of railroad can be included in the program and still be feasible and, at an effectiveness rate of 2000 per mile, we find that the railroad system can yield an effectiveness level of 200,000. Since this is clearly superior to that of the highway network, we are strongly tempted to conclude that the transportation needs of the program should be met by using railroads rather than highways. But if we make this conclusion, we would be wrong again. The problem is that we have not yet considered a mixed program comprised of both highways and railroads.

Suppose that we are considering construction of a 100-mile railroad system, a quantity that is feasible in terms of both constraints, and that will serve 200,000 users. But let us examine the possibility of replacing the last 2 railroad miles with 1 highway mile. The result will be not only that this program is still feasible, it will also serve more users than the "pure" railroad program. Let us examine whether we can feasibly substitute 10 highway miles for 20 railroad miles.

Following the budget restraint, we multiply 10 highway miles times the cost per highway mile ($1 million) to give a total highway cost of $10 million. We do the same for 80 railroad miles at a cost of $.5 million per mile to get a total railroad cost of $40 million. Adding the two together gives a total cost of $50 million, which is precisely equal to the available budget:

$$\$1,000,000(10) + \$500,000(80) = \$50,000,000$$

Following the same procedure for the air pollution constraint, we find that 10 highway miles will increase the air quality index by $.4(10) = 4$, while 80 railroad miles will increase the air quality index $.05(80) = 4$. Adding the two together, we find that the combined program will increase the air quality index by a total of 8, which is clearly feasible:

$$.4(10) + .05(80) \leq 10$$

Thus the combined program is feasible in terms of both constraints. Now we compute the total effectiveness level of this program. Ten highway miles with an effectiveness rate of 5000 per mile indicates that 50,000 users can be served via the highway network. Eighty railroad miles with an effectiveness rate of 2000 per mile indicates that 160,000 users can be served via the railroad system. Adding these together yields a total program effectiveness of 210,000 as shown in the objective function:

$$5000(10) + 2000(80) = 210,000$$

This feasible program, consisting of 10 highway miles and 80 railroad miles, is much more effective than any program considered thus far. If we continued this way by trial and error, admittedly an arduous and time-consuming procedure, we would find that the maximum feasible program consists of $16\frac{2}{3}$ highway miles and $66\frac{2}{3}$ railroad miles, with an effectiveness level of 216,690. Fortunately, however, a mathematical technique called linear programming is available that has the capability of solving this problem directly not only for the case where there are only two alternative programs and just two inequality constraints but also for cases requiring the evaluation of large numbers of alternative programs subject to many constraints.

We can illustrate how the solution to our linear programming problem may be obtained via diagrammatic means. First, we write the problem mathematically as objective function:

$$\text{Max } E = 5000x_H + 2000x_R \qquad \qquad 6.3\text{a}$$

subject to:

Budget constraint $\qquad\qquad\qquad x_H + \quad .5x_R \leq 50 \qquad\qquad 6.3\text{b}$

Air quality constraint $\qquad\qquad .4x_H + \quad .05x_R \leq 10 \qquad\qquad 6.3\text{c}$

and $\qquad\qquad\qquad\qquad\qquad\qquad x_H, \qquad x_R \geq 0 \qquad\qquad\qquad 6.3\text{d}$

(where the budget constraint has been divided through by \$1 million).

In Figure 6.2 we show the budget constraint as the area below the line BB: any planned combination of x_H (highway miles) and x_R (railroad miles) lying above BB would require more funds than the budget affords. Similarly, the air quality constraint is shown as the area below the line AA. Furthermore, since both x_H and x_R are constrained to be nonnegative, we find that

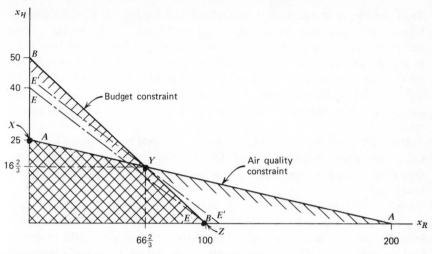

FIGURE 6.2   Graphical solution of linear programming problem.

the only feasible programs, that is, combinations of x_H and x_R that do not violate any constraints, are those lying in the hatched area of Figure 6.2.

But our task is not merely to find a feasible program: we want to solve for the one that maximizes program effectiveness. How can this be done? It is a theorem of linear programming that, to find an optimal solution, all we must do is evaluate the corners of the feasible space to see which one maximizes the objective function. In Figure 6.2 we only have three corners to consider: X, Y, and Z. Our method for evaluating them will be as follows:

Arbitrarily, we start with the corner Z, having the values ($x_H = 0$, $x_R = 100$). We insert these values into the objective function, and find that if the solution were at this corner, $E = 5000(0) + 2000(100) = 200,000$. We can then represent the objective function as a straight line in Figure 6.2 if we determine the point on the X_H axis at which E also equals 200,000. Setting $x_R = 0$, we find $x_H = 200,000/5000 = 40$. We are therefore able to connect the two points ($x_H = 40$, $x_R = 0$) and ($x_H = 0$, $x_R = 100$) with the line EE, which is our objective function at the value $E = 200,000$.

Notice first that line EE lies above the corner X. This means that X cannot possibly be the optimal corner—it is inferior to Z. Next, notice that line EE cuts through a part of the feasible space, and that the corner Y is the only corner lying above line EE. If we now move the line parallel to itself and upward, we shall reach the corner Y. At this point, the objective function does not cut through the feasible space, but touches it at Y. Furthermore, if the objective function were moved upward somewhat more, it would no longer touch the feasible space, that is, it would yield infeasible programs.

Thus the objective function is maximized and feasible at Y, the values of which can be read off the diagram as ($x_H = 16\frac{2}{3}$, $x_R = 66\frac{2}{3}$). Further, these values maximize program effectiveness at $E = 216{,}690$ on the line $E'E'$. It should be noted, however, that if the objective function had different effectiveness coefficients, then the optimal program might well have been at a different corner. For example, if e_H were 5000 as before but e_R were 4000 (instead of 2000), then the optimal corner is found at Z, as the reader should verify.

Although small problems of the size just described can be easily solved by hand, most linear programming problems are solved by computer, and books describing computational methods for solving linear programs are widely available.[21]

Instead of requiring a goal to be maximized, objective functions often require a goal, such as total program costs, to be minimized. In this case, the inequalities would all be written as lower rather than upper limits, requiring that the program levels minimizing costs at least attain stated goals expressed as constraints.

If either incidence of program impacts or externalities appear in the objective function, then the effectiveness rates (e_j) are replaced with the weighted effectiveness rates ($\bar{E}_j$) obtained in equation 6.2.

Finally, if project indivisibilities exist, then the integer constraint equation 6.1d must be included, while if project packages, including groupings of complementary projects, are limited to one each, then in addition to the integer constraint equation 6.1d, the constraint equation 6.1e that limits the number of projects (j) to zero or one ($0 \leq x_j \leq 1$) is also required. In either case, instead of solving the problem via linear programming methods, the addition of constraint equation 6.1d requires the use of *integer programming* methods.[22]

These quantitative techniques, known collectively as mathematical programming, have a great deal of appeal for many people because of their capacity for concisely stating many kinds of planning problems. Explicitly stated are the objectives to be optimized, the alternatives that are available for this end, the resources they use, the side effects they generate, and the resource scarcities and other constraints that affect the degree to which the

[21] See, for example, W. J. Baumol, *Economic Theory and Operations Analysis*, second edition (Englewood Cliffs, N.J.: Prentice-Hall, 1965), Chapter 5; and G. Hadley, *Linear Programming* (Reading, Mass.: Addison-Wesley Publishing, 1962).

[22] Refer to Baumol, Chapter 8 on integer programming and Chapter 19 on capital budgeting; also Martin Weingartner, *Mathematical Programming and the Analysis of Capital Budgeting Problems*, Englewood Cliffs, N.J.: Prentice-Hall, 1963, and his article "Capital Budgeting of Interrelated Projects," *Management Science, 12*, March 1966, 485–516.

goals can feasibly be attained. So why are not these techniques used more frequently? We indicated the main reason in the very first section of this chapter: because their use requires that all of the coefficients for each and every program alternative must have already been satisfactorily quantified, and this just has not been done. True, there are some programs (usually public works projects) with limited and well-defined impacts where all the necessary information can be obtained. In these instances, mathematical programming may provide significant improvements in program selection. But for most urban programs it is doubtful that the quantified information needs ever will be satisfied. Nonetheless, the principles of programming methods provide an extensive and sound *conceptual* basis for improving the program evaluation and selection process.

6.3 COST EFFECTIVENESS ANALYSIS: LONG TERM

Thus far, our analyses have made use of the assumption that all future program impacts and costs either do not exist or can be ignored. In this sense, our analyses have been short term in nature. But very few goal-oriented programs fit this assumption. Most generate a long time span of program impacts; and most involve ongoing costs and are therefore long term in nature. To evaluate long-term programs, our analytic technique must take into account the program impacts and costs that will exist during each time period over a long-term planning future. To do this requires that two conditions be met: first, the analyst must be able to estimate program impacts and costs for each period up to the planning horizon. Second, a method must be available for weighing the importance of a future impact or cost relative to impacts or costs that occur in the immediate future. We assume that methods for estimating future impacts and costs are available, and concentrate instead on the second problem—weighing future program impacts and costs.

6.3.1 DISCOUNTING

Suppose there are two programs, A and B, that generate exactly the same goal impacts, but A's impacts occur right away, while B's do not occur until next year. Which program is to be preferred? A, of course (why wait if you do not have to?). But there is some amount by which B's impacts might increase relative to A's that would cause the two to be of equal value. For example, if B's delayed impacts were to increase so that they exceeded A's impacts by $r\%$, we might be just enough satisfied with this "payment for waiting the entire year" so that we would have a hard time choosing among the two.

$$A_{t(0)}(1 + r) = B_{t(1)} \qquad 6.4$$

If we already know the value of r, then we can easily convert an impact occurring one or more years from now into an equivalent value today. For example B's superior impacts that occur in period $t(1)$ would be of equal value with another project yielding returns today $[t(0)]$ if these current returns were

$$A_{t(0)} = \left(\frac{1}{1+r}\right)B_{t(1)}$$

Similarly, if program C's impacts occurred a year after B's, they would also have to be $r\%$ more than B's to be valued the same as B

$$B_{t(1)}(1+r) = C_{t(2)}$$

which implies, from equation 6.4, that

$$A_{t(0)}(1+r)(1+r) = C_{t(2)}$$

or, in terms of A's impacts two years earlier,

$$A_{t(0)} = \left[\frac{1}{(1+r)^2}\right]C_{t(2)}$$

Translating future returns into equivalently valued current ones is called discounting, and r is referred to as the discount rate.[23] The logic can be extended to determine the present value of an impact occurring n years from now:

$$A_{t(0)} = \left[\frac{1}{(1+r)^n}\right]G_{t(n)}$$

Suppose, to be more realistic, that a project V generates impacts V_t over each of the next n years rather than in just one of those years. How can we determine a single impact measure for that project for use in comparison with another project? We just add up the returns for each of the n years, where the returns are first discounted back to the present.

$$V = \frac{V_1}{1+r} + \frac{V_2}{(1+r)^2} + \cdots + \frac{V_n}{(1+r)^n} = \sum_{t=1}^{n}\frac{V_t}{(1+r)^t} \qquad 6.5$$

Someone might ask, "this is all very well in theory, but is discounting really used, and how would anyone be able to estimate the value of r, which after all is nothing but a charge for delay?" Indeed, discounting is used in practice, especially in benefit-cost analysis, as described in the first section of this chapter. And how might the discount rate be measured? One way is simply to use the bank rate of interest. For instance, note that equation 6.4,

[23] An excellent discussion of discounting is in Haveman, pp. 157–162.

instead of comparing two projects, might have been stating that "if a sum A is currently deposited in an interest-bearing bank account earning $r\%$ per year, it will be worth $A(1+r)$ or B at the end of one year." And note the logical possibilities offered by this measure. Suppose that while B is the return on a project one year hence, A represents the money available to spend on project B or any other project. We can say that since the money can simply be deposited in an interest-bearing account and will be worth exactly $A(1 + r)$ a year later, the project B must yield at least this much before it gets selected

$$A_{t(0)}(1 + r) \leq B_{t(1)}$$

If the impacts B were also stated in money terms (more characteristic of benefit-cost rather than effectiveness-cost analysis we could write, by rearranging terms,

$$r \leq \frac{B_{t(1)} - A_{t(0)}}{A_{t(0)}}$$

This is to say that a criterion for project selection is to select only if the rate of return from the project is at least as great as the interest rate that could otherwise have been earned. We see then that the interest rate represents the *opportunity cost* of program funds—the returns that could have readily been obtained by those funds if they were *not* used for the program.

The problem is that the bank rate of interest, or what is more commonly used, the interest rate on riskless government bonds, is not a good measure of the opportunity cost of the program funds. Since these funds are typically raised via taxation, for example, by simply removing them from the private sectors of the economy, their opportunity cost is the rate of return that could have been earned in the private sectors—these earnings being a contribution to social welfare. Baumol has shown[24] that if an industry needs to earn at least the return offered on riskless government bonds before it further expands production, but that its returns (profits) are taxed rather heavily, then the return that it actually has to worry about is the pretax rate of return. For example, if government bonds pay 5% interest and if business profits are taxed at the rate of 50%, then the industry really has to have a 10% rate of return before investing in another project. Baumol has also shown that a good measure of the opportunity cost of funds to be used in the public sector can be obtained as a weighted average of the pretax rates of return in each of the private sectors, and that in the above example the discount rate would therefore be a lot closer to 10% rather than to 5%.[25]

[24] William J. Baumol, "On the Discount Rate for Public Projects," in Haveman and Margolis, pp. 273–290.
[25] Baumol, p. 280.

However, we should indicate that Baumol, like others, placed a certain modification on the derivation of the discount rate.

If, in the productive activities of the private sectors that contribute to the social welfare, certain uncompensated costs to society are also generated (water and air pollution, for example), to base the discount rate on private sector returns alone is to overstate the private sector's contribution to society and, consequently, the discount rate. The negative externalities as well as any positive ones should also be taken into account. Hence, the modification needed in calculating the discount rate is an adjustment to take account of the externalities generated in the private sector—the proper discount rate measures the *social* opportunity cost in removing the funds from the private sector.

We can now proceed to evaluate projects with both future impacts (stated in effectiveness terms) and future costs. We first consider programs with multiperiod impacts, reserving the combined case until later.

6.3.2 LONG-TERM PROGRAM EVALUATION WITH ZERO FUTURE COSTS

Consider a program in which impacts occur over many years in the future but in which all program costs are borne currently, and are subject to a limited budget. For example, suppose a federal agency exists that has the goal of reducing recidivism among convicts released from prison. The agency's mode of operation is to provide one-time grants-in-aid to municipal authorities that operate antirecidivism programs. The federal agency wants to know which of two alternative antirecidivism programs to fund within its given budget so as to obtain the greatest program effectiveness in response to its grants-in-aid.

The measure of effectiveness will be based on the number of ex-convicts who are not again convicted of a crime as a result of each program's receiving a federal grant-in-aid. Many of these programs might have been operated by the municipality even without the grant-in-aid. The information that is needed is the increase in each program's effectiveness that could only have occurred with the grant-in-aid. A further difficulty in measuring effectiveness is that one program (program A) may take several years after the receipt of federal funding before it becomes effective after which time each ex-convict treated will be permanently rehabilitated, while another program (program B) may be immediately effective, but may lose its effect after just a few years. Thus the measure of effectiveness should take into account not only the number of ex-convicts that are rehabilitated but also the length of time for which they are rehabilitated and also how much time passes before the rehabilitation occurs.

Suppose that program A consists of halfway houses to serve as homes for ex-convicts located within urban residential communities complete with staff psychiatrists, educational and job training facilities, and the like. It is estimated that for each $100,000 grant-in-aid for a halfway house, 50 ex-convicts will be rehabilitated for the remainder of their lives (an average of 25 years) who would not have been rehabilitated except for the grant. However, it will take three years before the ex-convicts become effectively rehabilitated.

Program B consists of job training centers, oriented to the needs of ex-convicts, operated by local boards of education. It will take $200,000 to stimulate a municipal authority to establish a job training center, and each center will rehabilitate 100 ex-convicts; but it is expected that the effect will not be permanent, lasting for an average of only three years.

If unit effectiveness-cost ratios are calculated for each program with timing of impacts ignored, one might conclude that both programs are equally efficient. Instead, it is necessary to calculate unit effectiveness rates based on the discounted stream of program impacts. Assume that the discount rate is 10%. We calculate the current value of impacts for B first over the three years of its effectiveness:

$$e_B = \frac{e_{t(1)}}{1 + r} + \frac{e_{t(2)}}{(1 + r)^2} + \frac{e_{t(3)}}{(1 + r)^3}$$

$$= \frac{100}{1 + .10} + \frac{100}{(1 + .10)^2} + \frac{100}{(1 + .10)^3}$$

$$= 91 + 83 + 75 = 249$$

Dividing the unit effectiveness rate ($e_B = 249$) by unit cost ($C_B = \$200,000$) gives an efficiency rate (e_B/C_B) of .0014.[26] Repeating this procedure for program A, we find that

$$e_A = \frac{50}{(1 + .10)^3} + \frac{50}{(1 + .10)^4} + \frac{50}{(1 + .10)^5} + \cdots + \frac{50}{(1 + .10)^{25}}$$

If we calculate only the first five years of this expression, we would obtain a unit effectiveness rate of

$$e_{A(3-7)} = 157$$

which, when divided by a unit cost of $100,000, gives an efficiency rate of .0016, which already exceeds that of program B. If we had included all 25 years of program A's impacts in the effectiveness rate, its efficiency rate

[26] A case can be made for including all costs of establishing and maintaining the alternative programs rather than considering only the federal grant. But the federal administrator who is charting a course to best achieve the goals mandated for his agency is not likely to feel that the necessary institutional conditions exist for considering all program impacts.

would have greatly exceeded that of program B. Thus program A should be given priority for the federal agency's grant-in-aid.

As in the instances we have discussed earlier, if problems of project indivisibilities and complementarities exist, or if additional valued objèctives exist giving rise to questions of incidence or externalities, then we should apply as indicated the appropriate analytic method.

6.3.3 LONG-TERM EVALUATION WITH FUTURE COSTS: BENEFIT-COST ANALYSIS

In the preceding section, we considered the evaluation of programs with multiperiod impacts. In this section, we add to our analysis multiperiod costs. Such costs are the result of several factors, including the administrative and operating costs that arise in running an ongoing program. Another factor giving rise to multiperiod costs is associated with the nature of capital-intensive programs. After a large initial outlay for public investments such as roads, housing, water and sewer facilities, hydro-power dams, and the like, the stream of goal-attaining impacts generated by these programs depends on the condition of the capital stock. But the condition of capital stock tends to deteriorate both with usage and with time and, as a result, the impacts of capital stock tend to decline over time thereby depreciating the stock's value. To offset the effects of deterioration, capital stock must be repaired and replaced over time, and this gives rise to ongoing costs.[27]

To treat the ongoing program costs $[C_{t(1)}, \ldots, C_{t(T)}]$, over a T year program life following the initial outlay $[C_{t(0)}]$, a difficulty arises that is generally not encountered in the treatment of the initial cost. Since the outlay of initial costs are usually subject to a fixed and known budget, their effects on the total effectiveness of a program can be assessed through a budget constraint inequality as has been the procedure throughout most of this chapter.

However, future budgets are generally unknown and, in any case, the future programs that would compete for inclusion in the future budgets are not known. Hence, instead of working with future budget constraints, essentially what we do is to assume that future program costs will not use enough of future budgets for us to worry about, or else we assume that ongoing costs can be financed outside of the budget (a most inappropriate assumption!). We then obtain the current value of all program impacts over time, and the current value of all costs over time, for each program. Then we

---

[27] A sizeable literature has developed relating to initial costs and maintenance costs in the determination of the optimal economic life span of capital stock. See P. Masse, *Optimal Investment Decision* (Englewood Cliffs, N.J.: Prentice-Hall, 1962); and C. E. Churchman, R. L. Ackoff, and E. L. Arnoff, *Introduction to Operation Research* (New York: Wiley, 1957), Chapter 17, "Replacement Theory."

select the program with the greatest current value of impacts relative to the current value of costs, the current budget constraint considered.

When the total weighted impacts for a given program estimated for each time period include external as well as primary impacts (incidence of impacts should also be considered), and when the weights we multiply them with are prices (recall our discussion of these weights in Section 6.2.6 on externalities, and footnote 17), the sum of the weighted impacts in period t are called benefits, B_t. Since benefits are stated in money terms, it is possible to subtract the costs incurred in period t (C_t) to obtain a measure of net benefits for the program in period t

$$b_t = B_t - C_t$$

If we then discount period t net benefits and sum over all periods, we obtain the current value of the net benefit stream generated by the project.[28]

$$b = \sum_{t=0}^{n} \frac{b_t}{(1 + r)^t} \qquad\qquad 6.6$$

Assuming a budget constraint, we select projects in decreasing order of their b values until the budget is used up, project indivisibilities and complementarities considered. If the program is such that many project units can be included under each program (recall the library or the antilead poisoning examples), the b measure is calculated on a unit basis, just as were the effectiveness rates, in the earlier examples. We then seek to maximize the net benefits of the entire program plan over all programs i

$$\text{Max } V = \sum_i b_i x_i$$

subject to

$$\sum_i C_{t(0)i} x_i \le K_{t(0)}$$

and

$$x_i \ge 0 \qquad \text{for all } i$$

In cases where budget [$K_{t(0)}$] does not constrain program size (financing from money markets may be possible as in the sale of municipal bonds, if the requisite interest rates are paid), the criterion for program selection is simply that the current value of the net benefit stream—equation 6.6—be

[28] In equation 6.6, we begin our summation with period 0 instead of period 1 because we suppose that while both benefits and ongoing costs commence in period 1, when the program is open, there will be a prior period in which all initial costs (for construction, organizing, etc.) are incurred. There may also be a scrap value to the program at the end of the nth period, which should also be included.

greater than zero. This implies that

$$\frac{\sum_{t=0}^{n} \dfrac{B_t}{(1+r)^t}}{\sum_{t=0}^{n} \dfrac{C_t}{(1+r)^t}} > 1 \qquad\qquad 6.7$$

which is to say that the benefit-cost ratio must be greater than one for any program included in the budget. However, there is a strange implication here. We have been assuming that costs, effectiveness rates, and benefit rates remain constant. The implication is that the benefit-cost ratio is also constant; hence, programs with a positive benefit-cost ratio would not only be included in the plan, they would also be expanded without limit. This absurd result has an explanation. The benefit-cost ratio should not be assumed constant over very large cost levels. Actually, the ratio would begin to move lower and lower as each addition to the program size brought fewer impacts and also began to force up prices and, therefore, program costs. The assumption of a constant ratio, however, is useful for programs that do not become so large that they begin to affect the economy and its prices.

PROBLEMS

1. A certain school district has decided to provide bus service for the children going to schools within the district. It is considering whether to purchase the expensive standard size bus that seats 40 or the inexpensive "mini-bus" that seats 8. Counting interest and amortization, annual maintenance costs, insurance, and bus driver's salaries, the large bus costs $30,000 per year each, while the small one costs $10,000 each. There is a budget of $2.7 million for the program.
   (a) Which of the two buses should be purchased to maximize the number of children served (indicate the number of children)?
   (b) Make the decision on the basis of effectiveness/cost ratios; is it the same?
   (c) Suppose, in addition, that there are 4000 children who should be served; now which is the best program? What would you recommend in this situation?

2. A community development program in one neighborhood of a large city has decided to build park space to serve the neighborhood children and elderly. It has budgeted $1 million for the purchase of land and the construction of park and recreation facilities. Two large empty lots are

available for purchase in the neighborhood. Lot A would cost $750,000 to buy and fully equip; lot B would cost $900,000. It is estimated that lot A would serve 3500 residents while lot B, with a somewhat superior location, would serve 4000. Which lot should be developed?

3. A municipality is deciding whether to spend a $10 million budget on a manpower training center or low income housing. For each $20,000 it spends on manpower training it can expect to successfully train and employ one person in a job with earnings above the poverty level. However, an indirect effect of this person's new spending is to raise local earnings, thereby raising yet one additional person from poverty. In addition, in a study of 10,000 formerly poor but employable persons who were living in substandard housing and who were, on finding employment, raised out of poverty, 8000 were found to have moved up to acceptable quality housing and to have brought an additional 10,000 family members with them. That is to say, an indirect effect of raising two persons out of poverty is to raise the housing quality for 3.6 persons. On the other hand, it takes $15,000 to house 4 persons in a low-income housing unit, while another study has shown that of 4,000 people who moved from substandard to above standard housing, an indirect effect was that 80 who would otherwise have remained unemployed were so affected by the new environment that they found acceptable jobs. Suppose that the job training program can be built at any size over a minimum of $30,000, but new housing units cost $15,000 each. Furthermore, a survey indicates that the community values decent housing half again as much as it values a non-poverty level job. All this information is summarized in the following table.

GOAL		EFFECTIVENESS PER UNIT		COST PER UNIT
		INCOME	HOUSING	
PROGRAM	WEIGHT	1	1.5	(in DOLLARS)
Manpower training		2.0	3.6	20,000
Housing		.08	4.0	15,000

(a) How many units of each program should be constructed to maximize program effectiveness?

(b) Suppose that through a change in attitudes, income and housing are now valued equally (e.g., the weights are both unity). Now what is the effectiveness maximizing program?

4. In the above example, the federal government, aware of the general preference of municipalities for housing rather than for income upgrading

programs, decides to establish a grant-in-aid program to encourage greater municipal activity in the latter type of program. Furthermore, the government is aware that municipalities never, in practice, calculate indirect effects when evaluating programs. For example, municipalities assume that the effects of a manpower training program on housing goals are zero, and assume likewise for the effects of a housing program on income goals. Recompute effectiveness to reflect these biases.

(a) Determine what is the smallest "percentage of total manpower training costs" that the federal government must pay to get the municipal government to choose the manpower program rather than the housing program (assume, again, the weights 1 for income and 1.5 for housing).

(b) Instead of a grand-in-aid program, the federal government decides to use a revenue sharing program. This merely has the effect of increasing the municipality's budget by the amount of the inter-governmental transfer. How much must the federal government increase the municipality's $10 million budget to cause it to switch from housing to manpower?

(c) What is your position on federal grant-in-aid programs versus revenue sharing? Feel free to bring in other issues not discussed here

5. Let us look at the antirecidivism problem (the last example in the chapter) from the municipality's point of view and with a few changes. We consider only program A, with the same 2-year lag but add that the half-way house would operate for ten years and the average remaining life of persons treated would be 16 years. It will cost the municipality $600,000 to construct and equip the halfway house before operation begins. In addition, after taking into account the small rent each resident will be charged to help defray costs, it will cost $100,000 annually to maintain the house and program. However, an analysis of the value of permanently rehabilitating 50 people shows that society would benefit by $50,000 annually because of the increased productivity of the people, the savings in prison, court, and law-enforcement costs, and the savings in damages that would have been wrought by them had they remained criminals. The analysis must consider that 50 persons are rehabilitated in each period of the facility's life beginning with t = 3.

(a) Assuming a discount rate of 10%, should the city construct and operate the half-way house?

(b) Now make this decision assuming a discount rate of 16%.

Note: the formula for the present value of program A

$$A_{t(o)} = -C_{t(o)} + \sum_{t=1}^{25} \frac{B_t - C_t}{(1 + r)^t}$$

is to be calculated over all 16 expected years of social benefits generated by each of the eight consecutive groups of people rehabilitated during $3 = t = 10$. The use of Appendix VIII can simplify the computations.

BIBLIOGRAPHY

Ackoff, Russell L. "Toward Quantitative Evaluation of Urban Services," In *Public Expenditures in the Urban Community*, Howard G. Schaller (ed.), pp. 91–117. Washington D.C.: Resources for the Future, 1963.

Baumol, W. J. *Economic Theory and Operations Analysis*, second edition. Englewood Cliffs, N.J.: Prentice-Hall, 1965.

Churchman, C. W., R. L. Ackoff, and E. L. Arnoff. *Introduction to Operations Research*. New York: Wiley, 1957.

Crecine, John P. "Financing the Metropolis." Vol. 4. *Urban Affairs Annual Review*. Beverly Hills, Cal.: Sage Publications, 1970.

Depuit, Jules. "On the Measurement of the Utility of Public Works." In *Readings in Welfare Economics*, K. Arrow and T. Scitovsky (eds.), pp. 225–283. Homewood, Ill. Richard P. Irwin, 1969.

Dorfman, Robert. *Measuring Benefits of Government Investments*. Washington, D.C.: Brooking Institution, 1965.

Eckstein, Otto. *Water Resource Development*. Cambridge, Mass.: Harvard University Press, 1958.

Friedmann, John. "Planning as Innovation: the Chilean Case," *Journal of the American Institute of Planners*, 32 (July 1966), 194–204.

Hadley, G. *Linear Programming*. Reading, Mass.: Addison-Wesley, 1962.

Hanssmann, Fred. *Operations Research Techniques for Capital Investment*. New York: Wiley, 1968.

Haveman, Robert. *The Economics of the Public Sector*. New York: Wiley, 1970.

Haveman, Robert, and Julius Margolis (eds). *Public Expenditures and Policy Analysis*. Chicago: Markham, 1970.

Hirsch, Werner. *The Economics of State and Local Government*. New York: McGraw-Hill, 1970.

Kneese, Allen V., and Blair Bower. *Managing Water Quality: Economics, Technology, Institutions*. Baltimore: Resources for the Future and Johns Hopkins Press, 1968.

Krutilla, John V., and Otto Eckstein. *Multiple Purpose River Development.*
Baltimore: Resources for the Future and Johns Hopkins Press, 1958.

Marglin, Stephen A. *Public Investment Criteria.* Cambridge, Mass.: The
M.I.T. Press, 1967.

Margolis, Julius (ed). *The Public Economy of Urban Communities.* Washington,
D.C.: Resources for the Future, 1965.

Margolis, Julius. "Secondary Benefits, External Economies, and the Justification of Public Investment," *Review of Economics and Statistics, 39*
(1957), 284–91.

Masse, P. *Optimal Investment Decision.* Englewood Cliffs, N.J.: Prentice
Hall, 1962.

Prest, A. R., and R. Turvey. "Cost-Benefit Analysis: A Survey," *Economic
Journal, 75* (1965), 683–735.

Weingartner, Martin. "Capital Budgeting of Interrelated Projects," *Management Science, 12* (March 1966), 485–516.

———. *Mathematical Programming and the Analysis of Capital Budgeting
Problems.* Englewood Cliffs, N.J.: Prentice-Hall, 1963.

William J. Baumol's *Economic Theory and Operations Analysis* is an
invaluable book for explaining many of the complicated concepts in modern
economic analysis. Its clarity makes the reading seem almost easy.

John P. Crecine's *Financing the Metropolis* is a book of readings in which
numerous urban-level issues are discussed from the economist's point-of-view.
The subject material is not limited to financing as the title seems to indicate,
but includes papers on urban and ghetto economic structures, housing,
public services, and PPB.

Robert H. Haveman's *The Economics of the Public Sector* is a nontechnical
but thoroughgoing presentation of this relatively new area of economic
analysis.

Haveman and Margolis' *Public Expenditures and Policy Analysis* is an
excellent collection of articles covering key conceptual and implementation-
related issues in benefit-cost analysis and PPB.

Werner Z. Hirsch's *The Economics of State and Local Government* presents
almost every kind of analytic apparatus available for analyzing almost every
aspect of governmental structure that is involved in the provision of public
services, including the assessment of demand, financing, production, distribution, and budgeting—this volume is complete with lots of capsule summaries of actual applications of the analytic methods.

CHAPTER 7

Program Scheduling

7.1 INTRODUCTION

After we have solved the problems in the planning process discussed in the previous chapters, we must still actually implement the planned project or program. There remains the problem of actually scheduling the components of the program over time, of allocating program resources to the parts, and of keeping track of progress and rescheduling activities as conditions change and feedback accumulates. In community development and urban planning these scheduling problems are often not of the kind where it is possible to determine how they have been done in the past or how they have been handled in other places. We are most often in a situation where what we are going to do has not been done before, at least not in quite the way that we want to do it or under the same conditions and constraints. Therefore, we need a technique to estimate the best way of proceeding. Here, we examine two related techniques for doing this. The first technique is called PERT (Program Evaluation and Review Technique). It is a tool for setting a schedule for a complex project composed of many interrelated tasks and for carefully monitoring progress and periodically readjusting the schedule to efficiently deal with difficulties and unforseen changes in conditions. The second technique is called CPM (Critical Path Method), a technique for discovering the most efficient ways to speed up, or crash, a project. These two techniques are variations on the same theme.

PERT involves the definition of the various tasks that must be executed as part of a project or plan, linking these together in sequences, and then using time estimates for the completion of each task to study the possible ways of reallocating time resources among the tasks to expedite completion of the whole project. CPM works with both time and cost estimates to adjust schedules efficiently under crash conditions. We demonstrate both of these techniques with a typical but small-scale community project, the construction of a community park.

7.2 USING PERT—PROGRAM EVALUATION AND REVIEW TECHNIQUE

Step One

Consider that we now have a decision to implement the construction of the community park. Four community groups each have a limited pool of volunteer workers to contribute to the project. Our problem is to schedule the work. The first step in applying PERT to this problem is to define the tasks or activities that must be executed to build the park. Suppose that we determine that there are four: (1) cleaning out the junk and trash on the park site, (2) collecting usable materials to build playthings, benches, protective fences, and the like, (3) landscaping the site, and (4) building and installing the equipment. We assume that each of the four community groups that are cooperating in this project has agreed to take as its share of the project one of these tasks.

Step Two

The next step in PERT is to sequence these activities, illustrating the functional succession of events over time. To do this, representatives from each of the task groups should meet to work out the task interconnections. Our example is fairly simple. We can see immediately that collection of materials must precede their use in building and that the cleaning out of junk and trash must precede landscaping. We assume, for a while, that no other interdependencies exist. We now have two parallel sequences as are shown in Figure 7.1. Lines, with arrowheads at their ends, like the four in Figure 7.1, represent *activities* in PERT networks. Activities are components of the project that consume resources such as the time and money. The beginnings and endings of activities are called *events*. Every activity has a beginning event and an ending event. Every project as a whole begins with a single beginning event and ends with a single ending event. Activities in

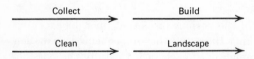

FIGURE 7.1 Four defined activities.

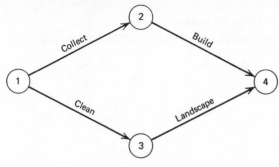

FIGURE 7.2   A sequence of activities and events.

a sequence share events; the ending event for the prior activity is the beginning event for the subsequent activity. The events needed to complete the PERT network for our park are inserted in Figure 7.2. The numbers assigned to events are arbitrary, and their numerical order has no particular significance.

Step Three

Our next step is to get from each of the work groups some estimates of the time that they expect to require to complete their activities. Since a single estimate of the time required is chancy, we also require information about the range of possible times it could take to complete each activity. This will allow us to take account of the probable deviations from expected values a little later. In PERT we require three time estimates for each activity: a, b, and m. They are defined as follows:

$a =$ most optimistic time, the shortest time that could be expected to occur under the best of luck and conditions—having a probability of about one out of 100.

$b =$ most pessimistic time, the longest time that could be required under the worst of luck and conditions—having a probability of about one out of 100.

$m =$ most likely time, the modal time, the time you expect to most often require if the activity were to be executed many many times under randomly varying conditions.

These estimates are then algebraically combined to calculate the mean time that we could expect, or the expected elapsed time for each activity. It is calculated as

$$t_e = \frac{a + 4m + b}{6} \qquad 7.1$$

TABLE 7.1
Time Estimates

Activities	Events		Times			
	Beginning	Ending	a	m	b	t_e
Collect materials	1	2	1	3	5	3
Clean out junk	1	3	1	2	3	2
Build equipment	2	4	2	3	4	3
Landscape	3	4	3	6	9	6

Suppose, then, that we obtain for our park construction activities the time estimates from each group as shown in Table 7.1. The last column contains the expected times calculated by the above formula for t_e. It is only coincidence, in our problem, that t_e values are the same as the m values. This happened because our m values in each case fall exactly half way between a and b. If m was closer to a than to b, or vice versa, the implied distribution of finish times would not be symmetrical and thus the mean (t_e) would not be equal to the mode (m). For example, if we had $a = 1$ week, $m =$ two weeks, and $b =$ nine weeks due to a really far out possibility of a very long delay, say, due to bad weather, then

$$t_e = \frac{1 + 4(2) + 9}{6} = 3$$

Step Four

Our next step is to use these expected times to figure out the earliest expected date at which we can expect to finish each activity and, in turn, finally to arrive at the completion of the project. We begin by assigning the t_e values to the network as in Figure 7.3. We are now going to determine a time T_E for each event, which is the earliest expected time for arriving at each event. We begin with the start event and assign it a $T_E = 0$ and work through from there. The expected time for getting from event 1 to event 2 is $t_e = 3$. Therefore, the earliest expected time for arriving at event 2 is at the end of three weeks. Thus for event 2, $T_E = 3$ (see Figure 7.4). Similarly the earliest expected time for arriving at event 3 is $T_E = 2$, after completion of the cleanup activity in the expected time of two-weeks. We now must determine the T_E for event 4. By the route from event 2 we can say that the earliest expected time of getting to event 2 is three weeks and if we add to that the expected three weeks for building activity, we would expect to arrive at event 4 after six weeks. But, coming at event 4 from event 3, we see that it takes two weeks to arrive at event 3 and, when we add to this the

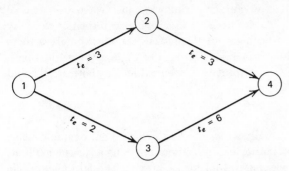

FIGURE 7.3   The network with t_e values assigned.

six expected weeks to complete landscaping, we arrive at event 4 at the end of eight weeks. The question now is, which date constitutes the earliest expected date for completion of the whole project, which is what event 4 is by definition. The answer is $T_E = 8$ because the lower path, cleanup, and landscaping, would not be finished after the six-week date. We can state a general rule for this choice which is worth remembering. When calculating the earliest expected arrival date (T_E) for an event and faced with more than one route to that event and thus more than one possible value for T_E, you always assign the latest of the alternatives. This assures you that all, even the most time consuming, of the prerequisites to the event can be expected to be completed. See our calculations in Figure 7.4.

We can already see in this simple network that there is a critical path. The term, critical path, is used in both PERT and CPM. It is the longest one through the network, from event 1 to event 3 to event 4, that determines the earliest expected completion date for the whole project. The path is critical because any delays along it will delay the whole project and require a change

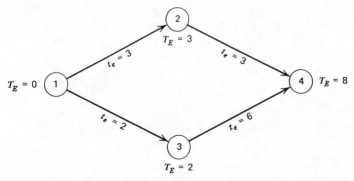

FIGURE 7.4   The network with earliest expected arrival times T_E.

in the whole schedule. The advantage of knowing just where the critical path lies is that progress on those critical path activities can then be carefully monitored while slack in other parts of the system can absorb delays there without upsetting the whole schedule. This idea of finding the critical path and doing various things to control it is the central idea in both PERT and CPM.

Step Five

The critical path is not usually so easy to find as it is in our example. Thus PERT offers a way of systematically finding it and making adjustments to it. Our next step in this process is to find for each event the latest allowable time (T_L) for leaving an event and still not delaying the project completion. To do this, we work backward through the network, first setting a scheduled completion date for the whole project. In our example we might set this at eight weeks, since that is our earliest expected completion time. If we were under pressure to finish sooner, we would set it earlier. We set T_L for the end event equal to this schedule date of eight weeks. See Figure 7.5. We now work backward by subtracting t_e values from T_L values. The T_L for event 2 equals the T_L of 8 minus the t_e of three weeks for building; that is, if the latest allowable time for being at event 4 is eight weeks and we expect it to take three weeks to get from event 2 to event 4, then the latest allowable time for leaving event 2 and still making it to event 4 on time is five weeks $(8 - 3)$. Thus $T_{L2} = 5$.

By the same reasoning the latest allowable time for leaving event 3 and expecting to make it to event 4 on time is two weeks $(8 - 6)$. Thus $T_{L3} = 2$.

To get the correct T_L for event 1 again involves a choice. Coming from event 2, we get $T_{L2} - t_{e1-2} = T_{L1} = 5 - 3 = 2$. But coming from the other path, we get $T_{L3} - t_{e1-3} = T'_{L1} = 2 - 2 = 0$. Which should we

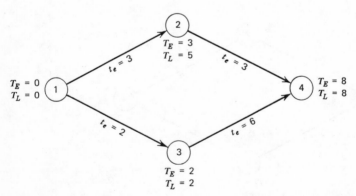

FIGURE 7.5 The network with latest allowable times for leaving T_L.

choose? The correct one is $T_{L1} = 0$ because if we delay two weeks from now (0) before starting any activities, we cannot expect to finish eight weeks from now. But if we start now, we can expect to make it. Thus the latest allowable time for starting is now. Again this process gives rise to a rule worth remembering. When we are calculating the latest allowable leaving time, T_L, for an event and are faced with more than one possible route for leaving and thus alternative values for T_L, we always assign the earliest of the alternatives. This assures us that there will be enough time left, subsequent to that event, to complete the whole project on time. These computations give us Figure 7.5.

Step Six

We are now in a position to define the critical path in very precise terms. We do this first by defining *slack* time. Slack time is the amount of play or free time associated with an event and is calculated as the difference between the earliest expected time for arriving at an event and the latest allowable time for leaving it. Slack time, then, for each event is $T_L - T_E$. Slack times for our project are calculated as in Table 7.2 and are displayed in Figure 7.6.

Figure 7.6 shows the critical path for this network, the longest path through, or the path with the least or lowest slack time. Slack time may be positive, zero, or negative. The two weeks of slack time associated with event 2 imply that either the collecting or the building activity could take two weeks longer than expected and still not delay the completion, on time, of the whole park.

We have now clearly established the project-wide implications of the original time estimates. But time estimates contain the possibility of variation. We know that the 8-week estimate for the final event could be off. It would be nice to be able to say, for example, how probable it is that the

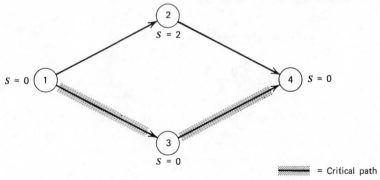

FIGURE 7.6　Network with slack times and critical path.

TABLE 7.2
Calculation of Slack Times

Event	T_L	$-$	T_E	$=$	S (Slack)
1	0		0		0
2	5		3		2
3	2		2		0
4	8		8		0

project would take more than 10 weeks, or how confident we can be that we will not vary more than 2 weeks in either direction from the expected completion date.

Step Seven

We can calculate these probabilities. Using the estimates of a and b for each activity, we estimate the standard deviation of each activity on the critical path—a measure of how much, on the average (if the project were executed many times), deviation from expected time, t_e, would be. The standard deviation is estimated as one sixth of the range or

$$\sigma_{i-j} = \frac{b_{i-j} - a_{i-j}}{6} \qquad \text{where } i\text{'s and } j\text{'s are events} \qquad 7.2$$

These standard deviations can then be pooled, in the manner of equation 7.3 below, to get a standard deviation of the final event by taking the square root of the sum of squared standard deviations of all activities on the critical path. In Figure 7.6 activities 1 to 3 and 3 to 4 were on the critical path. The probability calculations would be as follows.

$$\sigma_{1-3} = \frac{3 - 1}{6} = \frac{2}{6} = .33$$

$$\sigma_{3-4} = \frac{9 - 3}{6} = \frac{6}{6} = 1.00$$

$$\sigma T_{E4} = \sqrt{(\sigma_{1-3})^2 + (\sigma_{3-4})^2} \qquad 7.3$$

$$= \sqrt{(.33)^2 + (1.00)^2}$$

$$= \sqrt{.11 + 1.00}$$

$$\sigma T_{E4} = 1.05$$

To interpret these in terms of confidence limits or probabilities the following assumptions are made:

1. For 68% of the time the project will be completed somewhere within plus or minus *one* standard deviation from the earliest expected completion time. Thus with a $T_{E4} = 8$ weeks, we can be 68% confident that, in fact, it will be completed somewhere between 6.95 weeks and 9.05 weeks.
2. For 95% of the time the project will be completed somewhere within plus or minus *two* standard deviations from the earliest expected completion time of the final event. Thus we can be 95% confident that our park will be completed no sooner than in 5.90 weeks and no later than 10.10 weeks.
3. For 99.7% of the time the project will be completed somewhere within plus or minus *three* standard deviations from the earliest expected completion time of the final event. Thus we can be 99.7% confident that the project will be completed somewhere between 4.85 and 11.15 weeks.

In effect, these assumptions amount to assuming that the distribution of completion times approximates a "normal" bell-shaped curve.

Step Eight

Now the point of going to all this trouble is that we may decide that being 99.7% sure of finishing within 11.15 weeks is not good enough. We may feel that with warm weather coming soon we would like to speed things up so that the park can be available when it is most needed. This is typically accomplished in PERT analysis by shifting the allocation of resources from slack activities to activities on the critical path. We could complete our park more quickly, for example, if we could get some of the people who are in the group that is going to build equipment to put their time into landscaping instead. We then might get some revised time estimates like those in Table 7.3.

Recalculating the T_E and T_L values and slack times with these revised data gives us the result of Figure 7.7. We can see that the effect of this replanning of resources is that all paths have become critical and that the

TABLE 7.3
Revised Time Estimates

Activity	Beginning	Ending	a	m	b	t_e	σ
Collect materials	1	2	1	3	5	3	.66
Cleanup	1	3	1	2	3	2	.33
Build (revised)	2	4	3	4	5	4	.33
Landscape (revised)	3	4	2	5	8	5	1.00

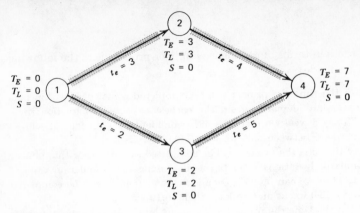

FIGURE 7.7   Network analysis based on revised times.

T_{E4} now is reduced to seven weeks rather than eight weeks. Meanwhile what has happened to our probability estimates? If we take the critical path of events 1, 3, and 4 we get

$$\sigma T_{E4} = \sqrt{(.33)^2 + (1.00)^2} = 1.05$$

That is the same as we had before replanning. If we take the other critical path through events 1, 2, and 4 we get

$$\sigma T'_{E4} = \sqrt{(.33)^2 + (.66)^2} = .74$$

Which calculation should we accept as the proper estimate of the standard deviation of the project? We must choose the larger, as it represents the outside limits of risk. It should be clear that the standard deviation of the project easily could have changed as a result of the time reallocation if the range between a and b changed as a result of the reallocation in either the building activity or the landscaping activity.

What we have done to schedule the implementation of the park plan may seem an incredibly needless complication. In fact, it was. Many people could probably have visualized much of this work in their heads. We chose such a simple problem purposely so that the technique could be learned on a problem where the result could be intuitively verified. Precisely the same procedures can be applied to much larger problems, with hundreds of activities and complex linkages. We would simply follow the rules we have set out. We had only four community groups working together for a few weeks. The first major use of PERT was in the 1950s in the United States Navy's Polaris submarine construction project with 250 prime contractors and more than 9000 subcontracts.

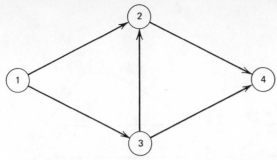

FIGURE 7.8   Network with a dummy activity added.

7.3   DUMMY ACTIVITIES

We may have considered that in the construction of the park it would be desirable not only to collect all materials before building but also to have all of the junk cleaned out so that some construction could take place in its final position, for instance, fences, paving, and the like. This would be expressed in the network as an activity arrow between events 3 and 2, as in Figure 7.8.

Activity 3-2 is really not an activity, it is simply an expression of the precedence of activities. It consumes no resources. Links such as this are called dummy activities and always have a $t_e = 0$. Aside from the designation of precedence, dummy activities are also used in the following way. Suppose we have two parallel activities that have the same beginning event and also share the same ending event, as with activities A and B in Figure 7.9. Instead of working with the verbal descriptions of activities, we find it more convenient to refer to an activity only by the numbers of its beginning and ending events. This is especially necessary in computerized analysis. But this poses a problem because it is impossible to differentiate A from B in Figure 7.9. They would both be referred to as 1-2. To solve this dilemma a dummy activity is inserted arbitrarily to supply an additional number. Figure 7.10 shows four different ways, all equally valid, in which this could be done to alter Figure 7.9. Note that, as we pointed out previously, the numbers assigned to events are quite arbitrary and do not need to represent a temporal sequence.

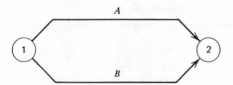

FIGURE 7.9   Two parallel activities.

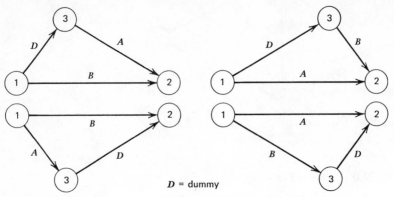

FIGURE 7.10 Four alternative configurations using a dummy.

7.4 CPM—CRITICAL PATH METHOD

Step One

The purpose of the critical path method is to use estimates of activity costs, as well as time estimates, to find the most efficient way of crashing a project—completing it in the minimum feasible time with no costs spared, but also none wasted. Such a solution is called the optimal solution. The estimates needed to conduct this analysis are, for each activity, a normal time and a crash time and a normal cost and a crash cost. We demonstrate CPM by using our park problem, but this time we include the dummy activity inserted in the previous section. We use as our basic data those given in Table 7.4.

TABLE 7.4
Time and Cost Data for Five Activities

Activity	Begins	Ends	Times (in weeks)		Costs (in dollars)	
			Crash	Normal	Crash	Normal
Collect	1	2	1	3	200	50
Cleanup	1	3	$\frac{1}{2}$	2	100	0
Build	2	4	2	3	300	100
Dummy	3	2	0	0	0	0
Landscape	3	4	1	6	150	0

TABLE 7.5
Costs per Week to Crash

Activity	Weeks Saved by Crashing	Added Funds Needed To Crash (in dollars)	Cost per Week To Crash (in dollars)
Collect	2	150	75
Cleanup	1½	100	67
Build	1	200	200
Dummy	0	0	0
Landscape	5	150	30

Step Two

The next step is to calculate for each activity what it would cost, over and above normal cost, to crash it; how much time, over and above normal, would be saved on each activity if it were crashed; and then, by dividing the added cost by the time saved, we derive a cost per week to crash for each activity. The CPM uses this cost per week value to systematically crash the project, one activity at a time, cheapest first, to sequentially find the least cost, minimum time schedule. Our cost per week estimates are derived in Table 7.5 based entirely on the data in Table 7.4.

Step Three

The next step is to construct the project network and, by using normal times as t_e values, calculate values for T_E, T_L, Slack, and then determine the critical path, just as in the PERT routine. This gives us the result shown in Figure 7.11.

Step Four

The critical path is from event 1, through event 3 to event 4. To shorten completion time for the project as a whole, we know that we must shorten the critical path because it, by definition, is the longest path through the project. That means, in this case, that we must crash either the cleanup activity or the landscaping activity. (Crashing in our park construction means using and paying for professional services rather than using local volunteers). Which one should we crash? The cheapest one. Our reasoning goes like this. Why pay $67 to gain a week's time (the cost of crashing cleanup) when you can get the same time for only $30 (the cost per week of crashing the landscaping)? Thus we choose to crash landscaping first. This gives us a new time estimate for that activity.

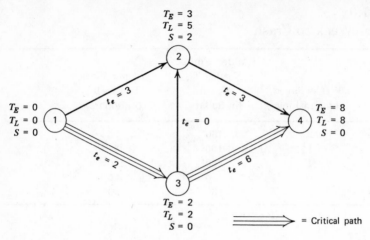

FIGURE 7.11   Initial critical path analysis.

Step Five

We now recalculate the network, using this new time estimate to get a new critical path as is shown in Figure 7.12.

Notice that although we reduced the time for landscaping by five weeks, the total project time is only reduced by two weeks. Why not five weeks? Because as we crashed the landscaping activity, the critical path shifted on us. As shown in Figure 7.12, it now runs from event 1 through event 2 to event 4.

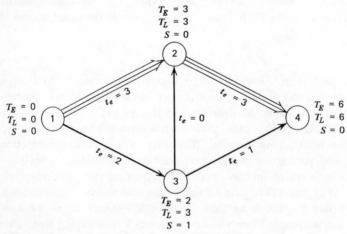

FIGURE 7.12   Second critical path analysis.

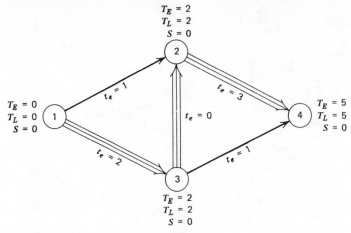

FIGURE 7.13   Third critical path analysis.

Step Six

The next move is now to reduce total completion time further by reducing the length of the new critical path. We do this by crashing the least expensive activity on the critical path again. Collection, according to Table 7.5, costs $75 per week and building activities cost $200 per week. Thus we crash the collection activity and recalculate the new critical path (it shifted again) as in Figure 7.13.

Step Seven

Again we choose to crash that activity on the new critical path that gives us a shortened total completion time at the lowest cost. This time it is the cleaning activity at $67 per week, reducing time for that task to one-half week. Substituting the new time and recalculating the critical path gives us Figure 7.14.

Step Eight

Now the critical path is back up on the path from event 1 through event 2 to event 4. We want to crash further but the collection activity was previously crashed. Thus the only remaining choice is to crash the building activity down to two weeks. This is done in Figure 7.15.

But now the critical path is still through events 1, 2, and 4. This time, however, there are no remaining uncrashed activities on it. This then constitutes the shortest possible critical path for the project and thus represents minimum feasible project completion time.

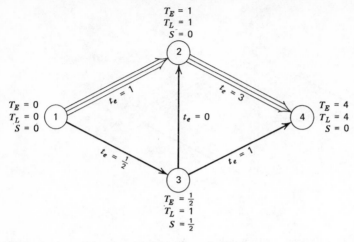

FIGURE 7.14   Fourth critical path analysis.

Step Nine

Now notice that slack time exists at event 3. This means that we have paid to crash an activity further than was necessary. Our next step then is to ease up on the crashed activities that do not lie on the critical path, easing up just to the point that they become critical. This will yield a project schedule of minimum feasible length at minimum expense. Thus we must now work through the noncritical parts of the schedule, easing up wherever we

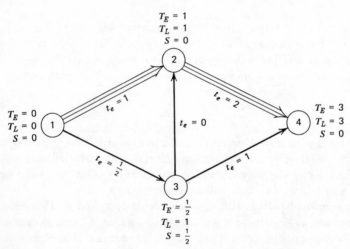

FIGURE 7.15   Fifth critical path analysis: all crashed.

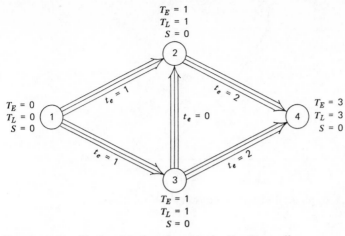

$T_E = 1$
$T_L = 1$
$S = 0$

$T_E = 0$
$T_L = 0$
$S = 0$

$T_E = 3$
$T_L = 3$
$S = 0$

$t_e = 1$

$t_e = 2$

$t_e = 0$

$t_e = 1$

$t_e = 2$

$T_E = 1$
$T_L = 1$
$S = 0$

FIGURE 7.16   Sixth critical path analysis: "optimum."

can. First we study the alternatives and their costs. Easing up on cleanup activity can save us $67 per week. Easing up on landscaping can save us $30 per week. Naturally, since we prefer to save more money rather than less, we ease up on cleanup activities as much as possible first. The maximum amount that cleanup can be lengthened is one-half week, at which point it becomes critical. Next, landscaping can be lengthened by one more week, at which it, too, becomes critical. The resulting schedule with all activities critical is shown in Figure 7.16.

One might wonder if this is not the long way round to get to this solution. Would it not be more direct simply to begin the analysis by crashing all activities, determining the critical path, and then easing up on the non-critical activities thereby eliminating several tedious steps? That would be a more sensible routine if only we could be sure of two things: (1) that the only schedule we are interested in is the quickest one—which is to say that we are confident that we will be able to bear the expense of all of the crashes needed to reach that point; and (2) that we are reasonably sure that the optimum solution is closer to the condition where all activities are crashed than it is to the condition where all activities are normal. Because of the considerable uncertainty of both of these assumptions, especially where projects are large and expensive, the normally prescribed routine of analysis described with our park example in detail is the preferred method. This allows the schedule planner to offer the decision maker a range of completion times from the very minimum to the completely normal and the costs associated with each alternative.

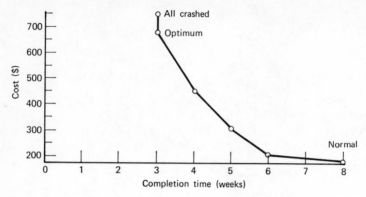

FIGURE 7.17   A graph of alternative solution times and costs.

Step Ten

To get the costs associated with each of the intermediate steps one would have to, at each juncture, uncrash those activities not on the critical path up to the point where they all become critical, as was done for Figure 7.16, to determine the minimum cost associated with each intermediate step. In that manner we are able to determine from Table 7.5 and Figures 7.11 to 7.16 the costs that are displayed in Table 7.6 and are graphed in Figure 7.17.

TABLE 7.6
Time and Cost Data for Alternative Critical Path Solutions

Completion Times of Alternative Solutions (in weeks)	Minimum Cost (after Uncrashing) (in dollars)	Alternative	Figure No.
Normal = 8	150	Initial	7.11
6	210	Second	7.12
5	315	Third	7.13
4	457	Fourth	7.14
Optimal = 3	687	Sixth	7.16
All crashed = 3	750	Fifth	7.15

7.5   THE ASSUMPTIONS OF PERT AND CPM

The fundamental assumption of both PERT and CPM is that the project is definable by activities that have distinct beginning and ending points. A related assumption is that there is significant temporal interdependence among the activities. Without this, there would be little need for the techniques.

Another set of assumptions pertaining to PERT are those about the underlying probability distributions of time estimates. The formulas used to calculate t_e values and standard deviations assume a beta distribution of events while the probability criteria used to interpret confidence levels assume a normal distribution. The theory of PERT is ambiguous about these distributions.[1]

A third major assumption of PERT is that resources are capable of being shifted from one activity to another. This is often not possible and must be carefully considered in network replanning. The classic example occurs in housebuilding where an excess of plumbers cannot be shifted to do the work of electricians, and vice versa. In a public project requiring the cooperation of, say, the federal office of Housing and Urban Development in Washington, D.C. and the local government of a small town in Tennessee it is virtually impossible to shift personnel from one agency's activities to those of others.

The additional assumptions required to execute CPM are strikingly similar to those made in the simpler forms of cost-effectiveness and then relaxed later in Chapter 6. This should not be too surprising, since this present Chapter and Chapter 6 deal with costs allocated over time. There is another link between these methods that should be mentioned. The technique of linear programming used in budget allocation problems in Chapter 6 can also be applied to project scheduling with limited resources.[2] One of these assumptions is that there is no lumpiness in the activities, such that, for example, it is practically feasible to execute an activity at any speed in between normal and crash time. Similarly, we assume that cost is a direct linear function of time. Consider the following example in which these assumptions would not hold true. Suppose the activity under consideration involved many complex statistical calculations. Doing them on a desk calculator might take five weeks, but on an electronic computer might only take four hours of preparation and five minutes of machine time. But there is no feasible in-between time. This, incidentally, is also a case where crash cost might be less than normal cost, not greater.

Another assumption made in CPM is that there is no discounting of costs over time. It could be introduced, however, using the techniques of Chapter 6.

---

[1] For an examination of the implications of these distribution assumptions see K. R. MacCrimmon, and C. A. Ryavec, "Analytical Study of the PERT Assumptions," *Operations Research, 12* (January 1964), 16–37.

[2] For a presentation of linear programming applied to scheduling problems see Jerome D. Wiest, and Ferdinand K. Levy, *A Management Guide to PERT/CPM* (Englewood Cliffs, N.J.: Prentice-Hall, 1969).

Finally we assume no indirect costs or time benefits are entering the calculations.

We point out one more parallel to Chapter 6. Similar to the way in which incidence groups were treated there is the consideration of different task groups in PERT and CPM. Different sets of actors, agencies, and organizations are very frequently distinguished in both techniques. The techniques, in fact, are instruments of management coordination designed in large part for this very purpose.

PROBLEMS

1. Draw and label the networks for the following three projects. No activity lines should cross. It will probably be necessary to do rough sketches before preparing the final networks.

(A) Project I

ACTIVITY	BEGINNING EVENT	ENDING EVENT
A	1	2
B	1	3
C	2	4
D	3	4
E	2	5
F	4	5

(B) Project II

ACTIVITY	BEGINNING EVENT	ENDING EVENT
A	1	2
B	1	3
C	2	4
D	3	4
E	3	5
F	4	5
G	2	6
H	4	7
I	5	7
J	6	7
K	6	8
L	5	9
M	7	9
N	8	9

(C)   Project III

ACTIVITY	BEGINNING EVENT	ENDING EVENT
A	0	15
B	15	11
C	11	12
D	12	14
E	14	3
F	12	2
G	2	3
H	0	11
I	0	4
J	4	7
K	7	8
L	8	6
M	6	3
N	12	13
O	13	3
P	15	12
Q	4	5
R	5	6
S	0	1
T	1	2
U	0	9
V	9	10
W	10	6

2. In the network below:
   (a) Which events are on the critical path?
   (b) Which of the following represent reallocations of resources among activities that may get the project completed sooner.

---

   (1) transfer of resources from G to B
   (2) transfer of resources from D to H
   (3) transfer of resources from H to F
   (4) transfer of resources from C to E
   (5) transfer of resources from F to A
   (6) transfer of resources from G to H

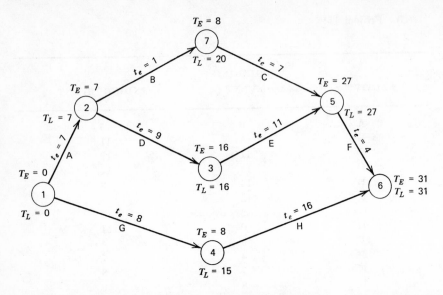

3. Use the following data on two planning projects, develop the needed additional information, and apply CPM to the networks, deriving the full range of completion times and the appropriate costs associated with each alternative. Show all of the steps and standard computations of the technique. Finally, explain how the results might be useful to a project administrator.

ACTIVITY	BEGINS	ENDS	CRASH TIME (IN WEEKS)	NORMAL TIME (IN WEEKS)	CRASH COST	NORMAL COST
A	1	2	1	2	$200	$100
B	2	3	4	6	250	200
C	1	3	1	3	140	100

ACTIVITY	BEGINS	ENDS	CRASH TIME (IN WEEKS)	NORMAL TIME (IN WEEKS)	CRASH COST	NORMAL COST
X	1	2	2	4	$150	$100
Y	2	3	0	0	0	0
Z	1	3	1	3	200	100

4. Consider the following data set:

ACTIVITY	BEGINS	ENDS	a	m	b
A	1	2	3	9	12
B	1	3	8	10	16
C	2	4	1	6	8
D	2	5	3	6	10
E	3	5	1	5	10
F	4	6	4	6	8
G	5	6	5	13	15

Sequence the events into a network, compute t_e, T_E, T_L, Slack time, and the standard deviation of the critical path. Interpret the results.

5. For the same project, substitute the following time and cost data for CPM analysis.

ACTIVITY	CRASH TIME	NORMAL TIME	CRASH COST	NORMAL COST
A	3	8	$6000	$3000
B	8	12	10000	8000
C	1	3	10000	7000
D	3	6	9000	3000
E	1	6	6000	4000
F	4	7	6000	3900
G	5	11	16000	10600

Apply the critical Path Method including a graphic plot of the alternative time and cost data.

6. Consider a situation where you might be running several independent and simultaneous projects, wanting to most efficiently spend your "crash" funds among the several projects. How might you employ critical path method to help you manage this problem?

BIBLIOGRAPHY

Apgar, Mahlon, IV. "Systems Management in the New City: Columbia, Maryland," in Richard S. Rosenbloom and John R. Russell. *New Tools for Urban Management*. Boston: Graduate School of Business Administration, Harvard University, 1971.

Archibald, Russell D., and Richard L. Villoria. *Network-Based Management Systems (PERT/CPM)*. New York: Wiley, 1968.

Brennan, Maribeth. *PERT and CPM: A Selected Bibliography*, Exchange Bibliography 53. Monticello, Ill.: Council of Planning Librarians, June 1968.

Candueb, Isadore. "Critical Path Method Can Be Tool for Effective, Efficient Execution of Renewal Projects," *Journal of Housing*, *23* (October 1966), 508–510.

Federal Electric Corporation. *A Programmed Introduction to PERT*. New York: Wiley, 1967.

George, Stephen, Jr., and Clyde E. Pyers. "The Application of Critical Path Programming to Large-Scale Transportation Studies," *Highway Research News*, *12* (June 1966), 51–66.

Levin, Richard I., and Charles A. Kirkpatrick. *Planning and Control With PERT/CPM*. New York: McGraw-Hill, 1966.

Logan, George H. "A Suggested Approach to Sophisticated Problem Solving for Cities," *Western City*, *43* (August 1967), 19–22 *passim*.

MacCrimmon, K. R., and C. A. Ryavec. "Analytical Study of the PERT Assumptions," *Operations Research*, *12* (January 1964), 16–37.

Merten, Walter. "PERT (Program Evaluation and Review Technique) and Planning for Health Programs," *Public Health Reports*, *81* (May 1966), 449–454.

Ontario Department of Municipal Affairs, Community Planning Branch. *Network Diagrams and the Official Plan*. Toronto: Ontario Department of Community Affairs, 1968.

Price, W. L. *Graphs and Networks*. Princeton, N.J.: Auerbach, 1971.

Roberts, Paul O. "Selecting and Staging Additions to a Transport Network," in John R. Meyer and Mahlon R. Straszheim. *Pricing and Project Evaluation*. Washington, D.C.: The Brookings Institution, 1971, pp. 251–275.

Rogers, Andrei. *Matrix Methods in Urban and Regional Analysis*. San Francisco: Holden-Day, 1971, Chapter 6.

Vaughan, Richard D. "Use of the Critical Path Method in a Pollution Control Program," *Journal of the American Water Works Association*, (September 1964), 1092–96.

Vazsonyi, Andrew. "L'Histoire de Grandeur et la Décadence de la Méthode PERT," *Management Science*, *16* (April 1970), B-449-455.

Wiest, Jerome D., and Ferdinand K. Levy. *A Management Guide to PERT/CPM*. Englewood Cliffs, N.J.: Prentice-Hall, 1969.

Woodgate, H. S. *Planning by Network*, second edition. London: Business Publications Ltd., 1967.

Five items in this bibliography are about general management scheduling techniques. The ones by the Federal Electric Corporation and by Levin and Kirkpatrick are the easiest. Woodgate is at an intermediate level. Archibald and Villoria and the book by Wiest and Levy are more advanced.

The little book by Price and the article by MacCrimmon and Ryavec are quite technical examinations of the theory underlying scheduling techniques.

Applications in the area of urban planning are discussed in Apgar, Candueb, George and Pyers, Logan, Merten, Roberts, Vaughan, and Rogers. Additional applications are beautifully illustrated in the publication of the Ontario Department of Municipal Affairs. Applications also can be found in the bibliography by Brennan.

Vazsonyi's paper is in English and is a candid and humorous treat that should not be missed.

PART II
Models

CHAPTER 8

Projecting Population

8.1 INTRODUCTION

This chapter is about techniques for estimating the growth or decline of populations over time. By population, we mean the number of people living in a place: a city, state, neighborhood, or the like. In the first part of this chapter we discuss simple projection techniques for estimating changes in total population size over time. In the second part we consider projection models that deal with components of the population separately. We do not attempt to survey comprehensively the field of population studies. The purpose of this chapter is to introduce the fundamental models, and to teach the mathematics and assumptions on which they operate, introducing these topics in a practical context.

We will use the terms projection, prediction, and forecasting interchangeably, although philosophical distinctions can be made. What all these terms signify are reasoned quantitative techniques for finding estimates of future population levels that can be used as the basis for plans and policy decisions. Knowledge about past populations and assumptions about future populations are fundamental to planning decisions in every aspect of community life.

8.2 SIMPLE POPULATION FORECASTING MODELS

The simple population forecasting models study past trends of growth and extrapolate these trends into the future. We present the six most frequently used elementary models. They are: (1) the linear model, (2) the exponential, (3) the modified exponential, (4) the Gompertz curve, (5) the comparative method, and (6) the ratio method. We first describe each of these techniques and then discuss some techniques for fitting them into practice with real data.

8.2.1 THE LINEAR (STRAIGHT-LINE) MODEL

This model is used when the population of the area being studied has exhibited a history of nearly equal absolute increments of population growth per year, decade, or other unit of time, and the assumption is made that this pattern will persist into the future. Mathematically this is the same linear model that we used in correlation and regression analysis of the general form:

$$\text{pop } Y = a + bX \quad \overset{\text{base pop}}{} \overset{\text{time}}{}$$

Here, however, the dependent variable is population and the independent variable is time; the b coefficient is the average annual increment of growth; and a is the population at the base year from which we are extrapolating. Our linear forecasting model looks like this:

$$P_{t+n} = P_t + b(n) \qquad\qquad 8.1$$

where

$P =$ population

$t =$ a time index (for instance, years, or decades)

$P_{t+n} =$ population (n) units of time from (t)

$n =$ number of units of time (in years, decades, etc.)

$b =$ average growth increment per unit of time.

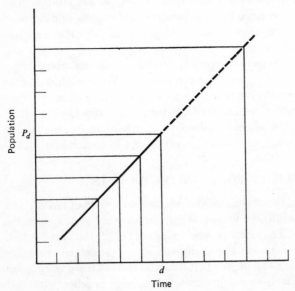

FIGURE 8.1 The linear model.

Algebraically we can define this as

$$b = \frac{\sum\limits_{t=2}^{d} (P_t - P_{t-1})}{m}$$

8.2

where

$m =$ the number of historical intervals over which the average is calculated

$d =$ the date of the latest data in the historical record being analyzed.

Graphically it looks like Figure 8.1. Suppose, then, that for our community we had the following historical information:

POPULATION	TIME	
	YEAR (t)	
6,000	1967 (1)	
11,000	1968 (2)	
16,000	1969 (3)	
21,000	1970 (4)	

There are two simple ways we could approach the data to fit a straight line to them. One is simply to graph the data as in Figure 8.2, to observe that, indeed, the historical trend is linear (not significantly curved or irregular), and to take a straightedge and a pencil and to extend the line as the dotted segment has been extended in Figure 8.2. The other approach would be to

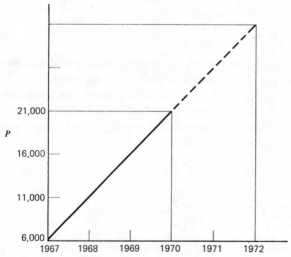

FIGURE 8.2   A graphic linear projection.

calculate the differences in absolute growth for the historical period to determine if they were equal, or nearly so, as below:

Absolute Annual Change

$$P_{68} - P_{67} = 5000$$

$$P_{69} - P_{68} = 5000$$

$$P_{70} - P_{69} = 5000$$

such that

$$b = \frac{\sum\limits_{t=1968}^{1970} (P_t - P_{t-1})}{m}$$

$$b = \frac{(P_{1970} - P_{1969}) + (P_{1969} - P_{1968}) + (P_{1968} - P_{1967})}{3}$$

$$b = \frac{5000 + 5000 + 5000}{3}$$

$$b = \frac{15,000}{3} = 5000$$

Thus we can now project from 1970 to 1972 using the formula as

$$P_{t+2} = P_t + 5000(n)$$

$$P_{1970+2} = P_{1970} + 5000(2)$$

$$P_{1972} = 21,000 + 10,000 = 31,000$$

8.2.2 EXPONENTIAL CURVE PROJECTIONS – Geometric

Thomas Malthus, an English scholar whom everyone talks about and few have read, claimed that population tends to grow at a geometric rate. It compounds, like interest on money. The exponential curve portrays this idea, growth at a constant rate or percentage, which means that with each unit of time, the absolute addition to population gets bigger and bigger and bigger. The projection model takes this form:

where

$$P_{t+n} = P_t(1 + r)^n \qquad\qquad 8.3$$

$$r = \frac{1}{m} \sum_{t=2}^{d} \frac{P_t - P_{t-1}}{P_{t-1}} \qquad\qquad 8.4$$

and: P, t, and m are defined as in equations 8.1 and 8.2. This is shown graphically in Figure 8.3. In this case we might have historical data that

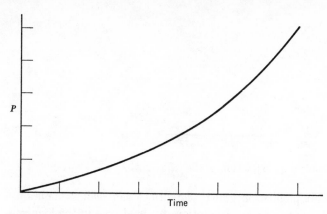

FIGURE 8.3   The exponential curve ($r = .3$).

reads as follows:

POPULATION	YEAR
10,000	1967
13,000	1968
16,900	1969
21,970	1970

The graphic solution to this projection is illustrated in Figure 8.4. The rate of change (r) can be estimated by studying the percentage increases each time period as

$$\frac{P_{1968} - P_{1967}}{P_{1967}} = \frac{13,000 - 10,000}{10,000} = .30$$

$$\frac{P_{1969} - P_{1968}}{P_{1968}} = \frac{16,900 - 13,000}{13,000} = .30$$

$$\frac{P_{1970} - P_{1969}}{P_{1969}} = \frac{21,970 - 16,900}{16,900} = .30$$

We can then use the mathematical formula to project from 1970 to 1972 as

$$P_{t+2} = P_t(1 + .30)^2$$
$$P_{1972} = P_{1970}(1.69)$$
$$P_{1972} = 21,970(1.69)$$
$$P_{1972} = 37,129$$

The proof that this form of prediction equation expresses a constant percentage increase is exactly the same as that used in Chapter 6 to derive the formula for interest and discount rates. It should be clear from the graph

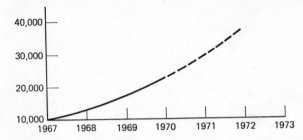

FIGURE 8.4 A graphic approximation of the exponential.

of this function that population growth conditions can seldom maintain a situation where this exponential assumption can hold true in the long run. It leads to scarry predictions of fatal overpopulation in the very long run.

8.2.3 THE MODIFIED EXPONENTIAL - Exponential

A sometimes more reasonable curve of the exponential family of mathematical functions is one with a declining pace of growth approaching an upper capacity limit. Graphically the curve looks like that shown in Figure 8.5.[1] The prediction formula states that the population in time $t + n$ is found by taking the maximum limit, a capacity (K), and subtracting from it some portion, $(v)^n$, of the unused capacity, $(K - P_t)$. The further in time one projects, the smaller the amount that is subtracted from K, expressing

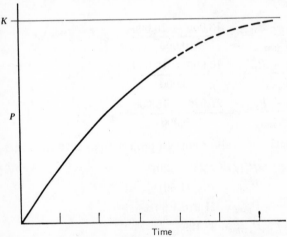

FIGURE 8.5 The modified exponential.

[1] See also Frederick E. Croxton, Dudley J. Cowden, and Sidney Klein, *Applied General Statistics* (Englewood Cliffs, N.J.: Prentice-Hall, 1967), pp. 262–267.

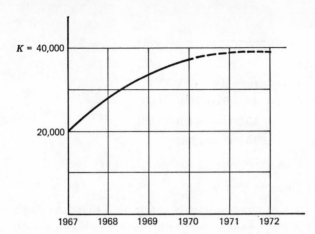

FIGURE 8.6   The plot of solution to the modified exponential.

this approach of P to K in a manner where average annual percentage of unused capacity (e.g. vacant land) that does not get used up in each successive time period is a constant, (v). The formula is

$$P_{t+n} = K - [(K - P_t)(v)^n]$$ 8.5

where
$$K = \text{upper limit of capacity}$$

and
$$v = \frac{1}{m} \sum_{t=2}^{d} \frac{K - P_t}{K - P_{t-1}}$$ 8.6

The following data can be graphically or mathematically projected as shown in Figure 8.6 and estimated for projection below:

POPULATION	TIME YEAR (t)
20,000	1967 (1)
28,000	1968 (2)
32,800	1969 (3)
35,600	1970 (4)

$$\frac{K - P_{1968}}{K - P_{1967}} = \frac{40,000 - 28,000}{40,000 - 20,000} = \frac{12,000}{20,000} = .60$$

$$\frac{K - P_{1969}}{K - P_{1968}} = \frac{40,000 - 32,800}{40,000 - 28,000} = \frac{7200}{12,000} = .60$$

$$\frac{K - P_{1970}}{K - P_{1969}} = \frac{40,000 - 35,600}{40,000 - 32,800} = \frac{4400}{7200} = .60$$

Then

$$v = \frac{.60 + .60 + .60}{3} = .60$$

and

$$P_{t+2} = K - [(K - P_t)(v)^2]$$
$$P_{1972} = 40,000 - [(4,400)(.60)^2]$$
$$= 40,000 - [(4,400)(.36)]$$
$$= 40,000 - 1,584$$
$$P_{1972} = 38,416$$

8.2.4 THE GOMPERTZ GROWTH CURVE

This curve is also of the exponential family and is an S-shape, having a lower limit and an upper limit, K. It is shown in Figure 8.7 with its general algebraic formula in equation 8.7.

$$P_{t+n} = Ka^{b^n} \qquad\qquad 8.7$$

The assumptions implied are that growth begins slowly with increasing momentum until it reaches an inflection point and begins to increase in growth increments of decreasing size. We do not carry this more complex formula into a numerical example.[2]

8.2.5 THE COMPARATIVE METHOD

The above four techniques each assume that future growth is predictable on the basis of knowledge of past growth trends of an area, a very tenuous

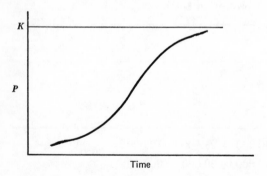

FIGURE 8.7   The Gompertz curve.

[2] For further discussion see Carrothers and Isard, Chapter 2, in Walter Isard, *Methods of Regional Analysis* (New York: The Technology Press of M.I.T. and Wiley, 1960); and Croxton, Cowden, and Klein, pp. 267–282.

assumption in many cases. The comparative technique asserts that future growth of an area, call it area C, is predictable on the basis of historical trends in a different area, call it area D. The latter area is called the pattern area. We assume that the origins of D and C are similar and that their histories form a similar pattern but that D is ahead of C and thus can be used as a pattern to predict the future of C. The idea is seldom expressed mathematically, but it could take the form

$$_CP_{t+n} = {}_DP_{(t-10)+n}$$

suggesting a 10-year lag time for C behind the population of D. The idea might be expressed more generally as

$$_CP_{t+n} = (p)\ _DP_{(t-l)+n} \qquad\qquad 8.8$$

where l = a time lag and p = some proportion of $_DP$. The tendency might be graphically illustrated as in Figure 8.8. If we have some reason to believe that our study area and some pattern area have shared a common sequence of change influences and that, while the study area experienced them later, the parallel pattern theory is still convincing, then a comparative forecast can be made. In the past, this technique was often applied to whole cities, assuming one whole city to follow the pattern of another. It never worked very well that way, but it can be applied with some confidence to project growth patterns of certain types of subareas in a city. Suburbs on an urban fringe, for example, tend to follow a comparable pattern of filling up the land once it is "ripe" for development, as was already suggested in the modified exponential. Central business districts (CBD's) and their immediate environs also have tended, in United States cities, to follow comparable patterns of population change.

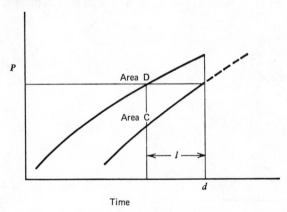

FIGURE 8.8   An example of the comparative method.
Proportion $(p) = 1$.

8.2.6 FORECASTS WITH RATIOS

The basic idea of the ratio technique is represented in the following example. We assume that population growth in the study area, say a community (C), is highly dependent on what happens to population in its surrounding region, say the state in which it is located (S). If we are willing to assume that the nature of this real interdependence is likely to persist into the near future, and if we have at hand population projections for the state, then by assuming that the ratio between the two populations will remain constant, we can calculate the community's share of the state's projected total.

These assumptions take the form of the algebraic equality:

$$\frac{{}_C P_{t+n}}{{}_S P_{t+n}} = \frac{{}_C P_t}{{}_S P_t}$$

For projection purposes the terms are rearranged by multiplying both sides by ${}_S P_{t+n}$ yielding:

$$_C P_{t+n} = \left(\frac{{}_C P_t}{{}_S P_t}\right) {}_S P_{t+n} \qquad\qquad 8.9$$

It simply says that the future size of the community $({}_C P_{t+n})$ will be some constant fraction $({}_C P_t / {}_S P_t)$ of the future size of the state $({}_S P_{t+n})$.

The equation should appear similar to the linear model, because it is. It is, in fact, the linear model of general form $y = a + bX$ where a, the intercept, is assumed to be zero, and the independent variable is the size of the state population, and the b coefficient is the ratio of population sizes. It is shown graphically in Figure 8.9. The only historical data required is the size of the community and of the state at one point in time. That point is plotted, a line is drawn from it to the (0, 0) point at the origin, and then is extrapolated

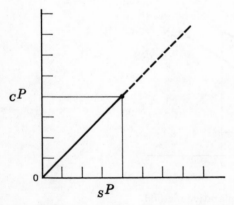

FIGURE 8.9 A graph of the ratio model, city correlated with state.

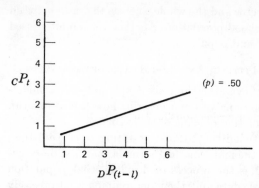

FIGURE 8.10   A graph of the comparative model as a form of the ratio model.

into the future. Thus it should be clear that the technique, on statistical grounds, is inferior to the linear model based on a series of historical data. If, to counter this criticism, we improve the ratio technique by looking at several points in time and take an average or trend of ratios, then we are mathematically doing the same thing we were doing in the linear and various exponential types of curves.

The only remaining difference is that our causal variable still differs, and very well may be superior as it is considerably more convincing to expect a community's future to be heavily determined by the larger system of which it is socially, economically, politically, and physically an integral part. On the other hand, the problem of defining the appropriate region to serve as the defining context for a community is a knotty problem, at least, in theory. In practice, one is severely limited by the few regions for which reliable forecasts are already available, and most theoretical considerations, unfortunately, get lost in the shuffle. The ratio technique is quite popular, unlike the comparative method. It permits the planner to utilize estimates made with far more sophisticated techniques as inputs to his local projections.

You might also notice that the ratio technique and the comparative technique are also algebraically almost identical. The independent variable there is the population of another community, time lagged. For any given time lag the population of the study community can be expressed as a ratio of the population of the pattern area. This relationship, as expressed in equation 8.8, could then be graphed as in Figure 8.10, also a linear or ratio function. There are many variations on the ratio technique. We might reverse the roles, saying for example, that the future growth of a smaller component, say California, might be used to project the future growth of the western United States, or that the growth of a typical sector of a city might be used to project the whole SMSA. Another variation is to use the ratio between a nongeographic subsector and the whole, such as the ratio between school enrollment and neighborhood population. Another version often used is a ratio between employment and population.

8.2.7 EQUATION SELECTION, FITTING, AND LOG TRANSFORMATIONS

In this section we show how several of these six simple projection models can be fitted by using regression analysis and describe how logarithms can be used to simplify the extrapolation of some of these curves.

First, what is meant by equation fitting? Equation-fitting, or curve-fitting, is simply the process of finding the mathematical formula that best describes a given set of data. For us, it is the process of deciding what population growth curve best fits our historic data and, then, determining what precisely the coefficients of that equation should be in order to make projections with it.

The first critical problem one faces in using these models is choosing among them. The most direct method of approach is to plot the data we have and to look for regularities. If we have only historical data on the study community as a whole, then we have little choice but to plot these data against time and try to determine if there appears to be a tendency of a linear, or nonlinear variety in them. If we also have data for, say, the region or comparable study areas, then we should explore these patterns, visually at first, in these data. Not only the relative goodness-of-fit of the different functions must be considered. More important, the acceptability of the assumption implicit in those formulas must be judged and weighed in the context of other knowledge. If, however, and this is unlikely, we find that in the light of all considerations we cannot choose one technique over another and both seem reasonable, then by all means we should choose the one that is mathematically simpler—the one for which it is easier, computationally, to determine the appropriate coefficients.

Now let us turn to the task of estimating the coefficients, such as, b in the linear model and r in the exponential. We have already pointed out that three of the six models presented above are alternate forms of the linear equation. They are the linear model itself, the comparative model, and the ratio model, each simply using different independent variables. Because this is true, then it is also true that regression analysis, as presented in Chapter 5, can be used to find the appropriate projection parameters, values for the intercepts and slopes of the best fitting straight lines. Why should we go to all that trouble? Why not just, in the linear case, say, average the differences that are in the historical data and plug into the given formula? One reason is that the formula for b as given in equation 8.2 assumes that the data available are for equal time periods. Usually this is not true—there are often gaps in the data series so that the calculation of b has to be adjusted for them. Regression analysis automatically does this. A second reason is

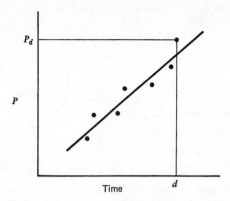

FIGURE 8.11   A straight-line fit to a scatter of points.

that, in the real world, population will never be perfectly linear. Even though a trend may be clearly linear, there is going to be variation about that trend. Thus we are in the same situation as we were in regression analysis when we were attempting to fit a line to a *scatter* of points, not a line of points. In the best of reality the data would still range about the straight line as in Figure 8.11. Where P_d lies in Figure 8.11, it is not on the trend line, it is above it. This means that if we use P_d as the value for P_t in the linear equation $[P_{t+n} = P_t + b(n)]$, our projection will be too high, not a true extension of the trend (see Figure 8.12). Thus it should be clear that the projection formulas presented in equations 8.1, 8.3, 8.5, and 8.7 to 8.9 for each technique

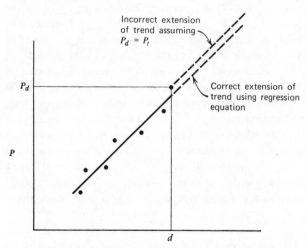

FIGURE 8.12   Regression analysis as an extrapolation technique.

are theoretical forms or models, and that great care must be taken in translating them from the world of perfect data to that of real data and real-world variations.[3]

Log Transformations

What we want to show next is how even a fourth equation, the exponential, can be translated into terms that allow the use of linear regression estimation.

Formally logs, or logarithms, are defined as follows:

$$\text{If } N = a^x \qquad \text{then } \log_a N = x$$

This says that if a number N can be expressed as some other positive number a (not $= 1$) raised to a power, then we may express the log of N, to the base a, as x.

For example:

if
$$10 = 10^1 \qquad \text{then } \log_{10} 10 = 1$$
and if
$$100 = 10^2 \qquad \text{then } \log_{10} 100 = 2$$
and if
$$1000 = 10^3 \qquad \text{then } \log_{10} 1000 = 3$$
and if
$$10,000 = 10^4 \qquad \text{then } \log_{10} 10,000 = 4$$
and if
$$100,000 = 10^5 \qquad \text{then } \log_{10} 100,000 = 5, \text{ etc.}$$

Thus logs, to the base 10, represent a scale that transforms numbers (N's) between 100 and 1000 to numbers (logs) between 2 and 3, and transforms numbers between 1000 and 10,000 to numbers (logs) between 3 and 4, and so on. Notice that the effect of this transformation is to dampen the effects of higher numbers, relative to lower ones. Thus a change in real population from 10 to 100, an absolute increase of *90* persons, is represented in logs as a change of one, from 1 to 2. Then a change from 100 to 1000, a change of *900* (10 times as much as before), is also represented as only a change of one, from 2 to 3. Likewise a change in population from 1000 to 10,000, an increase of *9000* (10 times as much as before), again is represented in logs as a change of one, from 3 to 4. Thus the log transformation is taking an exponential growth in N (a constant percentage $= 1000\%$ in this example) and systematically is translating it into a scale that represents these changes as equal absolute changes. An exponential change pattern is transformed into a linear change pattern.

---

[3] A useful set of rules for selecting the proper trend equation to apply to a set of data are in Croxton, Cowden, and Klein, pp. 282–284.

TABLE 8.1
How Logs Transform Exponential
Data into a Linear Function

t	P	ΔP	$\text{Log}_{10} P$	$\Delta \log_{10} P$
0	20,000		4.301	
		5,000		.097
1	25,000		4.398	
		6,250		.097
2	31,250		4.495	
		7,813		.097
3	39,063		4.592	
		9,766		.097
4	48,829		4.689	
		12,206		.097
5	61,036		4.786	
		15,277		.097
6	76,313		4.883	
		19,078		.097
7	95,391		4.980	

Let us look at an example (Table 8.1 represents data on population and its change) first in regular interval-scale measurements, and second in log-transformed terms.

The left-hand side of Table 8.1 was derived by taking the absolute differences. Since we see that they get bigger each time, we suspect that the data would take an exponential form on normal graph paper. To fit this equation we would have to calculate percentage changes and, if they turned out fairly constant, we could average them to get r.

The right-hand side of Table 8.1 shows the logs of the population figure—the powers to which 10 would have to be raised to equal the population. Since all of the population figures are between 10,000 and 100,000, their logs all fall between 4.0 and 5.0. These logs can be found in any standard table of logarithms. Such a table is presented in Appendix IX of this book. Notice now that the changes in log values ($\Delta \log_{10} P$) are constantly equal. This regularity now makes the plot of the $\log_{10} P$ against time a straight line. Graphically we move from Figure 8.13 to Figure 8.14.

The virtue of introducing logarithms is that, as a result the data we previously expressed in an exponential equation can now be expressed in a linear equation and thus its parameters a and b can also be estimated with regression analysis, which is desirable here for exactly the same reasons that it was desirable with the originally linear data.

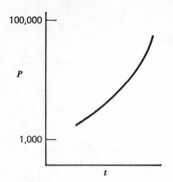 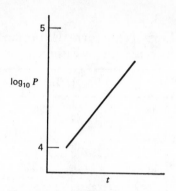

FIGURE 8.13   An exponential example.   FIGURE 8.14   The log transformation of the exponential example.

The procedure is (1) translate population into logs, (2) estimate equation, (3) project equation (still in log terms), (4) translate projection out of logs back into original number scale. The log transform of the exponential equation is written

$$\log_{10} P_{t+n} = \log a + (n) \log b$$

or

$$\log_{10} P_{t+n} = \log_{10} P_t + (n) \log_{10} (1 + r)$$

whereas the original form was

$$P_{t+n} = P_t(1 + r)^n$$

The use of logarithms in one other transformation is of some value. If the Gompertz equation is transformed from its normal form into logs, it takes on, not a linear form, but a modified exponential form. The graphs of its two forms and the appropriate equations are given in Figures 8.15 and 8.16. One can see that the lower half of the curve, like the exponential, gets straightened out in log form and that the curvature of the upper half has become somewhat accelerated.

We conclude this section by making one summary observation. The six basic projection equations presented in this chapter, we now see, can be expressed either directly or through transformation as one of two different curves—the linear, and the modified exponential. Yet each of the six makes radically differing assertions about the behavior of population size. What we hope has been made clear is that the fundamental differences among these six techniques are not that they stem from radically different mathematical routines but, instead, from very different ways of interpreting a set of quite closely related, sometimes identical, abstract algebraic forms.

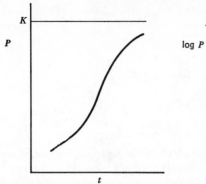

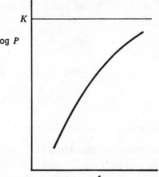

FIGURE 8.15 $P_{t+n} = Ka^{b^n}$ FIGURE 8.16 $\text{Log } P_{t+n} = \text{Log } K + (\text{Log } a)b^n.$

8.3   COMPOSITE POPULATION FORECASTING MODELS

There are two principal shortcomings in the previous models. First, they are grossly simple minded in their causal structure. They assume, respectively, that future population of a community is caused by past growth of that community, by past growth of some other community, or by growth of the region. Now almost no one using these models really believes these assumptions literally. Rather, they are usually in the position where they have to accept these causal variables as the best for which information is available or as reasonable proxies for the complex set of real causes of population change. The first shortcoming of the simpler models is causal structure.

A second major shortcoming is the monolithic, aggregate nature of the projection they produce. It would be helpful, for planning purposes, to project much more than just the total size of a community's population. It would be helpful to know the breakdown by ages, sex, cultural background, income, and the like of that one aggregate projection of size.

A chief virtue of the simpler models, in addition to their simplicity in use, is that they are the building blocks of the more complex models that attempt to meet these shortcomings.

The true causes of population change have long been recognized as being natural increase and migration. Natural increase is composed of new births into the population and the effects of removals by death. Migration is concerned with the effect of individuals moving into an area, minus the number moving out, which is called net migration. In this section of the chapter we consider these two components, natural increase and net migration, separately. The thrust of our presentation will first be a composite model of natural increase called cohort-survival analysis. We then discuss the additional component of net migration. The general form of the total components model is

$$P_{t+n} = P_t + N + M \qquad\qquad 8.10$$

where

$$N = \text{natural increase}$$

$$M = \text{net migration}$$

8.3.1 The Cohort-Survival Model

This model of natural increase when used by itself as a projection technique assumes that net migration is equal to zero. It begins by breaking the total population into age groups, called cohorts. Each cohort is further subdivided into a male cohort and a female cohort. The age breakdown most frequently used is that of the United States Census which has 5-year intervals up to age 84, and one final group for those 85 and older. Thus there are 18 age cohorts of males and 18 of females, 36 in all. These can be displayed in a graph called an age-sex pyramid, as shown in Figure 8.17.

Cohort-survival analysis takes each of these 36 cohorts and projects them separately. For example, the number of male persons age 0–4, in say, 1970 is multiplied by some survival rate (1 − death rate), to find the number of people in the male age group 5–9 in 1975. Historical data show that these age-specific survival rates change very slowly so that we are fairly safe in assuming that they remain constant, although different for each cohort. Algebraically we would write

$$_{5-9}P_{t+5} = _{0-4}(S)_{0-4}P_t$$

where

$$S = (1 - D)$$

$$D = \text{death rate}$$

The death rate is also called the crude death rate and is equal to the number of deaths in a time period divided by the population at the middle of that period. This must be determined from historical records.

The effect of mortality rates then is modeled in cohort-survival analysis by what is essentially a set of 36 separate linear equations, each solved independently. Since the survival rates will always be less than 1 (some always die), a given cohort of people projected through time will tend to become smaller and smaller.

The other major element of the analysis deals with births, constantly, over time, supplying the new cohort in each time period. These are projected by the use of cohort-specific birthrates applied to the cohorts of women of childbearing age. The whole process, pictorially, might look like the age-sex

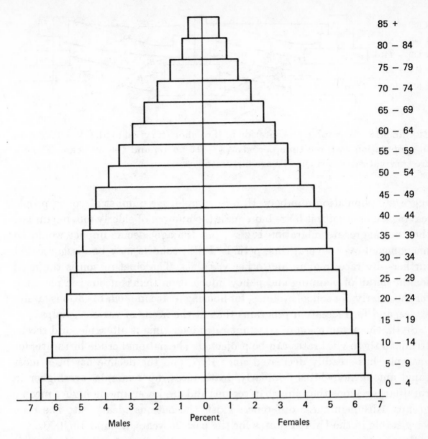

FIGURE 8.17   An age-sex pyramid.

pyramid of Figure 8.18 as it moves through time. Figure 8.18 lumps age groups together and makes bigger time jumps than normal to illustrate the process.

A few further clarifications must be made to make our presentation fully accurate. First, the calculation of new births normally uses the female cohorts between the ages of 15 and 44. Births below or above those limits are rare and can be included in the calculation of the birthrate for the nearest cohort. Second, the birthrates specified must be live-birth rates adjusted for the number of births which may be expected to survive for their first 5 years. Third, once the projected births have been derived, they must be divided into those expected to be male and those expected to be female. Fourth, our assumption of no net migration must apply to every cohort, not just to the

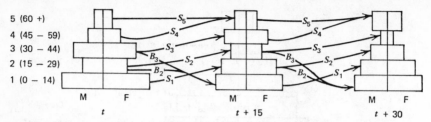

FIGURE 8.18   A graphic presentation of the cohort survival model. We have here the population at three time periods t, $t + 15$ years, and $t + 30$ years. The S's are survival rates and the B's are birthrates.

aggregate population numbers. If, for example, the number of young people leaving a community is large but equals the number of elderly moving into it, then net aggregate migration is zero, but the age-specific impact would be phenomenal over several time periods. Fifth, cohorts may be disaggregated further—by race, region, and other variables. The chief reason is the need for the detail of planning and policy information that is needed in planning for the elderly, for school systems, for housing to accommodate various family styles, and for recreation programs that fit the needs of various groups.

Sixth, the assumption of constant rates over time is alterable, and recent trends in these vital rates can be projected. The national crude birthrate, for example, has steadily decreased since 1957, and the decline has been most rapid among nonwhites. Similarly death rates, for example, are higher in rural-farm regions than in urban regions and are lower among higher income groups. Although these differences exist, the national death rate has been very stable in the United States for the past 20 years, around 10/1000.

Seven, a reminder about aggregating and disaggregation of rates is appropriate. If we have an annual death rate and we want to convert it to a 5-year survival rate, we do not multiply the death rate by 5 and subtract from one, as some might be tempted to do. We just subtract it from one to get an annual survival rate which is then raised to the fifth power. The difference is shown below, assuming an annual death rate of .10. To demonstrate this principle of using rates, which also applied previously in this chapter in the exponential, consider a cohort of, say, 100 people, and apply a

WRONG	RIGHT
$S = 1 - 5(d)$	$S = (1 - d)^5$
$S = 1 - 5(.10)$	$S = (1 - .10)^5$
$S = 1 - .50$	$S = (.90)^5$
$S = .50$	$S = .59$

survival rate of .90 to it 5 years in succession and see what percentage is left at the end of 5 years. By the same reasoning a 10-year survival rate is converted to a 5-year rate not by dividing it in two but by taking its square root.

Finally, in Table 8.2 a sample cohort survival projection has been worked through. The uppermost section of this table gives all of the data and assumed rates that are required to make the calculation. The middle portion lays out all calculation formulas for projecting the male cohorts and, using the given data, projects ahead one 15-year time period. The lower portion does the same thing for the female cohorts. The aggregate population projection is summed at the base of the table. The 10 cohort projection formulas presented would produce the next period projection by adding 1 to all time subscripts.

8.3.2 MIGRATION

This component of population growth and change is the most difficult to forecast. Data on historical trends are very scanty and research has not been prolific in offering models of accuracy comparable to the natural increase method. Some limited data are available in the United States Census of Population. We concentrate here on two kinds of models for estimating and projecting migration. They are:

1. Simple forecasting models using residuals.
2. Complex models of migration.

Simple Forecasts of Residuals

The residual technique makes use of the general formulation, equation 8.10, that says population changes because of natural increase and migration. Thus, if we know or can estimate the portion of historical growth of a community that is attributable to natural increase, we must consider the difference between this natural increase and the amount by which the population actually grew as migration. Algebraically, for example, we can rewrite equation 8.10 as

$$N_{1960-1970} + M_{1960-1970} = P_{1970} - P_{1960}$$

where

$$N = \text{natural increase}$$

$$M = \text{migration}$$

$$P = \text{total population}$$

And, by rearranging the terms, we get equation 8.21.

$$M_{1960-1970} = (P_{1970} - P_{1960}) - N_{1960-1970} \qquad 8.21$$

TABLE 8.2
Basic Data and Equations for a Cohort-Survival Example

Cohort	Age Group	Survival Rates ^mS	Survival Rates ^fS	Surviving Birthrates B	Male Cohort Size at Time t (in 1000's)	Female Cohort Size at Time t (in 1000's)
5	60 +	.20	.40		3	3
4	45-59	.50	.60		5	5
3	30-44	.65	.70	.90	12	12
2	15-29	.75	.80	2.00	10	10
1	0-14	.85	.90		20	20

Proportion of males 0–14 $= p(m) = .51; \; p(f) = 1 - p(m)$

Assume 1 time interval $= 15$ years Total $P_t = 100,000$

Projection of Male Cohorts to $t + 1$

Equation 8.11 $\quad ^m_5P_{t+1} = {}^m_4S({}^m_4P_t) + {}^m_5S({}^m_5P_t) \qquad = .5(5) + .2(3) \qquad = 3.1$

Equation 8.12 $\quad ^m_4P_{t+1} = {}^m_3S({}^m_3P_t) \qquad\qquad\qquad = .65(12) \qquad\qquad = 7.8$

Equation 8.13 $\quad ^m_3P_{t+1} = {}^m_2S({}^m_2P_t) \qquad\qquad\qquad = .75(10) \qquad\qquad = 7.5$

Equation 8.14 $\quad ^m_2P_{t+1} = {}^m_1S({}^m_1P_t) \qquad\qquad\qquad = .85(20) \qquad\qquad = 17.0$

Equation 8.15 $\quad ^m_1P_{t+1} = [B_2({}^f_2P_t) + B_3({}^f_3P_t)]p(m) = [2(10) + .9(12)].51 = 15.7$

Projection of Female Cohorts to $t + 1$

Equation 8.16 $\quad ^f_5P_{t+1} = {}^f_4S({}_4P_t) + {}^f_5S({}^f_5P_t) \qquad = .6(5) + .4(3) \qquad = 4.2$

Equation 8.17 $\quad ^f_4P_{t+1} = {}^f_3S({}^f_3P_t) \qquad\qquad\qquad = .7(12) \qquad\qquad = 8.4$

Equation 8.18 $\quad ^f_3P_{t+1} = {}^f_2S({}^f_2P_t) \qquad\qquad\qquad = .8(10) \qquad\qquad = 8.0$

Equation 8.19 $\quad ^f_2P_{t+1} = {}^f_1S({}^f_1P_t) \qquad\qquad\qquad = .9(20) \qquad\qquad = 18.0$

Equation 8.20 $\quad ^f_1P_{t+1} = [B_2({}^f_2P_t) + B_3({}^f_3P_t)]p(f) = [2(10) + .9(12)].49 = 15.1$

Total population $= P_{t+1} = \sum_{i=1}^{n} ({}^m_iP_{t+1} + {}^f_iP_{t+1}) = 104,800$

By the same technique, a series of historical migration figures can be derived as, say,

$$M_{1950-1960} = (P_{1960} - P_{1950}) - N_{1950-1960}$$
$$M_{1940-1950} = (P_{1950} - P_{1940}) - N_{1940-1950}$$

$$\cdot \qquad \cdot$$
$$\cdot \qquad \cdot$$
$$\cdot \qquad \cdot$$

etc.   etc.

These data can then be analyzed for trends of a linear or curvilinear nature with the same analytic tools that we presented above under simple population forecasting models.

Ratio techniques can also be used and are often considered better. In general, a relation such as equation 8.22 is assumed.

$$\frac{M_{1970-1980}}{P^*_{1980}} = \frac{M_{1960-1970}}{P^*_{1970}} \qquad \qquad 8.22$$

where

$$P^*_{1970} = P_{1960} + N_{1960-1970}$$

This is rewritten for projection purposes as

$$M_{1970-1980} = \frac{M_{1960-1970}}{P^*_{1970}} P^*_{1980} \qquad \qquad 8.23$$

where

$$M_{1960-1970} = (P_{1970} - P_{1960}) - N_{1960-1970}$$

so that, finally,

$$P_{1980} = P^*_{1980} + M_{1970-1980}$$

Several variations of this technique are possible. One, of course, is to assume a ratio between community migration and regional migration, assuming a constant city share. Another possible innovation is to disaggregate migration by age cohorts, sex, and other variables.

Complex Models of Migration

The simple models of migration use as the causal or independent variable past trends in population growth and its components. The more complex models ask the question: Why do people move? The most sophisticated models of migration are usually tied to some notions of economic push and pull as the prime determinant of migration.

Variables that indicate economic opportunity can usefully be studied with multiple regression analysis in conjunction with data of past migration changes. Most of these will take a form that relates migration between two regions or places as a function of the relative economic opportunities in the two areas and some indicators of the accessibility of those opportunities.

This can be stated generally as

$$M_{ij} = f(E, A) \qquad 8.24$$

where

$M_{ij} =$ migration between i and j

$E =$ economic opportunity

$A =$ accessibility

$f =$ some (unspecified) functional relationship.

To elaborate, we might say that we expect the amount of migration between two places to vary with the relative size of the two places (a measure of potential opportunities), the relative unemployment in the two places (a measure of real opportunities), the relative wage and salary levels of the two places (a measure of benefits), the relative costs of living in the two places (a measure of cost), and the distance between the two places (a measure of the cost of moving). We can write this as

$$M_{ij} = f(P_i, P_j; U_i, U_j; WS_i, WS_j; CL_i, CL_j; D_{ij}) \qquad 8.25$$

where

$M_{ij} =$ migration between i and j

$P =$ population size

$U =$ unemployment level

$WS =$ wage and salary level

$CL =$ cost of living

$D =$ distance

Models of this general form have been developed and calibrated, using multiple regression analysis, by Lowry, Rogers, and others with reasonable success. We learn in the next two chapters that such a model can be considered as a variation on a general model of trip-making. It is considered in depth in those chapters. Techniques for sophisticated economic projections are extensively treated in Chapter 12.

PROBLEMS

1. Given the following data, use the linear model to project population to 1975.

$$P_{1950} = 29,000$$
$$P_{1955} = 25,000$$
$$P_{1960} = 24,000$$
$$P_{1965} = 20,000$$
$$P_{1970} = 19,000$$

2. Given the following data, use the exponential model to project population to 1973.

$$P_{1950} = 15,000$$
$$P_{1955} = 16,000$$
$$P_{1960} = 18,000$$
$$P_{1965} = 20,000$$
$$P_{1970} = 23,000$$

3. Given the following data, use the modified exponential model to project population to 1974. Assume $K = 20,000$.

$$P_{1966} = 16,000$$
$$P_{1967} = 17,000$$
$$P_{1968} = 17,750$$
$$P_{1969} = 18,313$$
$$P_{1970} = 18,735$$

4. Consider the following data on the minor civil divisions (MCD) of a county.

YEAR	MCD 1	MCD 2	MCD 3	MCD 4	MCD 5	TOTAL COUNTY
1930	100	100	100	100	100	500
1940	190	130	100	95	60	575
1950	240	169	100	90	45	644
1960	270	220	100	70	35	695
1970	290	290	100	30	30	740

(a) Project the population of each of the MCD's by decade to the year 2010, using the exponential model. Plot the results and evaluate the fit of the model to the data.

(b) Select the model that you feel would best fit the data of each MCD and apply the models to project to 2010 again. Plot these results and compare them to (a) above.

(c) Suppose that you are given a set of projections for the county as a whole which are:

YEAR	TOTAL COUNTY
1980	780
1990	830
2000	880
2010	925

Adjust both of your projection sets, (a) and (b), proportionally, by ratios, to these county totals. Plot the results and compare the differences between the two sets of adjusted projections.

5. Below we have the data for the age-sex profiles of five separate communities. What kind of community would you expect that we have in each case, based on your interpretation of this data? What planning problems might you expect each to have? Assuming net migration for each cohort to be zero in the future, how would you expect these communities to develop in the future?

AGE COHORT	COMMUNITY 1 MALE	FEMALE	COMMUNITY 2 MALE	FEMALE	COMMUNITY 3 MALE	FEMALE
70 +	1%	2%	0%	0%	0%	0%
60-69	10	10	0	0	2	1
50-59	6	5	2	3	2	3
40-49	3	3	4	4	11	10
30-39	2	3	5	5	19	18
20-29	4	5	7	8	9	10
10-19	7	8	11	12	4	5
0-9	16	15	19	20	3	3

COMMUNITY 4 MALE	FEMALE	COMMUNITY 5 MALE	FEMALE
0%	1%	0%	0%
1	2	1	0
2	6	3	1
3	8	20	2
1	9	34	3
1	14	24	6
10	10	2	2
16	16	1	1

6. Using the cohort-survival data and equations of Table 8.2:
   (a) Carry out the complete set of calculations for time periods $t + 2$ and $t + 3$.
   (b) Graph the age-sex pyramids for this problem for t, $t + 1$, $t + 2$, and $t + 3$, and interpret what is happening to this population.

BIBLIOGRAPHY

Beshers, James M. (ed). *Computer Methods in the Analysis of Large-Scale Social Systems*, second edition. Cambridge, Mass.: The M.I.T. Press, 1968, Part III. "Demographic Applications of Computer Models."

Bogue, Donald J. *Principles of Demography*. New York: Wiley, 1969.

Bouvier, Leon F. "Estimating Post-Censal Populations of Counties," *Journal of the American Institute of Planners, 37* (January 1971), 45–46.

Chapin, F. Stuart, Jr. *Urban Land Use Planning*, second edition. Urbana, Ill.: University of Illinois Press, 1965, Chapter 5.

Commission on Population Growth and the American Future. *Population and the American Future: The Report of the Commission on Population Growth and the American Future*. Washington, D.C.: U.S. Government Printing Office, 1972.

Croxton, Frederick E., Dudley J. Cowden, and Sidney Klein. Applied General Statistics. Englewood Cliffs, N.J.: Prentice-Hall, 1967.

Demko, George J., Harold M. Rose, and George A. Schnell (eds). *Population Geography: A Reader*. New York: McGraw-Hill, 1970.

Greenberg, Michael R. "An Application of Probability Matrices to Demographic and Socioeconomic Changes in Ethnic Concentrations: The Case of New York City," *The New York Statistician, 22* (September-October 1970), 3–6.

———. "A Test of Combinations of Models for Projecting the Population of Minor Civil Divisions," *Economic Geography, 48* (April 1972), 179–188.

Greenberg, Michael R., Donald A. Krueckeberg, and Richard Mautner. *Long-Range Population Projections for Minor Civil Divisions: Computer Programs and User's Manual*. New Brunswick, N.J.: Center for Urban Policy Research, 1973.

Hightower, Henry C. "Population Studies," in W. I. Goodman and E. C. Freund (eds). *Principles and Practice of Urban Planning*. Washington, D.C.: International City Managers' Association, 1968, pp. 51–75.

Isard, W. *Methods of Regional Analysis*. New York: The Technology Press of M.I.T. and Wiley, 1960, Chapters 2 and 3.

Jaffe, A. J. *Handbook of Statistical Procedures for Long-Range Projections of Public School Enrollment.* Washington, D.C.: U.S. Government Printing Office, 1969.

Keyfitz, Nathan. "On Future Population," *Journal of the American Statistical Association, 67* (June 1972), 347–363.

McGimsey, George. "The 1970 Census: Changes and Innovations," *Journal of the American Institute of Planners, 36* (May 1970), 198–203.

Morrison, Peter A. *Demographic Information for Cities: A Manual for Estimating and Projecting Local Population Characteristics.* A Report Prepared for Department of Housing and Urban Development, R-618-HUD. Santa Monica, Cal.: The Rand Corporation, June 1971.

Orcutt, G. H., Martin Greenberger, John Korbel, and Alice M. Rivlin. *Microanalysis of Socioeconomic Systems: A Simulation Study.* New York: Harper and Brothers, 1961.

Post, Arnold R. "Mobility Analysis," *Journal of the American Institute of Planners, 35* (November 1969), 417–421.

Rogers, Andrei. *Matrix Analysis of Interregional Population Growth and Distribution.* Berkeley, Cal.: University of California Press, 1968.

Siegel, Jacob S. "Development and Accuracy of Projections of Population and Households in the United States," *Demography, 9* (February 1972), 51–68.

United States Bureau of the Census. *1970 Census Users' Guide, Parts 1 and 2.* Washington, D.C.: U.S. Government Printing Office, October 1970.

———. *Current Population Reports.* Series P-25, No. 461, "Components of Population Change by County: 1960–1970." Washington, D.C.: U.S. Government Printing Office, June 1971.

———. *Current Population Reports.* Series P-25, No. 480, "Illustrative Population Projections for the U.S.: The Demographic Effects of Alternative Paths to Zero Growth." Washington, D.C.: U.S. Government Printing Office, April 1972.

———. *Current Population Reports.* Series P-25, No. 454, "Inventory of State and Local Agencies Preparing Population Estimates: Survey of 1969." Washington, D.C.: U.S. Government Printing Office, December 1970.

———. *The Methods and Materials of Demography.* Washington, D.C.: U.S. Government Printing Office, 1971.

———. *Current Population Reports.* Series P-25, No. 477, "Preliminary Projections of the Populations of the States: 1975–1990." Washington, D.C.: U.S. Government Printing Office, March 1972.

United States Bureau of the Census. *Current Population Reports*, Series P-25, No. 493, "Projections of the Population of the United States, by Age and Sex: 1972–2020." Washington, D.C.: U.S. Government Printing Office, December 1972.

Bogue, The Commission on Population Growth and the American Future Report, Isard, Keyfitz, and Siegel represent a variety of good general references on demography. Applications to planning are discussed in Bouvier, Chapin, Greenberg (1972), Hightower, McGimsey, and Post, and are considered at more advanced, research-oriented levels in Demko, Greenberg (1970), and Rogers. The book by Morrison, the United States Bureau of the Census' *Methods and Materials of Demography*, and the books by Jaffe, and Greenberg, Krueckeberg, and Mautner each serve as operational handbooks, the latter including computer programs. The use of the computer is also discussed in Beshers and in Orcutt. The other United States Bureau of the Census reports represent a sampling of highly useful documents for the practicing analyst.

CHAPTER 9

Location and Travel Behavior

9.1 INTRODUCTION

A city planning department of a certain city is confronted with the following three problems.

1. A regional shopping center is being planned by a private developer for construction in a sparsely settled area of the city. The developers submit to the City Planning Commission a request for a zoning variance and for a new access road, the cost of which is to be borne by the city. In making their decision, the commissioners want to know if the location of the proposed shopping center would be unfavorable for the area's long-term pattern of development. Considerations in this judgement include the possibility that the location has already been reserved for future recreational or other desirable land use, or that it might be sufficiently inaccessible to the area's current and future shoppers as to invite the construction of additional regional centers in the same area which are more conveniently located to shoppers. In the opinion of the commissioners, if additional centers proliferated, the proposed shopping center might fail in the competition, not only causing the city's road investment to be wasted but also resulting in a wasteful commercial development pattern. In this event, the city would not want to grant the zoning change or to bear the cost of an access road.

2. A long-range development plan is being prepared in which the location and activity mix of new public facilities must be specified where required, and improvements in both the physical stock and activity mix of existing facilities must also be considered. Agencies are included in the planning process that are responsible for administering the several types of public service activities. One of these public services is the library system.

Several sites located in the less densely settled parts of the city are being considered by library planners as locations for new facilities. In addition, in a number of inner-city neighborhoods within the service area of the main downtown library facility, community representatives have expressed interest in the potential use of the informal and voluntary learning atmosphere that a library could provide to less educated residents, and they have suggested that several small and highly accessible facilities be added that have collections more appropriate to the interests of the inner-city residents. However, several library administrators have been reluctant to locate additional facilities in these neighborhoods because too few of their residents would come to utilize the expensive reference collections and the other costly basic services that are provided in the typical library. They further argue that books of interest to the people of these neighborhoods are already available in the downtown facility and that to provide additional facilities within the service area of the downtown facility would be wasteful.

The library planners involved in the long-range planning process agree that the appropriate measure of the effectiveness of the city's library system is not the number of areas of the city that are within the service area of some facility but, instead, the frequency of usage made by the city's residents on all the facilities of that system over a given period of time. Given the available future budgets, the planners want to vary locations, collection mix, and size of facility to arrive at a library facilities plan that would maximize usage of the facilities, taking account of needs and usage rates not only in the less densely settled parts of the city but also in the older and densely settled inner-city neighborhoods.

3. Decisions about the location and capacity of all public facilities depend on the amount of population growth that each residential area of the city will experience over the future period of time with which the plan is concerned. Therefore, a forecast is needed of the residential development that is expected to occur in each area of the city over this future.

In each of these three cases, urban planning decisions depend strongly on a knowledge of the relationship between activity locations and the travel behavior of the users of these activities. In the first case, the long-term viability of a shopping center depends on the trip-making accessibility of its location to its user (shopping) population relative to the accessibility of other locations to the same user population that may be developed by competitors in the future. In the second case, the usage of the library system as a whole depends on the usage of each facility in the system. This, in turn depends on the willingness of user populations to make trips to a library, which depends not only on the size and collection mix of the library relative to the reading characteristics of the local population but also on the accessibility of the facility to that population. Finally, in the case of small-area forecasts of the city's future residential populations, the number of families that will want to reside in a given area will depend, to a great extent, on the relative trip-making accessibility of that area to other activity locations, particularly to centers of employment, to which the residing population will regularly travel.

What is needed is an analytic technique for relating the travel or usage rates made by a given user population to an activity or commodity (housing) provided at a given location, where the effect on travel rates of the distance separating a user population from an activity location is considered. Location analysts have long been concerned with the development and empirical implementation of such a technique. The most frequently used technique is known as the "gravity model," and this, together with several variants, is the subject of this chapter. In addition to the conceptual antecedents of this approach, and its structure as a probability model, we focus attention on empirical estimation, and it is here, as we learn, that the operational power and appeal of this technique can be demonstrated. We make use of the three examples above in our description of the model: the use of the gravity model in evaluating commercial location, public facilities location, and residential location.

9.2 CONCEPTUAL ANTECEDENTS

9.2.1 THE PURE GRAVITY MODEL

Empirical studies made in the 1940s by George Kingsley Zipf[1] and, quite independently, by John Q. Stewart[2] showed that a surprising array of human phenomena involving interaction over space at the macroscopic level could be predicted by the laws used in Newtonian physics. One such law is the "inverse square of distance" formula for the gravitational attraction F_{AB} exerted by two celestial bodies, A and B, on each other

$$F_{AB} = K \frac{P_A P_B}{d^2} \qquad 9.1$$

where P_A is the mass of A, P_B is the mass of B, d is the distance between A and B, and K is a constant. It was found that if, instead of the mass of two celestial bodies, the population of two cities A and B were inserted in the formula with d representing the distance between the two cities, it was possible to predict with unexpected accuracy diverse examples of human interaction over space such as the number of people traveling by bus, train, or airplane between pairs of cities, the number of telephone calls, the volume in tons of railway express shipments between cities,[3] and the number of students from each state in the nation enrolled at Princeton University.[4]

---

[1] George Kingsley Zipf, *Human Behaviour and the Principle of Least Effort: an Introduction to Human Ecology* (Cambridge, Mass.: Addison-Wesley, 1949).

[2] John Q. Stewart, "Empirical Mathematical Rules Concerning the Distribution and Equilibrium of Population," *Geographical Review, 37* (1947), 461–485.

[3] Zipf, op. cit. Acutally, Zipf's calculations made use of the relation $K(P_A P_B/d)^\lambda$ where λ was empirically determined.

[4] John Q. Stewart, "The Gravity of the Princeton Family," *Princeton Alumni Weekly, 40* (1940).

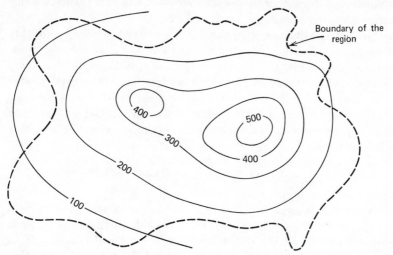

Boundary of the region

FIGURE 9.1 Isopotential contours over a region.

In addition, the formula for the gravitational potential V_A exerted by all masses at point A,

$$V_A = K \sum_{i \neq A} \frac{P_i}{d_{Ai}} \qquad\qquad 9.2$$

where, instead of mass, the population, P, of each city, i, and of the distance, d_{Ai}, from city A to city i are used, yields a measure that Stewart called the "population potential" of city A.[5] This measure could be plotted on a map such as is shown in Figure 9.1.[6] By connecting with a line all cities having equal measures of population potential, the resulting "isopotential contour" provides a visual presentation of the intensity of human activity or urbanization over the map of a region or nation. The measure of population potential has been found to be correlated with demographic and socioeconomic patterns

[5] For a review of these aspects of the gravity model see W. Isard et al., *Methods of Regional Analysis* (New York: Wiley, 1960), Chapter 11. Also see G. Olsson, *Distance and Human Interaction* (Philadelphia: Regional Science Research Institute 1965), and G. A. P. Carrothers, "An Historical Review of the Gravity and Potential Concepts of Human Interaction, *Journal of the American Institute of Planners*, 22 (Spring 1956) 94–102.

[6] John Q. Stewart, "The Potential of Population and Its Relationship to Marketing," in Reavis Cox and Wroe Alderson (eds.), *Theory in Marketing* (Chicago: Irwin, 1950), pp. 19–40.

such as population density, land rents, and sales of a newspaper from a city to its surrounding counties.[7]

Although Zipf and Stewart were the first theorists to explore thoroughly the analogy between mechanics in physics and human macro-behavior, they were by no means the first to make use of this analogy. An earlier, but again not the first, use was made in 1929 by a market research analyst named William J. Reilly to delineate market areas around retail towns, a use that, as we shall see, was the basis for the kinds of planning-related analyses that we wish to apply to provide answers to the questions posed at the beginning of this chapter.

9.2.2 REILLY'S LAW AND THE MAPPING OF TRADE AREAS

Consider the following problem.

Town A contains a large department store that attracts customers from many smaller nearby towns. However, it is believed that shoppers living in towns located beyond a certain distance from town A will not shop in its department store but, instead, will shop in another town, town B, which happens to be more accessible. The manager of the store in town A wants to identify this cutoff distance, or market boundary, at all points around his town as a basis for determining his advertising campaign.

Reilly suggested that there exists a relationship—which came to be known as Reilly's law of retail gravitation—by which the market boundary between the two retail towns could be identified.[8] According to his hypothesis, shoppers living at any point between the two towns A and B will be attracted to the towns in accordance with the relative populations, P, of the two towns (P_A/P_B) and inversely with the square of the relative distance d of that point from the two towns $[(d_B/d_A)^2]$. However, they will shop only in the town with the stronger overall attraction. The problem then reduces to that of identifying the point between the two towns for which these two forces are equalized, the point at which

$$\left(\frac{P_A}{P_B}\right)\left(\frac{d_B}{d_A}\right)^2 = 1 \qquad\qquad 9.3$$

Shoppers living at this point will be attracted to the two retail towns equally, and this point, therefore must lie on the market boundary.

Suppose this point lies on a straight line that connects the two towns, as is shown in Figure 9.2. In this case, we need only identify d_A, the distance of

---

[7] John Q. Stewart, and W. Warntz, "Physics of Population Distribution," *Journal of Regional Science*, 1 (1958), 99–123.

[8] William J. Reilly, "Methods for the Study of Retail Relationships," *University of Texas Bulletin*, No. 2944 (1929).

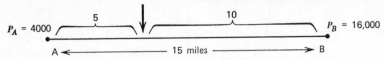

$P_A = 4000$ ⟍⟍ 5 ⟍⟍ ↓ ⟋ 10 ⟋ $P_B = 16{,}000$

A ⟵————————— 15 miles —————————⟶ B

FIGURE 9.2   A market boundary lying on a line connecting two towns.

this point from town A. The distance of d_B of that point from town B is then, simply, the total distance between the two towns d_{AB} less the distance d_A of that point from town A

$$d_B = d_{AB} - d_A$$

Substituting this into equation 9.3, we have

$$\frac{P_A}{P_B}\left(\frac{d_{AB} - d_A}{d_A}\right)^2 = 1$$

Multiplying both sides of this expression by P_B/P_A and taking the square root of both sides, we have

$$\frac{d_{AB}}{d_A} - 1 = \sqrt{\frac{P_B}{P_A}}$$

Adding one to both sides and multiplying both sides by $d_A/(1 + \sqrt{P_B/P_A})$ gives

$$d_A = \frac{d_{AB}}{1 + \sqrt{\dfrac{P_B}{P_A}}} \qquad\qquad 9.4$$

Making use of equation 9.4, we can easily identify the market boundary d_A lying on a straight line between any two retail towns A and B, and this result depends only on knowledge of the distance separating the two towns, d_{AB}, and their populations, P_A and P_B. Suppose, for example, that town A has a population of 4000, and town B has a population of 16,000, and the two towns are 15 miles apart. Then

$$d_A = \frac{15}{1 + \sqrt{\dfrac{16{,}000}{4000}}} = \frac{15}{1 + \sqrt{4}} = 5$$

which is to say that town A's market boundary lies five miles away on the line connecting A and B—town B's market boundary is 10 miles away.

This application of Reilly's law yields discontinuous trade areas as is exemplified in the map of Figure 9.3. With discontinuous trade areas, all shoppers living within the trade area of a given retail town are predicted to make all of their purchases in that retail town and none in any other town.

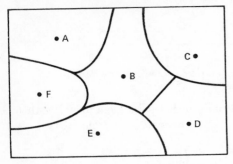

FIGURE 9.3   A map of trade areas for retail towns.

However, a more general application of the gravity model does not yield discontinuous trade areas,[9] as we demonstrate in the next section.

9.2.3   ADDITIONAL EMPIRICAL REALITIES

In fact, empirical studies like those made by Brian Berry[10] have shown that trade areas for retail centers are not discontinuous—there is not a point or line in space whereby residents living on one side of the line make all their purchases in that retail town and residents living on the other side make all their purchases in another. Instead, at any given residential point between two centers, some residents shop at one center and some at another and, as any shopper knows, the same resident may from time to time shop at one center and then at another. But what is empirically evident is that the probability that residents will shop at a given center increases, the closer the point of residence is to that center and the more distant that point is from other centers, the size of centers being held constant. This is illustrated in Figure 9.4 in which the lines represent shopping trips made from points of

[9] The more deductive approach to trade area analysis of location theory, in contrast to the more empirical and aggregative approach of the gravity model, also predicts discontinuous trade areas. A. Losch, *The Economics of Location* (New Haven, Conn.: Yale University Press, 1954), Chapters 9–12; E. F. Hoover, *The Location of Economic Activity* (New York, McGraw-Hill, 1948), Chapter 4; and W. Isard, *Location and Space Economy* (New York; jointly by the Technology Press of M.I.T. and Wiley, 1956). Also refer to H. Hotelling, "Stability in Competition," *Economic Journal, 39* (1929), 41–57; F. Fetter, "The Economic Law of Market Areas," *The Quarterly Journal of Economics, 39* (1924), 520–529; and C. D. Hyson and W. P. Hyson, "The Economic Law of Market Areas," *The Quarterly Journal of Economics, 64* (1950), 319–324; all of which are reprinted in R. Dean, W. Leahy, and D. McKee (eds.), *Spatial Economic Theory* (New York: The Free Press, 1970).

[10] See Brian J. L. Berry, *Geography of Market Centers and Retail Distribution* (Englewood Cliffs, N.J.: Prentice-Hall, 1967), especially pp. 10–20, for a very thorough and readable synthesis of Berry's extensively published empirical work.

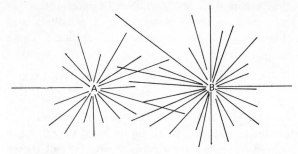

FIGURE 9.4 Shopping travel patterns.

residence to one of the two retail centers, A and B. Residents living nearer a given center are shown as being more likely to shop at that center, but some residents travel long distances and shop at the more distant center. Center B, being the larger of the two centers, attracts more shoppers living nearer to center A than center A attracts of those living nearer center B.

In contrast with a model that predicts a constant number of shopping trips to a given center up to a certain maximum distance or market boundary and no trips to that center beyond that boundary, as is shown in Figure 9.5a, what would be better is a model that predicts a decreasing number of trips to a given center as the distance from that center increases and as the distance from another center decreases, as is shown in Figure 9.5b. Just such a model is described in the rest of this chapter.

9.3 THE GRAVITY MODEL AS A PROBABILITY ALLOCATION MODEL

9.3.1 DERIVING THE MODEL

The number of trips (T) over any given time period made from households living at location i to a center at location j increases with the number of

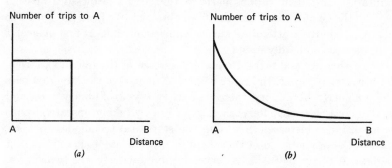

FIGURE 9.5 Two approaches to trip prediction.

trip-makers (H) at location i and with the number of opportunities (S) available at the center j for satisfying the demands of the trip-makers, and decreases with the cost of traveling (D) from location i to location j. These relationships are shown in equation 9.5

$$T_{ij} = K \frac{H_i^{\alpha} S_j^{\beta}}{D_{ij}^{\lambda}} \qquad 9.5$$

where K is a constant, the value of which will be indicated below, and α, β, and λ are empirically determined constants. This relation has the form of the gravity model. It may be used to predict trips made to any type of center supplying needed goods or services, where the decisions of residents to make a trip and to choose a center are voluntary. Types of centers that have been analyzed by this model include shopping centers, libraries, hospitals, and recreation centers or parks.

The variables that serve as measures for H_i, the number of trip-makers at i, may include the population or the number of households at i. If, instead of trips, T_{ij}, we are predicting the value of purchases made by residents of i at shopping center j, then the aggregate income available for purchases at i is inserted for H_i. The variable inserted for S_j, the number of opportunities available at the center at j, depends on the type of center. If it is a retail shopping center, the variable used may be the floor area of the center, the size of the inventory, or the sales at j.

In the remainder of this section, we show how variations of the gravity model may be used to evaluate public facilities, retail shopping centers, and residential location behavior. Then, in the next section, we examine methods for statistically estimating the parameters (i.e., K, α, β, and λ) of the model.

9.3.2 The Unconstrained Gravity Model

Data have been obtained for a certain neighborhood in a large city that show the number of trips per month made from that neighborhood to each of 10 libraries located in various parts of the city. The distance of each library from the neighborhood has also been obtained. We have plotted these two sets of data in the scatter diagram shown in Figure 9.6. At first glance, it seems that a relation hardly exists.

However, when we add a third variable, the size of the library, a strong relation becomes apparent. In Figure 9.6, we have marked the large libraries with the symbol S^+ (in this city, there are only two types of library, large and small). It now is clear that for each class of library taken separately, trips decline as distance increases. By using the statistical techniques that are described in the next section of this chapter, we estimate a curve that best fits the data. We have plotted this curve, or more precisely, the two curves, S^+ for large libraries and S^- for small ones, in Figure 9.7. The mathematical

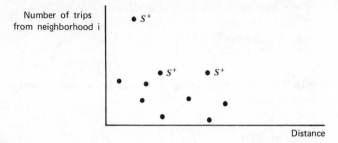

FIGURE 9.6   A scatter diagram showing trips to libraries and distance to libraries.

expression from which these curves are derived is, not surprisingly, the gravity model.[11] What the curves state is just what the model states. By using equation 9.5, and assuming that our statistical analysis has yielded the convenient result that $\alpha = \beta = 1$, that $\lambda = 2$ and that $K = .003$, we can "plug in" some numbers to illustrate this.

Suppose that the variable H_i is measured by the number of households residing in neighborhood i, that library size S_j^- is measured by the number of books at library j, and that distance from i to j is measured in miles. Then if $H_i = 1000$, and $S_j^- = 1000$, we can calculate that a small library located

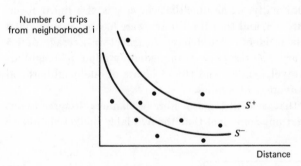

FIGURE 9.7   The relationship between number of trips and distance to library, size of library held constant.

[11] For applications of the gravity model to the evaluation of public facilities, see Jack B. Ellis and Carlton S. VanDoren, "A Comparative Evaluation of Gravity and System Theory Models for Statewide Recreational Traffic Flows," *Journal of Regional Science, 6* (1966), 57–70; and J. B. Schneider. "Measuring the Locational Efficiency of the Urban Hospital," Philadelphia: Regional Science Research Institute, Discussion Paper No. 11 (1967).

an average distance of one mile from residents of i will result in

$$T_{ij} = .003\left(\frac{1000 \cdot 1000}{1^2}\right) = 3000$$

or 3000 trips per month made by residents of i. Similarly, a small library located 10 miles from i will result in

$$T_{ij} = .003\left(\frac{1000 \cdot 1000}{10^2}\right) = 30$$

or only 30 trips per month. Inserting now $S_j^+ = 2000$, into this equation, verify that the model predicts that a large library will generate 6000 trips per month if it is located only one mile from i, or 60 trips if it is located 10 miles from i.

We can now use the model to show how the gravity model can be applied for evaluating public facilities plans, as was promised at the beginning of this chapter.[12]

Suppose that our city is made up of only three neighborhoods, $i = 1$, 2, and 3. To simplify calculations and also to make it easier to see what the model is "doing," we assume that each neighborhood contains the same number of households: $H_1 = H_2 = H_3 = 1000$. For the moment, we retain our assumptions that $\alpha = \beta = 1$, that $\lambda = 2$, that $K = .003$, and that $S_j^- = 1000$; $S_j^+ = 2000$. Finally, we assume that the city is of a linear form, as is illustrated in Figure 9.8, and that if a library were located in any given single neighborhood, its residents would have to travel an average of 1.5 miles to get to the library, the residents of immediately adjacent neighborhoods would have to travel 4 miles, and the residents of one neighborhood may have to travel an average of 8 miles.

Let us suppose now that a small team of library planners disagree about the issue of decentralization. Some feel that the available budget should be

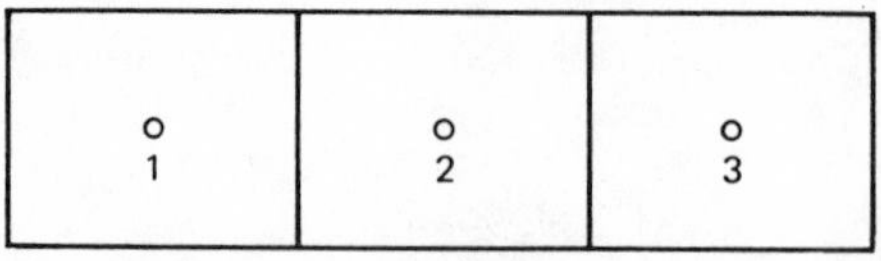

FIGURE 9.8   A linear city with three neighborhoods.

---

[12] For a general analytic treatment of this problem, see Michael Teitz, "Toward a Theory of Urban Public Facility Location," *Papers, The Regional Science Association, 21* (1968), 35–51.

used to construct small libraries scattered around the various neighborhoods of the city. Their point of view is supported by the argument that a decentralized pattern of facilities will reduce the average distance each city resident would have to travel to get to the nearest library and, in consequence, the limited library budget would yield more library users. Others in the group take the opposite view. They insist that a central facility pattern is the more effective. They agree that a decentralized pattern will, indeed, reduce the average distance of residents to the nearest library. Their argument, however, is that the centralized plan minimizes the average distance of residents to the "average valued" book. It is not the distance to the *nearest* book but the distance to the *needed* book that generates users, and since the need for a given type of book varies from person to person, it would be more effective to use the limited budget to locate a diverse collection of books in one central place so as to increase the likelihood of a user's finding the right book at the nearest (the central) facility. Unfortunately, both arguments have merit to some extent, but the question of merit cannot be resolved on a priori grounds. Empirical knowledge is needed of trip-making behavior in response to distance and to size of library collection.

Of course, if the budget is large enough, then we could satisfy both groups and not worry about empirical knowledge. We could put one large facility at the center and two small ones in the other two neighborhoods. But it is more realistic to assume a limited budget, and this we do. However, to permit concentration on the role of location behavior in settling our planners' controversy, we suppose that one large library costs the same as two small facilities, where each is one half the size of the large one, that is, there are no economies of scale in construction or operation.

To evaluate the two alternative plans—one large library in neighborhood no. 2 versus two small libraries, one each in neighborhoods nos. 1 and 3—all we need to do is compute the total amount of library usage in the city, measured by total trips, T, generated by each plan. This becomes the effectiveness measure of each plan, and since the two plans require identical budgets, the plan with the greatest effectiveness is the plan of choice.

For the decentralized plan, total trips $T^{(-)}$ will be

$$T^{(-)} = \sum_i \sum_j T_{ij}^{(-)} = \sum_i \sum_j .003 \frac{H_i^1 S_j^1}{D_{ij}^2}$$

which may be written as the sum of the total trips made from each of the three neighborhoods to each of the two facilities:

$$T^{(-)} = \left[\sum_j T_{1j}^{(-)} \right] + \left[\sum_j T_{2j}^{(-)} \right] + \left[\sum_j T_{3j}^{(-)} \right]$$

where

$$\sum_j T_{1j}^{(-)} = .003 \left[\frac{1000(1000)}{(1.5)^2} + \frac{1000(1000)}{8^2} \right] = 1380$$

$$\sum_j T_{2j}^{(-)} = .003 \left[\frac{1000(1000)}{4^2} + \frac{1000(1000)}{4^2} \right] = 375$$

and

$$\sum_j T_{3j}^{(-)} = .003 \left[\frac{1000(1000)}{8^2} + \frac{1000(1000)}{(1.5)^2} \right] = 1380$$

Therefore

$$T^{(-)} = 1380 + 375 + 1380 = 3135$$

which is to say that the decentralized plan will have a usage rate of 3135 trips per month throughout the city.

It should be apparent that it is not difficult to apply the gravity model for estimating either the usage rate of a single facility or of an entire plan—the only difficulty is that there are numerous calculations to be made. Familiarity with both the application and nature of the gravity model can be obtained quickly by doing some of the problems at the end of the chapter.

9.3.3 THE CONSTRAINED GRAVITY MODEL

In the application of the gravity model we have just described, an overall increase in the attractiveness of the various facilities will have the effect of increasing the total number of trips made by the residents of any given neighborhood. It was this characteristic of the model that we used in evaluating alternative facilities location plans. But not all types of trip-generating activities have this effect. For example, the quantity of goods purchased by households to fill their consumption needs may not depend on the locational pattern of shopping centers but, instead, on exogenous conditions such as average income and family size. Where this is true, we would want to take the total number of trips originating in each neighborhood as already given, perhaps as predicted by the average family income and size in each neighborhood.

Our model is now constrained to assure that the combined number of trips made to the various centers j from a given neighborhood i, no matter how attractive these centers, remain constant at the fixed level $\bar{T}_i$. The constraining equation

$$\bar{T}_i = \sum_j T_{ij} \qquad 9.6$$

must now be included in our model along with equation 9.5. Substituting equation 9.5 for the T_{ij} in equation 9.6, we may write

$$\bar{T}_i = \sum_j K \frac{H_i{}^{\alpha}S_j{}^{\beta}}{D_{ij}^{\lambda}}$$

But note that in this summation, both K and $H_i{}^{\alpha}$ remain constant as j varies from center to center. These two constants may, therefore, be shifted to the left of the summation sign.

$$\bar{T}_i = KH_i{}^{\alpha} \sum_j \frac{S_j{}^{\beta}}{D_{ij}^{\lambda}}$$

We see that K is now required to be equal to

$$K = \frac{\bar{T}_i}{H_i{}^{\alpha} \sum_j \dfrac{S_j{}^{\beta}}{D_{ij}^{\lambda}}} \qquad 9.7$$

and that it contains the total attraction of all centers on the trip-making decisions of residents at location i, $(\sum_j S_j{}^{\beta}/D_{ij}^{\lambda})$.

If we substitute this constraint for the constant K in equation 9.5, we obtain

$$T_{ij} = \bar{T}_i \frac{\dfrac{H_i{}^{\alpha}S_j{}^{\beta}}{D_{ij}^{\lambda}}}{H_i{}^{\alpha} \sum_j \dfrac{S_j{}^{\beta}}{D_{ij}^{\lambda}}}$$

However, since the $H_i{}^{\alpha}$ cancels out, this expression reduces to

$$T_{ij} = \bar{T}_i \frac{\dfrac{S_j{}^{\beta}}{D_{ij}^{\lambda}}}{\sum_j \dfrac{S_j{}^{\beta}}{D_{ij}^{\lambda}}} \qquad 9.8$$

and we see that the attraction of center j $(S_j{}^{\beta}/D_{ij}^{\lambda})$ is normalized by the total attraction of all centers; that is to say, the model considers the effects of competition.[13] Here, although we no longer require the variable H_i, we now must have the total number of trips from i, $\bar{T}_i$.

[13] Note that if in place of the proxy H_i for the number of trip-makers in K in equation 9.5 we had used the number of trips $\bar{T}_i$ from i, then K is simply

$$K = \frac{1}{\sum S_j{}^{\beta}/D_{ij}^{\lambda}}$$

and equation 9.8 results directly. This is the approach used in M. C. Hayes and A. G. Wilson, "Spatial Interaction," *Socio-Economic Planning Sciences, 5* (1971), 73–95.

Notice that this relation may be rewritten as

$$\frac{T_{ij}}{\overline{T}_i} = \frac{\dfrac{S_j{}^{\beta}}{D_{ij}^{\lambda}}}{\sum\limits_j \dfrac{S_j{}^{\beta}}{D_{ij}^{\lambda}}}$$

Since the terms on each side of the equal sign lie between zero and one, and since the sum of these terms over all centers j is equal to one, they are both probabilities. Further, if the T_{ij} and $\overline{T}_i$ have already occurred and are observations rather than predictions, then $T_{ij}/\overline{T}_i$ is also an empirical probability. In any case, either term may be written as the probability $p(j \mid i)$, which is the probability that a trip will be made to center j given that the trip is to be made by a resident of location i.

$$p(j \mid i) = \frac{\dfrac{S_j{}^{\beta}}{D_{ij}^{\lambda}}}{\sum\limits_j \dfrac{S_j{}^{\beta}}{D_{ij}^{\lambda}}} \qquad\qquad 9.9$$

from which equation 9.8 may be written more simply as[14]

$$T_{ij} = p(j \mid i)\overline{T}_i \qquad\qquad 9.10$$

The term $p(j \mid i)$ may alternatively be thought of as a market share (to recall the problem of discontinuous versus probabilistic trade areas discussed in a preceding section)—the share of the market at i held by the center j. Thus the constrained gravity model, equation 9.10, predicts the number of trips from i to j by allocating the given total at i ($\overline{T}_i$) to each center j. It does this via the probability $p(j \mid i)$ obtained in equation 9.9, in which the probability depends on the opportunities supplied at a given center (S_j), the distance of the center to residents at i (D_{ij}), and the attraction held by all competing centers on residents at i ($\sum\limits_j S_j{}^{\beta}/D_{ij}^{\lambda}$).

We now apply the constrained gravity model to a problem described at the beginning of this chapter. We cast the problem as follows:

Suppose four neighborhoods are located adjacent to each other in our linear city as in Figure 9.9. At present, there is just one large (2000 sq ft) shopping center located in neighborhood no. 1. Aware that land prices in

[14] One of the earliest to use the gravity model as a probability model was David Huff, "A Probabilistic Analysis of Shopping Center Trade Areas," *Land Economics, 39* (1963), 81–90; and David Huff, *Determination of Inter-Urban Retail Trade Areas* (Los Angeles: Real Estate Research Program, Graduate School of Business Administration, Division of Research, University of California, Los Angeles, 1966).

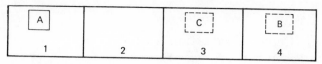

FIGURE 9.9 Four neighborhoods in a linear city with a shopping center, A and a proposed small center, B, and a possible large center, C.

neighborhood no. 4 are low, a shopping center developer wants to construct a small (1000 sq ft) facility at a location in that neighborhood which, at present, is zoned for residential use. He applies to the City Planning Commission for a variance, and requests that certain public investments be made. Should the City Planning Commission comply with the developer's request, or should they discourage him?

Of foremost concern to the commissioners is the stability of the proposed center against the likelihood of future competition. For example, if a large center were to be constructed at a future date in neighborhood no. 3, the stability of the proposed small center and, therefore, the future value of the requested public investments, would be in doubt. Of secondary concern to the commissioners is the desire to encourage a commercial development pattern that is most beneficial to the city as a whole, and they would therefor like to identify appropriate locations for commercial development.

We recast the constrained gravity model in terms of purchases Y_{ij} made by residents of neighborhood i at shopping center j, rather than trips T_{ij} so that equation 9.10 now appears as

$$Y_{ij} = p(j \mid i)\overline{Y}_i$$

where $\overline{Y}_i$ is total consumer expenditures per time period in neighborhood i, and $p(j \mid i)$ is as stated in equation 9.9. To simplify the arithmetic, we suppose that each neighborhood has a total of $\overline{Y}_i = \$1000$ to spend each month on consumer purchases. As previously, we assume $\beta = 1$, $\lambda = 2$, and that distances between neighborhoods are the same; we need only add the distance to a neighborhood two neighborhoods removed, which is 12 miles. We summarize the data in Table 9.1.

First, we calculate the total sales that the proposed center B can expect, given that its only competitor is center A. Then the question of whether the proposed center B could withstand the competition of a possible large center C located in neighborhood no. 3. The criterion for stability will be that a small center must have at least $1000 in monthly sales to cover costs or else it will fail.

Our first step will be to calculate the attraction measures S_j/D_{ij}^λ for each neighborhood i and center j. These ratios are shown in Table 9.2. For example,

TABLE 9.1
Data for Shopping Center Evaluation

Neighborhood	Total Consumer Expenditures $\overline{Y}_i$	Distance (D_{ij}) from		
		Center A	Proposed Center B	Possible Center C
1	$1000	1.5	12	8
2	$1000	4	8	4
3	$1000	8	4	1.5
4	$1000	12	1.5	4
Size of center in square feet		2000	1000	2000

this ratio for center A and neighborhood no. 2 is

$$\frac{S_A}{D_{2A}^2} = \frac{2000}{4^2} = 125$$

Next, we compute the total attraction that the two centers would have for the residents of each neighborhood ($\sum_j S_j/D_{ij}^\lambda$), which is shown in the "total" column of Table 9.2, that is, it is the total of columns A and B.

Our third step is to compute the probabilities $p(j \mid i)$. This is done by dividing the attraction measure of a given row and column of Table 9.2 by the total attraction measure found in the same row in the "total" column. The probabilities, or "relative attraction" measures, are shown in Table 9.3.

Finally, to find the predicted quantity of purchases Y_{ij}, we multiply the total purchases of neighborhood i ($\overline{Y}_i$) by the probability $p(j \mid i)$. These predictions are shown in Table 9.4.

TABLE 9.2
The S_j/D_{ij}^2 Matrix

Neighborhood \ Center	A	B	Total
1	888.8	7.0	895.8
2	125.	15.6	140.6
3	31.2	62.5	93.7
4	14.0	444.4	458.4

TABLE 9.3
The $p(j \mid i)$ matrix

Center Neighborhood	A	B
1	.99	.01
2	.89	.11
3	.33	.67
4	.03	.97

Adding up the purchases made at a given center from each neighborhood i, we obtain a prediction of the total sales at each center j ($Y_j = \sum_i Y_{ij}$). We see that the proposed center B is projected to do a volume of about \$1760, or about 80% of center A's sales. Given that this center is only half the size of center A and that it is planned for location in neighborhood no. 4 because of the supply of cheaper land, we might suppose that the proposed center will indeed be a profitable investment—at least, until it gets some strong nearby competition. The reader is now equipped to analyze this question and related policy questions in problems 5, 6, and 7 at the end of this chapter.

9.3.4 A GRAVITY FORMULATION OF RESIDENTIAL LOCATION

The projection of the residential expansion of urban areas also often relies on some variation of the gravity model, asserting that population growth, other things being equal, will be attracted to areas on the basis of their relative capacity to accommodate population growth. We present a general

TABLE 9.4
Predicted Purchases and Total Sales

Center Neighborhood	A	B	Total Purchases of i
1	\$990	\$ 10	\$1000
2	890	110	1000
3	330	670	1000
4	30	970	1000
Total sales at j	\$2240	\$1760	\$4000

form of this model. Simple variations of it have been developed by Hansen,[15] Lowry,[16] and others.[17]

The gravity model of residential location asserts that population growth in a subarea or zone j of the city will be some portion of total population growth of the city. That portion is a function of vacant (developable) land in each zone and the accessibility of each zone to the centers of employment in the city. Thus each zone develops an index of accessibility as

$$A_j = \sum_{i=1}^{n} \frac{E_i}{D_{ij}^{\lambda}} \qquad i \neq j \qquad\qquad 9.11$$

where

E_i = size of employment in zone i

D_{ij} = time distance from i to j

Growth is then allocated according to equation 9.12.

$$G_j = G_t \left(\frac{L_j A_j}{\sum\limits_{i=1}^{n} L_i A_i} \right) \qquad\qquad 9.12$$

where

G_j = the residential population growth of zone j

G_t = total population growth for city

L_j = some measure of unused capacity, such as vacant land

A_j = accessibility to employment as in equation 9.11

Several qualifications are needed. First, other variables might be added. For example, L_j might be modified to include an effect of zoned density differences among areas and price differences among areas, and the like. Second, access to employment is used as a proxy. We should really expect people to evaluate accessibility as some weighted combination of attraction and distance to a whole range of use types based on frequency of interaction, value of time, and so forth. Employment is used primarily because it is, for most people, the least flexible trip and also because, when models of residential location are linked with models of transportation systems, the journey

[15] Walter G. Hansen, "How Accessibility Shapes Land Use," *Journal of the American Institute of Planners*, 25 (1959), 73–76.

[16] Ira S. Lowry, *A Model of Metropolis* (Santa Monica, Cal.: The Rand Corporation, RM-4125-RC, 1964).

[17] For a thorough discussion of the various analytic models, see Britton Harris, "Quantitative Models of Urban Development: Their Role in Metropolitan Policy-Making," in H. Perloff and L. Wingo (eds.), *Issues in Urban Economics* (Baltimore: Johns Hopkins Press and Resources for the Future, 1968).

to work is the dominant trip type at peak-load times on the system and, therefore, the critical trip type in evaluating the capacity of alternative transport systems to cope with demand.

9.4 EMPIRICAL ESTIMATION

In this section we show how the gravity model may be made operational by (1) the use of multiple regression analysis for estimating the model's parameters, (2) calculation of the constant K, (3) a useful modification of the distance function, and (4) the inclusion of additional variables.

9.4.1 METHODS FOR PARAMETER ESTIMATION

When the gravity model (equation 9.5) is estimated for use in unconstrained form and a separate model is estimated for each residential location i, the variable H_i will be constant with only the variables T_{ij}, S_j, and D_{ij} varying from observation to observation. Therefore, it will not be necessary to gather data for H_i. Instead, it will be subsumed in the constant K. Alternatively, if the constrained gravity model is to be used, then the variable H_i cancels out (as is shown in equations 9.7 and 9.8 and the paragraph between them). We therefore write our basic equation as

$$T_{ij} = K_i \frac{S_j^{\beta,i}}{D_{ij}^{\lambda,i}}$$

$$= K_i S_j^{\beta,i} D_{ij}^{-\lambda,i} \qquad\qquad 9.13$$

where the constant K_i and the exponents β_i and λ_i are specific to each residential location i.

Taking the logarithms of this equation, we have

$$\log T_{ij} = \log K_i + \beta_i(\log S_j) - \lambda_i(\log D_{ij}) \qquad\qquad 9.14$$

This equation is linear in the logs of the variables T_{ij}, S_j, and D_{ij}. Therefore, if we have current or historical cross-section data on these three variables for a set of towns or neighborhoods, we merely convert them into their logarithms and run a multiple regression on them in the following form.

$$\log T_{ij} = a + b_1 \log S_j + b_2 \log D_{ij}$$

The regression coefficient b_1 will be an unbiased estimate of β_i, and the regression coefficient b_2 will be an unbiased estimate of $-\lambda_i$. In addition, the regression will provide measures of the quality of these estimates by providing the t-values of these coefficients as well as measures of correlation. Typically, on the basis of past experience, we shall obtain values of the parameter β

that are quite small but positive, perhaps smaller than one; values of λ are usually in the range $1 < \lambda < 3$ (which is to say that our regression coefficient b_2 will be in the range $-3 < b_2 < -1$).

However, a problem arises in attempting to use the constant of regression a to derive an estimate of K. It develops that the antilog of a yields an overestimate of K.[18] It is systematically biased and, therefore, should not be used as the estimate of K. The question now arises: How then are we to estimate K? Recalling our discussion concerning the use of a constraint, we may already have an idea in mind. Let us denote the observed values of the variables by putting a little hat on top—$\hat{T}_{ij}$, $\hat{S}_j$, and $\hat{D}_{ij}$. Using our unbiased estimates of β_i and λ_i from the regression, we now proceed as follows.

If K_i is unbiased, then since the other coefficients are also unbiased, the model written in equation 9.13 will yield estimates T_{ij}^*, which are also unbiased. This implies that the expected value of the estimates obtained from the model $E(T_{ij}^*)$ must be equal to the average value of the observed $\hat{T}_{ij}$. Inserting the observed values $\hat{S}_j$ and $\hat{D}_{ij}$ into equation 9.13, summing over the n observations ($j = 1, \ldots, n$), and dividing by n, we have

$$E(T_{ij}^*) = \frac{\sum\limits_{j}^{n} \hat{T}_{ij}}{n} = \frac{K_i \sum\limits_{j}^{n} \hat{S}_j^{\beta,i} \hat{D}_{ij}^{-\lambda,i}}{n}$$

Our estimate of K_i is now obtained as

$$K_i = \frac{\sum\limits_{j} \hat{T}_{ij}}{\sum\limits_{j} \hat{S}_j^{\beta,i} \hat{D}_{ij}^{-\lambda,i}} \qquad\qquad 9.15$$

where the n's cancel out. Thus our unbiased estimate of K_i has the form of equation 9.7 derived previously with the variable H_i deleted.

However, when K_i is to be used with the unconstrained gravity model for predicting the T_{ij}, only the observed values $\hat{T}_{ij}$, $\hat{S}_j$, and $\hat{D}_{ij}$ should be used for the derivation as is shown in equation 9.15 above. This ratio is expected to remain constant for each location i. The reason for this is that, in using the unconstrained model, we are assuming that the total number of trips made from i increases as aggregate access increases, that is

$$\sum_{j} T_{ij} = g_i \sum_{j} S_j^{\beta,i} D_{ij}^{-\lambda,i} \qquad\qquad 9.16$$

so that if this is substituted for $\sum\limits_{j} \hat{T}_{ij}$ in equation 9.15, we would have $K_j = g_i$, a constant.

[18] Refer to Arthur S. Goldberger, *Econometric Theory* (New York: Wiley, 1964), pp. 217–218.

In contrast, when we are using the constrained gravity model for predictions, we have reason to believe that the total number of trips is uncorrelated with aggregate access, for example, that $g = 0$, so that equation 9.16 cannot be substituted for $\sum_j \hat{T}_{ij}$ in equation 9.15. Instead, a projection of $\bar{T}_i$ is required, perhaps, as a function of population, family size, and income. Therefore, instead of using the observed values of the T, S, and D variables in equation 9.15, we use their projected values. Inserting the value of K_i thus obtained into equation 9.13, we have what was derived in Section 9.3.3 above

$$T_{ij} = \bar{T}_i \frac{S_j^{\beta,i} D_{ij}^{-\lambda,i}}{\sum_j S_j^{\beta,i} D_{ij}^{-\lambda,i}} \qquad 9.8$$

or, more simply,

$$T_{ij} = p(j \mid i)\bar{T}_i \qquad 9.10$$

Thus, unlike the other coefficients of the constrained model, K_i does not remain constant when the model is used for forecasting purposes. Not only may the total number of trips (T_i) change but also the number of competing centers and, therefore, the quantity $\sum S_j^{\beta} D_{ij}^{-\lambda}$ may change. But we have completed our effort to show how the model should be estimated, and we may now point out two additional ways to improve the model.

9.4.2 Modifications and Extensions

An Alternative Distance Attenuator

First, in equation 9.13, we show that the effect of distance on trip-making behavior is inverse, to the power λ. However, as the distance between i and j becomes smaller and smaller (approaching zero), the number of trips the model predicts becomes larger and larger (approaching infinity). To avoid this problem, analysts have frequently suggested that a better function of distance would be the negative exponential, where instead of writing $D_{ij}^{-\lambda}$, we would write $e^{-\lambda D, ij}$ where e is the constant $2.718 \cdots$. Instead of appearing as is shown in Figure 9.10*a*, this function predicts a finite zero distance trip frequency, as is shown in Figure 9.10*b*. This may be of analytic use, since it shows the effects of all influences other than distance on trip-making behavior.

If we are to use the negative exponential function in our model, equation 9.13 becomes

$$T_{ij} = KS_j^{\beta} e^{-\lambda D, ij} \qquad 9.17$$

This time, if we are to estimate the β and λ coefficients, we should use Naperian logarithms for our transform which, in logs to the base e, gives

$$\log T_{ij} = \log K + \beta(\log S_j) - \lambda D_{ij} \qquad 9.18$$

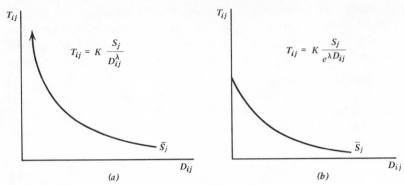

FIGURE 9.10   Two functions relating trips to distance.

Our approach to estimation now differs from our previous one in that we now take the logs (to the base e) only of T_{ij} and S_j; the distance variable is not transformed. Thus, the regression

$$\log T_{ij} = a + b_1 \log S_j + b_2 D_{ij}$$

yields the coefficient b_1, our unbiased estimate of β, and b_2, our unbiased estimate of $-\lambda$. As before, K_i is estimated as

$$K_i = \frac{T_i}{\sum S_j{}^\beta e^{-\lambda D, ij}}$$

which, when inserted into equation 9.17, gives the probability model of equation 9.10. Which of these two formulations is better? We should try them both and use the t-values and r^2's to make our choice.

Our last suggestion concerns the introduction of additional variables, and modifications of the dependent variable T_{ij} to make the analysis more specific.

Modifications in the Variables

Additional variables. Our gravity model predicts trips from i to j by taking only three variables as independent: the total number of trips from i, the size of center j, and the distance from i to j. But in reality, the number of trips made from a given residential location to a given center depends on many other attributes of the trip-makers than just the total number of trips they make, on many other attributes of the centers than just its size, and on additional attributes of travel cost other than just distance.

Consider the attributes of the trip-makers. Residents of locations in which automobile ownership per family is high will travel more frequently to shopping centers located near highways; where automobile ownership is low, relatively more trips will be made to centers served by mass transit. Differences between locations in characteristics of the trip-makers will be picked up in the coefficients K_i, β_i, and λ_i, since a separate equation is to be estimated for each residential location. But in some cases, as we learn later, it will not be possible to make a separate regression analysis for each residential location. Instead, the data must be pooled, and just one equation will be calculated for use with any residential location. In this instance, the socioeconomic characteristics that affect travel behavior must be explicitly incorporated into the model as additional variables. Not only might an automobile ownership variable be included, but also should per capita income, age and education levels, variables that underlie buying power and tastes, be included.

When the various attributes that account for the relative attractive power of a given shopping center are considered, we find that size of centers may not be much more important in predicting trips than is the age of the center and, perhaps, will be less important than whether or not a big name department store such as Macy's is included in the center.[19] If instead of shopping centers, we are predicting trips to a public facility such as a library, in addition to the size of the library (perhaps as measured by total number of books), the average age of the collection, the number of periodicals and journals, and the number of staff personnel available for aiding students and other readers are important determinants of usage. Also, the type of collection, perhaps as measured by the proportion of the collection in specialized titles, or children's books, is also an important determinant of trips to the library and should be included.

Finally, in our measure of distance we might use actual travel times or costs instead of miles, thereby to include the effects of traffic congestion or fast highways. We might even measure the effects of on-site parking facilities by including in a time-distance measure the time required to obtain a parking space.

In addition to improving the explanatory power of our model, the inclusion of all these additional variables allows the inclusion of a number of controllable variables that can be affected by policy in a planning context. The size and type of collection mix and other facility characteristics that are included as variables in the model are all subject to the control of planners and policymakers, and their inclusion in the model allows the model to be used for evaluating alternative policies.

---

[19] This type of variable introduces a new twist to the analysis. All other variables so far considered have been of the interval scale type. "Whether or not a major name department store is in the center" is a yes or no variable, an example of a nominally scaled variable. This is treated in regression analysis as a "dummy" variable in which "yes" is given the value 1 and "no" is given the value 0. Refer to J. Johnston, *Econometric Methods* (New York: McGraw-Hill, 1963), pp. 221–228; also R. Wonnacott and T. Wonnacott, *Econmetrics* (New York: Wiley, 1970), pp. 68–75.

Disaggregating the trip-makers. Instead of lumping all trip-makers together in residential location i and using the model to predict their trip-making behavior in the aggregate, we might use the model to predict the number of trips made by each of several relatively homogeneous groups of trip-makers from that location. For example, we might predict the number of trips made from i to j by subgroup k (T_{ijk}). The trip-makers, for example, may be disaggregated into subgroups on the basis of age—we might want to predict the number of library trips made by students of high school age or younger separately from the rest of the population because we may need specific information on the determinants of the library usage rates of the local school-age population.

Instead of disaggregation on the basis of the demographic characteristics of the trip-makers, we may disaggregate the trip-makers according to the transportation mode they use.

For example, the travel behavior of trip-makers who use automobiles is quite different from those who rely on mass transit. To consider them together leaves out a possible policy dimension—libraries located near transit stops serve different populations than do libraries located with orientation to the automobile.

When we disaggregate the trip-makers in this fashion, we construct a separate equation for each subgroup. If we also include the additional variables discussed immediately above, our model takes the following form:

$$T_{ijk} = K_{ik}S_{1j}^{\beta,1}S_{2j}^{\beta,2}\cdots S_{rj}^{\beta,r}D_{ijk}^{-\lambda} \qquad 9.19$$

In the case of the constrained model, this can be written as

$$T_{ijk} = P(j \mid ik)\bar{T}_{ik}$$

As previously, the coefficients may be estimated via multiple regression in the logs of the variables[20]

$$\log T_{ijk} = \log K_{ik} + \sum_{h}^{r} \beta_{hi} \log S_{hj} - \lambda \log D_{ijk}$$

where there are r different variables S describing the characteristics of centers at j and where our distance measure is to the mode k (time distance is now the appropriate measure of D_{ijk}).

At this point, with the addition of all these new variables, we ought to step back from the details and consider two problems that now arise. The first concerns the model's accuracy. We are now dealing with a model that hardly resembles the pure gravity model as explored by Stewart. There are

[20] As before, the antilog of K_{ik}, where $\log K_{ik}$ is obtained via multiple regression, is biased, so we use the type of calculation shown in equation 9.15 to obtain K_{ik}.

now many variables, and the many coefficients are all empirically derived. One would expect that with all these refinements, our model would yield a much higher degree of estimating accuracy than does Stewart's pure model. But, as surprising as it may seem (to us perhaps, but undoubtedly it was not to Stewart), studies have shown that these refined models are less accurate![21] The simple but more elegant formulation of equation 9.1 still is the best description of trip-making behavior between large concentrations of people. Why then even discuss the more cumbersome apparatus such as is given in equation 9.19? The answer is, simply, that although we want the most accurate estimates possible, the pure gravity model does not give us estimates about the kinds of things we usually want to know. When we insert the additional variable S_{2j}, where S_2 may stand for the type of collection mix available at a library at j, and when we disaggregate the trip-makers into say, students and nonstudents, it is because we want to make a policy decision about the type of collection mix a library in a certain location should have; and we want to use the model to give us some information to help us make this decision: namely, how variations in S_{2j} affect the usage rates of students versus nonstudents.

The second problem that is posed by these additional variables is, in estimating the model's coefficients via multiple regression analysis, we may run into difficulties of data scarcity. The greater the number of additional variables included, the greater the number of observations needed of trips to centers j made from location i via mode k to retain the statistical reliability of the estimated coefficients. This is the problem of "degrees of freedom," described in Chapters 4 and 5, needed to evaluate the significance of an estimate, in this case the regression coefficients b.

As the degrees of freedom decline, the likelihood of obtaining statistically significant regression coefficients also declines. The number of degrees of freedom (df) is obtained as

$$df = n - q$$

where n is the number of observations included in the regression and q is the number of separate variables to be included in the regression. We see therefore, that as the number of variables increases, the number of degrees of freedom and, consequently, the statistical reliability of the model decreases. For example, if for a given neighborhood i and mode k we have observations of the number of trips to 20 centers and there are six variables in the regression (including the dependent variable), then there are only 14 degrees of freedom, which may be too few for acceptable results.

---

[21] Roger E. Alcaly, "Aggregation and Gravity Models: Some Empirical Evidence," *Journal of Regional Science*, 7 (1967) 61–72.

One way around this problem is not to calculate a separate regression for each residential location i but, instead, to pool the observations and construct a model that predicts both the number of trips made from each neighborhood i and the centers j to which these trips are made. Such a model would reincorporate a set of variables $\{H_{1i}, \ldots, H_{ui}\}$, the number of tripmakers at i, and their characteristics. The model would have the following form

$$T_{ijk} = K_k H_{1i}^{\alpha,1} \cdots H_{ui}^{\alpha,u} S_{1j}^{\beta,1} \cdots S_{rj}^{\beta,r} D_{ijk}^{-\lambda} \qquad 9.20$$

which, in the case of the constrained model, may be written as

$$T_{ijk} = p(ij \mid k)\overline{T}_k$$

In the latter case, the model estimates the joint probability distribution of trips by both origin i and destination j, with mode k taken as given. Although projections of total trips by mode $\overline{T}_k$ need not be disaggregated to origin i, there are now required a very large number of projections of the variables $\{H_{1i}, \ldots, H_{ui}; S_{1j}, \ldots, S_{rj}; D_{ijk}\}$.

Continuing in this vein should demonstrate that if measures describing the characteristics of the various transport modes are also included as variables in the model (for example, travel fares, frequency of service, and perhaps passenger comfort by mode k and from i to j) the model would now predict the modal split[22]—the relative usage of each mode—as well as the number of trips from i to j.

PROBLEMS

1. Using equation 9.3, show that the market boundary predicted by Reilly's law will be a curved line bending back toward town A, with respect to Figure 9.2.
2. Develop the calculations for the centralized library plan discussed in Section 9.3.2 of this chapter and indicate which is the better plan.
3. Wait! Don't generalize yet. Suppose that our empirical estimates of the model's behavioral coefficients indicate that $\beta = \frac{1}{2}$ instead of $\beta = 1$, all other coefficients remaining the same. Using this as the exponent of

[22] The model developed by Quandt and Baumol, known as the "abstract mode" model, is an unconstrained model that allows the total number of trips to depend on the number of modes and both their absolute and relative characteristics. In addition, in predicting the number of trips from i to j, the model makes use of the kinds of variables appearing in the pure gravity model (population at i, population at j, etc.). See Richard E. Quandt and William J. Baumol, "The Demand for Abstract Transport Modes: Theory and Measurement," *Journal of Regional Science, 6* (1966), 13–26.

collection size (e.g., we now write $S^\beta = \sqrt{S}$), reevaluate both plans and indicate which plan is now the better one. Interpret the role of the coefficient β in relating S to T_{ij}.

4. Suppose now that neighborhood no. 1 is a low-income, low education community, and that its library usage rates are relatively low. This may be indicated by the coefficient K, which may differ from one neighborhood to the next (as may the other coefficients). Suppose that $K_1 = .001$ but that $K_2 = K_3 = .003$ as before. Again, using $\beta = \frac{1}{2}$, $\alpha = 1$, and $\lambda = 2$, now evaluate the two plans. After making the evaluation, consider the effects of a goal that the plan be such that no fewer than 10% of all trips be made from neighborhood no. 1.

5. In regard to the problem discussed in Section 9.3.3, above, if a large center does locate in neighborhood no. 3, will the proposed center B survive (as indicated earlier, the break-even point for a small center is $1000 per month)? What would you recommend to the commissioners?

6. Suppose that a private developer, seeing that center A is the only facility, decides that another larger center should be constructed. Given that he wants to maximize profits, which neighborhood nos. 2, 3, or 4 would be chosen for his center? Assume (a) that he ignores the possibility of future entry of additional competition; (b) that land prices in the three neighborhoods are the same so that the only reason for preferring one neighborhood over another is superior access to markets; and (c) that profits are proportional to sales.

7. Is the commercial development pattern resulting from the private locational decision of the preceding problem a good pattern from the community's point of view?[23] Where would you have a new center located? Suppose it has been agreed that an appropriate criterion by which to evaluate the effectiveness of alternative commercial development pattern is the measure

$$\sum_i \sum_j K_i \frac{H_i S_j}{D_{ij}^2}$$

where $K_1 = .001$, $K_2 = .008$, $K_3 = .03$, and $K_4 = .07$; also where H_i is 1000 for each i and $S_j = 2000$ for each j. Assuming that center A is fixed at neighborhood no. 1, in which neighborhood would a new large shopping center lead to the highest value of this "aggregate access" measure?[24]

[23] Refer to Hotelling's classic analysis of this type of problem in H. Hotelling, "Stability in Competition."

[24] For an application of the constrained gravity model for the planning of Metrotowns, see T. R. Lakshmanan, and W. G. Hansen, "A Retail Market Potential Model," *Journal of the American Institute of Planners, 31* (May 1965), 134–143.

BIBLIOGRAPHY

Alcaly, Roger E. "Aggregation and Gravity Models: Some Empirical Evidence," *Journal of Regional Science*, 7 (1967), 61–72.

Berry, Brian J. L. *Geography of Market Centers and Retail Distribution.* Englewood Cliffs, N.J.: Prentice-Hall, 1967.

Carrothers, G. A. P. "An Historical Review of the Gravity and Potential Concepts of Human Interaction," *Journal of the American Institute of Planners*, *22* (Spring 1965), 94–102.

Dean, R., W. Leahy, and D. McKee (eds). *Spatial Economic Theory.* New York: The Free Press, 1970.

Ellis, Jack B., and Carlton S. VanDoren. "A Comparative Evaluation of Gravity and System Theory Models for Statewide Recreational Traffic Flows," *Journal of Regional Science*, *6* (1966), 57–70.

Fetter, F. "The Economic Law of Market Areas," *The Quarterly Journal of Economics*, *39* (1924), 520–529.

Goldberger, Arthur S. *Econometric Theory.* New York: Wiley, 1964.

Hansen, Walter G. "How Accessibility Shapes Land Use," *Journal of the American Institute of Planners*, *25* (1959), 73–76.

Harris, Britton. "Quantitative Models of Urban Development: Their Role in Metropolitan Policy-Making." in H. Perloff and L. Wingo (eds). *Issues in Urban Economics.* Baltimore: The Johns Hopkins Press and Resources for the Future, 1968.

Hayes, M. C., and A. G. Wilson. "Spatial Interaction," *Socio-Economic Planning Sciences*, *5* (1971), 73–95.

Hoover, E. M. *The Location of Economic Activity.* New York: McGraw-Hill, 1948.

Hotelling, H. "Stability in Competition," *Economic Journal*, *39* (1929), 41–57.

Huff, David. *Determination of Inter-Urban Retail Trade Areas.* Los Angeles: Real Estate Research Program, Graduate School of Business Administration, Division of Research, University of California, Los Angeles, 1966.

———. "A Probabilistic Analysis of Shopping Center Trade Areas," *Land Economics*, *39* (1963), 81–90.

Hyson, C. D., and W. P. Hyson. "The Economic Law of Market Areas," *The Quarterly Journal of Economics*, *64* (1950), 319–324.

Isard, W. *Location and Space Economy.* New York: The MIT Press and Wiley, 1956.

Isard, W. et al. *Methods of Regional Analysis.* New York: Wiley, 1960.

Johnston, J. *Econometric Methods*. New York: McGraw-Hill, 1963.

Lakshmanan, T. R., and W. G. Hansen. "A Retail Market Potential Model," *Journal of the American Institute of Planners, 31* (May 1965), 134–143.

Losch, A. *The Economics of Location*. New Haven, Conn.: Yale University Press, 1954.

Lowry, Ira. *A Model of Metropolis*. Santa Monica, Cal.: The Rand Corporation, RM-4125-RC, 1964.

Olsson, G. *Distance and Human Interaction*. Philadelphia: Regional Science Research Institute, 1965.

Quandt, Richard E., and William J. Baumol. "The Demand for Abstract Transport Modes: Theory and Measurement," *Journal of Regional Science, 6* (1966), 13–26.

Reilly, William J. "Methods for the Study of Retail Relationships," *University of Texas Bulletin*, No. 2944 (1929).

Schneider, J. B. "Measuring the Locational Efficiency of the Urban Hospital," Philadelphia: Regional Science Research Institute, Discussion Paper No. 11 (1967).

Stewart, John Q. "Empirical Mathematical Rules Concerning the Distribution and Equilibrium of Population," *Geographical Review, 37* (1947), 461–485.

Stewart, John Q. "The Gravity of the Princeton Family," *Princeton Alumni Weekly, 40* (1940).

———, and W. Warntz. "Physics of Population Distribution," *Journal of Regional Science, 1* (1958), 99–123.

———. "The Potential of Population and Its Relation to Marketing," in Reavis Cox and Wroe Alderson (eds). *Theory in Marketing*. Chicago: Irwin, 1950, 19–40.

Teitz, Michael. "Toward a Theory of Urban Public Facility Location," *Papers, The Regional Science Association, 21* (1968), 35–51.

Wonnacott, R., and T. Wonnacott. *Econometrics*. New York: Wiley, 1970.

Zipf, George Kingsley. *Human Behavior and the Principle of Least Effort: an Introduction to Human Ecology*. Cambridge, Mass.: Addison-Wesley Press, 1949.

The volume by Berry provides a good introduction to the ideas of this chapter and to related applications and theories. Some recent advances in this area are discussed in the paper by Hayes and Wilson. One of the most complete bibliographies on the subject is contained in the volume by Olsson. Nearly all of the items in our bibliography are cited in the footnotes of this chapter.

CHAPTER 10

Land Use and Transportation Models

10.1 INTRODUCTION

A proposal has been made to locate an expressway on the southeastern perimeter of a city. Many groups within the city are concerned with the implications of this proposal. Initial reactions are varied. The school board feels that the expressway may reduce through traffic on major arteries near schools, which is highly desirable, but also realizes that the city's population may then spread to the southeast into new suburbs requiring new school buildings, and more teachers, a development that current financial conditions would not permit. The traffic safety commission and staff hope that the expressway will result in fewer accident hazards because of its limited access design. Downtown merchants fear that if rapid suburbanization develops, it will spawn a large suburban shopping center, competing with their establishments and depressing central city land values. The housing authority is concerned with the many homes that will be razed for the right-of-way and for the displaced families in a housing market already short of supply. Local homebuilders, realtors, and banks, however, view transportation as a stimulus to the local economy, hoping that this link with the Interstate Highway System will induce industrial development and a new demand for housing and jobs. The public transit company opposes the highway. Their ridership is dwindling, and they believe that the money should be spent on mass transit to offer improved levels of service, thus diverting people from highways to transit and making the expressway unnecessary. The state highway department urges the city to support the proposal. They assert that the public will certainly buy more cars and spend more time traveling in the future than they do now, and all of that will be cheaper with the expressway than without it, and the sooner it is built the better.

There are other implications of the proposal that can be anticipated as issues. These might include the impact of increased commuting costs on workers who now live in the center of the city. Their jobs may suburbanize if the highway is built and they will be forced into reverse commutation. Also, the concentration of large volumes of auto traffic on the expressway may unduly concentrate hydrocarbons and oxides of nitrogen, as opposed to diffusing this pollution over the existing street system or to reducing it through increased reliance on a noncombustion powered public transit system.

The city commissioners must ultimately act for all local interests and must accept or reject the proposal; the grounds for such a decision would clearly encompass a broad spectrum of social, political, economic, and technical considerations. The feature common of many of the issues that we focus on in this chapter, is the set of underlying assumptions and projections of land use and traffic—questions such as: "What volume of traffic can be expected in 1980 on Plum Street if the expressway is built, and how much if not?" "How many people will ride the transit system if the expressway is built, and how many if not?" "How many new dwelling units will be built in the southeast section if the expressway is built?" "Where will new homes be built if there is no expressway?" "How would improvement of the transit system affect the location of new jobs?" Each question considers either some impact of the transportation system on future land use or some impact of land use development on the future transportation system. In this chapter we examine a set of models and techniques for estimating and forecasting the type, magnitude, and distribution of these mutual impacts.

10.2 A GENERAL STRATEGY OF LAND USE AND TRANSPORTATION FORECASTS

The objective in forecasting land use and transportation is to capture in an analytic model the interrelatedness and interdependence of these two urban systems. Some models of this interdependence are developed in the previous chapter on location and travel behavior, where we study how, for example, the locations of a set of libraries (land uses) are selected in large part because of the accessibility of the sites (transportation) and how the locations of the libraries and their users, in turn, determine the magnitude of travel among those locations. Our objective in this chapter is to estimate these relationships for the whole of an urban area, accounting for several types of land use, and many locations, linked to one another by numerous access routes and competing modes.

Ideally we would like a model that could evaluate all possible configurations of land use and transportation and tell us which is best. But no such model exists. The best efforts that analysts of the problem have been able to devise consist of models that separately forecast various pieces of the systems. These models, set in sequence, attempt to simulate a succession of limited changes in these interacting systems, as they might happen over time. Figure 10.1 represents a common configuration of these analytic procedures. The main line of analysis is represented in the chain of linked land use models and transportation models. These are fed by forecasts or assumptions about selected exogenous variables—variables whose values are determined by some process outside of the main stream of this analysis (for example, aggregate population projections for the city) or a policy alternative for the transportation system (for example, the expressway proposal). There are, within each of the cells of Figure 10.1, several different ways of modeling the components of land use and transportation. We examine some of the major alternative techniques in this chapter, beginning with some of the problems of defining and measuring the existing system. We then review both general and specific land use forecasting models, and consider traffic forecasting techniques.

10.3 DEFINING AND MEASURING THE SYSTEMS

In this section we examine three general kinds of problems of definition and measurement that must be resolved before one can actually begin to apply land use and transportation models to a problem. First, the region being studied must be defined in terms of its geographic limits and then must be partitioned in units of observation or zones. Second, a set of land use variables must be defined to serve as the descriptors and indexes of change in land use. Third, a set of transportation variables must be defined to serve as descriptors and indexes of change in the transportation system. These choices are not wholly independent of one another, but are, in fact, highly interdependent with each other and with the choices among alternative land use and transportation models—because it is, of course, the function of those models to capture and to manipulate these variables that we are here defining for the set of geographic places that we define. However, since we cannot discuss everything at once we review the general nature of these definitions and measurement problems here and allow the later discussion of specific models to serve as a vehicle for their elaboration.

10.3.1 THE STUDY REGION AND ZONES

The problem of setting the geographic boundary of the study region is usually solved by a compromise among three principles. The first principle is a technical guide that says the region should constitute the commuter-shed— a region that is self-contained in terms of origins and destinations of trips to and from jobs. Much of the focus of transportation planning is concerned with the demand for travel at peak hours of the day and most of the traffic

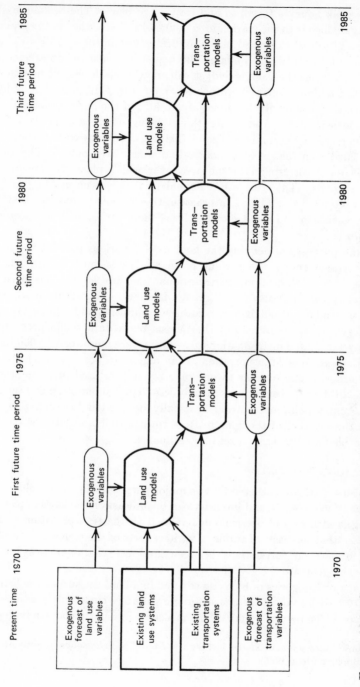

FIGURE 10.1 General forecasting sequence of land use and transportation models.

at these peak hours is travel to and from work places. The commuter-shed notion is analogous to the market area defined by Reilly's law in the previous chapter and to the watershed in the natural environment.

The second principle for defining the region is economic—the region can only be as large as the study's budget will allow. Considering the fact that in large multimillion dollar metropolitan land use transportation studies, data gathering commonly consumes about 60% of the budget, this is a very serious consideration. And, other things being equal, as the size of the region increases or the number of zones increases, so do the costs of the study.

The third principle is of a political-administrative nature. The region defined should correspond to the area over which planning concern and control extends. That is to say it should fit the decision-making unit the study is intended to address. In practice, the region's boundaries therefore usually correspond to some set of political boundaries, such as those of a cluster of counties.

For the purposes of defining the land uses of various parts of the region and the travel among the various parts, the parts must be defined. The smallest unit of observation in traditional land use studies has been the separately owned parcels of land. Such a fine level of detail, for most transportation studies, would be economically prohibitive and computationally unmanageable. Even Bureau of the Census block data would prove to be unwieldy for a large metropolitan area—there were more than 49,000 blocks in the Chicago Area Transportation Study region. In practice, a set of zones on the order of one quarter to one mile square are used in these studies, yielding a total number of zones usually less than 700 but often greater than 200. A center point or centroid is usually designated for each zone and defines the location of the zone relative to longitude and latitude or some comparable two-dimensional set of coordinates.

10.3.2 Land Use Data

Land use data are gathered for two major purposes; (1) so that changes in land use type, location, and intensity can be forecast on the basis of past and existing land uses and determinants related to the transportation system, and (2) so that forecasts of traffic in various parts of the region can be made, based in part on correlations between land use characteristics and the traffic they generate.

The major categories of land use covered in a land use survey are listed in Table 10.1 with some of the characteristic variables commonly measured for each type.[1] The precise variables one measures in a particular study depend

[1] See Marion Clawson and Charles L. Stewart, *Land Use Information* (Baltimore: The Johns Hopkins Press, 1965).

TABLE 10.1

Standard Land Use Codes and Commonly Measured Characteristics[2]

	Standard Land Use Code	Commonly Measured Characteristics
1000	Residential	Population, density, car owner- ship, income, family size, number of dwelling units
2000	Manufacturing	Number of employees, acres, shipments
3000	Manufacturing (cont.)	
4000	Transportation, communications, and utilities	Employees, acres, parking capacity, berths
5000	Trade (e.g., wholesale, retail)	Employees, floor area, acres, parking capacity
6000	Services (e.g., medical, educational)	Acres, attendance, capacity, employees
7000	Cultural, entertainment and recreational	Acres, attendance, capacity
8000	Resource production and ex- traction (e.g., agriculture, mining)	Acres, employees, shipments
9000	Undeveloped land and water areas	Acres, development and capacity, zoned use.

on the data requirements of the land use and transportation models selected. In practice, this choice is usually a compromise of mutual adjustment. The available, workable models limit the kinds of data that can be used while the limited resources for data collection are a restraint on the types of models that one can practically use.

10.3.3 THE TRANSPORTATION SYSTEM

Data used to describe the transportation system are of two kinds: (1) data describing the physical components of the system, and (2) data describing the system's use and performance in use.

The physical system is described as a network consisting of nodes, which are usually points of street or route intersection, and links, which are the

---

[2] These codes are those of the Urban Renewal Administration and Bureau of Public Roads, *Standard Land Use Coding Manual* (Washington, D.C.: U.S. Government Printing Office, 1965). The numbers (1000, 2000, . . .) refer to a four-digit classification code. The Manual can also be found reproduced in full in Clawson, Appendix I.

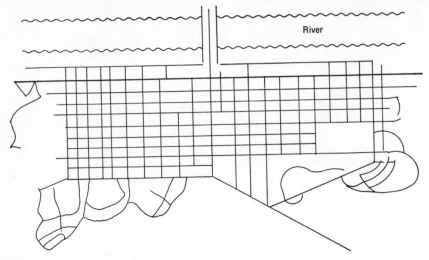

FIGURE 10.2   A hypothetical small city.

facilities connecting nodes with one another. Each analysis zone in the study area must contain, at least, one transport node. If there are several nodes in a zone, one is designated as the prime node or centroid, and these centroids serve as the interface between the area-based land use characteristics of the zones and the network-based characteristics of the transportation system. Traffic flows entering or leaving the network are assumed to originate and to terminate at these centroids, and the type and quantity of this traffic is assumed to be a function of the links entering and leaving the node, the zone surrounding the central node, and these sets of characteristics for all other centroids and zones to which the node is linked.

For a simplified example of this process of abstracting a set of nodes, links, and zones, we might consider a city like that shown in Figure 10.2 and its possible representation in analytic terms, shown in Figure 10.3.

The chief properties of the links that are measured are their capacities to carry traffic and their existing levels of use and service. Capacity is generally defined as the maximum number of vehicles one could reasonably expect to pass over a given section of a roadway during a given time period (say, 1 hr) under prevailing roadway and traffic conditions. The capacities of various types of roadways under many conditions have been extensively studied by traffic engineers, and a standard set of estimating procedures is available.[3]

[3] For definition and estimating procedures see Highway Research Board, *Highway Capacity Manual*, Special Report No. 87 (Washington D.C.: National Academy of Sciences, 1965).

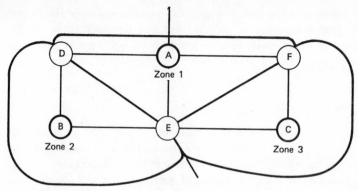

FIGURE 10.3 An abstraction of the hypothetical small city into six nodes, seven links, and three zones of analysis.

In addition to capacity, some measure of existing usage levels is needed to assess the extent of capacity presently being consumed, and to estimate current facility performance, which is partially a function of usage. Changes in performance, often measured as average speed, might be expected as we increase or decrease future loadings on a link. Statistical studies have shown that, for various types of traffic ways, speed, capacity, and volume of flow are systematically interrelated in a function like that shown in Figure 10.4. As the ratio of volume to capacity increases, or as volume approaches capacity, speed declines. In Figure 10.4 there is little decline until volume reaches 60% of capacity, beyond which point speed declines at an exponential rate.[4]

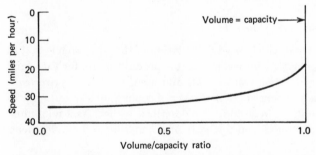

FIGURE 10.4 The general relationship between speed, volume, and capacity.

[4] A good general introduction to this theory is in W. R. Blunden, *The Land-Use Transport System* (New York: Pergamon Press, 1971), Chapters 3 and 5. An advanced discussion and critique of Highway Capacity Manual methods is found in Martin Wohl and Brian V. Martin, *Traffic Systems Analysis for Engineers and Planners* (New York: McGraw-Hill, 1967), Chapters 6 and 10 to 14.

Surveys of traffic and the travel behavior of persons consume the largest share of data gathering resources in land use and transportation studies. These surveys, largely conducted on a sample basis, are usually known as origin and destination (O and D) studies.[5]

10.4 LAND USE MODELS

The purpose of the land use models that we discuss is to forecast land developments for the zones of an urban area, taking into account in this process certain assumptions about the influence of the transportation system in the determination of future patterns of location. We first discuss two general approaches to land use forecasts and then examine models in each of three broad sectors of land use: basic employment, residences, and services.

10.4.1 GENERAL APPROACHES TO LAND USE FORECASTING

One general approach to land use forecasting might be called the *planned requirements approach*. A traditional method, it derives from a precomputer technology and is strongly influenced by notions of analysis developed in the design professions. It is mathematically simple and highly judgemental. The second general approach is the *market simulation approach* which derives from a computer technology. It is often mathematically complex, and its judgemental components are more explicit and allow less latitude. In the planned requirements approach, transportation plays a more loosely defined role than in the market simulation models.

The Planned Requirements Approach

The most complete and widely used formulation of this approach is that of Chapin.[6] The main analytic components of this procedure are, for each land use category, a set of *location requirements* and a set of *space requirements*. Phase I of this procedure consists of a number of tooling-up studies, some of which are like the land use inventories we described earlier. As a minimum, Chapin prescribes inventories and forecasts of population and employment,

---

[5] For a review of the methods of these studies, see Richard M. Zettel and Richard R. Carll, *Summary Review of Major Metropolitan Area Transportation Studies in the United States* (Berkeley: Institute for Traffic and Transportation Studies, 1962); and Walter Y. Oi and Paul W. Shuldiner, *An Analysis of Urban Travel Demands* (Evanston, Ill.: The Transportation Center, 1962), Chapter 3.

[6] F. Stuart Chapin, Jr., *Urban Land Use Planning*, second edition (Urbana, Ill.: University of Illinois Press, 1965). First published by Harper and Brothers, 1957.

inventories of vacant and renewal land, and of existing and substandard dwelling units.

In phase II there is a two-stage process for estimating future land requirements. First, a set of location requirements is defined, comprising verbal or semi-quantitative principles for the location of various types of land use. Such principles state, for example, that manufacturing should be located on reasonably level land of not more than 5% slope, and elementary schools should serve districts of, say, not greater than one-half mile in diameter. Principles of this nature are used to allocate land using activities to available land in the region, and the resulting distribution is designated a *schematic land use diagram*.

A distinction is drawn between *region-serving* activities, such as manufacturing and wholesaling, and *local* activities, which include housing, local shopping, schools, churches, and recreation areas. Land is allocated for region serving users first, and then housing and local activities are distributed. Each round of allocations assumes certain features of the existing and future transportation system, and many of the location requirements enumerated by Chapin directly address the access needs of the land uses.

The second stage of phase II takes the schematic land use diagram generated above and then applies specific numerical space requirements or standards, translating all activities into land area requirements. These standards state, for example, the amount of square feet per industrial employee, the number of acres per person for parks of different kinds, the minimum number of acres per school, and the like. The product of this stage is a trial distribution of space requirements.

The third phase of the procedure is a design phase in which spatial conflicts among different land uses for the same location, and between the land use system and the transportation system, are "ironed out" and resolved by manipulating the land use pattern and transportation assumptions to get a good fit among the competing considerations of "activity patterns," "livability," "cost-revenue considerations," "land values," "physiographic and visual factors," and their "transportation implications."[7]

Specific rules for the resolution of conflicts among these competing land uses for a site are not defined by the method. These judgements must be made by the analyst, based on the given principles and standards, the special

---

[7] It is important to recognize the contribution Chapin made. The work stands as a major synthesis and systematization, advancing the state of practice theretofore embodied in the prescriptions of works such as *Action for Cities: A Guide for Community Planning* (Chicago: Public Administration Service, 1943); and American Public Health Association, *Planning the Neighborhood* (Chicago: Public Administration Services, 1948); and a disparate literature of piecemeal techniques.

knowledge of local conditions, and what is considered to be in the best interest of the public.[8]

The Market Simulation Approach

The archetype of urban market simulation models was developed in the early 1960s by Ira Lowry of the Rand Corporation, working with the Pittsburgh Regional Planning Association. The general structure of the Lowry model, which has since been imitated, altered, and expanded many times, considers three major land use categories:

1. A *basic sector* of establishments whose clients are predominantly nonlocal and, consequently, their site selection process is not constrained by the requirements of access to local markets.
2. A *household sector* of residential population whose location is assumed to be strongly influenced by the locations of basic sector jobs.
3. A *retail sector* of public and private enterprises that primarily service households and whose location choice is oriented to the household sector.[9]

The simulation assumes that future basic employment is given and thus known for all zones in the region. Households are generated then as a direct function of employment and located by a model that assigns households to zones primarily determined by the number of jobs attracting workers to each zone. After households are located, constrained by preassigned density ceilings in each zone, the retail employment and land uses required by the households are generated, subject to certain minimum size constraints (e.g., so many students are needed to justify constructing a school) and land availability. But it does not stop there. Since the initial resident population is assigned to a zone because of the basic jobs available, by creating retail service centers we have created more jobs; thus, there must be more residents to fill those jobs and, hence, a second round of household allocations. Then those new households will demand a new increment of retail services, and then new households, and round and around, bit by bit, until the increments are small enough to be ignored. The entire analytic process is handled in mathematical form on electronic computers.

[8] For another presentation of this method, longer than ours but shorter than Chapin's see Shirely F. Weiss, "Land Use Studies," in William I. Goodman and Eric C. Freund (eds.), *Principles and Practice of Urban Planning* (Washington, D.C.: International City Manager's Association, 1968).

[9] The primary Lowry document is Ira S. Lowry, *A Model of Metropolis* (Santa Monica, California: The Rand Corporation, August 1964), available through the U.S. Department of Commerce, Clearinghouse for Federal Scientific and Technical Information, Washington, D.C., document AD 603670. Also see William Goldner, "The Lowry Model Heritage," *Journal of the American Institute of Planners*, 37 (March 1971), 100–110, for a review of successors to the Lowry model.

Clearly, both the Chapin and Lowry approaches draw somewhat similar distinctions among region-serving or basic and residential and household oriented sectors. Both make assumptions about the role of influence of the transportation system. The Chapin requirements model leaves much latitude for judgement. The Lowry simulation model, as we shall see, is highly specified. One of the greatest differences between them is in what the builders claim for their approaches. The output objective of the planned requirements approach is a desirable plan, a prescription for what ought to develop from the point of view of the public good. Lowry and other market simulators disclaim any normative implications, and claim only, and at best, to be forecasting an economic growth process, extrapolating patterns of economic market behaviors. This difference is more apparent than real, however, and was resolved quite nicely in 1960 by Britton Harris.[10] The distinction between plan and projection dissolves when one considers both processes as ones that work out the implications of a set of assumptions about standards, preferences, technology, and behaviors. We have the requirements-planner saying that the assumptions are desirable policies and the market-projectors saying that the assumptions are simply realistic expectations of what will happen.

Clearly significant methodological differences exist between the two approaches. The simulation approach tends to be more replicable, explicit, and amenable to controlled (paper) experiments; the traditional requirements approach tends to be more judgmental and sensitive to dealing with non-routine problems. Most developments in method in the last decade have carried through with the simulation approach but, as we learn as we now consider some specific land use models, the differences we are talking about are sometimes more formal than substantive.[11]

10.4.2 BASIC SECTOR LAND USE MODELS

By the term basic land use we refer to activities that are neither households nor household-oriented. (It is not a particularly good term but it is short and

---

[10] See Britton Harris, "Plan or Projection: An Examination of the Use of Models in Planning," *Journal of the American Institute of Planners, 26* (November 1960), 265–272. For a sample of the less sympathetic viewpoint see William L. Weismantel, "Dante's Inferno: The First Land Use Model," *Journal of the American Institute of Planners, 25* (November 1959), 175–179.

[11] Indeed, Chapin himself has made some very significant direct contributions to simulation research. See, for example, F. Stuart Chapin, Jr., and Shirley F. Weiss, *Factors Influencing Land Development* (Chapel Hill, N.C.: Institute for Research in Social Science, August 1962). The question of the proper role of judgements in analysis is by no means a well-settled one, however; see Jerry B. Schneider, "Solving Urban Location Problems: Human Intuition Versus the Computer," *Journal of the American Institute of Planners, 37* (March 1971), 95–99.

is generally used.) As a class of activities this includes industry, finance, insurance, real estate, some education, government, wholesaling, regional recreation and regional shopping centers, and certain fairly unique facilities such as airports or sports arenas. Models of intraurban location for many of these activities are not well developed and have been the subject of considerably less research and effort than have residential location models and models of residence-serving activities. These activities are frequently left to judgement or to "exogenous" analysis by major land use transportation simulation studies.

The best efforts in this area have been applied to the distribution of manufacturing employment. We present two models that have been developed: one for the Puget Sound Study (Washington), and one for the Bay Area Simulation Study (BASS) in the San Francisco area.

The Puget Sound Model

This was designed and used in the Puget Sound Regional Transportation Study about 1964 for the region surrounding Seattle and Tacoma,Washington.[12] Exogenous industrial employment forecasts were available for 16 major industrial sectors. Two different land use patterns (policies) were being evaluated, and in this model they differed in terms of the land areas considered available for industrial location. The following procedure was used to allocate industrial employment, by sector, under the two different available land distribution assumptions to the various zones of the region. First, each of the 16 sectors or industrial classes was classified as stable, declining, or growing. The stable sector industries were assumed to remain at their existing locations and employment levels for the future. The declining industries were treated next, and for these employment sectors the existing sector employment in each zone was reduced in proportion to the projected total sector decline—a simple across-the-board proportional reduction. This leaves the growing industrial employment sectors, which were handled in two stages. First, the existing firms in these sectors were interviewed to ascertain their intentions for expansion. These plans of the private firms were accepted as reliable projections, and increments of the projected regional growth were allocated to zones in accord with these reported intentions. But there was still an amount of unclaimed growth that had to be allocated.

The final increments of future growth were allocated by attempting in a qualitative, judgemental manner to match up the characteristics of the remaining available sites with the remaining increments by industrial type.

[12] For an excellent summary of this and the other Puget Sound Models, see H. James Brown et al., *Empirical Models of Urban Land Use: Suggestions on Research Objectives and Organization* (New York: National Bureau of Economic Research, 1972), pp. 30–37.

Each site and industry was qualitatively scored and matched on the basis of the following *location requirement* factors:

1. Freeway proximity.
2. Water transport proximity.
3. Rail transport proximity.
4. Access to labor.
5. General desirability.

The BASS Model (Bay Area Simulation Study).

This industrial location submodel was designed and used for the allocation of manufacturing, trucking and warehousing, and wholesale trade employment to 777 zones of the 13-county region around San Francisco Bay.[13] It is similar in general structure to the Puget Sound procedure but is more formalized (less judgemental) in its evaluation of location. The projection period is very long, 55 years, done in 5-year cycles or increments, with interaction taking place among employment models, housing models, and transportation models in every cycle.

For each time period there was a pool of "new" employees to be allocated. One source of employees in this pool was the exogenous growth forecast. A second source was from a simulated migration of industries out of high density zones into the pool of employees to be allocated to new locations. This is achieved by calculating a density (employment plus population) per square mile for each zone. Then, on the basis of studies of historical changes in density it was decided that for any zone with a density of 30 per acre or more, 10% of each industry's employment would be removed—assumed to migrate out of the zone. A linear function over the density range of 10 to 30 was assumed between density and migration rate; such that a density of 20 per acre implied 5% migration, and a density of 10 per acre implied the level at or below which there was no migration.

The third source of employment in the pool to be newly allocated came from a set of procedures for distributing decline that had been projected in the exogeneous regional employment forecasts. The share of regional decline that is assigned (deducted, actually) to each zone assumes that decline will be a function of the relative share of that industry's employment already in the zone and of the zone's density. In other words, if two zones have equal shares of the declining industry now, but one zone is more dense, then the more dense zone will lose a greater share than the less dense zone. First a

---

[13] The full report is *Jobs, People and Land: Bay Area Simulation Study* (Berkeley, Cal.: Center for Real Estate and Urban Economics, 1968). A summary can be found in Brown et al., pp. 60–67.

percentage decline (PCDECL) for each zone is calculated as:

$$\mathrm{PCDECL}_j{}^k = \frac{\mathrm{EMP}_j{}^k \cdot \mathrm{DEN}_j^{1/2}}{\sum_m \mathrm{EMP}_m{}^k \cdot \mathrm{DEN}_m^{1/2}} \qquad 10.1$$

where EMP is employment, k is the industry group, j is one of m zones, and DEN is density.[14]

The actual employment loss was then assumed to be 20% greater than this share and was calculated as

$$\mathrm{EMPLOS}_j{}^k = \mathrm{PCDECL}_j{}^k \cdot (1.20 \cdot \Delta \mathrm{EMP}^k) \qquad 10.2$$

where, of course, ΔEMP is a negative number equal to total regional decline projected. This extra 20% is apparently a simulated snowballing or local multiplier effect. This extra 20% is not considered lost to the region but goes into the pool of employees and is reallocated. The pool now has in it, projected employee growth, employees relocating due to industry migration spurred by high densities, and relocating employees spurred by industrial decline.

The pool of new or relocating employees is now allocated by calculating a score for each zone. Each tract has, in fact, a separate score, like an attractiveness measure, for each industrial group k. Hence, by industry, scores are calculated, the tract with the highest score is allocated a firm (an average number employees for firms of that industrial type), and then scores are recalculated, the highest scoring zone gets a new firm, and so on, until all employees of that industrial type are located.

The zone scores are calculated as

$$S_j{}^k = \sum_i W_i{}^k \cdot I_j{}^i \qquad 10.3$$

where I is the index for factor i in tract j and W is a weight for the factor i for industry type k. There were a total of 39 possible industrial location factors, one of which, for example, was an index of restaurants in each tract. Each tract's index score was calculated as

$$I_j{}^i = \frac{X_j{}^i - \min^i}{\max^i - \min^i} \qquad 10.4$$

Thus the best zone, with regard to restaurants (X^i) would have a restaurant index ($I_j{}^i$) of 1.0, and the worst would have an index of zero. Among the 39 factors was the existing number of employees in each of 20 different employment groups, measures of transport facilities by rail, freeway, and water, the

[14] Our BASS formulas tend to follow the simplifications of Brown et al.

number of employees in certain industrial types within 30 minutes of the zone, and region-wide measures of accessibility of the zone to all other zones, of the general gravitational form presented in the previous chapter, where

$$A_j = \sum_{i=1}^{n} \frac{E_i}{D_{ij}^{\lambda}}$$ 10.5

Each of these indexes was assigned a weight W_i^k, which was different for each industry type. Thus there was a different score for each industry type in each zone, depending on the set of weights applied to the location factors. The weights were determined by applying multiple regression analysis to recent historical data with employment in an industry group as the dependent variable, and with all of the other factors as independent variables. This was done by using the regression coefficients b as weights, and adjusting them by using expert judgement to account for anticipated changes over time in the importance of factors that were judged to be inadequately represented by the historical (regression) analysis.

A dynamic feature of this model is found in the employee size of firms allocated. Studies of changing mean size of firms for each industry revealed differences, and these were used to set rates of change by industry, so that with each five-year cycle, the size of the "firm" allocated in the growth model changed systematically. Finally, the newly allocated employees were translated into acres of land required, by the application of land absorption coefficients which also vary over time and by industry.[15]

10.4.3   RESIDENTIAL DISTRIBUTION MODELS

Intraurban residential location models attempt to simulate the housing market by taking into account varying salient features of supply—such as existing housing stock, land availability, price, housing type, accessibility to jobs and community services, and deterioration; and demand—such as family sizes, incomes, work places, life cycle, and competition for sites.[16] We present and discuss two operational models of residential location. The first is the Hansen model, a gravity model; the second is the BASS model.

[15] For an excellent review of approaches to models of the general type discussed in this section see: Stephan H. Putman, "Intraurban Employment Forecasting Models: A Review and a Suggested New Model Construct," *Journal of the American Institute of Planners, 38* (July 1972), 216–230.

[16] Two good reference works in the theory and research of residential location are: William Alonso, *Location and Land Use* (Cambridge, Mass.: Harvard University Press, 1964); and Alfred N. Page and Warren R. Seyfried (eds.), *Urban Analysis* (Glenview, Ill.: Scott, Foreman & Co., 1970).

The Gravity Model

The gravity model of residential distribution presented briefly in Chapter 9 has been widely used in various forms. In its usual form, the Hansen formulation, it states that

$$G_j = G_t\left(\frac{L_j A_j}{\sum_i L_i A_i}\right) \qquad\qquad 10.6$$

In words, the population growth increment allocated to a zone G_j is equal to some portion of the total growth increment for the city G_t, and that proportion is determined by the land available in that zone L_j times an index of accessibility of the zone to all other zones A_j, relative to (divided by) the sum of this product for all zones i in the city. The accessibility index most often used is of the form

$$A_j = \sum_{i=1}^{n} \frac{E_i}{D_{ij}^{\lambda}} \qquad\qquad 10.7$$

Where E_i is the size of employment in zones i and D_{ij} is the distance to that zone. Thus the index is an index of accessibility to jobs. If we look at the model as an attempt to simulate a housing market it is rather simplistic.

Total demand, G_t, is usually estimated exogenously either by translating employment into population by a factor, as Lowry did, or by independently forecasting population. In either case, total demand in a place is seldom allowed to be influenced by housing supply. This demand is then distributed over the zones in proportion to the relative supply of land on which housing may be built, and the relative demand for each zone as reflected in the relative transport savings it offers a worker locating in the zone. The model makes good sense—at least, in terms of an individual locator's behavior. People do make a trade-off between land and travel costs, at least in theory, but there is good reason to believe that many other things such as schools, neighbors, recreation access, and urban renewal also influence location decisions, and these factors are poorly explained by the gravity model.[17] Calibrating the model is not straightforward. It is done by experimentally assigning various exponents to distance and by running it on historical data and comparing the modeled outcomes with the known historical outcomes, and thus, by successive approximations, finding a "best-fitting" exponent. Exponents are usually in the neighborhood of 2, and some studies have simply adopted the exponents derived from other studies rather than go through the difficulties of calibration.

[17] For more critical discussion of this form of gravity model, see Michael A. Stegman, "Accessibility Models and Residential Location," *Journal of the American Institute of Planners, 36* (January 1969), 22–29; and Anthony J. Catanese, "Home and Work-place Separation in Four Urban Regions," *Journal of the American Institute of Planners, 37* (September 1971), 331–337.

The appropriate measure of distance is also a subject of considerable variation in practice. Lowry used airline distance in miles, others have used time-distance—either average peak-hour travel time by the shortest route, or a weighted average of transit and highway route times.

The BASS Residential Location Model

The Bay Area Simulation Study's residential location models combine the gravity model with several other models that appear to improve the chances that the simulation results replicate behavior of the housing market.[18] The BASS model first disaggregates housing supply and demand into k submarkets. There are six of these and numbers 1, 2, and 3 are single family— high, middle, and low value, respectively; and numbers 4, 5, and 6 are multiple family—high, middle, and low value, respectively. Each iteration of the model (five-year cycle) is run on each submarket. Demand is composed of new households, forecast exogenously in the population forecast, and relocating households, displaced by housing demolition, which is forecast in a demolitions model. Supply consists of a housing stock, which is devalued in a filtering model and new construction. Demand, finally, is allocated to supply via an accessibility to employment model.

The demolition model estimates the number of housing units to be demolished by type k and by zone j. The basic equation is

$$D_j{}^k = \text{Tot } D \left[\frac{(DR^k \cdot H^k)}{\sum\limits_{k=1}^{6}(DR^k \cdot H^k)} \right] \left[\frac{(DR_j{}^k \cdot H_j{}^k)}{\sum\limits_{j=1}^{n}(DR_j{}^k \cdot H_j{}^k)} \right] \qquad 10.8$$

This states that demolitions by type, by zone $(D_j{}^k)$ equal total demolitions times a proportion to be allocated to type k (the middle term of the right-hand side of the equation), times a proportion to be allocated to zone j. The notational terms are:

$\text{Tot } D$ = Total demolitions rate (exogenously set) times total housing units in the region

DR^k = A preset demolition rate for each housing type, the relative values for $k = 1, 2, 3$ are 1, 2, 4, respectively, and for $k = 4, 5, 6$ are 2, 4, 8, respectively

H^k = is the existing housing stock by type

$H_j{}^k$ = is H^k by zone

$$DR_j^{k=1,2,3} = \frac{(DD_j)^{1/4} \cdot (PM_j)^{1/2}}{HV_j}$$

[18] See note 13 above.

where

$$DD_j = \text{a density measure in zone } j$$
$$PM_j = \text{the proportion of housing units that}$$
$$\text{are multiple in zone } j$$
$$HV_j = \text{an index of housing value} = (2 \cdot \text{high}$$
$$\text{value} + \text{middle value/total housing}$$
$$\text{units})$$

$$DR_j^{k=4,5,6} = (DR_j^{k=1,2,3})^{1/2}$$

Thus we see that both of the ratio terms in equation 10.8 find that the rate of demolition is higher where density is higher, multiple family housing is more prevalent, and land values are lower. The final output of this model has a supply effect, reducing the housing stock, and a demand effect, dislocating households that must be relocated along with new households derived from the population projections.

The filtering process model attempts to simulate how some housing units depreciate over time and shift or filter down to a lower level of value.[19] Single and multiple unit types are filtered separately. Type 1's become type 2's and type 2's become type 3's and, similarly type 4's become type 5's and type 5's become type 6's. Removals, filtering out, so to speak, are handled separately in the demolition model. The basic filtering equations are

$$FIL_j^{k=1,2} = FIL^k \left[\frac{(PM_j^{1/2} \cdot HV_j \cdot H_j^{\,k}}{\sum_j (PM_j^{1/2} \cdot HV_j \cdot H_j^{\,k})} \right] \qquad 10.9$$

$$FIL_j^{k=4,5} = FIL^k \left[\frac{(H_j^{\,k}/HV_j)}{\sum_j (H_j^{\,k}/HV_j)} \right] \qquad 10.10$$

where

$$FIL^k = \text{the number of units to be filtered from the stock}$$
$$\text{of } H^k = \text{a set rate of filtering } (FR^k) \text{ times } H^k,$$
$$\text{the number of units of a given housing type}$$
$$PM_j = \text{the proportion of housing units that are multiple}$$
$$\text{in zone } j$$
$$HV_j = \text{the index of housing value in zone } j$$
$$H_j^{\,k} = \text{the housing stock of type } k \text{ in zone } j$$

The total potential number of new housing units to be constructed is generated exogenously. There is a very complex series of calculations and

[19] For an excellent discussion of filtering theory, see William Grigsby, *Housing Markets and Public Policy* (Philadelphia: University of Pennsylvania Press, 1963).

assumptions used to disaggregate this into the number of each type and then to disaggregate the number of each type in each zone. We verbally describe this rather than elaborate the various equations and their notation.

The total potential supply is first split into single and multiple family housing in each tract on the basis of the existing proportional split (with a potential percentage calculated) and on tract density. The latter consideration, density, is given twice the weight of the former consideration. Next, each of these sectors is broken down into one of the three value classes, based on value, density, and slope-of-the-land variables. Additional adjustments in potential supply are based on the outcomes of the filtering estimates, the set requirements for the proportion of supply in different value classes, and the land absorption coefficients of different housing types.

10.4.4 RETAIL AND LOCAL SERVICE ACTIVITY LOCATION MODELS

The theory and development of empirical modeling in this area are covered extensively in the previous chapter, Chapter 9. The model of spending at shopping centers described in Chapter 9 can be summarized in equation form as

$$Y_j = \sum_{i=1}^{m} Y_{ij} \qquad 10.11$$

$$Y_{ij} = \bar{Y}_i \left(\frac{\dfrac{S_j^{\beta}}{D_{ij}^{\lambda}}}{\sum_{j=1}^{n} \dfrac{S_j^{\beta}}{D_{ij}^{\lambda}}} \right) \qquad 10.12$$

Equation 10.11 says that the income of shops in zone $j(Y_j)$ equals the sum of spending from all zones i in j, or Y_{ij}. And spending from i in $j(Y_{ij})$ is equal to some function (the ratio in brackets) of total shopping dollars spent by the residents of $i(\bar{Y}_i)$. That ratio or proportion is the relative attractiveness S_j and accessibility D_{ij}^{λ} of zone j. To translate these dollars into acres of employees would be a fairly easy task, using some calculated land absorption coefficients or employee ratios. A major difficulty of the model is that it assumes a certain homogeneity about what is termed shopping goods. Suppose, for example, only enough dollars were forecast to a zone to rent one small building and to hire two clerks. What do we presume they are doing, or in terms of the transportation system, what kind of traffic will they generate. That may vary greatly between, say, selling diamonds and selling newspapers. The point is that there are hierarchies of different kinds of shopping goods, and geographic specialization takes place. The Lowry model, which we describe next, attempts to reflect this reality.

The Lowry model partitions service activities into three groups:

1. *Neighborhood facilities*, including food stores, drug stores, gas stations, elementary and secondary schools, and similar functions.
2. *Local facilities*, including restaurants, medical facilities, churches, recreation facilities, department and variety stores, and similar functions.
3. *Metropolitan facilities*, including parts of many categories that are also listed above under local with "large shares of department stores, financial services, lodgings, business services, and public administration."

The total number of employees for each type for the region is estimated (E^k) as a product of the number of projected households (N) and the number of retail employees, by type, per household (a^k):

$$E^k = a^k N \qquad (k = 1, 2, 3) \qquad\qquad 10.13$$

A potential share of these employee groups for each zone was then calculated by a modified gravity model as

$$E_j^{\ k} = b^k \left(\sum_{i=1}^{n} \frac{c^k N_i}{T_{ij}^k} + d^k E_j \right) \qquad\qquad 10.14$$

N is the number of household or potential customers in various zones i which can be expected to decrease with distance from j, (T_{ij}^k). This distance function is different for each facility type k and is approximated by a function of airline distance r between zones as

$$T_{ij}^k = \frac{\alpha^k - \beta^k r + \gamma^k r^2}{2\pi r} \qquad\qquad 10.15$$

E_j is the total employment in the zone, the potential shoppers who shop from work rather than from home, and c^k and d^k are the weights or relative proportions of the potential market assumed to derive from home-based shoppers as opposed to work-based shoppers. These weights are .90, .10 for neighborhood facilities ($k = 1$), are .70, .30 for $k = 2$, and are .50, .50 for $k = 3$. Finally, b^k is a scaling factor representing the proportion of all retail employees that are expected to be of type k.

Employees are then distributed to zones in accord with the potential ($E_j^{\ k}$) subject to two constraints. The first is that there must be a minimum potential for a facility before it will, in reality, appear. There are thresholds of 30 employees for $k = 1$, 250 for $k = 2$, and 20,000 for $k = 3$. Until a zone meets these minimum requirements (Z^k), its potential is shipped elsewhere and pooled with that of other zones. Thus either

$$E_j^{\ k} \geq Z^k$$

or

$$E_j^{\ k} = 0$$

The other constraint is on available land. Land for retail functions $A_j{}^R$ is calculated using certain land absorption factors e^k as

$$A_j{}^R = \sum_{k=1}^{3} e^k E_j{}^k \qquad 10.16$$

and for any zone this cannot exceed the land in the zone A_j minus the unusable land $A_j{}^u$ and the basic industries land $A_j{}^B$. Thus

$$A_j{}^R \leq A_j - A_j{}^u - A_j{}^B \qquad 10.17$$

In other words, only unusable and basic industrial land takes priority over land for shopping. Retail sector land can and will displace housing as the model advances growth from one cycle to the next, and within each cycle from iteration to iteration, in working through the multiplier-type process of the Lowry estimating procedure described earlier in this chapter.[20]

10.5 TRAFFIC FORECASTING MODELS

10.5.1 GENERAL APPROACHES

Traffic forecasting models attempt to estimate the future volume of traffic by person trips or vehicles for a particular facility or system. We can distinguish among three general approaches to this problem, corresponding generally with their historical development. All three approaches are currently in use.

The first approach is the simple projection of a historical trend, through the application of a growth rate to existing volumes of traffic. Formally, we say that the volume of traffic T from one point i to another point j by a particular mode k (say automobile) on a particular route l will increase or decrease by a given rate of change, based perhaps on studies of historical rates of change. We can write this, in general form, as

$$(T_{ijkl})_{t+n} = r_n (T_{ijkl})_t \qquad 10.18$$

---

[20] An especially important contribution to commercial activity simulation, for which we lack sufficient groundwork and space to present adequately here, is Brian J. L. Berry, *Commercial Structure and Commercial Blight* (Chicago: University of Chicago, Dept. of Geography, 1963).

Other important coverage of land use models can be found in two special issues of the *Journal of the American Institute of Planners*, Vol. 25 (May, 1959) and Vol. 31 (May, 1965) and in Highway Research Board, *Urban Development Models*, Special Report 97 (Washington, D.C.: National Academy of Sciences, 1968); and, of course, in H. James Brown *et al.*

where

$$t = \text{existing time period}$$
$$t + n = \text{some future time}$$
$$r_n = \text{some rate of future change}$$

The technique is simple and direct, but it is causally naive. The techniques that apply to this general approach are those of curve fitting, essentially the same techniques as those we applied to population growth in Chapter 8.

A second approach to traffic forecasting breaks down the aggregate term T_{ijkl} into component parts. First T_i is estimated. The models used here are known as *trip generation* models, and they attempt to project the volume of trips generated by a place, usually based on characteristics of that place's population and land use. Next the portion of those trips generated at i that might go to $j (T_{ij})$ is estimated as a function of T_i and the characteristics of zone j. This gives the total volume of traffic desiring to go from i to j. This second phase is called *trip distribution*. Next come models that attempt to estimate how the travel from i to j will be split among the various modes of travel k, for example, automobile versus transit. These models are called *modal split* models. Finally, there are models that assign portions of trips from i to j by mode k to a particular route or facility l that links i to j. These models are called *assignment models*. With the exception of modal split, the models are applied in the above order. Modal split, however, is usually handled in conjunction with one of the other three models such as separately generating trips by mode or separately distributing them by mode. The sequence is illustrated in Figure 10.5 below.

These models of the second approach, which we review in more detail below, have always been considered weakest in their ability to handle satisfactorily the modal split problem, a weakness one might surmise from the seemingly indecisive nature of the problem's location in the sequence of analysis.

Recent research in travel behavior and forecasting has attempted to focus on the modal split problem, and represents the third general approach to traffic forecasting. These are typified by various "abstract-mode" models of the type presented at the end of Chapter 9. They represent a return to a

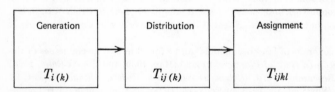

FIGURE 10.5 The sequential traffic forecasting scheme.

one-step model as in the first general approach to traffic forecasting discussed above. But, now, more truly causal variables have replaced the historical trend variables of the naive one-step model. These abstract mode models directly project T_{ijk} as a product of a multiple regression equation or equations, using independent variables such as population at i and j, income at i and j, travel time, cost, measures of comfort of travel, and the like. These models have been developed and used primarily to forecast travel between cities in situations where a specific mode k is equivalent to a specific route l, rather than within cities, but they do represent one of the current frontiers of research and can be expected to expand their range of future application.[21]

The majority of the better land use and transportation planning studies utilize some version of the second general approach described above. For the balance of our discussion we focus on some of the principal models and techniques used in this sequential approach to traffic forecasting.

10.5.2 TRIP GENERATION

Trip generation refers to the process of estimating the number of trips made by the residents, or generated by the activities, of a zone. Several terms must be defined, including what a trip is, who or what is making the trip, and when the trip is occurring.

In common everyday speech we speak of a trip in terms of a round trip—to the grocery and home again. We define a trip as a movement between an origin land use and a destination. If one goes from home to work, after work drives to a shopping center, and then returns home, that would constitute three trips. But some trip-generation analyses focus not on the projection of trips, let alone round trips, but on *trip ends*. Every trip, of course, has two ends, an origin-end and a destination-end.

Let us look at a simple illustration of this. Suppose that we had three isolated locations, as in Figure 10.6, a residential center, an employment center, and a commercial center. Person no. 1 leaves the residential area, goes to employment, and returns directly at the end of the day. Person no. 2 leaves home, goes to work, from there goes shopping, and then returns home. Person no. 3 goes from home to shopping and back home. These movements shown in Figure 10.6 can be measured as 3 round trips from home: or as 7 trips, or as 14 trip ends—6 generated by residential land use, 4 by employment land use, and 4 by commercial land use. The phenomenon observed, whereby in the course of a given day the number of trips entering a zone

---

[21] In addition to the Quandt and Baumol reference of Chapter 9, see John R. Meyer and Mahlon R. Straszheim, *Pricing and Project Evaluation* (Washington, D.C.: The Brookings Institution, 1971), Chapter 9; and Richard Quandt (ed.), *The Demand for Travel: Theory and Measurement* (Lexington, Mass.: Heath, Lexington Books, 1970).

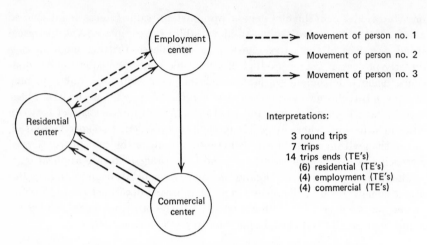

Interpretations:

3 round trips
7 trips
14 trips ends (TE's)
(6) residential (TE's)
(4) employment (TE's)
(4) commercial (TE's)

FIGURE 10.6   An illustration of round trips, trips, and trip ends.

tends to equal the number leaving, is known as the "directional symmetry of travel."

We must also distinguish among person trips and vehicle trips. While many projections are made in person-trip units these must, at some stage of the study, be translated into vehicles, using some persons-per-vehicle rate or set of rates to determine the fit between the vehicular capacity of a route, and the vehicles demanding space on it. Furthermore a time period must be assumed. The time unit for a volume of trips one usually uses is either an average day, corresponding in vehicle terms to the volume of average daily traffic (ADT), or an annual average day's traffic (AADT). The common alternative to daily units is peak-hour volume, sometimes estimated as a percentage of ADT. Given these definitions, we now review three types of trip generation techniques: one based on land use ratios, one based on regression analysis, and one which combines these two approaches to introduce modal split.

The Land Use Ratio Model

This technique, first developed in the Detroit Area Transportation Study (DATS) in the early 1950s, first establishes a set of land use categories. Then, from O and D survey data, trip origins associated with each land use category are counted, and an average rate, such as trips per acre, is calculated for each land use category. These rates are then used in conjunction with land use forecasts to estimate future trip generation for each zone. Commercial land use trip origins are often stated as so many trips per square foot of retail space; manufacturing trips are stated as so many per employee or 100 employees, and residential trip origins are stated as so many per acre.[22] The technique has been elaborated in many instances to include variations in the distance of land use from the Central Business District (CBD), and variations in residential density.

The underlying statistical structure of this sort of analysis conforms to an analysis of variance design when one attempts to explain variation in a continuous variable (trips generated) by a discontinuous set of nominal categories (land use types) or ordinal categories (e.g., categories of residential density). The assumption, therefore, being made in applying the various trip generation rates derived from sample data is that a statistically significant variation in mean rates exists among land use categories and that these differences are stable from zone to zone and over time.

Household Regression Models

A major effort to improve on the land use ratio models has been in the use of multiple regression models within the residential-based trip generation land use category. Among the advantages in this move has been switching to a behavioral unit of analysis, the household (acres do not really make trips, households and their parts do), and to a continuous variable statistical model, more sensitive to variations in the independent variables than is the categorical or analysis of variance format of land use ratio technique. This has been especially desirable within the category of household-based trip origins as they, by far, account for the largest portion of all trip origins, about 40%.

The principal independent variables used in these models of household trip making are

1. Household size.
2. Car ownership.
3. Distance to the CBD.
4. Population density.
5. Income.

Studies have repeatedly shown that a dominant factor is car ownership; the number of vehicles the family has available for use. One of the most complete analyses of household trip generation was done by Oi and Shuldiner, reanalyzing data for Modesto, California and Chicago, Illinois.[23] They found that both car ownership and persons per household were clearly the strongest variables in explaining variation in the number of "from home" trips. Their

[22] Much of the theoretical support for this technique was developed in Robert B. Mitchell and Chester Rapkin, *Urban Traffic: A Function of Land Use* (New York: Columbia University Press, 1954).

[23] See Oi and Shuldiner, Chapter 4, for an excellent presentation of the analysis.

linear regression equations, below, for Modesto illustrate to some extent the relative power of these variables and are of the form of the projection equations often used in these studies.[24]

$$T = .65 + 1.9(v) \qquad R^2 = .49 \qquad 10.19$$

$$T = -.63 + 1.2(p) \qquad R^2 = .67 \qquad 10.20$$

$$T = -.65 + .96(p) + .61(v) \qquad R^2 = .69 \qquad 10.21$$

where

T = average number of from home vehicle trips per dwelling unit (DU)

p = person per DU

v = vehicles per DU

While equations of this sort are widely used in traffic studies for projection purposes, the work of Oi and Shuldiner consistently points out that often these relationships are, in fact, not linear, and that the assumptions of regression analysis are usually not met. The result is a bias in the projections.

Generation with Modal Split

We describe here briefly the techniques used in Pittsburgh in 1958.[25] In studies where modal split is handled as part of trip generation, this model and variations on it are commonly used, employing a principle of separately treating transit trips to the CBD and all other transit trips.

The first step was to forecast total future person trips for each zone. Next, the portion of these destined for the CBD was estimated for each zone and separated from non-CBD trips. Then, based on past behavior, the portions of CBD trips expected to use transit was calculated, leaving a balance of CBD trips to the automobile mode.

Next, transit trips to school were estimated, using an equation fit from historical data that was

$$\text{Log } Y = 3.3 - .91(\log X) \qquad R^2 = .56 \qquad 10.22$$

where

Y = school transit trips per 1000 persons

and

X = net residential density

[24] From Oi & Shuldiner, p. 216, based on unweighted average values for 58 traffic census zones in Modesto (also see pp. 86 and 266).

[25] See, Martin J. Fertal et al., *Modal Split: Documentation of Nine Methods for Estimating Transit Usage* (Washington, D.C.: U.S. Department of Transportation, December 1966), reprinted October 1970.

indicating that lower density zones produce more children using transit services to get to school.

All other transit trips were estimated by regression equations, based on net residential density and cars per household. Thus for each zone, one derived finally

1. The CBD transit trips.
2. The school transit trips.
3. The "other" transit trips.
4. A residual of automobile person trips.

10.5.3 Trip Distribution

The principal task for a trip distribution model is to take the number of future trip ends generated for a zone T_i and to estimate how many of the trips leaving a zone will desire to go to each of the other zones T_{ij}, and to forecast these interzonal transfers for every zone. In this section we present three different trip distribution models: one of a family of growth factor models known as the Detroit model, a gravity model, and a modal split model.

The Detroit Growth Factor Model

This model is one of a number of models whose essential nature is to measure existing movements from one zone to another and to project by multiplying the existing volume by a growth factor. The Detroit model was developed from an earlier model by Fratar.[26]

The Detroit model says that trips from zone i will increase by a rate F_i and will be attracted to zone j in proportion to the relative growth rate of trip-making at j, relative to the city as a whole, or F_j/F. This can be written as

$$T_{ij} = \left(t_{i \to j} \frac{(F_i \cdot F_j)}{F} + t_{j \to i} \frac{(F_j \cdot F_i)}{F} \right) \qquad 10.23$$

or

$$T_{ij} = t_{ij} \frac{(F_i \cdot F_j)}{F} \qquad 10.24$$

[26] For a review of these models see Brian V. Martin, Frederick W. Memmott, III, and Alexander J. Bone, *Principles and Techniques of Predicting Future Demand for Urban Area Transportation* (Cambridge, Mass.: The M.I.T. Press, 1961); and Nigel D. Finney, "Trip Distribution Models," in Anthony J. Catanese (ed.), *New Perspectives in Urban Transportation Research* (Lexington, Mass.: Lexington Books, 1972), pp. 63–146.

where

$$T_{ij} = \text{future total trips between } i \text{ and } j$$
(both directions)

$$t_{ij} = \text{existing total trips between } i \text{ and } j$$

$$t_{i \to j} = \text{existing trips from } i \text{ to } j$$

$$F_i = \frac{T_i}{t_i}, \quad T_i = \text{projected trip ends at } i$$

$$t_i = \text{existing trip ends at } i$$

$$F_j = \frac{T_j}{t_j}$$

$$F = \frac{T}{t} \quad \text{(city or study area totals)}$$

One of the complicating factors in this model, as well as in the gravity model (which follows) is that while the basic formulas are simple, the methods do not give an accurate result the first time. The formulas must be applied, then some adjustment factors must be constructed, and then the principal formulas must be recalculated; this is often done several times over until, by a process of successive approximations, an acceptable solution is produced. We use a small example to demonstrate the process.

Suppose in our three-zoned city, our origin-destination survey revealed the following interzonal flows, shown both graphically and in Table 10.2.

On the right-hand side of the table we enter projected trip ends for each zone, and the city as a whole (we will assume these are derived from a trip-generation analysis) and then calculate the various F-values needed for the

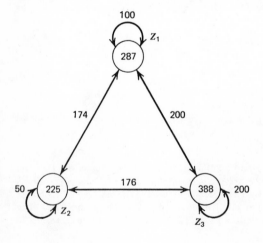

TABLE 10.2
Flows in a Three-Zone City

From \ To	1970 Flows Z_1	Z_2	Z_3	1970 Total City t_i	Projected Totals 1980 $T_i(g)$	F_i
Z_1	100	87	100	287	574	2
Z_2	87	50	88	225	675	3
Z_3	100	88	200	388	388	1
				$t = 900$	$T = 1637$	$F = 1.8$

Detroit model. Now we can apply equation 10.24 as follows:

$$T_{ij} = t_{ij} \frac{(F_i \cdot F_j)}{F}$$

$$T_{11} = 100 \cdot \frac{2 \cdot 2}{1.8} = 222$$

$$T_{12} = 174 \cdot \frac{2 \cdot 3}{1.8} = 580$$

$$T_{13} = 200 \cdot \frac{2 \cdot 1}{1.8} = 222$$

$$T_{22} = 50 \cdot \frac{3 \cdot 3}{1.8} = 250$$

$$T_{23} = 176 \cdot \frac{3 \cdot 1}{1.8} = 293$$

$$T_{33} = 200 \cdot \frac{1 \cdot 1}{1.8} = \underline{111}$$

$$1678$$

Assuming directional symmetry of flows, we then can construct Table 10.3. But the resulting T_i's do not match the generated $T_i(g)$ trips. We therefore calculate a set of correcting growth factors as

$$\text{(a)} \quad F_i' = \frac{T_{ig}}{T_i} \quad \text{and} \quad \text{(b)} \quad F' = \frac{T_g}{T} \qquad 10.25$$

and, shown in the far right-hand column of Table 10.3, these new F's are

TABLE 10.3
First Round of Trip Distribution Estimates

	1	2	3	T_i	$T_i(g)$	F'_i
1	222	290	111	623	574	.92
2	290	250	146.5	686.5	675	.98
3	111	146.5	111	368.5	388	1.05
				$T = 1678$	$T_g = 1637$	$F' = .976$

then used in the adjustment equation that is shown below and executed for a second round of estimated values (T'_{ij}), displayed in Table 10.4.

$$T'_{ij} = T_{ij} \frac{F'_i \cdot F'_j}{F'} \qquad\qquad 10.26$$

Notice that the total is 1629, which is now slightly less than $T_{(g)}$ but is closer to it than is the first round value of 1678, indeed, very close. The adjustment routine can be repeated for successive rounds until one gets as

TABLE 10.4
Second Round of Trip Distribution Estimates

$$T'_{11} = 222 \cdot \frac{.92 \cdot .92}{.976} = 193$$

$$T'_{12} = 580 \cdot \frac{.92 \cdot .98}{.976} = 536$$

$$T'_{13} = 222 \cdot \frac{.92 \cdot 1.05}{.976} = 220$$

$$T'_{22} = 250 \cdot \frac{.98 \cdot .98}{.976} = 246$$

$$T'_{23} = 293 \cdot \frac{.98 \cdot 1.05}{.976} = 309$$

$$T'_{33} = 111 \cdot \frac{1.05 \cdot 1.05}{.976} = 125$$

$$= 1629$$

close to $T_{(g)}$ as seems within reason. In our example, being within eight trips, one-half of 1%, is probably close enough.

The Gravity Model

The gravity model applied to trip distribution embodies the familiar gravitational notion of movements being a function of attractiveness and an inverse function of friction due to distance. Tests have proved that it is considerably more accurate than the growth-factor models. Its usual form is

$$T_{ij} = T_i \left(\frac{T_j K_{ij} F_{ij}}{\sum_{j=1}^{n} T_j K_{ij} F_{ij}} \right) \qquad 10.27$$

where

T_{ij} = the number of trips from i to j (one directional)
T_i = the future number of trips generated, originating at i (one half total trip ends projected at i)
T_j = the number of future trips generated, having as their destination zone j (one half total trip ends projected at j)
F_{ij} = an exponentially determined "travel time factor" that expresses an average area wide effect of spatial separation that approximates $1/D_{ij}^{\lambda}$ where λ varies with D_{ij}
K_{ij} = a zone-to-zone adjustment factor

The K_{ij} and F_{ij} values are calibrated as follows. First a trip distribution table based on surveys of current behavior is constructed of known true values t_{ij}. Then current measures of time distance and attraction (say, employment) are plugged into a model to generate a modeled distribution of T_{ij}'s, where the T_i's correspond to those of the survey table. The table of true values and modeled values are compared by plotting the frequency distribution of trip lengths. Values of time distance in the model are then altered, and the model is recalculated to generate a frequency distribution of trip lengths as close to the true distribution as possible. These adjusted distance factors are our F_{ij} values.

Now, although there may be very good correspondence between the true and modeled frequencies of trip lengths for the city as a whole, there may remain cell-by-cell, zone-to-zone, discrepancies between the true and the modeled distribution tables. Based on these differences, correction factors, K_{ij}, are derived to bring finally the model results into conformance with true values. These F_{ij} and K_{ij} factors are then held constant for projection purposes while T_j's and T_i's change.[27]

As with the Detroit model, the first round results may not be satisfactory and may require the iterative application of correction factors to successively approximate an acceptable solution. We might get as a first approximation, for example, a result as is shown in Table 10.5. The problem is that the distributed arrivals to zones, $T_{j(d)}$, are not equal to the generated arrivals T_j used in the first run to get the trip distribution table—which in this case are, respectively, 203, 174, 235 [in other words, equal to $T_{i(g)}$]. What must be done to correct for this is to compute an adjusted T'_j and to rerun the model where[28]

$$T'_j = \frac{T_j}{T_{j(d)}} \cdot T_j \qquad\qquad 10.28$$

so that for example,

$$T'_{j=2} = \frac{174}{215} \cdot 174 = 141$$

The gravity model is widely used and relatively accurate in tests where it has been used to forecast known values. Under similar test conditions the growth factor models have produced results that averaged errors of 130% while gravity models averaged errors in the vicinity of 15%.

TABLE 10.5
Hypothetical Result from First Run of Gravity Model

From \ To	1	2	3	$T_{i(g)}$
1	171	26	6	203
2	11	160	3	174
3	25	29	181	235
$T_{j(d)}$	207	215	190	612

[27] Equation 10.27 has precisely the form of the constrained gravity model discussed at length in Chapter 9. Estimates of K and λ may also be estimated with those techniques that are described in Chapter 9. For further discussion, see Bureau of Public Roads, *Calibrating and Testing a Gravity Model for Any Size Urban Area* (Washington, D.C.: U.S. Department of Commerce, 1965); Blunden, Chapter 8; and Finney.
[28] For a demonstration see Blunden, pp. 247–250.

The main task of a modal split model introduced at this juncture is to forecast the share of interzonal transfers that will select each mode of travel. If we assume, for example, two modes, automobile and transit, the product of this analysis will be two matrices or trip-distribution tables, one for each mode.

This particular model was developed for the Buffalo, New York region in the mid 1960s by the Niagara Frontier Transportation Study. This model has three phases.

Phase I establishes a minimum and a maximum of expected number of total trips between each pair of zones. Phase II applies a weighted averaging technique to select a value between that minimum and maximum as the expected volume of total interzonal transfers. Phase III then finally divides this total expected volume between the two modes in accord with the weights of Phase II. We give an example.

In the first phase a distance-sensitive distribution model is employed, such as the gravity model. Separate trip generation estimates must be available for work trips and nonwork trips. First, it is assumed that all trips will be made by automobile. The gravity model is applied by using distance or travel time factors that are based on the streets and highways. This produces a set of trip distributions.

Next, we do the same job again, this time assuming that all travel must take place on the transit system. Thus the travel times used in the gravity model this time are solely based on that system.[29] This produces a second set of interzonal transfers. The true total of interzonal transfers is assumed to be somewhere between these two separate estimates.

In the second phase a set of relative weights or proportions is derived. The proportion of total trips assigned to a particular mode is considered to be a function of four variables:

1. The trip purpose of trip-maker.
2. The automobile availability to trip-maker.
3. The relative quality of service of mode.
4. The trip length.

We already indicated that two trip-purpose classes are employed—work and nonwork. For each we also have a binary split on the automobile availability—available and not available. Households with no cars will have none available for either trip type; households with one car are assumed to have it available for work, but then there will be none available for nonwork

---

[29] Actually the gravity model was not used. Instead an "opportunity model" was used, which is similarly sensitive to distance. Either could be used.

trips (at least, during certain periods of the day). Households with two or more cars available are presumed to have a car available for both trip types. Thus for each zone and set of trip origins from that zone, we have a projected number of trips that are work, and nonwork, and for each category a further breakdown into automobile available, and automobile not-available trips.

A quality ratio is calculated for each pair of zones which is the ratio of automobile-to-transit travel time indices. The automobile index is terminal time plus the accumulated link time plus a measure of parking costs where 2 cents equals one minute. The transit index is terminal time plus accumulated link and transfer times. Lastly, trip lengths, zone to zone, are considered, a difference easily lost in the travel-time ratios, as it affects the choice of travel mode.

These four variables are then tabulated and graphed on the basis of historical data against the variable "transit usage proportion" to estimate their joint effects on choice of mode, resulting in a set of graphs such as in Figure 10.7. These curves are sometimes called "diversion curves," as they indicate the share of travel diverted to an alternative mode.

These transit shares (and implied automobile shares assuming the sum of the two equals 100%) are then used as the weights in taking portions of transit-only distributed trips and automobile only distributed trips and in

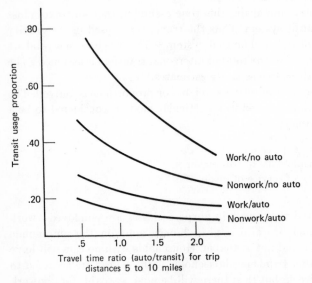

FIGURE 10.7   Sample diversion curves, Niagara Frontier model.[30]

[30] See Fertal et al., p. 126.

pooling these as the "interpolated" final estimate of total trips. The transit proportions category is then applied again to this pooled total to get the final model split, Transit/Automobile. A sample set of computations for this type of model is shown in Figure 10.8, for illustrative purposes.

10.5.4 TRAFFIC ASSIGNMENT

In this section we discuss techniques for assigning the interzonal transfers to specific facilities and routes that link together the various zones.

The simplest assignment technique is called the all-or-nothing method because it first determines the shortest path (set of links) between each pair of zones and then assigns all traffic between a pair of zones to that minimum path, and nothing to the other, nonminimum, paths. The technique is illustrated in Figure 10.9 and in Table 10.6. Figure 10.9 shows our hypothetical sample city with its seven arterial links and a time assigned to each. The minimum time paths are indicated by the arrows.[31] In Table 10.6 the assignments are made, using the "both-way" trip distribution which we previously used in illustrating the Detroit model (Table 10.4). Notice that when a path consists of more than one link, as in T_{2-3}, all trips are assigned to each link on the path. Intrazonal trips have been assigned in direct proportion to link time-length. The sums of the columns give us total link loads.

The next step in such an analysis would be to translate these volumes into design terms, and to compare the level of demand, represented by these assigned volumes, with the level of supply—either existing capacities or an assumed set, whichever was used in determining the distance and transport related parameters of the earlier models of the analysis sequence. Thus we might find that we have assigned a peak-hour volume of 45,000 vehicles to a link that has a capacity of only 20,000. We might conclude, therefore, that our planning analysis shows a need to increase the capacity of this link by 125%. But such a conclusion also demonstrates an inherent problem in relying on this technique. As the loading table of Table 10.6 shows, loadings on the system are very uneven, ranging from 64 to 950 trips. Yet the time differences among the alternative routes between zones are not very large, at least between A and B and A and C, when one compares the shortest path with the next shortest. The point is that, given alternative routes like these, people do not behave in an all-or-nothing manner. We might expect people to rather quickly learn that A-E is very crowded and that A-D and A-F are not. Indeed, the more crowded A-E becomes, the slower it becomes, and

---

[31] The minimum paths are easy to find here, but not on largescale complex systems. A technique for doing this by computer, in fact, did not exist until the discoveries of Dantzig and Morris in 1957. See Meyer and Straszheim, p. 137.

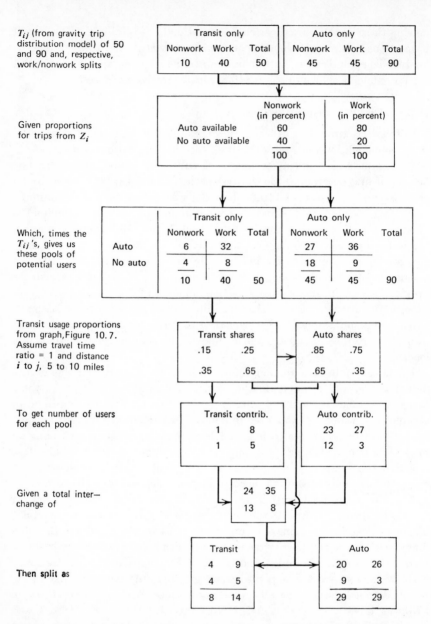

T_{ij} (from gravity trip distribution model) of 50 and 90 and, respective, work/nonwork splits

Transit only			Auto only		
Nonwork	Work	Total	Nonwork	Work	Total
10	40	50	45	45	90

Given proportions for trips from Z_i

	Nonwork (in percent)	Work (in percent)
Auto available	60	80
No auto available	40	20
	100	100

Which, times the T_{ij}'s, gives us these pools of potential users

	Transit only			Auto only		
	Nonwork	Work	Total	Nonwork	Work	Total
Auto	6	32		27	36	
No auto	4	8		18	9	
	10	40	50	45	45	90

Transit usage proportions from graph, Figure 10.7. Assume travel time ratio = 1 and distance i to j, 5 to 10 miles

Transit shares		Auto shares	
.15	.25	.85	.75
.35	.65	.65	.35

To get number of users for each pool

Transit contrib.		Auto contrib.	
1	8	23	27
1	5	12	3

Given a total inter—change of

24	35
13	8

Then split as

Transit		Auto	
4	9	20	26
4	5	9	3
8	14	29	29

FIGURE 10.8   A sample set of computations for the Niagara Frontier model.

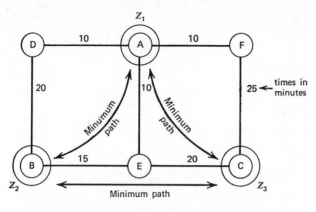

FIGURE 10.9   Minimum time paths, sample city.

how long can it thus remain the shortest time path? This brings us to the introduction of capacity constraints into the assignment model.

Previously in this chapter we introduced a general relationship between volume, capacity, and speed (from which, when given the physical length of a link, we can compute time-distance). This is shown again in Figure 10.10. Assignment with capacity constraints can work in several different ways. One technique is to set an absolute capacity on each link, and then to assign in an all-or-nothing manner, filling up to capacity the shortest routes first and, as each fills, to move to the next shortest route, filling it up, and so on.

An alternative use of capacity constraints is as follows. A zone is chosen. Its traffic is loaded on the minimum time paths, then all time paths are

TABLE 10.6
Simple All-or-Nothing Trip Assignment Table Assuming
Proportional Intrazonal Assignments

Pathways		Links						
T_{ij}	Total	A-D	A-E	A-F	B-D	B-E	C-E	C-F
1-1	193	64	64	64				
1-2	536		536			536		
1-3	220		220				220	
2-2	246				141	105		
2-3	309					309	309	
3-3	125						56	69
Total Link Loads		64	756	64	141	950	585	69

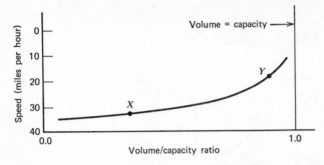

FIGURE 10.10   The general relationship between speed, volume, and capacity.

recalculated, adjusting times upward on those links just loaded, in accord with some traffic impedence function, such as is shown in Figure 10.10. If, for example, the loading moved a link's volume/capacity ratio from point X to point Y, it would have reduced average speed on that link from, say, 35 to 20 miles per hour; and if the link was 3 miles long, it would have increased its time-distance from about 5 minutes to about 9 minutes.[32] A second zone is chosen. Its traffic is allocated to a new set of minimum paths. Then the minimum paths are recalculated, and so on. One of the difficulties of the method is in the choosing of the zones. The order in which zones are chosen does not seriously affect the actual volumes of loadings that result, but it will affect the average trip length. In other words, it has an implication as to who gets preference for the shorter routes. This is a difficulty because the average trip length in a system is a criterion on which the system will be judged by some decision makers, and the average trip length resulting from this assignment routine is an artifact of the technique. A random selection of zones has been used by some studies to minimize this difficulty.

Another variation commonly used in assignment routines is the diversion curve. These curves, similar to those of Figure 10.7 are used most frequently to determine a split between an expressway route and a nonexpressway route that links two nodes, based on relative measures of time saved, distance, or another indication of performance attractiveness.[33]

---

[32] We calculated this as $T = (60 \cdot D)/S$, where T = time in minutes, $D=$ distance, and S = speed.

[33] For further discussion, especially of assignment under modal split conditions in a policy context, see Roger L. Creighton, *Urban Transportation Planning* (Urbana, Ill.: University of Illinois Press, 1970), pp. 245–353. For technical reference and computer programs, see Bureau of Public Roads, *Traffic Assignment Manual* (Washington, D.C.: U.S. Department of Commerce, 1964); and Bureau of Public Roads, *Traffic Assignment and Distribution for Small Urban Areas* (Washington, D.C.: U.S. Department of Commerce, 1965).

PROBLEMS

1. A good way to test one's understanding of a model and to determine if all of the necessary components are in their proper order is to draw a flow diagram of boxes and arrows, specifying the various steps and the ways in which they are interlinked. First try doing this for the general form of the Lowry model in Section 10.4.1 and then do this for the Puget Sound and BASS models of Section 10.4.2.

2. Using the gravity model of residential location in equations 10.6 and 10.7, what would be the 1980 population of zones 1, 2, and 3, given the following data?

Minimum Travel Times From \ To	Z_1	Z_2	Z_3
Z_1	15	25	30
Z_2	25	15	35
Z_3	30	35	15
1980 Employment	4000	6000	2000
1970 Vacant Residential Land	50 Acres	500 Acres	2000 Acres
1970 Population	15,000	10,000	5000

Assume a growth increment of 20,000 population and a distance exponent $(\lambda) = 2$.

3. Consider the distance function in Lowry's retail model, equation 10.15. Given below the set of coefficients that he used, values of α, β, and γ, for each of the three levels of facilities, k, what behavioral implications are embodied in the functions? What is T_{ij} doing differently for each facility type when its values get plugged into equation 10.14? How would you compare these functions with the "distance-squared" terms of a gravity model?

   Suggestion: Calculate T_{ij} for $r = 1, 3, 7$, and 10, or some similar sample of values for each of the classes k.

		α	β	γ
$k = 1$	(neighborhood facilities)	.5107	.7400	.2699
$k = 2$	(local facilities)	.0116	.0012	.0202
$k = 3$	(metropolitan facilities)	.0664	.0442	.0156

4. Assume two possible alternative transportation systems for 1980, represented by the following minimum time-distances.

ALTERNATIVE A (NO EXPRESSWAY)				ALTERNATIVE B (WITH AN EXPRESSWAY)			
To From	Z_1	Z_2	Z_3	To From	Z_1	Z_2	Z_3
Z_1	15	25	30	Z_1	12	15	20
Z_2	25	15	35	Z_2	15	12	15
Z_3	30	35	15	Z_3	20	15	12

Use the gravity model, equation 10.27, to distribute trips to these two systems. Assuming that $T_i = T_j$, such that $T_{1j} = 203$, $T_{2j} = 174$, $T_{3j} = 235$; all $K_{ij} = 1$, and F_{ij} are as follows:

MINUTES OF TIME DISTANCE	F_{ij}
0 to 4	50.0
5 to 9	31.0
10 to 14	20.0
15 to 19	11.0
20 to 24	8.0
25 to 29	5.0
30 to 34	3.4
35 to 39	2.7

How could you compare the outcomes and what would you conclude about the model's sensitivity to alternatives?

5. Assign the trips distributed under the two alternatives above to the network of Figure 10.9 (the no-expressway alternative) and the network

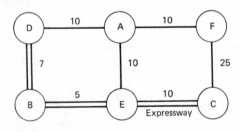

below (the expressway alternative), using the all-or-nothing method, with no capacity constraints. What difference does the expressway make in the distribution of trips, assuming that the future loadings are not exceeding capacities? What is the average trip length (in minutes) under each of the two systems? How would you intuitively estimate the future travel to be distributed if capacities of the three expressway links were all equal, and twice that of arterials (the nonexpressway links)? What other information would you need to answer this question adequately?

BIBLIOGRAPHY

Alonso, William. *Location and Land Use*. Cambridge, Mass.: Harvard University Press, 1964.

American Public Health Association. *Planning the Neighborhood*. Chicago: Public Administration Service, 1948.

Bay Area Simulation Study. *Jobs, People and Land: Bay Area Simulation Study (BASS)*. Berkeley: Center for Real Estate and Urban Economics, 1968.

Berry, Brian J. L. *Commercial Structure and Commercial Blight*. Chicago: University of Chicago, Department of Geography, 1963.

Blunden, W. R. *The Land-Use Transport System*. New York: Pergamon, 1971.

Brown, H. James, R. Royce Ginn, Franklin I. James, John F. Kain, and Mahlon R. Straszheim. *Empirical Models of Urban Land Use: Suggestions on Research Objectives and Organization*. New York: National Bureau of Economic Research, 1972.

Bureau of Public Roads. *Calibrating and Testing a Gravity Model for Any Size Urban Area*. Washington, D.C.: U.S. Department of Commerce, 1965.

Bureau of Public Roads. *Traffic Assignment and Distribution for Small Urban Areas*. Washington, D.C.: U.S. Department of Commerce, September, 1965.

Bureau of Public Roads. *Traffic Assignment Manual, For Application with a Large, High Speed Computer*. Washington, D.C.: U.S. Department of Commerce, June 1964.

Catanese, Anthony J. "Home and Workplace Separation in Four Urban Regions," *Journal of the American Institute of Planners, 37* (September 1971), 331–337.

Chapin, F. Stuart, Jr. *Urban Land Use Planning*, Second edition, Urbana, Ill.: University of Illinois Press, 1965.

Chapin, F. Stuart, Jr., and Shirley F. Weiss. *Factors Influencing Land Development*. Chapel Hill: Institute for Research in Social Science, August 1962.

Clawson, Marion, and Charles L. Stewart. *Land Use Information*. Baltimore: The Johns Hopkins Press, 1965.

Creighton, Roger L. *Urban Transportation Planning*. Urbana, Ill.: University of Illinois Press, 1970.

Fertal, Martin O., Edward Weiner, Arthur J. Balek, and Ali F. Sevin. *Modal Split: Documentation of Nine Methods for Estimating Transit Usage*. Washington, D.C.: U.S. Department of Transportation, 1966.

Finney, Nigel D. "Trip Distribution Models," in Anthony J. Catanese (ed). *New Perspectives in Urban Transportation Research*. Lexington, Mass.: Lexington Books, 1972.

Goldner, William. "The Lowry Model Heritage," *Journal of the American Institute of Planners, 37* (March 1971), 100–110.

Grigsby, William. *Housing Markets and Public Policy*. Philadelphia: University of Pennsylvania Press, 1963.

Harris, Britton. "Plan or Projection: An Examination of the Use of Models in Planning", *Journal of the American Institute of Planners, 26* (November 1960), 265–272.

Harris, Britton (ed). *Urban Development Models: New Tools for Planning*, A Special Issue of the *Journal of the American Institute of Planners, 31* (May 1965).

Highway Research Board. *Highway Capacity Manual*, Special Report No. 87. Washington, D.C.: National Academy of Sciences, 1965.

———, *Urban Development Models*, Special Report No. 97. Washington, D.C.: National Academy of Sciences, 1968.

Kilbridge, Maurice, Robert O'Block, and Paul Teplitz. *Urban Analysis*. Cambridge, Mass.: Graduate School of Business Administration, Harvard University, 1971.

Lowry, Ira S. *A Model of Metropolis*. Santa Monica, Cal.: The Rand Corporation, 1964.

Martin, Brian V., Frederick W. Memmott, III, and Alexander J. Bone. *Principles and Techniques of Predicting Future Demand for Urban Area Transportation*. Cambridge, Mass.: The M.I.T. Press, 1961.

Meyer, John R., and Mahlon R. Straszheim. *Pricing and Project Evaluation*. Washington, D.C.: The Brookings Institution, 1971.

Mills, Edwin S. *Studies in the Structure of the Urban Economy*. Baltimore: The Johns Hopkins Press and Resources for the Future, 1972.

Mitchell, Robert B., and Chester Rapkin. *Urban Traffic: A Function of Land Use.* New York: Columbia University Press, 1954.

Oi, Walter Y., and Paul W. Shuldiner. *An Analysis of Urban Travel Demands.* Evanston, Ill.: The Transportation Center, 1962.

Page, Alfred N., and Warren R. Seyfried (eds). *Urban Analysis.* Glenview, Ill.: Scott, Foresman, 1970.

Public Administration Service. *Action for Cities: A Guide for Community Planning.* Chicago: Public Administration Service, 1943.

Putman, Stephan H. "Intraurban Employment Forecasting Models: A Review and a Suggested New Model Construct," *Journal of the American Institute of Planners, 38* (July 1972), 216–230.

Quandt, Richard (ed). *The Demand for Travel: Theory and Measurement.* Lexington, Mass.: Heath Lexington Books, 1970.

Schneider, Jerry B. "Solving Urban Location Problems: Human Intuition Versus the Computer," *Journal of the American Institute of Planners, 37* (March 1971), 95–99.

Stegman, Michael A. "Accessibility Models and Residential Location," *Journal of the American Institute of Planners, 35* (January 1969).

Voorhees, Alan M. (ed). *Land Use and Traffic Models: A Progress Report.* A Special Issue of the *Journal of the American Institute of Planners, 25* (May 1959).

Weismantel, William L. "Dante's Inferno: The First Land Use Model," *Journal of the American Institute of Planners, 25* (November 1959), 175–179.

Weiss, Shirley F. "Land Use Studies," in William I. Goodman and Eric C. Freund (eds). *Principles and Practice of Urban Planning.* Washington, D.C.: International City Manager's Association, 1968.

Wohl, Martin, and Brian V. Martin. *Traffic Systems Analysis for Engineers and Planners.* New York: McGraw-Hill, 1967.

Zettel, Richard M., and Richard R. Carll. *Summary Review of Major Metropolitan Area Transportation Studies in the United States.* Berkeley: Institute for Traffic and Transportation Studies, 1962.

Nearly all of the items in this bibliography are cited in the footnotes for this chapter. It is extremely difficult to specify works of special merit or value, but at the risk of offending some (not to mention the many excellent works we have not cited at all), we refer the reader who is in search of a next step in his studies, or in search of general reference works in this area to the books by Blunden; Brown et al.; Creighton; and the Highway Research Board's *Urban Development Models.*

CHAPTER 11

An Algebra for Linear Systems

11.1 INTRODUCTION

As we are by now aware, the algebra involved in analyzing most activity systems in our urbanized society is often quite cumbersome. Because a sizeable number of variables enter into the analysis, and because the sub-scripting notation can become complicated, the logic of the analytic procedure often becomes submerged. This makes difficult the task not only of evaluating the plausibility of the procedure, but also of simplifying it.

For these reasons, an algebra specifically suited for handling the computations of large systems would be a valued tool. Since it is the subject of this chapter, it should not come as a surprise that this tool has already been developed. It is called *linear algebra* or, frequently, matrix algebra. Its contribution to the analytic process is indicated in the following example.

Suppose that a government agency is concerned with the attainment of two social goals for low-income families: the improvement of housing and of health conditions. In an analysis of the determinants of these two goals, it is agreed that better housing not only contributes to the housing goal but, by improving safety and sanitation and by reducing crowding, also contributes to the health goal. However, better housing is costly and, to the extent that low income families can afford higher rents, the better the housing program that can be attained. This is not to say that improved income, perhaps as a result of an improvement in the availability of jobs, is the only source of financing. Another is government funds. First, government income transfers, perhaps in the form of family welfare payments or as rent subsidies, can supplement a family's income and rent-paying-ability. But government budgets can also be allocated to programs in direct attainment of goals. Outright grants or low-interest loans can be made to construct or to improve

362

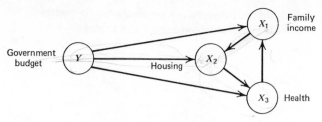

FIGURE 11.1 Four linked variables.

housing and to construct health facilities and to provide health services. But here, the system being analyzed takes a complicating turn. To the extent that the health goal is attained, individuals will become capable of productive activity and, as a result, their earned income from employment may increase. This type of "feedback" linkage will have a multiplier effect on the further attainment of both housing and health goals. This relationship as well as the others that have been indicated are shown in the flow diagram in Figure 11.1.

If the impact can be estimated of each of these variables on the other variables that it is believed to determine, then it is reasonable to represent this system of relationships mathematically. Let us suppose that after some inquiry, it is found that all relationships are linear and additive. Then the system can be represented by the following linear equations, where X_1 is family income, X_2 is the number of units of acceptable quality housing, and X_3 is a health status index, and Y is the government budget;

$$X_1 = \qquad\qquad a_{13}X_3 + b_1 Y \qquad\qquad 11.1$$

$$X_2 = a_{21}X_1 \qquad\qquad + b_2 Y \qquad\qquad 11.2$$

$$X_3 = \qquad a_{32}X_2 \qquad + b_3 Y \qquad\qquad 11.3$$

This is a set of three simultaneous linear equations, and if the coefficients a_{ij} and b_i have all been estimated, this system may be solved by substituting equation 11.1 for X_1 in equation 11.2, and then substituting the result for X_2 in equation 11.3.

$$X_3 = \left(\frac{a_{32}a_{21}b_1 + a_{32}b_2 + b_3}{1 - a_{32}a_{21}a_{13}} \right) Y$$

which is to say that X_3 is linearly proportionate to Y. Once X_3 is obtained, we can insert its value into equation 11.1 to solve for X_1. Since X_3 depends on Y, so does X_1. Finally, the value of X_2 may be obtained by inserting the value of X_1 into equation 11.2. In sum, we see that the entire system depends on the level of the government budget Y.

The algebra required to obtain this result is cumbersome. In contrast, we could have made use of matrix algebra to solve for the vector:

$$X = \begin{bmatrix} X_1 \\ X_2 \\ X_3 \end{bmatrix}$$

as follows

$$X = [I - A]^{-1}BY \qquad\qquad 11.4$$

and we see immediately that the system depends on the level of Y, given the two sets of coefficients A and B. How this result can be derived and how numerical results may be obtained therefrom requires knowledge of only the elements of matrix algebra, and it is to the task of obtaining this knowledge that we now turn.

11.2 ADDITION AND SUBTRACTION

11.2.1 VECTORS

Suppose that a chain of grocery stores sells apples, milk, and salami. Store A has sold 20 apples, 15 quarts of milk, and 10 salamis, while Store B has sold 45 apples, 5 quarts of milk, and 11 salamis. How many of each item was sold by the entire chain?

Let us put the quantity of each item sold in a column—one column for each store.

		Store A A	Store B B
Quantity sold by each store	Apples	20	45
	Milk	15	5
	Salamis	10	11

Instead of calling these columns just "columns," let us call them "column vectors." In that way we feel justified in calling our new tool an algebra! We may now add the two column vectors together to get a new column vector that gives quantities of each item sold for the entire chain.

$$A \quad + \quad B \quad = \quad C$$

or

$$\begin{bmatrix} 20 \\ 15 \\ 10 \end{bmatrix} + \begin{bmatrix} 45 \\ 5 \\ 11 \end{bmatrix} = \begin{bmatrix} 65 \\ 20 \\ 21 \end{bmatrix}$$

This not-very-difficult procedure is called vector addition. In general, two vectors A and B yield the vector C by adding

$$\begin{bmatrix} a_1 \\ a_2 \\ a_3 \end{bmatrix} + \begin{bmatrix} b_1 \\ b_2 \\ b_3 \end{bmatrix} = \begin{bmatrix} c_1 \\ c_2 \\ c_3 \end{bmatrix}$$

or, written another way,

$$[a_j] + [b_j] = [c_j], \qquad j = 1, 2, 3$$

Two rules constrain this procedure, however. The first is that both vectors being added must be column vectors, or they must be two row vectors

$$[20 \quad 15 \quad 20] + [45 \quad 5 \quad 1] = [65 \quad 20 \quad 21]$$

But we *cannot add a row vector to a column vector.*

The second requirement is that *the vectors being added must have the same number of components.* Thus one vector has three components ($j = 1, 2, 3$), the other must also have three. The addition of vectors with different numbers of components is not defined.

11.2.2 MATRICES

Suppose now that in a certain city, there are two hospitals, A and B. Each hospital has an outpatient, a maternity, and a surgery wing. Figures have been collected during the year showing the number of persons treated in each wing of each hospital. Because of certain policy implications, the data have been tabulated to indicate whether the person treated was under the age of 18. These figures are shown in Table 11.1.

TABLE 11.1
Number of Patients Treated in Each City
Hospital by Age and Type of Treatment

Hospital	Age \ Wing	Outpatient	Maternity	Surgery
A	<18	120	25	5
	≥18	85	90	70
B	<18	80	5	10
	≥18	50	60	65

These figures can be added together in several ways depending on the type of information needed. For example, if all we want to know is the total number of patients treated by A and B, respectively, then we would add across the rows and down the columns for the two hospitals separately to find that 395 persons were treated by A and 270 were treated by B. Instead, we may not care which hospital provided the treatment but are concerned with the total number of persons in the city requiring each of the three types of treatment according to whether or not the person treated was under 18. To obtain this information, we merely add the number in a given row and column of Table 11.1 for hospital A to the number in the same row and column for hospital B. Doing this for each row and column gives Table 11.2.

Few who have ever done clerical work will find the procedure for calculating Table 11.2 unfamiliar. What is not likely to be familiar, however, is the fact that we have performed matrix addition. A matrix is nothing more than a set of numbers arranged in rows and columns such as is shown in Tables 11.1 and 11.2. For example, we lift the rows and columns for hospital A from Table 11.1 and designate it as the A matrix

$$A = \begin{bmatrix} 120 & 25 & 5 \\ 85 & 90 & 70 \end{bmatrix}$$

Similarly, we obtain the B matrix:

$$B = \begin{bmatrix} 80 & 5 & 10 \\ 50 & 60 & 65 \end{bmatrix}$$

Adding the two matrices together, we obtain the matrix C

$$A + B = C$$

or

$$\begin{bmatrix} 120 & 25 & 5 \\ 85 & 90 & 70 \end{bmatrix} + \begin{bmatrix} 80 & 5 & 10 \\ 50 & 60 & 65 \end{bmatrix} = \begin{bmatrix} 200 & 30 & 15 \\ 135 & 150 & 135 \end{bmatrix}$$

TABLE 11.2
Number of Patients Treated City-Wide by Age and Type of Treatment

Age \ Wing	Outpatient	Maternity	Surgery
<18	200	30	15
≥18	135	150	135

where the matrix C contains the same entries as in Table 11.2. In general, two matrices, A and B, yield the matrix C by adding

$$\begin{bmatrix} a_{11} & a_{12} & a_{13} \\ a_{21} & a_{22} & a_{23} \end{bmatrix} + \begin{bmatrix} b_{11} & b_{12} & b_{13} \\ b_{21} & b_{22} & b_{23} \end{bmatrix} = \begin{bmatrix} c_{11} & c_{12} & c_{13} \\ c_{21} & c_{22} & c_{23} \end{bmatrix}$$

or, written another way,

$$[a_{ij}] + [b_{ij}] = [c_{ij}] \qquad i = 1, 2; \quad j = 1, 2, 3$$

The requirement for matrix addition is that both matrices being added must be of the same order. The order of a matrix is stated in terms of the numbers of rows and the number of columns, in that order. In the preceding example, matrix A has two rows and three columns—its order is (2×3), read "two by three." Since matrix B is of the same order, the two matrices are said to be *conformable* for addition, and their summation yields the matrix C, which is also of order (2×3).

It may be noted that a matrix of order (3×1) has another name. It is the entity we encountered earlier—a column vector with three components. A matrix of order (1×3) is a three-component row vector. And to complete this set of "jargon," a matrix of order (1×1), which is nothing more than our old friend, the number, is called a *scalar*.

The procedure for matrix subtraction follows the same rules as for matrix addition. If matrix B is to be subtracted from matrix A, it must be of the same order. For example, if we wanted to know how many more persons were treated by hospital A than by hospital B, maintaining detail on type of treatment and age, we find the matrix as

$$A - B = C$$

or

$$[a_{ij}] - [b_{ij}] = [c_{ij}], \qquad i = 1, 2; \quad j = 1, 2, 3$$

or

$$\begin{bmatrix} 120 & 25 & 5 \\ 85 & 90 & 70 \end{bmatrix} - \begin{bmatrix} 80 & 5 & 10 \\ 50 & 60 & 65 \end{bmatrix} = \begin{bmatrix} 40 & 20 & -5 \\ 35 & 30 & 5 \end{bmatrix}$$

11.3 MULTIPLICATION

11.3.1 VECTORS

In our example of the chain of grocery stores, the total number of each item sold was shown in the vector C. We now want to know a single figure—total sales. This can be obtained if we know the price of each item.

Let the price of apples be 5 cents each, let milk be 30 cents per quart, and salamis 80 cents each. These prices can be arranged in the row vector P.

$$P = [.05 \quad .30 \quad .80]$$

Then, if we multiply the quantity of each item sold by its unit price and add, the total will give the one figure of total sales s.

$PC = s$

$$= [.05 \quad .30 \quad .80] \begin{bmatrix} 65 \\ 20 \\ 21 \end{bmatrix}$$

$$= [(.05)(65) + (30)(.20) + (.80)(21)] = [3.25 + 6.00 + 16.80]$$

$$= 26.05$$

we see that total sales were \$26.05. This procedure, which few have not done many times in the past, is vector multiplication.

In general, two vectors will yield a single figure s by multiplying

$$[p_1 \quad p_2 \quad p_3] \begin{bmatrix} c_1 \\ c_2 \\ c_3 \end{bmatrix} = s$$

or, written another way,

$$\sum_{j=1}^{3} p_j c_j = s$$

The rules constraining vector multiplication can be readily extracted from the procedures we have just followed. First, the jth elements of each vector are multiplied together and the resulting products, for all values of j, are added. Second, both vectors must have the same number of components. In the above example, both vectors have three components. Third, the row vector is always to the left of the column vector, assuming that only the single scalar (s in the example above) is to be derived. What happens when the vectors are reversed and then multiplied will be indicated when we treat matrix multiplication. But before we consider this we note that, since $A + B = C$, the following are all equivalent:

$$s = PC$$
$$= P(A + B)$$
$$= PA + PB$$

Hence, if we were initially asked to multiply P first by A, then by B, and then add the result to get s, we should know that P could first be factored out to give $P(A + B)$, thereby saving a step in vector multiplication.

11.3.2 VECTORS AND MATRICES MULTIPLIED BY A SCALAR

Before continuing with matrix multiplication, we consider the multiplication of a vector by a scalar, and of a matrix by a scalar.

Let us suppose that prices have doubled. Then each element of the P vector should be doubled. This can be shown as

$$2P = 2[.05 \quad .30 \quad .80] = [.10 \quad .60 \quad 1.60]$$

In general, a scaler m multiplied by a vector P gives

$$mP = m[p_1 \quad p_2 \quad p_3] = [mp_1 \quad mp_2 \quad mp_3]$$

Now suppose that the number of patients treated by all city hospitals, shown in the matrix above, is expected to uniformly increase by 10%. The new matrix can then be obtained by multiplying each element of the C matrix by 1.1

$$1.1C = 1.1\begin{bmatrix} 200 & 30 & 15 \\ 135 & 150 & 135 \end{bmatrix} = \begin{bmatrix} 220 & 33 & 16.5 \\ 148.5 & 165 & 148.5 \end{bmatrix}$$

In general, a scalar m multiplied by a matrix C gives

$$mC = m\begin{bmatrix} c_{11} & c_{12} & c_{13} \\ c_{21} & c_{22} & c_{23} \end{bmatrix} = \begin{bmatrix} mc_{11} & mc_{12} & mc_{13} \\ mc_{21} & mc_{22} & mc_{23} \end{bmatrix}$$

11.3.3 MULTIPLYING A MATRIX BY A VECTOR

We now show two examples that involve the multiplication of a matrix by a vector. The first entails the computation of construction costs for three types of housing renewal alternatives.

Suppose that if an existing building is to be retained rather than demolished, it may be rehabilitated to a certain quality standard through low-cost construction techniques that may extend the life of the building only for a short time span, thereby requiring high annual maintenance costs; or it may be rehabilitated with expensive but durable construction techniques that require low annual maintenance costs. But if the building is too deteriorated to be rehabilitated, then it must be demolished and replaced with new construction. In our example, we compute initial costs only, although we recognize that a more complete cost analysis would require inclusion of annual maintenance costs for each alternative.

Table 11.3
Construction Requirements per Dwelling Unit

Alternative Inputs per Dwelling Unit	Cans of Paint	Feet of Lumber	Bags of Concrete	Labor
Short life rehabilitation	5	10	2	10
Long life rehabilitation	5	15	4	20
New construction	6	20	8	25

In Table 11.3 we show for each of the three renewal alternatives the amount of each construction item required per dwelling unit.

To compute the total initial cost for each alternative, we require the unit cost for each construction item. Suppose that paint costs \$4 per can, lumber costs \$1 per foot, concrete costs \$3 per bag, and labor costs \$5 per worker. These unit costs are arrayed in the vector C.

$$C = \begin{bmatrix} 4 \\ 1 \\ 3 \\ 5 \end{bmatrix}$$

If the figures in Table 11.3 are shown as the matrix A, then a vector F showing the total initial outlay for each alternative may be calculated as

$$AC = F$$

$$= \begin{bmatrix} 5 & 10 & 2 & 10 \\ 5 & 15 & 4 & 20 \\ 6 & 20 & 8 & 25 \end{bmatrix} \begin{bmatrix} 4 \\ 1 \\ 3 \\ 5 \end{bmatrix}$$

$$= \begin{bmatrix} (5)(4) + (10)(1) + (2)(3) + (10)(5) \\ (5)(4) + (15)(1) + (4)(3) + (20)(5) \\ (6)(4) + (20)(1) + (8)(3) + (25)(5) \end{bmatrix} = \begin{bmatrix} 86 \\ 147 \\ 193 \end{bmatrix}$$

We see that short-life rehabilitation will require an initial outlay of \$86 per dwelling unit, long-life rehabilitation will require \$147, and new construction will require \$193.

In general, a matrix multiplied by a vector will yield another vector

$$\begin{bmatrix} a_{11} & a_{12} & a_{13} & a_{14} \\ a_{21} & a_{22} & a_{23} & a_{24} \\ a_{31} & a_{32} & a_{33} & a_{34} \end{bmatrix} \begin{bmatrix} c_1 \\ c_2 \\ c_3 \\ c_4 \end{bmatrix} = \begin{bmatrix} f_1 \\ f_2 \\ f_3 \end{bmatrix}$$

$$(3 \times 4) \qquad (4 \times 1)\ (3 \times 1)$$

or, written another way,

$$\sum_{j=1}^{4} a_{ij}c_j = f_i; \qquad i = 1, 2, 3$$

col = rows

The rules governing the multiplication of a matrix by a vector are quite similar to those that apply to vector multiplication. Assuming that the vector is to the right of the matrix, the number of columns in the matrix must equal the number of components in the vector. In our example above, there are four columns in the matrix, and four components in the vector, and they are therefore *conformable* for multiplication.

We can simplify the rule for conformability by treating the vector as a matrix with one column. Our first step is then to write the order of each matrix under each matrix as we have done above. The order of matrix A is (3×4) and of matrix C is (4×1). They are conformable for multiplication if the two inner numbers are the same, as is shown below:

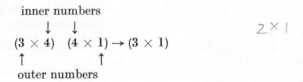

inner numbers
↓ ↓
$$(3 \times 4) \quad (4 \times 1) \to (3 \times 1)$$
↑ ↑
outer numbers

2 × 1

Since this requirement is satisfied, they may be multiplied, and will yield the three element vector F shown above. That this is true can be ascertained by checking the two outer numbers of order statements. They are 3 and 1, respectively, which can be written as the order of the new vector F. That the vector in the example above must be to the right of the matrix can be seen by noting that if it were not, the order statements would be

inner numbers
↓ ↓
$$(4 \times 1) \quad (3 \times 4)$$

The two inner numbers differ, so that the matrices are now not conformable for multiplication. Of course, it is possible that the vector may be to the left of the matrix, if the problem were so structured, but again these orders must be such that conformability exists. For example, a two-component row vector may be multiplied by a matrix of order (2 × 3) to yield another row vector of order (1 × 3).

Assuming now that the matrices are conformable for multiplication and that the vector is to the right of the matrix, the jth component of the vector is multiplied by the number in the jth column of the first row of the matrix. Proceeding in this way for each value of j—in the above example, $j = 1, \ldots, 4$—the resulting products are summed to give the first component of the new vector. This procedure is then repeated for the second row of the matrix to give the second component of the new vector, and so on, until the procedure has been applied for every row of the matrix. We now apply this procedure to a second example taken from decision theory.

Suppose that three housing programs are being considered. Program 1 consists of all short-life rehabilitation, program 2 consists of all long-life rehabilitation, and program 3 consists of all new construction. In reality, programs would contain various mixtures of these three, but we are simplifying the presentation. It is forecasted that if program 1 is applied now, 70 housing units will remain in acceptable condition after 10 years. If program 2 is applied now, 90 units will remain, and if program 3 is chosen, 80 units will remain.

However, it is noted that this forecast depends on certain critical assumptions. First, it assumes that the average real income level will be increased with new prosperity, and second, that international tensions are such that the nation will not be enmeshed in a war. But several other future environments are possible—in fact, we should consider four such futures:

FUTURE	PROBABILITY
Prosperity, no war	.15
Prosperity, war	.25
No Prosperity, no war	.20
No Prosperity, war	.40
	1.00

After we consult with political scientists and economists about these possibilities, the probability that each of these four alternative futures will materialize is calculated as is shown above (note that the sum of these probabilities must equal 100%).

A forecast for each of the three possible futures in addition to the "prosperity, no war" future is now computed, and all four forecasts are shown in the four columns of Table 11.4.

TABLE 11.4
Number of Housing Units Remaining
in Standard Condition After 10 Years,
Given Four Future Environments

Program \ Futures	Prosperity		No Prosperity	
	No War	War	No War	War
1	70	60	60	50
2	90	45	40	20
3	80	20	70	15

Taking these possible futures together with their respective probabilities into account, we may compute for each program the expected number of units remaining 10 years hence by multiplying the forecast for a given program for each future by the probability of that future and adding. Using matrix notation, with Table 11.4 shown as the matrix A and the probabilities shown as the vector P,

$$AP = E$$

$$
\begin{bmatrix}
70 & 60 & 60 & 50 \\
90 & 45 & 40 & 20 \\
80 & 20 & 70 & 15
\end{bmatrix}
\begin{bmatrix}
.15 \\
.25 \\
.20 \\
.40
\end{bmatrix}
= E
$$

$$(3 \times 4) \qquad (4 \times 1) \quad (3 \times 1)$$

We check the orders of the matrices and note (1) that they are conformable for multiplication, and (2) that they will yield a three-component column vector. Multiplying, we have

$$
E = \begin{bmatrix}
70(.15) + 60(.25) + 60(.20) + 50(.40) \\
90(.15) + 45(.25) + 40(.20) + 20(.40) \\
80(.15) + 20(.25) + 70(.20) + 15(.40)
\end{bmatrix}
$$

or

$$
E = \begin{bmatrix}
57.50 \\
40.75 \\
37.00
\end{bmatrix}
$$

TABLE 11.5
Distribution of Expenditures by
Commodity and Income Group

Purchase Group	Food	Clothing	Housing
Poor	.40	.10	.50
Rich	.20	.25	.30

If we are willing to base our decision upon expected values, and assuming that the three programs use up the same budget, we would choose program 1, which gives the highest expected number of units remaining 10 years hence: $57\frac{1}{2}$. We now consider the multiplication of a matrix by another matrix.

11.3.4 MATRIX MULTIPLICATION

Suppose that a community is partitioned into two groups, poor and rich, and that available data show that of the income earned by the poor, 40% is spent on food, 10% is spent on clothing, and 50% is spent on housing. In contrast, the rich spend 20% of their income on food, 25% on clothing, and 30% on housing (the remaining 25% is saved). These data are recorded in Table 11.5.

Additional information shows that of the total income earned as wages or profits in the food industries, 70% were earned by the poor and 30% was earned by the rich; earnings in the clothing industry were 50% to the poor and 50% to the rich; in the housing industry, 40% was earned by the poor and 60% was earned by the rich. These data are recorded in Table 11.6.

TABLE 11.6
Distribution of Earnings
by Industry and Income
Group

Industry	Group Poor	Rich
Food	.70	.30
Clothing	.50	.50
Housing	.40	.60

Let the data in Table 11.5 be represented by the matrix A, and in Table 11.6 be represented by the matrix B. If we multiply the two matrices, we obtain a new matrix C, which is of some interest.

$$\begin{array}{ccc} A & B & = & C \\ (2 \times 3) & (3 \times 2) & & (2 \times 2) \end{array}$$

Checking the orders of the matrices, we see that the inner numbers are the same so that they are conformable for multiplication. The order of the new matrix C is (2×2), which is referred to as a *square matrix* because it has the same number of rows as columns. Multiplying, we have

$$\begin{array}{cc} A & B \end{array}$$

$$\begin{bmatrix} .40 & .10 & .50 \\ .20 & .25 & .30 \end{bmatrix} \begin{bmatrix} .70 & .30 \\ .50 & .50 \\ .40 & .60 \end{bmatrix}$$

$$= \begin{bmatrix} .40(.70) + .10(.50) + .50(.40) & .40(.30) + .10(.50) + .50(.60) \\ .20(.70) + .25(.50) + .30(.40) & .20(.30) + .25(.50) + .30(.60) \end{bmatrix}$$

$$= \begin{bmatrix} .530 & .470 \\ .385 & .365 \end{bmatrix} = C$$

To obtain this result, the first row of matrix A was multiplied by the first column of matrix B to obtain the number .53, shown in row 1, column 1, of matrix C. Then we multiplied the second row of matrix A by the first column of matrix B to obtain .385 shown in row 2, column 1, of matrix C. Thus far, we have proceeded as if the A matrix were being multiplied by a column vector, the result being that shown in column 1 of matrix C. We obtain the results shown in column 2 of matrix C by multiplying the A matrix by the second column of matrix B.

Let us now interpret matrix C. The entries in this matrix show the probability that a dollar spent by income group i will be earned by income group k: if the poor spend \$1, then 47 cents of it will become the earnings of the rich, while if the rich spend \$1, only $38\frac{1}{2}$ cents will become the earnings of the poor. This is the result of the first round of spending that can be traced by the "income multiplier," the mechanics of which are described in Chapter 12.

In general, a matrix of order $(m \times r)$, when multiplied by a second matrix of order $(r \times s)$, will yield a third matrix of order $(m \times s)$:

$$\begin{bmatrix} a_{11} & a_{12} & a_{13} \\ a_{21} & a_{22} & a_{23} \end{bmatrix} \begin{bmatrix} b_{11} & b_{12} \\ b_{21} & b_{22} \\ b_{31} & b_{32} \end{bmatrix} = \begin{bmatrix} c_{11} & c_{12} \\ c_{21} & c_{22} \end{bmatrix}$$

where the elements of the C matrix are obtained by multiplying the shaded rows and columns of the two matrices as shown below

$$\begin{bmatrix} a_{11} & a_{12} & a_{13} \\ a_{21} & a_{22} & a_{23} \end{bmatrix} \begin{bmatrix} b_{11} & b_{12} \\ b_{21} & b_{22} \\ b_{31} & b_{32} \end{bmatrix} = \begin{bmatrix} c_{11} & c_{12} \\ c_{21} & c_{22} \end{bmatrix}$$

$$\begin{bmatrix} a_{11} & a_{12} & a_{13} \\ a_{21} & a_{22} & a_{23} \end{bmatrix} \begin{bmatrix} b_{11} & b_{12} \\ b_{21} & b_{22} \\ b_{31} & b_{32} \end{bmatrix} = \begin{bmatrix} c_{11} & c_{12} \\ c_{21} & c_{22} \end{bmatrix}$$

$$\begin{bmatrix} a_{11} & a_{12} & a_{13} \\ a_{21} & a_{22} & a_{23} \end{bmatrix} \begin{bmatrix} b_{11} & b_{12} \\ b_{21} & b_{22} \\ b_{31} & b_{32} \end{bmatrix} = \begin{bmatrix} c_{11} & c_{12} \\ c_{21} & c_{22} \end{bmatrix}$$

$$\begin{bmatrix} a_{11} & a_{12} & a_{13} \\ a_{21} & a_{22} & a_{23} \end{bmatrix} \begin{bmatrix} b_{11} & b_{12} \\ b_{21} & b_{22} \\ b_{31} & b_{32} \end{bmatrix} = \begin{bmatrix} c_{11} & c_{12} \\ c_{21} & c_{22} \end{bmatrix}$$

or written another way,

$$\sum_{j=1}^{3} a_{ij} b_{jk} = c_{ik}; \qquad i = 1, 2; \quad k = 1, 2$$

The i,kth element in the matrix C is obtained by multiplying the ith row of the matrix A by the kth column of the matrix B.

Some additional rules governing matrix multiplication can now be indicated.

1. In general, $AB \neq BA$.

2. If two matrices A and B are conformable for addition and also for multiplication by the matrix C, then

$$AC + BC = (A + B)C$$

An obvious exception to the first of these two rules is where the matrix B is the same as A, so that in reality we are multiplying A by itself, or squaring it:

$$AA = A^2$$

For example, if we were to square the matrix C that we just computed, we would obtain

$$CC = C^2$$

$$\begin{bmatrix} .530 & .470 \\ .385 & .365 \end{bmatrix} \begin{bmatrix} .530 & .470 \\ .385 & .365 \end{bmatrix} = \begin{bmatrix} .462 & .421 \\ .345 & .304 \end{bmatrix}$$

$$(2 \times 2) \qquad (2 \times 2) \qquad (2 \times 2)$$

The elements of the matrix C^2 indicate the probability that a dollar spent by income group i will be earned by income group k in the second round of spending—that is, after being spent by i, it is earned by some group that spends it again.

Proceeding in this way, the C matrix may be raised to any power. Now, observing the direction of change in the elements of C^2 relative to C, try to guess the magnitude of the elements of the matrix C^∞.

11.4 SIMULTANEOUS EQUATIONS AND MATRIX INVERSION

In Chapter 6 we were confronted with a problem in cost-effectiveness analysis in which the sizes of two alternative programs were to be determined such that two equations were satisfied, where program A consists of highway construction and program B consists of railroad construction. Specifically, we were given that: (1) each mile of highway costs $1 million, each mile of railroad costs $\frac{1}{2}$ million, and the total program budget is $50 million; and that (2) each mile of highway will raise an air pollution index by .4, each mile of railroad will raise the index by .05, and the air pollution index must not be raised by more than 10 points. By using a trial and error approach, we found that the budget and air quality constraints would be satisfied if $16\frac{2}{3}$ miles of highway and $66\frac{2}{3}$ miles of railroad were constructed. We now show a more direct method of solving this problem, with x_1 representing the number of highway miles and x_2 the number of railroad miles, both of which are initially unknown.

The information given above may be summarized in the following set of simultaneous equations:

$$1,000,000(x_1) + 500,000(x_2) = 50,000,000$$

$$.4(x_1) + \qquad .05(x_2) = 10$$

Without affecting the result, we may divide the first equation through by

1 million so as to simplify our later calculations. The equation system reduces to

$$x_1 + .5x_2 = 50$$

$$.4x_1 + .05x_2 = 10$$

We show three techniques for solving for x_1 and x_2, the first of which is usually taught in second-year high school algebra, and the second two of which make use of matrix algebra.

11.4.1 SOLVING TWO EQUATIONS IN TWO UNKNOWNS

The first method requires that one or both equations be multiplied by some number so that when the resulting two equations are added together, one of the unknowns (x_1 or x_2) cancels out, leaving one equation in one unknown. Let us multiply the first equation by -1 and the second equation by $+10$. This gives

$$-x_1 - .5x_2 = -50$$

$$4x_1 + .5x_2 = 100$$

Adding the two equations together gives

$$3x_1 = 50$$

Dividing both sides of this equation by three gives

$$x_1 = 16\tfrac{2}{3}$$

and we have solved for the value of x_1. To solve for the other unknown, x_2, we insert the value of x_1 ($16\tfrac{2}{3}$) into any of the original equations again to give one equation in one unknown. Let us use the first equation:

$$16\tfrac{2}{3} + .5x_2 = 50$$

Subtracting $16\tfrac{2}{3}$ from both sides gives

$$.5x_2 = 33\tfrac{1}{3}$$

and dividing both sides by .5 gives

$$x_2 = 66\tfrac{2}{3}$$

Thus we have derived the same result that is obtained in Chapter 6.

11.4.2 CRAMER'S RULE

The second technique for obtaining this result requires the calculation of *determinants*, a number which can be obtained for any square matrix. Our first step is to write the equation system in matrix form where

$$AX = B$$

$$A = \begin{bmatrix} 1 & .5 \\ .4 & .05 \end{bmatrix} \quad \text{and} \quad B = \begin{bmatrix} 50 \\ 10 \end{bmatrix}$$

or

$$\begin{bmatrix} 1 & .5 \\ .4 & .05 \end{bmatrix} \begin{bmatrix} x_1 \\ x_2 \end{bmatrix} = \begin{bmatrix} 50 \\ 10 \end{bmatrix}$$

That this way of writing the equation system is the same as the original system can be seen by actually multiplying the A matrix by the X vector.

Our second step is to calculate the *determinant* of the matrix A. For a matrix of order (2×2), this is a very simple procedure. The determinant of the matrix A, denoted by the symbol Δ or by the use of a straight line on either side of the matrix rather than brackets, is

$$\Delta = \begin{vmatrix} 1 & 5 \\ .4 & .05 \end{vmatrix} = 1(.05) - .5(.4) = -.15$$

All that was done to obtain $\Delta = -.15$ was to multiply the two numbers lying on each of the two diagonal lines drawn through the matrix. From the product lying on the diagonal falling from left to right, we subtract the product lying on the diagonal falling from right to left. This procedure applies to any square matrix of order (2×2). Methods for calculating the determinant of larger matrices will be described below.

The third step is to form a new matrix by deleting the column number that corresponds to the subscript number of the X vector. For example, if we wish to solve for x_1, we delete column 1, and if we wish to solve for x_2, we delete column 2. In place of the deleted column, we insert the B vector, and then calculate the determinant of the resulting revised matrix. This determinant is denoted by the symbol Δ_i, where i stands for the number of the deleted column. For example,

$$\Delta_1 = \begin{vmatrix} 50 & .5 \\ 10 & .05 \end{vmatrix} = 50(.05) - .5(10) = -2.5$$

and

$$\Delta_2 = \begin{vmatrix} 1 & 50 \\ .4 & 10 \end{vmatrix} = 1(10) - 50(.4) = -10.0$$

The fourth and final step is to divide Δ_i by Δ to obtain the value of x_i.

$$x_i = \frac{\Delta_i}{\Delta}$$

For example,

$$x_1 = \frac{\Delta_1}{\Delta} = \frac{-2.5}{-.15} = 16.67$$

$$x_2 = \frac{\Delta_2}{\Delta} = \frac{-10.0}{-.15} = 66.67$$

This technique, known as Cramer's rule, has yielded the same result as obtained previously.

11.4.3 MATRIX INVERSION FOR MATRICES OF ORDER (2×2)

Finally, our third technique entails the calculation of a matrix inverse. Although this approach is somewhat more time-consuming than the use of Cramer's rule, in many instances where the constraints (or goals) are being varied, it can be considerably more time-saving in the long run.

Briefly, the technique makes use of the notion that if

$$AX = B$$

where both A and B are given, then it should be possible to solve for the vector X with both A and B on the right-hand side of the equation. For example, in ordinary algebra, if we have two givens, 5 and 10, in the equation,

$$5Y = 10$$

then dividing both sides by 5 puts both givens on the right side

$$Y = (\tfrac{1}{5})10 = 2$$

However, matrix algebra does not include matrix division. But it does include an operation similar to the use of reciprocals in ordinary algebra. For example the reciprocal of 5 is $\tfrac{1}{5} = .2$, so that 10 can be multiplied by the reciprocal of 5 to give the above result

$$Y = (.2)10 = 2$$

In matrix algebra, the analogue to the reciprocal is the matrix inverse. Here the inverse of the matrix A is A-inverse, written A^{-1}. To understand how this is used, it is necessary to employ one additional concept—the identity.

In ordinary algebra, the number 1 is an identity for multiplication, since any number, when multiplied by 1, remains identically the same.

$$5(1) = 5; \qquad 37(1) = 37$$

In matrix algebra, the analogue to the number 1 is the identity matrix denoted by the capital letter I. This is a matrix with 1's on the main diagonal—the elements lying on a straight line drawn from the extreme upper left-hand corner of the matrix down to the extreme lower right-hand corner—and zeroes elsewhere. Thus an identity matrix is always square. For example, an identity matrix or order (4×4) is

$$\underset{(4 \times 4)}{I} = \begin{bmatrix} 1 & 0 & 0 & 0 \\ 0 & 1 & 0 & 0 \\ 0 & 0 & 1 & 0 \\ 0 & 0 & 0 & 1 \end{bmatrix}$$

The identity matrix has the property that if it is multiplied by any other matrix, it yields identically the same matrix. The reader should determine that the A matrix of the cost-effectiveness example, when multiplied by an identity matrix of order (2×2), remains unchanged $(AI = IA = A)$:

$$\begin{bmatrix} 1 & .5 \\ .4 & .05 \end{bmatrix} \begin{bmatrix} 1 & 0 \\ 0 & 1 \end{bmatrix} = \begin{bmatrix} 1 & .5 \\ .4 & .05 \end{bmatrix}$$

Now in ordinary algebra, if any number is multiplied by its own reciprocal, the result is equal to the number 1

$$5(\tfrac{1}{5}) = 5(.2) = 1$$

Similarly, in matrix algebra if any matrix is multiplied by its own inverse, the result is equal to the identity matrix

$$A^{-1}A = I$$

This result, which we demonstrate later, can be used to solve for the X vector. Premultiplying both sides of the equation $AX = B$ by A^{-1},

$$A^{-1}AX = A^{-1}B$$

But, since $A^{-1}A = I$ and $IX = X$, we have

$$X = A^{-1}B$$

With this approach, once we have calculated the A^{-1}, to solve for the X vector is simply a matter of matrix multiplication. If the program goals given in the B vector should change, assuming that the A matrix remains unchanged, we can readily compute a new X vector by using the new B vector and the unchanged A^{-1}. We now proceed to calculate the inverse of the A matrix. This approach applies only to matrices of order (2×2).

The first step is to interchange the elements along the main diagonal. The second step is to multiply the other two elements by -1. The resulting matrix is known as the adjoint of the matrix A, written $AdjA$

$$AdjA = \begin{bmatrix} .05 & -.5 \\ -.4 & 1 \end{bmatrix}$$

The third step is to compute the determinant of the A matrix. This was done previously when we made use of Cramer's rule. There we found that

$$\Delta = -.15$$

Our last step is to multiply each element of $AdjA$ by $1/\Delta$. The result gives A^{-1}

$$A^{-1} = \frac{1}{\Delta}(AdjA) = \frac{1}{-.15}\begin{bmatrix} .05 & -.5 \\ -.4 & 1 \end{bmatrix} = \begin{bmatrix} -.333 & 3.333 \\ 2.667 & -6.667 \end{bmatrix}$$

To prove that this result is correct, we need only multiply it by A, and if the result is equal to I, then A^{-1} is the true inverse of A

$$\begin{bmatrix} 1 & .5 \\ .4 & .05 \end{bmatrix}\begin{bmatrix} -.333 & 3.333 \\ 2.667 & -6.667 \end{bmatrix} = \begin{bmatrix} 1 & 0 \\ 0 & 1 \end{bmatrix}$$

Thus we have demonstrated that $A^{-1}A = I$. It should be noted that this result cannot always be obtained. This will happen when $\Delta = 0$, as shown in the matrix below

$$K = \begin{bmatrix} 1 & 2 \\ 3 & 6 \end{bmatrix} \quad \text{and} \quad \Delta = 6 - 6 = 0$$

In this case, K^{-1} cannot be calculated, and the matrix K is said to be *singular*, in contrast to the matrix A for which $\Delta \neq 0$. The matrix A is said to be *nonsingular*.

We may now proceed to calculate the vector X with the matrix A^{-1}.

$$X = A^{-1}B$$

$$= \begin{bmatrix} -.333 & 3.333 \\ 2.667 & -6.667 \end{bmatrix}\begin{bmatrix} 50 \\ 10 \end{bmatrix}$$

$$= \begin{bmatrix} 16.68 \\ 66.68 \end{bmatrix}$$

a result that differs from the results obtained from the other two methods by .01 because of rounding error. The advantage of this approach can be seen by assuming that political forces have caused the budget of the original equation system to increase by 10 and the air quality constraint to decrease by 2.

Now calculate the new X vector by each of the three methods, making use of the A^{-1} matrix that has already been calculated for the third of those methods.

11.4.4 Matrix Inversion for Matrices of Order (3 × 3)

We now show how to calculate a determinant and a matrix inverse for a matrix of order (3 × 3). This procedure can in principle be applied to larger order matrices. However, large equation systems are rarely solved by hand, since electronic computers are generally available to solve those systems quite rapidly.

To calculate the determinant of a matrix of order (3 × 3), our first step is to calculate a new entity called a *cofactor*. We calculate one cofactor for each of the three elements lying in any one row or column. Suppose that we choose to calculate the cofactors for the elements b_{1j} of the first row of the B matrix shown below. We then delete the first row and the jth column of B and calculate the (2 × 2) determinant of the remaining four elements, which we denote with the symbol Δ_{1j}. We start with column 1. If the matrix B is

$$B = \begin{bmatrix} 1 & 0 & 5 \\ 3 & 2 & 7 \\ 2 & 4 & 0 \end{bmatrix}$$

Then the cofactor Δ_{11} is

$$\Delta_{11} = 2(0) - 4(7) = -28$$

To determine the sign of the cofactor, we multiply Δ_{1j} by the term $(-1)^{i+j}$. For the element b_{11}, we multiply Δ_{11} by

$$(-1)^{1+1} = (-1)^2 = +1$$

Thus the cofactor of the element b_{11} is $+1(-28) = -28$.

Proceeding in this fashion, we obtain the cofactors of b_{12} and b_{13}:

$$\text{cofactor of } b_{12} = (-1)^{1+2}[\Delta_{12}]$$

$$\Delta_{12} = \begin{vmatrix} 1 & 0 & 5 \\ 3 & 2 & 7 \\ 2 & 4 & 0 \end{vmatrix} \qquad \begin{aligned} &= (-1)^3[3(0) - 7(2)] \\ &= -1[-14] = +14 \end{aligned}$$

$$\text{cofactor of } b_{13} = (-1)^{1+3}[\Delta_{13}]$$

$$\Delta_{13} = \begin{vmatrix} 1 & 0 & 5 \\ 3 & 2 & 7 \\ 2 & 4 & 0 \end{vmatrix} \qquad \begin{aligned} &= (-1)^4[3(4) - 2(2)] \\ &= +1[8] = +8 \end{aligned}$$

The second step, which is the last step, is then to multiply these three cofactors of the elements b_{1j} by b_{1j} and to sum the resulting products

$$\Delta = b_{11}(\text{cofactor of } b_{11}) + b_{12}(\text{cofactor of } b_{12})$$
$$+ b_{13}(\text{cofactor of } b_{13})$$
$$= 1(-28) + 0(14) + 5(8) = 12$$

Thus the determinant of B is 12.

This technique, as we noted above, can also be used to evaluate the determinant of a matrix of order (4×4) and larger. For the (4×4), this would be done by calculating the four cofactors for the elements along any one row or column, where these cofactors are $(-1)^{i+j}[\Delta_{ij}]$, Δ_{ij} being of order (3×3) and obtained by the cofactor expansion method described above.

The determinant obtained via the cofactor expansion method can be used in conjunction with Cramer's rule, or it can be used to calculate a matrix inverse. The latter, however, requires that the adjoint be calculated, and it is to this that we now turn.

To compute the adjoint of a matrix of order (3×3), we first replace each element of the matrix by its cofactor. For example, if we replace each element of the B matrix with its respective cofactor, we would have

$$\text{cofactor matrix of } B = \begin{bmatrix} -28 & 14 & 8 \\ 20 & -10 & -4 \\ -10 & 8 & 2 \end{bmatrix}$$

$$\text{cofactor of } b_{ij} = (-1)^{i+j}[\Delta_{ij}]$$

where Δ_{ij} is obtained by deleting the ith column and the jth row of the B matrix and by calculating the (2×2) determinant of the remaining elements.

The last step required for calculating the adjoint of B makes use of an additional procedure. We must *transpose* the cofactor matrix of B. This is the easiest of the several matrix operations to accomplish—it entails replacing the ijth element with the jith element. For example, the transpose of the A matrix that we used in our cost-effectiveness example, which is denoted as A^T, is

$$A^T = \begin{bmatrix} 1 & .4 \\ .5 & .05 \end{bmatrix} \quad \text{where} \quad A = \begin{bmatrix} 1 & .5 \\ .4 & .05 \end{bmatrix}$$

Since the elements along the main diagonal remain unchanged, we have merely reversed the positions of .4 and .5. Another way of visualizing this procedure is to pretend that we are holding the matrix along its main diagonal and that we flip the matrix over so that what was the upper right-hand corner is now the lower left-hand corner. We now transpose the cofactor matrix of B, and thereby obtain the adjoint of the B matrix

$$AdjB = \begin{bmatrix} -28 & 14 & 8 \\ 20 & -10 & -4 \\ -10 & 8 & 2 \end{bmatrix}^T = \begin{bmatrix} -28 & 20 & -10 \\ 14 & -10 & 8 \\ 8 & -4 & 2 \end{bmatrix}$$

Finally, to obtain the inverse of B, we multiply each element of $AdjB$ by $1/\Delta$, where Δ is the determinant of B that we calculated previously via the cofactor expansion method:

$$B^{-1} = \frac{1}{\Delta} AdjB$$

$$= \frac{1}{12} \begin{bmatrix} -28 & 20 & -10 \\ 14 & -10 & 8 \\ 8 & -4 & 2 \end{bmatrix}$$

$$= \begin{bmatrix} -2.333 & 1.667 & -.833 \\ 1.167 & -.833 & .667 \\ .667 & -.333 & .167 \end{bmatrix}$$

PROBLEMS

SECTION 11.2   (ADDITION AND SUBTRACTION)

Given the vectors

$$A = \begin{bmatrix} 1 \\ 0 \\ 5 \end{bmatrix} \qquad\qquad B = \begin{bmatrix} 6 & 2 \end{bmatrix}$$

$$C = \begin{bmatrix} 5 & 9 \end{bmatrix} \qquad\qquad D = \begin{bmatrix} 3 \\ 7 \\ 1 \end{bmatrix}$$

$$E = \begin{bmatrix} 9 \\ 2 \end{bmatrix} \qquad\qquad F = \begin{bmatrix} 3 \\ 6 \\ 5 \end{bmatrix}$$

Find:

1. $B + C =$
2. $A + B =$
3. $A + D + F =$
4. $D + E =$
5. $F - D =$

Given the matrices

$$G = \begin{bmatrix} 1 & 4 & 3 \\ 6 & 2 & 5 \end{bmatrix} \qquad H = \begin{bmatrix} 0 & 5 \\ 3 & 2 \end{bmatrix}$$

$$K = \begin{bmatrix} 2 & 5 \\ 7 & 4 \\ 1 & 6 \end{bmatrix} \qquad L = \begin{bmatrix} 4 & 0 & 8 \\ 1 & 9 & 3 \end{bmatrix}$$

$$M = \begin{bmatrix} 6 & 2 \\ 18 & 6 \end{bmatrix} \qquad N = \begin{bmatrix} 1 & 6 & 2 \\ 4 & 0 & 1 \\ 7 & 5 & 3 \end{bmatrix}$$

Find:

6. $H + M =$
7. $K + G =$
8. $L - G =$
9. $N + L =$

SECTION 11.3 (MULTIPLICATION)

Use the vectors and matrices given above to find:

Vectors

10. $CE =$ 12. $DF =$ 13. $EB =$

Multiplication by a scalar

14. $6A =$ 15. $7G =$

Multiplication of matrices by vectors

16. $HE =$ 17. $LD =$ 18. $CG =$
19. $EN =$ 20. $KF =$ 21. $BHE =$

Matrices

22. $LK =$ 23. $HG =$ 24. $MH =$
25. $HM =$ 26. $EB =$ 27. $NK =$
28. $H^3 =$

Two equations in two unknowns

29. $4x + 10y = 20$
    $7x + 3y = 15$
    Solve for x and y

Cramer's rule

Use the vectors and matrices given above to find:

30. $HX = E$; find X
31. $MX = E$; find X
32. $KX = F$; find X

Matrix inversion

33. $H^{-1} =$
34. $[I - M]^{-1} =$
35. $X - HX = E$; find X
36. $N^{-1} =$

BIBLIOGRAPHY

Catanese, Anthony J. *Scientific Methods of Urban Analysis*. Urbana, Ill.: University of Illinois Press, 1972, Chapter 2.

Garin, Robert A. "A Matrix Formulation of the Lowry Model for Intra-metropolitan Activity Allocation," *Journal of the American Institute of Planners, 32* (November 1966), 361–366.

Hadley, G. *Linear Algebra*. Reading, Mass.: Addison-Wesley, 1961.

Isard, W., and T. Reiner. "Aspects of Decision-making Theory and Regional Science," *Papers and Proceedings of the Regional Science Association, 9* (1962), 25–33.

Kemeny, J. G., J. L. Snell, and G. L. Thompson. *Introduction to Finite Mathematics*. Englewood Cliffs, N.J.: Prentice-Hall, 1957, Chapter 5.

Leontief, W. W. *The Structure of the American Economy, 1919–1939*. New York: Oxford University Press, 1941.

Lipschutz, S. *Theory and Problems of Finite Mathematics, Schaum's Outline Series*. New York: McGraw-Hill, 1966, Chapters 9 to 12.

Rogers, Andrei. "Matrix Methods of Population Analysis," *Journal of the American Institute of Planners, 32* (January 1966), 40–44.

Rogers, Andrei. *Matrix Methods in Urban and Regional Analysis*. San Francisco: Holden-Day, 1971.

School Mathematics Study Group. *Introduction to Matrix Algebra, Student's Text*. New Haven: Yale University Press, 1961.

Silvers, Arthur L. "The Structure of Community Income Circulation in an Incidence Multiplier for Development Planning," *Journal of Regional Science*, *10* (1970), 175–189.

Theil, H., J. C. G. Boot, and T. Kloek. *Operations Research and Quantitative Economics. An Elementary Introduction*. New York: McGraw-Hill, 1965, Chapters 1 and 3.

The books by the School Mathematics Study Group and Lipschutz are both excellent introductions with numerous clear examples and many problems with answers. Hadley is a more advanced mathematics textbook. Kemeny, Snell, and Thompson is also introductory.

The other bibliographic entries represent applications to a variety of practical problems. Andrei Rogers' *Matrix Methods of Urban and Regional Analysis* is the most comprehensive and thorough reference work available on the application of matrix algebra to urban and regional problems.

CHAPTER 12

Regional Income and Employment Analysis

12.1 INTRODUCTION

A municipality is preparing a program plan for the next several years. To be included are a job training program and a land use and transportation plan. The size of the job training program over the next five years depends not only on the effect of population growth in expanding the local labor force but also on the number and kinds of jobs created in the local and nearby economies in which local workers will seek employment. Similarly, in designing the land use and transportation plan, planners want estimates of the number and spatial pattern of jobs and population that will locate in the area in the relevant future. Finally, the size of future municipal budgets will depend to some degree on receipts of local sales and other taxes, and in preparing their budget forecasts, planners will want estimates of these future tax receipts.

In each of these cases, the planning task requires an analysis of future economic activity that will take place both within a community or municipality as well as in adjacent or other nearby areas. These areas must be included in the projections because they strongly affect the planning problem. Their residents regularly make trips to the municipality to work and to shop, while residents of the municipality itself can be employed in these communities. All of this interaction results in intensive use of the transportation and other public facilities located in one community by residents of a different but nearby community, as is shown in Figure 12.1. Because community economic activity is so strongly dependent on spatial interaction, meaningful economic analysis cannot be done without including all of the

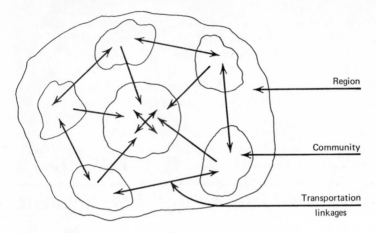

Region

Community

Transportation
linkages

FIGURE 12.1   A region of interacting communities.

communities that are strongly interconnected in terms of regular shopping or employment travel. Although this requirement suggests a very complex "intermunicipality" economic analysis, the practical way to meet this requirement is to carry out the economic analysis at the level of the entire region that comprises the several interconnected communities, and then to allocate the regional totals to the component communities and municipalities by techniques like those described in Chapters 9 and 10. In highly urbanized areas, this means that the most appropriate unit for economic analysis is at the level of the *metropolitan region* or, in terms used by the Census Bureau, the SMSA (Standard Metropolitan Statistical Area). In rural areas, the appropriate unit would be a group of one or more counties that could properly be thought of as a commuting shed or labor market.[1] The directness and practicality of the regional approach is even clearer when we note that the economic future of a given community depends on the array of resources to which it has access and its advantages in using them in producing goods for shipment to the rest of the nation. But since the other communities in the same region will have access to the same array of resources, the economic impacts of these resources will be operating at the regional level. For these reasons, the techniques to be described in this chapter belong to the realm of "regional economic analysis," and will not include methods already indicated

[1] Refer to the concept of "functional economic area" developed by Karl Fox. See K. Fox and T. Krishna Kumar, "The Functional Economic Area: Delineation and Implications for Economic Analysis and Policy," *Papers, The Regional Science Association, 15* (1965). Also C. L. Leven, J. B. Legler, and P. Shapiro, *An Analytical Framework for Regional Development Policy* (Cambridge: The M. I. T. Press, 1970), Chapter IV.

for distributing regional totals to subregions, municipalities, communities, or other spatial units comprising the basic functional economic region.[2]

We begin with the basic multiplier model and its close relative, the economic base model, both of which are easy to learn but could result in sizeable and unnecessary research outlays. Next, we describe the input-output model, which is costly to implement in its proper form, and somewhat more difficult to learn (but using our methods of the preceding chapter, the difficulty should be minimal). The method is widely known and is often applied with expectations that considerably exceed its relatively limited but, in the right places, quite useful capacities. Then, we describe a series of ratio techniques that, if used with reasonable caution, can produce good projections at very low research cost. Included among these methods are those based on the well-known "shift and share" analysis. Finally, we present, as optional reading, an illustration of a regional econometric model—a forecasting technique that is extremely versatile, increasingly encountered in urban and regional work and, if properly executed, relatively inexpensive. However, the implementation of this approach is very technical and requires considerably more training than is offered here, which is the reason why we present no more than a brief introduction of it.

Thus our objective in this chapter is to provide the planning analyst with several projection techniques that can be directly applied, as well as to give him a basis for understanding the capacities and limitations of several of the more complex but operational techniques. This is important because planners are instrumental in the decision to use these techniques and should be in a position to evaluate when a given technique would be appropriate, unrealistic, or too costly for a given research objective.

12.2 SOME DEFINITIONS AND ACCOUNTING IDENTITIES

Economists have, over the years, developed a set of definitions and measurement rules (more colloquially, a jargon) that will be unfamiliar to those who have not previously worked with economists. Because a knowledge of some of this jargon is essential for those who want to understand economic models, or who want to use economic data published in sources such as the United States Census of Manufactures, or both, we briefly explain some of the more frequently used terms and measurement rules.

---

[2] An excellent review of methods for allocating regional employment totals to small areas within the region is provided by Steven Putman, "Intraurban Employment Forecasting Models: A Review and a Suggested New Model Construct," *Journal of the American Institute of Planners, 38* (July 1972), 216–230. These were introduced in this volume in Chapter 10, where additional references can be found.

1. *Final versus intermediate goods.* A large portion of the goods purchased within a region are purchased by local firms for resale. These goods may take the form of raw materials to be further fabricated, or perhaps of already finished goods to be displayed in small quantities and retailed. Since the intent of those who purchase them is simply to resell them, such goods are called intermediate goods. In contrast, goods that are purchased for final use locally—say, food to be eaten by local households, machinery for productive use by local manufacturers, paper for use by local government—or, at least, not for resale locally because they leave the region as exports, are called final goods. The reason we distinguish between final and intermediate goods will quickly be explained.

2. *Regional product.* This is a measure of the quantity of final goods and services produced over a time period (say, a year) by the various businesses, governments, and individuals that do the daily work of a regional economy. The term is used interchangeably here with "regional output"—in a way, it is an indicator of region-wide effort. However, the indicator does not measure only physical output. How can we add the containers of milk sold by the supermarket together with the paintings sold by an artist? We have to multiply the quantity sold of each good by the price of each good to get the value of milk and of paintings sold, and then we add them. Hence, the indicator shows regional output in *money* terms. Since prices may vary between regions or for a single region at different time periods, the regional product measure does not always tell us what we want it to. However, there are methods that are used to adjust for price differences so as to make the regional product measure a more useful indicator of physical output activity for comparative purposes. We call the measure, when adjusted for price differences, the regional product in *real* terms.

In adding up the sales of the different regional activities, we must remember not to include the local sales of intermediate goods. This is because the value of intermediate goods are already reflected in the prices of the final goods. If we added (1) the price of the bottles sold to the milk distributor by the local bottle manufacturer, to the (2) price of the milk sold to the local supermarket by the milk distributor, to (3) the price of the bottle of milk sold by the supermarket for final use to the local consumer, and added all this into our regional output measure, we would have counted the value of the bottle three times and the milk itself two times. To avoid this "double counting," we leave out the region's intermediate sales and count only the final goods sold.

But there is one more problem. We want our regional product measure to be an indicator of the actual productive work that took place in the region. Much of the value of final goods, however, may consist of the value of materials produced in other regions, for example, imports. For example, a pair of imported shoes sold in a local retail store for $20 should not increase regional product by $20 because the effort involved in producing the shoes took place in a different region and, in fact, has already been counted as part of the regional product of that region. Thus the retail store's cost for the shoes, say $12, should be deducted, and the remainder should be included in the regional product measure as reflecting the local shoe store's efforts in storing, showing, and selling the shoes. Even if the shoes were made locally, the leather to make them would have been imported; the cost of the leather would have to be deducted. And if the local consumer had purchased the shoes directly in another region, then the entire price of the shoes should be left out of the local regional product measure. Thus, whether they occur directly or indirectly, imports are excluded from the regional product measure.

3. *Value added.* In the shoe store example, suppose that the year's sales of the store were $300,000. However, the cost of intermediate goods and services—the shoes, accountant's services, window dressing services, and the like, amounted to $200,000. The remaining $100,000 went to pay salaries, rent, interest on loans, and for profit. The cost of all intermediate goods and services is deducted from sales, and what is left over is called *value added.* It is the amount paid to the four ← *factors of production*: labor (receives wages and salaries), land (receives rent), capital (receives interest), and entrepreneurship (receives profits).

4. *Regional income.* This is the amount of income earned by all the region's productive factors during a time period (say, a year). It may be calculated two ways. We may visit business and government, and count up the value added of every productive activity of the region regardless of whether intermediate or final goods were sold. Or, we may visit households and count up the earnings of the four factors of production: we add up the wages and profits earned by labor and entrepreneurs, and also the interest and rent earned by the owners of capital and land. Well, we may not be able to get all this information from households (undistributed business profits, interest, and the like), but the distinction between the two methods should be clear. And the regional income total will very nearly equal the regional product total, as well it should, since the income would have been earned in producing that product. The major difference between the two measures is that some of the region's income is received from productive activities elsewhere: some local laborers commute to nearby regions for work; some local residents own land and capital located in other regions for which they receive income; local government may receive transfers from other governments. And the reverse is also true: some portion of the regional product is used to pay owners of locally used factors who reside elsewhere.

5. *Sectoring.* It is not .possible to analyze the determinants of the level of regional product by tracing the activity of each and every producing and purchasing unit in the region. Hence, we split up the regional product total according to the groups of producing or purchasing activities that have the most similar income-generating behavior. We then seek to analyze the behavior of each such group, or sector, as it is more usually termed. For example, among producers, we may lump together diverse firms such as an electric can-opener manufacturer and an automobile manufacturer and call this the "consumer durables sector." It will be easier to follow the producing behavior of all such firms in the group because there is much that they have in common (they are all dependent on the economic conditions that affect consumers' willingness to buy costly durables). And we might group all the different purchasers in the region into just four sectors: governmental units, household consumers, business firms that invest in plant and

equipment, and external markets to which the region exports, since the purchasers within each of these four groups base their purchasing decisions on conditions that are more similar than do purchasers in different groups. It follows that our analytic strategy will seek to analyze and, perhaps, to project the level of regional income and product by the determinants of the output decision of each producing sector and of the buying decision of each purchasing sector.

Now that these definitions have introduced the material, let us consider more specifically the sectoring scheme that partitions regional product by type of buyer. Buyers that have similar demand patterns in purchasing the region's final goods and services are grouped together, and regional product is partitioned likewise. Thus regional product denoted as RP, is the sum of the purchases made by four final demand sectors: consumption, C, investment, I,[3] government, G, and exports, X, remembering that imports, M, must be deducted from the total.

$$RP \equiv C + I + G + X - M \qquad 12.1$$

Although this regional product identity (when something is true by definition we use the identity sign $\equiv$) has simplicity in its favor, it is not as helpful as it might be for the purpose of tracing the sources of regional income. One seemingly modest adjustment, however, will do the trick. We disaggregate imports according to the final demand sector in which they occurred, either directly or indirectly (recall our discussion of this issue in the last paragraph of our definition of regional product). Hence, our regional product identity is rewritten as

$$RP \equiv (C - M_C) + (I - M_I) + (G - M_G) + (X - M_X) \qquad 12.1'$$

Each term in brackets now shows the amount of regional income earned in the production and sale of goods to each final demand sector. Thus

$$\left. \begin{aligned} Y_C &\equiv C - M_C \\ Y_I &\equiv I - M_I \\ Y_G &\equiv G - M_G \\ Y_X &\equiv X - M_X \end{aligned} \right\} \qquad 12.2$$

which states the income earned in the consumption sector, Y_C, the investment sector, Y_I, the government sector, Y_G, and the export sector, Y_X,

---

[3] By investments, we do not mean only the purchases of plant and equipment by local business. Any commodity that is purchased locally that cannot be used up during the time period under analysis (say, a given year) is to be thought of as investment. A house built by a local family is an example.

respectively. To simplify our presentation of regional economic models, we assume that all income generated (produced) in the region is identically equal to the income received (earned) in the region, so that regional product, RP, is equal to regional income, which we denote as Y.[4] Working now in terms of regional income, equation 12.1 becomes

$$Y \equiv Y_C + Y_I + Y_G + Y_X \qquad 12.3$$

This equation is a very fundamental accounting identity in regional economic analysis. It is not used in every regional income study—very likely, it would not be seen even in the majority of regional studies. But the quality of every such study can be evaluated in terms of this regional income identity because underlying every model of regional output, income, or employment is a relation that reflects income generation and income flows, whether the equation is stated in income terms explicitly or by an income proxy—such as employment levels.[5] The reason an equation such as equation 12.3 is found more often in the advanced rather than in the simpler regional analyses is, in large part, because of the difficulty in (1) obtaining regional income data, and (2) sectoring the income data into even two, let alone the four, final demand sectors of the identity. Income data for many industries are available from published sources, particularly, the value-added data published in the United States Census of Manufactures. But this gives income by producing sector (the steel industry, the textile industry, etc.) and not by final demand sector. And in the general case, the problem cannot be side-stepped simply by lumping industries together that "quite nearly" conform to final demand sectors because most industries sell either directly or indirectly to more than one final demand sector. (Locally produced textiles, for example, may be in a shirt made locally that you, as a member of the consumption sector, purchased locally, and also in the upholstery of the locally made furniture that was exported.) And while we might go out and try to use survey questionnaires to measure all these transactions, the task may in theory involve an infinite number of visits to trace the value added earned in each producing sector

---

[4] In fact, the two measures are not equal, and in actual regional analysis, the need to adjust for net income received from other regions, positive or negative, should be given explicit treatment. It may be noted, however, that the ratio of Y to RP may be fairly constant over time, a relation that would simplify the analysis. See Frederick W. Bell, "An Econometric Forecasting Model for a Region," *Journal of Regional Science*, 7 (Winter 1967), 112.

[5] More complete discussions of regional accounts are to be found in Walter Isard, *Methods of Regional Analysis* (Cambridge, Mass.: Technology Press of M.I.T. and Wiley, 1960); and Charles Leven, "Regional Income and Product Accounts: Construction and Applications," in Werner Hochwald (ed.), *Design of Regional Accounts* (Baltimore: The Johns Hopkins Press and Resources for the Future, 1961).

to the final demand sector in which the produced good ended up. But this is not meant to discourage further interest in the subject, for regional economists are often a resourceful bunch. They have developed a "bag of tools" to resolve the problem. Two such tools are the "location quotient" and the "minimum requirement" method. These are extremely popular and easy to use, an advantage, however, that might quickly fade when we learn that they are also extremely inaccurate. A third method that does the job properly makes use of the "input-output" model, a tool that is difficult and expensive to use but that, nevertheless, is quite popular. However, it is necessary to delay our discussion of input-output analysis until a little later.

12.3 SECTORING METHODS

The first step in the sectoring process is usually to reduce the number of sectors by "getting rid" of two of them. The government sector is often split into local government and nonlocal government. Purchases made by local government are then lumped in with the purchases of the consumption sector, while those made by local offices of nonlocal government are lumped in with the export sector. This practice will not usually create problems later because local government generally provides services to local consumers and is probably quite responsive to the usual determinants of consumer demand (such as increasing population); while the purchases of nonlocal government depend on revenues that come from outside the region (such as federal procurement), so that it makes sense to treat them the same as exports. The other sector to be merged away is the investment sector, which is lumped in with consumption. This practice is defensible if the objective of the regional economic analysis is to make long-term rather than short-term projections because investment in the short term (say one to five years) depends on conditions that are quite different than those underlying consumer demand. This leaves us with just two sectors, consumption and export, so that equation 12.1 becomes

$$RP \equiv (C - M_C) + (X - M_X) \qquad 12.1'$$

while equation 12.3 becomes

$$Y \equiv Y_C + Y_X \qquad 12.3'$$

Now we did say earlier that, in the general case, we cannot group industries together that quite nearly conform to final demand sectors. But there is a special case when we can, and that is when the region under analysis is not heavily industrialized. For example, in a rural region, the mining, agricultural, and the few manufacturing industries that exist might sell all output to other regions and also might purchase all their interindustry inputs from other regions, so that these industries can be quite reasonably lumped together as the "export sector." All remaining productive activity, such as retailing and services, becomes the consumption sector. However, as the region develops a stronger industrial and urban structure, interindustry interdependencies develop that make this approach to the sectoring problem undesirable. We might then resort to one of the frequently used methods such as the location quotient or the minimum requirements method.

The notion on which these two methods are based is that there exists some "standard" geographic area over which a "normal" quantity of a given good is produced and is entirely consumed within its borders. In the case of industry j, the normal quantity, which is stated in relative terms, is Y_{*j}/Y_*— that is, value added in industry j as a percentage of the total final output of the "standard" geographic area, this area being denoted with an asterisk.

For the region under analysis, say region R, we then compare its industry j output as a percentage of its total output—(Y_{Rj}/Y_R), with the "normal" percentage of the "standard" region. If the two percentages are equal, then region R is thought to be producing just enough to satisfy its own local demand. If, for some industry, region R's ratio is lower than "normal," then region R is thought to be importing some of that commodity, and if its ratio is higher than "normal," region R is thought to be exporting that commodity.

In the typical application of these methods, the output proportions are more frequently calculated with employment data rather than with value added or sales data because employment data are easier to obtain.

In the case in which the "standard" geographic area is the entire nation (N), we divide region R's output proportion for industry j by the nation's output proportion for that industry. The resulting ratio is called the *location quotient*. If we calculate it in employment, E, terms, it is

$$\frac{\dfrac{E_{Rj}}{E_R}}{\dfrac{E_{Nj}}{E_N}} \gtrless 1$$

If the calculated value exceeds unity, then the industry is presumed to be an exporter, while if it is less than unity, imports are implied.[6]

---

[6] It should be noted that some analysts require the location quotient to be considerably higher than unity (in one case, 1.51) before an industry is classified as an exporter. See George Hildebrand and Arthur Mace, "The Employment Multiplier in an Expanding Industrial Market: Los Angeles County, 1940–47," *Review of Economics and Statistics*, 32 (August 1950), 241–249; and Michael R. Greenberg, "A Test of Alternative Models for Projecting County Industrial Production at the 2, 3, and 4 Digit Standard Industrial Code Levels," *Regional and Urban Economics*, 1 (February 1972), 397–418.

In the case of the "minimum requirements" method, we choose an industry j and then select from among all the regions R of the nation, the region to be denoted by an asterisk (*) that has the lowest proportion of output in that industry $[Y_{*j}/Y_* = \min_R (Y_{Rj}/Y_R)]$. Thus the region chosen as standard will vary from industry to industry. In having the lowest output proportion for an industry, the region is thought to be producing an amount that would just justify its own internal requirements. The other regions that produce more than their "minimum requirement" are thought to export the "excess."

Regardless of which of these two techniques is used, the level of region R's exports for industry j will be estimated as follows. We first calculate region R's internal demand for commodity j by multiplying region R's total output by "normal" output percentage for that industry. We can view the result as an estimate of industry j's contribution to the region's value added in consumption $_c\hat{Y}_{Rj}$ (the hat over the Y is to indicate an estimate of the quantity rather than an actual measurement of it):

$$_c\hat{Y}_{Rj} = \left(\frac{Y_{*j}}{Y_*}\right) Y_R$$

If the amount estimated as being produced for local consumption is subtracted from the total value added of industry j, the result is an estimate of industry j's output produced for export $_x\hat{Y}_{Rj}$

$$_x\hat{Y}_{Rj} = Y_{Rj} - {}_c\hat{Y}_{Rj}$$

We then sector region R's total output into the consumption and export sectors by summing the consumption and export estimates over all industries

$$Y_R \equiv {}_c\hat{Y}_R + {}_x\hat{Y}_R$$

where

$$_c\hat{Y}_R \equiv \sum_j {}_c\hat{Y}_{Rj}$$

and

$$_x\hat{Y}_R \equiv \sum_j {}_x\hat{Y}_{Rj}$$

including in the summation only those industries for which $_xY_{Rj} > 0$.

Instead of sectoring regional product, we might have been working with employment data so that we would have sectored total regional employment as

$$E_R \equiv {}_c\hat{E}_R + {}_x\hat{E}_R$$

This identity serves as the basis of the "economic base" model, to which we return later. In either case, the two sectoring tools are easy to use. Which one is more appropriate? There are two criteria for choosing: the logic underlying the tool and its *ex post* track record for accuracy.

The logic underlying the location quotient method is more reasonable than that of the minimum requirements method. In the United States, for example, the entire nation is a reasonable geographic unit to choose as the standard because almost all of what is produced there is also consumed there: only 4 % of the national product is exported. Furthermore, if all regions have consumption patterns identical with the nation, we might expect regions to specialize in the production of certain commodities in which they have cost advantages and then to trade the excess over local needs with other regions to get their standard consumption mix. What is wrong is that so many commodities are produced in a region that, in the form produced, they are not demanded locally at all. For example, iron ore is not consumed as iron ore. All of local production will be exported to steel mill regions. And perhaps the steel mill regions will export all local production to automobile producing regions. Furthermore, all regions should not be thought of as having similar consumption patterns. Regions in the South undoubtedly consume relatively less in home-heating systems and winter clothing than do regions in the North. Finally, in those industries that do export from the nation, a region with a location quotient equal to one should be thought of as exporting some of the output of that industry. In all these cases, our location quotient would yield an underestimate of regional exports.

The minimum requirements method also assumes that all regions have identical consumption patterns, but it does not suffer as much from the other criticisms cited for the location quotient technique. Instead, it suffers from some internal inconsistencies. The relative consumption of each local industry output in each region is taken as less than the national average, which is inconsistent with the fact that a national average must be equivalent to the weighted summation of regional averages. Likewise, if all but the "standard" region produces just enough for its own needs, it seems that there are not any regions that import what all those exporting regions export. All very unreasonable. But in terms of the other criterion—statistical accuracy—the minimum requirements method is way out in front.

Tiebout[7] made a study in which the percentage of industry output exported in each of six cities was computed via the location quotient and then was compared with the percentage actually measured via survey. The results for one of these cities, which is typical of the rest, are shown in Table 12.1.

In another study, Greytak[8] used data at the state and multistate level for seven such regional units in the United States. Against actual "exports

[7] Charles M. Tiebout, *The Community Economic Base Study* (New York: Committee for Economic Development, 1962), p. 49.
[8] David Greytak, "A Statistical Analysis of Regional Export Estimating Techniques," *Journal of Regional Science, 9* (December 1969), 387–395.

TABLE 12.1
Location Quotient Results for Industry Export Estimates
Decatur, Illinois

Industry	Loc. Quot.	Survey	Industry	Loc. Quot.	Survey
Food	71	87	Nonelectrical machinery	74	97
Chemicals	44	98			
Primary metals	20	97	Transport equipment	45	100

as a percentage of shipments data" obtained from the *1963 Census of Transportation*, he compared the accuracy of location quotient estimates made with both an employment and a population base, and also minimum requirements estimates. His indicator of "average error of estimation" shows that the average error of both types of location quotient estimates was approximately 90% of the mean of the actual values. The minimum requirements method fared much better: it had an average error of about 60% of the mean of the actual values. This is better, but still extremely inaccurate.

A different approach to the sectoring problem was developed by Czamanski.[9] He avoided the final demand sector framework, using a framework that was suggested from location theory. He grouped industries into those that normally locate outside of their markets, which he termed "geographically-oriented" industries; those that locate in proximity to the geographically-oriented industries, which he termed "complementary" industries, and those that tend to locate in urban centers, which he termed "urban-oriented" industries. To go along with his sectoring scheme, Czamanski devised a predictive model that is relatively easy to implement. We do not consider this model here, but examine now some of the models that depend on final demand sectoring.

12.4 THE MULTIPLIER MODEL

The reason we choose to sector regional product by final demand markets, as indicated previously, is because we have some theories that explain the level of final demand for one or more sectors. The sector most amenable to modeling is the consumption sector. Theory tells us that the quantity spent on consumption in a region depends on the aggregate of the incomes earned

[9] Stanislaw Czamanski, "A Model of Urban Growth," *Papers, The Regional Science Association, 13* (1964), 177–200.

in the regions. Numerous empirical studies have been made of this relationship, known as the consumption function, and it has been found that an acceptable way (albeit not necessarily the best way) to represent the relation is as a proportionate (linear) one

$$C = cY \qquad 12.4$$

where the coefficient c is the share of regional income spent on consumption (the rest is saved). Furthermore, theory tells us that some proportion of consumer outlays will be spent on consumer imports. Part of these imports will be made by local consumers *directly* in other regions, and part will be made *indirectly* insofar as goods purchased from local retail shops will have been produced elsewhere; and if not, then some of the parts of the goods produced and sold locally will have been produced elsewhere. At the empirical level, we may lump both the direct and indirect consumer imports together and assume, with good reason, that they will be proportionate with the level of local consumer expenditures

$$M_C = mC \qquad 12.5$$

As we learn later, the indirect imports can also be estimated via the more detailed input-output model. However, because the mix of consumer imports will not vary greatly among regions of similar size, the more refined approach will only yield a marginal improvement in accuracy.[10]

Recall from equations 12.2 that when consumer imports M_C, are subtracted from final consumer sales, C, the result yields income earned in the consumption sector

$$Y_C = C - M_C$$

Substituting our expressions (12.4) and (12.5) for the two variables on the right-side of this expression, we have

$$Y_C = cY - mcY$$

or, more simply,

$$Y_C = c(1 - m)Y \qquad 12.6$$

That is, income earned in the consumption sector is proportionate to the level of regional income.

We now enter our regional income identity (equation 12.3') into the analysis. Substituting equation 12.6 for Y_C in this identity, we have

$$Y = c(1 - m)Y + Y_X$$

---

[10] See W. Isard, and S. Czamanski, "Techniques for Estimating Multiplier Effects of Major Government Programs," *Papers, Peace Research Society (International)*, *3* (1965), 19–45.

The expression for Y_C on the right side can be shifted to the left side of this equation so that Y can be factored out. This gives

$$Y[1 - c(1 - m)] = Y_X$$

and we now solve for Y, the regional income level, as

$$Y = \left[\frac{1}{1 - c(1 - m)}\right] Y_X \qquad 12.7$$

The bracketed term is called the multiplier. If the coefficients c and m have been estimated via empirical methods (if data exists for C, M_C, and Y, then we calculate $c = C/Y$ and $m = M_C/C$ which are average propensities, or what is better, if time series data are available, the coefficients may be estimated as marginal propensities via regression analysis).[11]

To use this multiplier model for projecting the level of regional income in the future, we first estimate the multiplier by using current or historical data and then assume that the multiplier will remain constant into the future. Then, if a projection of income to be earned in the region's export sector is available, we simply multiply the export income projection by the multiplier to get the regional income projection. However, as it develops, the multiplier effect can be incorporated without the cost of actually estimating the multiplier. This we see in Section 12.5 below. But in either case, we need estimates of future export sector earnings. Techniques for obtaining these estimates are described in Section 12.6.

In the remainder of this section, we consider the theoretical basis for believing that an increase in exports should yield the multiplier effect, and then we discuss some practical issues associated with the use of a multiplier for projecting regional income.

An increase in regional export sales (X) to other regions will, on deducting the imports involved in producing the exported goods (M_X), directly increase regional income (Y) via the increase within the export sector (Y_X). We see in the next section how the input-output model can be used to delete these imports from export sales to yield the export sector income estimate. Some portion of the direct regional income increase earned in the export sector will be spent on consumption sector earnings as is shown in equation 12.6. This increase, of course, is added to the direct regional income increase—it is the first round of the multiplier process induced by the export earnings increase. Those who earn income in the consumption sector have to eat: they spend their induced income increase on more consumption, a part of this flow circulating once again to the hands of those who earn their income in the

[11] An excellent discussion of the regional multiplier model is in Charles Tiebout's, *The Community Economic Base Study*, Chapter 6.

consumption sector—the second round of induced consumption sector earnings. In theory, there are an infinite number of rounds triggered by this process, but each succeeding round adds less and less to the regional income increase because part of the income earned in each round is not spent (it is saved), and another part leaves the region as imports. A diagram showing how this multiplier or feedback process works, together with the saving and import *leakages* that cause the income flow process to converge at a specific and finite increase as estimated by the multiplier model is shown in Figure 12.2.

Thus, if 90% of regional income is spent on consumption (10% saved) and if one third of every dollar spent on consumption is spent directly or indirectly on imports, our coefficients to the multiplier are $c = .9$ and $m = .333$. We may then calculate the multiplier as

$$\left[\frac{1}{1 - .9(1 - .333)} = \frac{1}{1 - .6} = 2.5 \right]$$

$\$ 2.50$ $Consumption$ $Imports$ Y_X $(= \$1.00)$

Via our multiplier model, equation 12.7, we can say that if export sector earnings increase by one dollar, and if the multiplier is 2.5, then regional income will increase by 2.5 dollars. One dollar of this increase is the direct export sector increase and the remaining 1.5 dollars is the induced consumption sector increase due to the multiplier process.

$impt$

Suppose we have a five year projection of export sector earnings showing that Y_X will be $1 million. Then, via equation 12.7, regional income is

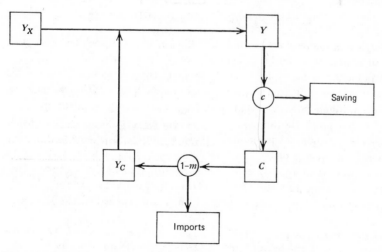

FIGURE 12.2   The income circulation process underlying the multiplier effect.

projected as
$$Y = (2.5)\$1,000,000 = \$2,500,000$$

In addition, if we want to project the region's employment level five years hence, we need an equation that converts income into employment. More advanced methods include the use of an input-output model (to be described in the next section) that computes employment by industry based on the projected output of each industry; another method that uses a nonlinear production function to take account of capital and technology changes is described in the last section of the chapter. But here, we base our employment projection on a simple projection of income per employee (Y/E). Suppose that in five years this ratio is projected to be \$5000. Then given the above regional income projection, our regional employment projection is

$$E = \left(\frac{1}{Y/E}\right) Y = \left(\frac{1}{\$5000}\right)(\$2,500,000) = 500 \qquad \longleftarrow$$

Finally, as part of a forecast of the region's governmental budget, suppose that a projection is needed of the receipts (T) expected from a local 5% tax on all consumer sales. Then, in addition to subtracting from the consumer sales level C the import level M_C, we also subtract

$$T = tC = .05C$$
to obtain
$$Y_C = c(1 - m - t)Y = .9(1 - .333 - .05)Y \qquad 12.6'$$

Our revised income multiplier then yields a regional income estimate of

$$Y = (2.25)\$1,000,000 = \$2,250,000$$

from which consumer sales would be \$2,025,000 from which sales tax receipts of \$101,250 would be collected,[12] as the reader should verify.

To implement the multiplier model, we need the estimates of income by sector. But as we indicated earlier, employment data, which are easier to obtain, are frequently used instead. In fact, the earliest applications of a model of this type at the regional level were stated in employment terms. Known as the "economic base model," regional employment was partitioned into exports and consumption sectors, as is indicated previously, with all the difficulties involved in apportioning industry employment figures to the two final demand sectors. But the export sector was referred to as the "basic" sector, denoted as E_B, and the consumption sector was called the nonbasic

---

[12] For a more thorough discussion of tax base and fiscal outlook analysis, see W. Hirsch, *The Economics of State and Local Government* (New York: McGraw-Hill, 1970), 49–81 and 277–290.

sector E_N.[13] Instead of depending on total employment, the size of the nonbasic sector was shown as proportionate to the size of the basic sector

$$E_N = \left(\frac{E_N}{E_B}\right)E_B \qquad\qquad 12.8$$

Consum

where the coefficient E_N/E_B, called the "base ratio," was assumed constant over time. When inserted for E_N in the total employment identity, we have

$$E = \left(\frac{E_N}{E_B}\right)E_B + E_B$$

Base ratio

or

$$E = \left(1 + \frac{E_N}{E_B}\right)E_B \qquad\qquad 12.9$$

Thus, as previously, a regional activity total depends on the level of activity of the export or basic sector, where the activity level is measured in employment terms. That the multiplier is of the form shown does not make the model structurally different from the income multiplier. By replacing the one in the multiplier by E_B/E_B, then E_B in the denominator by $E - E_N$, and dividing both the numerator and denominator of the resulting expression by E, equation 12.9 could also be written as

$$E = \left(\frac{1}{1 - \dfrac{E_N}{E}}\right)E_B$$

This form is quite the same as that of the income multiplier of equation 12.7 and would have been derived if nonbasic employment were shown as proportionate to regional employment in equation 12.8 instead of basic employment. Thus the economic base model is seen to have the same theoretical base as the income multiplier. But in the multiplier process, employment does not flow through income earners' hands as does income, which is to say that employment is little more than a proxy for income in this model. But there is a danger in using employment as a proxy. Although a given level of value added (e.g., income paid out) in a certain industry may well reflect a certain amount of employment in that industry at one point in time, the income/employment ratio may not at all remain constant over time as technology progresses to increase the ratio, and as certain industries substitute capital for labor over time. Since technology and capital substitution

---

[13] The development of this technique is credited to Homer Hoyt who applied it during the 1930s for projecting employment in small cities.

proceed at different rates in different industries, we have less grounds for expecting an employment multiplier to remain constant than we have for an income multiplier.

This is not to say that the income multiplier as shown in equation 12.7 is free from criticism. At the very least, we should recall that when we lumped local investment and local government in with the consumption sector, our use of the multiplier model as shown in equation 12.7 assumes that the growth of these two "lumped out" sectors is proportionate with the growth of regional income, as is indicated by equation 12.6. We have already discussed this point at the beginning of Section 12.3 on sectoring and have indicated that for short-term projection purposes, the proportionality assumption does not reasonably reflect investment behavior. On the other hand, the use of the income multiplier for long-term purposes is objectionable because the import propensity (m) is sure to change as new local-oriented industries locate in the region, resulting in what we call "import substitution," and also as relative prices between regions change, causing imports to be more or less desirable.[14] Some of the objections to the multiplier both in employment and in income terms will be countered at the end of this chapter when we describe some of the more advanced econometric models that currently are being used for regional analysis.

12.5 INPUT-OUTPUT ANALYSIS

From our discussion of the income multiplier model, it seems that regional income and product magnitudes are best projected in terms of the behavior of the markets to which the region sells, and this implies that regional output should be partitioned into the final demand sectors that reflect these markets. But it also seems that a number of regional magnitudes are best projected by the output levels of the specific industries by which they are generated. For example, since the region's indirect imports consist of intermediate goods purchased by local industry, a projection of indirect imports would be facilitated by first projecting the output levels of the region's industries. Another example: if we wish to project the occupational composition of the region's employed labor force, we would best approach this problem by first projecting the output levels of the various regional industries because if certain industries grow faster than others, then the occupational skills needed in the faster growing industries will also grow faster than the others, resulting in a change in the region's occupational composition of employment.

[14] Additional discussion of both the employment and income multipliers can be found in Isard, *Methods of Regional Analysis*, pp. 189–205; Charles Tiebout; and in Ralph W. Phouts (ed.), *The Techniques of Urban Economic Analysis* (West Trenton: Chandler-Davis, 1960).

What is needed is a way to translate regional output levels in each of the final demand sectors into output levels by industrial sector. That is, we want a method to show how much each of the region's industrial sectors would have had to produce in order that a given final demand sector could have made the sales that it did. And if such a method were available, we could use it to solve the sectoring problem we described earlier—the problem of estimating the amount of direct and indirect imports that should be deducted from the sales of each final demand sector so as to arrive at the level of income earned in each final demand sector (see equation 12.2).

The method we want, if it has not been guessed, is the *input-output model*.[15] After showing the accounting table containing the data required to set up the model, we proceed to show how it works.

The first step is to decide on an appropriate sectoring frame in which to group the region's many business firms and other producers of the region's output. We may feel that the behavior of all such producers can be adequately analyzed if they were combined into only 10 homogeneous sectors, or we might be determined to have plenty of detail so that no fewer than 200 sectors would do. But because we want to simplify the presentation, we include all these producers in just two sectors: manufacturing and commercial. We also retain the simplifying assumption that the investment and local government sectors are included with consumption.

Via a direct survey of local producers (firms, individuals, and governments), we learn that all those classified as "manufacturing" had a sales volume of $280 during the past year. (OK, so the region is a little small; but would it seem preferable to learn this while doing calculations with more realistic figures like $280,374,562.28?) Of this total, they had to spend $120 on purchases of materials from other local firms also classed as "manufacturing," and $60 on materials from the commercial sector. So much for the manufacturing sector's local purchases of intermediate goods. But they also imported $30 worth of intermediate goods from other regions. The total of all these purchases amounted to $210, so that from a sales total of $280, they had $70 left over as value added, which was paid out as salaries, interest, rent, and profits. This is the kind of accounting data we need to do an input-output analysis, and it is shown in the first column of Table 12.2 under the heading MFG. A similar set of data is shown for the commercial sector in the

---

[15] An alternative model, known as "intersectoral flows analysis" is also available. Described by Tiebout, Chapter 4, the method requires a less costly field survey than does "input-output." However, a key assumption underlying this technique (known as "row coefficient" stability) is less realistic. The assumption was shown to yield inferior results. See Karen R. Polensky, "An Empirical Test of Interregional Input-Output Models: Estimation of 1963 Japanese Production," *American Economic Review*, 53 (May 1970), 76–82.

TABLE 12.2
Regional Interindustry and Income Accounts

Purchases

Sales

		Intermediate Demand Sectors		Final Demand Sectors		
Output	Input	MFG.	COMM.	Consumption	Exports	Total sales
MFG.		120	80	20	60	280
COMM.		60	10	80	30	180
Imports		30	40	25	—	95
Value added		70	50	—	—	120
Total purchases		280	180	125	90	675

column labeled COMM. But there is also some additional data shown in Table 12.2. In addition to asking local producers to account for their purchases, we also have asked them to account for their sales. Specifically, for the manufacturing sector, we found that of the $280 total, $60 went to outside markets (export) and $20 went to local markets (consumption). The remaining $200 went to other local industries as sales of intermediate goods to other local industries: $80 went to the commercial sector, $120 went to firms within the manufacturing sector (note that we have already filled in the cells for local intermediate goods transactions with our earlier data on purchases; but the sales data provide a useful cross-check). There is one entry in the table, however, that we have not yet explained. Since our survey thus far has only involved local business and not local households, how would we have learned that local consumers directly imported $25 worth of goods and services in shopping trips to other regions? Unfortunately, to measure these direct consumer imports, a local household survey will be needed. But even if this information is not obtained, we are still able to use the accounts table for the input-output analysis, as we shall see.

In practice, many analysts do not even use a survey to get the numbers for the table. Instead, they use a shortcut technique whereby a national accounts table is adjusted to reflect the industrial composition of a specific region. In practice, which is the better approach? It depends on how much the local planning process depends on accurate estimates, and on how much public investment would be wasted if it were based on mistaken projections. If a great deal would be lost, then it is more reasonable to spend more on more accurate research, which implies the survey approach. If very little would be lost, then shortcut methods are reasonable even though they have been shown to be quite inaccurate.[16]

We now proceed to explain how the input-output model can translate sales by final demand sector into output by industrial sector. What we need to convert the accounts table into a model is a behavioral regularity between two variables that can be measured statistically. Theorizing that the inputs used by a given industry to produce a unit of output will follow a regular pattern as dictated by technology, much as the inputs used to make one kind of soup follow a regular pattern dictated by its recipe, W. Leontief formulated and estimated an input-output model for the United States economy.[17] The regularity that we assume is that the quantity of purchases (Q) made by industry i from industry j are in the proportion a_{ij} with the level of output of industry i:

$$Q_{ij} = a_{ij}Q_i \qquad\qquad 12.10$$

To estimate our "interindustry coefficients," a_{ij}, all we need are measures of Q_{ij} and Q_i, so that

$$a_{ij} = \frac{Q_{ij}}{Q_i} \qquad\qquad 12.11$$

The measures we need are all to be found in our table of interindustry and income accounts, Table 12.2. For example, we see that the commercial sector buys \$80 of inputs from the manufacturing sector to produce \$180 worth of output, so that

$$a_{12} = \frac{80}{180} = .444$$

Similarly, \$10 worth of inputs are purchased internally by the commercial sector, so that

$$a_{22} = \frac{10}{180} = .056$$

We have now completed estimating the input-output coefficients for the commercial sector, accounting for 50% of the purchases of that sector. Of the remaining 50%, 22% is accounted for by imports

$$m_2 = .222$$

[16] Refer to Stanislaw Czamanaski and Emil Malizia, "Applicability and Limitations in the Use of National Input-Output Tables for Regional Studies"; the "Comments" by Morris Goldman and William Miernyk; and William Schaffer and Kong Chu, "Non-survey Techniques for Constructing Regional Interindustry Models," all in *Papers, The Regional Science Association, 23* (1969), 65–101.

[17] W. W. Leontief, *The Structure of the American Economy* (New York: Oxford University Press, 1951).

and the remaining 28% is paid to value added

$$v_2 = .278$$

Having obtained the interindustry coefficients (a_{i2}), the import coefficient (m_2), and the value added coefficient (v_2) for the second column of our accounts table, we continue by estimating these same coefficients for the remaining columns in the industrial part of the table which, in this case, is just the first column. The resulting "input coefficient matrix" is shown as Table 12.3.

It should be noted that the assumptions involved in the regional input coefficient matrix differ somewhat from those envisioned by Leontief for a national coefficient matrix. In the latter, the interindustry coefficients (a_{ij}) assume only constant input-proportions based on constant technology. But in this regional matrix, the coefficient a_{ij} reflects only those intermediates purchased within the region. Intermediates purchased elsewhere are combined together as imports. Thus the regional interindustry coefficient is also based on the assumption of constant import patterns by type of input.

We now proceed to construct our model. We subtract from the sales of each industry (Q_i) the sales of intermediate goods to each local industrial sector (Q_{ij}) to obtain the sales of final goods to the consumption (C_i) and export (X_i) sectors

$$Q_1 - Q_{11} - Q_{12} = C_1 + X_1$$

$$Q_2 - Q_{21} - Q_{22} = C_2 + X_2$$

12.12

But recall that the Q_{ij} can, via equation 12.10, be predicted by the Q_i, so

TABLE 12.3
Regional Input-Coefficient
Matrix

Output \ Input	MFG.	COMM.
a_{ij} { MFG.	.429	.444
COMM.	.214	.056
m_j Imports	.107	.222
v_j Value added	.250	.278
Total	1.000	1.000

that this system may be rewritten as

$$Q_1 - a_{11}Q_1 - a_{12}Q_2 = C_1 + X_1$$
$$Q_2 - a_{21}Q_1 - a_{22}Q_2 = C_2 + X_2$$

12.13

We may factor the $(Q_i - a_{ij}Q_i)$, where $i = j$, into $(1 - a_{ij})Q_i$. Then, given the level of sales in the final demand sectors (the C_i and the X_i), we may solve for the industrial output levels needed for this final demand by treating the Q_i as two unknowns to be solved by the two linear equations 12.13. Or, recalling our matrix algebra from Chapter 11, we may write equations 12.13 in matrix form as

$$\begin{bmatrix} Q_1 \\ Q_2 \end{bmatrix} - \begin{bmatrix} a_{11} & a_{12} \\ a_{21} & a_{22} \end{bmatrix} \begin{bmatrix} Q_1 \\ Q_2 \end{bmatrix} = \begin{bmatrix} C_1 + X_1 \\ C_2 + X_2 \end{bmatrix}$$

or, more simply, as

$$Q - AQ = C + X$$

where

$$Q = \begin{bmatrix} Q_1 \\ Q_2 \end{bmatrix}; \quad A = \begin{bmatrix} a_{11} & a_{12} \\ a_{21} & a_{22} \end{bmatrix}; \quad C + X = \begin{bmatrix} C_1 + X_1 \\ C_2 + X_2 \end{bmatrix}$$

Factoring out the Q vector, this becomes

$$[I - A]Q = C + X$$

Finally, if we multiply both sides by $[I - A]^{-1}$, we have

$$[I - A]^{-1}[I - A]Q = [I - A]^{-1}[C + X]$$

which is the same as

$$IQ = [I - A]^{-1}[C + X]$$

or, more simply,

$$Q = [I - A]^{-1}[C + X]$$

12.14

Since all the terms on the right-hand side of equation 12.14 are given, we may solve for the components of the Q sector. But to do this requires that the inverse matrix $[I - A]^{-1}$ be calculated. This matrix is referred to as the Leontief matrix, and is assumed to remain constant over time, for use with projections of $C + X$ that may be given over time. And the equation is what we call the *input-output* model.[18] We now proceed to implement the model with the data from our input coefficient matrix.

[18] The two major references on regional input-output models are W. Isard et al., *Methods of Regional Analysis*, Chapter 8; and W. Miernyk, *The Elements of Input-Output Analysis* (New York: Random House, 1965).

Since the A matrix is of order (2×2), the I matrix must be of the same order. Inserting the numerical values of the A matrix from the interindustry section of Table 12.3, we have

$$[I - A] = \begin{bmatrix} 1 & 0 \\ 0 & 1 \end{bmatrix} - \begin{bmatrix} .429 & .444 \\ .214 & .056 \end{bmatrix}$$

$$= \begin{bmatrix} .571 & -.444 \\ -.214 & .944 \end{bmatrix}$$

The determinant of this matrix is

$$\Delta = (.571)(.944) - (-.444)(-.214) = .444$$

Interchanging the elements along the main diagonal and reversing the sign of the other two elements, we obtain the adjoint of the $[I - A]$ matrix

$$\text{Adj}[I - A] = \begin{bmatrix} .944 & .444 \\ .214 & .571 \end{bmatrix}$$

We now calculate the Leontief inverse by multiplying $\text{Adj}[I - A]$ by $1/\Delta$

$$[I - A]^{-1} = \frac{1}{\Delta} \, Adj[I - A]$$

$$= \frac{1}{.444} \begin{bmatrix} .944 & .444 \\ .214 & .571 \end{bmatrix}$$

$$= \begin{bmatrix} 2.126 & 1.000 \\ .482 & 1.286 \end{bmatrix}$$

What do these elements of the Leontief inverse signify? They show how much output must be produced in a given industrial sector in order that $1 of final demand sales can be made. This production not only includes the $1 of final goods sold *directly* by the industrial sector to a final demand sector, but also the dollar value of goods sold indirectly to that final demand sector, these being the intermediate goods produced locally to be incorporated in the final goods. We give an example: an electric can opener sold to a local consumer gives rise to the direct sale of the final good in the local commercial sector. That sale depended on the production of the can opener as an intermediate good by the local manufacturing sector (which indirectly sells to the local consumer); the production of which depended on the production of an electric motor, also by the local manufacturing sector (a second-order indirect sale to the local consumer). As shown in the inverse matrix, a dollar of final sales by the manufacturing sector gives rise to $1 direct manufacturing sector sales plus $2.126 - $1 = 1.126 worth of indirect manufacturing sector sales, and also to $.482 worth of indirect commercial sector sales.

Given the amount of final goods that actually were sold by each industrial sector (as is shown in Table 12.2), we can make use of the Leontief inverse to calculate the output level that must have been produced by each industrial sector in the region. Since our final goods were assumed sold to only two final demand sectors, consumption and exports, we seek to calculate the vector of industry outputs that served the vector of export demands

$$X = \begin{bmatrix} \$60 \\ \$30 \end{bmatrix}$$

and the vector of local consumption demands

$$C = \begin{bmatrix} \$20 \\ \$80 \end{bmatrix}$$

as were stated in Table 12.2. We label the export-determined output vector Q_X and the consumption-determined output vector Q_C. If our input-output model can properly translate sales by final demand sector into output by industrial sector, then we expect to find that the sum of the two output vectors Q_X and Q_C equal the original output vector Q in which the manufacturing sector produced $280 and the commercial sector produced $180.

Via equation 12.14,

$$Q_X = [I - A]^{-1}X$$
$$= \begin{bmatrix} 2.126 & 1.000 \\ .482 & 1.286 \end{bmatrix}\begin{bmatrix} \$60 \\ \$30 \end{bmatrix}$$
$$= \begin{bmatrix} \$157.56 \\ \$67.50 \end{bmatrix}$$

and

$$Q_C = [I - A]^{-1}C$$
$$= \begin{bmatrix} 2.126 & 1.000 \\ .482 & 1.286 \end{bmatrix}\begin{bmatrix} \$20 \\ \$80 \end{bmatrix}$$
$$= \begin{bmatrix} \$122.52 \\ \$112.52 \end{bmatrix}$$

Summing these two vectors to check our results, we find that

$$Q_X + Q_C = \begin{bmatrix} \$280.08 \\ \$180.02 \end{bmatrix}$$

which is rather close to the actual output levels (the overestimate of 8 cents and 2 cents, respectively, in the two sectors is due to rounding error).[19]

Now it seems that since the output vectors Q_X and Q_C are each considerably greater than their respective final demand vectors X and C, the input-output model must be reflecting an interindustry multiplier process akin to the income multiplier process of equation 12.7. In a certain sense, this is true. It is a sales multiplier, and reflects the impact of the sales of final goods on the internal generation of sales of intermediate goods. But recall that in the determination of regional income and product, sales of intermediate goods were not included in the calculations because to do so would result in double counting: the value of these intermediates is already included in the value of the final goods sold. And, in fact, the sales level of final goods will be greater than is the amount of regional income that they actually yield because, as is indicated in equation 12.2, it includes the cost of direct and indirect imports. And recall the difficulties that we encountered when we tried to find ways to obtain measures of income by final demand sector. But it is in the resolution of this problem that the input-output model is able to make a very useful contribution. It can be used to "shrink" the sales level of each final demand sector into the income level earned in each such sector—a task that is rather contrary to the concept of a multiplier.

To show how this is done, recall that we calculated a vector of value-added coefficients as part of our input-coefficient matrix in Table 12.3. Each value-added coefficient (v_j) shows the percentage of an industry's total sales that is paid out as income (or value added). Hence, now that we know how much of each industry's output goes directly and indirectly to a given final demand sector, we are only one step away from deriving the income earned by that final demand sector. We can multiply the output level of each industry, generated by a given final demand sector, by it's value added coefficient to obtain the income paid by each industry in serving that final demand sector, and then sum over all local industries to get our long sought measure of "income" by sector of final demand. In the process, we have excluded the direct and indirect imports from our result. Thus

$$Y_X = VQ_X$$

$$Y_C = VQ_C$$

12.15

From Table 12.3, our value added vector is

$$V = [.250 \quad .278]$$

[19] It should be noted that as the size of the matrix increases, the size of the rounding error can be kept to a minimum by increasing the number of decimal points to which the calculations are carried.

so that

$$Y_X = [.250 \quad .278] \begin{bmatrix} \$157.56 \\ \$67.50 \end{bmatrix}$$
$$= \$58.16$$

which, in excluding intermediate imports, is quite a bit less than total export sales ($X_1 + X_2 = \$90$); and

$$Y_C = [.250 \quad .278] \begin{bmatrix} \$122.52 \\ \$112.52 \end{bmatrix}$$
$$= \$61.91$$

which is also less than total consumption sales made locally ($C_1 + C_2 = \$100$; note that local consumers also directly imported another \$25 worth of goods) by the amount of indirect consumer imports. And the estimated income earnings in each final demand sector sums to just about the actual amount shown in Table 12.2 as value added:

$$Y = Y_X + Y_C = \$120.07$$

whereas actually from Table 12.2 we have

$$Y = V_{\text{MFG}} + V_{\text{COMM}} = \$70 + \$50 = \$120$$

The slight error of 7 cents is again due to rounding error.

Now we discuss using the model for regional income and employment projections. Given the export/consumption sectoring scheme, with all the assumptions indicated, and if we have as given a projection of future export sales by industrial sector, we may arrive at a projection of regional income by any of several methods. The first is to translate sectoral export sales (X) into export income (Y_X) via equation 12.15. We may then enter this figure into our income multiplier equation 12.7 to obtain a regional income projection. Instead, we may modify the import function (equation 12.5) so that it estimates only direct imports M_D. The level of local consumer expenditures C_L would then be

$$C_L = c(1 - m_D)Y$$

and, if C_L can be expressed in vector form reflecting the purchases of consumers from each industry [implying that $c(1 - m_D)$ is a vector], then income earned in the consumption sector Y_C can be obtained by using the input-output model to exclude indirect consumer imports

$$Y_C = V[I - A]^{-1}C_L = V[I - A]^{-1}c(1 - m_D)Y$$

A projection of regional income, given a vector of projected exports, and the export sector earnings as derived via the input-output inverse and the value-added vector can then be estimated as

$$Y = \left(\frac{1}{1 - V[I - A]^{-1}c(1 - m_D)} \right) Y_X \qquad 12.16$$

However, as we indicated before, the income-multiplier effect can be more easily calculated via less costly means as is indicated in Section 12.6 below.

Finally, in more elegant form, we might "close" the model with respect to consumption by including both the value-added (households) coefficient vector and a vector of consumption coefficients within the matrix to be inverted. The resulting "closed" Leontief inverse, when multiplied by the export vector, will incorporate the income-multiplier effect.[20]

If our objective is to obtain employment rather than income projections, instead of multiplying the projected industry output vector Q, as derived from equation 12.14, by the value-added coefficient vector, we may form a vector E of employment-to-output ratios, one for each industry. Then, total regional employment is estimated by multiplying the E vector by the Q vector. Similarly, if what we want is employment by type of occupation, we might assume that a unit of output in a given industry requires a given number of workers from each occupation (available in the *U.S. Census of Population*). Forming a matrix of number of workers per unit output by occupation and by industry, we may again multiply this matrix by the projected Q vector to get a projection of employment by occupation.

But all this has assumed export sales (X) as given. How can exports by industrial sector be projected? We describe two widely used methods for making those estimates in the next section.

12.6 PROJECTIONS: RATIO METHODS

The Constant Share Method

The export sales of locally produced goods to regions in the rest of the nation that "import" them depends to a great extent on the growth of those regions. If the local region is able to maintain intact its relative advantages as a supplier, then as the nation's importing regions grow, the exporting region's share in supplying this growth will remain constant. To simplify the analysis, it is usual to identify a region's export market area as coterminous with the nation as a whole. We write the growth in the nation's "import" demand for industry i as ΔM_{iN}. If the region R's share in the national production in industry i is s_{iR}, then this region's growth in export sales will be

$$\Delta X_{iR} = s_{iR} \Delta M_{iN} \qquad\qquad 12.17$$

The assumption of constant shares implies that region j's current share of the national market is also s_{iR}, so that currently

$$X_{iR} = s_{iR} M_{iN}$$

---

[20] Refer to Miernyk, or to H. Chenery and P. Clark, *Interindustry Economics* (New York: Wiley, 1959).

Dividing equation 12.17 by this expression, the share coefficient drops out

$$\frac{\Delta X_{iR}}{X_{iR}} = \frac{\Delta M_{iN}}{M_{iN}}$$ 12.18

so that to assume constant regional shares is to assume that region R's exports for industry i grows at the same rate as the growth of the national "import" demand for that industry's output. If exogenous projections of national "import" demand are available, then via equation 12.18, regional export growth is known. Of course, these national commodity-specific "import" demands are not measured and, therefore, these growth rates are unknown. Instead, we use available projections of national commodity-specific output growth rates $(\Delta Q_{iN}/Q_{iN})$ as a proxy.[21] Regional commodity i export growth is then projected as

$$\Delta X_{iR} = \left(\frac{\Delta Q_{iN}}{Q_{iN}}\right) X_{iR}$$ 12.19

But this still requires a set of estimates of current export levels for each regional industry. And this again raises the question of whether to use the shortcut methods that we have described previously to estimate industry exports from industry output data, or to use the more accurate and costly field survey approach. We suppose here that a survey has been made yielding all the information of Table 12.2.

We learn that projections have been made of the national growth rates over the next five years for all manufacturing industries combined, and also for industries classified as commercial. They are as shown in Table 12.4. Since the region's current industrial sector exports have been measured by survey as \$60 for the manufacturing and as \$30 for the commercial sector, we project the region's five-year growth in industrial sector exports according

TABLE 12.4
National Sectoral Growth Rate
Projections (Illustrative)

Sector	Five-Year Growth Rate
Manufacturing	.276
Commercial	.402

[21] Such projections are made by the Bureau of Labor Statistics, U.S. Department of Labor, *The U.S. Economy in 1980, A Summary of BLS Projections, Bulletin 1673* (Washington, D.C.: U.S. Government Printing Office, 1970).

to equation 12.19 as

$$\Delta X_{\text{MFG}.R} = (.276)\$60 = \$16.56$$

$$\Delta X_{\text{COMM}.R} = (.402)\$30 = \$12.06$$

In practice, this procedure is typically modified to avoid the necessity of measuring the current export levels of all regional industries. Instead, a shortcut sectoring technique such as the location quotient is used to identify those regional industries that produce at least partly for export markets (the criterion being that an industry's location quotient must exceed unity, or perhaps some number greater than unity adjudged to more conservatively discriminate export from nonexport industries). Total output changes (ΔQ_{iR}), rather than export change, are then projected by the constant share method, so that the total output of such industries (Q_{iR}), instead of just their export output (X_{iR}), is used as the base in equation 12.19 to be multiplied by the industry-specific national growth rates.

Shift and Share Analysis: the Constant Shift Method

A given region may grow at a rate slower (faster) than the national average if (1) the region has a mix of industries strongly weighted toward the slow (fast) growth type; or (2) if the region's internal supply advantages have declined (improved) in relation to those offered in other regions, thus making it less (more) competitive as an industrial location. It would be helpful for those concerned with development planning to identify which of these two effects has been responsible for the region's recent relative growth rate. A simple technique for measuring the *industry mix effect* and the *competitive effect* was applied by Edgar Dunn[22] to the 48 states of the continental United States, and it provided an easily grasped historical summary of how and why each state grew the way it did.[23]

To use this procedure, known as *shift-and-share analysis*, national and regional output, value-added, or employment data, by industry, must be obtained for two periods in the recent past (say years t and $t - n$). Assuming that output data are used, the first task is to calculate the region's output increase for each industry that would have occurred if that industry had grown at the same rate as total national output,[24] as measured by

[22] Edgar S. Dunn, Jr., "A Statistical and Analytical Technique for Regional Analysis," *Papers, The Regional Science Association*, 6 (1960), 97–112.

[23] H. Perloff et al., *Regions, Resources, and Economic Growth* (Baltimore: The Johns Hopkins Press and Resources for the Future, 1960).

[24] We are showing the technique in output change-terms rather than in output level-terms, as is more typically done. Without affecting the results yielded by the method, the presentation in change terms better relates to other methods shown in this chapter.

$(\Delta Q_N/Q_{N,t-n})Q_{iR,t-n}$, where $\Delta Q_N \equiv Q_{N,t} - Q_{N,t-n}$. Subtracting the industry's hypothetical growth from the growth that actually occurred (ΔQ_{iR}), we obtain a measure that can be called the industry's *total shift* S_{iR}:

$$S_{iR} \equiv \Delta Q_{iR} - \left(\frac{\Delta Q_N}{Q_{N,t-n}}\right)Q_{iR,t-n} \qquad 12.20$$

We want to determine whether the magnitude of this shift was due to forces operating on the industry at the national level, such as changes in national demand patterns or relative industry technological progress, or at the regional level such as changes in the quality of the region's labor supply. To do this, we split the total shift into two parts: one part called a *proportionality shift*

$$P_{iR} \equiv \left(\frac{\Delta Q_{iN}}{Q_{iN,t-n}} - \frac{\Delta Q_N}{Q_{N,t-n}}\right)Q_{iR,t-n} \qquad 12.21$$

depending on the difference between the total national growth rate and the industry's national growth rate; and another part called the *differential shift*

$$D_{iR} \equiv \left(\frac{\Delta Q_{iR}}{Q_{iR,t-n}} - \frac{\Delta Q_{iN}}{Q_{iN,t-n}}\right)Q_{iR,t-n} \qquad 12.22$$

depending on the difference between the industry's regional growth rate and its national growth rate.

If the bracketed term in the proportional shift is positive, it means that our region has a rapid growth industry, while if the bracketed term in the differential shift is positive, it means that the industry finds the local region to be a better environment than it does the nation in general. Thus the proportional shift measures the industry mix effect, while the differential shift measures the competitive effect. That the two measures equal the total shift can be seen by adding them

$$P_{iR} + D_{iR} \equiv \left(\frac{\Delta Q_{iN}}{Q_{iN,t-n}} - \frac{\Delta Q_N}{Q_{N,t-n}}\right)Q_{iR,t-n}$$

$$+ \left(\frac{\Delta Q_{iR}}{Q_{iR\ t-n}} - \frac{\Delta Q_{iN}}{Q_{iN,t-n}}\right)Q_{iR,t-n}$$

$$\equiv \left(\frac{\Delta Q_{iR}}{Q_{iR,t-n}} - \frac{\Delta Q_N}{Q_{N,t-n}}\right)Q_{iR,t-n}$$

$$\equiv \Delta Q_{iR} - \left(\frac{\Delta Q_N}{Q_{N,t-n}}\right)Q_{iR,t-n} \equiv S_{iR}$$

If we sum the resulting calculated measures over all industries in a region, we obtain

$$\sum_i S_{iR} \equiv \sum_i P_{iR} + \sum_i D_{iR} \qquad 12.23$$

Observe that $\sum_i S_{iR}$ can be written from equation 12.20 as

$$S_R \equiv \sum_i S_{iR} \equiv \sum_i \left[\Delta Q_{iR} - \left(\frac{\Delta Q_N}{Q_{N,t-n}} \right) Q_{iR,t-n} \right]$$

$$\equiv \Delta Q_R - \sum_i \left(\frac{\Delta Q_N}{Q_{N,t-n}} \right) Q_{iR,t-n}$$

$$\equiv \Delta Q_R - \left(\frac{\Delta Q_N}{Q_{N,t-n}} \right) Q_{R,t-n}$$

Thus, the total regional shift S_R, is a measure of the region's overall growth (ΔQ_R) in comparison to the growth it would have made if it grew at the same rate as the nation as a whole. Equation 12.23 shows whether this total regional shift, either positive or negative, was due more to the region's particular industry mix ($\sum P_{iR}$) or to the region's internal conditions ($\sum D_{iR}$). And that's what shift-share analysis is all about—a very useful approach for getting an idea of the causes of recent regional change.

The method has also been adapted for use in projecting the growth of a region's industries. To do this requires three steps. First, we divide equation 12.22 by $Q_{iR,t-n}$ to obtain

$$\frac{D_{iR}}{Q_{iR,t-n}} = \frac{\Delta Q_{iR}}{Q_{iR,t-n}} - \frac{\Delta Q_{iN}}{Q_{iN,t-n}} \qquad 12.24$$

This gives the differential growth rate that industry i recently experienced in the region: it is the difference between the industry's recent regional and national growth rates. Second, relocating the national growth-rate term to the same side as the differential growth-rate term, and again multiplying both sides by $Q_{iR,t-n}$, we write

$$\Delta Q_{iR} = \left(\frac{\Delta Q_{iN}}{Q_{iN,t-n}} + \frac{D_{iR}}{Q_{iR,t-n}} \right) Q_{iR,t-n} \qquad 12.25$$

Then, we obtain projections over the next n years for each industry's national growth rate ($\Delta Q_{iN}/Q_{iN,t}$) where now $\Delta Q_{iN} = Q_{iN,t+n} - Q_{iN,t}$) which is inserted in place of the industry's growth rate in the recent past. Third, assuming the industry's recent past differential growth rate as measured by equation 12.24 to remain constant into the future, we add the national industry projected growth rate to recent past differential growth rate and multiply by the industry's current regional output level ($Q_{iR,t}$). The result of this "constant-shift" method gives the projected growth for industry i in region R over the next n years.

$$\Delta Q_{iR} = \left(\frac{\Delta Q_{iN}}{Q_{iN,t}} + \frac{D_{iR}}{Q_{iR,t-n}}\right)Q_{iR,t} \qquad 12.26$$

Note that the constant-shift method differs from the constant-share method only by the addition of the differential growth rate to the national industry growth rate, and that, like the constant-share method, the variable being projected is typically a region's industrial output total rather than its industrial exports. Let us consider an example.

Step One. We find that during the past five years region R's manufacturing sector grew somewhat less rapidly than did manufacturing nationwide by 1.6%. Region R's commercial sector, in contrast, had a growth rate that exceeded that of the nation's by 3.8%.

Step Two. We obtain national five-year projections for both sectors from Table 12.4.

Step Three. We add the national growth rate projections to the region's recent differential growth rates to obtain projected five-year regional growth rates, and multiply the result by the region's current sectoral output levels (shown in Table 12.2 as $280 and $180 for the manufacturing and commercial sectors, respectively). The five-year growth projections are

$$\Delta Q_{\text{MFG},R} = (.276 - .016)\$280 = (.26)\$280 = \$72.8$$

$$\Delta Q_{\text{COMM},R} = (.402 + .038)\$180 = (.44)\$180 = \$79.2$$

The constant-shift method, in taking account of the possibility that regional shares may shift, appears more reasonable than the constant-share method. And it is not very much more difficult to apply. Therefore, should we not conclude that it is the better technique? No, not at all. The acid test of any analytic technique is how well it performs in practice. There have been a number of evaluations of the two methods, and we indicate the results of two of them. Both, it should be noted, evaluate the methods by their accuracy in projecting industry output levels, instead of export levels, over a relatively short term, from the base year 1958 to the year 1963, where the actual 1963 levels were already known.

Using manufacturing employment data for 16 SMSA's, Brown[25] found that the constant-share method produced consistently and measurably

---

[25] H. James Brown, "Shift and Share Projections of Regional Economic Growth: an Empirical Test," *Journal of Regional Science, 9* (April 1969), 1–18.

less expected error[26] (roughly one third less) than did the constant-shift method. Using value-added data for only industries that he classified as export-oriented (via a modified location quotient) for the 23-county New York metropolitan region, Greenberg[27] found the constant-share technique to produce far less expected error (almost 50% less via the same error measurement technique as used by Brown) than did the constant-shift method.

What has been more damaging to the constant-shift method is Brown's finding that the industry-specific differential growth rates as measured by equation 12.24 are completely unstable from one period to the next (a conclusion obtained via chi-square and t-tests of the difference-between-means).[28] He showed that it is because of its instability that the inclusion of the differential growth rates of the recent past as a proxy for projected differential growth rates actually reduces the accuracy of the simpler constant-share method.

The conclusion is unavoidable. The constant-share method is better than the constant-shift method. But it is not the best that can be done with the shift and share approach.[29]

Shift and Share Analysis: the Projected Shift Method

Instead of augmenting the constant differential growth rate, Greenberg incorporated a projection of the region's changing population share. His projecting equation which is used for projecting the future industry value added levels, $Y_{iR,t+n}$, rather than output or value added change, ΔY_{iR}, of export-oriented industry may be written as follows[30]

$$Y_{iR,t+n} = \left(1 + \frac{\Delta Y_{iN}}{Y_{iN,t}}\right)\left[\frac{1 + \Delta P_R/P_{R,t-1}}{1 + \Delta P_N/P_{N,t-1}}\right] Y_{iR,t} \qquad 12.27$$

[26] The measure of expected error is Theil's u-statistic, and it is obtained by subtracting the actual 1963 values from the "projected" 1963 values, taking the mean of the squares of these differences, dividing this by the mean of the squared actual values, and taking the square root of the result.

[27] Michael R. Greenberg, p. 407.

[28] Brown, pp. 10–13. However, it has been shown that the aggregated differential growth rate for the region as a whole is quite stable from one time period to the next. See C. C. Paraskevopoulos, "The Stability of the Regional Share Component: An Empirical Test," *Journal of Regional Science*, 11 (April 1971), 107–112.

[29] The last piece of analysis that Brown included in his paper was a regression of the differential growth rate of all industries and regions on a set of possible causal variables. In failing to find correlates, Brown concluded that the shift and share approach is not useful for regional analysis. This conclusion cannot be drawn from Brown's analysis, however, for the very reason that he offered: the regression was not a proper test of the model because the model is industry-specific while his regression cut across industries.

[30] Greenberg, pp. 406–409.

where the term in brackets is one plus the region's projected n-year population growth rate, starting with a one-year lag from the current period, relative to the nation's projected population growth rate plus one, also lagged one year. Once the two sets of projections are made (national-industry and regional-national population growth rates), the regional projections are easily calculated. Greenberg found that when the basis of the region's shifting share is explicitly projected, as in his equation 12.27, the expected projection error was reduced by almost one third relative to the best alternative—the constant-share method.

More recently, Silvers has found that an equation written in a form similar to equation 12.25 reasonably reflects the short-term dynamic equilibrium behavior of regional industry in response to changing national demand and to changing relative supply conditions.[31] However, (1) the dependent variable to be projected should be a given industry's export output change rather than its total output change, and (2) the differential growth rate term should not be assumed constant, but should be a projection of the growth rates of regional resources supplies (such as skilled labor or social overhead capital) relative to the aggregated growth rate of similar resources in all regions together that export the output by the given industry. Specifically, for the case in which just one resource such as labor (L) is scarce, the region's export growth for industry i would be projected as

$$\Delta X_{iR} = \left(\frac{\Delta Q_{iN}}{Q_{iN,t}} + \frac{D_{iR}}{X_{iR,t}}\right) X_{iR,t} \qquad 12.28$$

The differential growth rate is defined, in this case,[32] as

$$\frac{D_{iR}}{X_{iR,t}} \equiv \frac{\Delta L_R}{L_{R,t}} - \frac{\Delta L_N}{L_{N,t}} \qquad 12.29$$

[31] Arthur L. Silvers, "Export Base Analysis in Practice and in Theory" (Belo Horizonte, Brazil: Resources for the Future and Centro de Desenvolvimento e Planejamento Regional, Universidade Federal de Minas Gerais, 1972).

[32] For the general case with m scarce resources (Z_h) and only n of the nation's regions exporting the output of industry i, the projected differential growth rate is written (with the subscript i implicit):

$$\frac{D_R}{X_{R,t}} \equiv \sum_{h=1}^{m} b_h \frac{\Delta Z_{hR}}{Z_{hR,t}} - \sum_{R=1}^{n} \frac{X_{Rt}}{M_{N,t}} \left(\sum_{h=1}^{m} b_h \frac{\Delta Z_{hR}}{Z_{hR,t}}\right) \qquad 12.29'$$

where the b_h are weights required for adding the growth rates of unlike resources (and can be estimated via regression analysis), and the $X_{R,t}/M_{N,t}$ are the percentage of region R's share in the national "import" demand for industry i.

where $\Delta L_R/L_{R,t}$ and $\Delta L_N/L_{N,t}$ are projections of the growth rates of regional and national labor supplies, respectively.[33]

That this formulation of the shift and share approach for use in regional projections will yield acceptable results is given support by noticing that the equation found most accurate by Greenberg, equation 12.27, can be closely approximated as[34]

$$\Delta Y_{iR} = a_t \left[\frac{\Delta Y_{iN}}{Y_{iN,t}} + \left(\frac{\Delta P_R}{P_{R,t}} - \frac{\Delta P_N}{P_{N,t}} \right) \right] Y_{iR,t} \qquad 12.27'$$

Here, the dependent variable is the total value added of export-oriented industries. Assuming industry value added to be proportionate to the industry output, the form of the projection equation is the same as that of the shift and share identity of equation 12.25 with the current rather than prior years as the base of all ratios, as it should be for projecting purposes. The growth rate difference in projected regional and national populations is of the form recommended in equation 12.28 and, since population is an extremely close correlate of labor supply, the population growth rate differential will, in part, be reflecting the effect of the relative growth in the region's labor supply. What is different is that the entire expression is multiplied by the coefficient a_t which, however, over the relatively short run will not differ greatly from unity.

Completing the Regional Income Projections

To derive aggregate regional income, we must next consider the multiplier effect by which export sector earnings induce earnings in the rest of the regional economy. However, as we indicated earlier, the multiplier effect as derived by the simple multiplier in equation 12.7 or the complex one of

---

[33] This autonomous labor supply "push" effect on regional growth has been put forth as the key determinant of regional growth differential in the celebrated work by George Borts and Jerome Stein, *Economic Growth in a Free Market* (New York: Columbia University Press, 1964).

[34] Writing $Y_{iR,t+n} = \Delta Y_{iR} + Y_{iR,t}$ subtract $Y_{iR,t}$ from both sides of equation 12.27. After factoring the $Y_{iR,t}$ and multiplying the term in parentheses by the numerator of the bracketed term, equation 12.27 becomes

$$\Delta Y_{iR} = \left[\frac{1 + \dfrac{\Delta Y_N}{Y_{N,t}} + \dfrac{\Delta P_R}{P_{R,t-1}} + \dfrac{\Delta Y_N}{Y_{N,t}} \dfrac{\Delta P_R}{P_{R,t-1}}}{1 + \Delta P_N/P_{N,t-1}} - 1 \right] Y_{iR,t}$$

Deleting the term $(\Delta Y_N/Y_{N,t})(\Delta P_R/P_{R,t-1})$, since two short-term growth rates when multiplied together approximate zero, and ignoring the one-period lag in the population growth rate projections, the resulting expression with the denominator $1/(1 + \Delta P_N/ P_N) = a_t$ being regionally invariant, can be written as is shown in equation 12.27'.

equation 12.16 can be obtained by more direct and less costly means. Both multipliers reduce to a scalar coefficient that can be denoted by the coefficient b, so that regardless of the complexity of effort involved in calculating b, we can write the income multiplier equation as

$$Y_{R,t} = b Y_{XR,t}$$

Also, a projection of regional income growth ΔY can be written as

$$\Delta Y_R = b \, \Delta Y_{XR}$$

Dividing this equation by the preceding one, we obtain

$$\frac{\Delta Y_R}{Y_{R,t}} = \frac{\Delta Y_{XR}}{Y_{XR,t}}$$

The multiplier term b has dropped out, and we see that it is not necessary to calculate it at all! The very concept of a constant scalar multiplier implies that aggregate regional income grows at the same rate as does the exogenous variable which, in the model as shown, is regional export income. Hence, to project the growth in regional income (ΔY_R), all we need to do is multiply the region's current income level $(Y_{R,t})$ by the projected growth rate of its export income $(\Delta Y_{XR}/Y_{XR,t})$:

$$\Delta Y_R = \left(\frac{\Delta Y_{XR}}{Y_{XR,t}} \right) Y_{R,t} \qquad\qquad 12.30$$

But we still must project the region's export earnings growth (ΔY_{XR}) to have the needed projected export earnings growth rate, and to do this, the input-output model is the tool of choice. To see why this is so, consider the approach that projects industry output or value-added or employment *totals* $(Q_{iR,t+n})$ rather than industry *exports* $(X_{iR,t+n})$. This approach, while more pragmatic, ignores the fact that many regional industries produce for internal markets to meet local interindustry demand in addition to producing for export markets. Although this effect may be insignificant in regions with lower industrialization levels (small towns and rural areas), it is certain to be significant in more highly industrialized regions. Thus an industry's future regional output $(Q_{iR,t+n})$ will include production for export $(X_{iR,t+n})$ *plus* local interindustry demand $(Q_{iR,t+n} - X_{iR,t+n})$. But the level of this part of the industry's output is unlikely to be proportionate with its total output. Instead, it is likely to vary as the export growth in *other* regional industries varies: as outlined in Section 12.4, this output constitutes the *indirect exports* generated by the export sales to other industries. This being the case, it is no wonder that Brown found the shift and share approach to be unsuitable for projecting an industry's *total* regional output level. Unless great care is taken to assure that the shift and share approach is applied for projecting the output levels of industries that produce almost entirely for export markets (as Greenberg seems to have done), the method is, indeed, conceptually and statistically unsuitable for the task. Better to apply it to what it is reasonably suited to do, and that limits it to projecting the export part of industry output. To project the remaining indirect export output is just what the input-output model is structured to do.

Thus once the vector, (ΔX_R), giving each industry's regional export increase, has been projected, the vector giving each industry's total output increase (ΔQ_{XR})[35] is obtained, via equation 12.14, as

$$\Delta Q_{XR} = [I - A]^{-1} \Delta X_R \qquad 12.31$$

From this, the export sector's income increase is projected, via equation 12.15, as

$$\Delta Y_{XR} = V \Delta Q_{XR} \qquad 12.32$$

Given the current export sector earnings level $(Y_{XR.t})$, the export sector earnings growth rate is computed and, together with the region's current income level, we obtain via equation 12.30 our regional income growth projection.

In the more usual case in which the total output growth of export industries is projected, the input-output approach is not applicable. Nevertheless, equation 12.30 can be used to project total regional income growth if, from the industrial output growth projections of export industries value-added growth (ΔY_{XR}) can be obtained. This can be done by inserting the vector of projected total output increase, by export industry, into equation 12.32, and proceeding as before.

If regional employment growth projections (ΔE_R) are also desired, we multiply the export output vector ΔQ_{XR} by a vector giving each industry's employment-to-output ratio, sum the resulting employment increase projections to get the regional export employment increase, and insert in an equation of the same form as equation 12.30 stated in employment terms to obtain the projected total regional employment increase. Instead, if a ratio method such as this is believed to ignore unrealistically additional determinants of regional employment (such as capital substitution and technological progress), we might use some of the more advanced equipment to be described in the next (and final) section of this chapter. But before we consider the more advanced material, we summarize our projection methods in Figure 12.3.

---

[35] This assumes that a given industry does not also directly or indirectly serve local consumption-demand. If this assumption is wrong, then equation 12.31 projects only that part of an industry's output produced directly or indirectly for export.

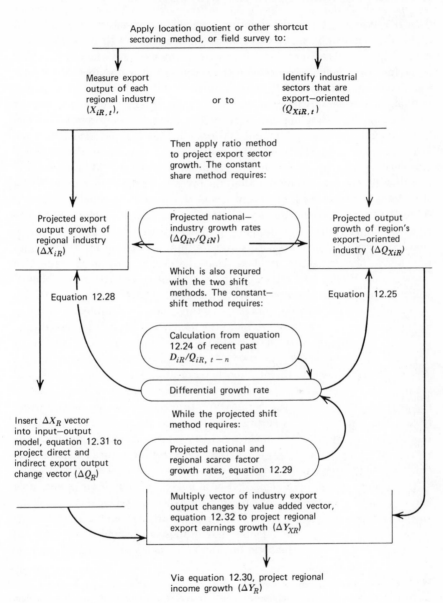

Apply location quotient or other shortcut
sectoring method, or field survey to:

Measure export
output of each
regional industry
$(X_{iR,t})$,

or to

Identify industrial
sectors that are
export–oriented
$(Q_{XiR,t})$

Then apply ratio method
to project export sector
growth. The constant
share method requires:

Projected export
output growth of
regional industry
(ΔX_{iR})

Projected national–
industry growth rates
$(\Delta Q_{iN}/Q_{iN})$

Projected output
growth of region's
export–oriented
industry (ΔQ_{XiR})

Equation 12.28

Which is also requred
with the two shift
methods. The constant–
shift method requires:

Equation 12.25

Calculation from equation
12.24 of recent past
$D_{iR}/Q_{iR,\,t-n}$

Differential growth rate

Insert ΔX_R vector
into input–output
model, equation 12.31 to
project direct and
indirect export output
change vector (ΔQ_R)

While the projected shift
method requires:

Projected national and
regional scarce factor
growth rates, equation 12.29

Multiply vector of industry export
output changes by value added vector,
equation 12.32 to project regional
export earnings growth (ΔY_{XR})

Via equation 12.30, project regional
income growth (ΔY_R)

FIGURE 12.3   Ratio methods for projecting regional income growth.

12.7 PROJECTIONS: ECONOMETRIC METHODS

In recent years, the multi-equation econometric models used to describe national economies have become increasingly attractive to regional economists. The reasons are not difficult to find: many analysts who have studied economics have included an econometrics course in their studies. They may well have found that theory and method in national econometric model building is considerably more advanced than the regional counterpart and, in addition, books describing the state of the art are widely available. The lengthy experience built up and recorded in national econometric work provides detailed information to the analyst about what to do. For example, alternative specifications for the consumption function should be considered as well as for the production function, the investment function, and functions that describe inventory investment, wage and price determination, foreign trade, and many others. Finally, all this sophisticated work comes to the analyst complete with computer package programs that provide the necessary simultaneous equations estimators and routines for testing for autocorrelation and other statistical problems that the econometrician is trained to know about. When the model is built, the output presented to the "client" will include a set of charts that trace the path of each important variable over time, perhaps, in increments of every three months. Employing the same historical data that were used to build the model, the model's predicted time path can be compared with the actual time path so that a visual idea can be obtained about the model's accuracy. And it is nearly always accurate, with R^2's that might hover in the neighborhood of .997. All very impressive, and what is most impressive is that the cost of constructing these models at the regional level, so long as the necessary data can be obtained or "derived" from published sources, is surprisingly low. But are regional econometric models necessarily better than the even less costly ratio methods? Like the ratio models we have discussed, actual measures of sectoral exports and calculations of inter-industry demands are not usually included. Nonetheless, *if* the model is built by a *competent* econometrician and *if the proper data* can be obtained, there are strong reasons for expecting regional econometrics to yield a superior projection tool.[36] The reasons are (1) a much broader range of variables that determine regional magnitudes can be and *is* included; (2) more complex and more realistic functional forms can be included, such as

---

[36] We cannot include as an example of good econometrics the multiple equation "industrial dynamics" approach as found in Jay Forrester's *Urban Dynamics* (Cambridge, Mass.: The M.I.T. Press, 1969) and other urban-regional models patterned on this otherwise provocative approach, for reasons to be found in Edwin Mills, *Studies in the Structure of the Urban Economy* (Baltimore: The Johns Hopkins Press and Resources for the Future, 1972), p. 80.

multivariate linear or nonlinear equations; and (3) the statistical methods used are specifically structured to minimize error, and the analyst is cognizant of the need to take account of such sources of estimation bias as spurious correlation (due to misspecification of the model) and coefficient identification problems (due to the possibility of reverse causality among the variables). Also by including controllable exogenous variables, these models can project the impact on regional growth of a variety of public policies.

Regional econometric models have been built for a number of regions in the United States and in other countries. Among the more interesting of those constructed in the United States are the models of the Philadelphia and St. Louis metropolitan regions, the states of Massachusetts, Iowa, and Ohio, and the Northeast Corridor region.[37]

Because of their complexity, we do not attempt to describe or compare them here. However, a recommendation on how a good regional model should be structured has been provided by Lawrence Klein, a foremost econometrician who has constructed many national models to whom the reader is referred.[38]

In what follows, we present an example of an extremely simple, one-sector model with all prices excluded. The first four equations are already familiar: the regional product identity equation 12.1,[39] the consumption function equation 12.4, the import function equation 12.5, and the (constant share) export function, equation 12.17.

income $\quad\quad Y_t = C_t + I_t + G_t + X_t - M_t$

consumption $\quad C_t = a_C + b_C Y_t$

imports $\quad\quad M_t = a_M + b_M Y_t$

exports $\quad\quad X_t = a_X + b_X (\text{GNP}_t)$

---

[37] In the order indicated, refer to Norman Glickman, "An Econometric Forecasting Model of the Philadelphia Region," *Journal of Regional Science*, *11* (April 1971), 15–32. CONSAD Research Corporation, *Final Version of the CONSAD Regional Econometric Model as Applied to the St. Louis SMSA* (Pittsburgh: CONSAD, 1969) (the model was constructed by Fu-chen Lo); Frederick W. Bell, "An Econometric Forecasting Model for a Region," *Journal of Regional Science*, *7* (Winter 1967), 109–128; Wilbur R. Maki et al., *Simulation of Regional Product and Income with Emphasis on Iowa, 1954–1974*, *Agricultural and Home Economics Experiment Station Research Bulletin 548* (Ames: Iowa State University, 1966); W. L. L'Esperance et al., "Gross State Product and an Econometric Model of a State," *American Statistical Association Journal*, *64* (September 1969), 787–807; and Robert Thomas Crow, *An Econometric Model of the Northeast Corridor of the United States* (Springfield, Va.: Clearinghouse for Federal Scientific and Technical Information, March 1969).

[38] Lawrence R. Klein, "The Specification of Regional Econometric Models," *Papers, The Regional Science Association*, *23* (1969), 105–116.

[39] We assume regional product to be the same as regional income.

(where GNP_t in the last equation is the current gross national product), and the fifth merely states that government sector outlays are exogenously determined:

$$\text{government} \qquad G_t \equiv \bar{G}_t$$

Of the six remaining equations, three are identities. The first two equations are new, and we explain them now.

The first is the investment function. Much work has been done in the theory and practice of investment function formulation, but we use a very simple one. We assume that the current level of investment (which is actually the increase in the capital supply ($I_t \equiv \Delta K$), depends linearly on the current output level (Y_t) less the capital supply already on hand (K_{t-1}). The idea here is that if output is high and capital low, then the existing capital supply is inadequate relative to the production level, and increased investment purchases would therefore be observed.

$$\text{investment} \qquad I_t = a_I + b_I Y_t - c_I K_{t-1}$$

At this point, if all the coefficients of these equations have been estimated (via regression techniques including ordinary and two-stage least squares), we may insert into the income identity all the other equations to derive an income-multiplier equation that is conceptually the same as equation 12.7 above[40]

$$Y_t = \frac{a}{1-b} + \frac{1}{1-b}\,(\bar{G}_t + b_X\,GNP_t - c_I K_{t-1})$$

We see that current income rises if government expenditures in the region rise, if current GNP rises, but that it is less if the region had had lots of capital on hand at the beginning of the period, which would have discouraged investment.

The second new equation is the production function. A production function shows how much industrial output will be produced, given the quantity of the different inputs used and given current technology. In this sense, we are already familiar with production functions: every column vector in the technical coefficient matrix (A) of the input-output model is a production function. But in econometric work, something at once simpler and more complex is usually employed: simpler because it does not include a host of interdependently determined interindustry inputs but, usually, only labor and capital, and more complex because the equation is nonlinear and carries in its background both books and articles that might number in the thousands which describe its theoretical and empirical properties. The one most popularly used is known as the Cobb-Douglas production function and may be

---

[40] The coefficients $a = a_C + a_I + a_X - a_M$ and $b = b_C + b_I - b_M$, respectively.

written as

$$\text{production function} \qquad Y = A(1 + r)^t E_t^\alpha K_t^\beta$$

where E_t and K_t are the current levels of employment and capital, respectively, and the term $A(1 + r)^t$ is the effect of technology, which progresses at the rate r per year.[41] In the usual case, the coefficients α and β are positive and are expected to sum to unity, which reflects the assumptions of positive marginal productivity on inputs with constant returns to scale. One method for estimating the coefficients of the Cobb-Douglas function is to take its logarithm and to estimate, via regression analysis, the equation

$$\log Y = a + b_1 t + b_2 \log E + b_3 \log K$$

where b_1, b_2, and b_3 are unbiased estimates of $\log (1 + r)$, and α and β, respectively, although a is a biased estimate of A.[42]

Once the production function is estimated, we can use it, together with the income multiplier and investment equations to determine the regional employment level. We insert the values of $\bar{G}_t$, GNP_t, and K_{t-1} into the income multiplier to solve for Y_t. This, together with K_{t-1}, is inserted in the investment function to solve for I_t. Via our next equation, an identity, we obtain the current capital supply:

$$\text{capital} \qquad K_t = K_{t-1} + I_t$$

Then the estimated levels of Y_t and K_t are inserted into the production function, and E_t, the employment level, is determined as a residual. How this may be done is readily seen if we state the production function in terms of E_t instead of Y_t:

$$E_t = [A(1 + r)^t]^{-1/\alpha} Y_t^{1/\alpha} K_t^{-\beta/\alpha}$$

This says that whatever the income level, the employment level will be lower than it would be otherwise if the rate of technological progress (r) or the capital supply (K_t) should increase.

The last three equations concern the region's labor force and its unemployment. The first is a labor force equation. This has been formulated many ways, and may be structured to take account of natural population growth (birth, aging, and death rates) which we have already discussed in Chapter 8,

[41] A very clear and thorough discussion of production functions is provided by R. G. D. Allen, *Macroeconomic Theory* (London: Macmillan, 1968); while an excellent discussion of how to estimate them is in Lawrence Klein, *An Introduction to Econometrics* (Englewood Cliffs, N.J.: Prentice-Hall, 1962).

[42] See Arthur Goldberger, *Econometric Theory* (New York: Wiley, 1964), pp. 217–218. Recall our discussion in Chapter 9 of this problem in relation to the estimation of the coefficient K.

as well as net migration in response to wage and unemployment differentials among regions. We illustrate these effects as follows[43]

$$\text{labor force} \qquad L_t = a_L + b_L t + c_L u_{t-1}$$

where L_t is the current labor force, the term $b_L t$ shows the effect of natural increase over time (t), and the term $c_L u_{t-1}$ shows the effect of the last period's unemployment rate (u_{t-1} reflecting labor market tightness) on net migration. Then, the region's current unemployment level is obtained as

$$\text{unemployment} \qquad U_t = L_t - E_t$$

from which the current unemployment rate is obtained as

$$\text{unemployment rate} \qquad u_t = U_t/L_t$$

which can be inserted in the labor force equation to determine next period's labor force.

And that completes our regional econometric model: 11 equations, of which 5 are identities, with just 3 exogenous variables (time, government expenditures, and gross national product). If annual projections for 2 of the exogenous variables ($\bar{G}_t$ and GNP_t) are available, then we can test the effect of public policy on the time path of such goal variables as total income (Y), employment (E), unemployment rate (u), and even per capita income as measured by Y/L. For example, suppose $\bar{G}_t$ can be affected by a federal revenue-sharing program. We can show how various inflows of revenue, in affecting $\bar{G}$, will affect the goal variables.[44] If the investment function had been formulated to include the effect of profits on investment, then the effect on those goal variables of a low interest business loan program or of an air pollution control program can be projected.[45]

It should be noted, however, that the regional econometric approach is not at all beyond criticism. A model is no better than the strength of its conceptual structure and the significance and stability of its estimated parameters and, on both counts, these models may be criticized.

At the conceptual level, the model we have shown leaves aside the possibility that an improvement in the region's location advantage can improve its exports—the very basis for regional development programs. Regional exports

---

[43] This equation is only illustrative. Much work has been done on this relation, and the reader is referred to the regional econometric models already mentioned.

[44] This has been done by Glickman for Philadelphia.

[45] This was the use to which the CONSAD model for St. Louis was put.

are determined via what is essentially a constant share model. But, we have already indicated the conceptual superiority of a projected share approach in which an exogenously determined differential growth rate reflecting internal supply improvements can improve regional exports and, thereby, all the target variables. To be sure, a regional model can be formulated to reflect these more complicated relations, and Klein's specification is an example.[46] But this makes more difficult the econometric work, and for this reason, most regional econometric models reflect the structure we have illustrated.

On the statistical level, since most of the variables in a time series model tend to move together, multicollinearity may cause the coefficients of two collinear variables included in the same equation to be biased, and will also make it quite difficult to tell whether a given selection of explanatory variables forms a better specification for a given equation than another. There are other statistical problems that also beset the use of regional econometric models for projection purposes. After constructing such a model for the Coastal Plains states, Charles Richter[47] cited the above two, as well as problems of autocorrelation, measurement errors in the time series data, the delineation of appropriate regional boundaries, the long-term instability of the structural coefficients, and the practice of using such models for long-term projections (say, 20 years), for which they are unsuited, instead of for short-term projections (up to an upper limit of 5 years).[48] After suggesting that some of these problems could be countered via the use of cross section rather than (perhaps, in addition to?) time series data, he concludes "that these models yield information which may be better than nothing at all, and that there still are no better techniques available."[49]

PROBLEMS

1. Below is a set of data for the Nation of Atopia, with figures disaggregated into three regions, A, B, and C. Suppose that you are a planner for region C and that the data show employment levels.

---

[46] See Klein.
[47] Charles Richter, "Some Limitations of Regional Econometric Models," *The Annals of Regional Science*, 6 (June 1972), 28–34.
[48] Glickman cites additional problems as well, and indicates what might be done about them.
[49] Richter, p. 34.

YEAR	INDUSTRY	REGION A	REGION B	REGION C	NATION
1965	Mfg.	50	100	100	250
	Comm.	100	100	50	250
	Total	150	200	150	500
1970	Mfg.	100	150	150	400
	Comm.	250	250	100	600
	Total	350	400	250	1000

Source: Atopia, Bureau of the Census.

(a) Calculate total export employment for region C for both 1965 and 1970 via the location quotient and the minimum requirements method.

(b) Can you think of ways to upgrade the accuracy of these estimates?

2. Again, for region C, using the location quotient estimates:

(a) Calculate the employment multiplier for 1970 (using the economic base model) making use of the export and local data derived from the location quotient in problem 1.

(b) In what ways does the magnitude of this multiplier differ from one that would have been provided by a Keynesian-type income multiplier?

3. The following input-output inverse matrix and value added vector have been estimated for region C:

$$[I - A]^{-1} = \begin{bmatrix} 2 & 1 \\ .5 & 1.5 \end{bmatrix}$$

$$V = [.20 \quad .25]$$

(a) Can you use these matrices with the "census" data above to estimate export-sector earnings (Y_X)?

(b) Suppose a vector of export sales were available:

$$X = \begin{bmatrix} 100 \\ 200 \end{bmatrix}$$

(c) Calculate Y_X.

(d) What methods can you think of to estimate this X vector?

(e) What analytic process is implicit in the matrix equation $Y_X = V[I - A]^{-1}X$ that yields the Y_X estimate superior to that provided by the location quotient and minimum requirements methods?

4. Again for region C, but this time assuming that the census data above is in "value-added" rather than "employment" terms:
   (a) Use the "constant-shift" model to project the increase in exports over the five-year period 1970 to 1975. Using first the "census data" and then your export-local estimates, calculate the forecast, first, in terms of the increased output of export industry and, then, in terms of export increases following the schema of Figure 12.3. To help you, the following national growth rate projections for 1970 to 1972 are supplied:

$$\text{Mfg.} = .50$$

$$\text{Comm.} = .75$$

   (b) Using the multiplier or equivalent, project the total income growth for the same five-year period.
5. Now suppose that you have obtained a better job as planner with the national government and must think of all three regions together. Using shift and share analysis:
   (a) Evaluate the total rate of growth of each region relative to that of the nation (e.g., the total shifts).
   (b) Then, via the differential and proportional shift measures, indicate for each region whether the causes of these shifts were due to internal or external causes.
   (c) Would your thinking about what policies ought to be used to improve region C's growth pattern differ from what they would have been had you remained employed as region C's planner?

BIBLIOGRAPHY

Allen, R. G. D. *Macroeconomic Theory*. London: Macmillan, 1968.

Bell, Frederick W. "An Econometric Forecasting Model for a Region," *Journal of Regional Science*, 7 (Winter 1967), 109–128.

Brown, H. James. "Shift and Share Projections of Regional Economic Growth: An Empirical Test," *Journal of Regional Science*, 9 (April 1969), 1–18.

Bureau of Labor Statistics, U.S. Department of Labor. *The U.S. Economy in 1980, A Summary of BLS Projections, Bulletin 1673*. Washington, D.C.: U.S. Government Printing Office, 1970.

Chenery, H., and P. Clark. *Interindustry Economics*. New York: Wiley, 1959.

CONSAD Research Corporation. *Final Version of the CONSAD Regional Econometric Model as Applied to the St. Louis SMSA*. Pittsburgh: CONSAD, 1969.

Crow, Robert Thomas. *An Econometric Model of the Northeast Corridor of the United States*. Springfield, Va.: Clearinghouse for Federal Scientific and Technical Information, March 1969.

Czamanski, Stanislaw. "A Model of Urban Growth," *Papers, The Regional Science Association, 13* (1964), 177–200.

Czamanski, S., and Emil Milizia. "Applicability and Limitations in the Use of National Input-Output Tables for Regional Studies, *Papers, The Regional Science Association, 23* (1969), 65–77.

Dunn, Edgar S., Jr. "A Statistical and Analytical Technique for Regional Analysis," *Papers, The Regional Science Association, 6* (1960), 97–112.

Forrester, Jay. *Urban Dynamics*. Cambridge, Mass: The M.I.T. Press, 1969.

Fox, Karl, and T. Krishna Kumar. "The Functional Economic Area: Delineation and Implications for Economic Analysis and Policy," *Papers, the Regional Science Association, 15* (1965), 57–85.

Glickman, Norman. "An Econometric Forecasting Model of the Philadelphia Region," *Journal of Regional Science, 11* (April 1971), 15–32.

Goldberger, Arthur. *Econometric Theory*. New York: Wiley, 1964.

Greenberg, Michael R. "A Test of Alternative Models for Projecting County Industrial Production at the 2, 3, and 4 Digit Standard Industrial Code Levels," *Regional and Urban Economics, 1* (February 1972), 397–418.

Greytak, David. "A Statistical Analysis of Regional Export Estimating Techniques," *Journal of Regional Science, 9* (December 1969), 387–395.

Hildebrand, George, and Arthur Mace. "The Employment Multiplier in an Expanding Industrial Market: Los Angeles County, 1940–1947," *Review of Economics and Statistics, 32* (August 1950), 241–249.

Hirsch, W. *The Economics of State and Local Government*. New York: McGraw-Hill, 1970.

Isard, Walter. *Methods of Regional Analysis*. Cambridge, Mass.: Technology Press of M.I.T. and Wiley, 1960.

Isard, W., and S. Czamanski. "Techniques for Estimating Multiplier Effects of Major Government Programs," *Papers, Peace Research Society (International), 3* (1965), 19–45.

Klein, Lawrence R. *An Introduction to Econometrics*. Englewood Cliffs, N.J.: Prentice-Hall, 1962.

————. "The Specification of Regional Econometric Models," *Papers, The Regional Science Association, 23* (1969), 105–116.

Leontief, W. W. *The Structure of the American Economy*. New York: Oxford University Press, 1951.

L'Esperance, W. L. et al. "Gross State Product and an Econometric Model of a State," *American Statistical Association Journal, 64* (September 1969), 787–807.

Leven, Charles. "Regional Income and Product Accounts: Construction and Applications," in Werner Hochwald (ed). *Design of Regional Accounts*. Baltimore: The Johns Hopkins Press and Resources for the Future, 1961.

Leven, C. L., J. B. Legler, and P. Shapiro. *An Analytic Framework for Regional Development Policy*. Cambridge, Mass.: The M.I.T. Press, 1970.

Maki, Wilbur R. et al. *Simulation of Regional Product and Income with Emphasis on Iowa, 1954–1974, Agricultural and Home Economics Experiment Station Research Bulletin 548*. Ames: Iowa State University, 1966.

Miernyk, W. *The Elements of Input-Output Analysis*. New York: Random House, 1965.

Mills, Edwin. *Studies in the Structure of the Urban Economy*. Baltimore: The Johns Hopkins Press and Resources for the Future, 1972.

Paraskevopoulos, C. C. "The Stability of the Regional Share Component: An Empirical Test," *Journal of Regional Science, 11* (April 1971), 107–112.

Perloff, Harvey S., Edgar S. Dunn, Jr., Eric C. Lampard, and Richard F. Muth. *Regions, Resources, and Economic Growth*. Baltimore: The Johns Hopkins Press and Resources for the Future, 1960.

Phouts, Ralph W. *The Techniques of Urban Economic Analysis*. West Trenton: Chandler-Davis, 1960.

Polensky, Karen R. "An Empirical Test of Interregional Input-Output Models: Estimation of 1963 Japanese Production," *American Economic Review, 53* (May 1970), 76–82.

Putman, Steven. "Intraurban Employment Forecasting Models: A Review and a Suggested New Model Construct," *Journal of the American Institute of Planners, 38* (July 1972), 216–230.

Richter, Charles. "Some Limitations of Regional Econometric Models," *The Annals of Regional Science, 6* (June 1972), 28–34.

Schaffer, William, and Kong Chu, "Non-survey Techniques for Constructing Regional Interindustry Models," *Papers, The Regional Science Association, 23* (1969), 83–101.

Silvers, Arthur L. "Export Base Analysis in Practice and in Theory," Belo

Horizonte, Brazil: Resources for the Future and Centro de Desenvolvimento e Planejamento Regional, Universidade Federal de Minas Gerais, 1972.

Tiebout, Charles. *The Community Economic Base Study*. New York: Committee for Economic Development, 1962.

As general references we might suggest Isard, Tiebout, Phouts, and Miernyk.

Isard's *Methods of Regional Analysis* is a broad survey of the state of the art in regional economic analysis until 1960. It includes chapters on regional social accounting, the location quotient, multipliers and economic base analysis, input-output analysis, and an array of additional methods.

Tiebout's 84-page monograph was written for laymen by one of the field's outstanding analysts who was one of the first to create interest in the use of Keynesian tools of analysis for regional work. The monograph presents the practical side of doing a multiplier analysis as well as a highly readable presentation of the theoretical and empirical problems involved.

The articles in the book by Phouts trace the development of economic base and regional multiplier analysis during the 1950s. Included are some that show how the techniques should be applied, and some that criticize the assumptions involved.

Miernyk's book is available in paperback and is an extensive but highly readable presentation of the input-output model, including both elementary and more advanced applications, and a variety of modifications that are possible.

Appendices

I. *Review of Algebraic Operations.*

II. *Random Digits.* Reprinted by permission from Paul G. Hoel, *Introduction to Mathematical Statistics*, fourth edition (New York: Wiley, 1971), pp. 98–99.

III. *Squares and Square Roots.* Reprinted by permission from Paul G. Hoel, *Introduction to Mathematical Statistics*, fourth edition (New York: Wiley, 1971), pp. 382–390.

IV. *Areas of a Standard Normal Distribution.* Reprinted by permission from Paul G. Hoel, *Introduction to Mathematical Statistics*, fourth edition (New York: Wiley, 1971), p. 391.

V. *Student's "t" Distribution.* Reprinted by permission from Paul G. Hoel, *Introduction to Mathematical Statistics*, fourth edition (New York: Wiley, 1971), p. 393.

VI. X^2 *Distribution.* Reprinted by permission from Catherine M. Thompson, "Tables of the Percentage Points of the X^2 Distribution," *Biometrika*, *32* (1941), 188–189, and in D. A. S. Fraser, *Statistics: An Introduction* (New York: Wiley, 1958), p. 394. Values have been corrected to E. S. Pearson and H. O. Hartley (eds.), *Biometrika Tables for Statisticians*, Volume I, third edition (Cambridge, Eng.: The University Press, 1966), pp. 136–137.

VII. *F Distribution* Reprinted by permission from George W. Snedecor, *Statistical Methods*, fifth edition (Ames, Iowa: Iowa State University Press, 1956), pp. 246–249.

VIII. *Present value of 1.*

IX. *Mantissas for Common Logarithms.* Reprinted by permission from H. C. Fryer, *Elements of Statistics* (New York: Wiley, 1954), pp. 247–248.

439

Review of Algebraic Operations

1. $a + b = b + a$

2. $a \cdot b = b \cdot a$

3. $a + (b + c) = (a + b) + c$

4. $a \cdot (b \cdot c) = (a \cdot b) \cdot c$

5. $a \cdot (b + c) = a \cdot b + a \cdot c$

6. $a - (b + c) = a - b - c$

7. $\dfrac{a}{b} \cdot \dfrac{c}{d} = \dfrac{ac}{bd}$

8. $\dfrac{a/b}{c/d} = \dfrac{a}{b} \cdot \dfrac{d}{c} = \dfrac{ad}{bc}$

9. $\dfrac{a + b}{c} = \dfrac{a}{c} + \dfrac{b}{c}$

10. $a^m \cdot a^n = a^{m+n}$

11. $\dfrac{a^m}{a^n} = a^{m-n}$

12. $a^{-n} = \dfrac{1}{a^n}$

13. $(a^m)^n = a^{m \cdot n}$

14. $(a \cdot b)^n = a^n \cdot b^n$

15. $\left(\dfrac{a}{b}\right)^n = \dfrac{a^n}{b^n}$

16. $a^0 = 1$

17. $a^{1/n} = \sqrt[n]{a}$

18. $a^{m/n} = (\sqrt[n]{a})^m$

19. $(a + b)^2 = a^2 + 2ab + b^2$

20. $(a - b)^2 = a^2 - 2ab + b^2$

21. $(a + b)^3 = a^3 + 3a^2b + 3ab^2 + b^3$

22. $(a - b)^3 = a^3 - 3a^2b + 3ab^2 - b^3$

23. $(a + b)(a - b) = a^2 - b^2$

24. If $a^x = N$ then $x = \log_a N$

25. $\log_a (M \cdot N) = \log_a M + \log_a N$

26. $\log_a \dfrac{M}{N} = \log_a M - \log_a N$

27. $\log_a N^p = p \cdot \log_a N$

28. $\displaystyle\sum_{i=1}^{N} a_i = a_1 + a_2 + a_3 + \cdots + a_N$

29. $\displaystyle\sum_{i=1}^{N} a_i^2 = a_1^2 + a_2^2 + a_3^2 + \cdots + a_N^2$

30. $\displaystyle\sum_{i=1}^{N} a_i b_i = a_1 b_1 + a_2 b_2 + a_3 b_3$
$$+ \cdots + a_N b_N$$

31. $\displaystyle\sum_{i=1}^{N} (a_i + b_i) = (a_1 + b_1) + (a_2 + b_2)$
$$+ (a_3 + b_3) + \cdots + (a_N + b_N)$$
$$= \sum_{i=1}^{N} a_i + \sum_{i=1}^{N} b_i$$

32. $\displaystyle\sum_{i=1}^{N} (a_i + b_i)^2 = \sum_{i=1}^{N} (a_i^2 + 2a_i b_i + b_i^2)$
$$= \sum_{i=1}^{N} a_i^2 + \sum_{i=1}^{N} 2a_i b_i + \sum_{i=1}^{N} b_i^2$$

33. $\displaystyle\sum_{i=1}^{N} k a_i = k \sum_{i=1}^{N} a_i$ where k is a constant

34. $\displaystyle\sum_{i=1}^{N}\sum_{j=1}^{M} a_{ij} = \sum_{j=1}^{M} a_{1j} + \sum_{j=1}^{M} a_{2j}$
$$+ \cdots + \sum_{j=1}^{M} a_{Nj}$$

Random Digits

03991	10461	93716	16894	98953	73231	39528	72484	82474	25593
38555	95554	32886	59780	09958	18065	81616	18711	53342	44276
17546	73704	92052	46215	15917	06253	07586	16120	82641	22820
32643	52861	95819	06831	19640	99413	90767	04235	13574	17200
69572	68777	39510	35905	85244	35159	40188	28193	29593	88627
24122	66591	27699	06494	03152	19121	34414	82157	86887	55087
61196	30231	92962	61773	22109	78508	63439	75363	44989	16822
30532	21704	10274	12202	94205	20380	67049	09070	93399	45547
03788	97599	75867	20717	82037	10268	79495	04146	52162	90286
48228	63379	85783	47619	87481	37220	91704	30552	04737	21031
88618	19161	41290	67312	71857	15957	48545	35247	18619	13674
71299	23853	05870	01119	92784	26340	75122	11724	74627	73707
27954	58909	82444	99005	04921	73701	92904	13141	32392	19763
80863	00514	20247	81759	45197	25332	69902	63742	78464	22501
33564	60780	48460	85558	15191	18782	94972	11598	62095	36787
90899	75754	60833	25983	01291	41349	19152	00023	12302	80783
78038	70267	43529	06318	38384	74761	36024	00867	76378	41605
55986	66485	88722	56736	66164	49431	94458	74284	05041	49807
87539	08823	94813	31900	54155	83436	54158	34243	46978	35482
16818	60311	74457	90561	72848	11834	75051	93029	47665	64382
34677	58300	74910	64345	19325	81549	60365	94653	35075	33949
45305	07521	61318	31855	14413	70951	83799	42402	56623	34442
59747	67277	76503	34513	39663	77544	32960	07405	36409	83232
16520	69676	11654	99893	02181	68161	19322	53845	57620	52606
68652	27376	92852	55866	88448	03584	11220	94747	07399	37408

79375	95220	01159	63267	10622	48391	31751	57260	68980	05339
33521	26665	55823	47641	86225	31704	88492	99382	14454	04504
59589	49067	66821	41575	49767	04037	30934	47744	07481	83828
20554	91409	96277	48257	50816	97616	22888	48893	27499	98748
59404	72059	43947	51680	43852	59693	78212	16993	35902	91386
42614	29297	01918	28316	25163	01889	70014	15021	68971	11403
34994	41374	70071	14736	65251	07629	37239	33295	18477	65622
99385	41600	11133	07586	36815	43625	18637	37509	14707	93997
66497	68646	78138	66559	64397	11692	05327	82162	83745	22567
48509	23929	27482	45476	04515	25624	95096	67946	16930	33361
15470	48355	88651	22596	83761	60873	43253	84145	20368	07126
20094	98977	74843	93413	14387	06345	80854	09279	41196	37480
73788	06533	28597	20405	51321	92246	80088	77074	66919	31678
60530	45128	74022	84617	72472	00008	80890	18002	35352	54131
44372	15486	65741	14014	05466	55306	93128	18464	79982	68416
18611	19241	66083	24653	84609	58232	41849	84547	46850	52326
58319	15997	08355	60860	29735	47762	46352	33049	69248	93460
61199	67940	55121	29281	59076	07936	11087	96294	14013	31792
18627	90872	00911	98936	76355	93779	52701	08337	56303	87315
00441	58997	14060	40619	29549	69616	57275	36898	81304	48585
32624	68691	14845	46672	61958	77100	20857	73156	70284	24326
65961	73488	41839	55382	17267	70943	15633	84924	90415	93614
20288	34060	39685	23309	10061	68829	92694	48297	39904	02115
59362	95938	74416	53166	35208	33374	77613	19019	88152	00080
99782	93478	53152	67433	35663	52972	38688	32486	45134	63545
27767	43584	85301	88977	29490	69714	94015	64874	32444	48277
13025	14338	54066	15243	47724	66733	74108	88222	88570	74015
80217	36292	98525	24335	24432	24896	62880	87873	95160	59221
10875	62004	90391	61105	57411	06368	11748	12102	80580	41867
54127	57326	26629	19087	24472	88779	17944	05600	60478	03343
60311	42824	37301	42678	45990	43242	66067	42792	95043	52680
49739	71484	92003	98086	76668	73209	54244	91030	45547	70818
78626	51594	16453	94614	39014	97066	30945	57589	31732	57260
66692	13986	99837	00582	81232	44987	69170	37403	86995	90307
44071	28091	07362	97703	76447	42537	08345	88975	35841	85771
59820	96163	78851	16499	87064	13075	73035	41207	74699	09310
25704	91035	26313	77463	55387	72681	47431	43905	31048	56699
22304	90314	78438	66276	18396	73538	43277	58874	11466	16082
17710	59621	15292	76139	59526	52113	53856	30743	08670	84741
25852	58905	55018	56374	35824	71708	30540	27886	61732	75454

46780	56487	75211	10271	36633	68424	17374	52003	70707	70214
59849	96169	87195	46092	26787	60939	59202	11973	02902	33250
47670	07654	30342	40277	11049	72049	83012	09832	25571	77628
94304	71803	73465	09819	58869	35220	09504	96412	90193	79568
08105	59987	21437	36786	49226	77837	98524	97831	65704	09514
64281	61826	18555	64937	64654	25843	41145	42820	14924	39650
66847	70495	32350	02985	01755	14750	48968	38603	70312	05682
72461	33230	21529	53424	72877	17334	39283	04149	90850	64618
21032	91050	13058	16218	06554	07850	73950	79552	24781	89683
95362	67011	06651	16136	57216	39618	49856	99326	40902	05069
49712	97380	10404	55452	09971	59481	37006	22186	72682	07385
58275	61764	97586	54716	61459	21647	87417	17198	21443	41808
89514	11788	68224	23417	46376	25366	94746	49580	01176	28838
15472	50669	48139	36732	26825	05511	12459	91314	80582	71944
12120	86124	51247	44302	87112	21476	14713	71181	13177	55292
95294	00556	70481	06905	21785	41101	49386	54480	23604	23554
66986	34099	74474	20740	47458	64809	06312	88940	15995	69321
80620	51790	11436	38072	40405	68032	60942	00307	11897	92674
55411	85667	77535	99892	71209	92061	92329	98932	78284	46347
95083	06783	28102	57816	85561	29671	77936	63574	31384	51924
90726	57166	98884	08583	95889	57067	38101	77756	11657	13897
68984	83620	89747	98882	92613	89719	39641	69457	91339	22502
36421	16489	18059	51061	67667	60631	84054	40455	99396	63680
92638	40333	67054	16067	24700	71594	47468	03577	57649	63266
21036	82808	77501	97427	76479	68562	43321	31370	28977	23896
13173	33365	41468	85149	49554	17994	91178	10174	29420	90438
86716	38746	94559	37559	49678	53119	98189	81851	29651	84215
92581	02262	41615	70360	64114	58660	96717	54244	10701	41393
12470	56500	50273	93113	41794	86861	39448	93136	25722	08564
01016	00857	41396	80504	90670	08289	58137	17820	22751	36518
34030	60726	25807	24260	71529	78920	47648	13885	70669	93406
50259	46345	06170	97965	88302	98041	11947	56203	19324	20504
73959	76145	60808	54444	74412	81105	69181	96845	38525	11600
46874	37088	80940	44893	10408	36222	14004	23153	69249	05747
60883	52109	19516	90120	46759	71643	62342	07589	08899	05985

APPENDIX III

Squares and Square Roots

USE OF THE TABLE

The square roots of all numbers from 1.00 to 10.0 can be found directly in the columns labeled $\sqrt{N}$. The square roots of numbers from 10.0 to 100 can be found directly in the columns labeled $\sqrt{10N}$. The square roots of other numbers from .00100 to 10,000 can be found by applying the following rules. An example is given for each rule.

Rules	Examples for $N = 1.26$
$\sqrt{1000N} = 10\sqrt{10N}$	$\sqrt{1260} = 35.4965$
$\sqrt{100N} = 10\sqrt{N}$	$\sqrt{126} = 11.2250$
$\sqrt{10N} = $ see table	$\sqrt{12.6} = 3.54965$
$\sqrt{N} = $ see table	$\sqrt{1.26} = 1.12250$
$\sqrt{\frac{1}{10}N} = \frac{1}{10}\sqrt{10N}$	$\sqrt{.126} = .354965$
$\sqrt{\frac{1}{100}N} = \frac{1}{10}\sqrt{N}$	$\sqrt{.0126} = .112250$
$\sqrt{\frac{1}{1000}N} = \frac{1}{100}\sqrt{10N}$	$\sqrt{.00126} = .0354965$

N	N²	√N̄	√10N̄		N	N²	√N̄	√10N̄
1.00	1.0000	1.00000	3.16228		1.50	2.2500	1.22474	3.87298
1.01	1.0201	1.00499	3.17805		1.51	2.2801	1.22882	3.88587
1.02	1.0404	1.00995	3.19374		1.52	2.3104	1.23288	3.89872
1.03	1.0609	1.01489	3.20936		1.53	2.3409	1.23693	3.91152
1.04	1.0816	1.01980	3.22490		1.54	2.3716	1.24097	3.92428
1.05	1.1025	1.02470	3.24037		1.55	2.4025	1.24499	3.93700
1.06	1.1236	1.02956	3.25576		1.56	2.4336	1.24900	3.94968
1.07	1.1449	1.03441	3.27109		1.57	2.4649	1.25300	3.96232
1.08	1.1664	1.03923	3.28634		1.58	2.4964	1.25698	3.97492
1.09	1.1881	1.04403	3.30151		1.59	2.5281	1.26095	3.98748
1.10	1.2100	1.04881	3.31662		1.60	2.5600	1.26491	4.00000
1.11	1.2321	1.05357	3.33167		1.61	2.5921	1.26886	4.01248
1.12	1.2544	1.05830	3.34664		1.62	2.6244	1.27279	4.02492
1.13	1.2769	1.06301	3.36155		1.63	2.6569	1.27671	4.03733
1.14	1.2996	1.06771	3.37639		1.64	2.6896	1.28062	4.04969
1.15	1.3225	1.07238	3.39116		1.65	2.7225	1.28452	4.06202
1.16	1.3456	1.07703	3.40588		1.66	2.7556	1.28841	4.07431
1.17	1.3689	1.08167	3.42053		1.67	2.7889	1.29228	4.08656
1.18	1.3924	1.08628	3.43511		1.68	2.8224	1.29615	4.09878
1.19	1.4161	1.09087	3.44964		1.69	2.8561	1.30000	4.11096
1.20	1.4400	1.09545	3.46410		1.70	2.8900	1.30384	4.12311
1.21	1.4641	1.10000	3.47851		1.71	2.9241	1.30767	4.13521
1.22	1.4884	1.10454	3.49285		1.72	2.9584	1.31149	4.14729
1.23	1.5129	1.10905	3.50714		1.73	2.9929	1.31529	4.15933
1.24	1.5376	1.11355	3.52136		1.74	3.0276	1.31909	4.17133
1.25	1.5625	1.11803	3.53553		1.75	3.0625	1.32288	4.18330
1.26	1.5876	1.12250	3.54965		1.76	3.0976	1.32665	4.19524
1.27	1.6129	1.12694	3.56371		1.77	3.1329	1.33041	4.20714
1.28	1.6384	1.13137	3.57771		1.78	3.1684	1.33417	4.21900
1.29	1.6641	1.13578	3.59166		1.79	3.2041	1.33791	4.23084
1.30	1.6900	1.14018	3.60555		1.80	3.2400	1.34164	4.24264
1.31	1.7161	1.14455	3.61939		1.81	3.2761	1.34536	4.25441
1.32	1.7424	1.14891	3.63318		1.82	3.3124	1.34907	4.26615
1.33	1.7689	1.15326	3.64692		1.83	3.3489	1.35277	4.27785
1.34	1.7956	1.15758	3.66060		1.84	3.3856	1.35647	4.28952
1.35	1.8225	1.16190	3.67423		1.85	3.4225	1.36015	4.30116
1.36	1.8496	1.16619	3.68782		1.86	3.4596	1.36382	4.31277
1.37	1.8769	1.17047	3.70135		1.87	3.4969	1.36748	4.32435
1.38	1.9044	1.17473	3.71484		1.88	3.5344	1.37113	4.33590
1.39	1.9321	1.17898	3.72827		1.89	3.5721	1.37477	4.34741
1.40	1.9600	1.18322	3.74166		1.90	3.6100	1.37840	4.35890
1.41	1.9881	1.18743	3.75500		1.91	3.6481	1.38203	4.37035
1.42	2.0164	1.19164	3.76829		1.92	3.6864	1.38564	4.38178
1.43	2.0449	1.19583	3.78153		1.93	3.7249	1.38924	4.39318
1.44	2.0736	1.20000	3.79473		1.94	3.7636	1.39284	4.40454
1.45	2.1025	1.20416	3.80789		1.95	3.8025	1.39642	4.41588
1.46	2.1316	1.20830	3.82099		1.96	3.8416	1.40000	4.42719
1.47	2.1609	1.21244	3.83406		1.97	3.8809	1.40357	4.43847
1.48	2.1904	1.21655	3.84708		1.98	3.9204	1.40712	4.44972
1.49	2.2201	1.22066	3.86005		1.99	3.9601	1.41067	4.46094
1.50	2.2500	1.22474	3.87298		2.00	4.0000	1.41421	4.47214
N	N²	√N̄	√10N̄		N	N²	√N̄	√10N̄

N	N²	√N̄	√10N̄
2.00	4.0000	1.41421	4.47214
2.01	4.0401	1.41774	4.48330
2.02	4.0804	1.42127	4.49444
2.03	4.1209	1.42478	4.50555
2.04	4.1616	1.42829	4.51664
2.05	4.2025	1.43178	4.52769
2.06	4.2436	1.43527	4.53872
2.07	4.2849	1.43875	4.54973
2.08	4.3264	1.44222	4.56070
2.09	4.3681	1.44568	4.57165
2.10	4.4100	1.44914	4.58258
2.11	4.4521	1.45258	4.59347
2.12	4.4944	1.45602	4.60435
2.13	4.5369	1.45945	4.61519
2.14	4.5796	1.46287	4.62601
2.15	4.6225	1.46629	4.63681
2.16	4.6656	1.46969	4.64758
2.17	4.7089	1.47309	4.65833
2.18	4.7524	1.47648	4.66905
2.19	4.7961	1.47986	4.67974
2.20	4.8400	1.48324	4.69042
2.21	4.8841	1.48661	4.70106
2.22	4.9284	1.48997	4.71169
2.23	4.9729	1.49332	4.72229
2.24	5.0176	1.49666	4.73286
2.25	5.0625	1.50000	4.74342
2.26	5.1076	1.50333	4.75395
2.27	5.1529	1.50665	4.76445
2.28	5.1984	1.50997	4.77493
2.29	5.2441	1.51327	4.78539
2.30	5.2900	1.51658	4.79583
2.31	5.3361	1.51987	4.80625
2.32	5.3824	1.52315	4.81664
2.33	5.4289	1.52643	4.82701
2.34	5.4756	1.52971	4.83735
2.35	5.5225	1.53297	4.84768
2.36	5.5696	1.53623	4.85798
2.37	5.6169	1.53948	4.86826
2.38	5.6644	1.54272	4.87852
2.39	5.7121	1.54596	4.88876
2.40	5.7600	1.54919	4.89898
2.41	5.8081	1.55252	4.90918
2.42	5.8564	1.55563	4.91935
2.43	5.9049	1.55885	4.92950
2.44	5.9536	1.56205	4.93964
2.45	6.0025	1.56525	4.94975
2.46	6.0516	1.56844	4.95984
2.47	6.1009	1.57162	4.96991
2.48	6.1054	1.57480	4.97996
2.49	6.2001	1.57797	4.98999
2.50	6.2500	1.58114	5.00000

N	N²	√N̄	√10N̄
2.50	6.2500	1.58114	5.00000
2.51	6.3001	1.58430	5.00999
2.52	6.3504	1.58745	5.01996
2.53	6.4009	1.59060	5.02991
2.54	6.4516	1.59374	5.03984
2.55	6.5025	1.59687	5.04975
2.56	6.5536	1.60000	5.05964
2.57	6.6049	1.60312	5.06952
2.58	6.6564	1.60624	5.07937
2.59	6.7081	1.60935	5.08920
2.60	6.7600	1.61245	5.09902
2.61	6.8121	1.61555	5.10882
2.62	6.8644	1.61864	5.11859
2.63	6.9169	1.62173	5.12835
2.64	6.9696	1.62481	5.13809
2.65	7.0225	1.62788	5.14782
2.66	7.0756	1.63095	5.15752
2.67	7.1289	1.63401	5.16720
2.68	7.1824	1.63707	5.17687
2.69	7.2361	1.64012	5.18652
2.70	7.2900	1.64317	5.19615
2.71	7.3441	1.64621	5.20577
2.72	7.3984	1.64924	5.21536
2.73	7.4529	1.65227	5.22494
2.74	7.5076	1.65529	5.23450
2.75	7.5625	1.65831	5.24404
2.76	7.6176	1.66132	5.25357
2.77	7.6729	1.66433	5.26308
2.78	7.7284	1.66733	5.27257
2.79	7.7841	1.67033	5.28205
2.80	7.8400	1.67332	5.29150
2.81	7.8961	1.67631	5.30094
2.82	7.9524	1.67929	5.31037
2.83	8.0089	1.68226	5.31977
2.84	8.0656	1.68523	5.32917
2.85	8.1225	1.68819	5.33854
2.86	8.1796	1.69115	5.34790
2.87	8.2369	1.69411	5.35724
2.88	8.2944	1.69706	5.36656
2.89	8.3521	1.70000	5.37587
2.90	8.4100	1.70294	5.38516
2.91	8.4681	1.70587	5.39444
2.92	8.5264	1.70880	5.40370
2.93	8.5849	1.71172	5.41295
2.94	8.6436	1.71464	5.42218
2.95	8.7025	1.71756	5.43139
2.96	8.7616	1.72047	5.44059
2.97	8.8209	1.72337	5.44977
2.98	8.8804	1.72627	5.45894
2.99	8.9401	1.72916	5.46809
3.00	9.0000	1.73205	5.47723
N	N²	√N̄	√10N̄

N	N²	√N	√10N	N	N²	√N	√10N
3.00	9.0000	1.73205	5.47723	**3.50**	12.2500	1.87083	5.91608
3.01	9.0601	1.73494	5.48635	3.51	12.3201	1.87350	5.92453
3.02	9.1204	1.73781	5.49545	3.52	12.3904	1.87617	5.93296
3.03	9.1809	1.74069	5.50454	3.53	12.4609	1.87883	5.94138
3.04	9.2416	1.74356	5.51362	3.54	12.5316	1.88149	5.94979
3.05	9.3025	1.74642	5.52268	3.55	12.6025	1.88414	5.95819
3.06	9.3636	1.74929	5.53173	3.56	12.6736	1.88680	5.96657
3.07	9.4249	1.75214	5.54076	3.57	12.7449	1.88944	5.97495
3.08	9.4864	1.75499	5.54977	3.58	12.8164	1.89209	5.98331
3.09	9.5481	1.75784	5.55878	3.59	12.8881	1.89473	5.99166
3.10	9.6100	1.76068	5.56776	**3.60**	12.9600	1.89737	6.00000
3.11	9.6721	1.76352	5.57674	3.61	13.0321	1.90000	6.00833
3.12	9.7344	1.76635	5.58570	3.62	13.1044	1.90263	6.01664
3.13	9.7969	1.76918	5.59464	3.63	13.1769	1.90526	6.02495
3.14	9.8596	1.77200	5.60357	3.64	13.2496	1.90788	6.03324
3.15	9.9225	1.77482	5.61249	3.65	13.3225	1.91050	6.04152
3.16	9.9856	1.77764	5.62139	3.66	13.3956	1.91311	6.04949
3.17	10.0489	1.78045	5.63028	3.67	13.4689	1.91572	6.05805
3.18	10.1124	1.78326	5.63915	3.68	13.5424	1.91833	6.06630
3.19	10.1761	1.78606	5.64801	3.69	13.6161	1.92094	6.07454
3.20	10.2400	1.78885	5.65685	**3.70**	13.6900	1.92354	6.08276
3.21	10.3041	1.79165	5.66569	3.71	13.7641	1.92614	6.09098
3.22	10.3684	1.79444	5.67450	3.72	13.8384	1.92873	6.09918
3.23	10.4329	1.79722	5.68331	3.73	13.9129	1.93132	6.10737
3.24	10.4976	1.80000	5.69210	3.74	13.9876	1.93391	6.11555
3.25	10.5625	1.80278	5.70088	3.75	14.0625	1.93649	6.12372
3.26	10.6276	1.80555	5.70964	3.76	14.1376	1.93907	6.13188
3.27	10.6929	1.80831	5.71839	3.77	14.2129	1.94165	6.14003
3.28	10.7584	1.81108	5.72713	3.78	14.2884	1.94422	6.14817
3.29	10.8241	1.81384	5.73585	3.79	14.3641	1.94679	6.15630
3.30	10.8900	1.81659	5.74456	**3.80**	14.4400	1.94936	6.16441
3.31	10.9561	1.81934	5.75326	3.81	14.5161	1.95192	6.17252
3.32	10.0224	1.82209	5.76194	3.82	14.5924	1.95448	6.18061
3.33	11.0889	1.82483	5.77062	3.83	14.6689	1.95704	6.18870
3.34	11.1556	1.82757	5.77927	3.84	14.7456	1.95959	6.19677
3.35	11.2225	1.83030	5.78792	3.85	14.8225	1.96214	6.20484
3.36	11.2896	1.83303	5.79655	3.86	14.8996	1.96469	6.21289
3.37	11.3569	1.83576	5.80517	3.87	14.9769	1.96723	6.22093
3.38	11.4244	1.83848	5.81378	3.88	15.0544	1.96977	6.22896
3.39	11.4921	1.84120	5.82237	3.89	15.1321	1.97231	6.23699
3.40	11.5600	1.84391	5.83095	**3.90**	15.2100	1.97484	6.24500
3.41	11.6281	1.84662	5.83952	3.91	15.2881	1.97737	6.25300
3.42	11.6964	1.84932	5.84808	3.92	15.3664	1.97990	6.26099
3.43	11.7649	1.85203	5.85662	3.93	15.4449	1.98242	6.26897
3.44	11.8336	1.85472	5.86515	3.94	15.5236	1.98494	6.27694
3.45	11.9025	1.85742	5.87367	3.95	15.6025	1.98746	6.28490
3.46	11.9716	1.86011	5.88218	3.96	15.6816	1.98997	6.29285
3.47	12.0409	1.86279	5.89067	3.97	15.7609	1.99249	6.30079
3.48	12.1104	1.86548	5.89915	3.98	15.8404	1.99499	6.30872
3.49	12.1801	1.86815	5.90762	3.99	15.9201	1.99750	6.31644
3.50	12.2500	1.87083	5.91608	**4.00**	16.0000	2.00000	6.32456
N	N²	√N	√10N	N	N²	√N	√10N

N	N²	√N̄	√10N̄	N	N²	√N̄	√10N̄
4.00	16.0000	2.00000	6.32456	**4.50**	20.2500	2.12132	6.70820
4.01	16.0801	2.00250	6.33246	4.51	20.3401	2.12368	6.71565
4.02	16.1604	2.00499	6.34035	4.52	20.4304	2.12603	6.72309
4.03	16.2409	2.00749	6.34823	4.53	20.5209	2.12838	6.73053
4.04	16.3216	2.00998	6.35610	4.54	20.6116	2.13073	6.73795
4.05	16.4025	2.01246	6.36396	4.55	20.7025	2.13307	6.74537
4.06	16.4836	2.01494	6.37181	4.56	20.7936	2.13542	6.75278
4.07	16.5649	2.01742	6.37966	4.57	20.8849	2.13776	6.76018
4.08	16.6464	2.01990	6.38749	4.58	20.9764	2.14009	6.76757
4.09	16.7281	2.02237	6.39531	4.59	21.0681	2.14243	6.77495
4.10	16.8100	2.02485	6.40312	**4.60**	21.1600	2.14476	6.78233
4.11	16.8921	2.02731	6.41093	4.61	21.2521	2.14709	6.78970
4.12	16.9744	2.02978	6.41872	4.62	21.3444	2.14942	6.79706
4.13	17.0569	2.03224	6.42651	4.63	21.4369	2.15174	6.80441
4.14	17.1396	2.03470	6.43428	4.64	21.5296	2.15407	6.81175
4.15	17.2225	2.03715	6.44205	4.65	21.6225	2.15639	6.81909
4.16	17.3056	2.03961	6.44981	4.66	21.7156	2.15870	6.82642
4.17	17.3889	2.04206	6.45755	4.67	21.8089	2.16102	6.83374
4.18	17.4724	2.04450	6.46529	4.68	21.9024	2.16333	6.84105
4.19	17.5561	2.04695	6.47302	4.69	21.9961	2.16564	6.84836
4.20	17.6400	2.04939	6.48074	**4.70**	22.0900	2.16795	6.85565
4.21	17.7241	2.05183	6.48845	4.71	22.1841	2.17025	6.86294
4.22	17.8084	2.05426	6.49615	4.72	22.2784	2.17256	6.87023
4.23	17.8929	2.05670	6.50384	4.73	22.3729	2.17486	6.87750
4.24	17.9776	2.05913	6.51153	4.74	22.4676	2.17715	6.88477
4.25	18.0625	2.06155	6.51920	4.75	22.5625	2.17945	6.89202
4.26	18.1476	2.06398	6.52687	4.76	22.6576	2.18174	6.89928
4.27	18.2329	2.06640	6.53452	4.77	22.7529	2.18403	6.90652
4.28	18.3184	2.06882	6.54217	4.78	22.8484	2.18632	6.91375
4.29	18.4041	2.07123	6.54981	4.79	22.9441	2.18861	6.92098
4.30	18.4900	2.07364	6.55744	**4.80**	23.0400	2.19089	6.92820
4.31	18.5761	2.07605	6.56506	4.81	23.1361	2.19317	6.93542
4.32	18.6624	2.07846	6.57267	4.82	23.2324	2.19545	6.94262
4.33	18.7489	2.08087	6.58027	4.83	23.3289	2.19773	6.94982
4.34	18.8356	2.08327	6.58787	4.84	23.4256	2.20000	6.95701
4.35	18.9225	2.08567	6.59545	4.85	23.5225	2.20227	6.96419
4.36	19.0096	2.08806	6.60303	4.86	23.6196	2.20454	6.97137
4.37	19.0969	2.09045	6.61060	4.87	23.7169	2.20681	6.97854
4.38	19.1844	2.09284	6.61816	4.88	23.8144	2.20907	6.98570
4.39	19.2721	2.09523	6.62571	4.89	23.9121	2.21133	6.99285
4.40	19.3600	2.09762	6.63325	**4.90**	24.0100	2.21359	7.00000
4.41	19.4481	2.10000	6.64078	4.91	24.1081	2.21585	7.00714
4.42	19.5364	2.10238	6.64831	4.92	24.2064	2.21811	7.01427
4.43	19.6249	2.10476	6.65582	4.93	24.3049	2.22036	7.02140
4.44	19.7136	2.10713	6.66333	4.94	24.4036	2.22261	7.02851
4.45	19.8025	2.10950	6.67083	4.95	24.5025	2.22486	7.03562
4.46	19.8916	2.11187	6.67832	4.96	24.6016	2.22711	7.04273
4.47	19.9809	2.11424	6.68581	4.97	24.7009	2.22935	7.04982
4.48	20.0704	2.11660	6.69328	4.98	24.8004	2.23159	7.05691
4.49	20.1601	2.11896	6.70075	4.99	24.9001	2.23383	7.06399
4.50	20.2500	2.12132	6.70820	**5.00**	25.0000	2.23607	7.07107
N	N²	√N̄	√10N̄	N	N²	√N̄	√10N̄

N	N²	√N̄	√10N̄	N	N²	√N̄	√10N̄
5.00	25.0000	2.23607	7.07107	**5.50**	30.2500	2.34521	7.41620
5.01	25.1001	2.23830	7.07814	5.51	30.3601	2.34734	7.42294
5.02	25.2004	2.24054	7.08520	5.52	30.4704	2.34947	7.42967
5.03	25.3009	2.24277	7.09225	5.53	30.5809	2.35160	7.43640
5.04	25.4016	2.24499	7.09930	5.54	30.6916	2.35372	7.44312
5.05	25.5025	2.24722	7.10634	5.55	30.8025	2.35584	7.44983
5.06	25.6036	2.24944	7.11337	5.56	30.9136	2.35797	7.45654
5.07	25.7049	2.25167	7.12039	5.57	31.0249	2.36008	7.46324
5.08	25.8064	2.25389	7.12741	5.58	31.1364	2.36220	7.46994
5.09	25.9081	2.25610	7.13442	5.59	31.2481	2.36432	7.47663
5.10	26.0100	2.25832	7.14143	**5.60**	31.3600	2.36643	7.48331
5.11	26.1121	2.26053	7.14843	5.61	31.4721	2.36854	7.48999
5.12	26.2144	2.26274	7.15542	5.62	31.5844	2.37065	7.49667
5.13	26.3169	2.26495	7.16240	5.63	31.6969	2.37276	7.50333
5.14	26.4196	2.26716	7.16938	5.64	31.8096	2.37487	7.50999
5.15	26.5225	2.26936	7.17635	5.65	31.9225	2.37697	7.51665
5.16	26.6256	2.27156	7.18331	5.66	32.0356	2.37908	7.52330
5.17	26.7289	2.27376	7.19027	5.67	32.1489	2.38118	7.52994
5.18	26.8324	2.27596	7.19722	5.68	32.2624	2.38328	7.53658
5.19	26.9361	2.27816	7.20417	5.69	32.3761	2.38537	7.54321
5.20	27.0400	2.28035	7.21110	**5.70**	32.4900	2.38747	7.54983
5.21	27.1441	2.28254	7.21803	5.71	32.6041	2.38956	7.55645
5.22	27.2484	2.28473	7.22496	5.72	32.7184	2.39165	7.56307
5.23	27.3529	2.28692	7.23187	5.73	32.8329	2.39374	7.56968
5.24	27.4576	2.28910	7.23838	5.74	32.9476	2.39583	7.57628
5.25	27.5625	2.29129	7.24569	5.75	33.0625	2.39792	7.58288
5.26	27.6676	2.29347	7.25259	5.76	33.1776	2.40000	7.58947
5.27	27.7729	2.29565	7.25948	5.77	33.2929	2.40208	7.59605
5.28	27.8784	2.29783	7.26636	5.78	33.4084	2.40416	7.60263
5.29	27.9841	2.30000	7.27324	5.79	33.5241	2.40624	7.60920
5.30	28.0900	2.30217	7.28011	**5.80**	33.6400	2.40832	7.61577
5.31	28.1961	2.30434	7.28697	5.81	33.7561	2.41039	7.62234
5.32	28.3024	2.30651	7.29383	5.82	33.8724	2.41247	7.62889
5.33	28.4089	2.30868	7.30068	5.83	33.9889	2.41454	7.63544
5.34	28.5156	2.31084	7.30753	5.84	34.1056	2.41661	7.64199
5.35	28.6225	2.31301	7.31437	5.85	34.2225	2.41868	7.64853
5.36	28.7296	2.31517	7.32120	5.86	34.3396	2.42074	7.65506
5.37	28.8369	2.31733	7.32803	5.87	34.4569	2.42281	7.66159
5.38	28.9444	2.31948	7.33485	5.88	34.5744	2.42487	7.66812
5.39	29.0521	2.32164	7.34166	5.89	34.6921	2.42693	7.67463
5.40	29.1600	2.32379	7.34847	**5.90**	34.8100	2.42899	7.68115
5.41	29.2681	2.32594	7.35527	5.91	34.9281	2.43105	7.68765
5.42	29.3764	2.32809	7.36206	5.92	35.0464	2.43311	7.69415
5.43	29.4849	2.33024	7.36885	5.93	35.1649	2.43516	7.70065
5.44	29.5936	2.33238	7.37564	5.94	35.2836	2.43721	7.70714
5.45	29.7025	2.33452	7.38241	5.95	35.4025	2.43926	7.71362
5.46	29.8116	2.33666	7.38918	5.96	35.5216	2.44131	7.72010
5.47	29.9209	2.33880	7.39594	5.97	35.6409	2.44336	7.72658
5.48	30.0304	2.34094	7.40270	5.98	35.7604	2.44540	7.73305
5.49	30.1401	2.34307	7.40945	5.99	35.8801	2.44745	7.73951
5.50	30.2500	2.34521	7.41620	**6.00**	36.0000	2.44949	7.74597
N	N²	√N̄.	√10N̄	N	N²	√N̄	√10N̄

N	N²	√N	√10N
6.00	36.0000	2.44949	7.74597
6.01	36.1201	2.45153	7.75242
6.02	36.2404	2.45357	7.75887
6.03	36.3609	2.45561	7.76531
6.04	36.4816	2.45764	7.77174
6.05	36.6025	2.45967	7.77817
6.06	36.7236	2.46171	7.78460
6.07	36.8449	2.46374	7.79102
6.08	36.9664	2.46577	7.79744
6.09	37.0881	2.46779	7.80385
6.10	37.2100	2.46982	7.81025
6.11	37.3321	2.47184	7.81665
6.12	37.4544	2.47386	7.82304
6.13	37.5769	2.47588	7.82943
6.14	37.6996	2.47790	7.83582
6.15	37.8225	2.47992	7.84219
6.16	37.9456	2.48193	7.84857
6.17	38.0689	2.48395	7.85493
6.18	38.1924	2.48596	7.86130
6.19	38.3161	2.48797	7.86766
6.20	38.4400	2.48998	7.87401
6.21	38.5641	2.49199	7.88036
6.22	38.6884	2.49399	7.88670
6.23	38.8129	2.49600	7.89303
6.24	38.9376	2.49800	7.89937
6.25	39.0625	2.50000	7.90569
6.26	39.1876	2.50200	7.91202
6.27	39.3129	2.50400	7.91833
6.28	39.4384	2.50599	7.92465
6.29	39.5641	2.50799	7.93095
6.30	39.6900	2.50998	7.93725
6.31	39.8161	2.51197	7.94355
6.32	39.9424	2.51396	7.94984
6.33	40.0689	2.51595	7.95613
6.34	40.1956	2.51794	7.96241
6.35	40.3225	2.51992	7.96869
6.36	40.4496	2.52190	7.97476
6.37	40.5769	2.52389	7.98123
6.38	40.7044	2.52587	7.98749
6.39	40.8321	2.52784	7.99375
6.40	40.9600	2.52982	8.00000
6.41	41.0881	2.53180	8.00625
6.42	41.2164	2.53377	8.01249
6.43	41.3449	2.53574	8.01873
6.44	41.4736	2.53772	8.02496
6.45	41.6025	2.53969	8.03119
6.46	41.7316	2.54165	8.03741
6.47	41.8609	2.54362	8.04363
6.48	41.9904	2.54558	8.04984
6.49	42.1201	2.54755	8.05605
6.50	42.2500	2.54951	8.06226
N	N²	√N	√10N

N	N²	√N	√10N
6.50	42.2500	2.54951	8.06226
6.51	42.3801	2.55147	8.06846
6.52	42.5104	2.55343	8.07465
6.53	42.6409	2.55539	8.08084
6.54	42.7716	2.55734	8.08703
6.55	42.9025	2.55930	8.09321
6.56	43.0336	2.56125	8.09938
6.57	43.1649	2.56320	8.10555
6.58	43.2964	2.56515	8.11172
6.59	43.4281	2.56710	8.11788
6.60	43.5600	2.56905	8.12404
6.61	43.6921	2.57099	8.13019
6.62	43.8244	2.57294	8.13634
6.63	43.9569	2.57488	8.14248
6.64	44.0896	2.57682	8.14862
6.65	44.2225	2.57876	8.15475
6.66	44.3556	2.58070	8.16088
6.67	44.4889	2.58263	8.16701
6.68	44.6224	2.58457	8.17313
6.69	44.7561	2.58650	8.17924
6.70	44.8900	2.58844	8.18535
6.71	45.0241	2.59037	8.19146
6.72	45.1584	2.59230	8.19756
6.73	45.2929	2.59422	8.20366
6.74	45.4276	2.59615	8.20975
6.75	45.5625	2.59808	8.21584
6.76	45.6976	2.60000	8.22192
6.77	45.8329	2.60192	8.22800
6.78	45.9684	2.60384	8.23408
6.79	46.1041	2.60576	8.24015
6.80	46.2400	2.60768	8.24621
6.81	46.3761	2.60960	8.25227
6.82	46.5124	2.61151	8.25833
6.83	46.6489	2.61343	8.26438
6.84	46.7856	2.61534	8.27043
6.85	46.9225	2.61725	8.27647
6.86	47.0596	2.61916	8.28251
6.87	47.1969	2.62107	8.28855
6.88	47.3344	2.62298	8.29458
6.89	47.4721	2.62488	8.30060
6.90	47.6100	2.62679	8.30662
6.91	47.7481	2.62869	8.31264
6.92	47.8864	2.63059	8.31865
6.93	48.0249	2.63249	8.32466
6.94	48.1636	2.63439	8.33067
6.95	48.3025	2.63629	8.33667
6.96	48.4416	2.63818	8.34266
6.97	48.5809	2.64008	8.34865
6.98	48.7204	2.64197	8.35464
6.99	48.8601	2.64386	8.36062
7.00	49.0000	2.64575	8.36660
N	N²	√N	√10N

N	N²	√N	√10N
7.00	49.0000	2.64575	8.36660
7.01	49.1401	2.64764	8.37257
7.02	49.2804	2.64953	8.37854
7.03	49.4209	2.65141	8.38451
7.04	49.5616	2.65330	8.39047
7.05	49.7025	2.65518	8.39643
7.06	49.8436	2.65707	8.40238
7.07	49.9849	2.65895	8.40833
7.08	50.1264	2.66083	8.41427
7.09	50.2681	2.66271	8.42021
7.10	50.4100	2.66458	8.42615
7.11	50.5521	2.66646	8.43208
7.12	50.6944	2.66833	8.43801
7.13	50.8369	2.67021	8.44393
7.14	50.9796	2.67208	8.44985
7.15	51.1225	2.67395	8.45577
7.16	51.2656	2.67582	8.46168
7.17	51.4089	2.67769	8.46759
7.18	51.5524	2.67955	8.47349
7.19	51.6961	2.68142	8.47939
7.20	51.8400	2.68328	8.48528
7.21	51.9841	2.68514	8.49117
7.22	52.1284	2.68701	8.49706
7.23	52.2729	2.68887	8.50294
7.24	52.4176	2.69072	8.50882
7.25	52.5625	2.69258	8.51469
7.26	52.7076	2.69444	8.52056
7.27	52.8529	2.69629	8.52643
7.28	52.9984	2.69815	8.53229
7.29	53.1441	2.70000	8.53815
7.30	53.2900	2.70185	8.54400
7.31	53.4361	2.70370	8.54985
7.32	53.5824	2.70555	8.55570
7.33	53.7289	2.70740	8.56154
7.34	53.8756	2.70924	8.56738
7.35	54.0225	2.71109	8.57321
7.36	54.1696	2.71293	8.57904
7.37	54.3169	2.71477	8.58487
7.38	54.4644	2.71662	8.59069
7.39	54.6121	2.71846	8.59651
7.40	54.7600	2.72029	8.60233
7.41	54.9081	2.72213	8.60814
7.42	55.0564	2.72397	8.61394
7.43	55.2049	2.72580	8.61974
7.44	55.3536	2.72764	8.62554
7.45	55.5025	2.72947	8.63134
7.46	55.6516	2.73130	8.63713
7.47	55.8009	2.73313	8.64292
7.48	55.9504	2.73496	8.64870
7.49	56.1001	2.73679	8.65448
7.50	56.2500	2.73861	8.66025
N	N²	√N	√10N

N	N²	√N	√10N
7.50	56.2500	2.73861	8.66025
7.51	56.4001	2.74044	8.66603
7.52	56.5504	2.74226	8.67179
7.53	56.7009	2.74408	8.67756
7.54	56.8516	2.74591	8.68332
7.55	57.0025	2.74773	8.68907
7.56	57.1536	2.74955	8.69483
7.57	57.3049	2.75136	8.70057
7.58	57.4564	2.75318	8.70632
7.59	57.6081	2.75500	8.71206
7.60	57.7600	2.75681	8.71780
7.61	57.9121	2.75862	8.72353
7.62	58.0644	2.76043	8.72926
7.63	58.2169	2.76225	8.73499
7.64	58.3696	2.76405	8.74071
7.65	58.5225	2.76586	8.74643
7.66	58.6756	2.76767	8.75214
7.67	58.8289	2.76948	8.75785
7.68	58.9824	2.77128	8.76356
7.69	59.1361	2.77308	8.76926
7.70	59.2900	2.77489	8.77496
7.71	59.4441	2.77669	8.78066
7.72	59.5984	2.77849	8.78635
7.73	59.7529	2.78029	8.79204
7.74	59.9076	2.78209	8.79773
7.75	60.0625	2.78388	8.80341
7.76	60.2176	2.78568	8.80909
7.77	60.3729	2.78747	8.81476
7.78	60.5284	2.78927	8.82043
7.79	60.6841	2.79106	8.82610
7.80	60.8400	2.79285	8.83176
7.81	60.9961	2.79464	8.83742
7.82	61.1524	2.79643	8.84308
7.83	61.3089	2.79821	8.84873
7.84	61.4656	2.80000	8.85438
7.85	61.6225	2.80179	8.86002
7.86	61.7796	2.80357	8.86566
7.87	61.9369	2.80535	8.87130
7.88	62.0944	2.80713	8.87694
7.89	62.2521	2.80891	8.88257
7.90	62.4100	2.81069	8.88819
7.91	62.5681	2.81247	8.89382
7.92	62.7264	2.81425	8.89944
7.93	62.8849	2.81603	8.90505
7.94	63.0436	2.81780	8.91067
7.95	63.2025	2.81957	8.91628
7.96	63.3616	2.82135	8.92188
7.97	63.5209	2.82312	8.92749
7.98	63.6804	2.82489	8.93308
7.99	63.8401	2.82666	8.93868
8.00	64.0000	2.82843	8.94427
N	N²	√N	√10N

N	N²	√N	√10N	N	N²	√N	√10N
8.00	64.0000	2.82843	8.94427	**8.50**	72.2500	2.91548	9.21954
8.01	64.1601	2.83019	8.94986	8.51	72.4201	2.91719	9.22497
8.02	64.3204	2.83196	8.95545	8.52	72.5904	2.91890	9.23038
8.03	64.4809	2.83373	8.96103	8.53	72.7609	2.92062	9.23580
8.04	64.6416	2.83549	8.96660	8.54	72.9316	2.92233	9.24121
8.05	64.8025	2.83725	8.97218	8.55	73.1025	2.92404	9.24662
8.06	64.9636	2.83901	8.97775	8.56	73.2736	2.92575	9.25203
8.07	65.1249	2.84077	8.98332	8.57	73.4449	2.92746	9.25743
8.08	65.2864	2.84253	8.98888	8.58	73.6164	2.92916	9.26283
8.09	65.4481	2.84429	8.99444	8.59	73.7881	2.93087	9.26823
8.10	65.6100	2.84605	9.00000	**8.60**	73.9600	2.93258	9.27362
8.11	65.7721	2.84781	9.00555	8.61	74.1321	2.93428	9.27901
8.12	65.9344	2.84956	9.01110	8.62	74.3044	2.93598	9.28440
8.13	66.0969	2.85132	9.01665	8.63	74.4769	2.93769	9.28978
8.14	66.2596	2.85307	9.02219	8.64	74.6496	2.93939	9.29516
8.15	66.4225	2.85482	9.02774	8.65	74.8225	2.94109	9.30054
8.16	66.5856	2.85657	9.03327	8.66	74.9956	2.94279	9.30591
8.17	66.7489	2.85832	9.03881	8.67	75.1689	2.94449	9.31128
8.18	66.9124	2.86007	9.04434	8.68	75.3424	2.94618	9.31665
8.19	67.0761	2.86182	9.04986	8.69	75.5161	2.94788	9.32202
8.20	67.2400	2.86356	9.05539	**8.70**	75.6900	2.94958	9.32738
8.21	67.4041	2.86531	9.06091	8.71	75.8641	2.95127	9.33274
8.22	67.5684	2.86705	9.06642	8.72	76.0384	2.95296	9.33809
8.23	67.7329	2.86880	9.07193	8.73	76.2129	2.95466	9.34354
8.24	67.8976	2.87054	9.07744	8.74	76.3876	2.95635	9.34880
8.25	68.0625	2.87228	9.08295	8.75	76.5625	2.95804	9.35414
8.26	68.2276	2.87402	9.08845	8.76	76.7376	2.95973	9.35949
8.27	68.3929	2.87576	9.09395	8.77	76.9129	2.96142	9.36483
8.28	68.5584	2.87750	9.09945	8.78	77.0884	2.96311	9.37017
8.29	68.7241	2.87924	9.10494	8.79	77.2641	2.96479	9.37550
8.30	68.8900	2.88097	9.11045	**8.80**	77.4400	2.96648	9.38083
8.31	69.0561	2.88271	9.11592	8.81	77.6161	2.96816	9.38616
8.32	69.2224	2.88444	9.12140	8.82	77.7924	2.96985	9.39149
8.33	69.3889	2.88617	9.12688	8.83	77.9689	2.97153	9.39681
8.34	69.5556	2.88791	9.13236	8.84	78.1456	2.97321	9.40213
8.35	69.7225	2.88964	9.13783	8.85	78.3225	2.97489	9.40744
8.36	69.8896	2.89137	9.14330	8.86	78.4996	2.97658	9.41276
8.37	70.0569	2.89310	9.14877	8.87	78.6769	2.97825	9.41807
8.38	70.2244	2.89482	9.15423	8.88	78.8544	2.97993	9.42338
8.39	70.3921	2.89655	9.15969	8.89	79.0321	2.98161	9.42868
8.40	70.5600	2.89828	9.16515	**8.90**	79.2100	2.98329	9.43398
8.41	70.7281	2.90000	9.17061	8.91	79.3881	2.98496	9.43928
8.42	70.8964	2.90172	9.17606	8.92	79.5664	2.98664	9.44458
8.43	71.0649	2.90345	9.18150	8.93	79.7449	2.98831	9.44987
8.44	71.2336	2.90517	9.18695	8.94	79.9236	2.98998	9.45516
8.45	71.4025	2.90689	9.19239	8.95	80.1025	2.99166	9.46044
8.46	71.5716	2.90861	9.19783	8.96	80.2816	2.99333	9.46573
8.47	71.7409	2.91033	9.20326	8.97	80.4609	2.99500	9.47101
8.48	71.9104	2.91204	9.20869	8.98	80.6404	2.99666	9.47629
8.49	72.0801	2.91376	9.21412	8.99	80.8201	2.99833	9.48156
8.50	72.2500	2.91548	9.21954	**9.00**	81.0000	3.00000	9.48683
N	N²	√N	√10N	N	N²	√N	√10N

N	N^2	$\sqrt{N}$	$\sqrt{10N}$	N	N^2	$\sqrt{N}$	$\sqrt{10N}$
9.00	81.0000	3.00000	9.48683	**9.50**	90.2500	3.08221	9.74679
9.01	81.1801	3.00167	9.49210	9.51	90.4401	3.08383	9.75192
9.02	81.3604	3.00333	9.49737	9.52	90.6304	3.08545	9.75705
9.03	81.5409	3.00500	9.50263	9.53	90.8209	3.08707	9.76217
9.04	81.7216	3.00666	9.50789	9.54	91.0116	3.08869	9.76729
9.05	81.9025	3.00832	9.51315	9.55	91.2025	3.09031	9.77241
9.06	82.0836	3.00998	9.51840	9.56	91.3936	3.09192	9.77753
9.07	82.2649	3.01164	9.52365	9.57	91.5849	3.09354	9.78264
9.08	82.4464	3.01330	9.52890	9.58	91.7764	3.09516	9.78775
9.09	82.6281	3.01496	9.53415	9.59	91.9681	3.09677	9.79285
9.10	82.8100	3.01662	9.53939	**9.60**	92.1600	3.09839	9.79796
9.11	82.9921	3.01828	9.54463	9.61	92.3521	3.10000	9.80306
9.12	83.1744	3.01993	9.54987	9.62	92.5444	3.10161	9.80816
9.13	83.3569	3.02159	9.55510	9.63	92.7369	3.10322	9.81326
9.14	83.5396	3.02324	9.56033	9.64	92.9296	3.10483	9.81835
9.15	83.7225	3.02490	9.56556	9.65	93.1225	3.10644	9.82344
9.16	83.9056	3.02655	9.57079	9.66	93.3156	3.10805	9.82853
9.17	84.0889	3.02820	9.57601	9.67	93.5089	3.10966	9.83362
9.18	84.2724	3.02985	9.58123	9.68	93.7024	3.11127	9.83870
9.19	84.4561	3.03150	9.58645	9.69	93.8961	3.11288	9.84378
9.20	84.6400	3.03315	9.59166	**9.70**	94.0900	3.11448	9.84886
9.21	84.8241	3.03480	9.59687	9.71	94.2841	3.11609	9.85393
9.22	85.0084	3.03645	9.60208	9.72	94.4784	3.11769	9.85901
9.23	85.1929	3.03809	9.60729	9.73	94.6729	3.11929	9.86408
9.24	85.3776	3.03974	9.61249	9.74	94.8676	3.12090	9.86914
9.25	85.5625	3.04138	9.61769	9.75	95.0625	3.12250	9.87421
9.26	85.7476	3.04302	9.62289	9.76	95.2576	3.12410	9.87927
9.27	85.9329	3.04467	9.62808	9.77	95.4529	3.12570	9.88433
9.28	86.1184	3.04631	9.63328	9.78	95.6484	3.12730	9.88939
9.29	86.3041	3.04795	9.63846	9.79	95.8441	3.12890	9.89444
9.30	86.4900	3.04959	9.64365	**9.80**	96.0400	3.13050	9.89949
9.31	86.6761	3 05123	9.64883	9.81	96.2361	3.13209	9.90454
9.32	86.8624	3 05287	9.65401	9.82	96.4324	3.13369	9.90959
9.33	87.0489	3.05450	9.65919	9.83	96.6289	3.13528	9.91464
9.34	87.2356	3.05614	9.66437	9.84	96.8256	3.13688	9.91968
9.35	87.4225	3 05778	9 66954	9.85	97.0225	3.13847	9.92472
9.36	87.6096	3.05941	9.67471	9.86	97.2196	3.14006	9.92975
9.37	87.7969	3.06105	9.67988	9.87	97.4169	3.14166	9.93479
9.38	87.9844	3.06268	9.68504	9.88	97.6144	3.14325	9.93982
9.39	88.1721	3.06431	9.69020	9.89	97.8121	3.14484	9.94485
9.40	88.3600	3.06594	9.69536	**9.90**	98.0100	3.14643	9.94987
9.41	88.5481	3.06757	9.70052	9.91	98.2081	3.14802	9.95490
9.42	88.7364	3.06920	9.70567	9.92	98.4064	3.14960	9.95992
9.43	88.9249	3.07083	9.71082	9.93	98.6049	3.15119	9.96494
9.44	89.1136	3.07246	9.71597	9.94	98.8036	3.15278	9.96995
9.45	89.3025	3.07409	9.72111	9.95	99.0025	3.15436	9.97497
9.46	89.4916	3.07571	9.72625	9.96	99.2016	3.15595	9.97998
9.47	89.6809	3.07734	9.73139	9.97	99.4009	3.15753	9.98499
9.48	89.8704	3.07896	9.73653	9.98	99.6004	3.15911	9.98999
9.49	90.0601	3.08058	9.74166	9.99	99.8001	3.16070	9.99500
9.50	90.2500	3.08221	9.74679	**10.0**	100.000	3.16228	10.0000
N	N^2	$\sqrt{N}$	$\sqrt{10N}$	N	N^2	$\sqrt{N}$	$\sqrt{10N}$

Areas of a Standard Normal Distribution

An entry in the table is the proportion under the entire curve which is between $z = 0$ and a positive value of z. Areas for negative values of z are obtained by symmetry.

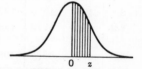

z	.00	.01	.02	.03	.04	.05	.06	.07	.08	.09
0.0	.0000	.0040	.0080	.0120	.0160	.0199	.0239	.0279	.0319	.0359
0.1	.0398	.0438	.0478	.0517	.0557	.0596	.0636	.0675	.0714	.0753
0.2	.0793	.0832	.0871	.0910	.0948	.0987	.1026	.1064	.1103	.1141
0.3	.1179	.1217	.1255	.1293	.1331	.1368	.1406	.1443	.1480	.1517
0.4	.1554	.1591	.1628	.1664	.1700	.1736	.1772	.1808	.1844	.1879
0.5	.1915	.1950	.1985	.2019	.2054	.2088	.2123	.2157	.2190	.2224
0.6	.2257	.2291	.2324	.2357	.2389	.2422	.2454	.2486	.2517	.2549
0.7	.2580	.2611	.2642	.2673	.2703	.2734	.2764	.2794	.2823	.2852
0.8	.2881	.2910	.2939	.2967	.2995	.3023	.3051	.3078	.3106	.3133
0.9	.3159	.3186	.3212	.3238	.3264	.3289	.3315	.3340	.3365	.3389
1.0	.3413	.3438	.3461	.3485	.3508	.3531	.3554	.3577	.3599	.3621
1.1	.3643	.3665	.3686	.3708	.3729	.3749	.3770	.3790	.3810	.3830
1.2	.3849	.3869	.3888	.3907	.3925	.3944	.3962	.3980	.3997	.4015
1.3	.4032	.4049	.4066	.4082	.4099	.4115	.4131	.4147	.4162	.4177
1.4	.4192	.4207	.4222	.4236	.4251	.4265	.4279	.4292	.4306	.4319

z	.00	.01	.02	.03	.04	.05	.06	.07	.08	.09
1.5	.4332	.4345	.4357	.4370	.4382	.4394	.4406	.4418	.4429	.4441
1.6	.4452	.4463	.4474	.4484	.4495	.4505	.4515	.4525	.4535	.4545
1.7	.4554	.4564	.4573	.4582	.4591	.4599	.4608	.4616	.4625	.4633
1.8	.4641	.4649	.4656	.4664	.4671	.4678	.4686	.4693	.4699	.4706
1.9	.4713	.4719	.4726	.4732	.4738	.4744	.4750	.4756	.4761	.4767
2.0	.4772	.4778	.4783	.4788	.4793	.4798	.4803	.4808	.4812	.4817
2.1	.4821	.4826	.4830	.4834	.4838	.4842	.4846	.4850	.4854	.4857
2.2	.4861	.4864	.4868	.4871	.4875	.4878	.4881	.4884	.4887	.4890
2.3	.4893	.4896	.4898	.4901	.4904	.4906	.4909	.4911	.4913	.4916
2.4	.4918	.4920	.4922	.4925	.4927	.4929	.4931	.4932	.4934	.4936
2.5	.4938	.4940	.4941	.4943	.4945	.4946	.4948	.4949	.4951	.4952
2.6	.4953	.4955	.4956	.4957	.4959	.4960	.4961	.4962	.4963	.4964
2.7	.4965	.4966	.4967	.4968	.4969	.4970	.4971	.4972	.4973	.4974
2.8	.4974	.4975	.4976	.4977	.4977	.4978	.4979	.4979	.4980	.4981
2.9	.4981	.4982	.4982	.4983	.4984	.4984	.4985	.4985	.4986	.4986
3.0	.4987	.4987	.4987	.4988	.4988	.4989	.4989	.4989	.4990	.4990

Student's t-Distribution

The first column lists the number of degrees of freedom (ν). The headings of the other columns give probabilities (P) for t to exceed the entry value. Use symmetry for negative t values.

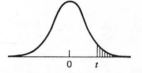

ν \ P	.10	.05	.025	.01	.005
1	3.078	6.314	12.706	31.821	63.657
2	1.886	2.920	4.303	6.965	9.925
3	1.638	2.353	3.182	4.541	5.841
4	1.533	2.132	2.776	3.747	4.604
5	1.476	2.015	2.571	3.365	4.032
6	1.440	1.943	2.447	3.143	3.707
7	1.415	1.895	2.365	2.998	3.499
8	1.397	1.860	2.306	2.896	3.355
9	1.383	1.833	2.262	1.821	3.250
10	1.372	1.812	2.228	2.764	3.169
11	1.363	1.796	2.201	2.718	3.106
12	1.356	1.782	2.179	2.681	3.055
13	1.350	1.771	2.160	2.650	3.012
14	1.345	1.761	2.145	2.624	2.977
15	1.341	1.753	2.131	2.602	2.947

ν \ P	.10	.05	.025	.01	.005
16	1.337	1.746	2.120	2.583	2.921
17	1.333	1.740	2.110	2.567	2.898
18	1.330	1.734	2.101	2.552	2.878
19	1.328	1.729	2.093	2.539	2.861
20	1.325	1.725	2.086	2.528	2.845
21	1.323	1.721	2.080	2.518	2.831
22	1.321	1.717	2.074	2.508	2.819
23	1.319	1.714	2.069	2.500	2.807
24	1.318	1.711	2.064	2.492	2.797
25	1.316	1.708	2.060	2.485	2.787
26	1.315	1.706	2.056	2.479	2.779
27	1.314	1.703	2.052	2.473	2.771
28	1.313	1.701	2.048	2.467	2.763
29	1.311	1.699	2.045	2.462	2.756
30	1.310	1.697	2.042	2.457	2.750
40	1.303	1.684	2.021	2.423	2.704
60	1.296	1.671	2.000	2.390	2.660
120	1.289	1.658	1.980	2.358	2.617
∞	1.282	1.645	1.960	2.326	2.576

APPENDIX VI

The X² Distribution

The first column lists the number of degrees of freedom (ν). The headings of the other columns give probabilities (P) for χ^2 to exceed the entry value. For $\nu > 100$, treat $\sqrt{2\chi^2} - \sqrt{2\nu - 1}$ as a standard normal variable.

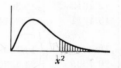

x^2

ν \ P	0.995	0.975	0.050	0.025	0.010	0.005
1	$392704 \cdot 10^{-10}$	$982069 \cdot 10^{-9}$	3.84146	5.02389	6.63490	7.87944
2	0.0100251	0.0506356	5.99146	7.37776	9.21034	10.5966
3	0.0717218	0.215795	7.81473	9.34840	11.3449	12.8382
4	0.206989	0.484419	9.48773	11.1433	13.2767	14.8603
5	0.411742	0.831212	11.0705	12.8325	15.0863	16.7496
6	0.675727	1.23734	12.5916	14.4494	16.8119	18.5476
7	0.989256	1.68987	14.0671	16.0128	18.4753	20.2777
8	1.34441	2.17973	15.5073	17.5345	20.0902	21.9550
9	1.73493	2.70039	16.9190	19.0228	21.6660	23.5894
10	2.15586	3.24697	18.3070	20.4832	23.2093	25.1882
11	2.60322	3.81575	19.6751	21.9200	24.7250	26.7568
12	3.07382	4.40379	21.0261	23.3367	26.2170	28.2995
13	3.56503	5.00875	22.3620	24.7356	27.6882	29.8195
14	4.07467	5.62873	23.6848	26.1189	29.1412	31.3194

ν \ P	0.995	0.975	0.050	0.025	0.010	0.005
15	4.60092	6.26214	24.9958	27.4884	30.5779	32.8013
16	5.14221	6.90766	26.2962	28.8454	31.9999	34.2672
17	5.69722	7.56419	27.5871	30.1910	33.4087	35.7185
18	6.26480	8.23075	28.8693	31.5264	34.8053	37.1565
19	6.84397	8.90652	30.1435	32.8523	36.1909	38.5823
20	7.43384	9.59078	31.4104	34.1696	37.5662	39.9968
21	8.03365	10.28293	32.6706	35.4789	38.9322	41.4011
22	8.64272	10.9823	33.9244	36.7807	40.2894	42.7957
23	9.26043	11.6886	35.1725	38.0756	41.6384	44.1813
24	9.88623	12.4012	36.4150	39.3641	42.9798	45.5585
25	10.5197	13.1197	37.6525	40.6465	44.3141	46.9279
26	11.1602	13.8439	38.8851	41.9232	45.6417	48.2899
27	11.8076	14.5734	40.1133	43.1945	46.9629	49.6449
28	12.4613	15.3079	41.3371	44.4608	48.2782	50.9934
29	13.1211	16.0471	42.5570	45.7223	49.5879	52.3356
30	13.7867	16.7908	43.7730	46.9792	50.8922	53.6720
40	20.7065	24.4330	55.7585	59.3417	63.6907	66.7660
50	27.9907	32.3574	67.5048	71.4202	76.1539	79.4900
60	35.5345	40.4817	79.0819	83.2977	88.3794	91.9517
70	43.2752	48.7576	90.5312	95.0232	100.425	104.215
80	51.1719	57.1532	101.879	106.629	112.329	116.321
90	59.1963	65.6466	113.145	118.136	124.116	128.299
100	67.3276	74.2219	124.342	129.561	135.807	140.169

APPENDIX VII

F-Distribution

5% (Roman Type) and 1% (Bold-Face Type) Points for the Distribution of F

Degrees of freedom for numerator (v_1)

Each cell shows the 5% point (Roman) over the 1% point (Bold-Face).

Degrees of freedom for denomi- nator (v_2)	1	2	3	4	5	6	7	8	9	10	11	12	14	16	20	24	30	40	50	75	100	200	500	∞
1	161 / 4052	200 / 4999	216 / 5403	225 / 5625	230 / 5764	234 / 5859	237 / 5928	239 / 5981	241 / 6022	242 / 6056	243 / 6082	244 / 6106	245 / 6142	246 / 6169	248 / 6208	249 / 6234	250 / 6258	251 / 6286	252 / 6302	253 / 6323	253 / 6334	254 / 6352	254 / 6361	254 / 6366
2	18.51 / 98.49	19.00 / 99.01	19.16 / 99.17	19.25 / 99.25	19.30 / 99.30	19.33 / 99.33	19.36 / 99.34	19.37 / 99.36	19.38 / 99.38	19.39 / 99.40	19.40 / 99.41	19.41 / 99.42	19.42 / 99.43	19.43 / 99.44	19.44 / 99.45	19.45 / 99.46	19.46 / 99.47	19.47 / 99.48	19.47 / 99.48	19.48 / 99.49	19.49 / 99.49	19.49 / 99.49	19.50 / 99.50	19.50 / 99.50
3	10.13 / 34.12	9.55 / 30.81	9.28 / 29.46	9.12 / 28.71	9.01 / 28.24	8.94 / 27.91	8.88 / 27.67	8.84 / 27.49	8.81 / 27.34	8.78 / 27.23	8.76 / 27.13	8.74 / 27.05	8.71 / 26.92	8.69 / 26.83	8.66 / 26.69	8.64 / 26.60	8.62 / 26.50	8.60 / 26.41	8.58 / 26.30	8.57 / 26.27	8.56 / 26.23	8.54 / 26.18	8.54 / 26.14	8.53 / 26.12
4	7.71 / 21.20	6.94 / 18.00	6.59 / 16.69	6.39 / 15.98	6.26 / 15.52	6.16 / 15.21	6.09 / 14.98	6.04 / 14.80	6.00 / 14.66	5.96 / 14.54	5.93 / 14.45	5.91 / 14.37	5.87 / 14.24	5.84 / 14.15	5.80 / 14.02	5.77 / 13.93	5.74 / 13.83	5.71 / 13.74	5.70 / 13.69	5.68 / 13.61	5.66 / 13.57	5.65 / 13.52	5.64 / 13.48	5.63 / 13.46
5	6.61 / 16.26	5.79 / 13.27	5.41 / 12.06	5.19 / 11.39	5.05 / 10.97	4.95 / 10.67	4.88 / 10.45	4.82 / 10.27	4.78 / 10.15	4.74 / 10.05	4.70 / 9.96	4.68 / 9.89	4.64 / 9.77	4.60 / 9.68	4.56 / 9.55	4.53 / 9.47	4.50 / 9.38	4.46 / 9.29	4.44 / 9.24	4.42 / 9.17	4.40 / 9.13	4.38 / 9.07	4.37 / 9.04	4.36 / 9.02
6	5.99 / 13.74	5.14 / 10.92	4.76 / 9.78	4.53 / 9.15	4.39 / 8.75	4.28 / 8.47	4.21 / 8.26	4.15 / 8.10	4.10 / 7.98	4.06 / 7.87	4.03 / 7.79	4.00 / 7.72	3.96 / 7.60	3.92 / 7.52	3.87 / 7.39	3.84 / 7.31	3.81 / 7.23	3.77 / 7.14	3.75 / 7.09	3.72 / 7.02	3.71 / 6.99	3.69 / 6.94	3.68 / 6.90	3.67 / 6.88
7	5.59 / 12.25	4.74 / 9.55	4.35 / 8.45	4.12 / 7.85	3.97 / 7.46	3.87 / 7.19	3.79 / 7.00	3.73 / 6.84	3.68 / 6.71	3.63 / 6.62	3.60 / 6.54	3.57 / 6.47	3.52 / 6.35	3.49 / 6.27	3.44 / 6.15	3.41 / 6.07	3.38 / 5.98	3.34 / 5.90	3.32 / 5.85	3.29 / 5.78	3.28 / 5.75	3.25 / 5.70	3.24 / 5.67	3.23 / 5.65
8	5.32 / 11.26	4.46 / 8.65	4.07 / 7.59	3.84 / 7.01	3.69 / 6.63	3.58 / 6.37	3.50 / 6.19	3.44 / 6.03	3.39 / 5.91	3.34 / 5.82	3.31 / 5.74	3.28 / 5.67	3.23 / 5.56	3.20 / 5.48	3.15 / 5.36	3.12 / 5.28	3.08 / 5.20	3.05 / 5.11	3.03 / 5.06	3.00 / 5.00	2.98 / 4.96	2.95 / 4.91	2.94 / 4.88	2.93 / 4.86
9	5.12 / 10.56	4.26 / 8.02	3.86 / 6.99	3.63 / 6.42	3.48 / 6.06	3.37 / 5.80	3.29 / 5.62	3.23 / 5.47	3.18 / 5.35	3.13 / 5.26	3.10 / 5.18	3.07 / 5.11	3.02 / 5.00	2.98 / 4.92	2.93 / 4.80	2.90 / 4.73	2.86 / 4.64	2.82 / 4.56	2.80 / 4.51	2.77 / 4.45	2.76 / 4.41	2.73 / 4.36	2.72 / 4.33	2.71 / 4.31
10	4.96 / 10.04	4.10 / 7.56	3.71 / 6.55	3.48 / 5.99	3.33 / 5.64	3.22 / 5.39	3.14 / 5.21	3.07 / 5.06	3.02 / 4.95	2.97 / 4.85	2.94 / 4.78	2.91 / 4.71	2.86 / 4.60	2.82 / 4.52	2.77 / 4.41	2.74 / 4.33	2.70 / 4.25	2.67 / 4.17	2.64 / 4.12	2.61 / 4.05	2.59 / 4.01	2.56 / 3.96	2.55 / 3.93	2.54 / 3.91
11	4.84 / 9.65	3.98 / 7.20	3.59 / 6.22	3.36 / 5.67	3.20 / 5.32	3.09 / 5.07	3.01 / 4.88	2.95 / 4.74	2.90 / 4.63	2.94 / 4.54	2.82 / 4.46	2.79 / 4.40	2.74 / 4.29	2.70 / 4.21	2.65 / 4.10	2.61 / 4.02	2.57 / 3.94	2.53 / 3.86	2.50 / 3.80	2.47 / 3.74	2.45 / 3.70	2.42 / 3.66	2.41 / 3.62	2.40 / 3.60
12	4.75 / 9.33	3.88 / 6.93	3.49 / 5.95	3.26 / 5.41	3.11 / 5.06	3.00 / 4.82	2.92 / 4.65	2.85 / 4.50	2.80 / 4.39	2.76 / 4.30	2.72 / 4.22	2.69 / 4.16	2.64 / 4.05	2.60 / 3.98	2.54 / 3.86	2.50 / 3.78	2.46 / 3.70	2.42 / 3.61	2.40 / 3.56	2.36 / 3.49	2.35 / 3.46	2.32 / 3.41	2.31 / 3.38	2.30 / 3.36
13	4.67 / 9.07	3.80 / 6.70	3.41 / 5.74	3.18 / 5.20	3.02 / 4.86	2.92 / 4.62	2.84 / 4.44	2.77 / 4.30	2.72 / 4.19	2.67 / 4.10	2.63 / 4.02	2.60 / 3.96	2.55 / 3.85	2.51 / 3.78	2.46 / 3.67	2.42 / 3.59	2.38 / 3.51	2.34 / 3.42	2.32 / 3.37	2.28 / 3.30	2.26 / 3.27	2.24 / 3.21	2.22 / 3.18	2.21 / 3.16
14	4.60 / 8.86	3.74 / 6.51	3.34 / 5.56	3.11 / 5.03	2.96 / 4.69	2.85 / 4.46	2.77 / 4.28	2.70 / 4.14	2.65 / 4.03	2.60 / 3.94	2.56 / 3.86	2.53 / 3.80	2.48 / 3.70	2.44 / 3.62	2.39 / 3.51	2.35 / 3.43	2.31 / 3.34	2.27 / 3.26	2.24 / 3.21	2.21 / 3.14	2.19 / 3.11	2.16 / 3.06	2.14 / 3.02	2.13 / 3.00

15	4.54	3.68	3.29	3.06	2.90	2.79	2.70	2.64	2.59	2.55	2.51	2.48	2.43	2.39	2.33	2.29	2.25	2.21	2.18	2.15	2.12	2.10	2.08	2.07
	8.68	**6.36**	**5.42**	**4.89**	**4.56**	**4.32**	**4.14**	**4.00**	**3.89**	**3.80**	**3.73**	**3.67**	**3.56**	**3.48**	**3.36**	**3.29**	**3.20**	**3.12**	**3.07**	**3.00**	**2.97**	**2.92**	**2.89**	**2.87**
16	4.49	3.63	3.24	3.01	2.85	2.74	2.66	2.59	2.54	2.49	2.45	2.42	2.37	2.33	2.28	2.24	2.20	2.16	2.13	2.09	2.07	2.04	2.02	2.01
	8.53	**6.23**	**5.29**	**4.77**	**4.44**	**4.20**	**4.03**	**3.89**	**3.78**	**3.69**	**3.61**	**3.55**	**3.45**	**3.37**	**3.25**	**3.18**	**3.10**	**3.01**	**2.96**	**2.89**	**2.86**	**2.80**	**2.77**	**2.75**
17	4.45	3.59	3.20	2.96	2.81	2.70	2.62	2.55	2.50	2.45	2.41	2.38	2.33	2.29	2.23	2.19	2.15	2.11	2.08	2.04	2.02	1.99	1.97	1.96
	8.40	**6.11**	**5.18**	**4.67**	**4.34**	**4.10**	**3.93**	**3.79**	**3.68**	**3.59**	**3.52**	**3.45**	**3.35**	**3.27**	**3.16**	**3.08**	**3.00**	**2.92**	**2.86**	**2.79**	**2.76**	**2.70**	**2.67**	**2.65**
18	4.41	3.55	3.16	2.93	2.77	2.66	2.58	2.51	2.46	2.41	2.37	2.34	2.29	2.25	2.19	2.15	2.11	2.07	2.04	2.00	1.98	1.95	1.93	1.92
	8.28	**6.01**	**5.09**	**4.58**	**4.25**	**4.01**	**3.85**	**3.71**	**3.60**	**3.51**	**3.44**	**3.37**	**3.27**	**3.19**	**3.07**	**3.00**	**2.91**	**2.83**	**2.78**	**2.71**	**2.68**	**2.62**	**2.59**	**2.57**
19	4.38	3.52	3.13	2.90	2.74	2.63	2.55	2.48	2.43	2.38	2.34	2.31	2.26	2.21	2.15	2.11	2.07	2.02	2.00	1.96	1.94	1.91	1.90	1.88
	8.18	**5.93**	**5.01**	**4.50**	**4.17**	**3.94**	**3.77**	**3.63**	**3.52**	**3.43**	**3.36**	**3.30**	**3.19**	**3.12**	**3.00**	**2.92**	**2.84**	**2.76**	**2.70**	**2.63**	**2.60**	**2.54**	**2.51**	**2.49**
20	4.35	3.49	3.10	2.87	2.71	2.60	2.52	2.45	2.40	2.35	2.31	2.28	2.23	2.18	2.12	2.08	2.04	1.99	1.96	1.92	1.90	1.87	1.85	1.84
	8.10	**5.85**	**4.94**	**4.43**	**4.10**	**3.87**	**3.71**	**3.56**	**3.45**	**3.37**	**3.30**	**3.23**	**3.13**	**3.05**	**2.94**	**2.86**	**2.77**	**2.69**	**2.63**	**2.56**	**2.53**	**2.47**	**2.44**	**2.42**
21	4.32	3.47	3.07	2.84	2.68	2.57	2.49	2.42	2.37	2.32	2.28	2.25	2.20	2.15	2.09	2.05	2.00	1.96	1.93	1.89	1.87	1.84	1.82	1.81
	8.02	**5.78**	**4.87**	**4.37**	**4.04**	**3.81**	**3.65**	**3.51**	**3.40**	**3.31**	**3.24**	**3.17**	**3.07**	**2.99**	**2.88**	**2.80**	**2.72**	**2.63**	**2.58**	**2.51**	**2.47**	**2.42**	**2.38**	**2.36**
22	4.30	3.44	3.05	2.82	2.66	2.55	2.47	2.40	2.35	2.30	2.26	2.23	2.18	2.13	2.07	2.03	1.98	1.93	1.91	1.87	1.84	1.81	1.80	1.78
	7.94	**5.72**	**4.82**	**4.31**	**3.99**	**3.76**	**3.59**	**3.45**	**3.35**	**3.26**	**3.18**	**3.12**	**3.02**	**2.94**	**2.83**	**2.75**	**2.67**	**2.58**	**2.53**	**2.46**	**2.42**	**2.37**	**2.33**	**2.31**
23	4.28	3.42	3.03	2.80	2.64	2.53	2.45	2.38	2.32	2.28	2.24	2.20	2.14	2.10	2.04	2.00	1.96	1.91	1.88	1.84	1.82	1.79	1.77	1.76
	7.88	**5.66**	**4.76**	**4.26**	**3.94**	**3.71**	**3.54**	**3.41**	**3.30**	**3.21**	**3.14**	**3.07**	**2.97**	**2.89**	**2.78**	**2.70**	**2.62**	**2.53**	**2.48**	**2.41**	**2.37**	**2.32**	**2.28**	**2.26**
24	4.26	3.40	3.01	2.78	2.62	2.51	2.43	2.36	2.30	2.26	2.22	2.18	2.13	2.09	2.02	1.98	1.94	1.89	1.86	1.82	1.80	1.76	1.74	1.73
	7.82	**5.61**	**4.72**	**4.22**	**3.90**	**3.67**	**3.50**	**3.36**	**3.25**	**3.17**	**3.09**	**3.03**	**2.93**	**2.85**	**2.74**	**2.66**	**2.58**	**2.49**	**2.44**	**2.36**	**2.33**	**2.27**	**2.23**	**2.21**
25	4.24	3.38	2.99	2.76	2.60	2.49	2.41	2.34	2.28	2.24	2.20	2.16	2.11	2.06	2.00	1.96	1.92	1.87	1.84	1.80	1.77	1.74	1.72	1.71
	7.77	**5.57**	**4.68**	**4.18**	**3.86**	**3.63**	**3.46**	**3.32**	**3.21**	**3.13**	**3.05**	**2.99**	**2.89**	**2.81**	**2.70**	**2.62**	**2.54**	**2.45**	**2.40**	**2.32**	**2.29**	**2.23**	**2.19**	**2.17**
26	4.22	3.37	2.89	2.74	2.59	2.47	2.39	2.32	2.27	2.22	2.18	2.15	2.10	2.05	1.99	1.95	1.90	1.85	1.82	1.78	1.76	1.72	1.70	1.69
	7.72	**5.53**	**4.64**	**4.14**	**3.82**	**3.59**	**3.42**	**3.29**	**3.17**	**3.09**	**3.02**	**2.96**	**2.86**	**2.77**	**2.66**	**2.58**	**2.50**	**2.41**	**2.36**	**2.28**	**2.25**	**2.19**	**2.15**	**2.13**
27	4.21	3.35	2.96	2.73	2.57	2.46	2.37	2.30	2.25	2.20	2.16	2.13	2.08	2.03	1.97	1.93	1.88	1.84	1.80	1.76	1.74	1.71	1.68	1.67
	7.68	**5.49**	**4.60**	**4.11**	**3.79**	**3.56**	**3.39**	**3.26**	**3.14**	**3.06**	**2.98**	**2.93**	**2.83**	**2.74**	**2.63**	**2.55**	**2.47**	**2.38**	**2.33**	**2.25**	**2.21**	**2.16**	**2.12**	**2.10**
28	4.20	3.34	2.95	2.71	2.56	2.44	2.36	2.29	3.24	2.19	2.15	2.12	2.06	2.02	1.96	1.91	1.87	1.81	1.78	1.75	1.72	1.69	1.67	1.65
	7.64	**5.45**	**4.57**	**4.07**	**3.76**	**3.53**	**3.36**	**3.23**	**3.11**	**3.03**	**2.95**	**2.90**	**2.80**	**2.71**	**2.60**	**2.52**	**2.44**	**2.35**	**2.30**	**2.22**	**2.18**	**2.13**	**2.09**	**2.06**
29	4.18	3.33	2.93	2.70	2.54	2.43	2.35	2.28	2.22	2.18	2.14	2.10	2.05	2.00	1.94	1.90	1.85	1.80	1.77	1.73	1.71	1.68	1.65	1.64
	7.60	**5.52**	**4.54**	**4.04**	**3.73**	**3.50**	**3.33**	**3.20**	**3.08**	**3.00**	**2.92**	**2.87**	**2.77**	**2.68**	**2.57**	**2.49**	**2.41**	**2.32**	**2.27**	**2.19**	**2.15**	**2.10**	**2.06**	**2.03**
30	4.17	3.32	2.92	2.69	2.53	2.42	2.34	2.27	2.21	2.16	2.12	2.09	2.04	1.99	1.93	1.89	1.84	1.79	1.76	1.72	1.69	1.66	1.64	1.62
	7.56	**5.39**	**4.51**	**4.02**	**3.70**	**3.47**	**3.30**	**3.17**	**3.06**	**2.98**	**2.90**	**2.84**	**2.74**	**2.66**	**2.55**	**2.47**	**2.38**	**2.29**	**2.24**	**2.16**	**2.13**	**2.07**	**2.03**	**2.01**
32	4.15	3.30	2.90	2.67	2.51	2.40	2.32	2.25	2.19	2.14	2.10	2.07	2.02	1.97	1.91	1.86	1.82	1.76	1.74	1.69	1.67	1.64	1.61	1.59
	7.50	**5.34**	**4.46**	**3.97**	**3.66**	**3.42**	**3.25**	**3.12**	**3.01**	**2.94**	**2.86**	**2.80**	**2.70**	**2.62**	**2.51**	**2.42**	**2.34**	**2.25**	**2.20**	**2.12**	**2.08**	**2.02**	**1.98**	**1.96**
34	4.13	3.28	2.88	2.65	2.49	2.38	2.30	2.23	2.17	2.12	2.08	2.05	2.00	1.95	1.89	1.84	1.80	1.74	1.71	1.67	1.64	1.61	1.59	1.57
	7.44	**5.29**	**4.42**	**3.93**	**3.61**	**3.38**	**3.21**	**3.08**	**2.97**	**2.89**	**2.82**	**2.76**	**2.66**	**2.58**	**2.47**	**2.38**	**2.30**	**2.21**	**2.15**	**2.08**	**2.04**	**1.98**	**1.94**	**1.91**
36	4.11	3.26	2.86	2.63	2.48	2.36	2.28	2.21	2.15	2.10	2.06	2.03	1.89	1.93	1.87	1.82	1.78	1.72	1.69	1.65	1.62	1.59	1.56	1.55
	7.39	**5.25**	**4.38**	**3.89**	**3.58**	**3.35**	**3.18**	**3.04**	**2.94**	**2.86**	**2.78**	**2.72**	**2.62**	**2.54**	**2.43**	**2.35**	**2.26**	**2.17**	**2.12**	**2.04**	**2.00**	**1.94**	**1.90**	**1.87**
38	4.10	3.25	2.85	2.62	2.46	2.35	2.26	2.19	2.14	2.09	2.05	2.02	1.96	1.92	1.85	1.80	1.76	1.71	1.67	1.63	1.60	1.57	1.54	1.53
	7.35	**5.21**	**4.34**	**3.86**	**3.54**	**3.32**	**3.15**	**3.02**	**2.91**	**2.82**	**2.75**	**2.69**	**2.59**	**2.51**	**2.30**	**2.32**	**2.22**	**2.14**	**2.08**	**2.00**	**1.97**	**1.90**	**1.86**	**1.84**
40	4.08	3.23	2.84	2.61	2.45	2.34	2.25	2.18	2.12	2.07	2.04	2.00	1.95	1.90	1.84	1.79	1.74	1.69	1.66	1.61	1.59	1.55	1.53	1.51

Degrees of freedom for numerator (ν_1)

Degrees of freedom for denominator (ν_2)	1	2	3	4	5	6	7	8	9	10	11	12	14	16	20	24	30	40	50	75	100	200	500	∞
42	4.07 / 7.27	3.22 / 5.15	2.83 / 4.29	2.59 / 3.80	2.44 / 3.49	2.32 / 3.26	2.24 / 3.10	2.17 / 2.96	2.11 / 2.86	2.06 / 2.77	2.02 / 2.70	1.99 / 2.64	1.94 / 2.54	1.89 / 2.46	1.82 / 2.35	1.78 / 2.26	1.73 / 2.17	1.68 / 2.08	1.64 / 2.02	1.60 / 1.94	1.57 / 1.91	1.54 / 1.85	1.51 / 1.80	1.49 / 1.78
44	4.06 / 7.24	3.21 / 5.12	2.82 / 4.26	2.58 / 3.78	2.43 / 3.46	2.31 / 3.24	2.23 / 3.07	2.16 / 2.94	2.10 / 2.84	2.05 / 2.75	2.01 / 2.68	1.98 / 2.62	1.92 / 2.52	1.88 / 2.44	1.81 / 2.32	1.76 / 2.24	1.72 / 2.15	1.66 / 2.06	1.63 / 2.00	1.58 / 1.92	1.56 / 1.88	1.52 / 1.82	1.50 / 1.78	1.48 / 1.75
46	4.05 / 7.21	3.20 / 5.10	2.81 / 4.24	2.57 / 3.76	2.42 / 3.44	2.30 / 3.22	2.22 / 3.05	2.14 / 2.92	2.09 / 2.82	2.04 / 2.73	2.00 / 2.66	1.97 / 2.60	1.91 / 2.50	1.87 / 2.42	1.80 / 2.30	1.75 / 2.22	1.71 / 2.13	1.65 / 2.04	1.62 / 1.98	1.57 / 1.90	1.54 / 1.86	1.51 / 1.80	1.48 / 1.76	1.46 / 1.72
48	4.04 / 7.19	3.19 / 5.08	2.80 / 4.22	2.56 / 3.74	2.41 / 3.42	2.30 / 3.20	2.21 / 3.04	2.14 / 2.90	2.08 / 2.80	2.03 / 2.71	1.99 / 2.64	1.96 / 2.58	1.90 / 2.48	1.86 / 2.40	1.79 / 2.28	1.74 / 2.20	1.70 / 2.11	1.64 / 2.02	1.61 / 1.96	1.56 / 1.88	1.53 / 1.84	1.50 / 1.78	1.47 / 1.73	1.45 / 1.70
50	4.03 / 7.17	3.18 / 5.06	2.79 / 4.20	2.56 / 3.72	2.40 / 3.41	2.29 / 3.18	2.20 / 3.02	2.13 / 2.88	2.07 / 2.78	2.02 / 2.70	1.98 / 2.62	1.95 / 2.56	1.90 / 2.46	1.85 / 2.39	1.78 / 2.26	1.74 / 2.18	1.69 / 2.10	1.63 / 2.00	1.60 / 1.94	1.55 / 1.86	1.52 / 1.82	1.48 / 1.76	1.46 / 1.71	1.44 / 1.68
55	4.02 / 7.12	3.17 / 5.01	2.78 / 4.16	2.54 / 3.68	2.38 / 3.37	2.27 / 3.15	2.18 / 2.98	2.11 / 2.85	2.05 / 2.75	2.00 / 2.66	1.97 / 2.59	1.93 / 2.53	1.88 / 2.43	1.83 / 2.35	1.76 / 2.23	1.72 / 2.15	1.67 / 2.06	1.61 / 1.96	1.58 / 1.90	1.52 / 1.82	1.50 / 1.78	1.46 / 1.71	1.43 / 1.66	1.41 / 1.64
60	4.00 / 7.08	3.15 / 4.98	2.76 / 4.13	2.52 / 3.65	2.37 / 3.34	2.25 / 3.12	2.17 / 2.95	2.10 / 2.82	2.04 / 2.72	1.99 / 2.63	1.95 / 2.56	1.92 / 2.50	1.86 / 2.40	1.81 / 2.32	1.75 / 2.20	1.70 / 2.12	1.65 / 2.03	1.59 / 1.93	1.56 / 1.87	1.50 / 1.79	1.48 / 1.74	1.44 / 1.68	1.41 / 1.63	1.39 / 1.60
65	3.99 / 7.04	3.14 / 4.95	2.75 / 4.10	2.51 / 3.62	2.36 / 3.31	2.24 / 3.09	2.15 / 2.93	2.08 / 2.79	2.02 / 2.70	1.98 / 2.61	1.94 / 2.54	1.90 / 2.47	1.85 / 2.37	1.80 / 2.30	1.73 / 2.18	1.68 / 2.09	1.63 / 2.00	1.57 / 1.90	1.54 / 1.84	1.49 / 1.76	1.46 / 1.71	1.42 / 1.64	1.39 / 1.60	1.37 / 1.56
70	3.98 / 7.01	3.13 / 4.92	2.74 / 4.08	2.50 / 3.60	2.35 / 3.29	2.23 / 3.07	2.14 / 2.91	2.07 / 2.77	2.01 / 2.67	1.97 / 2.59	1.93 / 2.51	1.89 / 2.45	1.84 / 2.35	1.79 / 2.28	1.72 / 2.15	1.67 / 2.07	1.62 / 1.98	1.56 / 1.88	1.53 / 1.82	1.47 / 1.74	1.45 / 1.69	1.40 / 1.63	1.37 / 1.56	1.35 / 1.53
80	3.96 / 6.96	3.11 / 4.88	2.72 / 4.04	2.48 / 3.56	2.33 / 3.25	2.21 / 3.04	2.12 / 2.87	2.05 / 2.74	1.99 / 2.64	1.95 / 2.55	1.91 / 2.48	1.88 / 2.41	1.82 / 2.32	1.77 / 2.24	1.70 / 2.11	1.65 / 2.03	1.60 / 1.94	1.54 / 1.84	1.51 / 1.78	1.45 / 1.70	1.42 / 1.65	1.38 / 1.57	1.35 / 1.52	1.32 / 1.49
100	3.94 / 6.90	3.09 / 4.82	2.70 / 3.98	2.46 / 3.51	2.30 / 3.20	2.19 / 2.99	2.10 / 2.82	2.03 / 2.69	1.97 / 2.59	1.92 / 2.51	1.88 / 2.43	1.85 / 2.36	1.79 / 2.26	1.75 / 2.19	1.68 / 2.06	1.63 / 1.98	1.57 / 1.89	1.51 / 1.79	1.48 / 1.73	1.42 / 1.64	1.39 / 1.59	1.34 / 1.51	1.30 / 1.46	1.28 / 1.43
125	3.92 / 6.84	3.07 / 4.78	2.68 / 3.94	2.44 / 3.47	2.29 / 3.17	2.17 / 2.95	2.08 / 2.79	2.01 / 2.65	1.95 / 2.56	1.90 / 2.47	1.86 / 2.40	1.83 / 2.33	1.77 / 2.23	1.72 / 2.15	1.65 / 2.03	1.60 / 1.94	1.55 / 1.85	1.49 / 1.75	1.45 / 1.68	1.39 / 1.59	1.36 / 1.54	1.31 / 1.46	1.27 / 1.40	1.25 / 1.37
150	3.91 / 6.81	3.06 / 4.75	2.67 / 3.91	2.43 / 3.44	2.27 / 3.13	2.16 / 2.92	2.07 / 2.76	2.00 / 2.62	1.94 / 2.53	1.89 / 2.44	1.85 / 2.37	1.82 / 2.30	1.76 / 2.20	1.71 / 2.12	1.64 / 2.00	1.59 / 1.91	1.54 / 1.83	1.47 / 1.72	1.44 / 1.66	1.37 / 1.56	1.34 / 1.51	1.29 / 1.43	1.25 / 1.37	1.22 / 1.33
200	3.89 / 6.76	3.04 / 4.71	2.65 / 3.88	2.41 / 3.41	2.26 / 3.11	2.14 / 2.90	2.05 / 2.73	1.98 / 2.60	1.92 / 2.50	1.87 / 2.41	1.83 / 2.34	1.80 / 2.28	1.74 / 2.17	1.69 / 2.09	1.62 / 1.97	1.57 / 1.88	1.52 / 1.79	1.45 / 1.69	1.42 / 1.62	1.35 / 1.53	1.32 / 1.48	1.26 / 1.39	1.22 / 1.33	1.19 / 1.28
400	3.86 / 6.70	3.02 / 4.66	2.62 / 3.83	2.39 / 3.36	2.23 / 3.06	2.12 / 2.85	2.03 / 2.69	1.96 / 2.55	1.90 / 2.46	1.85 / 2.37	1.81 / 2.29	1.78 / 2.23	1.72 / 2.12	1.67 / 2.04	1.60 / 1.92	1.54 / 1.84	1.49 / 1.74	1.42 / 1.64	1.38 / 1.57	1.32 / 1.47	1.28 / 1.42	1.22 / 1.32	1.16 / 1.24	1.13 / 1.19
1000	3.85 / 6.66	3.00 / 4.62	2.61 / 3.80	2.38 / 3.34	2.22 / 3.04	2.10 / 2.82	2.02 / 2.66	1.95 / 2.53	1.89 / 2.43	1.84 / 2.34	1.80 / 2.26	1.76 / 2.20	1.70 / 2.09	1.65 / 2.01	1.58 / 1.89	1.53 / 1.81	1.47 / 1.71	1.41 / 1.61	1.36 / 1.54	1.30 / 1.44	1.26 / 1.38	1.19 / 1.28	1.13 / 1.19	1.08 / 1.11
∞	3.84 / 6.64	2.99 / 4.60	2.60 / 3.78	2.37 / 3.32	2.21 / 3.02	2.09 / 2.80	2.01 / 2.64	1.94 / 2.51	1.88 / 2.41	1.83 / 2.32	1.79 / 2.24	1.75 / 2.18	1.69 / 2.07	1.64 / 1.99	1.57 / 1.87	1.52 / 1.79	1.46 / 1.69	1.40 / 1.59	1.35 / 1.52	1.28 / 1.41	1.24 / 1.36	1.17 / 1.25	1.11 / 1.15	1.00 / 1.00

Present Value of 1

This table presents values of $(1 + i)^{-n}$ or $1/[(1 + i)^n]$ where i and n vary and i is the interest or discount rate and n is the number of years one is discounting.

Example. To find the present value of a \$1 million return 5 years from now from a program, by using a discount rate of 4%, the calculation can be written as follows:

$$R_0 = \frac{R_5}{(1 + i)^n}$$

or

$$R_0 = R_5(1 + i)^{-n}$$

where

$$R_0 = \text{present value}$$

and

$$R_5 = \text{value 5 years from now}$$

Substituting our values and using the table we find that

$$R_0 = \$1,000,000.(1 + .04)^{-5}$$
$$R_0 = \$1,000,000. \times .821927$$
$$R_0 = \$821,927.$$

For values of n greater than 25, we can make use of the rule $(a)^m.(a)^n = a^{m+n}$.

Example. For $(1 + i)^{-37}$, use $(1 + i)^{-25}.(1 + i)^{-12}$

$$(1 + i)^{-n}$$

n \ i	.035(3½%)	.040(4%)	.045(4½%)	.050(5%)	.055(5½%)
1	.966 184	.961 538	.956 938	.952 381	.947 867
2	.933 511	.924 556	.915 730	.907 029	.898 452
3	.901 943	.888 996	.876 297	.863 838	.851 614
4	.871 442	.854 804	.838 561	.822 702	.807 217
5	.841 973	.821 927	.802 451	.783 526	.765 134
6	.813 501	.790 315	.767 896	.746 215	.725 246
7	.785 991	.759 918	.734 828	.710 681	.687 437
8	.759 412	.730 690	.703 185	.676 839	.651 599
9	.733 731	.702 587	.672 904	.644 609	.617 629
10	.708 919	.675 564	.643 928	.613 913	.585 431
11	.684 946	.649 581	.616 199	584 679	.554 911
12	.661 783	.624 597	.589 664	.556 837	.525 982
13	.639 404	.600 574	.564 272	.530 321	.498 561
14	.617 782	.577 475	.539 973	.505 068	.472 569
15	.596 891	.555 265	.516 720	.481 017	.447 933
16	.576 706	.533 908	.494 469	.458 112	.424 581
17	.557 204	.513 373	.473 176	.436 297	.402 447
18	.538 361	.493 628	.452 800	.415 521	.381 466
19	.520 156	.474 642	.433 302	.395 734	.361 579
20	.502 566	.456 387	.414 643	.376 889	.342 729
21	.485 571	.438 834	.396 787	.358 942	.324 862
22	.469 151	.421 955	.379 701	.341 850	.307 926
23	.453 286	.405 726	.363 350	.325 571	.291 873
24	.437 957	.390 121	.347 703	.310 068	.276 657
25	.423 147	.375 117	.332 731	.295 303	.262 234

$$(1 + i)^{-n}$$

n \ i	.060(6%)	.065(6½%)	.070(7%)	.075(7½%)	.080(8%)
1	.943 396	.938 967	.934 579	.930 233	.925 926
2	.889 996	.881 659	.873 439	.865 333	.857 339
3	.839 619	.827 849	.816 298	.804 961	.793 832
4	.792 094	.777 323	.762 895	.748 801	.735 030
5	.747 258	.729 881	.712 986	.696 559	.680 583
6	.704 961	.685 334	.666 342	.647 962	.630 170
7	.665 057	.643 506	.622 750	.602 755	.583 490
8	.627 412	.604 231	.582 009	.560 702	.540 269
9	.591 898	.567 353	.543 934	.521 583	.500 249
10	.558 395	.532 726	.508 349	.485 194	.463 193
11	.526 788	.500 212	.475 093	.451 343	.428 883
12	.496 969	.469 683	.444 012	.419 854	.397 114
13	.468 839	.441 017	.414 964	.390 562	.367 698
14	.442 301	.414 100	.387 817	.363 313	.340 461
15	.417 265	.388 827	.362 446	.337 966	.315 242
16	.393 646	.365 095	.338 735	.314 387	.291 890
17	.371 364	.342 813	.316 574	.292 453	.270 269
18	.350 344	.321 890	.295 864	.272 049	.250 249
19	.330 513	.302 244	.276 508	.253 069	.231 712
20	.311 805	.283 797	.258 419	.235 413	.214 548
21	.294 155	.266 476	.241 513	.218 989	.198 656
22	.277 505	.250 212	.225 713	.203 711	.183 941
23	.261 797	.234 941	.210 947	.189 498	.170 315
24	.246 979	.220 602	.197 147	.176 277	.157 699
25	.232 999	.207 138	.184 249	.163 979	.146 018

$$(1 + i)^{-n}$$

n \ i	.085(8½%)	.090(9%)	.095(9½%)	.100(10%)	.120(12%)
1	.921 659	.917 431	.913 242	.909 091	.892 857
2	.849 455	.841 680	.834 011	.826 446	.797 194
3	.782 908	.772 183	.761 654	.751 315	.711 780
4	.721 574	.708 425	.695 574	.683 013	.635 518
5	.665 045	.649 931	.635 228	.620 921	.567 427
6	.612 945	.596 267	.580 117	.564 474	.506 631
7	.564 926	.547 034	.529 787	.513 158	.452 349
8	.520 669	.501 866	.483 824	.466 507	.403 883
9	.479 880	.460 428	.441 848	.424 098	.360 610
10	.442 285	.422 411	.403 514	.385 543	.321 973
11	.407 636	.387 533	.368 506	.350 494	.287 476
12	.375 702	.355 535	.336 535	.318 631	.256 675
13	.346 269	.326 179	.307 338	.289 664	.229 174
14	.319 142	.299 246	.280 674	.263 331	.204 620
15	.294 140	.274 538	.256 323	.239 392	.182 696
16	.271 097	.251 870	.234 085	.217 629	.163 122
17	.249 859	.231 073	.213 777	.197 845	.145 644
18	.230 285	.211 994	.195 230	.179 859	.130 040
19	.212 244	.194 490	.178 292	.163 508	.116 107
20	.195 616	.178 431	.162 824	.148 644	.103 667
21	.180 292	.163 698	.148 697	.135 131	.092 560
22	.166 167	.150 182	.135 797	.122 846	.082 643
23	.153 150	.137 781	.124 015	.111 678	.073 788
24	.141 152	.126 405	.113 256	.101 526	.065 882
25	.130 094	.115 968	.103 430	.092 296	.058 823

$$(1 + i)^{-n}$$

n \ i	.140(14%)	.160(16%)	.180(18%)	.200(20%)	.220(22%)
1	.877 193	.862 069	.847 458	.833 333	.819 672
2	.769 468	.743 163	.718 184	.694 444	.671 862
3	.674 972	.640 658	.608 631	.578 704	.550 707
4	.592 080	.552 291	.515 789	.482 253	.451 399
5	.519 369	.476 113	.437 109	.401 878	.369 999
6	.455 587	.410 442	.370 432	.334 898	.303 278
7	.399 637	.353 830	.313 925	.279 082	.248 589
8	.350 559	.305 025	.266 038	.232 568	.203 761
9	.307 508	.262 953	.225 456	.193 807	.167 017
10	.269 744	.226 684	.191 064	.161 506	.136 899
11	.236 617	.195 417	.161 919	.134 588	.112 213
12	.207 559	.168 463	.137 220	.112 157	.091 978
13	.182 069	.145 227	.116 288	.093 464	.075 391
14	.159 710	.125 195	.098 549	.077 887	.061 796
15	.140 096	.107 927	.083 516	.064 905	.050 653
16	.122 892	.093 041	.070 776	.054 088	.041 519
17	.107 800	.080 207	.059 980	.045 073	.034 032
18	.094 561	.069 144	.050 830	.037 561	.027 895
19	.082 948	.059 607	.043 077	.031 301	.022 865
20	.072 762	.051 385	.036 506	.026 084	.018 741
21	.063 826	.044 298	.030 937	.021 737	.015 362
22	.055 988	.038 188	.026 218	.018 114	.012 592
23	.049 112	.032 920	.022 218	.015 095	.010 321
24	.043 081	.028 380	.018 829	.012 579	.008 460
25	.037 790	.024 465	.015 957	.010 483	.006 934

APPENDIX IX

Mantissas for Common Logarithms

These are logarithms to the base 10. Logs for numbers from 1.00 to 9.99 can be read directly from the table, placing a decimal point to the left of the four digits. For example,

$$\log_{10} 1.80 = .2553$$

and

$$\log_{10} 2.93 = .4669$$

If the number for which you are seeking the log is larger or smaller than the given range of the table, then shift your number's decimal place until it falls within the range of 1.00 to 9.99; look up this number's log, and either add 1 to that log for each place you shifted the decimal left, or subtract 1 from that log for each place you shifted the decimal to the right. For example, if you want the log of 1800, shift the decimal 3 places to the left, find the log of 1.8 = .2553, and add 3 to it. Thus the log of 1800 = 3.2553. Likewise, the log of .0293 = .4669 − 2, which can also be written as 8.4669 − 10.

To obtain natural logarithms, multiply the common log by 2.3026.

Mantissas for Common Logarithms

N	0	1	2	3	4	5	6	7	8	9
1.0	0000	0043	0086	0128	0170	0212	0253	0294	0334	0374
1.1	0414	0453	0492	0531	0569	0607	0645	0682	0719	0755
1.2	0792	0828	0864	0899	0934	0969	1004	1038	1072	1106
1.3	1139	1173	1206	1239	1271	1303	1335	1367	1399	1430
1.4	1461	1492	1523	1553	1584	1614	1644	1673	1703	1732
1.5	1761	1790	1818	1847	1875	1903	1931	1959	1987	2014
1.6	2041	2068	2095	2122	2148	2175	2201	2227	2253	2279
1.7	2304	2330	2355	2380	2405	2430	2455	2480	2504	2529
1.8	2553	2577	2601	2625	2648	2672	2695	2718	2742	2765
1.9	2788	2810	2833	2856	2878	2900	2923	2945	2967	2989
2.0	3010	3032	3054	3075	3096	3118	3139	3160	3181	3201
2.1	3222	3243	3263	3284	3304	3324	3345	3365	3385	3404
2.2	3424	3444	3464	3483	3502	3522	3541	3560	3579	3598
2.3	3617	3636	3655	3674	3692	3711	3729	3747	3766	3784
2.4	3802	3820	3838	3856	3874	3892	3909	3927	3945	3962
2.5	3979	3997	4014	4031	4048	4065	4082	4099	4116	4133
2.6	4150	4166	4183	4200	4216	4232	4249	4265	4281	4298
2.7	4314	4330	4346	4362	4378	4393	4409	4425	4440	4456
2.8	4472	4487	4502	4518	4533	4548	4564	4579	4594	4609
2.9	4624	4639	4654	4669	4683	4698	4713	4728	4742	4757
3.0	4771	4786	4800	4814	4829	4843	4857	4871	4886	4900
3.1	4914	4928	4942	4955	4969	4983	4997	5011	5024	5038
3.2	5051	5065	5079	5092	5105	5119	5132	5145	5159	5172
3.3	5185	5198	5211	5224	5237	5250	5263	5276	5289	5302
3.4	5315	5328	5340	5353	5366	5378	5391	5403	5416	5428
3.5	5441	5453	5465	5478	5490	5502	5514	5527	5539	5551
3.6	5563	5575	5587	5599	5611	5623	5635	5647	5658	5670
3.7	5682	5694	5705	5717	5729	5740	5752	5763	5775	5786
3.8	5798	5809	5821	5832	5843	5855	5866	5877	5888	5899
3.9	5911	5922	5933	5944	5955	5966	5977	5988	5999	6010
4.0	6021	6031	6042	6053	6064	6075	6085	6096	6107	6117
4.1	6128	6138	6149	6160	6170	6180	6191	6201	6212	6222
4.2	6232	6243	6253	6263	6274	6284	6294	6304	6314	6325
4.3	6335	6345	6355	6365	6375	6385	6395	6405	6415	6425
4.4	6435	6444	6454	6464	6474	6484	6493	6503	6513	6522
4.5	6532	6542	6551	6561	6571	6580	6590	6599	6609	6618
4.6	6628	6637	6646	6656	6665	6675	6684	6693	6702	6712
4.7	6721	6730	6739	6749	6758	6767	6776	6785	6794	6803
4.8	6812	6821	6830	6839	6848	6857	6866	6875	6884	6893
4.9	6902	6911	6920	6928	6937	6946	6955	6964	6972	6981

N	0	1	2	3	4	5	6	7	8	9
5.0	6990	6998	7007	7016	7024	7033	7042	7050	7059	7067
5.1	7076	7084	7093	7101	7110	7118	7126	7135	7143	7152
5.2	7160	7168	7177	7185	7193	7202	7210	7218	7226	7235
5.3	7243	7251	7259	7267	7275	7284	7292	7300	7308	7316
5.4	7324	7332	7340	7348	7356	7364	7372	7380	7388	7396
5.5	7404	7412	7419	7427	7435	7443	7451	7459	7466	7474
5.6	7482	7490	7497	7505	7513	7520	7528	7536	7543	7551
5.7	7559	7566	7574	7582	7589	7597	7604	7612	7619	7627
5.8	7634	7642	7649	7657	7664	7672	7679	7686	7694	7701
5.9	7709	7716	7723	7731	7738	7745	7752	7760	7767	7774
6.0	7782	7789	7796	7803	7810	7818	7825	7832	7839	7846
6.1	7853	7860	7868	7875	7882	7889	7896	7903	7910	7917
6.2	7924	7931	7938	7945	7952	7959	7966	7973	7980	7987
6.3	7993	8000	8007	8014	8021	8028	8035	8041	8048	8055
6.4	8062	8069	8075	8082	8089	8096	8102	8109	8116	8122
6.5	8129	8136	8142	8149	8156	8162	8169	8176	8182	8189
6.6	8195	8202	8209	8215	8222	8228	8235	8241	8248	8254
6.7	8261	8267	8274	8280	8287	8293	8299	8306	8312	8319
6.8	8325	8331	8338	8344	8351	8357	8363	8370	8376	8382
6.9	8388	8395	8401	8407	8414	8420	8426	8432	8439	8445
7.0	8451	8457	8463	8470	8476	8482	8488	8494	8500	8506
7.1	8513	8519	8525	8531	8537	8543	8549	8555	8561	8567
7.2	8573	8579	8585	8591	8597	8603	8609	8615	8621	8627
7.3	8633	8639	8645	8651	8657	8663	8669	8675	8681	8686
7.4	8692	8698	8704	8710	8716	8722	8727	8733	8739	8745
7.5	8751	8756	8762	8768	8774	8779	8785	8791	8797	8802
7.6	8808	8814	8820	8825	8831	8837	8842	8848	8854	8859
7.7	8865	8871	8876	8882	8887	8893	8899	8904	8910	8915
7.8	8921	8927	8932	8938	8943	8949	8954	8960	8965	8971
7.9	8976	8982	8987	8993	8998	9004	9009	9015	9020	9025
8.0	9031	9036	9042	9047	9053	9058	9063	9069	9074	9079
8.1	9085	9090	9096	9101	9106	9112	9117	9122	9128	9133
8.2	9138	9143	9149	9154	9159	9165	9170	9175	9180	9186
8.3	9191	9196	9201	9206	9212	9217	9222	9227	9232	9238
8.4	9243	9248	9253	9258	9263	9269	9274	9279	9284	9289
8.5	9294	9299	9304	9309	9315	9320	9325	9330	9335	9340
8.6	9345	9350	9355	9360	9365	9370	9375	9380	9385	9390
8.7	9395	9400	9405	9410	9415	9420	9425	9430	9435	9440
8.8	9445	9450	9455	9460	9465	9469	9474	9479	9484	9489
8.9	9494	9499	9504	9509	9513	9518	9523	9528	9533	9538
9.0	9542	9547	9552	9557	9562	9566	9571	9576	9581	9586

N	0	1	2	3	4	5	6	7	8	9
9.1	9590	9595	9600	9605	9609	9614	9619	9624	9628	9633
9.2	9638	9643	9647	9652	9657	9661	9666	9671	9675	9680
9.3	9685	9689	9694	9699	9703	9708	9713	9717	9722	9727
9.4	9731	9736	9741	9745	9750	9754	9759	9763	9768	9773
9.5	9777	9782	9786	9791	9795	9800	9805	9809	9814	9818
9.6	9823	9827	9832	9836	9841	9845	9850	9854	9859	9863
9.7	9868	9872	9877	9881	9886	9890	9894	9899	9903	9908
9.8	9912	9917	9921	9926	9930	9934	9939	9943	9948	9952
9.9	9956	9961	9965	9969	9974	9978	9983	9987	9991	9996

Index